THE VOICES OF NIMES

SUZANNAH LIPSCOMB is Professor Emerita of History at the University of Roehampton and a Fellow of the Royal Historical Society. She received her DPhil in History from Balliol College, Oxford, and was formerly Research Curator at Hampton Court Palace, Lecturer in Early Modern History at the University of East Anglia, and Head of the Faculty of History and Senior Lecturer in Early Modern History at the New College of the Humanities. She is the author of four other books about the sixteenth century, and has presented historical documentaries on the BBC, ITV, and Channel Five.

Most of the women who ever lived left no trace of their existence on the record of history. Sixteenth- and seventeenth-century women of the middling and lower levels of society left no letters or diaries in which they expressed what they felt or thought. Criminal courts and magistrates kept few records of their testimonies, and no ecclesiastical court records are known to survive for the French Roman Catholic Church between 1540 and 1667. For the most part, we cannot hear the voices of ordinary French women—but this study allows us to do so.

Based on the evidence of 1,200 cases brought before the consistories—or moral courts—of the Protestant or Huguenot church of Languedoc between 1560 and 1615, this book allows us to access ordinary women's everyday lives: their speech, behaviour, attitudes, and narratives about faith, love, marriage, sex, and society. Women appeared frequently before the consistory because one of the chief functions of moral discipline was the regulation of sexuality, and women were thought to be primarily responsible for sexual sin. This means that the registers include over a thousand testimonies by and about women, most of whom left no other record to posterity.

Women also featured so prominently before the consistories because of an ironic, unintended consequence of the consistorial system: it empowered women. Women quickly learnt how to use the consistory: it became the ideal environment for women to initiate cases, seek redress, or denounce others. The registers therefore offer unrivalled evidence of women's agency, in this intensely patriarchal society, in a range of different contexts, such as their enjoyment of their sexuality, choice of marriage partners, or idiosyncratic spiritual engagement. The consistorial registers let us see how independent and self-determining women could be in an age when they had limited legal rights, little official authority, and few prospects. As a result, this book suggests we need to reconceptualize ordinary women's power in this era: it was not merely silent, manipulative, and devious, but also bold, public, and vocal.

The Praise for *The Voices of Nîmes*

'Suzannah Lipscomb's extraordinary *Voices of Nîmes* performs that miracle which only the most powerful historians can execute: using a dense archive to re-awaken lost lives: the women of 16th century Protestant Nimes. Here they are to the life, body and soul, faith and feeling, morally intense, and sensually driven; vocal, animated, and in their way eloquent. This is a beautiful book, grippingly written, and destined to be a classic of social history.'

Professor Sir Simon Schama

'In the world of feminist history, *The Voices of Nîmes* has the potential to shift the paradigms through which we talk about women and power. This is classic micro-history as case study... *The Voices of Nîmes* constitutes a substantive display of scholarly acumen. The women of Lipscomb's narrative... have been lucky to find such a gifted chronicler.'

Kate Malby, *Financial Times*

'An expert account... outstanding.... No reader can be left in any doubt about the scale of the archival achievement in reconstructing so many compelling and detailed stories about the lives of women in Nîmes from these consistory registers.'

Graeme Murdock, *History: The Journal of the Historical Association*

'This impressive study vividly re-animates the lived realities of ordinary women... an extraordinary and painstaking piece of scholarship... this book is nothing short of mastery of the material, and a robust response to existing scholarship... Lipscomb has done these women a great service in resurrecting their stories. This work is essential reading for specialists and students of gender...'

Linda Briggs, *French Studies*

'Captivating... Thanks to her meticulous research... the voices of women are heard in 2019 in a way that they were rarely listened to by the consistory courts of Languedoc.'

Lyndan Warner, *TLS*

'Based on exhaustive research in the archives of the Huguenot Church of 16th- and 17th-century Languedoc, it is an imaginative attempt to reconstruct the mental and social worlds of women who have otherwise left no discernible mark in the historical record... Lipscomb's painstaking study... offers new insights into everyday life and popular morality in Reformation France... A finely wrought and colourful mosaic... a brilliant and luminous image... richly satisfying.'

Alexandra Walsham, *Literary Review*

Frontispiece. Copper engraved and hand-coloured plate of Nîmes, from 1572, from Georg Braun and Frans Hogenberg, *Civitates Orbis Terrarum*

The Voices of Nîmes

*Women, Sex, and Marriage
in Reformation Languedoc*

SUZANNAH LIPSCOMB

OXFORD
UNIVERSITY PRESS

OXFORD

UNIVERSITY PRESS

Great Clarendon Street, Oxford, OX2 6DP,
United Kingdom

Oxford University Press is a department of the University of Oxford.
It furthers the University's objective of excellence in research, scholarship,
and education by publishing worldwide. Oxford is a registered trade mark of
Oxford University Press in the UK and in certain other countries

First published 2019
First published in paperback 2022

Impression: 1

Published in the United States of America by Oxford University Press
198 Madison Avenue, New York, NY 10016, United States of America

British Library Cataloguing in Publication Data
Data available

Library of Congress Cataloging in Publication Data
Data available

ISBN 978–0–19–879766–1 (Hbk.)
ISBN 978–0–19–879767–8 (Pbk.)

Printed and bound by
CPI Group (UK) Ltd, Croydon, CR0 4YY

For Robin;
for my godparents, Penny and Jeremy;
and
in memory of their sons,
John-Paul and Louis.

Acknowledgements

The initial research on which this book is based was completed during my doctorate, which was funded by the Arts and Humanities Research Council; a scholarship from Balliol College, Oxford; a research fellowship from The Institute of Historical Research; and my parents' generosity. I am deeply grateful to all the above for their financial provision—and to all the institutions who have employed me since—Kingston University and Historic Royal Palaces, the University of East Anglia, New College of the Humanities, and, latterly, the University of Roehampton. This has been a book that has been long in the making.

I wish to thank all the staff at the Archives nationales, Bibliothèque nationale de France at the Arsenal, Richelieu, and François Mitterand sites, and the Bibliothèque de la Société de l'Histoire du Protestantisme Français in Paris. My sincere thanks also go to the staff of the Bibliothèque de L'Eglise Réformée in Nîmes, especially Guy Combes, Pasteur Thierry Faye, and M. Villeneuve. I am especially grateful to the staff at the Archives départementales du Gard in Nîmes—how lovely you have been to me over the years—and at the Archives départementales de l'Hérault, and du Tarn-et-Garonne. Among all my friends in Nîmes, Elisabeth Hodoroaba deserves special mention for her kindness to a stranger. In London, I am grateful to the staff of the British Library and the London Library, where great chunks of the book have been written.

I owe much of my intellectual development—such as it is—to a great triumvirate of powers. Lyndal Roper has showed great enthusiasm towards this project, and extraordinary insight and acuity, that have profoundly shaped my thinking. Susan Brigden—a consummate historian of elegance and originality—has been my trusted counsellor, friend, and mentor for nearly twenty years. And from my first inspirational meeting with him as an undergraduate, until the present day, Robin Briggs has been my polestar. He has been unstintingly generous in both time and ideas, which have always been sharp, insightful, and nuanced. A case in point is that he made time to read this manuscript in draft, contributing immensely thoughtful and helpful suggestions to its argument, and even performing a thorough and much-appreciated copy-edit. I consider myself incredibly lucky to have been nurtured by their minds and their hearts.

My notes and bibliography acknowledge all my scholarly debts, but I wish to pay particular tribute to a number who have shaped and influenced my thoughts—some on page and in person, some simply through their work—including: Sarah Apetrei, Bernard Capp, Natalie Zemon Davis, James R. Farr, Janine Garrisson-Estèbe, Anthony Fletcher, Laura Gowing, Julie Hardwick, Kat Hill, Colin Jones, Robert M. Kingdon, Sonja Kmec, Sir Diarmaid MacCulloch, Graeme Murdock, Andrew Pettegree, David Parrott, Judith Pollmann, Nancy Lyman Roelker, Ulinka Rublack, Jacques Solé, Allan A. Tulchin, Manon Van der Heijden, Georges Vigarello, Jeffrey R. Watt, Merry E. Wiesner-Hanks, and John Witte, Jr, and, especially,

Philippe Chareyre, Philip Conner, Philip Benedict, Emmanuel Le Roy Ladurie, and Raymond A. Mentzer. I also owe a debt of gratitude to Randle Cotgrave, compiler of an invaluable seventeenth-century French–English dictionary; Léon Ménard, a great eighteenth-century chronicler of Nîmes; and Pasteur Louis Auzières, the nineteenth-century minister who diligently copied the surviving deliberations of the Nîmes consistory—whenever I could not read the (mostly lovely) hand of the consistorial scribes, he could. I have indeed stood on the shoulders of giants. Finally, Katarzyna Kosior compiled the chronological conspectus that accompanies this book online and Mollie Charge crunched the numbers on the overlap of elders and town councillors; I am very grateful to them for their hard work and assistance (any errors that remain are mine).

I have the loveliest and most talented of agents: Felicity Bryan, who has acted for me on this and other books, and my wonderful broadcast agents, Helen Purvis and Sue Ayton. Thank you to you all. I am grateful to illustrator Adrian Teal and designer Lisa Hunter for the illustrated maps of Languedoc and Nîmes, to Stephanie Ireland and Cathryn Steele at OUP for their forbearance and good will, and to the anonymous Readers of the proposal and manuscript for their helpful suggestions.

For those who helped me to get settled in Nîmes, I am endlessly grateful. My aunt and godmother, Penny Stevens, and my father, Nick, accompanied me on my first tremulous trip, and smoothed the way with their witty French; my brother, Tim, drove me down with a car full of possessions; and my godfather, Jeremy Pratt, stood guarantor for my beautiful flat (as well as putting me up in Paris on countless occasions). Thank you to Drake Lawhead for the sixteenth-century plate of Nîmes.

The love, support, and input of many have enabled me to complete this work. Olly Ayers, Sarah Churchwell, Hannah Dawson, Paul Golding, Naomi Goulder, Malcolm Guite, Dan Jones, Kate and Matt Kirkpatrick, Lars Kjær, David Mitchell, Edmund Neill, Estelle Paranque, Joanne Paul, Helen Rand, Pippa Rees, and Naomi and Joseph Steinberg have all helped, listened, commented, encouraged, or put up with 'my' sixteenth-century French women. Sir Simon Schama, my lodestone, and Lucy Mieli have listened to more than most. I am immensely grateful to you all.

My greatest debts are twofold. My kind and generous mother, Marguerite, read the whole manuscript in draft, and it was much improved by her comments and emendations. She even embraced the thankless task of bringing order to my notes, and blessed me with love, encouragement, and care as I wrote; I cannot thank her in a way that would equal her contribution. And my Tom, who has given me hope, courage, and resilience; who has talked through ideas and problems over countless meals; who has kept the rest of life running while I 'had to work on the book' (I hear the sound of washing-up as I type): for all these indications of your love, and many more besides—and for your companionship in life—I am deeply thankful.

Suzannah Lipscomb
London, 2018
SDG

Contents

List of Figures and Map

FIGURES

MAP

Abbreviations and Prefatory Notes

ADG	Archives départementales du Gard, Nîmes
ADH	Archives départementales de l'Hérault, Montpellier
ADTG	Archives départementales du Tarn-et-Garonne, Montauban
Arc.Not.	Archives notariales (at the Archives départementales du Gard, Nîmes)
Ars.	Bibliothèque de l'Arsenal, Paris
BN	Bibliothèque nationale de France, Paris
BSHPF	Bibliothèque de la Société du Protestantisme Français, Paris
BSHPF	*Le Bulletin de la Société du Protestantisme Français*
FHS	*French Historical Studies*
JIH	*Journal of Interdisciplinary History*
Ms	Manuscrit
Ms.fr.	Manuscrits français (at the Bibliothèque nationale de France, Paris)
SCJ	*Sixteenth Century Journal*

NAMES

In the absence of a first name, I have normally put the title appended to names, such as Sire or Sieur (Sir or Master, used as a title of honour for merchants, tradesmen, and so on, and not to indicate a knighthood); Monsieur or M. (also meaning Sir or Master, but used for an equal); Mademoiselle, Mlle, or Damoiselle (meaning gentlewoman, and not indicative of being unmarried), and Donne ('Dame', used for older or respected women, and not necessarily those of high social status).

Ordinary women in the sixteenth and seventeenth centuries did not generally take their husbands' surnames on marriage but retained their fathers' surnames with a feminine ending. Women of more elevated status (the daughter of a 'Sieur') generally did adopt their husband's surnames but retained the honorific title Mademoiselle or Damoiselle.

Many people acquired sobriquets, some of which give clues about them. Women's nicknames might describe a physical or temperamental characteristic, such as *La Poucette* ('little thumb'; the English equivalent might be 'Thumbelina'), for one of short stature, or reflect their employment or origin, such as *La Gasconne*, for one from Gascony.

Many forenames—such as Claude, Pierre, and Estienne—were unisex.

MONEY

France in this period used the Roman monetary system, which was complicated by the existence of two types of money: money of account, for which there existed no actual coins, and a real currency, whose coins varied in value compared to the money of account. So:

20 *sous* = 1 *livre tournois*, but no *livres* were minted
12 *denier* = 1 *sou*
écu d'or soleil = c.50 *sous*

but this varied over time, so:

1560–75   1 *écu* = 2 *l.* 10 *s.*
1575–1615   1 *écu* = 3 *l.*

A *franc* was a coin worth 1 *livre* and, although no longer minted, *franc* could be used interchangeably for *livre*.

In these records, *sols* (or *solz*) is often used in place of *sous*.

DATES

In France the year was considered to start on 25 March (Lady Day) until 1564, when King Charles IX ordained that the start of the year should be counted from 1 January, following the introduction of the Gregorian calendar. For simplicity, dates between 1560 and 1565 have been rendered in the new style (e.g. 1 Jan. 1562), but dates between 1 January and 24 March until 1564 should properly be considered as part of the preceding year in the old style.

THE CONSISTORY

Although technically a singular noun, to recognize that the consistory was not an ahistorical, monolithic entity, but composed, each new year, of a different group of men, with their own prejudices, preoccupations, and principles, I have often used the noun as if it were a plural.

They referred to their church as the *Église Réformée*; in this study, I use 'Reformed', 'Protestant', 'Calvinist', and 'Huguenot' interchangeably.

'As all historians know, the past is a great darkness, and filled with echoes. Voices may reach us from it; but what they say to us is imbued with the obscurity of the matrix out of which they come; and, try as we may, we cannot always decipher them precisely in the clearer light of our own day.'

Margaret Atwood, *The Handmaid's Tale*

'All happy families are alike; each unhappy family is unhappy in its own way.'

Leo Tolstoy, *Anna Karenina*

On trouve dans les textes ainsi rassemblés une dose de pointillisme et de vécu qu'on cherchait en vain dans les chartes ou même dans la documentation notariale.

Emmanuel Le Roy Ladurie, Montaillou, village occitan de 1294 à 1324

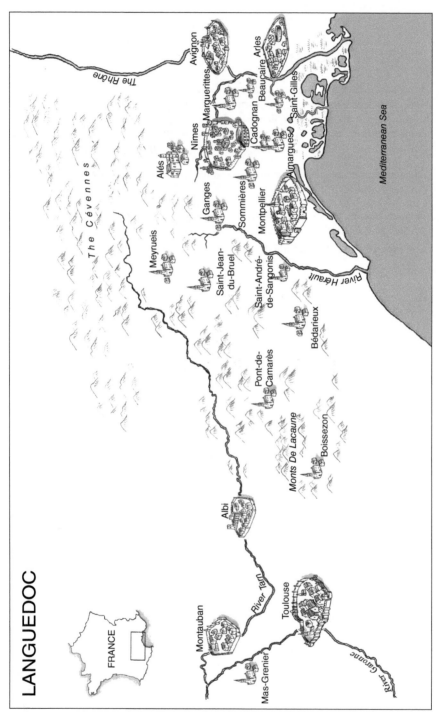

Map 1 Map of Languedoc, showing the principal cities, towns, and villages mentioned in this study (illustrator: Adrian Teal; designer: Lisa Hunter)

Introduction

In January 1580 Gillette de Girardet, an 18-year-old woman from Aigues-Mortes in southwestern France, said she could not be engaged to Anthoine Dumas because she was already married to Jesus Christ.

The case came before the consistory of the Protestant church in the city of Nîmes. Faced with conflicting statements—Anthoine said they were engaged, Gillette said they were not—the men of the consistory, which operated as the governing body and moral arbiter of the church, swung into operation. They began by questioning Gillette, who said that she was 'of the Christian religion'—by which she and the consistory meant Protestant—and that she promised to live and die in that religion. When exhorted to tell the truth about the marriage, she said that she submitted herself to the consistory and remitted her fate into their hands, but she denied that any promise of marriage or betrothal ceremony had passed between her and Anthoine Dumas. She was asked if she had received a ring from Dumas. She admitted that she had. Was it a gold ring? She said that she could not remember if it had been silver or gold. Did he say, 'This is a ring that I give to you in the name of marriage'? No, it had not been given in the name of marriage, but with the words, 'I give you this in good friendship and so that you will remember me', but as she thought it of little account, she said, she had thrown it on the table. The crucial statement came when she was asked why she had said that she was already married and to whom: she simply replied, 'to Jesus Christ'. She was suggesting that her relationship with God was sufficient defence against marrying a man she did not wish to wed.

It would be an understatement to say that such assertions were not to the consistory's liking. The consistory thought that God was on their side and that when it came to discerning His will in marital affairs they were best placed to judge. Earlier that same day when a woman called Loyse Mingaude had refused to marry her fiancé, a cobbler called M. Laurens, they had reprimanded her with the words, 'seeing her obstinacy . . . she should ask God to change and soften her heart'.

Gillette's story was also, unfortunately, soon to be discredited by the evidence of witnesses. The story these witnesses told indicates what might have been behind her reluctance to wed and why others were determined to make sure she did.

The web of relationships between Anthoine Dumas and the witnesses is the first clue. The most crucial witness, Raimond Dumas, was Anthoine's father's cousin. Raimond's son, Jehan Dumas—Anthoine's 'second cousin'—and his wife Françoise Gallande were also present, although neither said anything. In addition, Raimond's step-daughter's husband (effectively his son-in-law), Pierre Guerin, was a witness, as was Pierre Jullien, a town consul in Aigues-Mortes, who was related to Guerin and, therefore, to all the others, as his wife was Guerin's niece. Finally, also present was Anthoine's godfather , for whom he was named, Anthoine Jollie. Six people: all related to Anthoine Dumas and one an other, through blood, marriage, or spiritual ties.

The witnesses told the following tale. Raimond Dumas had business ties to the Girardet family: Gillette's father, Sire Pierre de Girardet, had rented a boat to Raimond Dumas and a few days before the alleged engagement Pierre de Girardet had died.[1] So a few days after her father's death Raimond had gone to visit Gillette to see if he would be able to continue to rent the boat, or if she wanted it to revert to her. He had taken Pierre Guerin with him and on their way they had passed Pierre Jullien's shop, and he had joined them. When they arrived Anthoine Dumas was, according to Raimond Dumas's testimony, already at Gillette's house.

Raimond's and Pierre Guerin's stories agreed on what had happened next: after speaking to Gillette about the lease, Raimond had asked her if she wanted the marriage between her and Anthoine—an idea which her late father had advocated— to go ahead. Raimond stated that Gillette's reply was:

> after her father's affliction, God wanted to provide her with a friend, and knowing that Anthoine Dumas had care of her affairs and that her late father had had a good friendship with him, it was her intention to follow the wishes of her father, if God ordained it, and take him in marriage.

The 40-year-old Pierre Guerin, however, remembered that she had said that she would marry 'at the hour God wishes it'.

According to Guerin, Raimond had then assured Gillette that he would make Anthoine give 1,000 *livres* or half of her father's possessions to her mother—Gillette would take the other half into the marriage as a dowry, and into the effective possession of the Dumas family, enriching them considerably.[2] Gillette had wanted further guarantees for her mother. Raimond had replied that the best way to guarantee provision for her mother would be a formal engagement ceremony between her and Anthoine. So, as both Raimond and Guerin reported, Raimond had asked Anthoine 'Do you give your body to Gillette here present?', to which he had replied 'Yes.' Raimond had asked the same question to Gillette, with the same affirmative reply. He had then asked each if they received the other's body and to this both also replied 'Yes.' Then Raimond had told Anthoine that he could kiss Gillette, which he did, and all the assembled company congratulated them. Asked if Gillette looked upset or cried at this point, Raimond said that on the contrary, she was very happy. Finally, according to Guerin, Gillette had asked all present to keep the engagement secret for a few days, which they had promised to do, and Anthoine

---

[1] '*Radelle*', Occitan for a raft or timber-boat.

[2] Possessions of this magnitude reveal that the Girardet family was comparatively wealthy in Nîmes society (and among those who came before the consistory). Both Gillette and Antoine were members of the local nobility—not technically true aristocrats, but from families who had been able to purchase noble land and seigneurial rights. Allan A. Tulchin finds that dowries among seigneurs-by-purchase averaged over 1,200 *livres*, while the next rank down of society—lawyers—had dowries averaging 900 *livres*: *That Men Would Praise the Lord: The Triumph of Protestantism in Nîmes, 1530–1570* (Oxford, 2010), 21.

to bring her some black fabric, from which she could make a mourning dress to wear for several days.

Raimond's version of events is Gillette's straightforward consent to marry. Pierre Guerin relates a more complex and believable tale, in which Gillette expresses concerns about God's consent to the match, the financial arrangements of the marriage, the public declaration of the union, and the need to appear in mourning for some time yet.

How should we interpret these events? Gillette was young, vulnerable, and grief-stricken when the engagement occurred: it happened just a few days after her father's death, when she was surrounded by a group of father figures: men far older than she, some with significant social standing and all related to the Dumas family. These men stood by while Raimond, the most vocal and persuasive of the group, urged her to marry in order to fulfil her father's dying wishes. Perhaps Raimond's motives were guileless, but there was also an economic imperative: Raimond rented that boat from the Girardets, and this marriage would bring it, and half their estate, into the possession of the Dumas family. He glossed over the financial arrangements of the match, including the provisions for her mother, that Gillette was so keen to settle. She was rushed into the decisive exchange of words, and only afterwards could and did she say that she wanted to pause a while before announcing the betrothal. She remembered decorum: that she ought to appear in mourning, and that it was not seemly to celebrate an engagement so soon after a bereavement. She had been caught off her guard, and the Dumas family had taken advantage of her.

In every version of events Gillette made reference to God's will. Both Raimond and Pierre recalled her use of phrases such as, 'if God had ordained it' and 'as God wishes'. Did God want her to marry? Not long after the event, she had made up her mind that He did not; that, in actual fact, she was married to Jesus Christ. When the consistory opened their questions to her by exhorting her 'to live and die in the Christian religion as she has promised to do' it confirmed her intention. At no point in her speech did Gillette stress her right to decide about marriage; for her this was a matter for God to decide. It may well be that this was her heart's conviction.

It could be, however, that her insistence that she was married to Jesus Christ was a deliberate attempt to persuade the consistory to her point of view. It seems that after Gillette had recovered from the absolute rawness of grief, she realized that this engagement was not what she wanted. The consistory had heard, from local rumour, that after the betrothal Gillette had told a female friend that 'she was pressed to marry' Anthoine, and that 'she could not be married to the said Dumas and if she took another then Dumas would not be her husband'. Did Gillette think that if she said she was married to Jesus Christ, she could break off her arrangement with Anthoine? If her appeal to God was an attempt to manipulate the religious authorities, it was in vain: they would brook no such subversion. If she had told them directly that she was 'pressed to marry' Anthoine she may have been on firmer ground: according to Calvinist regulations, engagements had to be made without compulsion, but Gillette never said this before the consistory. Instead, her choice of defence only provoked them: her presumption to know God's will better than they probably prejudiced her case from the start.

The last entry of this case in the registers, on 24 February 1580, is another attempt by Gillette to challenge the evidence given by the witnesses. Unfortunately for her, as all the evidence contradicted her account, the consistory concluded that 'the marriage will be achieved'.[3] By acting quickly while Gillette had been befuddled by grief, the men of the community had successfully manoeuvred to protect their financial interests and to keep valuable resources out of the hands of a young woman. The masterless woman had to be controlled, and the consistory helped them bring her into submission.

~

Most of the women who ever lived left no trace of their existence on the record of history. In Europe in the mid-sixteenth to early seventeenth centuries, it is likely that no more than 5 per cent of women were literate, and they were drawn from the landed elites. Women of the middling and lower levels of society left no letters, diaries, or notebooks in which they expressed what they felt or thought. They had few possessions to bequeath in wills and if married had diminished status under the law. Criminal courts and magistrates kept few records of their testimonies, and no ecclesiastical court records are known to survive for the French Roman Catholic Church between 1540 and 1667. For the most part, we cannot hear the voices of ordinary French women—but this study allows us to hear some: mediated, curtailed, but audible.

The case of Gillette de Girardet is an example of one of more than 1,200 cases brought before the Reformed consistories of Languedoc between 1561 and 1615, on which this book is based. It contains several features in common with a good number of the cases that arrived before the consistories: it pertained to the proper formation of marriage, was concerned with female faith, and involved an attempt to impose Protestant regulations on society. It also demonstrates a universal truth about the consistorial registers: they are unusually rich, for France in this period, in the glimpses they provide into everyday life, and the access they give us to ordinary women's speech, behaviour, and attitudes relating to love, faith, and marriage, as well as friendship and sex. Women appeared frequently before the consistory because one of the chief functions of moral discipline was the regulation of sexuality, and women were thought to be primarily responsible for sexual and other sins. This means that the registers include over a thousand testimonies by and about women, most of whom left no other record to posterity. In responding to charges of spiritual sin or in testifying against others, women offered descriptions of their daily lives and justifications for their behaviour.

Such testimonies are of great value because problems of evidence have dogged attempts to understand the lives of the ordinary people who made up sixteenth- and

---

[3] BN, Ms.fr. 8667, 91r, 92r, 95r, 99v–100r, 101v–102v, 104r, 16 Jan. 1580. A later Antoine Dumas (possibly even the same one) was the lieutenant of the judge at the nearby town of Saint-Gilles, suggesting again the high status of the Dumas family: ADG, Archives notariales, 2 E 1/256, Project de mise en nourrice, 21 May 1613.

seventeenth-century society. Women's voices, in particular, may be searched for in vain in the parish registers, notarial and judicial records, tax rolls, conduct books, and statutes that have constituted most of the evidence available to the historian. Such sources are too formulaic and prescriptive to allow much insight into the behaviour and mentalities of ordinary women—but the consistorial registers allow precisely that. Through them it is possible to explore the mental outlook and lived experience of poor to middling women in Languedoc, examining their actions, thoughts, feelings, motivations, values, beliefs, and strategies, and, in particular, considering their attitudes to, and experience of, gender, sexuality, marriage, and family. This study is concerned, above all, with how women understood their everyday lives, how they talked and thought about events, and how they sought to act when things went wrong. It provides new information about many aspects of social, marital, and sexual culture and also charts, in the gulf between ecclesiastical and popular attitudes, the slow nature of change in mentalities concerning marital and sexual morality.

Women also featured so prominently before the consistories because of an ironic, unintended consequence of the consistorial system: it empowered women. Women quickly learnt how to use the consistory: they denounced those who abused them, they deployed the consistory to force men to honour their promises, and they started rumours they knew would be followed up by the elders. The registers therefore offer unrivalled evidence of women's initiative, in this intensely patriarchal society, in a range of different contexts, such as their enjoyment of their sexuality, choice of marriage partners, or idiosyncratic spiritual engagement. The records testify to women's vociferously executed judgements on fiancés who abandoned them or husbands who failed them, on employers who assaulted them, or on other women who transgressed gender ideals. The consistorial registers, therefore, let us see how independent, self-determining, and vocal women could be in an age when they had limited legal rights, little official power, and few prospects. This is no heroic tale: women's suits were far from always successful, and women were frequently abused and assaulted, forced to do what they did not want to do, and punished for doing that which they did. Nevertheless, this study demands a reconceptualization of female power at this time, suggesting that it consisted not just of hidden, manipulative, and devious influence, but also of a far more public display of power than historians have previously recognized. The stories of the women in these pages reveal how gender was constructed and transformed in the heady days of early Protestantism and, equally strongly, the continuities in gender and social culture in France throughout this period.

The registers of the Reformed churches of Languedoc therefore provide an important new resource for the study of women and gender: new, because while the consistorial records have been used to explore the application of Reformed discipline, they have not been used before to fill the lacunae in the gender history of sixteenth- and seventeenth-century France. The women's voices heard through the consistories are those that appear almost nowhere else, because at the consistory women could initiate cases, as they could not before most criminal courts, and there was no fee to approach the consistory, so it was open to the poor. The survey of the historiography below makes clear how the consistories' witness to ordinary women's marital and sexual experiences greatly adds to existing knowledge.

THE SOURCES

The area under study is the ancient province of Languedoc, bordered by the Rhône river to the east, the Garonne river to the west, the Mediterranean Sea to the south, and the Massif Central, above the Tarn river, to the north. It is roughly equivalent to the modern French departments of Gard, Hérault, Tarn, Tarn-et-Garonne, Aveyron, and Lozère. The landscape and tumultuous history of the region in this period are considered in Chapter 1.

The consistorial records used here are those of ten cities and towns in Languedoc (Map 1, p. xvi), namely: Aimargues (two volumes, 1584–91, 1593–1602), Alès (three volumes, 1599–1612), Bédarieux (two volumes, 1579–86), Ganges (one volume 1588–1609), Meyrueis (one volume, 1587–92), Montauban (one volume, 1596–8), Nîmes (ten volumes, 1561–3, 1578–1615), Pont-de-Camarès (three volumes, 1574–8, 1580–96), Saint-André-de-Sangonis (one volume, 1585–1602), and Saint-Jean-du-Bruel (one volume, 1615). These twenty-five volumes total some 8,728 pages of registers. Among these, the survival of records from two great Protestant cities, Nîmes and Montauban, are especially important. The consistorial registers from Nîmes survive from 1561 to 1685, with the exception of the years 1564–77 (during which time it is possible that, as a result of Catholic restorations, the consistory did not meet), and are not only probably the best surviving collection of consistorial registers in existence but are among the best records of the way common people lived their lives in sixteenth- and seventeenth-century Europe. As such, they are the richest records used in this research, providing an abundance of cases that can be followed through to completion, and illustrating the limits of the possible for a Church at the height of its powers. The one surviving register for Montauban for 1595–8 is even richer in the material it offers, although over a comparatively short period of time; it is a great tragedy for historians that other registers from Montauban have not survived. The range of consistorial material from all the towns has provided an adequate check that the evidence from Nîmes is neither aberrant nor untypical, even if the consistory there was more consistently regular in meeting and loquacious in notation than most.

In an effort to join up the dots—to follow the threads of cases and people's lives as far as possible beyond the consistorial registers—I have turned to a number of other records in support of the consistorial research, with some satisfying and useful results. These have included evidence from the regional Protestant synods of Bas Languedoc (1561–82, 1596–1609) and the Reformed Church's national synods. For Bédarieux, I examined the Protestant baptismal and marriage register for 1574–1622. For Montauban, I read the deliberations of the consuls in Montauban for 1595 (they do not survive for 1596–1601), and the register of sentences pronounced in criminal matters by the town consuls of Montauban (1534–1606). For Nîmes, I examined the three Protestant baptismal and marriage registers covering

1571 to 1616. The register before 1571 no longer survives (in September 1604 Jeanne Marqueze returned from Provence and Orange, saying that she had been born in Nîmes, and the consistory noted that 'the book of baptisms from the time she was born has been burnt').[4] I also looked at the records of eight notaries in Nîmes (where possible choosing known Protestants) to find wills and marriage contracts, namely: Jean Ursi *le Jeune* (1582–1610), Michel Ursi (1595–1602), Jean Corniaret (1591–1615), Marcelin Bruguier (1591–6, 1608–15), Robert Restaurand (1580–2), Jacques Ursi (1561–79), Jean Mombel (1560–82), and Jean Guiran (1594–1615). I drew on Nîmes's civil council registers for 1559–1615 (although the years 1595–9 are missing), and on the communal archives, including documents relating to the religious troubles (1562–83, 1585–93), communal administration (1559–64), the policing of town (1586–1612), acts and contracts (1561–80), political acts (1613–15), and accounts of municipal and extraordinary spending. I spent some time with the criminal records of the council (1606–9) and the *sénéschal* court (from 1610), but they were haphazard, disorganized, and often barely legible (the first started at both ends, with later cases squeezed onto any remaining squares of parchment): a finer palaeographer than I pretend to be will have to brave these one day. Ultimately, however, I became aware that the testimony within them included very little material relating to the lives of women, which is unsurprising as the value of the consistorial records lies, at least in part, in the inclusion of, and comparative respect given, to women's testimonies.[5]

The temporal parameters for the study were chosen to reflect the period generating the richest source material. For the sixteenth century, the extant records of the consistories tend to date from the last three decades, following the founding of the Reformed Church in France in 1559. Despite the continuation of the Nîmes registers until 1685, Philippe Chareyre—the only scholar to date to work on the registers from 1561 through to 1685—concluded that 1578–1614 was the 'golden age of censure among Southern French Protestants'.[6] While it is hard to quantify change, there does appear to have been a decline in the quality of investigations into moral transgressions of a graver nature in the years after 1615, which has an effect upon the richness of the consistorial registers as source material.[7]

---

[4] ADG, 42 J 32, 250v, 3 Sept. 1604.

[5] Paul Ourliac, *Histoire du droit privé français de l'an mil au Code Civil* (Paris, 1985), 271; Ian Maclean, *The Renaissance Notion of Woman: A Study in the Fortunes of Scholasticism and Medical Science in European Intellectual Life* (Cambridge, 1980), 78; François Lebrun, *La vie conjugale sous l'Ancien Régime* (Paris, 1975), 79; Zoe A. Schneider, 'Women before the Bench: Female Litigants in Early Modern Normandy', *FHS* 23.1 (2000), 1–32, here 25.

[6] Philippe Chareyre, '"The Great Difficulties One Must Bear to Follow Jesus Christ": Morality at Sixteenth Century Nîmes', in *Sin and the Calvinists: Morals Control and the Consistory in the Reformed Tradition*, ed. Raymond A. Mentzer (Kirksville, MO, 1994), 64–5. See also Chareyre, *Le consistoire de Nîmes de 1561 à 1685*, 4 vols (Thèse de Doctorat d'État en Histoire: Université Paul-Valéry-Montpellier III, 1987); Solange Bertheau, 'Le consistoire dans les Églises Réformées du Moyen-Poitou au XVIIe Siècle', *BSHPF* 116 (1970), 332–59 and 513–49, here 527; Raymond A. Mentzer, 'Marking the Taboo: Excommunication in French Reformed Churches', in *Sin and the Calvinists: Morals Control and the Consistory in the Reformed Tradition*, ed. Raymond A. Mentzer (Kirksville, MO, 1994), 100.

[7] Chareyre attempts to list the number of cases before the consistory and finds for cases of sexuality and marriage this decline: 1585–94: 424 cases; 1595–1604: 293; 1604–14: 286; 1615–24: 151;

The consistory was at the heart of the local establishment of the Reformed Church, operating as the governing body of the Protestant Church but also acting in turns as an ecclesiastical tribunal, social mediator, and even marriage counsellor. Janine Garrisson-Estèbe suggested that 'the history of the French Protestant churches is also that of their consistories'.[8] The consistory was charged with imposing moral discipline on Protestant society, and material drawn from its cases naturally has an inherent bias towards transgressive and broken relationships. Such tales do not permit any claims of universality. Yet the moments of social breakdown represented by these cases, whether marital quarrels, illegitimate pregnancies, broken engagements, or malicious gossip, provide a window on to the attitudes of common people towards gender relations, sexuality, married life, and social networks.

Any information about women's lives gleaned from these registers has potentially been distorted by its transfer to posterity via the ministers, elders, and scribes of the consistories. The registers were shaped by the preoccupations, practices, and attitudes of those who made them. By defining what made it into the records, these concerns and procedures mediate women's words and lives to historians. The consistory is our constant companion: the window through which we behold and apprehend their world. To read the consistorial records is to be constantly drawn towards the consistory's obsessions and motivations: to examine the life of the interrogated one must read relentlessly against the grain. (It is surely for this reason that many scholars have used the consistories to write primarily about the ecclesiastical discipline itself, looking at the mentalities of the interrogators, not the interrogated.) Before attempting to analyse the insights found within the registers, it seems helpful, therefore, to read along the grain, and to consider the priorities, practices, and patriarchal attitudes of the consistory in recognition of the fact that these discourses construct a prism through which our understanding of women's lives is refracted. Chapter 2 explores the nature of the discipline, the Protestant moral code, and the consistory, including the Reformed perspective on women, as the backdrop for understanding the evidence used to examine women's lives in Chapters 3–7. At this stage, however, a word or two about the records themselves may be helpful.

Written on parchment and bound in vellum, the consistorial records were kept by scribes appointed for that purpose (Fig. I.1, p. 9). These men were often notaries, and legal language and devices intermittently shape the texts. Some had fine secretary hands, others were more scrawling and harder to decipher. They were among the most literate men in their society but by modern standards their literacy and eloquence leaves something to be desired. Pierre de la Barthe, for example, the royal notary who acted as scribe for the consistory in Montauban, wrote in a nice,

---

1624–34: 140; 1635–44: 53—suggesting a clear alteration around 1615 (*Le consistoire*, 20). The difficulties of compiling reliable statistics from the registers are considered below.

[8] Janine Garrison-Estèbe, *Les protestants du Midi, 1559–1598* (Toulouse, 1980), 92; Michael F. Graham, *The Uses of Reform: 'Godly Discipline' and Popular Behaviour in Scotland and Beyond, 1560–1610* (New York, 1996), 10–12.

Fig. I.1. Consistorial register for Nîmes 1595–1602, bound in vellum, *Registre des délibérations du consistoire de Nîmes, 1595–1602*, Archives départementales du Gard, 42 J 31, exterior

clear hand, but used no punctuation at all (see Fig. 6.1, p. 238). A common problem is that the subject of the verbs varies over the course of a sentence and it is often difficult to tell to whom a pronoun refers.

The consistories were conducted and transcribed in French. Emmanuel Le Roy Ladurie has charted the diffusion of French across the south by this period, arguing

that in Montpellier, for example, French was in general use by 1490.[9] In Montauban
in July 1595 a Spanish monk called Pierre Cardonne, who wanted to enter the
Protestant ministry, was told that he could not until he spoke French properly.[10]
Nevertheless, this was a French infused with Occitan, the language of the Languedoc.
Whole sentences are given in Occitan, as are countless individual words, as if the
Occitan word had infiltrated into daily French. These are listed in the glossary in
Appendix I, and mostly relate to quotidian, agricultural life, such *abeurador*
(a watering-place for livestock), *canebièra* (a hemp field), *capitèl* (a hut in a vineyard),
clapàs (a pile of stones), *mas* (a farm), *passadoire* (a sieve), and *prat* (a meadow), or
people's nicknames and insults, as can be seen in Chapters 1 and 3. Certain phrases
and idioms indicate the process of direct, 'live' transcription, although the scribes
hastily transferred testimonies into the third person. Although both rough and clean
copies of the consistorial minutes were probably made, with the exception of some
town council records from Nîmes (those from 1594–5) only fair copies survive of
all the manuscripts under study.[11]

HISTORIOGRAPHICAL OVERVIEW: WOMEN
IN EARLY MODERN FRANCE

There is surprisingly little scholarship on the behaviour, motivations, and beliefs of
women of the lower and middling levels of society in France in the late sixteenth
and early seventeenth centuries. The primary focus of scholarship has hitherto
been elite women and the structures of society, accessed primarily through prescriptive literature, such as literary and legal sources, and through notarial records.
Such material does not easily lend itself to recreating the narratives of ordinary
women. These narratives are important because they help balance out a picture of
French society that would otherwise be distorted in favour of the very different
world of the rich, powerful, and literate. They also, as Lyndal Roper found for
women's narratives arising out of witch-trials, allow us access into how women saw
sexual difference and how they made sense of their lives.[12] Scholarship on the episcopal and secular courts has allowed greater access to such narratives, but the late
sixteenth and early seventeenth centuries, while by no means entirely untouched,
have not been the subject of nearly as much analysis as either the late fifteenth
to early sixteenth centuries or, especially, the later seventeenth and eighteenth
centuries, largely because of an apparent lack of surviving records. In the light of
the overview that follows, it is evident that an analysis of the consistorial records

---

[9] Emmanuel Le Roy Ladurie, *Les paysans de Languedoc*, 2 vols (Paris, 1966), 169–70. Note that
Philip Conner concludes somewhat differently that French had made inroads into southern France
by the mid-sixteenth century, but that most people still predominantly spoke their mother tongue of
Occitan: *Huguenot Heartland: Montauban and Southern French Calvinism during the Wars of Religion*
(St Andrews, 2002).
[10] ADTG, I 1, 12r, 5 Jul. 1595.
[11] As suggested by Raymond Mentzer in conversation, 6 June 2006.
[12] Lyndal Roper, *Oedipus and the Devil: Witchcraft, Sexuality and Religion in Early Modern Europe*
(London and New York, 1994), 20.

of 1560 to 1615 to examine the behaviour and mentalities of low-status females could therefore substantially increase our understanding of the social realities of poor French women.

The doyenne of studies of gender and society in sixteenth-century France is Natalie Zemon Davis. Whether demonstrating how to read ritualized violence, carnivalesque disorder, pardon narratives in the letters of remission, a celebrated case of imposture, or a range of other issues, Davis has almost flawlessly reconstructed aspects of the religious, economic, and social lives of early modern women (though she has not been entirely without critics; see, for example, Robert Finlay, 'The Refashioning of Martin Guerre').[13] For a long time the stature of this pioneer, who seemed to have said it all, cast a shadow over continuing scholarship on gender and society in sixteenth-century France. A number of synthetic works further created the impression of completeness. Most notable among them were the five-volume *Histoire de la vie privée*, edited by Georges Duby and Philippe Ariès and another five-volume work, *Histoire des femmes en Occident*, written under the direction of Georges Duby and Michelle Perrot, with the volume on the sixteenth to eighteenth centuries edited by Davis and Arlette Farge.[14] Both collections of essays look at women's roles, powers, words, silence, representations, and relations although, as is the nature of overviews, minimal evidence is cited. Other similar works reinforced this impression of totality. Wendy Gibson's *Women in Seventeenth-Century France*, which is based on sources such as memoirs, *livres de raison* (commonplace books), and correspondence, offered (unproblematically) a picture true only to noblewomen's lives, while Danielle Haase-Dubosc and Eliane Viennot's 1991 volume sought to examine women in politics, law, religion, work, and the family over a broad sweep of time, from the sixteenth through to the eighteenth centuries.[15] More recently, Sharon Kettering and Mack P. Holt included good summary chapters on women, marriage, and the family in their surveys of Reformation France, while Susan Broomhall's study of *Women and Religion in Sixteenth-Century France* brought together some of her own archival research on female religious participation with the findings of existing secondary literature.[16] Despite its other merits, however, Broomhall's work assumes that poor women would have been unable to

---

[13] Natalie Zemon Davis, *Society and Culture in Early Modern Europe* (Cambridge, 1987), esp. 'The Rites of Violence', 'The Reasons of Misrule', 'Women on Top', and 'City Women and Religious Change'; *Fiction in the Archives: Pardon Tellers and Their Tales in Sixteenth Century France* (Stanford, 1987); *The Return of Martin Guerre* (Cambridge, MA, 1983); 'Ghosts, Kin and Progeny: Some Features of Family Life in Early Modern France', *Daedalus, Journal of the American Academy of Arts and Sciences* 106 (1977), 87–114; 'Women in the Crafts in Sixteenth-Century Lyon', *Feminist Studies* 8.1 (1982), 47–80; Robert Finlay, 'The Refashioning of Martin Guerre', *American Historical Review* 93.3 (1988), 553–71.

[14] Philippe Ariès and Georges Duby (eds), *Histoire de la vie privée*, 5 vols (Paris, 1985–7), vol. 3, Ariès et al., *De la Renaissance aux Lumières* (Paris, 1986); Georges Duby and Michelle Perrot (eds), *Histoire des femmes en Occident*, 5 vols (Paris, 1991–2), vol. 3, *XVIe–XVIIIe siècles*, ed. Davis and Arlette Farge (1991).

[15] Wendy Gibson, *Women in Seventeenth-Century France* (Basingstoke, 1989); Danielle Haase-Dubosc and Eliane Viennot (eds), *Femmes et pouvoirs sous l'Ancien Régime* (Paris, 1991).

[16] Sharon Kettering, *French Society 1589–1715* (Harlow, 2001), chs 1 and 2; Barbara B. Diefendorf 'Gender and the Family', in *Renaissance and Reformation France 1500–1648*, ed. Mack Holt (Oxford, 2002); Susan Broomhall, *Women and Religion in Sixteenth-Century France* (Basingstoke, 2006).

offer resistance to male ecclesiastical authorities—consistorial evidence suggests, very strongly, that this assumption is mistaken.[17] The idea that French women in this period have been comprehensively studied is misleading; there are still significant lacunae in our knowledge of the social realities experienced by women of the lower orders.[18]

Perhaps because of Davis's prominence, and undoubtedly also, as we shall see, as a reflection of the available source material, there are relatively few monographs on French women, gender, marriage, sexuality, or family for the sixteenth and early seventeenth centuries. Some of the best known (and oldest) focus their attention on demography, including Philippe Ariès's pioneer work, which argued that modern concepts of childhood, family sentiment, and structure did not exist in the medieval period, and Jean-Louis Flandrin's 1976 study of families, kinship, and households, where he charted important demographic trends such as the size and structure of families and their change over time.[19] Flandrin admitted that his work on attitudes and emotions was drawn mainly from prescriptive literature.[20] Similarly, François Lebrun drew on a mixture of demography and legal and ecclesiastical prescriptive sources to sketch key features of courtship, marriage, and sexuality.[21] René Pillorget's *La tige et le rameau* used extensive research on parish registers, notarial and judicial records, letters, conduct books, and literary works to produce a picture of marriage, household, patrimony, and family in France and England over the sixteenth to eighteenth centuries.[22] Like Pillorget, many French studies, including Lebrun and Flandrin's, consider a long period of history and have a tendency to conflate the findings of several centuries.[23] In practice this often means that eighteenth-century or nineteenth-century customs are projected back, which can create misleading assumptions about social relations in earlier periods. This is also the case with Claude Grimmer's investigation of prostitution, illicit love, and bastardy in France from the fourteenth to eighteenth centuries. Grimmer's study of illicit sexuality and illegitimacy derives from late seventeenth- and eighteenth-century norms, does not chart regional variation, and particularly focuses on the nobility and legal history.[24]

---

[17] Broomhall, *Women*, 44.

[18] As also commented by Scarlett Beauvalet-Boutouyrie in her *Etre veuve sous l'Ancien Régime* (Paris, 2001), 13.

[19] Ariès, Philippe, *L'enfant et la vie familiale sous l'Ancien Régime* (Paris, 1960); Jean-Louis Flandrin, *Familles: parenté, maison, sexualité dans l'ancienne société* (Paris, 1976), and *Les amours paysannes (XVIe–XIXe siècle): amour et sexualité dans les campagnes de l'ancienne France* (Paris, 1975)—a collection of edited texts annotated by Flandrin.

[20] Primarily Catholic moralists, Flandrin, *Familles*, 138–9.   [21] Lebrun, *La vie conjugale*.

[22] René Pillorget, *La tige et le rameau: familles anglaises et française 16e–18e siècle* (Paris, 1979).

[23] This is taken further in Martine Segalen's *Mari et femme dans la société paysanne* (Paris, 1980), which focused on peasant matrimonial life in nineteenth-century France very consciously in the light of what it could say about the twentieth century (9). Using ahistorical sources such as folklorist accounts and popular proverbs, Segalen argues that peasant society was based upon systems of production and only changed when they did, so her findings could be applied to previous centuries, despite hugely significant differences in the characteristics of the periods, for example, the average age at marriage.

[24] Claude Grimmer, *La femme et le bâtard: amours illégitimes et secrètes dans l'ancienne France* (Paris, 1983).

There have been several significant articles using prescriptive material to focus attention on social structures, drawing on literary, legal, and notarial sources. Aspects of customary laws, especially inheritance customs in various parts of France, were analysed by Emmanuel Le Roy Ladurie and Robert Wheaton.[25] Barbara B. Diefendorf used Parisian customary law and notarial documents to consider sixteenth-century widowhood in legal and economic terms.[26] Sarah Hanley's articles examining the royal legislation on clandestine marriage of 1556–1639 charted the important expansion of secular jurisdiction over marriage arrangements in this period, the enhancement of male power over women and children, and the compact between the family and the state in order to maintain the 'patriarchal hegemony' upon which both were based.[27] Notarial records were also used by Alain Collomp to outline the system of lineage, inheritance, and succession among the peasantry of the mountains of Haute-Provence, and by Annik Pardailhé-Galabrun, who studied Parisian households through the evidence of notarial inventories.[28] Most successfully, Davis, J. B. Collins, and Carol L. Loats used tax rolls, apprenticeship and service contracts, and other notarial evidence to examine women's economic importance and work identities in the sixteenth and seventeenth centuries.[29] There are also a number of articles that focus primarily on the experience of elite women. Among others, Roelker's classic studies exposed the role played by French noblewomen in fomenting Calvinism, Joan Davies explored the centrality of marriage in aristocratic family strategies, and Kristen B. Neuschel examined the ways in which noblewomen participated in warfare.[30]

Monographs have also, for the most part, maintained a focus on structures and elite women. Evelyne Berriot-Salvadore used literary sources, legal texts, wills, letters, and *livres de raison* to give an overview of the image and status of Renaissance

[25] Emmanuel Le Roy Ladurie, 'Système de la coutume: structures familiales et coutumes d'héritage en France au XVIe siècle', *Annales E.S.C.* 4–5 (1972), 825–46; Robert Wheaton, 'Affinity and Descent in Seventeenth-Century Bordeaux', in *Family and Sexuality in French History*, ed. Wheaton and Tamara K. Hareven (Philadelphia, PA, 1980).

[26] Barbara B. Diefendorf, 'Widowhood and Remarriage in Sixteenth-Century Paris', *Journal of Family History* 7 (1982), 379–95.

[27] Sarah Hanley, 'Family and State in Early Modern France: The Marriage Pact', in *Connecting Spheres: Women in the Western World, 1500 to the Present*, ed. Arilyn J. Boxer and Jean H. Quataert (New York and Oxford, 1987), and 'Engendering the State: Family Formation and State Building in Early Modern France', *FHS* 16 (1989), 4–27, here 15.

[28] Alain Collomp, *La maison du père: famille et village en Haute-Provence aux XVIIe et XVIIIe siècles* (Paris, 1983); Annik Pardailhé-Galabrun, *La naissance de l'intime: 3000 foyers parisiens XVIIe–XVIIIe siècles* (Paris, 1988).

[29] Loats and Davis disagree on the extent to which women had a role beyond the production of the household. Davis, 'Women in the Crafts'; J. B. Collins, 'The Economic Role of Women in Seventeenth-Century France', *FHS* 16 (1989), 436–70; Carol L. Loats, 'Gender, Guilds and Work Identity in Sixteenth-Century Paris', *FHS* 20.1 (1997), 15–30.

[30] Nancy L. Roelker, 'The Appeal of Calvinism to French Noblewomen in the Sixteenth Century', *JIH* 2.4 (1972), 391–418; Joan Davies, 'The Politics of the Marriage Bed', *French History* 6 (1992), 63–95; Kristen B. Neuschel, 'Noblewomen and War in Sixteenth-Century France', in *Changing Identities in Early Modern France*, ed. Michael Wolfe (Durham and London, 1996); see also Gayle K. Brunelle, 'Dangerous Liaisons: Mésalliance and Early Modern French Noblewomen', *FHS* 19 (1995), 75–103; and Sharon Kettering, 'The Patronage Power of Early Modern French Noblewomen', *Historical Journal* 32 (1989), 817–41 and 'The Household Service of Early Modern French Noblewomen', *FHS* 20.1 (1997), 67–78.

women, and their education, religion, and involvement in medicine, charity, and the literary world.[31] Information relating to women below the rank of merchants is scant, with the primary focus on highborn women, including grand dames such as Charlotte Duplessis-Mornay. This focus is maintained in Elizabeth Rapley's consideration of the role of women in the post-Tridentine Catholic Church of seventeenth-century France.[32] Rapley's history of the establishment and development of female congregations is also necessarily concerned more with structures than the narratives of the women involved.

By contrast, Scarlett Beauvalet-Boutouyrie's 1983 study of widowhood explicitly pointed out that knowledge of social realities for women was still insufficient. At least trying not to focus just on the elite, she used legal and literary texts and notarial records to consider the status, image, and role of widows and their legal and economic realities in Paris in the late seventeenth and eighteenth centuries.[33] Julie Hardwick also used notarial archives, together with judicial and parish records, to examine notaries and their households in Nantes in 1550–1650.[34] She considered the social functions of notaries and the nature of their households, including household management, property transmission, patterns of local sociability, and the daily practice of patriarchy. Unfortunately her source material, which drove her to focus primarily on structures, led to limited analysis of how this daily modification to the 'practice of patriarchy' played out, and while she states that she is looking at 'middling' families, they are in fact wealthy, with an average dowry of 2,000 *livres*.[35] Hardwick's thesis was that in practice patriarchy did not mean the exercise of power solely by men, and that authority in notarial households was shared, negotiated, and contested, with women's authority augmented by their contributions to family income. She states that by looking at daily interactions she has uncovered the complexity of forms that gender relations took as a result of day-to-day negotiations and demands, but contrasts apparent examples of 'complexity', such as women managing servants or the existence of solidarities between women, servants, and children 'who were all subordinated' with 'simple patriarchal oppression'.[36] As such, she works with a conventional concept of patriarchy, where patriarchy is

---

[31] Evelyne Berriot-Salvadore, *Les femmes dans la société française de la Renaissance* (Geneva, 1990); elites are the focus too in Carolyn Lougée, *Le paradis des femmes. Women, Salons and Social Stratification in Seventeenth-Century France* (Princeton, 1976); Sonja Kmec, *Noblewomen and Family Fortunes in Seventeenth-Century France and England: A Study of the Lives of the Duchesse de La Trémoïlle and her Sister-in-Law, the Countess of Derby* (D.Phil. thesis, University of Oxford, 2004).

[32] Elizabeth Rapley, *The Dévotes: Women and Church in Seventeenth-Century France* (London, 1990).

[33] Beauvalet-Boutouyrie, *Etre veuve*.

[34] Julie Hardwick, *The Practice of Patriarchy: Gender and the Politics of Household Authority in Early Modern France* (University Park, PA, 1998).

[35] Hardwick states that the average cash value of their dowries was 2,000 *livres* (58), compared with Tulchin's figures of 1,200 *livres* for the richest in Nîmes (seigneurs and judges), 900 *livres* for lawyers; 200 *livres* for wealthy merchants, and so on. Tulchin suggests that anyone with a dowry of 200 *livres* or above in sixteenth-century Nîmes was wealthy, see Tulchin, *That Men*, 21–2. Farr's finds dowries of 350 *livres* for master artisans and 135 *livres* for journeymen in Dijon, see James R. Farr, *Hands of Honor: Artisans and their World in Dijon, 1550–1650* (Ithaca, NY and London, 1988), 96. Dowries for the women I consider were often considerably smaller than this, see Chapter 4.

[36] Hardwick, *Practice*, ix, 87–90, 93.

an oppressive male system that women confront. Even though Hardwick opines that 'women could also hold each other responsible for keeping certain standards' (although this is unsupported by evidence and is later undermined by her suggestion that neighbours did not intervene in each other's domestic affairs), she does not consider what impact this could have on her definition of patriarchy. By contrast, my work suggests that the way women challenged patriarchy in the sixteenth and seventeenth centuries was as much a part of their participation in it as the ways in which they strengthened it, and that the successful maintenance of patriarchy among the Protestants of southern France relied on these challenges, as much as on women's collaboration with and inculcation of male domination, privilege, and control.

In the light of this difference of approach, it seems helpful to explain at this juncture how 'patriarchy' and 'gender' are conceptualized in this study. There has been debate about how useful 'patriarchy' is as an analytical category.[37] Early feminist use of the term has been criticized for suggesting an implacable, monolithic, and ahistorical oppressive ideological system in which the male domination of women is static, inflexible, and universal.[38] Sheila Rowbotham argued that the term 'patriarchy' is imprecise because it 'obscures the multiplicity of ways in which societies have defined gender' by returning us to biology.[39] The term has been discredited for making men into the enemy or oppressor, suggesting that patriarchy relies on men's consistent desire to dominate women, and obscuring how men and women work together to mutual benefit, and are reciprocally dependent.[40] Finally, it has been thought to focus more on women's oppression than their agency—their ability to act on their own behalf.[41]

In fact 'patriarchy' needs to be understood not as an external force imposed on women, but rather a dynamic process, involving both men and women, in which meanings are continually constructed and reshaped, constantly subject to change, and varied in form.[42] Here 'patriarchy' is, therefore, defined as a social system in which maleness and masculinity convey unearned privilege, which manifests itself in structural difference, so that men dominate in positions of power, rule, and influence, in cultural values and norms that favour men and masculinity, and in an obsessive control of women, who might otherwise threaten male privilege.[43]

---

[37] Anthony Fletcher, *Gender, Sex and Subordination in England 1500–1800* (New Haven, CT, 1995), xv–xvi; Anne Cranny-Francis, Wendy Waring, Pam Stavropoulous, and Joan Kirkby, *Gender Studies: Terms and Debates* (Basingstoke, 2003), 14–17; Michael Roper and John Tosh (eds), *Manful Assertions: Masculinity in Britain since 1800* (London and New York, 1991), 7–11; Sheila Rowbotham, 'The Trouble with Patriarchy' and Sally Alexander and Barbara Taylor, 'In Defence of "Patriarchy"', both in *People's History and Socialist Theory*, ed. Raphael Samuel (London, 1981); Joan Acker, 'The Problem with Patriarchy', *Sociology* 23.2 (1989), 235–40.

[38] An example of this early use is K. Millet, *Sexual Politics* (London, 1977). For a critique, see Rowbotham, 'The Trouble', 365; Roper and Tosh reject the term except to indicate 'father-rule'.

[39] Rowbotham, 'The Trouble', 365.

[40] Cranny-Francis et al., *Gender Studies*, 15; Rowbotham, 'The Trouble', 365–6; Fletcher, *Gender*, xvi.

[41] J. M. Bennett, 'Feminism and History', *Gender and History* 1 (1989), 251–72, here 259–63; Rowbotham, 'The Trouble', 365.

[42] Allan G. Johnson, *The Gender Knot: Unraveling our Patriarchal Legacy* (Philadelphia, PA, 2005), esp. 42–4; Bennett, 'Feminism and History', 251–72, esp. 259–63.

[43] Johnson, *Gender Knot*, 5, 6, 10, 14; Cranny-Francis et al., 15.

Patriarchy needs to be recognized as a cultural system in which both men and women participate and participated. The term 'participation' covers a whole range of ways in which women and men take part, whether through inculcation, collusion, or resistance—it therefore includes variance, both active domination by men and male uncertainty and unease about domination, and women colluding in patriarchy, as well as resisting it.[44] As Judith Bennett has pointed out, the dichotomy between women as victims under patriarchy and as self-directed agents is a false one.[45] In this way, use of the term 'patriarchy' should not be thought to minimize female agency or the nuanced nature of intra- and cross-gender interactions. In the sixteenth century, patriarchy was premised upon ideas about the subordination of women as a function of women's 'natural' physical and mental inferiority.

Gender is understood as the 'social organization of sexual difference'.[46] With Roper, it is recognized that sexual difference does have its own physiological and psychological reality, but there is also a very significant role played by social construction, where the dynamic meanings of biological differences—and with them the opportunities and experiences open to men and women—are established in each culture, social group, or epoch.[47] The work of gender historians is to examine how these meanings are produced and transformed across different situations in time. There remains a need for work on how the social organization of sexual difference in France in this period affected the lives of poor women, and in particular how this sexual difference was understood by these women.[48] This is especially interesting among the Calvinists in France in the late sixteenth century as some historians have identified the Reformation as a period exhibiting a crisis in men's control over women.[49] How gender hierarchy and meaning were constructed and legitimized in the early days of French Protestantism helps provide another answer to the question of the impact of the Reformation on women. The construction of gender is done primarily through challenge and response—the consistory's interactions with women were therefore the site of its construction.[50] Examining these interactions allows us to explore how gender was produced and transformed in this specific situation. The decision to focus on women's lives in this volume is not intended to suggest that the best way of studying gender is to examine women's and men's experiences separately nor to emphasize women's particularity in contrast to the universal experience of male subjects. It is simply a response to the sheer quantity (and quality) of material under study. In fact the chapters that follow focus very much on relations between women and men. What this study does not do, however, is explicitly examine ideas of maleness and masculinity in Protestant French communities, although there is much material here for study.[51]

---

[44] Johnson, *Gender Knot*, 29, 34, 43, 44.   [45] Bennett, 'Feminism and History', 262.
[46] Joan Wallach Scott, *Gender and the Politics of History* (New York, 1988); see also Scott, 'Gender: A Useful Category of Historical Analysis', *American Historical Review* 91 (1986), 1053–75.
[47] Roper, *Oedipus*, 4–5; Scott, *Gender*, 2, 5.   [48] Roper, *Oedipus*, 16, 19–20.
[49] Fletcher, *Gender*, xvi; Roper, *Oedipus*, 37–9.   [50] Scott, *Gender*, 5.
[51] Recent work on this area of research includes Scott H. Hendrix and Susan C. Karant-Nunn (eds), *Masculinity in the Reformation Era* (Kirksville, MO, 2008).

The works considered so far have provided an overview of the legal and theoretical framework for women's lives, good statistical analyses of demographic trends, insight into the lives of elite women, and in-depth knowledge of structures such as lineage and inheritance customs, but their sources are generally too formulaic and prescriptive to allow much insight into the mentalities or intentional behaviour of poorer women.[52] Such insight is important if we are to start to understand how such women experienced the world. As we have seen, illiteracy rates, especially for women, make diaries and letters from those of the lower sort rare, and the 'ego-literature' that survives from this period relates almost exclusively to the higher levels of society. Nevertheless, some historians have started to uncover the lives, narratives, and strategies of the lower classes: Davis used the letters of remission to access 'relatively uninterrupted narrative from the lips of the lower orders' and explored the narratives used by women in their pleas for pardon.[53] Broomhall has produced exciting analyses of the administrative records of municipal poor relief, including pauper letters from female supplicants.[54] Looking at the late seventeenth and eighteenth centuries, Georg'Ann Cattelona used the complaints and witness reports in the records of the *Hôpital du Refuge* in Marseille, where the city incarcerated disorderly women, to examine women's roles in regulating the sexual behaviour of others.[55]

There are two other categories of sources where historians have got close to hearing the voices of women of the lower orders: use of the *déclarations de grossesse* (declarations of pregnancy), and evidence from the *officialités* (Catholic episcopal tribunals) and lower criminal courts. Marie-Claude Phan and Jacques Depauw, among others, have studied the *déclarations de grossesse*—official statements made before municipal consuls by unmarried women pregnant with illegitimate children.[56] Although pertinent because often made by poor women (Phan finds that 70 per cent of deponents whose occupations are recorded were servants), these statements were very formulaic, and so scholarship has focused on the legal history of the *déclarations*,

---

[52] A problem identified by Robin Briggs, who pointed out the difficulty of using prescriptive Catholic material such as episcopal ordinances, confessors' manuals, works of devotion, and sermons, produced by those distanced from practical realities, as evidence of family behaviour, 'The Church and Family in Seventeenth-Century France', in *Communities of Belief: Cultural and Social Tension in Early Modern France* (Oxford, 1989), 236.

[53] Davis, *Fiction*, 5; cf. Arlette Farge and Michel Foucault (eds), *Le désordre des familles: lettres de cachet des archives de la Bastille aux XVIIIe siècle* (Paris, 1982). Davis also found some references to women's versions of their family history, blending sentiment and fact, in the *Livres de Raison*, but these exist only for higher-born women, 'Ghosts', 99.

[54] Susan Broomhall, '"Burdened with Small Children": Women Defining Poverty in Sixteenth-Century Tours', in *Women's Letters Across Europe, 1400–1700: Form and Persuasion*, ed. Jane Couchman and Ann Crabb (Aldershot, 2005), 'Understanding Household Limitation Strategies among the Sixteenth-Century Urban Poor in France', *French History* 20.2 (2006), 121–37 and 'Identity and Life Narratives among the Poor in Later Sixteenth-Century Tours', *Renaissance Quarterly* 57 (2004), 439–65.

[55] Georg'Ann Cattelona, 'Control and Collaboration: The Role of Women in Regulating Female Sexual Behaviour in Early Modern Marseille', *FHS* 18 (1993), 13–35.

[56] Marie-Claude Phan, 'Les déclarations de grossesse en France (XVIe–XVIIIe siecles): essai institutionnel', *Revue d'Histoire Moderne et Contemporaine* 22 (1975), 61–88 and *Les amours illégitimes: histoires de séduction en Languedoc (1676–1786)* (Paris, 1986); Jacques Depauw, 'Amour illégitime et société à Nantes au XVIII siècle', *Annales E.S.C.* 4–5 (1972), 1155–82; also Grimmer, *La femme*.

quantification, and, most interestingly, some analysis of circumstances in which the unmarried women became pregnant.[57] In addition, although as Phan notes *déclarations* were encouraged by the edict of 1556, the earliest surviving series of *déclarations* date from the 1640s, and most from the 1660s, leaving lacunae for the period under study.[58]

Records from the *officialités* have been consulted by a handful of historians. From 1556 royal legislation gave secular courts control over some aspects of marriage, especially forced or secret marriages, abductions, and property questions.[59] Contested separations were usually handled by the secular courts, and when it came to attempts to enforce promises of marriage, litigants seem to have found it effective to use the lower criminal courts and allege *rapt* (forceful abduction or seduction with the intention to marry without parental approval). However, the *officialités* continued to function for most people as the jurisdiction for obtaining dispensations for the prohibited degrees, cases where impotence was alleged, annulments, and formal separations—at least where humbler people were concerned—and where the parties were in agreement. This means that in principle, despite the reduction in their powers, the *officialités* ought to be an excellent source for attitudes and behaviour, and comparable, in the nature of the evidence, with the Reformed consistory. There has, however, been very poor record survival, and it is notable that three of the most prominent historians of the *officialités* have used the same source material: the records of the ecclesiastical tribunal of Troyes. André Burguière used these records to consider the rituals of marriage formation in 1480 to 1540, arguing that distinctions between popular and religious ritual can be easily over-emphasized.[60] Beatrice Gottlieb, examining cases in Troyes and Châlons-sur-Marne for 1455–94, considered the various meanings of 'clandestine marriage', while Jacques Solé has written an important book that investigates the behaviour, attitudes, and strategies of humble women at the turn of the sixteenth century, providing some scope for comparison between those before Reformed consistories and those in Catholic France—albeit for an earlier period.[61] As Burguière—who uses the *officialité* records up to 1540 and then again from 1667—makes clear, there is a gap in these records from the mid-sixteenth century to the mid-seventeenth century. In other areas where fragments of *officialité* records survive, they tend to be for the eighteenth century only. Alain Lottin has studied cases from the diocese of Cambrai in the late seventeenth and eighteenth centuries,

[57] Phan, *Les amours illégitimes*, 32, 43, 44; Depauw records 40 per cent of women as domestic servants, but notes only 18 per cent gave other occupations, 'Amour illégitime'.

[58] Phan, 'Les déclarations', 61, 65, 68, 69, 72.

[59] Hanley, 'Engendering the State', 9; Alain Lottin, 'Vie et mort du couple: difficultés conjugales et divorces dans le Nord de la France aux XVIIe et XVIII siècles', *XVIIe siècle* 102–3 (1974), 59–78, here 59–61; Julie Hardwick, 'Seeking Separations: Gender, Marriages, and Household Economies in Early Modern France', *FHS* 21.1 (1998), 157–80, here 159.

[60] André Burguière, 'Le rituel du marriage en France: pratiques ecclesiastiques et pratiques populaires', *Annales: E.S.C.* 33 (1978), 637–48.

[61] Beatrice Gottlieb, 'The Meaning of Clandestine Marriage', in *Family and Sexuality*, ed. Robert Wheaton and Tamara K. Hareven; Jacques Solé, *Etre femme en 1500: la vie quotidienne dans la diocèse de Troyes* (Paris, 2000).

where the Archbishop, in contrast to the rest of France, exceptionally retained control of matrimonial justice.[62]

These gaps in the *officialité* records suggest that more profitable work might have been done on the secular courts. One example is Hardwick's examination of 200 separation cases dealt with by the provost's court in Nantes in 1598–1710.[63] These cases provide little information on the poorer levels of society: Hardwick points out that the petitions relate to the middling social ranks, as the expense of taking out a court action deterred those below the artisanat. In addition, although she makes significant claims for her material, for example, that separation cases demonstrate how patriarchal power was negotiated, her findings are, at times, dissatisfying, as she reaches some odd conclusions by failing to consider the limitations and omissions of her sources.

James R. Farr's use of 3,024 *arrêts* (judicial decisions) from the criminal chambers of the *Parlement* (law court) of Burgundy from 1582 to 1730 to examine issues of *rapt*, prostitution, and marriage is much more substantial.[64] He states that the court trials for seduction and *rapt* 'were far from formulaic', and uses them to explore women's strategies to obtain marriage or deal with illegitimate pregnancies, extra-marital sexuality, courtship practices, and prostitution.[65] He recognizes, for instance, a tolerance towards pre-marital sexual activity, how women brought suits demanding the enforcement of marriage promises, and the importance of gifts in courtship rituals.[66] Like that of Solé, his work offers some grounds for comparison with evidence from the consistories and also exposes some gaps in knowledge, which my work on the consistories helps to fill. There are only two significant, though inevitable, limitations to Farr's important study. Farr focuses attention almost exclusively on women's strategies after marriage promises had been made or pregnancy had been discovered and does not really take account of consensual relationships—a consequence of the way cases were shaped for best results before the *Parlement*. Secondly, although Farr mentions that despite the costs involved some members of the lower orders (though not the very poor) used the courts, he admits that deponents were mostly drawn from the higher ranks of society.[67]

Aside from these two studies, much of the significant work on criminal courts is either from considerably earlier or later periods. Bronislaw Geremek's use of the judicial registers of the royal court under the provost of Paris and criminal records from seigneurial jurisdictions to explore marginality, criminality, and prostitution is situated in the late Middle Ages.[68] Work on the later period includes Zoë A. Schneider's study of female litigants in Normandy in the lower royal and seigneurial courts in 1680–1745 and Nicole Castan's work on family matters arising in

---

[62] Lottin, 'Vie' and *La désunion du couple sous l'Ancien Régime: l'exemple du Nord* (Paris, 1975).

[63] Hardwick, 'Seeking Separations'.

[64] Farr, *Authority and Sexuality in Early Modern Burgundy (1550–1730)* (New York and Oxford, 1995), 99.

[65] Farr, *Authority*, 115.   [66] Farr, *Authority*, 113, 114–15, 134, 144.

[67] Farr, *Authority*, 106–7.

[68] Bronislaw Geremek, *The Margins of Society in Late Medieval Paris*, trans. Jean Birrell (Paris and Cambridge, 1987).

criminal cases on appeal before the *Parlement* of Toulouse in 1690–1730.[69] It is worth noting in passing that other valuable work on French women, sexuality, marriage, and the family also falls either side of the period under study. Both Leah Otis-Cour's and Jacques Rossiaud's excellent studies of prostitution examine the medieval period, while there is a huge amount of important work on the eighteenth century, including that by Nicole and Yves Castan (on Languedoc), Cissie Fairchilds, David Garrioch, and Roderick Phillips, to name but a few.[70]

In summary, then, compared to the impression given by the surveys, there is actually very little material—beyond a handful of significant works—that examines the patterns of behaviour, motivations, beliefs, and scope for action of women of the lower and middling sorts in France in the late sixteenth and early seventeenth centuries.

Finally, especially as so much of the secondary literature has focused on social structures and the circumstances of elite women, it is briefly worth reviewing the existing state of knowledge about women's power and agency in the late sixteenth century. Many studies mention how women's legal status and theoretical power declined during the sixteenth century, before briefly cautioning against conflating ideological theory and lived reality by stressing that women did not experience unmitigated oppression.[71] As Haase-Dubosc and Viennot summarized it, early modern women could exercise '*non pas LE pouvoir, mais DU pouvoir*' ('not THE power, but SOME power').[72] Haase-Dubosc in 1991 criticized a previous '*misérabiliste*' (bleak) tendency to see the history of women as a litany of miseries and sufferings, instead directing the focus to women's capacity to act as subjects—but then only illustrating this with a single case of a famous elite woman.[73] Self-evident as it seems, only a few historians have actually examined any substantial evidence of women's agency in practice. Marcel Bernos explores the valiant efforts of female mystics to resist ecclesiastical authority, but sees this as exceptional behaviour.[74]

[69] Zoë A. Schneider, 'Women before the Bench: Female Litigants in Early Modern Normandy', *FHS* 23.1 (2000), 1–32; Nicole Castan, 'La criminalité familiale dans le ressort du Parlement de Toulouse, 1690–1730', in *Crimes et criminalité en France 17e–18e siècles*, ed. A. Abbiateci et al. (Paris, 1971), 'Les femmes devant la justice: Toulouse, XVIII siècle', in *Femmes et pouvoirs*, ed. Haase-Dubosc and Viennot.

[70] Leah Otis-Cour, *Prostitution in Medieval Society: The History of an Urban Institution in Languedoc* (Chicago, 1985); Jacques Rossiaud, *La prostitution médiévale* (Paris, 1988); Nicole Castan and Yves Castan (eds), *Vivre ensemble: ordre et désordre en Languedoc (XVIIe–XVIIIe siècles)* (Paris, 1981); Yves Castan, *Honnêteté et relations sociales en Languedoc (1715–1780)* (Paris, 1974); Cissie Fairchilds, 'Female Sexual Attitudes and the Rise of Illegitimacy: A Case Study', *JIH* 8.4 (1978), 627–67; *Domestic Enemies: Servants and their Masters in Old Regime France* (Baltimore, MD, 1984); David Garrioch, *Neighbourhood and Community in Paris, 1740–1790* (Cambridge, 1986); Roderick Phillips, 'Women, Neighborhood, and Family in the Late Eighteenth Century', *FHS* 18.1 (1993), 1–12; *Family Breakdown in Late Eighteenth-Century France: divorces in Rouen, 1792–1803* (Oxford and New York, 1980); also see Farge and Foucault, *Le désordre des familles*; and for the nineteenth century, Martine Segalen, *Mari et femme dans la société paysanne* (Paris, 1980).

[71] Duby and Perrot (eds), *Histoire des femmes*, vol. 3, 16; Diefendorf, 'Gender and the Family', 99–100; Lebrun, *La vie conjugale*, 81; Kettering, *French Society*, 21.

[72] Haase-Dubosc and Viennot (eds), *Femmes et pouvoirs*, 7.

[73] Haase-Dubosc and Viennot (eds), *Femmes et pouvoirs*, 147.

[74] Marcel Bernos, 'Résistances féminines à l'autorité ecclésiastique à l'époque moderne (XVIIe–XVIIIe siècles)', CLIO, Histoire, *Femmes et Sociétés* 15 (2002), 103–10.

Both Farr and Broomhall focus on women's strategies before the authorities, with the latter examining women's use of rhetorical strategies through creating credible narratives in their pursuit of poor relief.[75] Solé similarly explicitly focuses on women's autonomy and initiative—he says women could be '*chasseresses*' (hunters) as well as '*proies*' (prey).[76] Schneider, Lottin, and Castan all investigate how women pursued justice in the courts in a later period—whether resolving property issues, seeking separations from their spouses, or as witnesses influencing the outcomes of criminal trials.[77] Cattelona's work on women as witnesses before the Refuge also indicates how women initiated legal action.[78] Perhaps most memorably of all, Davis's characterization of Bertrande de Rols, the wife of Martin Guerre, describes a mode of interaction between women and men in sixteenth-century France based on independence, calculation, and manoeuvring to 'fashion' women's lives according to their own designs.[79] Finlay thinks Davis's reading of de Rols is overstated and implausible, and suggests that Davis makes de Rols an unconvincing 'proto-feminist of peasant culture'.[80] Does de Rols typify the behaviour of ordinary women in the period? Were women outwardly submissive but otherwise deviously man-oeuvring and strategizing? Was this a way of exercising private power to compensate for public powerlessness, as suggested elsewhere by Diefendorf?[81] Such a model of disguised, subtle, and apparently deceptive resistance by subordinate groups fits with anthropologist James C. Scott's analysis of domination and power relations.[82] More evidence is needed to put the case of Bertrande de Rols into context.

The fact that this evidence of women's agency spans such a long period of time suggests that women's activism in everyday matters was common. The women who presented themselves before the consistory were not particularly exceptional individuals, and much of their behaviour conforms to existing evidence of women's conduct—but this only makes the consistorial sources all the more important, because this sort of evidence for the responses of humble women to quotidian situations is sparse for the rest of France in the period under study. In addition, while these findings from Burgundy, Nantes, Marseille, and Troyes hint at the vast scope of action for women, they do not do so as systematically, nor on the basis of as much evidence, as this study offers. This allows us to pursue what Joan Wallach Scott has defined as the purpose of feminist history, 'not the recounting of great deeds performed by women but the exposure of the often silent and hidden operations of gender that are nonetheless present and defining forces in the organization of most societies'.[83]

---

[75] Farr, *Authority*; Broomhall, *Women*, 43–4, 'Burdened', 225–6, 230 and 'Understanding Household Limitation'.

[76] Solé, *Etre femme*, 111, see also 34, 72, 87, 147–8, 218, 251.

[77] Schneider, 'Women before the Bench'; Lottin, 'Vie'; N. Castan, 'Les femmes'.

[78] Cattelona, 'Control', 17, 21.   [79] Davis, *Martin Guerre*, 28, 31, 60.

[80] Finlay, 'The Refashioning', 557–60, 564, 570.

[81] Diefendorf, 'Gender and the Family', 117–18.

[82] James C. Scott, *Domination and the Arts of Resistance: Hidden Transcripts* (New Haven, CT, and London, 1990).

[83] Scott, *Gender*, 27.

This overview has shown that relatively few works consider the lives of ordinary women in France in the late sixteenth and early seventeenth centuries, and that work on the consistorial records to examine women's experience could provide balance in a historiography dominated by histories of the elites and by a focus on the eighteenth century. What has also emerged is that while it would be wonderful to compare systematically the experience of ordinary Protestant and Catholic women in France in the period, the evidence of women's narratives for this period of time and level of society is too patchy to make this possible. Nevertheless, the scholarship that exists, either for France in the period under study, or for earlier or later eras, helps to generate a series of questions and hypotheses about women's lives and experience that can be tested and explored through the witness of the consistories. Analysis of the consistorial records for the late sixteenth to the early seventeenth century to examine the behaviour and mentalities of the lower orders could therefore substantially add to our knowledge of the realities of poor French women's lives.

HISTORIOGRAPHICAL OVERVIEW: THE CONSISTORIES

Much of the work by scholars on consistorial records across Europe has assumed that the lack of a double standard in punishing sin means that the consistories have little to say about gender.[84] Janine Garrisson-Estèbe stated 'this is not...the place to talk about marriage, couples, and the family'.[85] Until recently scholarship on the consistories has tended to fall into one of two major categories: anecdotal or statistical.

In the early twentieth century historians focused on the colourful offences recorded in the consistories. Such an approach was adopted by Maurice Oudot de Dainville in 1932 to survey the sixteenth-century consistory in Ganges.[86] To highlight the consistory's disciplinary preoccupations, he focused on individual, often humorous, cases and the 'perverse curiosity' of the elders' enquiries into the private lives of their neighbours.[87] Although not especially analytical, Dainville made important observations about the workings of the consistory, noting, for example, that the consistory responded to general rumour. He also demonstrated that while men were sometimes reprimanded for their wives' sins, in matters of sexual impropriety women were especially targeted.[88]

This approach was continued into the 1970s by Frank Delteil, François Martin, and Solange Bertheau.[89] The latter considered the consistories of Moyen-Poitou in

---

[84] Keith Thomas, 'A Double Standard', *Journal of History of Ideas* 20 (1959), 195–216; Schilling stresses the balanced proportion of men and women in his 'Reform and Supervision of Family Life in Germany and the Netherlands', in *Sin*, ed. Mentzer, 33; Thomas, 'Double Standard'; Mentzer, 'Marking the Taboo', 123–5, 'Morals', 15; Graham, *The Uses*, 286–9.

[85] Garrisson, *Les protestants*, 108.

[86] Maurice Oudot de Dainville, 'Le consistoire de Ganges à la fin du XVIe siècle', *Revue d'historie de l'Église de France* 18 (1932).

[87] Dainville, 'Le consistoire', 466, 468, 469, 473, 477–82.

[88] Dainville, 'Le consistoire', 470, 471, 476.

[89] Frank Delteil, 'Institutions et vie de l'église réformée de Pont-de-Camarès (1574–1576)', in *Les Églises et leurs institutions au XVIeme siècle: hommage solennel à la mémoire du Professeur Jean Boisset,*

a similar if less sensational manner. Important points raised by Bertheau include the social composition of the elders, the focus on '*paillardise*' (etymologically, from 'straw' and therefore metaphorically, 'rolling in the hay', it meant illicit sex outside of marriage), intervention in relations between family and neighbours, and the recognition that there were two periods of application of the Discipline—a period of greater dogmatism and application until *c.*1630, and a period of gradual relaxation until 1685.[90] Her analysis, however, hesitates to pronounce on how these sources inform our knowledge of everyday life.

In 1972, Robert Kingdon called for historians to attempt a more systematic investigation of the consistories. He believed it would be possible to generate statistics on various deviations in order to establish which sins were most prevalent in Geneva, to examine the response of the consistory to these sins, the role of civil and religious authorities in punishment, and change over time.[91]

Historians responded with alacrity. E. William Monter, Raymond Mentzer, Heinz Schilling, Michael Graham, Philippe Chareyre, and Janine Garrisson-Estèbe produced quantitative analyses of the sins recorded in various consistorial registers in the hope of answering Kingdon's challenges.[92] Monter and Mentzer examined consistorial registers from Geneva, Nîmes, and Montauban, producing plentiful statistics to investigate individual sins and their division by gender.[93] Their findings for sins that concerned the consistories—quarrels, fornication, drunkenness, superstition, rebellion, and popular pastimes—support Dainville's earlier *précis*. Philippe Chareyre produced a four-volume doctoral thesis—a painstaking and comprehensive survey of the activity of the consistory at Nîmes between 1561 and 1685—which is invaluable as a reference guide, but contains relatively little qualitative analysis.[94] Mentzer demonstrated from his sample that women were not disciplined more than men, contrasting this with the clear gender bias of the municipal authorities.[95] In fact Mentzer's reiteration of the statistical evidence that French consistories excommunicated far more men than women is important because it implied that the consistorial registers were unlikely to be a rich historical source about women. This has probably been exaggerated by Schilling's conclusion, on the basis of ecclesiastical discipline in Emden and Groningen, that up to

---

ed. Michel Péronnet (Montpellier, 1978); François Martin, 'Ganges, action de son consistoire et vie de son église aux 16e et 17e siècle', *Études évangeliques* (Revue de théologie de la faculté libre de théologie protestante, Aix-en-Provence, 1942), 2; Bertheau, 'Le consistoire'.

[90] Bertheau, 'Le consistoire'.

[91] Robert M. Kingdon, 'The Control of Morals in Calvin's Geneva', in *The Social History of the Reformation*, ed. L. Buck and J. W. Zophy (Columbus, OH, 1972), 14.

[92] William Monter, 'The Consistory of Geneva, 1559–1569', *Bibliothèque d'Humanisme et Renaissance* 38 (1976); Raymond Mentzer, 'Disciplina', 'Morals and Moral Regulation in Protestant France', *JIH* 31 (2000), 'Le consistoire et la pacification du monde rural', *BSHPF* 135 (1989), and 'Marking the Taboo'; Heinz Schilling, 'Calvinism and the Making of the Modern Mind: Ecclesiastical Discipline of Public and Private Sin from the Sixteenth to the Nineteenth Century', in *Civic Calvinism in Northwestern Germany and the Netherlands* (Kirksville, MO, 1991); Graham, *The Uses*; Garrison, *Les protestants*, and with B. Vogler, 'La genèse d'une société protestante: étude comparée de quelques registres consistoriaux languedociens et palatins vers 1600', *Annales: E.S.C.* 31 (1976).

[93] Monter, 'The Consistory'; Mentzer, 'Disciplina', 'Morals'.   [94] Chareyre, *Le consistoire*.

[95] Mentzer, 'Morals', 4, 15, 'Disciplina', 109–11, 'Marking the Taboo', 123–5.

the mid-seventeenth century sexual offences played only a marginal role and the 'couple who violated Christian sexual standards had little to fear'.[96]

Schilling's work highlighted some of the weaknesses of the statistical method.[97] He admitted that interpretive categories provide little hope of comparability, and tried to chart change towards a more 'restrained, subdued society', yet confessed that the concept of success—discipline leading to a subsequent shift in behaviour—is not reliably indicated by statistics.[98]

Judith Pollmann questioned both the assumption that the consistorial registers form a representative record of disciplinary activity, and Kingdon's suggestion that they could be used to study the actual incidence of offences.[99] In comparing the registers of the consistory at Utrecht in 1622–8 with a surviving journal from an elder, Arnoldus Buchelius, Pollmann demonstrated the gap between actual events and the consistorial record, particularly when it came to sins by elites. She noted a process of consciously selective recording, not in response to the seriousness of each transgression, but because the consistory was disinclined to record information that might endanger the reputation of ministerial or elite families, in contrast to the optimistic concept of '*censura morum*' (censure of one's own conduct or life) expressed by Schilling and Dainville.[100] Lacunae also deliberately obscured conflict between secular and sacral authorities and, perhaps unintentionally, masked the vast number of issues—many most likely involving women—that were solved at the home-visit stage, before even reaching a consistorial trial.[101] This silence was also discovered by Monter in his analogous study of crime in Geneva in 1562, where by cross-referencing surviving criminal cases with a list of trials over one year, he concluded that the surviving trials were selected for preservation because of the severity of the sanction, the dangerousness of the accusations, or sheer curiosity value.[102] As such, statistical evidence of the trials alone may leave historians with an unduly vivid, sensational, and ruthless picture of Genevan justice. Margo Todd, in exploring Protestantism in Scotland, has also reminded historians that, as well as such deliberate excision, the level of detail given to each case varied with changing scribes and their diverse preoccupations, while the sheer fragility of the registers—damaged and faded with age and only infrequently surviving in complete runs—makes statistics derived from these sources unreliable.[103]

---

[96] Schilling, 'Calvinism', 62.   [97] Schilling, 'Calvinism', 45, and 'Reform'.

[98] Schilling, 'Calvinism', 45, 59; Graham, *The Uses*, 322–3, and 'Social Discipline in Scotland, 1560–1610', in *Sin*, ed. Mentzer, 138.

[99] J. S. Pollmann, 'Off the Record: Problems in the Quantification of Calvinist Church Discipline', *SCJ* 33.2 (2002), 424–38, 425.

[100] Pollmann, 'Off the Record', 430; Heinz Schilling, '"History of Crime" or "History of Sin"? Some Reflections on the Social History of Early Modern Church Discipline', in *Politics and Society in Reformation Europe: Essays for Sir Geoffrey Elton on His Sixty-Fifth Birthday*, ed. E. I. Kouri and Tom Scott (Basingstoke, 1987), 298; Dainville, 'Le consistoire', 465.

[101] Pollmann, 'Off the Record', 430, 433, 435.

[102] William Monter, 'Crime and Punishment in Calvin's Geneva, 1562', in his *Enforcing Morality in Early Modern Europe* (London, 1987), 281–4.

[103] Margo Todd, *The Culture of Protestantism in Early Modern Scotland* (New Haven, CT, and London, 2002), 16–17.

It might further be added that there are problems of comparability when it comes to counting cases, as one may be recorded in a brief two-line note, while others run to hundreds or thousands of words over many folios. This is especially relevant in cases of sexual immorality, which were often dealt with at some length— it is this discrepancy that makes it possible to claim that sexual sins occupied a small proportion of the cases dealt with by the consistory, without recognizing the time and effort expended on each one.[104] There are also questions about how to classify many cases.

To reflect the impossibility of collecting accurate or meaningful figures from these sources, and given the aim of highlighting mentalities and attitudes less easily elucidated by such figures, few statistics are provided in this study. The quantification here goes no further than stating that I have worked with around 1,200 cases (of varying lengths!), which are listed in full in a chronological conspectus that can be found online in PDF form; there I have provided the archival shelfmarks and foliation details of each case as an aid to future scholars.[105] I have also sometimes indicated in the chapters how many cases I have considered in any particular category to give the reader some sense of the sample size. There are, for example, over 200 fornication cases; nearly 150 cases of sexual assault; around 60 concerning magic; 110 concerning courtship and promises to marry; 90 cases or so of fights and disputes, around 80 adultery cases, nearly 50 cases of marital violence, and so on. I make no claim that these represent the incidence of these events in this period or even the totality of disciplinary activity on that theme; to the contrary, I am certain that they do not. There is no way of knowing how far these numbers were reflective and representative of behaviours in the population as a whole. This means it is very difficult to make reliable assertions about, or assessments of, social norms. What percentage of employers sexually harassed their maidservants? It is impossible to know, but that does not make the fact that many did, and the lived experience of the women who experienced it, any less compelling and important for our understanding of the period. What is likely is that these findings are the tip of an iceberg. Cases concerning illicit sex tended, for example, to be reported to the consistory or discovered only when the woman became pregnant or if the couple were caught in the act. Those who were 'luckier' or more discreet probably got away with it.

One of the early practitioners of statistical analysis has been among those who have identified the consistory as an exceptional source for 'exploring the contours of sociability and the mental outlook of ordinary people'.[106] Raymond Mentzer promoted a micro-historical analysis of individual encounters.[107] In his examination of the Calvinist campaign against papist superstition and idolatry, he compared doctrine to actual behaviour, and tried to reach beyond consistorial attitudes to the thoughts and behaviour of ordinary people. Taking one incident uncovered by

---

[104] e.g. Mentzer's allusion to the rarity of sexual crimes in Bédarieux, 'Le consistoire', 383.
[105] <http://suzannahlipscomb.com/the-voices-of-nimes-chronological-conspectus/>.
[106] Mentzer, 'Morals', 8.
[107] Mentzer, 'Morals', 9, 19; Clifford Geertz, *The Interpretation of Cultures* (New York, 1993), 6–7.

Dainville—that of two women at Ganges fighting in 1598 over access to the Lord's Table—he explored issues of social superiority and precedence invading sacramental occasions while, in another, he read cultural symbolism into a pilgrimage by three women in 1597 to dedicate an ailing infant to Saint-Pierre, noting the juxtaposition of Christian and non-Christian rituals (incidents considered in Chapter 3).[108] Mentzer's analysis situates individual events in knowledge of the culture and period, and he seeks to understand the incidents retold in the registers, while remaining conscious of the thick layer of interpretation through which these events reach the historian. His work suggests the possibility of using micro-historical analysis, although he has not applied this approach to a study of women or gender, beyond their place within the Church.[109] Meanwhile, similar models of gleaning sociological information and investigating attitudes have been employed by Jeffrey Watt and Karen Spierling to consider infant baptism, child-rearing, and education, and by Mark Valeri to consider social practice and attitudes towards usury and the economic market, all for sixteenth-century Geneva.[110] Most recently, Manon Van Der Heijden has examined criminal court records and consistory registers for early modern Holland from 1550 to 1800 to consider, among other things, alcohol abuse, and sexual and domestic violence.[111]

Finally, the consistory records of Montauban and Nîmes themselves have also been used recently by two historians of Church history. Philip Conner used the consistory records, among many other sources, to write an excellent history of Montauban's Calvinist church and of the political and church elites of that town during the Wars of Religion; his work alerted me to the surviving criminal register.[112] Allan A. Tulchin's invaluable examination of the early Calvinist Church in Nîmes drew on the first consistorial register of Nîmes, along with many other records, to explore the 'triumph of Protestantism' in Nîmes between 1530 and 1570.[113] In both cases, of course, their ends were very different from mine.

For despite the fact that the consistorial records are extraordinarily abundant in material about women, especially their marriages and sexualities, these sources have not previously been used to examine women's lives in Reformation France. This research is therefore novel in using the consistorial registers to gain insight

[108] Raymond A. Mentzer, 'The Persistence of "Superstition and Idolatry" among Rural French Calvinists', *Church History* 65 (1996), 220–33, 224–8.
[109] Raymond A. Mentzer, 'La place et le rôle des femmes dans les églises réformées', *Archives de Sciences Socials des Religions* 113 (2001).
[110] Jeffrey R. Watt, 'Calvinism, Childhood and Education: The Evidence from the Genevan Consistory', *SCJ* (2002), 440–1, 443, 445–6 and *The Making of Modern Marriage: Matrimonial Control and the Rise of Sentiment in Neuchâtel, 1550–1800* (New York, 1992); Karen E. Spierling, 'Insolence towards God? The Perpetuation of Catholic Baptismal Traditions in Sixteenth-Century Geneva', *Archive for Reformation History* 93 (2002), 97–125 and *Infant Baptism in Reformation Geneva: The Shaping of a Community, 1536–1564* (Aldershot and Burlington, ON, 2005); Mark Valeri, 'Religion, Discipline and the Economy in Calvin's Geneva', *SCJ* (1997).
[111] Manon Van der Heijden, 'Women as Victims of Sexual and Domestic Violence in Seventeenth-Century Holland', *Journal of Social History* 33.3 (2000), 623–44 and 'Domestic Violence, Alcohol Use and the Uses of Justice in Early Modern Holland', *Annales de Démographie Historique* 130 (2015), 69–85.
[112] Conner, *Huguenot Heartland*.   [113] Tulchin, *That Men*.

into lives of poor and middling women. Its primary concern is with the lives and attitudes of the women disciplined by the consistory, while remaining aware of the formative effect of the consistorial bias in filtering the information received.

MODELS AND METHODS

In the light of these substantial literature reviews on French women and the consistory, it is unnecessary to provide a comprehensive survey of the historiography of sixteenth- and seventeenth-century women outside France, but I wish to finish this introduction by mentioning, briefly, schools of thoughts and key works that have acted as models and influenced the methodology of this study.

An obvious influence has been the work of the *Annales* historians, specifically their preoccupation with mentalities—what founder Lucien Febvre described as the '*outillage mental*', or mental apparatus, of ordinary people.[114] The later *annalistes* also pioneered, along with historians such as Keith Thomas and Emmanuel Le Roy Ladurie, an approach that drew on the insights of different disciplines such as anthropology, sociology, and psychoanalysis.[115]

Ladurie is one of a number of historians who have used court depositions to reconstruct the events, relationships, and mental world of the past, and provide insight into the thoughts and feelings of ordinary men and women through their narratives.[116] His seminal work of 1975, *Montaillou*, explored the history of a Pyrenean village whose inhabitants were interrogated by Bishop Jacques Fournier, an Inquisitor in search of residual Cathar heresy in the late thirteenth

---

[114] The *Annales* were a broad school and several important characteristics of their approach—the focus on a long period (*la longue durée*); an attempt to write 'total history', incorporating all aspects of space and time; and a commitment to quantitative history—are not represented here, cf. Peter Burke, *The French Historical Revolution: The Annales School 1929–89* (Oxford, 1990); Fernand Braudel, 'Histoire et sciences sociales: la longue durée', *Annales: E.S.C.* 17 (1958), 725–53; an example of an attempt at 'total history' is *La Méditerranée et le monde méditerranéen à l'époque de Philippe II*, 2 vols (Paris, 1966); for quantitative history, Ladurie, *Les paysans*; and work by Pierre Chaunu, *Église, culture et société. Réforme et Contre-Réforme (1517–1620)* (Paris, 1980); Ernest Labrousse, *Histoire économique et sociale de la France*, 3 vols (Paris, 1970–9); and Pierre Goubert, *La vie quotidienne dans les campagnes françaises au XVIIe siècle* (Paris, 1982). This study takes inspiration from the work of *Annales* historians such as Marc Bloch, *Les rois thaumaturges* (1924, new edn Paris, 1983); Lucien Febvre, *Le problème de l'incroyance au XVIe siècle: la religion de Rabelais* (Paris, 1947); Philippe Ariès, *L'enfant et la vie familiale sous l'Ancien Régime* (Paris, 1960); Jacques Le Goff, *La naissance du purgatoire* (Paris, 1981); Jean-Louis Flandrin (ed.), *Les amours paysannes (XVIe–XIXe siècle): amour et sexualité dans les campagnes de l'ancienne France* (Paris, 1975), and *Familles: parenté, maison, sexualité dans l'ancienne société* (Paris, 1976); other scholars whose work has focused on *mentalités* include Jean Delumeau, Arlette Farge, Michèle Perrot, and Robert Muchembled.

[115] Keith Thomas, *Religion and the Decline of Magic* (Harmondsworth, 1971).

[116] J. A. Sharpe, *Defamation and Sexual Slander in Early Modern England: The Church Courts at York*, Borthwick Papers no. 58 (1980), see also his *Crime in Early Modern England 1550–1750* (1984, 2nd edn, London, 1999); Martin Ingram, *Church Courts, Sex and Marriage in England, 1570–1640* (Cambridge, 1987); Jenny Kermode and Garthine Walker (eds), *Women, Crime and the Courts in Early Modern England* (London, 1994); Robin Briggs, *Witches and Neighbours: The Social and Cultural Context of European Witchcraft*, 2nd edn (Oxford, 2002); Carlo Ginzburg, *The Cheese and the Worms: The Cosmos of a Sixteenth-Century Miller*, trans. John and Anne Tedeschi (London, 1980); Daniela Hacke, *Women, Sex and Marriage in Early Modern Venice* (Aldershot, 2004).

and early fourteenth centuries.[117] Ladurie demonstrated how it is possible to use the testimonies in court depositions to reconstruct the mentalities and ways of life of ordinary people—in this case medieval villagers—imaginatively and compellingly. In looking to *Montaillou* as an exemplar, it has also been important to listen to Ladurie's critics, who have had proper concerns about his accountability to, and relatively uncritical use of, his sources; his tendency to emphasize the 'curious and exotic'; his paraphrases of the original Latin in ways that distort its meaning; and his silence over the abstracting and distorting effects of the Inquisition's process of interrogation and transcription.[118] Such considerations are a reminder that inquisitorial records cannot be regarded as 'exact transcripts' (especially as the intermingling of the inquisitor's questions and the deponents' responses makes for a garbled and misleading final text).

It is crucial to use testimonies within their context—not extracting them from the circumstances of their creation—and to handle them with great care and integrity. The consistorial records seem not to have been translated in the process of recording (the presence of Occitan words helps assure us of that), and the questions of the interrogator (generally, the presiding minister) are foregrounded, but there was a process of transcription, a shift from first and second person into a third-person narrative, and a shape given by the consistory's questions, the latter explored more in Chapter 2. In writing about them, I have also necessarily translated the French and Occitan into English (although I contend that writing about them in modern French would involve a similar process of translation) and have tried to maximize my accountability by providing transcriptions of the original whenever it was in less-than-straightforward French or in Occitan. I remain optimistic, with Carlo Ginzburg, that it is possible, with careful handling of such records, to hear the voices of the past, even if we must remain aware at all times that any attempts to 'eavesdrop' are only as successful as eavesdropping on a telephone call with a poor connection being made in another room, or, to switch metaphors, that we only see the people of the past through a glass, darkly.[119]

Among other historians using court records, five have been particularly influential on my work. Bernard Capp used ecclesiastical and secular court records and prescriptive writings to explore the social behaviour of English women of the middling and lower orders in 1558–1714.[120] His particular interest was in how women might 'limit, evade or accommodate male domination' through subversive and hidden forms of defiance of patriarchy. Although he deliberately avoided the topic of courtship, much of his material—on the experience of marriage and service,

[117] Emmanuel Le Roy Ladurie, *Montaillou, village Occitan 1294 à 1324* (Paris, 1975).

[118] David Herlihy, 'Review: Ladurie, Montaillou', *Social History* 4.3, 517–20 suggests, ultimately, that the use Ladurie made of Fournier's register was 'sloppy and manipulative'; Leonard Boyle, 'Montaillou Revisited: *Mentalité* and Methodology', in *Pathways to Medieval Peasants*, ed. J. A. Raftis (Toronto, 1981), 121–31; Jessie Sherwood, 'The Inquisitor as Archivist, or Surprise, Fear, and Ruthless Efficiency in the Archives', *The American Archivist* 75.1 (2012), 56–80.

[119] Carlo Ginzburg, 'The Inquisitor as Anthropologist', in *Clues, Myths and Historical Method*, trans. John and Anne Tedeschi (Baltimore, MD, and London, 1989), 156–64.

[120] Bernard Capp, *When Gossips Meet: Women, Family and Neighbourhood in Early Modern England* (Oxford, 2003).

sexuality, gossip, and neighbourliness—provides direct grounds for comparison with the women before the French consistories. As church courts, like the consistories, provided a space for women to testify (or litigate), Capp also examines women's strategies of 'evasion, accommodation, negotiation and resistance', which have much in common with my findings from southern France.

Laura Gowing, also working with English women in a similar period (1560–1640), focused on the language and testimonies of people before the ecclesiastical courts where, in theory, women were allowed to litigate in their own names—although Gowing points out that in practice, women's words were not respected.[121] She examines the differing motives behind litigation, the high proportion of defamation cases brought by women, and the sexual nature of most insults, including the range of meanings of the word 'whore'.[122] She reiterates that sexual blame was thought, by women as well as men, to be almost entirely female, and highlights women's responsibility for governing household honour.[123] Her subjects are drawn from the middling ranks (she notes that the costs of going to court excluded servants and the poor), and she considers the types of narratives and modes of discourse they adopted.[124] An important conclusion is that sexual insult was one of the 'repetitious acts that constitute gender'.[125]

For Germany, Lyndal Roper and Ulinka Rublack have carried out equivalent, excellent work. Roper famously asserted that gender relations were at the crux of the Reformation itself.[126] By considering prostitution, the rites and rituals of weddings, transgressions of marriage, and gendered ecclesiastical roles before and after the Reformation, her goal was chiefly to examine the changing cultural framework around sexuality, gender, and work. As such, she recognizes important cultural shifts, such as the change from seeing prostitutes as a separate species of woman to conflating the categories of prostitute, fornicator, and adulteress after the Reformation, and equally significant continuity, by noting that the Reformed Council continued to support the right of husbands to chastize wives physically because it used violence as the ultimate sanction itself.[127]

Rublack drew on the trials of women before the criminal courts in sixteenth- and seventeenth-century Germany.[128] These interrogations provide insight into how women defended sexual honour and poor people's survival strategies, as well as the prevalent image of the insatiable woman, the sort of behaviours that women adopted to foster the impression of innocence, and neighbourly responses to cases of infanticide, marital quarrels, or gossip.[129] She states that she is not concerned with the response of authorities to bad marriages, the symbolism of insults, or women's representations of their problems in court—the themes explored by

---

[121] Laura Gowing, *Domestic Dangers: Women, Words and Sex in Early Modern London* (Oxford, 1996), 8, 10, 11, 38, 50–1.
[122] Gowing, *Domestic Dangers*, 36, 43, 61–2, 65, 74, 90–1, 116–18, 127.
[123] Gowing, *Domestic Dangers*, 2, 4, 65, 101.   [124] Gowing, *Domestic Dangers*, 61, 232–62.
[125] Gowing, *Domestic Dangers*, 125.
[126] Lyndal Roper, *The Holy Household: Women and Morals in Reformation Augsburg* (Oxford, 1989), 4.
[127] Roper, *The Holy Household*, 100, 112, 125, 130, 185, 193.
[128] Ulinka Rublack, *The Crimes of Women in Early Modern Germany* (Oxford, 1999).
[129] Rublack, *Crimes*, 2, 3, 22, 137, 119, 159, 57–66, 163ff., 200ff.

Roper and Gowing. Rublack concludes that the Reformation did not create a specifically Protestant social and moral order.[130] Of all her findings, those that are particularly relevant for comparison include finding a reluctance to denounce sexual offences, and that gossip was not gender-specific.[131] There are obviously also notable differences between her court records and those of the consistory—the German criminal courts regularly used torture in their interrogations, their range of punishments included the death sentence, and women were only allowed to bring accusations through husbands or guardians, unless they were widowed.[132]

In using court records, there is also much to learn from historians who have worked on witchcraft trials, and, among these, Robin Briggs' work on the duchy of Lorraine is pre-eminent in demonstrating how to handle difficult depositions with care and to interpret their rich material with sensitivity, empathy, and insight to create a convincing picture of the society in which both accused and accusers lived, and the mental world they inhabited.[133]

In short, these examples illustrate some of the best analysis that has been done on gender using court records. The consistorial registers rival the best surviving court and inquisitorial records in richness and insight. The chapters that follow unfold my findings from the consistorial records about ordinary French women's behaviour, thoughts, feelings, and values concerning all aspects of gender, and their marital, sexual, social, and religious identities. The study demonstrates the constantly imaginative methods that poorer women used to influence and direct the circumstances of their lives, the multiple ways in which the outworkings of gender affected women's realities, and how popular attitudes to marriage and sexuality remained distinct from those of the authorities. Above all, the study renews our understanding of women's mentalities and actions by re-conceiving the crucial intersection between challenge and collusion in women's participation in patriarchy. In the culture of Reformation France, ordinary women both challenged and participated in patriarchy, and even in the very acts of agency where women resisted or challenged the status quo, they ensured the successful maintenance of that patriarchy.

Finally, therefore, this study helps us to understand the impact of the Reformation on women. Gender was central to the Reformation not because there were radical new ideas about the position of women or new ways of relating between the sexes (cultural change was glacial, as Capp found, and popular attitudes about the social order, sexuality, and marriage were, in the short term, practically unchanged by Reformed moral codes, as Rublack concluded), but because the pattern of challenge and response in interactions between the Reformed institutions and ordinary women enabled and shaped both women's agency and patriarchy.[134] What the consistories give us is an unrivalled snapshot of how gender evolved in the torrid years of the early French Reformation.

---

[130] Rublack, *Crimes*, 258.   [131] Rublack, *Crimes*, 34, 22.
[132] Rublack, *Crimes*, 51, 54, 47.
[133] Briggs, *Witches and Neighbours* and *Witches of Lorraine* (Oxford, 2007).
[134] Roper, *The Holy Household*, 4; Capp, *When Gossips Meet*, 375; Rublack, *Crimes*, 258.

By recording moments of social fissure, whether the breakdown of neighbourly relations, illegitimate pregnancies, broken engagements, malicious gossip, or marital quarrels, these registers permit us to access the realities of society, family, and culture. Ladurie described the value of the testimonies of the villagers of Montaillou as '*pointillisme*'—tiny dots that together produce a great degree of luminosity and brilliance of colour. Taken together, the evidence from the registers of Languedoc also produces such luminosity and allows us to examine matters of love, morality, sex, belief, suffering, and social relationships among ordinary women living in an extraordinary age of violence and upheaval. Their voices, however distantly, can be heard again.

1

Landscape

LANGUEDOC AND THE WARS OF RELIGION

The Landscape

Sixteenth-century Languedoc was a land apart. The medieval autonomy of the Counts of Toulouse, who had ruled the ancient state of Languedoc, ceased with its annexation by the French crown in the aftermath of the thirteenth-century crusade against the Cathar heretics, but the Languedoc remained distinct in landscape, weather, and disposition. It was characteristic of the region that even as the *langue d'œil*—the French language—took root in the land that had once universally spoken the *langue d'oc*—the Occitan dialect—this very linguistic shift facilitated heterodoxy, quite at odds with the Roman Catholic culture of the Île-de-France.

At 17,500 square miles (45,325 km²), the province of Languedoc was larger than modern-day Switzerland or Denmark. It was bounded by the Rhône river to the east, the Mediterranean Sea to the south, by the Garonne river at its west, and to the north, beyond the Tarn, the Massif Central. The Haut-Languedoc enjoyed a warm and temperate climate, with frequent rains moderating the temperature. The Bas-Languedoc normally faced extreme heat in spring and summer: in early April 1586 it was so hot that the church in Nîmes substituted the midday service for one at the cooler hour of 5 a.m.[1] Although it was a land of sunshine, winters were cold; in Nîmes winter could bring the Mistral, a violent and icy wind from the north, and further west the northern Tramontane wind could also be powerful, cold, and dry.

The plains or *garrigues*—the semi-arid scrub between the Mediterranean and the mountains, where yellow-tipped gorse, cypress, and pine trees grew—were being transformed, by the sixteenth century, into wheat fields and olive groves. Vineyards—now such a feature of the Languedoc—seem, according to findings from Sérignan near Montpellier, likely to have covered only some 11 per cent of the land, as it was not really until the eighteenth century that Languedocian wine-growers discovered that harvesting grapes late increases both their sugar and

---

[1] ADG, 42 J 28, 221r, 9 Apr. 1586. Emmanuel Le Roy Ladurie has found that 'the number and intensity of hot summers diminished radically after 1560 and up to 1600', but contemporary evidence suggests that, even if comparatively cooler, these summers were experienced as hot: Emmanuel Le Roy Ladurie, *Times of Feast, Times of Famine: A History of Climate since the Year 1000*, trans. B. Bray (London, 1972), 242. The exception is the seven successive years of the 1590s (1591–7) in which the summers were cool; in 1594–7, 'rains fell incessantly all over Europe', causing wheat prices to soar: W. G. Hoskins, 'Harvest Fluctuations and English Economic History (XVIth/XVIIIth Centuries)', *Agricultural History Review* (1964), 28–46, here 38.

alcohol levels.[2] In the sixteenth and early seventeenth centuries the wines of Languedoc did not keep, and were not worth keeping.

To the south of Nîmes is the Camargues, a coastal plain of waterlogged marshland formed by the delta of the Rhône river. In the sixteenth century it was being drained, producing rich, fertile soil, but the mosquito-infested swamps exacted their price on the drainage workers.[3] It is likely many of them came from Aimargues, an ancient town of some several thousand people by 1500, which is situated next to the Petite Camargue by the Vidourle river. Until Louis XIII ordered their destruction, Aimargues was fortified by encompassing town walls.

At the centre of the Languedoc are the Cévennes mountains of granite and limestone. Deep, narrow gorges plunge from windswept plateaux, known as the *causses*, at heights of up to 5,000 feet (1,524 m). The flat *causses* provided pasture for sheep.[4] On the hillsides, olives were cultivated on terraces, but the dominant crops were white mulberry trees, to produce silk, and chestnut trees. Chestnuts are remarkably versatile—they can be milled into flour to provide a durable and nutritious substitute carbohydrate in the absence of grain, roasted as nuts, and juiced and fermented to produce sugar and beer. There were wild animals in these hills too—wild boar, wolves, stags, and even brown bears. These could be hunted as game, but sometimes hunted themselves: in Montauban in August 1595 wet-nurse Jeanne Pine applied for poor relief to cover her missing wages because the mother of the infant she was breastfeeding had been eaten by a wolf.[5] This was a world in which the landscape was being wrestled into submission, but not everything could be tamed.

Although the chief signs of human habitation in the high *causses* were isolated farms known as *mas*, there were clustered villages deep in the mountains. Of those that interest us, furthest north is Meyrueis. Resting between the foothills and the Causse Méjean at an altitude of 2,316 feet (706 m), Meyrueis was founded in the sixth century and is situated in a river valley, overshadowed by limestone cliffs. Slightly further south is Saint-Jean-du-Bruel. A town of then fewer than a thousand inhabitants, in a verdant valley at an altitude of 1,706 feet (520 m), Saint-Jean-du-Bruel boasts a single-arch twelfth-century bridge, spanning the Dourbie river. To the southwest, Pont-de-Camarès (known today simply as Camarès) is a hilltop village at 1,257 feet (383 m) at the foot of the Monts de Lacaune. It was famed in the sixteenth century for its red soil—*le rougier* (the clay saturated with iron oxide), thermal springs, and its medieval bridge, dating from 1311, over the Dourdou de Camarès river.

At the foot of the Cévennes are more substantial towns. The furthest south, Bédarieux in the Orb valley, was fortified with a fourteenth-century castle, *La Bastide*. Much further north, Ganges, at the confluence of the Hérault, Vis, and Rieutord rivers, and Alès, on the river Gardon 20 miles (40 km) north of Nîmes, were gateways

---

[2] Emmanuel Le Roy Ladurie, *Les Paysans de Languedoc* (Paris, 1969), 71–4.

[3] Ladurie, *Paysans*, 91–2.

[4] Allan A. Tulchin, *That Men Would Praise the Lord: The Triumph of Protestantism in Nîmes, 1530–1570* (Oxford, 2010), 8.

[5] ADTG, I 1, 33v, 82r, 23 Aug. 1595.

between the plains and the mountains. Both were medieval foundations; like Meyrueis, Alès can trace its origins to the sixth century.

These towns and villages built their artisanal economies on the pastoral and agricultural riches of the Cévennes, and their riverine positions. The villages of Meyrueis, Saint-Jean-du Bruel, and Pont-de-Camarès used wood from the chestnut trees to make wheels, clogs, and barrels. The *rougier* soil of Pont-de-Camarès made attractive pottery and varnished tiles. In all these towns and villages, animal prod-ucts were used to create consumer items.[6] Tanners treated animal skins to produce leather, which glovers, cobblers, and other craftsmen then transformed into clothes, shoes, and harnesses. Bédarieux became a centre of woollen cloth-weaving, while Ganges and Alès became famed for silk production.

Montauban, a twelfth-century city, was to the far west of the Languedoc. Some 30 miles (50 km)—or a long day's ride—north of Toulouse, the city had thick surrounding walls, a level bridge over the river Tarn dating from *c.*1336, and was surrounded by fertile alluvial plains. By 1600 it was a prosperous city with a popu-lation of around 17,000.[7]

At the east of the province stood the city of Nîmes. Twenty-five miles (40 km) from the sea, and a similar distance from Avignon and Montpellier, it had a popu-lation of some 13,700–15,000 in 1600, occupying the 80 acres (or just over 32 ha) within its shield-shaped medieval walls, and spilling into the *faubourgs*—suburbs—just outside its gates.[8] It had been a Roman city (called *Nemausus*) and still stand-ing at the apex of the city in the sixteenth century was *Les Arènes*, a remarkably well-preserved Roman amphitheatre, built around AD 70, which had been bricked up and was used as dwellings. The city also contained a quadrangular Roman tem-ple known as *La Maison Carrée*, and just outside were a temple dedicated to Diana and, at the top of a hill, a Roman watchtower, *La Tour Magne*. At the base of this hill was the town's fountain, an 'inexhaustible source of clear water' that was the best in the region, according to a visitor to the town in the 1590s.[9] All these Roman ruins remain today, and the footprint of the original walled city is easily traced.

Like the smaller towns, Montauban and Nîmes relied on agriculture and artisanal use of pastoral products. Allan A. Tulchin has calculated that something like a third of Nîmes's adult male population worked in the fields outside the city.[10] They are described as *laboureurs* and *travailleurs*, the first the equivalent of a yeoman, who owned his own land; the second a husbandman, who worked the land for others. Clothing manufacture was perhaps the next most populated occupation, the cities teeming with textile workers such as wool-carders, weavers, dyers, fullers, shearers, drapers, hosiers, tailors, and milliners.

---

[6] Tulchin, *That Men*, 8, 59; Ladurie, *Paysans*, 187–8.
[7] Philip Benedict, *The Huguenot Population of France, 1600–1685: The Demographic Customs and Fate of a Religious Minority* (Philadelphia, PA, 1991), 55.
[8] Benedict, *The Huguenot Population*, 55. The population had been between 10,000 and 12,000 in the mid-sixteenth century.
[9] Emmanuel Le Roy Ladurie and Francine-Dominique Liechtenhan (eds and trans.), *Le Siècle de Platter*, vol. 2, *Le voyage de Thomas Platter 1595–1599* (Paris, 2000), 147.
[10] Tulchin, *That Men*, 18.

Governance

Montauban was the seat of a *sénéchaussée* or royal court, whose conseillers adjudicated on civil and criminal cases affecting royal prerogatives. Nîmes had also been the seat of one of the most important *sénéchaussées* in Languedoc, but it had been replaced, in 1552, by a *présidial*—a court with some criminal and civil jurisdiction in relatively minor matters.[11] Constituted very similarly to the *sénéchaussée*, it comprised the *présidial* judges—known as *conseillers*, two *procureurs du roi* (king's prosecutors), and an *avocat du roi* (the king's lawyer). Their role was to deal with criminal justice and enforce royal ordinances. Such permanent royal offices carried great prestige and political advantage. The presence of the *présidial* meant that the city was unusually abundant in lawyers and notaries, and steeped in legal culture. Thomas Platter, visiting Nîmes in the 1590s, thought there were two thousand lawyers in the city, although Allan A. Tulchin suggests that four hundred would be a more realistic estimate.[12]

In both Nîmes and Montauban, the city was governed by four consuls. The consuls, who were selected every year from a list of nominees drawn up by the outgoing consuls—by lot in Nîmes and by an electoral college in Montauban—represented the social spectrum of the town. In Nîmes, the first consul was always a lawyer and was generally of noble status. The second was normally a *bourgeois*—a man who lived off his investments; one exception in Nîmes for the period under study was Bernard Arnaud, Seigneur de la Cassagne, second consul in 1570, but he was of a similar rank, being a noble and an equerry.[13] The third consul was normally a notary, artisan, or merchant.[14] The fourth was a *laboureur*, the highest rung of the agricultural trades, or, occasionally, a *jardinier*, a market-gardener of fruit and vegetables.[15] So, for example, on Sunday 7 January 1606, when the consuls in Nîmes for 1605 handed over responsibilities to their successors, the first consul went from being Jehan de Boyleau, Seigneur de Castelnau, to Jacques Bonhomme, *docteur en droictz* (doctor in law); the second consul from one *bourgeois*, Anthoine Duprix, to another, Claude Poujol; the third from Mathieu Lansard, *greffier* (clerk, a form of notary), to Jehan Rolland, merchant; and the fourth from *laboureur* Jacques Lombard, to his peer, *laboureur* Jacques Allier.[16] This pattern of drawing consuls from a range of social backgrounds was followed in very similar fashion in

---

[11] Platter thought that the *présidial* was in addition to the *sénéchaussée* (Ladurie and Liechtenhan, *Platter*, 154).

[12] Ladurie and Liechtenhan, *Platter*, 155; Tulchin, *That Men*, 11.

[13] ADG, E dépôt 36/128, 224r.

[14] Tulchin suggests that the third consul was always a notary or artisan (*That Men*, 12), but the third consul was a merchant in, at least, 1587, 1588, 1589, 1604, 1606, 1607, 1608, 1609, 1610, 1611, 1614, and 1615: ADG, E dépôt 36/131, 33r, 78r, 154v; E dépôt 36/134, 78r, 157r; E dépôt 36/135, 16r, 135v, 212v; E dépôt 36/136, 161v, 228v.

[15] The fourth consul was a *jardinier* in 1563, Jacques Guilhon (ADG, E dépôt 36/128, 1), and in 1588, François Trauquat (ADG, E dépôt 36/131, 78r).

[16] ADG, E dépôt 36/134, 157r. Jehan de Boyleau, Seigneur de Castelnau is elsewhere (e.g. ADG, E dépôt 36/131, 230r) recorded as Jean de Boyleau, Seigneur de Châteauneuf, a French translation of the Occitan.

Montauban, and was a peculiar characteristic of the governance of most southern French towns.[17]

In both Montauban and Nîmes, the consuls selected the town council (*conseil ordinaire*). Like the consuls, the councillors represented each of the four tiers of society, and new councillors would be nominated by previous incumbents.[18] In practice the size of the council in Nîmes seems to have varied greatly. Of a sample of thirty-three years (or 60 per cent) examined for 1560–1615, the number of councillors ranged between eleven and thirty-nine, the mean average being 18.6. The number fell below fifteen councillors in only nine of those thirty-three years and rose to twenty or above in fourteen years. Seventeen councillors, for example, attended the *conseil ordinaire* of 10 May 1614.[19]

Together with the consuls, the council had authority over all issues of municipal governance, including taxation, regulation of trades and guilds, licensing of taverns, upkeep of public buildings, the resolution of disputes, the setting of prices for meat and fish, the expulsion of vagabonds, and urban defence.[20] Each councillor also had specific responsibilities—as secretary, as auditor of accounts, for poor relief, for governing the clock tower, for keeping wages at the consular house, as apothecary, doctor, and surgeon of the hospital, for receiving and distributing emoluments, and so on.[21]

In Montauban the consulate also exercised civil and criminal jurisdiction, and could impose sentences and punishments. A 'Register of sentences pronounced in criminal matters by the consuls of the town of Montauban' survives for 1534 to 1606, and shows penalties imposed for crimes including theft, adultery, *paillardise* (fornication), murder, violence, fraud, vagrancy, perjury, and sedition.[22] These ranged from a public apology on one's knees before the community, through to flogging, exile from the city, the pillory, banishing to the galleys, and even execution. It is probable that the consuls of Nîmes had similar powers, although no similar register of sentences appears to survive.

In moments of urgent or important business, the council also held extraordinary council meetings, which were open to all the men of the city.[23] On 5 November 1563, it was at such an extraordinary council that the consuls of Nîmes announced the appointment of Henri de Montmorency, Seigneur de Damville, as royal Governor and Lieutenant-General of Languedoc and warned of his intention to visit the city (they were right to fear—on arrival he overthrew the Protestant consuls and

---

[17] Philip Connor, *Huguenot Heartland: Montauban and Southern French Calvinism during the Wars of Religion* (Aldershot, 2002), 25.

[18] ADG, E dépôt 36/131, 32v–33r, 2 Jan. 1587.

[19] ADG, E dépôt 36/136, 161v. Tulchin, *That Men*, 12, states that there were twelve *conseillers* in the Nîmes town council, but if this was true even in theory, it does not seem to have been observed in practice after 1560.

[20] See ADG, E dépôt 36/39, *Archives communales—Police de la ville et du territoire de Nîmes*.

[21] For the list of responsibilities assigned in 1587: ADG, E dépôt 36/131, 33r.

[22] ADTG, 5 FF 2, *Registre des sentences prononcees en matiere criminelle par les Consuls de la Ville de Montauban de 1534 à 1606*.

[23] For example, ADG, E dépôt 36/127, 248r, *conseil general et extraordinaire* on 13 November 1561.

replaced them with Catholics).[24] The scribe dutifully wrote down the names of those who attended—a tightly spaced list that runs to three full sides to record the hundreds who were present. When it came to critical affairs of civic governance, the citizens of Nîmes were enthusiastic participants in the political and legal life of their city.

Population, Pauperization, and the Plague

The late sixteenth and early seventeenth centuries were a period of economic hardship and real peril for many in Languedoc. The population of the province increased, on average, by 11.5 per cent per decade between 1500 and 1570 (it only slowed after this because of the devastating effect of the civil wars). Grain production proved entirely insufficient to meet the needs of this newly enlarged population, and the demand for bread began to outstrip supply. Grain prices sextupled between 1585 and 1600, while wages only tripled over the period, meaning that real wages declined dramatically.[25] The living standards of all workers reached their lowest level in the 1590s, but women suffered from this pauperization much more severely than their menfolk, as their wages—conventionally half the male wage—dropped to nearer a third.[26]

This structural impoverishment was exacerbated by almost inevitable short-term crises of subsistence. The 1590s were a time of severe dearth for people all over Europe, and Languedocians were no exception.[27] There were disastrous harvests in the south of France in 1590–3 and 1596–8, which quickly produced famine conditions for those living close to the bread line.[28] In January 1590 the church in Nîmes was moved to provide ten *sols* (double the usual poor-relief provision) for a 'poor woman...dying of hunger', and such individuals in need were not uncommon.[29]

Plague epidemics also broke out repeatedly; it has been calculated that a Europe-wide outbreak of plague occurred, on average, every nine years, and it is roughly with this frequency that it appeared in Languedoc.[30] Contemporaries saw epidemic disease as divine punishment for sin, prompting believers to prayer and repentance, and understandably so, because the plague was inexplicable, horrific, and arbitrary. Its lethality rate was terrifying: in Rennes in 1605, 20 per cent of the affected died within twenty-four hours, and 80 per cent within five days.[31] In the plague of 1628–30 Lyon lost half of its population of 70,000.[32] Nor could anyone forget the sheer awfulness of the symptoms: high fever, incessant vomiting, profound

---

[24] ADG, E dépôt 36/128, 1r–3r. [25] Ladurie, *Les paysans*, 189–96, 222, 277–9.
[26] Ladurie, *Les paysans*, 277.
[27] Lyndal Roper, *Witch Craze: Terror and Fantasy in Baroque Germany* (New Haven, CT, and London, 2004), 132; Andrew Cunningham and Ole Peter Grell, *The Four Horsemen of the Apocalypse: Religion, War, Famine and Death in Reformation Europe* (Cambridge, 2000).
[28] Cunningham and Grell, *Four Horsemen*, 235. [29] ADG, 42 J 29, 338, 31 Jan. 1590.
[30] Cunningham and Grell, *Four Horsemen*, 274.
[31] Colin Jones, 'Plague and its Metaphors in Early Modern France', *Representations* 53 (1996), 97–127, here 98.
[32] Jones, 'Plague', 99.

drowsiness without the ability to sleep, a blackened tongue, persistent thirst, difficult breathing, abscesses, and, of course, extremely painful buboes—tumours—in the neck, armpit, and groin.

The plague struck Nîmes in 1564–5, 1567, 1578–9, and 1589–90. In July 1564, when the epidemic returned after an absence of nine years, the town council ordered that the guards on the town gates be reinforced, and that those infected were to be received into the Sainte-Claire convent, in the western suburbs outside the city walls.[33] At the same time, fearing that the plague was worsening, the consuls drew up a contract with Master Surgeon Anthoine Vergier, promising to pay him handsomely if he remained in the city to serve the sick.[34] In May 1565 a list of extraordinary expenses in response to the plague—mostly providing for those reduced to poverty— runs to thousands of *livres*.[35] The disease resurfaced in early 1567. Wills of the period convey something of the terror that the pestilence inspired: Jacquette Delafont, 'fearing the danger of the plague', drew up her will in January 1567 because her husband had perished only a few days earlier.[36]

In December 1578 the plague broke out again in several quarters of the town, and in late December the consistory charged its elders to assess the needs of those poor and sick. The Christmas Eucharist was postponed and on 28 January 1579 public prayers were held to appeal to God for mercy.[37] At its height in this attack the plague killed a hundred people a day.[38] Several of the ongoing morality cases were abruptly truncated with the line 'dead of the plague, year 1579', and in May the consistory's own summoner (*advertisseur*), M. Maurin, died.[39] The inhabitants of Nîmes, including three of the consuls and the Protestant consistory, fled, leaving the town deserted. The consistory did not meet again until the plague had ceased in September, and prayers were said in October to thank God for His grace after such a 'great contagion of plague'.[40]

Less than a decade later, in January 1587, reports reached Nîmes of renewed plague in its immediate environs, and inhabitants from one infected area, Vaunage, were forbidden by the council from entering the city.[41] By October the plague had spread to Valleraugue in the Cévennes, and the consistory worried about the number of poor strangers coming into the town who might carry it with them, for they 'do not pray and recognize God and thus live like brute beasts', a statement which makes clear the perceived link between irreligion and the disease.[42] Public prayers were said to thank God for Nîmes's narrow escape, and it is probably no coincidence that consistorial fervour against sexual immorality seems to have been at its height in the late 1580s.[43] The plague continued in neighbouring towns

---

[33] ADG, E dépôt 36/128, 35v–36.   [34] ADG, E dépôt 36/84, 63r, 27 Jul. 1564.

[35] ADG, E dépôt 36/128, 82r.   [36] Arc.Not., 2 E/1 257 (Jacques Ursi), 9 Jan. 1567.

[37] BN, Ms.fr. 8667, 60v, 61v, 67r–v.

[38] Léon Ménard, *Histoire civile, ecclésiastique, et litteraire de la Ville de Nismes, avec des notes et les preuves, Suivie de dissertations historiques et critiques sur ses antiquités, et de diverses observations sur son histoire naturelle*, 7 vols (Paris, 1754), vol. 4, 364; vol. 5, 184–6.

[39] BN, Ms.fr. 8667, 65v, 68, 76v.

[40] Ménard, *Histoire*, vol. 5, 184–6; BN, Ms.fr. 8667, 76v, 77r, 78r.

[41] ADG, E dépôt 36/130, 34v.   [42] ADG, 42 J 28, 324v–325r, 28 Oct. 1587.

[43] ADG, 42 J 28, 354r, 27 Jan. 1588.

throughout the following year—the church organized a collection for the poor plague-ridden people of Uzès in November 1588, and two poor widows and their daughters took refuge from the plague in Montpellier in early 1588—before the disease returned to the city in the autumn of 1589.[44] It was a short bout and had passed by January 1590, but the sense of threat continued until May 1593, no doubt exacerbated by the poor harvests of these years.[45]

Precautions against the plague were also taken in 1605, 1606, and 1607, when reports of the pestilence at Toulouse persuaded the council to deny any non-residents entry to the city, and to forbid the innkeepers of the suburbs from hosting strangers.[46] It should never be forgotten that the domestic disputes and quotidian crises of these years were played out against a background of impoverishment and under the looming spectre of famine and plague.

Growth of Protestantism

From the mid-1530s ordinary men and women in France had started converting, in ever increasing numbers, to the strand of Protestantism named after its principal founder, Jean Calvin. The Calvinists rejected the authority of the Pope, abhorred the Mass, and deplored what they saw as the corruption, hypocrisy, and idolatry of the papal Church. Their Catholic enemies mocked them with the name 'Huguenots' (one suggestion for the etymology of this curious word is that when the Protestants gathered to sing psalms late at night in the city of Tours, they sounded like the ghost of a terrible scoundrel called King Huguet and other spirits, coming from purgatory to harm the living).[47] Under French law they were considered heretics who should be burnt at the stake—the first suspect for this heresy in Nîmes dates from 1537.[48] The Protestants remained a very small minority until the 1550s, when increasing numbers of conversions were accompanied by a crackdown on heresy. In the 1560s the Protestants of Nîmes would refer to this decade as 'the time of persecution'.[49]

Still the movement grew. In May 1559 the first national synod of the Reformed Church of France drew up a Confession of Faith that defined doctrine and a Discipline that outlined the structure of the Church—a system of ministers, deacons, and elders, with consistories, colloquies, and synods.

Protestantism spread especially fast in the south of France. In September 1559 pastor Guillaume Mauget was sent to Nîmes from the Calvinist mother-church in Geneva. In March 1561 two crucial events extended Protestant reach and appeal in Nîmes. On 15 March a radical Protestant *cahier de doléances* (book of grievances) was presented to the town council and consuls, with the support of 137 named citizens. In response to a worsening economic situation, it argued for controls on

---

[44] ADG, 42 J 29, 80, 120, 131, 284, 287, 313. Another refugee from the plague in Montpellier was an apothecary called Esprit Pin, ADG, 42 J 29, 131.

[45] ADG, 42 J 30, 173v; Ménard, *Histoire*, vol. 5, 242, 260.

[46] Ménard, *Histoire*, vol. 5, 337; ADG, E dépôt 36/134, 369r, 18 Oct. 1607.

[47] Natalie Zemon Davis, 'The Rites of Violence: Religious Riot in Sixteenth-Century France', *Past and Present* 59 (1973), 51–91, here 57; *Histoire ecclésiastique des Églises Réformées au Royaume de France*, ed. G. Baum and E. Cunitz, 3 vols (Paris, 1883–9), vol. 1, 308.

[48] Tulchin, *That Men*, 50.   [49] BN, Ms.fr. 8666, 31v, 48v, both from 1561.

royal power, the redirection of Catholic church revenues towards 'food for the poor', the future secular management of poor funds, and moral and religious reform, including prayers in the vernacular, freedom to read the Bible, the singing of hymns and psalms, and an end to dancing.[50] The *cahier* set the tone of the Protestant cause and was immensely popular—in the end, it was signed by over three hundred people and has been described as the 'closest Nîmes came to a referendum on the Reformation'.[51] The Protestants were quick to capitalize on the popular enthusiasm. Only eight days later, on 23 March 1561, the 'consistory of the Christian church of the town of Nîmes' met for the first time.[52] This governing body of the new church was established to ensure an equitable and efficient distribution of poor relief and, above all, to police the city's morals. One of its earliest acts, on 16 April 1561, was to establish a school of theology—the Reformed Academy of Nîmes—to train young men for the ministry.[53]

By the end of 1561 Catholic churches had been attacked by Protestant crowds on at least four occasions in an attempt to seize the churches for their own worship, and 8,000 people—roughly two-thirds of the population of the city—had gathered in Nîmes to hear the famous Protestant cleric, Pierre Viret, preach, when he was seconded to the city for a year. Some 50 per cent of Nîmes's population had converted to Calvinism—a staggeringly high proportion compared to, at most, 10 per cent of the twenty million population of France.[54] These converts included many from the local elites. By early 1562 60 per cent of the twenty-six judges of the *présidial* court were Protestant, and, by 1563 Protestants dominated the town council sufficiently to attempt to exclude Catholics.[55]

Such Protestant popularity was not unique in the Midi. In Toulouse it is estimated that one-seventh of the 35,000-strong population were Huguenot in 1562—but that number would soon decline rapidly.[56] The reason for this reversal was that, following Catherine de' Medici's granting of legal toleration to Protestantism in the Edict of Romorantin on 28 January 1562, a confrontation between a leading Catholic nobleman, François, duc de Guise, and a group of Protestant worshippers inside the walls of the small town of Vassy on 1 March 1562 degenerated into a massacre of fifty people—the first turn of the cycle of the deadly religious wars that would recur repeatedly across France over the next four decades. Toulouse was one of the cities where a Huguenot coup failed, to be followed by a persecution that guaranteed Catholic control. Nîmes and Montauban were exceptional, then, not

---

[50] Tulchin, *That Men*, 104–14.   [51] Tulchin, *That Men*, 113.

[52] BN, Ms.fr. 8666, 1r; Robert Sauzet, 'Huguenots et papists a Nîmes, du XVIe siècle au XVIIIe siècle', in *Histoire de Nîmes*, ed. Xavier Gutherz (et al.) (Aix, 1982), 151; Ménard, *Histoire*, vol. 4, 268.

[53] BN, Ms.fr. 8666, 4r, 16 Apr. 1561; Françoise Moreil, 'Le Collège et l'Académie réformée de Nîmes', *Bulletin de la Société de l'Histoire du Protestantisme Français* 122 (1976), 77–86, here 78.

[54] Ann H. Guggenheim, 'The Calvinist Notables of Nîmes during the Era of the Religious Wars', *SCJ* 3.1 (1972), 80–96, here 83; Menna Prestwich, 'Calvinism in France, 1555–1629', in *International Calvinism 1541–1715*, ed. Prestwich (Oxford, 1985), 73.

[55] Allan A. Tulchin, 'The Michelade in Nîmes, 1567', *FHS* 29.1 (2006), 1–36, 7; Ménard, *Histoire*, vol. 4, 357.

[56] Joan Davies, 'Persecution and Protestantism: Toulouse, 1562–1575', *HJ* 22.1 (1979), 31–51, here 34; J. Estèbe, 'Les Saint-Barthélemy des villes du midi', *Actes du colloque l'amiral de Coligny et son temps* (Paris, 1974), 718–19.

simply in becoming majority Protestant cities, but remaining so throughout the period despite the devastations of war.

Wars of Religion in the Languedoc

This was a time of great religious upheaval, war, and hardship across France. We know that Montauban was besieged three times in 1562 and, in September 1595, reports reached the city of a massacre of 120 of the 'faithful', both men and women, in the village of Ruffe, only 2.5 miles (4 km) from Montauban's walls.[57] The information available about Nîmes is, however, far more detailed and worth considering at some length as it provides the backdrop for all the analysis that follows.

Even before Vassy, Nîmes was put on a war footing. In November 1561, the city was created a state of defence: it was divided into four quarters, each commanded by a captain.[58] In June 1562 reports reached the council that the inhabitants of Avignon and other towns in Provence had turned on their neighbours, 'putting men, women, and children to the sword, [committing] rapes, and execrable inhumanities'. The council resolved to resist them by whatever means possible, even—considering the weakness of the city walls in the face of cannon—bravely deciding to make a 'rampart of flesh' in front of them to defend their town.[59] They also appointed two ministers to preach the gospel in the environs of Nîmes—a spiritual defence to add to the physical. By September 1562 the city was full of soldiers, and they had achieved their first victory—defeating the Catholics and massacring the clergy of Saint-Gilles, a small town some 10 miles (16 km) from Nîmes.[60] War had started to take its toll: the consistory started to make poor-relief provision for the widows of soldiers killed in the fighting.[61]

Following the Edict of Amboise of March 1563, Nîmes saw four years of peace, and an attempt to restore Catholicism. The royal government appointed a Catholic Governor and Lieutenant-General of Languedoc, Henri de Montmorency, Seigneur de Damville. Damville visited Nîmes in November 1563 and restored Catholic leadership in the town by replacing the Protestant consuls with Catholic alternatives. Catholic worship was re-established and on 22 December 1564 the king himself, Charles IX, made a solemn entry into Nîmes. His presence in the city during the month when consuls were elected was pivotal: the consuls for 1565, and again for 1566, were Catholics.[62] The one concession to the Protestants in these years was that they were permitted to construct a temple in Nîmes near the Maison Carrée, which was first used on 27 January 1566.[63]

Successive years of Catholic authority could not, however, quash the strength of Protestant sentiment in the town. On 30 September 1567, the festival of Saint Michel, the Nîmois Protestants staged an uprising that descended into a massacre.[64]

---

[57] ADTG, I 1, 55r, 21 Sept. 1595.   [58] ADG, E dépôt 36/127, 248r, 13 Nov. 1561.
[59] ADG, E dépôt 36/127, 8 Jun. 1562.   [60] ADG, E dépôt 36/17/1, 6 Sept. 1562.
[61] BN Ms.fr. 8666, 167r, 17 Oct. 1562.
[62] Sauzet, 'Huguenots', 155; Tulchin, 'Michelade', 10, Ménard, *Histoire* (1754), vol. 5, 2.
[63] Ménard, *Histoire*, vol. 4, 380; vol. 5, 2.
[64] The best accounts of the uprising and massacre are Tulchin, 'Michelade', and *That Men*, 161–79; Ménard, *Histoire*, vol. 5, 10–28.

Fomented by the Calvinist political elites of the town, rather than the ministers of the Reformed Church (who condemned the revolt), on 30 September Protestant crowds formed a militia and took to the streets, whipping up a frenzy of anger against Catholic rule. They were heard to shout, 'Kill! Kill the papists! New world!', an injunction tinged with millenarian hopes.[65]

Their first action was to seize the keys to the city gates from the first consul, Guy de Rochette, an act important for symbolic authority and practical control. They then arrested Rochette, Bernard d'Elbène, Bishop of Nîmes, and other leading Catholic political actors and priests, including at least half of the sixteen Catholic consuls who had served between 1564 and 1567.[66] The Catholics were imprisoned in humiliating circumstances, without food, and the rebels drew up lists of those who were to die, before murdering many. Contemporary estimates suggested that they massacred one hundred Catholics, although only a third of that number can be identified as victims.[67] Their bloody corpses were left to rot in the well at the bishop's palace. Among them was first consul Guy de Rochette. The Bishop narrowly managed to escape unharmed, but he was unable to return to Nîmes before his death in Arles a year later.[68] The rampaging Protestants also destroyed the cathedral, the bishop's palace, and all fifteen churches in Nîmes, except one, St. Eugénie (the façade of which still stands), and laid siege to the *château*. The town's leading chronicler, Léon Ménard, writing in the mid-eighteenth century, stated that by the end of 1567 the entire town of Nîmes 'was nothing more than a veritable image of terror and desolation'.[69]

This bloody affair, which became known as the Michelade, was an unusually large massacre of Catholics by Protestants. It stands in contrast with the later massacres of Protestants by Catholics on Saint Bartholomew's day in August 1572 throughout the rest of France (and Tulchin has argued that given the relative populations of Nîmes and Paris, the Michelade was proportionately nearly as bloody as the events of 1572).[70] Many historians have assumed that during the French wars of religion Protestants were less bloodthirsty than Catholics, directing their violence against objects rather than people; Nîmes is distinctive in proving that, given a majority, the Calvinists could be just as murderous towards their fellow humans.[71]

The Catholics fought back. In June 1568 royal troops entered the town and 100 people were condemned in March 1569 by the *Parlement* of Toulouse for their part in the Michelade. Most of the accused fled, but four offenders were arrested and taken to Toulouse to be executed. Their heads were sent back to Nîmes and mounted on the four principal gates of the town as a dire warning.[72] On Saint Michel's day 1569 the cathedral canons commemorated the Catholic dead, but it was a hubristic triumph. Two months later, on 15 November, the town

---

[65] Ménard, *Histoire*, vol. 5, 11.   [66] Tulchin, *That Men*, 165.
[67] Tulchin, *That Men*, 170.   [68] Ménard, *Histoire*, vol. 5, 10–24, 27–8.
[69] Ménard, *Histoire*, vol. 5, 33.   [70] Tulchin, 'Michelade', 2.
[71] Davis, 'The Rites', 76–7; Denis Crouzet, *Les guerriers de Dieu: la violence au temps de trouble de religion, vers 1525–vers 1610*, 2 vols (Paris, 1990), vol. 1, 600–1; see Tulchin, *That Men*, 175–9, for a fuller discussion.
[72] Ménard, *Histoire*, vol. 5, 42–5; Tulchin, 'Michelade', 26.

was re-occupied by Protestant forces and a second massacre ensued. Accounts suggest a death toll of another 100 or 150 Catholics. This time, the Protestant hold on the city would last.

By 1572 the town council, consulate, and *présidial* court of Nîmes were dominated by Calvinists, the leadership and governance of the city secure in Huguenot hands. Just like Montauban, Nîmes became a key bastion of the Huguenot confederation, the United Provinces of the Midi. Nearly a third of all Reformed provincial synods of Bas-Languedoc met in Nîmes during the religious wars, including one in May 1572.[73] Three months later news of the Saint Bartholomew's Day massacre—in which some 10,000 Huguenots in Paris and across France had been killed in episodes of brutal, sickening violence, over the space of four days—reached Nîmes. Stunned by the rumours, the council called an extraordinary meeting and made an extraordinary statement. The consuls—both Protestant and Catholic—declared that all the

> inhabitants of the present town, of the one and of the other religion, shall maintain and preserve in all safety and liberty persons and goods [so] that true citizens, inhabit-ants of the same town, may and will be, without permitting any of the said inhabitants to be subjected to any violence or force, which others shall be required to oppose with all their power, and in this respect have been taken into protection and kept safe without distinction of religion in order to maintain and preserve respectively the one and the other, according to the edict of pacification, under the obedience of the King and his justice.[74]

All present swore to abide by this, by the raising of their hands. This pacifying proclamation was vital to preventing imitative violence by Catholics or vengeful attacks by Protestants, and to maintaining the peace of Nîmes. When in the after-math of the massacre many erstwhile Protestants across France defected, in Nîmes 'the faithful' held strong.

Surrounded by, and regularly under attack from, Catholic forces, the city tried to survive with its religion intact in a hostile world. Its rebel status attracted many devastating assaults on the region. In 1573 Damville's troops attacked nearby Cauvisson and Montpesat, and besieged Sommières, some 16 miles (25 km) from Nîmes.[75] In July sixty Calvinists were killed in a skirmish with Damville between Nîmes and Millau.

Together with the fear this must have engendered, there were also practical implications to being at war. Protestants in the city and its surrounding villages were ordered to work on the fortifications of the town—a recurring theme over the following years.[76] In February 1573 all Protestants who owned olive trees within the city walls were ordered to cut them down, and contribute the branches towards the town's repair.[77] In 1573–4 all public monies—taxes, imports, and church revenues—were directed towards paying the expenses of war including the cost of

---

[73] BSHPF, Ms. 566; Guggenheim, 'Calvinist Notables', 90, n. 38; Ménard, *Histoire*, vol. 5, 66–70.
[74] ADG, E dépôt 36/129, 71v, 30 Aug. 1572.   [75] Ménard, *Histoire*, vol. 5, 86, 92.
[76] ADG, E dépôt 36/17/27, 24 Jan. 1574.   [77] ADG, E dépôt 36/17/10, 3 Feb. 1573.

fortifying the town and the provision of munitions.[78] The goods and perishables of Catholics and absentee Huguenots were sold to fund the fortifications, and contributions were levied on each household dependent on their wealth.[79] There was powder and saltpetre to buy (a loan for 1,000 *livres* was raised for this by the first consul in 1574) and injured soldiers to provide for.[80] In addition, the town gates were closed between 5 p.m. and sunrise and, in January 1574, a list was drawn up of inhabitants required to make daily rounds of the walls of the town.[81] In November 1574 the council extended this to every male household head, who were each required to take their turn guarding the town day and night—a measure that must have caused great inconvenience to daily life.[82]

There was a marked problem of absenteeism as men left the town to go and join companies of soldiers.[83] Such men were warned to return home to defend the town or find their possessions sold and their families put out of the town. Reformed women whose husbands had left the town were told to fortify themselves with arms.

There were also restrictions on Catholics. In January 1573 those Catholics who had carried arms or had any communication with the royal army, or those women who had mixed with the enemy were ordered to leave the city.[84] In June Catholics were ordered not to leave their houses once the evening alarm sounded (an injunction repeated a year later, suggesting it was being flouted), nor were they to climb the towers or any other high places of the city.[85] From 1574 they were not allowed to leave the town after curfew, to gather in groups of more than three, or to frequent the town's royalist Catholic enemies, under pain of flogging and banishment.

Food provisions for everyone were affected. In addition to the damage done to crops by ravaging troops, the fact that the countryside around Nîmes had become a theatre of war meant that nearby villagers had trouble getting to the city to sell at market (held in the city's main square) the wheat and other provisions necessary for the subsistence of the city.[86] In addition, much of what the townsfolk did have was requisitioned to feed troops, and lists were drawn up, such as that of June 1574, specifying the quantities of flour required from the 'principal inhabitants' of the city to be sent to the army camp just outside Nîmes at Caissargues.[87] Troops were also billeted within Nîmes. In 1574 each of the four captains of the town was put in charge of thirty mercenaries, bringing the total number to 120, and they needed accommodating.[88]

Even after Damville turned coat and allied with the Reformed in 1574, a new threat arose from Jacques de Crussol, duc d'Uzès, and Roger de Saint-Lary, maréchal de Bellegarde. In 1576 Damville rejoined the royal side, taking joint command of

[78] Ménard, *Histoire*, vol. 5, 76–7.
[79] ADG, E dépôt 36/129, 186r, 4 Nov. 1574 (advocates and gentlemen were to pay twenty *sols*; *bourgeois* and merchants fifteen *sols*; *laboureurs* ten *sols*; *travailleurs* five *sols*...).
[80] ADG, E dépôt 36/490, *Comptes des deniers municipaux et extraordinaires, 1564–1579.*
[81] ADG, E dépôt 36/17/26, 16 Jan. 1574.
[82] ADG, E dépôt 36/129, 186r, 4 Nov. 1574; Ménard, *Histoire*, vol. 5, pp. 123, 128, 230.
[83] Ménard, *Histoire*, vol. 5, 89.   [84] ADG, E dépôt 36/129, 96v, 12 Jan. 1573.
[85] ADG, E dépôt 36/17/12, 4 Jun. 1573; ADG, E dépôt 36/129, 186r, 4 Nov. 1574.
[86] Ménard, *Histoire*, vol. 5, 169.   [87] ADG, E dépôt 36/17/34, 6 Jun. 1574.
[88] ADG, E dépôt 36/129, 186r, 4 Nov. 1574.

the army in the Languedoc with Bellegarde the following year. Repeatedly between 1575 and 1578 Uzès and Bellegarde ravaged the agricultural holdings outside Nîmes, burning down windmills, scorching the wheat in the fields, and damaging vineyards.[89] In July 1575, for example, the authorities in Nîmes wrote to Uzès, complaining of the pillage, ravages, and extreme savagery of his troops.[90]

During this period the threat of a siege was perennial. Many peasants from the surrounding area, or Huguenots caught outside Nîmes, were robbed, killed, or taken prisoner. Ménard estimates that by 1576 so many had died in the wars that Nîmes had more than 1,000 widows.[91] Over the next decade many women would approach the consistory for help from the poor-relief fund because their husbands were missing, such as the breastfeeding mother from Baux in Provence who, in January 1586, pleaded that her poverty was a result of her spouse's absence, as he was off fighting in the war.[92]

Once again, materials for work on repairing the fortifications of the town, and wheat and flour, were requisitioned.[93] The furniture of those absent from the city, and of those who refused to contribute to the upkeep and subsistence of the soldiers of the town's garrison, was to be sold.[94] Possibly in order to provide for the soldiers, inhabitants of the town were forbidden in 1575 from eating and drinking in the inns and taverns, with fines to be imposed on erring landlords and their clientele.[95] The innkeepers were also ordered not to accommodate strangers, and there were further curtailments on the freedoms of Catholics too: in 1577 they were instructed not to leave their houses by day or night until commanded otherwise, or they would be 'exposed to the mercy of the soldiers and treated and ransomed as prisoners of war'.[96] Regular lists were also drawn up of people to be banished from the town and not to return while the war continued, under pain of flogging; many of them were women, some accompanied by children.[97] These restrictions remained in place until the peace, concluded in September 1577, was finally implemented in November 1578.

There followed eight years of relative peace, although during these years the nearby village of Marguerittes came under siege, and the council of Nîmes provided funds to move cannon to Marguerittes from Aigues-Mortes, to compensate soldiers injured by arquebuses, and other similar expenses, to the tune of a total 2,177 *écus* 7 *s.* by 1588.[98] After the formation of the Catholic League Nîmes was itself directly under threat again from 1586. Those living in the suburbs (specifically, the Faubourgs des Jacobins) were given three days to move their families inside the city walls.[99] In 1587 there were several bloody incursions by the Leaguers, who came right up to the ramparts at Nîmes. Inhabitants found outside the town were killed, several women and girls were raped, and many animals were stolen. Hostilities in the region continued sporadically after this, including attacks on the environs of

[89] Ménard, *Histoire*, vol. 5, 127, 164, 166, 169.   [90] ADG, E dépôt 36/17/53, 1 Jul. 1575.
[91] Ménard, *Histoire*, vol. 5, 148.   [92] ADG, 42 J 28, 258v, 28 Jan. 1586.
[93] ADG, E dépôt 36/17/42, 24 Jan. 1575.   [94] ADG, E dépôt 36/17/73, 1 Mar. 1576.
[95] ADG, E dépôt 36/17/43, 24 Jan. 1575.   [96] ADG, E dépôt 36/17/88, 11 Jun. 1577.
[97] e.g. ADG, E dépôt 36/17/44, 29 Jan. 1575, '*la femme de Pierre Temple dict Payant et ses enfans*'.
[98] ADG, E dépôt 36/490.   [99] ADG, E dépôt 36/18/156, 5 Sept. 1586.

Nîmes in 1592 and 1595.[100] The council continued to invest money into repairing the city walls whenever necessary, for instance mending a hole in the wall near the Saint-Antoine gate in 1596, at a cost of 307 *livres* 11 *s*. 6 *d*.[101]

In August 1587 two further companies of footmen and gendarmes were established at the expense of the community to keep watch over the safety of the town. By 1589 the situation was severe enough that the town council and consuls reinstituted their scheme to force citizens of the town to act as sentries. The townsfolk were instructed that each of them must take 'their turn, including at night', that they were not allowed to skip their shift, or put someone else in their place.[102] Gates were to be guarded against unknown persons, and the inns and taverns of Nîmes were instructed again not to host strangers. Such commands were reiterated: in 1593 it was ordered that all persons under the age of 50—of whatever quality or condition—were to do their part in the guarding of the town or be fined four *écus*.[103]

The consequences of being periodically at war were also felt in other, less obvious, ways. An industry of weapons manufacture grew up.[104] The soldiers garrisoned in the town could be rowdy, violent, and threatening; reports in November 1584 tell of one company seen whipping women and girls.[105] Outside the Saint-Antoine gate to the city in October 1585 certain soldiers were seen groping the breasts of maidservants, and the context suggests these were not mutually consensual caresses.[106] Other women were made pregnant by soldiers—in April 1581 Anne Maurine was reported to be carrying the child of a soldier known only as Renaurd, who 'lives in the present town as a soldier in the company of Monsieur de St. Cosme', while one woman, in early 1586, approached one of the elders of the consistory for assistance after her soldier died, leaving her with an illegitimate 2-year-old girl to feed.[107]

The presence of the soldiers made the Protestant Church alive to the possibilities for immorality. Reports reached the church of girls being frequented by soldiers in the town in 1589 (they were admonished and a church elder instructed to keep a watchful eye on them) and, even more alarmingly, there were rumours of women married to Protestant soldiers having affairs and becoming pregnant while their husbands were away at war.[108]

The atmosphere of suspicion extended to attitudes towards strangers. In 1586 the consistory drew up a list of all the strangers who had arrived in the town in the previous year.[109] Two years later, in the face of the growing number of the poor, they urged the consuls to expel these incomers 'who infect the town'.[110] In 1595 the consistory wanted Marcelin Blanc, landlord of the Three Crowns, to be expelled from the town as they suspected him of visiting Provence, and harbouring soldiers

---

[100] Ménard, *Histoire*, vol. 5, 230.   [101] ADG, E dépôt 36/490.
[102] ADG, E dépôt 36/131, 3, '*Garde et sûreté de la ville*', 2 Jan. 1587.
[103] ADG, E dépôt 36/18/175, 5 May 1593.
[104] ADG, 42 J 28, 164r, 20 Mar. 1585: Captain Lambert is recorded as '*faizeur d'armes de guerre*'.
[105] ADG, 42 J 28, 138r, 7 Nov. 1584.   [106] ADG, 42 J 28, 190r, 2 Oct. 1585.
[107] BN Ms.fr 8667, 205v, 19 Apr 1581; ADG, 42 J 28, 210v, 5 Feb. 1586.
[108] ADG, 42 J 29, 327, 10 Jan. 1590, and 586, 30 Jan. 1591.
[109] ADG, 42 J 28, 232v, 6 Aug. 1586.   [110] ADG, 42 J 29, 13, 20 Apr. 1588.

from La Motte, also in Provence. It was the fact that Blanc was Provençal himself that made him especially suspect as a Catholic sympathizer.[111]

Such hostility towards strangers came, in part, from a sense that the world outside Nîmes was not safe for Huguenots. Reports reached Nîmes in 1592 that their former minister, Jean de Serres, had been taken captive and imprisoned in Aix-en-Provence.[112] In January 1595 a 60-year-old man called Abraham Levite, a Jewish printer and merchant who had converted and been baptized 'at the beginning of the troubles', and his wife Jaqueline de la Molte, both from Lyon, reported that their 23-year-old son had been taken prisoner by the League at Rochefort near La Rochelle.[113] Later that year, the wife of M. Cornilhan asked the consistory's help to free her husband, who was imprisoned as a galley-slave in Marseille.[114] However difficult life within the city became during the wars, it was better than the alternatives.

These continued threats should, however, not obscure the fact that Nîmes did not experience uninterrupted warfare: for most of the last quarter of the sixteenth century, Nîmois Catholics and Protestants lived in a state of truce and coexistence. Despite the rhetoric of the early Reformed Church that characterized Roman Catholicism as a form of idolatry, devil-worship or 'spiritual fornication', and moments of extremism, such as the massacres of 1567 and 1569, the adherents of the two faiths continued, of necessity, to interact both socially and economically.[115] To the chagrin of the Calvinist authorities, mixed marriages were frequent. As Robert Sauzet identified, the 'frontier of Catholicism' ran through families.[116] This was a transitional religious world, and although the new generations of Calvinists in Nîmes enjoyed an acute sense of numerical and moral ascendancy, it remained the case that long-standing social relations, essential economic transactions, and even some deep-seated non-Protestant religious beliefs and customs (especially those for coping in times of crisis) could not be easily abandoned. Sauzet, therefore, insists that one must not imagine Nîmes as a 'Protestant city always in a state of alert'.[117]

Perhaps this explains, in part, how relatively seldom the war is mentioned in the pages of the consistory registers (though partly responsible, too, is the absence of records between 1563 and 1578). At first the paucity of obvious commentary on the progress of the war in the Church's records might seem odd, but it soon becomes apparent that the war is a red thread through the pages of the consistorial records, disappearing and reappearing throughout—men quarrel when on the watch, women widowed by the war need financial support, sexual immorality is a concern, and so on.[118] Rarely is the war foregrounded in the attention of the scribes and authorities; instead, it is the constant background noise, the *mise en scène* against which every other story plays out.

---

[111] ADG, 42 J 30, 359r, 363r, 17 May 1595.   [112] ADG, 42 J 30, 86v, 29 Jul. 1592.
[113] ADG, 42 J 30, 321v, 26 Jan. 1595.   [114] ADG, 42 J 31, 21v, 22 Dec. 1595.
[115] Sauzet, 'Huguenots', 155.
[116] Robert Sauzet, *Contre-Réforme et Réforme Catholique en Bas-Languedoc: le diocèse de Nîmes au XVIIe siècle* (Bruxelles, Louvain, and Paris, 1979), 167.
[117] Sauzet, *Contre-Réforme*, 165.
[118] See ADH, GG 24, 131v, 29 Aug. 1602, for an example of two men, Jacques Ferrier and Isaaq Parran, quarrelling while keeping guard.

After thirty-seven years, during which the Nîmois had experienced at least a decade of immediate threat, the Edict of Nantes in 1598 finally brought twenty years of peace in the region, confirming the rights of the Protestants in Nîmes to worship there. At this time, the population of Nîmes was composed of 11,000–12,000 Protestants and 3,000–4,000 Catholics; around 400–500 Protestant baptisms occurred each year, compared to the ninety annual Catholic baptisms.[119] The following years, however, saw a revival of Catholicism in the town. The Catholic bishopric in Nîmes had been effectively abandoned between 1567 and 1594, with the appointed successor to d'Elbène, Raymond Cavalesi, remaining absent. In 1598 a new bishop, Pierre de Valernod, was consecrated. He immediately took up residence in Nîmes and started to reinvigorate the Catholic church with all the zeal and enthusiasm of the Counter-Reformation.[120] Over the next decade Valernod oversaw the reconstruction of the cathedral, sent Jesuit missionaries into the Huguenot heartland of the Cévennes, established a Jesuit college in Nîmes, and refounded the confraternity of the *Saint-Sacrement*.[121] Such reforming activities alarmed the consistory, although it is worth remembering that even in these apparently Catholic endeavours, coexistence and collaboration between the confessions featured strongly: it was Huguenot architects who were first commissioned with rebuilding the Catholic cathedral.[122] Nevertheless, the Reformed church remained alert to the dangers. They noted that Catholics had been appointed to all the principal offices of the judiciary in the town, and petitioned the King to ensure that the last remaining office of criminal judge was given to a Protestant.[123] They worried about the fate of the nearby town of Beaucaire, where the Catholic consuls treated the Huguenots badly, and petitioned the *présidial* to stop the education of children by Jesuits, on the grounds that the Protestant college in the city was a royal foundation.[124] The civic authorities, too, were concerned, both during the illness of Henri IV, and on the news of his death, to make preparations to assure the tranquillity of the city.[125]

In fact, people continued to convert to Protestantism in significant numbers between 1600 and 1620, necessitating the engagement of a fourth pastor, even after the devastating blow of minister Jérémie Ferrier's conversion to Catholicism in 1613 and the humiliating insertion of the words 'supposedly reformed religion' into the Protestants' own register by the royal authorities.[126] It is possible, as Menna Prestwich suggests, that the confessions became more aggressive and suspicious of one another in early seventeenth-century Nîmes. Certainly the wars of religion recommenced in the spring of 1621—but that is beyond the temporal limits of this study.[127]

---

[119] Sauzet, *Contre-Réforme*, 151.
[120] Ménard, *Histoire*, vol. 5, 290; Sauzet, *Contre-Réforme*, 51.
[121] Ménard, *Histoire*, vol. 5, 290, 333; Sauzet, *Contre-Réforme*, 168, 185; Prestwich, 'Calvinism', 103.
[122] Prestwich, 'Calvinism', 101; Sauzet, *Contre-Réforme*, 168.
[123] ADG, 42 J 29, 462, 1 Aug. 1590.
[124] ADG, 42 J 33, 90r, 22 Feb. 1606; ADG, 42 J 34, 207v, 10 Apr. 1610.
[125] ADG, E dépôt 36/135, 22 May 1610.   [126] ADG, 42 J 34, 222v–226r.
[127] Prestwich, 'Calvinism', 103.

Throughout this tumultuous time, the only way for the people of the late sixteenth- and early seventeenth-century Protestant Church to cope was to adhere to a strict moral code that they believed would please God and save them from His wrath.

WOMEN'S LIVES

To set the cases that follow in some context, it is important to review the theoretical notions about, and practical realities of, women's lives in this period.

In theory women were supposed to be physically, morally, mentally, and emotionally weaker than men. Medical knowledge since the ancients had been based on humoral theory: the idea that the body contained four humours—blood, phlegm, black bile, and yellow bile—and that health depended on maintaining a balance of them. A natural conjunct of this was that men were thought to be hotter and drier than women, and therefore more rational; women's cold, moist bodies made them emotional and illogical. Women's lack of heat explained why they menstruated (men were thought to burn up any excess blood within them), why they did not grow bald (unlike men, who burned up their hair), and why they had wide hips and narrow shoulders (men's heat, by contrast, drove the matter in their bodies towards the sky).

Aristotle considered women's lack of heat in the process of generation to explain why they had failed to push their sexual organs outside of their body: women were imperfect or deformed men. This notion that women and men shared a physiology (if distorted in women) was not challenged until the late seventeenth century.[128] As Aristotle also believed that the imperfect would desire perfection, his theory explained, in part, the common belief of this period—that women were more sexually driven and lustful than men. Medical science went even further than that—sexual intercourse was thought to be a biological necessity for women, and those who ignored the natural imperative to reproduce were thought to risk terrible trouble.[129] The womb, if not satiated with sex and pregnancy, was believed by medical authorities to wander around the body, causing depression and irrational behaviour (the word 'hysteria' is cognate with 'uterus'). Women were, therefore, condemned biologically and inevitably to be temptresses of men.

Although the clitoris had been 'discovered' in 1548, the female ovum was not identified until 1827, and it was believed throughout this period that women needed a sexual climax to conceive.[130] This may have had positive consequences for loving sexual relations, but also suggested that a woman who became pregnant after rape had obviously not been raped.

---

[128] Thomas Gibson, *The Anatomy of Human Bodies Epitomised* (London, 1682).

[129] Sara Matthew Grieco, 'Amour et sexualité', in *Histoire des femmes en Occident*, ed. Georges Duby and Michelle Perrot, 5 vols (Paris, 1991), vol. 3, ed. Natalie Zemon Davis and Arlette Farge, 76.

[130] Thomas Vicary, *The Anatomy of the Body of Man* (London, 1548); also cf. Gabriele Falloppio's *Observationes Anatomicae* (Venice, 1561).

Women's physical and moral weakness was thought to extend beyond lechery to avarice, vanity, and garrulity, and had been demonstrated *in exemplum perfectum* by Eve, who had been the conduit by which evil entered the world.[131] One of the Church fathers, Tertullian, had called woman 'the devil's gateway', and female subjection was seen as a consequent corollary of Eve's sin (although even Calvin accepted that Eve had been inferior to Adam even before the Fall).[132] These may have been the beliefs of the elite, but many of them filtered down to the lower reaches of society and, even if they were challenged in practice, they created the mental space in which society functioned. Everyone at this time—including, we should assume, the women—believed that the female of the species was weaker than the male in body, mind, spirit, and resolve. More easily prone to temptation and sin, women needed men to provide them with a moral compass, physical protection, and intellectual direction. The seventeenth-century essayist, Pierre Nicole, compared women to vines: 'They do not know how to keep themselves standing upright, nor how to subsist by themselves; they need a prop, even more for their minds than for their bodies.'[133]

Women had no formal access to power: they were barred from public office and higher education; played no formal role in the Church, law, or government; and operated on the edges of the medical profession.[134] The subordinated place of women was also upheld in law. A married woman had no independent legal status apart from her husband: she was subject to him in all things. A contract signed by a married woman without her husband's signature was worthless. Her husband had possession of and responsibility for her goods and could dispose of them (her dowry aside) without the consent or knowledge of his wife.[135] A married woman could not technically own property, although wills from the period suggest that they did so in practice. Throughout the period women faced a worsening status under law: statutes were introduced to prevent marriage without parental consent and from February 1556 infanticide became a special case under French law.[136] This meant that if an unmarried woman concealed her pregnancy and secretly had a baby who died, she was automatically presumed guilty of child-murder, and sentenced to death. Barbara Diefendorf found that in Paris over the years 1565–1625 a total of 625 women received this sentence for infanticide.[137]

[131] Ian Maclean, *The Renaissance Notion of Woman: A Study in the Fortunes of Scholasticism and Medical Science in European Intellectual Life* (Cambridge, 1980), 16, 22.

[132] André Biéler, *L'homme et la femme dans la morale calviniste* (Geneva, 1963), 40; John Calvin, *Genesis*, Alister McGrath and J. I. Packer (eds), (Wheaton, IL, 2001), 52; John Calvin, *1, 2 Timothy and Titus*, Alister McGrath and J. I. Packer (eds), (Wheaton, IL, 1998), 49.

[133] Pierre Nicole, 'Pensées diverses', in *Essais de morale*, 6 vols (Desprez, 1755), vol. 6, 323.

[134] James R. Farr, *Authority and Sexuality in Early Modern Burgundy (1550–1730)* (New York and Oxford, 1995), 24.

[135] Paul Ourliac, *Histoire du droit privé francais de l'an mil au Code Civil* (Paris, 1985), 271; Merry E. Wiesner, *Women and Gender in Early Modern Europe* (Cambridge, 1993), 37; Barbara B. Diefendorf, 'Widowhood and Remarriage in Sixteenth-Century Paris', *Journal of Family History* 7.4 (1982), 379–95; Barbara B. Diefendorf, 'Gender and the Family', in *Renaissance and Reformation France, 1500–1648*, ed. Mack F. Holt (Oxford, 2002), 100.

[136] J. B. Collins, 'The Economic Role of Women in Seventeenth-Century France', *FHS* 16.2 (1989), 436–70, 439.

[137] Diefendorf, 'Gender', 116; Alfred Soman, 'Anatomy of an Infanticide Trial', *Changing Identities*, 252.

Life Cycle

At birth a baby had a 68-to 80-per-cent chance of making it through their first year of life: 200–300 children in every 1,000 died in their first twelve months. Fewer than half of all children born survived to the age of 20.[138] Robert Wheaton noted that in Bordeaux in 1647, of 142 married or widowed people's wills, 36 per cent showed there were no living children.[139]

At around the age of 12 or 13 most girls born to poor and middling families left home to start their working lives.[140] Over the next ten to fifteen years they saved money from their wages to enable them to build up or supplement their dowry, so that at some point in their 20s they could marry.[141] Young men enacted a similar pattern through apprenticeship.

For those of the lower orders, then, marriage happened relatively late, when a couple could afford to set up an independent household. The verb *s'établir* (to establish oneself) in French meant both to become economically independent and to marry.[142] Historians have variously estimated this to be at around 25 to 27 for women and 27 to 30 for men, although Allan A. Tulchin suggests that the age of first marriage was slightly lower in the south of France than the north, with women marrying in their early to mid-20s, or even late teens.[143] Mortality rates were such that at least one of the parents of these brides and grooms had probably already died: for seventeenth-century Bordeaux, Wheaton found that of 499 brides, fewer than a quarter still had both parents living, 42 per cent had lost one parent, and 35 per cent had lost both, while for Nîmes Tulchin finds that the parents of young adults were frequently absent when marriage contracts where drawn up.[144]

For most girls and women, at this time, marriage was their goal and ambition.[145] Being a wife and having access to those frequent social occasions when married women gathered to spin and gossip—known as the *veillées*—carried enormous amounts of social prestige. Young women still toiling to put aside a dowry could only look on with envy. To move from wearing one's hair down—displaying one's virginal spinster status—to putting one's hair up—as befitted a married woman—was a longed-for attainment. Few accepted that women could live alone outside the shelter of marriage.[146] For a woman to choose to remain single for life

[138] Jean-Louis Flandrin, *Familles: parenté, maison, sexualité dans l'ancienne société* (Paris, 1976), 54.

[139] Robert Wheaton, 'Affinity and Descent in Seventeenth-Century Bordeaux', in *Family and Sexuality in French History*, ed. Robert Wheaton and Tamara K. Hareven (Philadelphia, PA, 1980), 115.

[140] Olwen Hufton, 'Le travail et la famille', in *Histoire des femmes en Occident*, ed. Georges Duby and Michelle Perrot, 5 vols (Paris, 1991), vol. 3, ed. Davis and Arlette Farge, 17.

[141] Hufton, 'Le travail', 29–31; Collins, 'Economic Role', 440.

[142] Jean-Louis Flandrin, 'Repression and Change in the Sexual Life of Young People in Medieval and Modern Times', in *Family and Sexuality in French History*, ed. Robert Wheaton and Tamara K. Hareven (Philadelphia, PA, 1980), 31; Sharon Kettering, *French Society, 1589–1715* (Harlow, 2001), 9.

[143] Kettering, *French Society*, 9, says 25–7 for women, and 28–30 for men; Lebrun, *La vie conjugale*, 31, says 25–6 for women, 27–8 for men; Jean-Louis Flandrin suggests an average age for women of 24, *Familles: parenté, maison, sexualité dans l'ancienne société* (Paris, 1976), 54; Allan A. Tulchin, 'Low Dowries, Absent Parents: Marrying for Love in an Early Modern French Town', *SCJ* 44.3 (2013), 713–38, 724.

[144] Wheaton, 'Affinity', 115; Tulchin, 'Low Dowries', 715.

[145] Jacques Solé, *Etre femme en 1500: la vie quotidienne dans le diocèse de Troyes* (Paris, 2000), 80.

[146] Scarlett Beauvalet-Boutouyrie, *Etre veuve sous l'Ancien Régime* (Paris, 2001), 15.

was therefore so counter-cultural as to be thought perverse; for sixteenth- and seventeenth-century women, permanent spinsterhood was an unusual and very vulnerable situation.[147]

The most popular months of the year for a wedding were January and February.[148] Weddings were technically prohibited in Lent and Advent, roughly March and December (though did take place, for example, five in Nîmes in December 1593).[149] Most Protestants married on a Sunday in a blessing after the service, thus saving their friends and families from missing a day of work. In the south of France, the dowry that the bride brought to the marriage—however small—was considered practically obligatory. It remained, however, inalienable and was recuperated by a wife on the death of her spouse.[150]

Married women were, on average, pregnant every other year, filling the years of wedlock with the continual swell of pregnancy and the screams of new life.[151] Alayssette Forniere in Nîmes is a case in point: she gave birth to Jacob in April 1589, Jeanne in February 1591, Clemel in September 1593, Marie in February 1595, and Mathieu in September 1597—each interval just over or just under two years.[152] After marrying in 1571 Jehan Bertrand and Catherine Cheysse, from a small village near Ganges, had four children over the first ten years of their marriage.[153] By January 1595 Jaqueline de la Molthe and Abraham Levite had had nine children, of whom four were still alive.[154] In the Protestant baptismal and marriage register for Nîmes for 1585 to 1602, there are 350 weddings recorded and 7,603 births.[155] Tulchin has found that a quarter of all those marrying in notarial records for 1550–62 were not born in Nîmes, and estimated immigration to the city accounts for perhaps a third.[156] A small proportion of children were born outside marriage, and there were probably many couples who married in the Catholic church, but even so, this suggests an average of six to eight children born to each couple, of whom perhaps three or four died.[157] Women were pregnant so often that Lyndal Roper has suggested it even guided the ascetic of beauty: to be attractive was to be voluptuous, fleshy, and fecund.[158] It was not healthy, though: childbirth was painful, and dangerous. The rate of maternal death in childbirth ranged between sixteen and twenty-five women out of every thousand.[159]

Most women, even of the poor, inadvertently increased the incidence of childbirth by sending their infants to be breastfed by others, thereby losing out on the natural contraceptive benefits of breastfeeding. In May 1613 Françoise Surre arranged for her month-old child to be breastfed by another woman. She had hoped to work as a nurse herself for Antoine Dumas, a judge's lieutenant in Saint-Gilles, but as the

---

[147] François Lebrun, *La vie conjugale sous l'Ancien Régime* (Paris, 1975), 30.
[148] Tulchin, 'Low Dowries', 713–38, 720.   [149] ADG, E Dépôt 36/697, 522r (inverse).
[150] Lebrun, *La vie conjugale*, 76.
[151] Flandrin, *Familles*, 53, 57; Lebrun, *La vie conjugale*, 108; Hufton, 'Le travail', 46.
[152] ADG, E Dépôt 36/697, 90v, 133v, 205, 252r, 346r.
[153] ADG, 42 J 30, 84r–v, 85r–v, 27 Jul. 1592.   [154] ADG, 42 J 30, 321v, 26 Jan. 1595.
[155] ADG, E Dépôt 36/697.   [156] Tulchin, 'Low Dowries', 717.
[157] Flandrin, *Familles*, 53.   [158] Roper, *Witch Craze*, 146–50.
[159] Today, for comparison, in the United Kingdom, the maternal mortality ratio is 8.2 maternal deaths per 100,000 live births (it is double that in the United States).

child was so 'very young and tender' she feared that he might fall ill on the way or in Saint-Gilles' rumoured evil air, so she instead appointed the wife of Guillaume Delapierre, a weaver, as wet-nurse to her child at the generous rate of 21 *livres* for six months. The contract between Surre and the nurse contains a clause for pro-rata repayment if the baby died before the age of seven months.[160]

As the mortality rates of parents suggest, spousal death was also to be anticipated. Scarlett Beauvalet-Boutoyrie found that of 525 first-time marriages between 1650 and 1679, the average length of a marriage was a little under nineteen years. For 33 per cent of those couples, the union lasted for less than ten years, cut short not by divorce, but by death.[161] We should not imagine that the ubiquity of loss inured people to grief: in January 1584 the consistory in Nîmes noticed that Mademoiselle de Lansard had not been to church since the death of her husband and, when they sent one of their number to urge her to attend, she said she did not want to leave the house.[162]

Widowhood was a state, therefore, that women could possibly enter quite young, still with young children to raise. If the average age of marriage for a woman was around 25, and the average length of marriage nineteen years, then women could easily become widows in their early 40s or before. Beauvalet-Boutoyrie suggests that it was between 40 and 50 that most women risked becoming a widow.[163] Tax rolls indicate that widowed women headed up some 10 to 20 percent of all households and enterprises.[164] They were treated, in many ways, as head of the household: in May 1608 the widow of M. Ducros was summoned before the consistory in Nîmes as her daughter, Caterine, had committed fornication, and the widow was censured for not watching over her daughter 'as was her duty'.[165] A widow was answerable for the morality of the household—a task that otherwise fell on the male head.

Despite their prevalence, however, widows were not universally well-regarded. On the one hand, they were to be pitied; on the other, their untrammelled sexuality and power made them dangerous.[166] Emmanuel Le Roy Ladurie has suggested an added power was bestowed on women by the passing of the menopause (and post-menopausal women were certainly feared, as evidence from the witchcraft trials would suggest).[167] Many widows fell into poverty. Françoise de Guerin explained in December 1596 that her husband's death had left her in penury: 'she had no means of making a living because of her widowhood and also that she had nothing in the world.'[168] Dalphine Rodolousse asked the consistory in Montauban for assistance in October 1597, stating that she was in extreme poverty following the illness and death of her husband, and could not afford a wedding dress for her

---

[160] Arc.Not., 2 E 1/371, 21 May 1613; the 'evil air' might be a reference to disease, specifically, the plague, which was thought to be transmitted by corrupted, foul-smelling air.
[161] Beauvalet-Boutoyrie, *Etre veuve*, 149.
[162] ADG, 42 J 28, 72v, 11 Jan. 1584.   [163] Beauvalet-Boutoyrie, *Etre veuve*, 14, 337.
[164] Collins, 'Economic Role', 440; Diefendorf, 'Widowhood', 380.
[165] ADG, 42 J 34, 10r, 14 May 1608.   [166] Beauvalet-Boutoyrie, *Etre veuve*, 15.
[167] Emmanuel Le Roy Ladurie, *L'argent, l'amour et la mort en pays d'oc* (Paris, 1980), 50; also Roper, *Witch Craze*.
[168] ADTG, I 1, 215r–v, 28 Dec. 1596.

daughter.[169] Widows often featured on the church poor lists, such as a poor widow called *La Janasse* who was given wheat by the consistory of Pont-de-Camarès in March 1580, or the widow of Dermin Malefosse, who was helped by the consistory of Ganges with three *sous* in June 1587.[170] In March 1597 Ganges consistory's list of thirty-two donations to the poor included nine, or nearly 30 per cent, to widows.[171] Widows also appear in the lists of the poor receiving bequests in wills. In M. Dupin's will of 1605 he gave a large proportion of the 100 *livres* bequested to the poor to specific widows: 'twenty *livres* to Captain Boneti's widow, ten *livres* to [the widow] of Sainte-Marie, ten *livres* to her of Barthomyon Capelant.'[172] Widowed women often sought ways of making money, but their ambiguous situation meant that they needed to guard against accusations of immorality: a woman identified as 'the widow of the late Rogueffe' was chastised for letting soldiers sleep in her house in Pont-de-Camarès in April 1588—presumably as paying lodgers— and argued that she was 'truly poor'.[173] Marguerite de Barecou, widow of the provost Rouviere, was summoned to the consistory of Nîmes in 1602 for excessive usury, having received fifty *sous* for lending out ten *écus*—an interest rate of 10 per cent over four months.[174]

Remarriages, although not welcomed—because of fears of children being disinherited—were nonetheless common. One in every three or four marriages involved a widow, although the Reformed church required widows to wait at least seven and a half months after their husband's death before remarrying.[175] Evidence of these remarriages only made it into the pages of the consistories when there was some hiccup along the way. The opposition of Barthelemy Guarantz to the marriage of widow Marthe Pradonne with Anthoine Ballanoir in December 1581—on the grounds that she had previously promised to marry him—gives an interesting insight into the motivations, arrangements, and practicalities of a second marriage. Guarantz, himself a widower, recalled being asked by his friend, M. Fages, if he wanted to remain single, and replied that he would marry again if he could find someone and God wanted it. His friend had mentioned Marthe Pradonne, and Guarantz reflected that 'he knew the said Pradonne and if God wants it, he would be well at ease'. Guarantz subsequently arranged a time to meet Pradonne, and proposed to her saying, 'if God wants it, if she would take him as husband?' She replied, 'yes, if God wishes it'. They immediately discussed her dowry, which widows provided for themselves, and she said she could bring 100 *écus*, though for that she would have to sell her house in Arles. The split between them had occurred afterwards, when Guarantz had encountered problems with Pradonne's son, whom he described as 'really terrible', and they had both agreed to look elsewhere for a marriage partner,

[169] ADTG, I 1, 297r, 15 Oct. 1597.
[170] BN, Ars., Ms. 10434, 6r, 20 Mar. 1580; ADH, GG 24, 7v, 28 Jun. 1587.
[171] ADH, GG 24, 77r–v, 16 Mar. 1597.   [172] ADG, 42 J 33, 54r, 17 Aug. 1605.
[173] BN, Ars. Ms. 10434, 126v, 7 Apr. 1588.   [174] ADG, 42 J 32, 112r, 2 Oct. 1602.
[175] Kettering, *French Society*, 12; Collins, 'The Economic Role', 440; Beauvalet-Boutoyrie, *Etre veuve*, 38, 231; Wheaton, 'Affinity', 129; John Quick, *Synodicon in Gallia reformata* (London, 1692), 193; Jean Aymon, *Tous les synods nationaux des Églises réformées de France*, 2 vols (The Hague, 1710); Brian G. Armstrong, '*Semper Reformanda*: The Case of the French Reformed Church, 1559–1620', in *Later Calvinism*, 122.

though Guarantz had later, obviously, had second thoughts.[176] It is unsurprising that problems with children from a previous marriage hindered the match.

As mortality rates are so skewed by infant and child mortality, it is hard to estimate the average life expectancy if one reached the age of 20. It was certainly possible to live into one's 70s, 80s, or 90s: among those claiming poor relief in sixteenth-century Tours, Susan Broomhall found that, of those who mentioned old age as a cause of their poverty, the youngest was 72, and the oldest was 92.[177] Nevertheless, although it was possible to live up to a ripe old age, and although people achieved maturity and responsibility at a younger age than in modern culture, this was chiefly a society of young people, with all the attendant qualities of youth: boisterousness, certainty, intemperance, and optimism.

Wealth and Standards of Living

Tulchin examined 1,100 marriage contracts from Nîmes for 1550 to 1563 from which, using average dowry size, he established a hierarchy of occupational wealth. He showed that the wealthiest in Nîmes society were the seigneurs-by-purchase and judges of the *présidial* court, with dowries of over 1,200 *livres*, that lawyers received on average a dowry of 900 *livres*, bourgeois 500 *livres*, and wealthy merchants 200 *livres*. Anyone above this level, he concluded, could be considered wealthy. The upper-middling—with dowries of 100 to 200 *livres*—were yeomen, merchants, notaries, apothecaries, mercers, and embroiderers. The middling, with dowries of fifty to a hundred *livres*, were innkeepers and most highly skilled artisans (cloth-tradesmen, locksmiths, hatters, and carpenters), and those with an average of below fifty *livres* (the masons, labourers, and carters) were the poor.[178] A dowry of this size was still a year's salary for the very poorest in employment. Construction workers, such as masons, earned (in Paris) four to five *sous* a day, and worked 260 days a year, making an annual salary of between fifty-two and sixty-five *livres*, by comparison to a mason's average dowry of forty-five *livres*.[179] Women always earned significantly less than men. The rates of pay for nurses up until 1562 were as follows: a nursemaid providing childcare could expect twelve *sous* six *deniers* a month, making an annual salary of seven *livres* seven *sous*, while a wet-nurse could earn a somewhat greater seventeen *sous* six *deniers* a month, or an annual salary of ten *livres* seven *sous*.[180] Nurses generally received accommodation and subsistence as part of their role. Women working as day-labourers in agriculture—weeding grain fields, gathering olives—received a daily wage of two *sous* nine *deniers*, or an annual salary of thirty-five *livres* fifteen *sous* (although this supposes that they managed to

---

[176] BN, Ms.fr.8667, 269v–270r, 29 Dec. 1581.

[177] Susan Broomhall, "Burdened with Small Children": Woman Defining Poverty in Sixteenth-Century Tours', in *Women's Letters Across Europe, 1400–1700: Form and Persuasion*, ed. Jane Couchman and Ann Crabb (Aldershot, 2005), 232.

[178] Tulchin, *That Men*, 21–2; 'Low Dowries', 717. Cf. Beauvalet-Boutoyrie, *Etre veuve*, 245, who found, for 1660–70, dowries ranging between 62 *livres* for the daughter of a pastry-maker and 300,000 *livres* at the very top.

[179] Tulchin, 'Low Dowries', 726.   [180] Ladurie, *Paysans*, 127.

get work every day, which is unlikely).[181] Women's wages deteriorated in comparison to inflation as the sixteenth century progressed from around half to a third of a man's wage. It is therefore unsurprising that women had to work so long to raise a dowry, and that Tulchin also found, in a third of the marriage contracts he examined, that the dowry was simply listed as all the bride's goods—indicating a small amount that did not total, in value, tens of *livres*.[182]

This gives some sense of the social hierarchy of the town. Nearly every time a man was called before the consistory his occupation was recorded. Comparing these to Tulchin's figures for dowries, it is possible to list, in rough tiers of descending order of wealth and status, the professions represented before the consistory in Nîmes between 1561 and 1615:

seigneur	judge	lawyer (*advocat*)	bourgeois	
lawyer (*praticien*)	notary	merchant	surgeon	clerk
furrier	clothes-maker	saddler	apothecary	hosier
yeoman	carpenter	wainscotter	innkeeper	retailer	cordwainer/cobbler
hatter	tanner	student	goldsmith	wool-carder	locksmith
baker	market-gardener	weaver	farmer	master tailor	farrier
porter	furniture-maker	butcher	armourer	servant	husbandman
wood-worker	mason	roaster of meat	pastry-maker	labourer	

There are a handful of attendant professions not in Tulchin's list—glover, ropemaker, pin-maker, and so on—and one that was a newcomer in the mid- to late sixteenth century: master-gunsmith. In 1592 the consistory also drew up lists of different categories of occupation, which, with a few additional professions—printers, booksellers, painters, potters, and so on—broadly support this classification of Nîmois society and wealth.[183]

Dowries and wages can also be compared with the price of comestibles. The town consuls of Nîmes set the prices for bread, fish, and game in 1586, 1597, and 1600. In May 1586 white bread (although linked to the price of grain) went for seventeen *deniers*; brown bread for fourteen *deniers*—meaning that for those in the poorest trades, a loaf of bread cost almost a third of a day's wage.[184] The price of wheat went up in the 1590s. Fish was more expensive. The tariff of prices was as follows: two *sous* two *deniers* for a pound of sole or mullet; two *sous* for a pound of bass or grey mullet; one *sou* seven *deniers* for whiting, cod, and plaice (the latter two types of fish increased to two *sous* in 1600); and one *sou* for *melette* (a type of anchovy).[185] These prices were low, however, by comparison, to those for game: twenty *sous* for a pair of partridges, twelve *sous* for a hare or a pair of woodcocks,

---

[181] Ladurie, *Paysans*, 125.   [182] Tulchin, 'Low Dowries', 725.
[183] ADG, 42 J 30, 122v–123v, 18 Nov. 1592.
[184] ADG, E Dépôt 36/39, pièce 1, 28 May 1586.
[185] ADG, E Dépôt 36/39, 71v, 3 Jan. 1597, 120.

eight *sous* for a rabbit, and six *sous* for a duck.[186] Food could easily, therefore, eat up the vast majority of a wage: to buy a rabbit and a pound of cod in a week, and a loaf of bread each day, would cost nineteen *sous* seven *deniers*, out of a weekly wage for a mason for a six-day week of twenty-four to thirty *sous*: some 65 to 80 per cent. What was not spent on food would go on accommodation: cordwainer Anthonie Deleuse and Claude Rauelle rented a room to a woman called Fermine Relaissee in 1578 for twenty *sous* (or one *livre*) a month.[187]

In these circumstances it seems likely that poor to middling women owned few possessions of value. Wills allow us to build up a picture of what women possessed through what they left to their family and friends. Widow and impoverished noble Isabel de Folaquier left, in her will of July 1562, twelve *sous* to the poor and then money and goods to her three daughters, from two marriages. To her first daughter, Antonie Argentier, she bequeathed ten *livres*, two blouses, a violet corset, a petti-coat, a blanket, and the shoes and stockings she was wearing at the time she drew up the will. To her second daughter, Drivette Argentier, she left fifteen *livres* plus twelve sheets, a brown corset, a bolero jacket, and half of her jewels and small accessories. To her last daughter, Catherine Boisseron, she left five *livres* and a corset, a petticoat, and the other half of her accessories, clothes, and jewels.[188] In the same month Jaumette Raspail, the wife of an innkeeper, bequeathed to her servant, Marguerite Baldit, a linen dress, five blouses, six aprons, and six ruffs (or collars); to Marguerite Veyras, her blanket and three blouses; and to her sister Catherine Raspail, a ring of gold, worth one and a half *écus*, and a leather belt decorated with silver.[189] The items named in these wills probably did not represent all their possessions, but items considered by the testators sufficiently valuable to be mentioned, and they are few. We can also imagine, as we can learn from the inventory of the moveable possessions of Marie Vaurilhon, innkeeper at *La Croix Blanche* (The White Cross) at Générac from October 1613, that among a woman's household goods may have been platters, plates, dishes, an ewer, a salt-cellar, a bed made of wood, a mattress of wool or straw, sheets, and feather duvets with wool or linen exteriors, although, as the hostess of an inn, Vaurilhon had more of these things than most.[190]

Women's Work

Identifications were gendered.[191] When women were named before the consis-tory, their occupation was not generally asked for or offered. They tended to be identified by their relationship to a man, which means we nearly always know their marital status—a wife, a widow, or, if they are given as the daughter of so-and-so, still single.[192]

---

[186] ADG, E Dépôt 36/39, 72r.   [187] Bn, Ms.fr. 8667, 30r, 13 Aug. 1578.

[188] Arc. Not., 2 E 1/251, 11 Jul. 1562. '*Gounelles*' or '*gonnelles*' are petticoats made up of the bodices and skirts attached to each other; '*pellison*' is *pellisou*, a bolero jacket.

[189] Arc.Not., 2 E 1/251, 19 Jul. 1562. *Faudilh* ('*faudalz*') is Occitan for a small apron; '*coullaretz*' (*colaret* in Occitan, *collerette* in French) is a ruff or collar.

[190] Arc.Not., 2 E 1/371, 24 Oct. 1613.

[191] Carol L. Loats, 'Gender, Guilds, and Work Identity in Sixteenth-Century Paris', FHS 20.1 (1997), 15–30, here 18.

[192] Beatrice Gottlieb, 'The Meaning of Clandestine Marriage', in *Family and Sexuality in French History*, ed. Robert Wheaton and Tamara K. Hareven (Philadelphia, PA, 1980), 55.

In their teens and twenties many women worked as maidservants for employers who were effectively *in loco parentis*.[193] Many girls and young women travelled into major cities like Montauban and Nîmes in search of such work and were housed by their employers. Jehane Rate, from Alès, stated in May 1614 that she had stayed at the house of Sieur Verquiere for thirteen years before moving to Sieur Delicat's house, where she had remained for a year and a half.[194] Even modest households employed a servant or two, but I have come across only one maid described as a '*chambriere de chambre*' (literally a 'maidservant of the bedroom'), that is, a chambermaid or lady's maid: most were maids of all work and did everything from lighting fires, washing laundry, repairing clothes, cleaning dishes and floors, to fetching food from the market, taking out ordure, carrying in water, and preparing food.[195] Surviving wills from Nîmes in the period testify to legacies left to maidservants of clothes or money, for their 'good services'.[196] Nevertheless, it is true that the relationship between employer and maidservant exaggerated the issues of authority and subservience already present within the fabric of patriarchy, making servants more susceptible to mistreatment by their employers. Such abuse could involve, for instance, overwork, malnutrition, or the withholding of payment. In the 1580s the maidservants Jeanne Solière and Delphine Palatière complained to the consistory of Nîmes against their employers for the non-payment of their wages.[197] Jane Joubernesse from a village outside Alès complained to the consistory that her former employer, M. Bret, would not return her clothes.[198]

Women's occupations were not, however, limited to maid, nurse, or day-labourer. Many women joined their husbands in the trade that they practised, as important partners in their labour. For many professions, be it farming, inn-keeping, butchery, silk-making, or baking, a husband-wife team shared the labour and responsibilities of their joint trade, much of which was carried out within a workshop that formed part of the marital home.[199] Many women then continued this trade after their husband's death. Collins found that many widows in seventeenth-century Nantes had a prominent place in their trade guilds, and between 1620 and 1650 10 to 20 per cent of bakers mentioned in the archives, and 10 per cent of butchers, were women.[200] In sixteenth-century Rouen three of the forty-six richest merchants were women.[201] Collins and Loats have also found evidence, however, to suggest that women could adopt trades distinct from those of their husbands. In sixteenth-century Rouen twenty of thirty-six linen-merchants were women, and

---

[193] Flandrin, *Familles*, 62; Hufton, 'Le travail', 29; Sarah Maza, *Servants and Masters in Eighteenth-Century France: The Uses of Loyalty* (Princeton, 1983), 63; Diarmaid MacCulloch, *The Reformation: Europe's House Divided* (New York and London, 2003), 617; I. K. Hufton, *Adolescence and Youth in Early Modern England* (New Haven, CT, and London, 1994), 2.

[194] ADG, 42 J 35, 78v, 16 May 1614.   [195] Hufton, 'Le travail', 19–20.

[196] e.g. Arc.Not., 2 E 1/371, 26 Jun. 1596 (Jeanne Bonete); 2 E 1/251, 19 Jul. 1562 (Jaumette Raspail); 2 E 1/264, 24 Feb. 1576 (Jacques Maurin).

[197] ADG, 42 J 28, 274r, 312v, 8 Apr. 1587; BN, Ms.fr. 8667, 118r, 20 Apr. 1580.

[198] ADG, 42 J 30, 172r, 12 May 1593.

[199] Collins, 'The Economic Role', 451; Natalie Zemon Davis, 'Women in the Crafts in Sixteenth-Century Lyon', *Feminist Studies* 8.1 (1982), 47–80, here 48, 54.

[200] Collins, 'The Economic Role', 451.   [201] Collins, 'The Economic Role', 455.

not all were widows.[202] In a sample of 2,100 contracts for apprentices in Paris between 1540 and 1558, it is clear that women were providing the training in nearly 12 per cent of cases, while eighty-five cases clearly indicate that either two trades operated out of the household, or one or both of the partners worked outside the home.[203] Loats found that many women worked in making clothes and accessories, and their husbands included merchants, carpenters, masons, roofers, printers, cutlers, bakers, cobblers, lawyers, and farriers.[204]

The consistory records indicate that women in Languedoc worked in, at least, the following trades: the manufacture of clothes (cloth-trading, making nightcaps, manufacturing woollen cloth), the care and upkeep of clothes (laundry, bleaching linen), kneading bread, nursing and wet-nursing, printing, market-gardening, teaching, and one as a locksmith. Women also worked in the second-hand trade—buying items and selling them at a profit. Marguerite Deausee, Jehane Rousse, and Françoise Batutelle were regrators summoned to the consistory in February 1594 for having used false balances.[205] Above all women feature, in both the consistorial registers and town records, as innkeepers—in some cases, with their husbands, but often in sole charge of a tavern or lodging. In Nîmes alone, the records show that Bernardine Carreyron, widow of Jean Sauguier, was given a licence to continue to display a sign of Saint-Antoine above her inn in the *faubourgs* in February 1570.[206] A woman called Sarre was innkeeper of *Le Flascon* (The Flask) in September 1580 (and considered of ill repute).[207] In March 1583 Jehan Gaubin's widow was recorded as the landlady of an inn called Les Arènes (presumably in the amphitheatre itself).[208] Jane Fabresse was *hostesse*—landlady—of an unidentified tavern in October 1596 (and chucked out a group of men on the suspicion that they were accompanied by a prostitute disguised as a man).[209] Jehanne Bertanne was innkeeper of the *Chapeau Rouge* (The Red Hat) in November 1602, and, at the same time, Ysabel Cistie was recorded as running an unnamed tavern.[210] In 1605 Donne Anthonye Gille was *hostesse* of *La Teste Noyre* (The Black Head), while Pinhet's widow was landlady of *La Pomme* (The Apple).[211] These are isolated incidents, and there is no reason to think there were not more women in sole or joint charge of inns and taverns across Languedoc.

Time

Not everyone was asked their ages by the consistory; some who were proved able to give their age quite exactly: 28-year-old Bernardine Bermonde, 23-year-old scholar Anthoine Duplan, 20-year-old Isabel Lanteyresse, and a 64-year-old widow called Jeanne Roberte.[212] Most, however, gave a reckoning of their age that was more approximate. Marie Gibernesse was 'about 30 years old' when she came before the

[202] Collins, 'The Economic Role', 455; Loats, 'Gender', 15.   [203] Loats, 'Gender', 18, 23.
[204] Loats, 'Gender', 21–2.   [205] ADG, 42 J 30, 255v, 23 Feb. 1594.
[206] ADG, E Dépôt, 36/84, 194r, 3 Feb. 1570.   [207] BN, Ms.fr. 8667, 140r, 28 Sept. 1580.
[208] ADG, 42 J 28, 4r, 23 Mar. 1583.   [209] ADG, 42 J 31, 167r, 19 Feb. 1597.
[210] ADG, E Dépôt 36/39, 178r, 178v, 15 Nov. 1602.   [211] ADG, 42 J 33, 30r, 49v, 67r.
[212] BN, Ms.fr. 8667, 126r, 3 Jun. 1562; ADTG, I 1, 262r, 8 Jun. 1597.

consistory, as was Marthe de Praissac.[213] Gillette Franchilhonne was 'aged, as she said, 25 years or so'; Jehane Bugne was '45 years or about'; Marie Imberte was 'aged 20 years or so as she said'.[214]

The same is true when it came to describing how long something had lasted, or how long ago something had occurred. Sometimes the inexactitude makes sense: Isabel d'Asperes said she had heard rumours about an affair for 'four or five years'—it was a rumour and necessarily hazy.[215] Yet the same applies for events in women's lives: Jane Gibernesse said she had worked for Jacques Gardiol for 'around four years'; he later said she had worked for him for 'three years'.[216] Marthe Privade said she had lived and worked in Nîmes for 'nine or ten years'.[217] Catherine Coueffete said she had gone to the Mass 'for two years or more' (when it would have profited her not to exaggerate the time to the consistory).[218] A woman called Brunelle said her neighbour had beaten her 'some three years previously'; Ysabel Bonnete said she had not seen her husband 'for five or six years'.[219]

People only ever rarely—if at all—referred to the months of the year, and there is every reason to think that many people did not know them. Instead, the cardinal points of their calendar were high days and holy days—although people orientated by surprisingly few, spread over quite a circumscribed period of the year. The most common point of reference was Saint Madeleine (also spelled Saint Magdaleine), the day in honour of the saint known in English as Mary Magdalene, who was celebrated on 22 July. Saint Madeleine was the patron saint of repentant sinners, sexual temptation, and women, and legend had it that she, too, had lived in southern France. On that day a huge annual festival was held at Beaucaire, and it seems to have been a day of great festivities, much merriment, and untold transgressions. A woman called Simonne stated that she had been pregnant since three weeks before the 1581 Madeleine, Pierre Malbosque dated her pregnancy to nine or ten days after the last Madeleine in April 1583, and Marguerite Solière said in 1584 that she had been pregnant since 'around the time of the last Saint Magdaleine'.[220] The next most common date of reference was the feast-day of Saint Jean (or Saint Jehan), or Midsummer's Day, on 24 June. Catherine Daudeze stated in January 1595 that she had been pregnant since Saint Jean, and Anthonye Pradiere said she had been pregnant since seven or eight days after Saint Jehan.[221] In October 1602 Gillette Fabresse accused a man of trying to rape her on Saint Jean.[222] Lastly, people referred to Saint Michel—or Michaelmas (the day of the great massacre in 1567)—which was celebrated on 30 September. Catherine Doussaire in August 1589 said that 'about two years ago at the next Saint Michel, she had had a child', and Jane Gibernesse stated in January 1597 that she had been pregnant since the

[213] ADG, 42 J 31, 86v, 29 May 1596; ADTG, I 1, 59v, 8 Oct. 1595.
[214] ADG, 42 J 28, 357r–v, 360r, 3, 15 Feb. 1588.
[215] BN, Ms.fr. 8667, 126r, 3 Jun. 1562.   [216] ADG, 42 J 31, 155v, 160v, 15, 29 Jan. 1597.
[217] ADG, 42 J 30, 250r, 26 Jan. 1594.   [218] ADG, 42 J 29, 666, 2 Jun. 1591.
[219] ADG, 42 J 30, 139r, 12 Jan. 1593; 42 J 28, 114v, 18 Jul. 1584.
[220] BN, Ms.fr. 8667, 189r–190r, 17 Mar. 1581; ADG, 42 J 28, 9v, 27 Apr. 1583, and 76v, 1 Feb. 1584.
[221] ADG, 42 J 30, 319v, 18 Jan. 1595.   [222] ADG, 42 J 32, 116r, 23 Oct. 1602.

last Saint Michel.[223] As these dates only stretched across four months of the year, for the rest of the time people often used expressions like 'one evening that she could not at present remember', as Jehanne Bunhe did in February 1588.[224] At other times people linked their memory of events to a single dramatic event. Catherine Loise, for example, told the consistory that she had first had sex with Timothee Fabre 'the night when Boschet's brother was killed which she remembers very well'.[225] Their memories were sharp, but their modes of describing time—and, therefore, very probably, their conceptual framework for considering it—were imprecise.

Such information about the thoughts of and about women, and the realities of the lives of ordinary women among the poor to middling levels of French society helps provide a backdrop for the case-studies that follow.

[223] ADG, 42 J 29, 230, 6 Aug. 1589; 42 J 31, 155v, 15 Jan. 1597.
[224] ADG, 42 J 28, 357r, 3 Feb. 1588.   [225] ADG, 42 J 30, 3r, 2 Oct. 1591.

2

The Pursuit of Morality

THE PURPOSE OF MORAL DISCIPLINE

The mechanism for the imposition of morality, and for disciplinary action in the case of failure, was the consistory. Although it also functioned as the governing body and welfare centre of the local Reformed church, most of the consistory's time was absorbed in moral supervision, interrogation, and reprimand. This chapter explores the nature of that moral discipline and the functioning of the consistory, for it is only through it that we are able to examine women's lives in subsequent chapters.

The justification for, and model of, moral discipline was biblical precedent. In Matthew 18:15–17 Jesus explains how to deal with a fellow believer who has sinned through progressive public steps—address him individually, then before two or three witnesses, and, finally, if he refuses to listen, in front of the whole church. In Galatians 6:1–5 Paul urges believers to try to restore 'in a spirit of gentleness' those discovered in transgression, but to provide a salutary public warning to those who will not listen: 'for those who persist in sin, rebuke them in the presence of all, so that the rest may stand in fear' (1 Timothy 5:20). The ultimate sanction, for those who refused to reform, especially in matters of sexual immorality, was to cast them out from the church—'purge the evil person from among you' (1 Corinthians 5:1–2, 11–13).

Believing moral discipline to be 'the nerves of the body of the Church, as faith is the soul of it', Jean Calvin developed these injunctions into a system of discipline, following Johannes Oecolampadius and Martin Bucer.[1] Calvin prescribed three reasons for this: discipline would stop the name of God from being brought into disrepute and would prevent the faithful, otherwise so easily inclined to sin, from being corrupted by the influence and example of the wicked: 'Do you not know that a little leaven leavens the whole lump? Cleanse out the old leaven that you may be a new lump, as you really are unleavened.'[2] Thirdly, the practice of spiritual sanctions, such as suspension from the Lord's Supper, would prompt repentance and amendment in the life of sinners.[3] These reasons reveal a profound sense of the contaminating and corrosive power of sin but, at the same time, optimism that

---

[1] Michael F. Graham, *The Uses of Reform: 'Godly Discipline' and Popular Behaviour in Scotland and Beyond, 1560–1610* (New York, 1996), 11–12.

[2] 1 Corinthians 5:6–7.

[3] Janine Garrisson-Estèbe, *Les protestants du Midi, 1559–1598* (Toulouse, 1980), 90.

with the supervision and correction of a disciplining church, Christians could receive the help, education, and guidance necessary to resist.[4]

The goal of moral discipline in the French Calvinist Church was, therefore, to ensure that the Reformed congregations not only believed aright, but manifested this by living truly Christian lives, and were called back to the straight path whenever they strayed.[5] On seeing the behaviour of the Reformed population of Geneva, John Knox had remarked that he had never seen the Christian life lived so well: this was the desired outcome of discipline.[6] Reformed communities were to be set apart from their Catholic neighbours by behaviour that was visibly holy.[7]

The evidently sacred nature of the community made Protestantism attractive. Consistories in Protestant strongholds marooned in Catholic France did not fear to use excessive stringency lest they drive away potential converts, because the zeal and piety of moral discipline was actually a way of winning supporters. This surprising fact explains why the disciplined repeatedly returned to seek inclusion in the Calvinist community, why moral discipline functioned so successfully even though Protestantism never became the state religion of France, and, in part, why people continued to convert to Protestantism as the sixteenth century wore on.[8] Discipline may have served as a means of social control, but it was a voluntary yoke, and its success rested on people's choice to participate.[9] For individuals in a culture obsessed with honour, membership of the Reformed Church conveyed a highly desired association with respectability and moral probity. This was especially significant for women, for whom chastity remained a fraught indicator of moral standing.[10] Puritanical rigour characterized the new religion and created a strong sense of identity and validation.[11]

This is not to suggest that the consistories were always regarded positively. In Nîmes in 1606 the scribe noted that David Guiraud had used several 'piquant and irreverent' words that 'taxed the consistory's honour', but the words themselves go

---

[4] Garrisson-Estèbe, *Les protestants*, 89; Raymond A. Mentzer, 'Marking the Taboo: Excommunication in French Reformed Churches', in *Sin and the Calvinists: Morals Control and the Consistory in the Reformed Tradition*, ed. Raymond A. Mentzer (Kirksville, MO, 1994), 127.

[5] John Witte, Jr and Robert M. Kingdon, *Sex, Marriage and Family in John Calvin's Geneva*, vol. 1: *Courtship, Engagement and Marriage* (Grand Rapids, MI, 2005), 65.

[6] Knox, cited in Witte and Kingdon, *Sex, Marriage and Family*, 71.

[7] Graham, *The Uses*, 315; Raymond A. Mentzer, 'Notions of Sin and Penitence within the Reformed Community', in *Penitence in the Age of Reformations*, ed. Katharine Jackson Lualdi and Anne T. Thayer (Aldershot, 2000), 85.

[8] Graham, *The Uses*, 341.

[9] J. K. Cameron, 'Godly Nurture and Admonition in the Lord: Ecclesiastical Discipline in the Reformed Tradition', in *Die danische Reformation vor ihrem internationalen Hintergrund*, ed. Leif Grane and Kai Hørby (Göttingen, 1990), 272–3; Heinz Schilling, ' "History of Crime" or "History of Sin"? Some Reflections on the Social History of Early Modern Church Discipline', in *Politics and Society in Reformation Europe: Essays for Sir Geoffrey Elton on his Sixty-Fifth Birthday*, ed. E. I. Kouri and Tom Scott (Basingstoke, 1987), 295; Bruce Lenman, 'The Limits to Godly Discipline in the Early Modern Period with Particular Reference to England and Scotland', in *Religion and Society in Early Modern Europe 1500–1800*, ed. Kaspar von Greyerz (London, 1984), 142.

[10] J. S. Pollmann, 'Honor, Gender and Discipline in Dutch Reformed Churches', in *Dire l'interdit: The Vocabulary of Censure and Exclusion in the Early Modern Reformed Tradition*, ed. R. A. Mentzer, F. Moreil, and P. Chareyre (Leiden, 2010), 29–42.

[11] Graham, *The Uses*, 317, 342; Mentzer, 'Notions', 85.

unrecorded, suggesting a current of criticism which the registers only capture in part.[12] Nevertheless, even those aspersions that are recorded are fairly damning. Jehan Mombel, charged in September 1561 with idolatry, refused to make public reparation for his sin, stating that reparation was 'only a human invention...not found in the Bible' and that the consistory was made up of 'poor men, who have no money'.[13] Two months later, when summoned to appear before the consistory, Monsieur de Blauzau declared that he would 'rather submit himself to the auricular confession of the papists than the sermons of Monsieur Viret'.[14] Nor were these remarks merely growing pains. Roughly thirty years later, in April 1590, Anthoine Roguere, Seigneur de Clausonne—a leading member of Nîmois society—protested that the charges against him were 'false facts invented by the malevolence of certain of the present consistory, [who are] his enemies [and] who spread these rumours'.[15] In 1592 Loys Abram commented that the consistory at Nîmes had 'too much curiosity', and a year later M. Guiran complained in much stronger terms that the consistory was made up of 'incestuous parricides and others who live poorly'.[16] Nor were such comments confined to men: in 1586 Magdaleine Rotgiere, summoned to appear for having quarrelled with two other women, told her elder that 'she would resolutely never come to the consistory' although, after her deacon and a pastor were sent to speak to her, she did sheepishly arrive a month later.[17] Many protested when the discipline was used against them, but ultimately most submitted themselves to it.

The reason was that community unity was thought crucial. Moral discipline was, Calvin stated, the Church's 'sinews, through which the members of the body hold together'.[18] While Protestantism certainly promoted an unmediated, individual relationship with God, Calvinist faith in practice remained marked by covenantal theology and a sense of mutual responsibility for sin and morality.[19] This was reflected both in the way disciplinary matters came to the consistory's attention and the manner of restoration and reconciliation. Denunciations of others by the members of the congregation suggest a belief in the corporate nature of guilt and the right of the community to be involved in rectifying it, while reinstatement of sinners occurred in a context of public reparation that restored the moral integrity of the community and provided a remedial focus for public outrage. The community as a whole was purified by the repentance of sinners, and members were aware of their collective obligation to admonish and rebuke the straying believer and bring him or her to repentance and restored communion with God.[20] The success

---

[12] ADG, 42 J 33, 123v, 125v, 128r, 31 Aug. 1606.
[13] BN, Ms.fr. 8666, 32r, 5 Sept. 1561.   [14] BN, Ms.fr. 8666, 44v, 15 Nov. 1561.
[15] ADG, 42 J 29, 382, cf. ADG, E Dépôt 36/131, 73r from 27 Nov. 1594.
[16] ADG, 42 J 30, 98r, 26 Aug. 1592; 177v; his first name is not given, but many Guirans served as elders, adding to the interest of this remark.
[17] ADG, 42 J 28, 221v, 222v, 226r, 9 Apr. 1586.
[18] Calvin, *Institutes*, cited by Mark Valeri, 'Religion, Discipline and the Economy in Calvin's Geneva', *SCJ* (1997), 123–42, here 140.
[19] Lenman, 'The Limits', 129.
[20] Lenman, 'The Limits', 126; Mentzer, 'Notions', 84, 99; Graham, *The Uses*, 18.

of the discipline rested on the acceptance of this responsibility both at individual and community level.[21]

The holiness and integrity of the Christian community was paramount: according to Calvin, the critical measure of a well-ordered church was the devout celebration of the Eucharist, which must be pure and unsullied by the participation of an unworthy individual.[22] The Eucharist or the Lord's Supper, known in French—from the Latin *cena* (dinner, supper)—as the *cène*, was the central ritual and only participatory rite of the Calvinist Church, and was held in a commensurate degree of awe.[23] In advance of each quarterly celebration of the Eucharist, the congregation were warned to prepare themselves and to be reconciled with their neighbours.[24] Those found attending the Lord's Supper while in breach of the moral code were severely censured, like Jehanne Pueche and Jane Brugière, who in 1602 were rebuked by the consistory in Alès for having taken the Eucharist at the neighbouring town of Anduze while suspended for consulting sorcerers.[25] This need to protect the Lord's Supper meant ensuring that sinners were truly contrite and repentant, which manifested itself in a visual demonstration of humility and remorse.[26] It was vital that sinners came to a profound recognition of their shortcomings.[27] People who did not think they had done anything wrong—like M. Chalas, who as a witness in May 1583 had been complicit in an engagement made without parental consent—were sent away to reconsider and come to an acknowledgement of their sin.[28] The consistory sought an internalization of the discipline: recognition of one's faults, remorse, and repentance were crucial if the Lord's Supper was to remain truly pure.

In support of the discipline, Protestant life consisted of endeavours to inculcate practices and beliefs in line with Calvinist doctrine, primarily through preaching, catechizing, and the 'sung word'. In Nîmes sermons took place three times a week, once on Wednesdays and twice on Sundays.[29] The sermon was thought to be an effectual way of promoting change in people's lives. In April 1581, the minister was instructed to admonish the people in his sermon that in future they should

attend the services at 12 p.m. and 3 p.m., making their families come to the 12 p.m. service when the word of God is clearly manifested and the young may understand; keep their heads uncovered when the psalms are sung; not keep their shops open or

[21] Raymond A. Mentzer, 'Ecclesiastical Discipline and Communal Reorganisation among the Protestants of Southern France', *European History Quarterly* 21 (1991), 163–84, here 178.

[22] Graham, *The Uses*, 19.

[23] Calvin, 'Articles Concerning the Organization of the Church and of Worship at Geneva Proposed by the Ministers at the Council January 16, 1537', *Calvin: Theological Treatises*, trans. Rev. J. K. S. Reid (London, 1954), 48; Mentzer, 'Notions', 85.

[24] For example, ADTG I 1, 31v, 16 Aug. 1595, in advance of the sacrament to be celebrated on the first Sunday in September.

[25] ADG, I 1, 167r–v.

[26] Mentzer, 'Marking', 118; Graham, *The Uses*, 26; Mentzer, 'Notions', 85, 97; this is similar to the more developed idiom of later American Puritan conversion narratives where remorse and contrition were judged by a set of prescribed criteria, see Edmund Morgan, *Visible Saints: The History of the Puritan Idea* (New York, 1992).

[27] Mentzer, 'Notions', 97.   [28] ADG, 42 J 28, 10v.

[29] BN, Ms.fr. 8667, 142; ADG, 42 J 30, 280v.

sell merchandise on days of prayer during the service; not play games, neither in secret nor in public; nor eat or drink in inns and taverns, nor in their own houses during the service... [and] in all their actions, to comport themselves modestly and religiously as God commands us.[30]

Many of these measures were designed to enhance attendance at and respect for the sermon. Town gates were also closed at the time of each service, employers were responsible for ensuring the turnout of their servants, and in Montauban and maybe elsewhere lists were made of those who failed to show up.[31]

Together with the sermon, recitation of the catechism was thought to mould souls. The catechism was intoned each Sunday, and scholars at the Protestant Academy in Nîmes were among those required to learn the confession of faith by heart.[32] In addition psalm-singing, which has been described as the 'secret weapon of the Reformation', was considered valuable and efficacious.[33] The consistory in Nîmes employed a lead psalm-singer in 1604 for three years, paying him a starting fee of thirty-six *écus*, and an additional yearly salary of twenty-two *écus* (which had risen to twenty-seven *écus* a year by 1612).[34] The psalms were designed for the edification of those who sung or heard them sung: there was concern in Nîmes in 1608 that the cantor's voice was so low as to render the words hardly intelligible (he was instructed to stand up when singing and to repeat the psalms several times).[35] Another time the suitability of a man to be an elder was questioned in part because his daughter was grown up and able to read, but failed to carry a psalter with her to the service.[36] In Montauban, the congregation was urged to remain at church until the psalms had been sung, and to bring their psalters with them.[37] Here they also employed a scholar, one Foralguier Arguisan, to read the Bible at church for a salary of six *écus* a year.[38] The church was confident that feeding believers a steady diet of Bible-reading, sermons, catechisms, and psalms could not help but reform and redeem them from the inside out.

DISCIPLINARY PRIORITIES

The objective—a community visibly distinguished by holiness—meant that the consistories had specific disciplinary priorities. They wanted to stamp out obvious breaches of morality by eradicating superstition, suppressing irreligious forms of popular culture, containing and punishing illicit sexuality, ensuring marital and communal harmony, and disciplining transgressors for any other forms of public misconduct or

---

[30] BN, Ms.fr. 8667, 199v, 5 Apr. 1581.

[31] BN, Ms.fr. 8667, 197v, 335r; ADG, 42 J 29, 338; 42 J 30, 251v, 258r, 280v; ADTG I 1, 1v, 88v; these times varied when celebrating the Eucharist; cf. BN, Ms.fr. 8667, 142r.

[32] ADG, 42 J 30, 330v, 22 Feb. 1595; ADG, 42 J 32, 241v.

[33] Diarmaid MacCulloch, *The Reformation: Europe's House Divided* (New York and London, 2003), 298.

[34] ADG, 42 J 32, 249v, 25 Aug. 1604; ADG, 42 J 34, 393r, 22 Nov. 1612.

[35] ADG, 42 J 34, 51v, 17 Dec. 1608.   [36] ADG, 42 J 33, 136v, 8 Dec. 1606.

[37] ADTG I 1, 7v, 14 Jun. 1595.

[38] ADTG, I 1, 12v–14r; this also mentions the necessity of having someone to sing the psalms and someone to handle the finances, 5 Jul. 1595.

overt immorality. The consistory was therefore above all preoccupied by sins that would cause scandal, and necessarily focused more on behaviour than thought. Its members were often drawn into intervention in domestic situations when talk of private misconduct leaked into the public arena.[39]

Among its priorities was, firstly, spiritual purity. Calvinists were expected to keep the Sabbath holy, regularly attend services, and participate in the Eucharist. In Montauban in 1595 Benoict Massé and Jean Delbreilh, known as *Flandres*, were summoned to the consistory for having cut wheat on the previous Sunday to great scandal, seeing 'as it was a day of rest and that they did not attend church'.[40] Sermons frequently reminded people not to work 'in any way' on Sundays.[41] The consistory was also greatly vexed by the possibility that their congregation would be led astray through contact with Catholics.[42] Adam Farel was made to endure a severe censure and beg God's pardon while he knelt on the ground, because while visiting Tarascon in July 1593 he had raised his hat to a statue of Saint Martha (who, legend had it, had lived in Tarascon and tamed a dragon, the Tarasque, that terrorized the inhabitants).[43] Attendance at the Catholic Mass or baptizing a child in a Roman Catholic church were cause for fury, as was *ondoiement*—baptism by lay people. When elder Jehan Moulte performed an emergency baptism on a dying child in 1562 'to console the mother', he was strongly censured, deprived of the sacrament, suspended from his office as elder, and made to confess publicly to his sin.[44] Perhaps even more concerning was marrying in a Roman Catholic church (almost certainly to a non-Protestant). Interdenominational marriages were described as 'unequal', alluding to biblical texts such as 2 Corinthians 6:14–18, which proscribed the 'unequal yoking' of believers with unbelievers.[45] The synod of Bas Languedoc in Montpellier in 1591 ruled that parents who allowed their children to marry 'papists' would be publicly suspended.[46] The concern with contaminating spiritual influences was also felt in determining the education of children: parents who sent their children to Jesuit schools were pursued with vigour.[47]

The Church's concern with heterodoxy also manifested itself in resolute attitudes towards sorcery and magic, superstition, fortune-telling, blasphemy, and heresy. Women were frequently chastized for visiting the *bohémiens*—a word used from the fifteenth century to designate the wandering Romani peoples, known in English as gypsies—who offered medicine, spiritual healing, and divination.[48] Blasphemy met with serious consequences.

---

[39] Mentzer, 'Notions', 87, 91; Raymond Mentzer, ' "Disciplina nervus ecclesiae": The Calvinist Reform of Morals at Nîmes', *SCJ* 18 (1987), 13–39.

[40] ADTG, I 1, 19v, 19 Jul. 1595.

[41] ADG, 42 J 32, 97r, 28 Aug. 1602; see also ADG, 42 J 27, 197v; 42 J 28,152r; 42 J 29, 338; 42 J 30, 251v.

[42] Graham, *The Uses*, 315.

[43] ADG, 42 J 28, 27r, 30 Jul. 1583; a man called Lucquet was similarly chastised for honouring the idol in August 1583 (ADG, 42 J 28, 31r).

[44] BN, Ms.fr. 8666, 159r.   [45] ADG, 42 J 30, 293r; 42 J 35, 84v.

[46] ADG, 42 J 30, 388r; confirmed in 1614, ADG, 42 J 35, 84v.

[47] e.g. ADG, 42 J 33, 67r, 73v.   [48] e.g. ADG, 42 J 28, 35v, 24 Aug. 1583.

Defining themselves as holy also meant enforcing a code of behaviour that marked Protestants out from Catholics in their rejection of popular culture. Playing games was a cause for censure. The village of Ganges had a particularly spirited culture of gaming, or perhaps a consistory especially alive to its dangers, and regularly summoned men for playing skittles on the festival of Saint Madeleine, playing boules during the service, playing cards on a Sunday or otherwise, and gambling for rings, in various iterations during the decade for which we have records.[49] It is worth noting that the consistories were supported in this by the municipal authorities: in Nîmes in 1615, the consuls stepped in to prevent the playing of the 'scandalous game' of billiards, about which several of the town's inhabitants were said to have complained.[50]

Folk culture also came under attack. Carnivals, feast days, and festivals, which often marked saints' days and seasons of the Church year, were condemned as idolatrous.[51] Celebrations and revels of all kinds were suspect, and sometimes the reason for the church's angst is clear. In March 1583 Pierre Ysnard, Jacques Blanc, Mathieu Couston's son, and at least three other young men appeared at the wedding of M. les Favyers in Nîmes, wearing masks but otherwise totally naked.[52] The dancing that attended celebrations or weddings was thought dangerously sexual and so was a target of consistorial ire.[53] In Nîmes, Montauban, and Ganges, people— chiefly, but not exclusively, women—were repeatedly convoked for dancing, hosting dances, allowing their daughters to dance with young men, dancing on Sundays at the time of service, dancing in the street in broad daylight, dancing and masquing, dancing to the sound of musical instruments, dancing after having partaken of the Lord's Supper, and dancing on May Day and on Saint Madeleine.[54] The consistory maintained that dancing was 'dissolute and scandalous, tending to fornication', while the culprits, such as the wife of Sieur Finor, 'did not think she had done anything wrong'.[55]

The tendency of sexual sin to cause comment was one reason why fornication and adultery frequently appear in detail in the consistorial records.[56] The consistories

---

[49] ADH, GG 24, references include: 8v (Guillaume Barre for playing skittles, 3 Sept. 1587), 9v (François Olivie for playing games, 10 Sept. 1587), 15v (playing skittles, June 1591), 15v (boules during service, 13 Jul. 1591), 17v and 25v (Pierre Soulier, for playing on the Madeleine in 1591 and 1592), 70r (Uget Maury and Anthoine Janin for playing, 6 Oct. 1596), 71v (Pierre Cambon for gambling at cards for rings, 1 Dec. 1596), 74r (Micheu Barrau and Estienne Fabre for playing cards on a Sunday, 26 Dec. 1596), 75r (Estienne and Augier de Castel and Pierre Marty for playing cards, 2 Feb. 1597), 75v (Jehan Vassas for playing cards, 12 Feb. 1597), 83r (men playing cards, 29 May 1597).

[50] ADG, E dépôt 36/40, 23 Jan. 1615.   [51] e.g. BN, Ars. Ms. 6560, 66v.

[52] ADG, 42 J 28, 2r, 2v, 3r, 22v.

[53] Graeme Murdock, 'The Dancers of Nîmes: Moral Discipline, Gender and Reformed Religion in Late Sixteenth-Century France', unpublished paper.

[54] BN, Ms.fr. 8667, 30v, 56v, 118v, 154r, 203v, 207v; ADG, 42 J 28, 6v, 72v, 76r; ADG, 42 J 30, 169v, 258r, 261v, 275v; ADG, 42 J 31, 40v, 456r, 460r; ADTG, I 1, 4v, 20r, 24v, 28v, 29r, 30r, 92r, 94v; ADH, GG 24, 88r, 89r, 93r, 94r, 94v, 98v, 99r, 99v, 100v, 103v, 105v, 110r, 115r, 118v, 120v, 123v, 124r.

[55] ADG, 42 J 28, 72v, 11 Jan. 1584; ADG, 42 J 31, 456r, 23 Jan. 1602.

[56] Jean-Louis Flandrin, *Les amours paysannes (XVIe–XIXe siècle). Amour et sexualité dans les campagnes de l'ancienne France* (Paris, 1975), 225, 238; James R. Farr, *Authority and Sexuality in Early*

were deeply concerned with illicit sexuality, which covered a broad range of sexual activity outside heterosexual marriage—fornication, adultery, sexual assault, rape, prostitution, and procurement. There was no distinction in the punishment between consensual and non-consensual illicit sex. Pregnancies and illegitimate births often alerted the consistory to such behaviour, while they had an abiding fear of abortion, as reflected in the injunctions to many an unmarried pregnant woman to 'look after the fruit of her stomach', even though single mothers, orphans, and abandoned children necessitated financial commitments from both the church and the town. Fathers who paid for the upkeep of their illegitimate children became more culpable through this testament to their guilt, rather than being thought responsible. A merest whiff that men and women were interacting irregularly or over-familiarly could lead to suspicions of sexual activity. The accusation against Dimanche Fabresse of being a prostitute in 1591 simply emerged, she claimed, because a relative of her husband visited her house and stayed for several days, and Sieur Richant's son came to speak to her and gave her some money.[57] Even those who tolerated the sexually immoral were chastized, like Marguerite Pernière, who out of 'pity...and for charity' provided lodging in 1605 for an unmarried pregnant woman called Magdalene.[58]

The church was not alone in pursuing sexual misconduct. Contemporary secular authorities were also interested in the pursuit of *paillardise*: illicit sexual activity constitutes just under one-fifth, or sixty-two, of the total cases featured in Montauban's register of criminal sentences between 1561 and 1606.[59] Women bore the brunt of the blame: among those sixty-two sentences, forty-eight were against women, and fourteen against men, even though the identity of the man is recorded in several of the sentences against women.[60] The sentences for fornication were not light: the women concerned were required to make a public declaration of their crimes, and then were either given a substantial fine, as was Jammete Ruelle, who was fined nineteen *écus*, or banished from the town for one to three years, as were Jacmette La Molinaire, Marguerite Reyne, and Jehanne Cappelle (Fig. 2.1).[61] In 1597 Marye Barryere was sentenced by the seneschal court of Quercy to be whipped for her adultery, while Alyon Gironne, former wife of Robert Godin of Montauban, was condemned to death by judges in La Rochelle for 'her bad life and lewd misbehaviour'.[62] In Nîmes in October 1609 a woman called Seniere, who had given birth illegitimately, was condemned in an ordinance by the royal judicial officers to make public reparation and be whipped.[63] The church's interest in punishing and eradicating sexual sin was not, therefore, unusual at the time.

Modern Burgundy (1550–1730) (New York, Oxford, 1995), 112; Robin Briggs, *Communities of Belief: Cultural and Social Tension in Early Modern France* (Oxford, 1989), 270–1.

[57] ADG, 42 J 29, 699, 17 Jul. 1591.   [58] ADG, 42 J 33, 32r, 16 Mar. 1605.
[59] ADTG, 5 FF 2; Philip Conner, *Huguenot Heartland Montauban and Southern French Calvinism During the Wars of Religion* (Aldershot, 2002), 69.
[60] ADTG, 5 FF 2, 18v, 25v, 28r, 31r, 32r, 33r–v, 34v, 40v, 43r; Conner, *Huguenot Heartland*, 69.
[61] ADTG, 5 FF 2, 34v, 35r, 36v.   [62] ADTG, I 1, 231v, 229v, both 12 Feb. 1597.
[63] ADG, 42 J 34, 131v, 136r, 27 Oct. 1609.

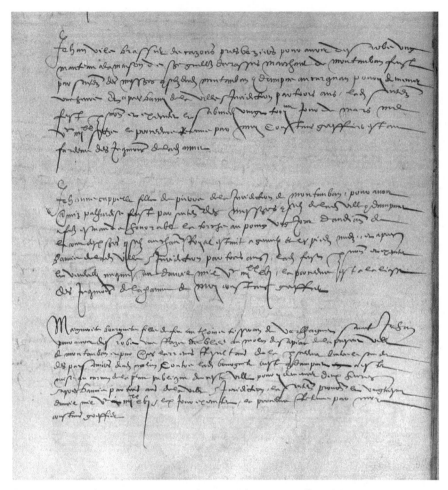

Fig. 2.1. Criminal sentences pronounced against Jehanne Cappelle and Marguerite Bourguete by the consuls of Montauban, *Registre des sentences prononcées en matière criminelle par les Consuls de la Ville de Montauban de 1534 à 1606*, Archives départementales du Tarn-et-Garonne, 5 FF 2, 35r (1596)

Divisions in society were another focus of consistorial attention. Quarrelling, fights, violence, defamation, and insults were all forms of behaviour that undermined communal harmony, and the consistory sought to heal such breaches. Marital strife and domestic disputes also attracted considerable interest. Divorce was not permitted under French law, but legal separations of 'possessions and body' were; nevertheless, the Protestant consistory consistently urged couples who were temporarily separated to re-establish their mutual household, almost irrespective of circumstance.

This preoccupation with upholding marriage also manifested itself in regulating the procedures of betrothal and espousal. Concerned with reinforcing patriarchy, the consistory held that parental consent and the presence of witnesses were necessary to validate engagement promises, which, once made, could not be dissolved by anything as whimsical as a mutual desire not to marry.[64] In this they echoed and anticipated the direction of the French law. Clandestine marriages were forbidden, while delaying a wedding after engagement was frowned upon. Yet despite the binding and irrevocable nature of the betrothal promises, consummation of the marriage was prohibited until after the wedding ceremony.

Some sins were, however, beyond the consistory's purview. Sodomy receives few mentions, probably partly because it was seldom discovered, and partly because its profound seriousness meant that the consistory quickly referred it to secular jurisdictions. In Pont-de-Camarès, on 28 August 1583, the consistory noted the 'detestable, abominable, and execrable act' committed by Jehan Guararde and Jehan Marc, and alerted the judiciary of the town to put them in prison and bring them to justice.[65] Even more seriously, in the one known case of 'incestuous fornication' in Nîmes, the name of the culprit is obscured and the consistory resolved to refuse to allow him to participate in the Lord's Supper, but otherwise to write to 'our fathers in Geneva' for advice on how to proceed.[66] Nor did the consistories ever attempt to investigate infanticide, the latter such a pressing concern for law courts around Europe in the seventeenth century, perhaps precisely because it was a criminal matter.[67] On the few occasions that people were accused of murder the consistory intervened only so far as to ensure the public suspension of the alleged culprits from the Eucharist, and otherwise stood back to allow the natural jurisdiction of the royal courts.[68]

In practice some consistorial objectives modified over time, as the consistories realized that there were limits to their powers to effect change. They discovered the unsurprising truth that the existence of moral rules does not guarantee compliance, and can even have perverse consequences. As Lyndal Roper notes, 'behavioural prohibitions can create...their own compulsion and transgressive possibilities'.[69] The existence of the discipline created new areas of prohibition and, simultaneously, of allure. The decline in the disciplining of family life after 1615 may well have come from waning confidence about their ability to instil moral values in an increasingly hostile exterior world.

---

[64] John Bossy, *Christianity in the West 1400–1700* (Oxford, 1975), 116.

[65] BN, Ars. Ms. 6563, 71v–72r, 28 Aug. 1583.

[66] BN, Ms.fr. 8666, 6v, 10 May 1561. See below for more examples of consultation between Reformed churches.

[67] For France, A. Soman, 'Sorcellerie, justice criminelle et société dans la France moderne', *Histoire, Économie et Société* 12 (1993), 177–217, and 'The Anatomy of an Infanticide Trial: The Case of Marie-Jeanne Bartonnet (1742)', in *Changing Identities in Early Modern France*, ed. Michael Wolfe (Durham and London, 1996); for a general European view, William L. Langer, 'Infanticide: A Historical Survey', *History of Childhood Quarterly 1* (1974), 353–65; for England, Laura Gowing, 'Secret Births and Infanticide in Seventeenth-Century England', *Past and Present* 156 (1997), 87–115; for Germany, R. Po Chia-Hsia, *Social Discipline*, 145 and Ulinka Rublack, *The Crimes of Women in Early Modern Germany* (Oxford, 1999), 163–96.

[68] ADG, 42 J 28, 186r (accusation of several murders by Captain Buon, 21 Sept. 1585); 42 J 30, 23v (accusation that master printer Sebastian Jaquy killed Jehan Boschet, 25 Dec. 1591), 376v, 387r (accusation that Nicolas Loys murdered Aymond Garanier, 12 Jul. 1595).

[69] Lyndal Roper, *Oedipus and the Devil: Witchcraft, Sexuality and Religion in Early Modern Europe* (London, 1994), 8.

THE MEMBERSHIP OF THE CONSISTORY

The consistories consisted of ministers, deacons, elders, a clerk, and a summoner. The pastors were preachers of God's word and ambassadors of God on earth. Within the consistory they directed proceedings and carried ultimate authority. Deacons (*diacres*) were appointed to oversee the administration of the poor list, to collect and distribute poor relief, and to visit the sick and imprisoned, each having responsibility for two adjoining districts. They also took an active part in consistorial meetings. The role of an elder (*ancien*) was to keep watch over the population of his district and report any misbehaviour or moral failings, to attend every meeting of the consistory, and to be involved in the administration of the Eucharist. The clerk (*greffier*) was the scribe or secretary for the consistory, responsible for keeping records of their meetings and their various lists (of people suspended from receiving the Lord's Supper, people who had been banished from the town, women who were sexually immoral, and so on). The role of summoner (*advertisseur*) was the only paid position. Originally twelve *livres* a year, by 1581 when cordwainer Guillaume Guiraud was appointed to be the summoner in Nîmes the annual salary had increased to twenty-five *livres*, payable monthly, with additional payments of five *sous* a week for acting as caretaker for the temple, and ten *sous* for setting out the apparatus at each celebration of the Eucharist.[70] The summoner was, in short, the consistory's general dogsbody.

In Montauban, in 1595, the consistory was made up of three ministers, fourteen elders, and one scribe—Pierre de la Barthe, a royal notary.[71] In later elections, only ten elders were chosen. The earliest consistory at Nîmes, in 1561, consisted of one minister, four deacons, ten elders, and a clerk, with a summoner for each district. By the 1580s this had normalized to three ministers, four deacons, nine elders, a clerk, and a single summoner, while in 1596–7 the number of deacons increased to five, and the elders again to ten.

Although the Reformed Church was distinct in its dependence on the laity, it still had a special place for pastors. As ministers of God's Word, pastors were recipients of a divine vocation that set them apart from the mass of the faithful. Pierre Viret, one of the first Protestant ministers in Nîmes, wrote:

> All must be concerned with the salvation of men, but only those who have been called by a special election of God can preach or administer the sacraments.[72]

In Calvin's *Institutes of the Christian Religion*, pastors were charged with a task 'similar to that which the Apostles had', namely, implementing ecclesiastical discipline, administering the sacraments, and expounding 'Scripture so that there may be a sound and pure doctrine preserved in the church'.[73] Thierry Wanegffelen

---

[70] BN, Ms.fr. 8666, 200r, 9 Jan. 1562/3; Ms.fr. 8667, 198r, 5 Apr. 1581.

[71] ADTG, I 1, 4v–5v, 7 Jun. 1595.

[72] Pierre Viret, *Du vray Ministère de la vraye Église de Jésus Christ et des vrais sacremens d'icelle, et des faus sacremens de l'église de l'Antechrist, et des additions adjoustées par les hommes au sacrement du baptesme* (Lyon, 1560), 7.

[73] Calvin, *Institution de la religion chrétienne* (1560 edn), IV, Ch. III, 4–5.

has highlighted the ontological change engendered by the rite of laying hands on the minister, which not only served to 'magnify the dignity of the ministry among the people', but to indicate to the pastor that 'he no longer belonged to himself, but was dedicated to the service of God and the Church'.[74] The pastor was an ambassador of God and the one who declared His will to the world: 'with the mouth of men, they [the ministers] speak to us as if of heaven.'[75]

The men who bore this high calling in late sixteenth-century Languedoc mostly came from the region, meaning that they were at home among the people and could surely speak the local variant of Occitan. Among the ministers in Nîmes, for example, Jacques Pineton de Chambrun, Sr (pastor 1562–1601) came from Marvejols, north of the Cévennes; Claude de Falguerolles (1577–88) from the Cévennes; and Jean de Serres (1580–1) from Villeneuve-de-Berg, to the west of Montélimar. Jérémie Ferrier (1600–13) came from Nîmes itself.[76] Many had received theological training in Geneva, including Pierre D'Airebaudouze (1564–70), Jehan de Falguerolles (1592–9), Pineton de Chambrun, Jr (1609–20), and Mardochée Suffren (1600–13); others, including de Serres and Ferrier, were professors at the Reformed academy at Nîmes. It appears that the consistory in Nîmes may have been keen to develop a ministerial dynasty: they funded the sons of pastors Jacques Pineton de Chambrun and Claude de Falguerolles through their studies in Switzerland.[77] The contract established between the church of Nîmes and Claude de Falguerolles's son, Jehan, in November 1587 is particularly interesting as it indicates that the consistory had originally planned to fund the studies of another son, Pierre, but, following his death, transferred this support to Jehan, suggesting how important they considered it to groom indigenous church leadership. The consistory was willing to invest quite heavily in this: they agreed to pay Jehan fifty *écus* a year, plus a further fifty *livres* for travel expenses and books, in return for his promise to 'consecrate himself to God and to the service of this church', a clause repeated three times.[78] In 1590 they granted him an additional 200 *livres* to help with his upkeep and his book purchases. The agreement put Jehan at risk: in 1589 he reported the great dangers and threats he experienced travelling between Nîmes and Geneva and a year later he fretted that his health was not robust enough for the job.[79] Nevertheless, he held to their agreement and returned after five years to serve as a pastor in Nîmes from 1592 (but he was right about his health: he died in late 1599, at around the age of 35).[80]

---

[74] Thierry Wanegffelen, 'Un cléricalisme réformé : le protestantisme français entre principe du sacerdoce universel et théologie de la vocation au ministère (XVIe–XVIIe siècles)', unpublished paper delivered at the *Reformation Studies Colloquium*, April 2004, citing Calvin, *Institution*, IV, Ch. III, 16.

[75] Calvin, *Institution*, IV, Ch. III, 16, 1.

[76] *Oeuvres des pasteurs de l'Église de Nîmes* (List of pastors 1559–1896), unpublished register, Bibliothèque de L'Église Réformée de Nîmes; cf. Eugène et Émile Haag, *La France protestante ou vies des protestants français qui se sont fait un nom dans l'histoire depuis les premiers temps de la Réformation jusqu'à la reconnaissance du principe de la liberté des cultes par l'Assemblée nationale*, 10 vols (Paris, 1846–59).

[77] ADG, 42 J 31, 437r; 42 J 29, 63–4.   [78] ADG, 42 J 29, 63–4, Nov. 1587.

[79] ADG, 42 J 29, 114, 441.   [80] ADG, 42 J 31, 321r, 343r.

One of the reasons why the consistory at Nîmes was so keen to train its own ministers and promote the ministry as a trade handed down from father to son appears to have been the enduring concern about ministerial availability and, more unfairly, reliability. The general shortage of ministers is indicated by examples such as minister Mardochée Suffren being lent to preach at the churches at Saint-Gilles and Bellegarde in 1601.[81]

Of the twenty-four pastors who served in Nîmes between 1560 and 1615, seventeen served for more than five years, and some far longer: Guillaume Mauget (1559–76) was a minister for seventeen years, Jean Moynier (1586–1610) for twenty-four years, Samuel Petit (1614–43) for twenty-nine years, and Jacques Pineton de Chambrun, Sr (1562–1601) for an exemplary thirty-nine years. Yet, they were not consistently well treated by the consistory. Pastors were instructed not to leave town without permission for fear of absenteeism or the more serious concern that they would be offered employment by another church, as the consistory of Nîmes itself had offered Jérémie Ferrier, minister at Alès, a post as 'perpetual pastor' in 1601 after his earlier visit to Nîmes.[82] For failing to comply with its commands, the consistory was happy to shame pastors in the consistorial record and to threaten disciplinary action, as exemplified by its dealings with Jehan de Falguerolles following his trip to Anduze 'without permission of the consistory' in October 1593.[83] In the folios concerning this affair, the consistory spoke in surprisingly strong terms against their minister—that he was 'without excuse', 'he had transgressed against the discipline', he would be 'greatly censured', and, that if it recurred, it would proceed against him 'rigorously'. Is it coincidental that over these pages the scribe also ceased to spell his name correctly, rendering it as 'Falgeyrolles' and 'Felgeirolles', returning to the correct spelling as he returned to grace?[84]

The consistory demonstrated similar brusqueness when demanding in 1589 that Jean de Serres relocate his family to Nîmes from their home in Orange, adding that unless he did so he would not 'bring the edification and contentment that the church requires of him'. Serres responded that could not afford to move his household because the church gave him 'such small means', and reminded the consistory of his frequent requests to be set at liberty from the Nîmes church.[85] His complaint about pitifully low wages was echoed at various points by Chambrun, Moynier, and Falguerolles, while Serres was not the only pastor to attempt, unsuccessfully, to leave the ministry in Nîmes.[86] In May 1585 Chambrun had declared to that year's consistory that he 'could and would no longer serve in this church', and that, in light of the 'indisposition to his person [and] the state of his affairs', he begged the consistory to remember his labour and give him his wages for the

---

[81] ADG, 42 J 31, 448.

[82] ADG, 42 J 32, 248v; 42 J 31, 400v; Haag and Haag, *La France protestante*, vol. 5, 93–7.

[83] ADG, 42 J 30, 223v.

[84] Although spelling was often erratic in sixteenth-century France, only 'Falgueyrolles' appears to have been a commonly accepted variant of his name, while these other spellings seldom appear elsewhere.

[85] ADG, 42 J 29, 267.   [86] ADG, 42 J 30, 316v; 42 J 33, 58r–9r.

previous year and the half of 1585 that had passed.[87] Not only were wages low, but they were withheld.

Similarly, Mardochée Suffren, who, like Jehan de Falguerolles, had returned to become a pastor in Nîmes after being trained in Geneva at the church's cost, petitioned the consistory just four years later to be 'given leave and set free' to serve at another church. He testified that he had spent the last year 'grievously sick', in part because of the extraordinary pressure put on him by the frequent absences of the other pastors. The consistory did not think he had legitimate cause to complain, and he remained in the service of the Reformed church of Nîmes until his death eight years later, in 1613.[88]

The picture that emerges is of the consistory consistently failing to pay adequate or timely wages, restricting ministers' liberty, and resulting unhappiness, complaint, overwork, stress-related illness, and even rebellion among the pastors. This was not only true in Nîmes—in Ganges, too, in 1597, the minister, M. Rogier, declared that he would not preach again until he had been paid his wages for that year.[89] Despite the apparent sense of unity conveyed in the practice of the discipline, the registers also reveal the degree of pressure and influence being exerted on the clergy by the laity, and how costly the task of being a Reformed minister was in the late sixteenth century.

In 1613 the church excommunicated one of its ministers at Nîmes, Jérémie Ferrier. There was cause: Ferrier had become politically active on behalf of the royal government, in defence of the limiting provisions of the Edict of Nantes on Protestants. This gave the national synod of the Reformed Church at Privas and colloquy at Lyon cause to investigate his behaviour, and they subsequently found that he had been negligent in his duties and had appropriated money, so forbade him from continuing his ministry in Languedoc. At first the consistory of Nîmes petitioned on behalf of their pastor, but when he accepted a position as a criminal assessor at the *présidial* court, they considered him to have deserted his post and condemned him as a 'scandalous man, incorrigible, impenitent, undisciplinable'.[90] Even before this sentence, the strength of feeling in the town against Ferrier—counting him as a traitor to the cause of Protestantism—had been such that the consuls had taken precautions to protect the lives of Ferrier and his family.[91]

In Montauban, the consistory demonstrated more loyalty and gratitude towards their ministers. In September 1595 the consistory organized an assembly of the consuls, lieutenant, and councillors of the *sénéchaussée* court, the King's lawyer, and other high-status people from the town to contest a ruling passed at a colloquy of ministers from the churches of Bas Quercy at Négrepleisse held several days earlier. The colloquy had ordered the dismissal of Montauban's second pastor, Bironis, noting his 'imbecility and weakness of voice'. Aware that this would leave them short-staffed and that Bironis had faithfully served the church for more than

---

[87] ADG, 42 J 28, 180v, 26 May 1585.   [88] ADG, 42 J 33, 58v, 7 Sept. 1605.
[89] Archives départementales de l'Hérault (hereafter ADH), GG 24, 81r, 13 Apr. 1597.
[90] ADG, 42 J 35, 13r–14r, 13 Sept. 1613; see also ADG, 42 J 34, 440v.
[91] ADG, E dépôt 36/136, 99r, 15 Jul. 1613.

twenty-six years, without previous complaint, the assembly moved to appeal the colloquy's resolution, terming it an act of ingratitude, 'against all form of law and justice' and Christian charity. They compared the relationship between the elderly Bironis and the church of Montauban to 'a wife with her husband, who, during the marriage, if the wife falls sick or has an accident, nevertheless, the husband cannot nor should not reject her'.[92]

As these incidents suggest, despite the status of the ministry, the power of the laity in the direction and running of the church was a peculiar feature of the Reformed Church in France in this period.[93] Even though few deacons or elders (apart from the semi-permanent post of summoner) served the church for more than two years consecutively, their power as a body of lay leaders was considerable and sustained. While ministers directed proceedings in the consistory, the proportion of pastors to deacons and elders meant ministerial voices could be outweighed, and Chareyre has rightly called deacons and elders 'the soul of the consistory'. [94] A substantial role existed for the laity in the practice of moral discipline.

Annually—in Nîmes, on the Wednesday following the first Sunday of December—deacons and elders were elected for the following calendar year. Election occurred by co-optation: in Montauban, the outgoing deacon or elder would nominate two candidates to succeed him, and the rest of the consistory would choose one of them to be elected.[95] In Nîmes, the outgoing elder put forward four names.[96] This process conformed to the church's guidelines, which stated that deacons and elders should be selected by the 'common voice' of the consistory.[97]

Co-optation meant that incoming deacons and elders had been recognized as worthy members of the Reformed community by their peers. At each election, the consistory read aloud 1 Timothy 3:1–13 and Titus 1:5–9, which describe the qualities essential to overseers and deacons of the church: as 'God's stewards', they should be 'above reproach...sober-minded, self-controlled, respectable, hospitable...not a drunkard, not violent but gentle, not quarrelsome...well thought of by outsiders', 'upright, holy, and disciplined', and able to manage their own households well.[98] The recitation served to guide the minds of those choosing their successors, and to remind the incoming consistory of their responsibilities. That these scriptural injunctions were used as a yardstick is indicated by the challenge to the election of M. Duprins in 1606 on the grounds that he was a quarreller with an appetite for revenge, who did not know the commandments, believed in purgatory, let his daughter attend the Mass with his sister in Beaucaire, and whose family was badly instructed in religion.[99] These allegations implied that Duprins failed, at each point, to match the standards of self-control, holiness, and good domestic patriarchy demanded by the Bible. Duprins protested that the allegations came from one of

---

[92] ADTG, I 1, 45r–50r, 14 Sept. 1595.

[93] Robert M. Kingdon, 'The Control of Morals by the Earliest Calvinists', in *Renaissance, Reformation, Resurgence*, ed. Peter De Klerk (Grand Rapids, MI, 1976), 105–6.

[94] Philippe Chareyre, *Le Consistoire de Nîmes 1561 à 1685*, 4 vols (Thèse de Doctorat d'État en Histoire: Université Paul-Valéry-Montpellier III, 1987), vol. 1, 106.

[95] ADTG, I 1, 4v.   [96] ADG, 42 J 29, 317.   [97] Chareyre, *Le Consistoire*, vol. 1, 121.

[98] BN, Ms.fr. 8666, 63v; ADTG, I 1, 91r; ADG, 42 J 29, 317.

[99] ADG, 42 J 33, 136v, 8 Dec. 1606.

his enemies who had invented them all, that he had been a Protestant for a decade, and, rather than believing in purgatory, his faith was in the ability of the blood of Christ to wash souls and purge all sins; he was eventually elected, but the allegation against him delayed this by twenty days.[100]

In the Nîmes election for 1581 the elected deacons, elders, and clerk were required to promise to:

> keep the things that are dealt with in the consistory secret, and not to reveal them or declare them anywhere except at the consistory, and to be vigilant as to the scandals that are committed by those of the church, so that by declaring their heedlessness and fault to the consistory, the church of God may not succumb and be diminished; [all of] which they promised to do diligently and to comport themselves like true children of God and to keep everything secret.[101]

The charge to the consistory was to ensure watchfulness, privacy, and holiness.

The election to deaconate or eldership conveyed, therefore, a high level of expectation, onerous responsibilities, and the corollary of significant prestige and status. Deacons and elders took their roles very seriously, and by joining the consistory, committed many hours to the service of the church—hours put in on top of their ordinary occupations.[102] Once elected, service for a year (during which time they were not to leave the town 'without sufficient excuse') appears to have been almost mandatory.[103] Elders who missed a meeting of the consistory without a legitimate reason were fined five *sous* for the benefit of the poor.[104] Acceptable excuses were of the order of being quarantined during a breakout of plague, and needing to bring in the harvest.[105]

Successive generations of elders needed to be reminded of the penalty and, in Nîmes, in 1609, the fine was even extended to those who were late to the consistory without good reason.[106]

Not everyone appreciated co-optation on to the consistory. In the earliest records of the Nîmes consistory, the clerk made lengthy notes about negotiations held following the January 1563 election, and these reveal a panoply of excuses proffered in an attempt to avoid serving. Mathieu Suau protested that he could not accept the position of summoner because he had responsibility for a sick father, and his wife and children; an elder from the previous year retorted that he too had a wife and four children. Anthoine Carrière, elected to serve as an elder for the Jacobins suburbs, said he could not do so because his poverty meant that he could not serve without wages. The consistory agreed to elect another in his place, but when his replacement, weaver Barthelemy Borniole, made the same excuse of poverty, they remonstrated with Borniole until he accepted. Lawyer Jaques Davin said that he did not want to take the role without his father's consent, so the consistory deputized

---

[100] ADG, 42 J 33, 158v.   [101] BN, Ms.fr. 8667, 150v, 7 Dec. 1580.

[102] Chareyre, *Le Consistoire*, vol. 1, 115; Margo Todd, *The Culture of Protestantism in Early Modern Scotland* (New Haven, CT, and London, 2002), 10.

[103] BN, Ms.fr. 8666, 72r.

[104] e.g. BN, Ms.fr. 8666, 31v; ADG, 42 J 30, 274v; ADG, 42 J 34, 59v.

[105] BN, Ms.fr. 8666, 61r; ADTG, I 1, 16r; GG 24, 91r.

[106] ADG, 42 J 28, 372v; 42 J 30, 274v; 42 J 34, 59v.

two men to go with him to extract it. Jehan Fontfroide argued that he would be unable to join the consistory because he had promised to support the new second consul, Sauveur Cappon; he was excused. Robert Agullonet, elected as an elder, said that there were many others more suitable for the role and, besides that, he had substantial business affairs in Toulouse and elsewhere; he was, nevertheless, persuaded to accept. Anthoine Cheyron said it was inconvenient for him as he had a shop and farm, but ultimately took the role. Mathieu Jan Jac, too, accepted the charge of elder after offering 'certain excuses'.[107] This means that out of sixteen men approached to serve in 1563, eight offered excuses not to serve, although at least five of these were, nevertheless, made to do so. Serving on the consistory seems to have been regarded by some as a burdensome and unattractive responsibility. With two individual exceptions (Maurice Blisson in 1599 and notary Michel Ursi in 1605), this is the only time the clerk recorded such reluctance to serve.[108] Perhaps being on the consistory became more appealing, but it seems more likely that a decision was made to exclude such objections from the record.

Despite an element of compulsion and the burden of their charge, deacons and elders were, for the most part, diligent in meeting their many responsibilities, as helpers to the poor and needy, overseers of the town's morality, and sustainers of the heritage of the church. In fact, many returned to serve repeatedly. Bertheau has found that this repetition of service meant the consistories of Moyen-Poitou 'fatally took on the appearance of a closed caste', while Chareyre has suggested that membership of the consistory in Nîmes was sometimes 'a family affair'.[109] In a thirty-year sample in Nîmes between 1585 and 1615 of 204 elders and deacons, 112 or 55 per cent served for more than one year, while thirty-one or 15 per cent served for more than four years, though seldom all consecutively. Some particularly long-serving members were M. Bosquier, who served as deacon nine times (1586–9, 1596, 1598–1601); Jehan Bourguet, who served as an elder and deacon seven times (1597, 1602–3, 1608–9, 1613–14); Tristan Brueis, Seigneur de Saint-Chapte, as deacon seven times (1603–6, 1610–12), and Antoine Cheyron, as elder and deacon, seven or eight times (1585?, 1586, 1591, 1597–1601). It was also quite common for certain families to be well represented on the consistory. Examples include the Dupin and Guiraud families: Jehan Dupin was an elder in 1588, Charles Dupin in 1592, and Anthoine Dupin in 1596, while an unidentified M. Dupin served as a deacon in 1589 and 1594; Claude Guiraud served as elder and clerk in 1590 and 1591, David Guiraud as an elder in 1602–3 and 1613–14, and Guillaume Guiraud as summoner from 1588 continuously to 1604.[110] Other notable examples of dynasties among the eldership include the DuVieux, Baudoin, Gregoire, Foucard, Davin, and Veyras families, while in 1613 Maurice Blisson was succeeded by his son, Daniel.[111]

[107] BN, Ms.fr. 8666, 199r–203v.   [108] ADG, 42 J 31, 317r; ADG, 42 J 33, 71r.
[109] Solange Bertheau, 'Le Consistoire dans les Églises Réformées du Moyen-Poitou au XVIIe Siècle', *BSHPF* 116 (1970), 332–59 and 513–49, here 350. Cf. also Graham, *The Uses*, 77–83; Raymond A. Mentzer, 'Le consistoire et la pacification du monde rural', *BSHPF* 135 (1989), 373–91, 376; Chareyre, *Le Consistoire*, vol. 1, 131.
[110] The Dupins and Guirauds were also well represented in the consulate.
[111] ADG, 42 J 35, 33r.

There are two caveats to bear in mind when considering this strong evidence of a caste of elders. Despite the considerable temporal and financial hardship imposed on those serving in the consistory, just as it was difficult to refuse an eldership, it was also difficult to step down if re-elected.[112] In addition, Chareyre has highlighted the institutional preference for continuity and the detrimental effect of continual change on the smooth functioning of the consistory.[113] This may explain why deacons, as overseers of elders, were re-elected less frequently and for longer time periods than elders. The manner of election, the continual reappearance of certain names, and their positions on the town consulate and council as well (see p. 82) do however suggest that deacons and elders would have been men of standing who shared a common background.

Evidence of the occupations of deacons and elders broadly confirms this. In Montauban, the figures show considerable under-representation of the lowest social strata.[114] Even the criteria necessary to become an elder militated against the involvement of peasants and unskilled workers: the moral conditions of orthodoxy and high standing were matched by the requirement of literacy in French.[115]

Chareyre identified a distinction between the occupational background of those serving as deacons, and those serving as elders between 1581 and 1619.[116] This is perhaps most easily understood in tabular form:

	Deacons		Elders	
	No.	%	No.	%
Seigneurs	49	28%		
Royal officials	1	0.5%		
Lawyers	90	50.5%		
Bourgeois	4	2%	84	20%
Doctors	7	4%		
Merchants			75	18%
Merchant-*bourgeois*			2	0.5%
Notaries etc.			59	14%
Yeomen etc.			33	8%
Artisans			36	9%
Health			18	4%
Unknown	27	15%	109	26.5%

These figures indicate that the deaconate was dominated by members of the urban rich, and the eldership was mainly composed of the upper-middling and middling

---

[112] See ADG, 42 J 33, 3–5.   [113] Chareyre, *Le Consistoire*, vol. 1, 124.

[114] Garrisson, *Les protestants*, 94.

[115] B. Vogler and J. Estèbe, 'La genèse d'une société protestante: étude comparée de quelques registres consistoriaux languedociens et palatins vers 1600', *Annales: Economies, Sociétés, Civilisations* 31 (1976), 364; Garrisson, *Les protestants*, 97. Signatures by the consistory at Aimargues in 1594 (ADG, E Dépôt GG 54, 52v) suggest that this literacy could, however, be quite limited: of twenty signatures, six are just initials; another seven written in ill-formed childish hands. The requirements were undoubtedly higher in larger cities such as Nîmes and Montauban.

[116] Chareyre, *Le Consistoire*, vol. 1, 142, 144, cf. his codification of states and professions, vol. 3, 185; cf. Allan A. Tulchin, *That Men Would Praise the Lord: The Triumph of Protestantism in Nîmes, 1530–1570* (Oxford, 2010), 21.

ranks of urban society. The roles and responsibilities of the deacons—handling money, visiting the sick and prisoners, and composing the public face of the church—reflected this higher degree of influence.[117] Although there was some overlap—some *bourgeois* did appear among the deaconate—most remained among the ranks of the elders, where they appeared to have formed the majority, accompanied by members of the well-respected juridical and health professions, artisans, and the higher ranks of the agricultural workers. Professions that do not appear to have been represented were those that were relatively poorer, involved being constantly on the move, or represented a position of inferiority under a master— servants, husbandmen, shepherds, retailers—or professions that carried some taint of pollution or had insufficient moral standing, such as butchers and innkeepers.[118] Those serving on the consistory needed to have a well-respected, influential status among their contemporaries in order to carry out their duties, while requiring a certain degree of flexibility in their work in order to devote a year or more to the service of the church, but they were not necessarily the richest or most elevated citizens of the town. In fact, the consistory demonstrated a very similar range of social backgrounds in their ecclesiastical governance to that seen in the composition of the consulate of the town.

It is, therefore, going too far to say, as Garrisson does, that there was a 'genuine confiscation of consistorial power by superior social classes in Calvinist towns and villages', while the consolidated evidence of the consistorial registers from Nîmes, Montauban, Ganges, and elsewhere does not support Mentzer's conclusion that the social status of the elders who sat in judgement (high) was almost diametrically opposed to those whom they chastized (modest).[119] The eldership of the consistory was drawn, in the main, from the middling ranks of urban society, and one of the surprising insights of the consistorial records is their pronounced tendency to challenge, on moral grounds, those of superior social status to their own. Nevertheless, it is possible to state that the combination of dynasties of elders, election by co-optation, the requirements of the role, and the occupational backgrounds from which they were drawn, created a cadre of deacons and elders with a shared mentality, ethos, and culture.

SACRED AND SECULAR GOVERNANCE

Pierre Viret explained at the establishment of the Lyon consistory in 1560 that the authority vested in the consistory was not intended to interfere with the functioning of secular government and justice, but, nevertheless, the significant power and authority of the consistories of cities such as Montauban and Nîmes created, in theory, potential for a conflict of interests to occur.[120] In practice, however, by

---

[117] Chareyre, *Le Consistoire* vol. 1, 132.   [118] Chareyre, *Le Consistoire* vol. 1, 152.
[119] Garrisson, *Les protestants*; Graham, *The Uses*, 77–83; Mentzer, 'Ecclesiastical Discipline', 166.
[120] Menna Prestwich (ed.), *International Calvinism 1541–1715* (Oxford, 1985); 'Calvinism', 84.

collaboration and co-operation, these religious and political elites appear to have formed an interlocking armour that was only occasionally breached.

In Nîmes the four consuls were in constant communication with the consistory. Consuls attended the consistory's extraordinary meetings, and the consistory frequently deputized elders to ask the consuls to help enforce decisions or solve problems.[121] In July 1595, for example, the consistory 'charged Captain Privat to speak to the consuls to make them close shops on Sundays'.[122] A common request was for the consuls to exile the degenerate: in April 1587 the consistory asked the consuls to expel Jehan de Nages from the town for 'playing the fool and lots of insolences', and five years later they wanted M. de Lachalade to be banished for being an 'atheist, tavern-goer, card player, magician, quarreller, and sodomite'.[123] It was decided as policy in June 1583 that when a non-married woman was found to be pregnant, a deacon would report her to the consuls and magistrates in the presence of two elders.[124] The purpose of this was for the consuls to evict the culprit from the town, as happened in 1595 when two elders were deputized to report a pregnant women to the second consul, Charles Dupin, so that she might be expelled.[125] A more wide-ranging decision, such as that of September 1598 to ask the consuls 'to expel the whores of the town', was also not uncommon.[126] In Ganges, too, the consistory instructed the town's consuls to expel Françoise Fabresse on the grounds of fornication.[127] When there were irreconcilable disputes or when accusations against individuals were serious, the consistory involved the consuls—as with two master tailors, one notorious for having poisoned his wife, the other for having fought for the Catholic League, who came to the consistory's attention in November 1595.[128] The frequency and confidence of such demands suggests they were met with co-operation. Information also went the other way. In February 1609 second consul Pierre Galafret appeared before the consistory to inform them of an ongoing court case involving maidservant Judict Arboussette, who claimed to be pregnant by a scholar from Dauphiné called M. Durant. It was understood as a call to action: the consistory immediately summoned her employer and wrote to Durant's home church.[129]

In Nîmes there were also close links between the consistory and the town council. In 1579 elders were sent from the consistory to speak to the consuls and the council about the financial upkeep of the pastors (further evidence of the issue of ministerial wages).[130] In October 1589 the council meeting was held 'in the temple of the Reformed religion of Nîmes'.[131] Members of the consistory regularly

[121] Jacques Boulenger, *Les protestants à Nîmes au temps de l'Edit de Nantes* (Paris, 1903), 105.
[122] ADG, 42 J 30, 372v, 10 Jul. 1595.
[123] ADG, 42 J 28, 277v, 29 Apr. 1587; 42 J 30, 43v, 18 Mar. 1592.
[124] ADG, 42 J 28, 20v, 8 Jun. 1583.   [125] ADG, 42 J 31, 12r, 22 Nov. 1595.
[126] ADG, 42 J 31, 301v, 5 Sept. 1599. See p. 103 for further discussion of the focus on expelling women for sexual sin.
[127] ADH, GG 24, 111r–v, 114v, 22 Aug. 1599.
[128] ADG, 42 J 28, 184v, 14 Aug. 1585, for an example of an irreconcilable dispute; 42 J 31, 9v, 8 Nov. 1595.
[129] ADG, 42 J 34, 69r, 18 Feb. 1609.   [130] BN, Ms.fr. 8667, 72r, 4 Mar. 1579.
[131] ADG, E dépôt 36/131, 173v, 31 Oct. 1589.

attended the extraordinary meetings of the council: in a sample of twelve years for which both consistory registers and town council records survive, there was always at least one representative of that year's consistory at such meetings, and an average of four of them.[132] In four of those years at least one minister of the church attended.[133]

In Montauban the consistory similarly forwarded to the consulate information about suspect people or incidents on which they were unable to act.[134] Here it is clear that the directives were mutual: the consuls told ministers what to preach—asking them to deliver a sermon admonishing the people of the city not to blaspheme the name of God, to attend each Sunday's catechisms, not to play games or engage in debauchery, not to haunt the town's taverns, to close their shops on Wednesday while the sermon was being given, and not to buy or sell during the hour of the service.[135] They also worked together on ecclesiastical decisions: it was an assembly of consuls, lawyers, and members of the consistory who defended minister Bironis in 1595.[136]

The survival in Montauban of both the consistorial records for 1595–8 and the register of criminal sentences for 1534–1616 means that it is possible to chart a relationship between ecclesiastical and secular justice in the overlapping years. Catherine Rosselle was, for example, sentenced by the consuls to make public reparation for *paillardise* on 2 March 1598, and two days later the consistory launched a full investigation into the charges against her, gathering witnesses and ultimately suspending her rapist, Gabriel Olivier, from the sacrament.[137] It seems highly likely that information was being passed from the consulate to the consistory.

This congruity of governance was undoubtedly partly a result of a large overlap in personnel. In Montauban Philip Conner found that 62 per cent of the elders who served on the consistory also served at one time or other on the town consulate.[138] Comparing the consistorial registers and town council records in Nîmes, a similar overlap can be observed between the make-up of the Nîmes consulate and town council, and the consistory. Taking a twenty-two-year sample from 1560–1615, or 40 per cent of the period under study, there were, in those years, in total, eighty-one consuls, 209 town councillors, and 207 elders.[139] In the

[132] ADG, E Dépôt 36/127, 207v; E Dépôt 36/128, 1r; E Dépôt 36/131, 154r–v, 199r; E Dépôt 36/132, 73r, 225v, 230r; E Dépôt 36/133, 22r, 102v, 108, 154r, 334r; E Dépôt 36/135, 135v, 136r.
[133] ADG, E Dépôt 36/131, 199r; E Dépôt 36/133, 102v, 108r, 154r; E Dépôt 36/135, 135r–v.
[134] Conner, *Huguenot Heartland*, 70; ADTG, I 1, 22r–23v, 174v, 336v, 339r–v. ADTG, I 1, 22r–23v, 174–v, 336v, 339r–v.
[135] ADTG, I 1, 90r, 10 Jan. 1596.   [136] See pp. 75–6. ADTG, I 1, 45r–50r, 14 Sept. 1595.
[137] ADTG, 5 FF 2, 37v, 2 Mar. 1598; ADTG, I 1, 328v, 329r–v, 332v, 4 Mar. 1598. Also noted by Conner, *Huguenot Heartland*, 70–1.
[138] Conner, *Huguenot Heartland*, 52.
[139] The following analysis is based on the consistorial registers (BN, Ms.fr. 8666; BN, Ms.fr. 8667; ADG, 42 J 28; ADG, 42 J 29; ADG, 42 J 30; ADG, 42 J 31; ADG, 42 J 32; ADG, 42 J 33; ADG, 42 J 34; ADG, 42 J 35) and the archives communales, containing the town council's deliberations (ADG, E dépôt 36/128, 9r; ADG, E dépôt 36/130, 69r, 79r, 140r, 184r, 201r, 263v; ADG, E dépôt 36/131, 6r, 33r, 78r–v, 267r, 343r; ADG, E dépôt 36/132, 126r; ADG, E dépôt 36/133, 253r–v, 257r; ADG, E dépôt 36/134, 4 Aug. 1605, 3 Sept. 1605, 13 Sept. 1605, 157r, 160r; ADG,

consistorial registers first names of the elders are not always provided and, for some surnames, this gives several possible candidates. The following statistics are based on using both certain and most probable candidates, with figures based only on those known for certain supplied in parentheses. I found that of 209 councillors, one hundred men or 48 per cent of councillors also served as elders (sixty-two or 30 per cent using only confirmed candidates). Of eighty-one consuls, fifty-three or 65 per cent served as elders (thirty-three or 41 per cent using only confirmed candidates). Or, to reverse this, of the 207 elders during these years, one hundred men or 48 per cent of elders served as councillors, and fifty-three men, or 26 per cent of elders, served as consuls. If 65 per cent of consuls and 48 per cent of councillors in this sample were, had been, or would be elders, then these findings differ markedly from Ann Guggenheim's conclusion that, in Nîmes, few members of the political elite belonged to the consistory.[140]

Conner argues that, for Montauban, 'being elected to an official church position was quickly regarded as an important role in the regulation of society and...a stepping-stone for many up-and-coming individuals', although sometimes established members of the elite also served on the consistory.[141] Conner charts at least three men who served as consuls and elders simultaneously.[142] In Nîmes there was a slight preference to serve as an elder before becoming a councillor or a consul. Thirty-nine men in the sample were simultaneously councillors and elders.[143] It was far less common to hold the consulate and eldership simultaneously—only one man in my sample of twenty years appears to have been both a serving consul and an elder—Jacques Davin in 1579—no doubt because of the level of work involved.[144] It was not unknown to move swiftly from one capacity to another: in 1593–4 Jacques Seren served as an elder and in 1595 he became a town consul; in 1606 Jacques Allier served as a consul, before becoming an elder for four years in 1608. Many people held both positions repeatedly, most notably nobleman Tristan de Brueis, Seigneur de Saint-Chapte, who was twice a consul (1595, 1601) and seven times a deacon (1603–6 and 1610–12). As with the eldership itself, the dominance of several key families in the consulate, for examples the Combes, Galafrès, and Guiraud families, is marked—only one of the important families on the consulate, the Lombards, is not represented at all in the eldership of the consistory in this period (maybe they were Catholic). This means that even when the members of the consistory did not hold coincident multiple offices in the governance of the church and town, there would have been a significant amount of personal

E dépôt 36/135, 16r, 212v–213r, 355v; ADG, E dépôt 36/136, 125v, 161v, 228v). There are breaks in the runs of consistorial registers between 1563 and 1578, and the town council records between 1595 and 1599.

[140] Ann H. Guggenheim, 'Calvinism and the Political Elite of Sixteenth-Century Nîmes', Ph.D. thesis (New York University, 1968), 274.

[141] Conner, *Huguenot Heartland*, 50.   [142] Conner, *Huguenot Heartland*, 51.

[143] Of the one hundred councillors, fifty-one were elders first, forty-four were councillors first, and five each became an elder and a councillor at the same time. Of the fifty-three consuls, thirty-one were elders first.

[144] Jacques Davin is, however, a probable candidate for the eldership that year, and cannot be definitively confirmed.

influence and unity of vision between the consistory, consulate, and council. In Ganges, when one consistory retired, the minister thanked the members for serving God and the church and instructed them to remember for the rest of their lives that they had had this honour in the church and to do nothing against all true Christians.[145] If the same ethos held in Montauban and Nîmes, we can imagine that a congruity of vision stretched well beyond any period of simultaneous service.

Besides the consulate and town council, the key figures in the municipal and judicial administration and governance of these cities were the royal judges or magistrates of the local *présidial* court.[146] Appointed for life by the king, these magistrates did not have an annual turnover like the consuls and, as a result, had far more permanent power and influence. The national synods of the French Reformed church tried to delineate the rights and responsibilities of the consistories and magistrates, while safeguarding the rights of the consistories to administer their own discipline.[147] In both Montauban and Nîmes the consistories were warned early in their existence not to encroach on the administration of royal justice.[148]

The consistory in Nîmes constantly tried to placate the magistrates, asking their advice and inviting them, along with the consuls, to attend their extraordinary meetings.[149] Certain cases of criminality were referred to the magistrates for trial.[150] In 1596, in Nîmes, the consistory called their attention to the 'night-time disorders and ribaldry that are ordinarily committed by young men' and, in 1604, deputized three elders to speak to the magistrates about two masons who persistently mistreated their wives, asking them 'to arrest them and put them in prison'.[151] In Montauban a cobbler called Solery who worked until 9 p.m. on a Sunday was reported to the magistrates.[152]

Like the consuls, the consistory expected the magistrates to implement their decisions: for instance, to ensure the gates of the town were closed during Sunday sermons and to banish immoral women from the town.[153] Consistorial directives occasionally impinged on the prerogatives of the magistrates, but there is little evidence of serious tension and, although any may have been deliberately obscured in consistorial records, the predominantly Protestant convictions of the magistrates appears to have meant that they were willing, for the most part, to bow to the authority of the church.[154] At other times the consistory gleaned information about immoral behaviour from the judiciary, as in 1587 when widow Magdaleine

[145] ADH, GG 24, 105v, 25 May 1599.
[146] Guggenheim, 'The Calvinist Notables of Nîmes During the Era of the Religious Wars', *SCJ* 3.1 (1972), 80–96, 84.
[147] Boulenger, *Les protestants*, 112–13; Jean Aymon, *Tous les synods nationaux des Églises réformées de France*, 2 vols (The Hague, 1710), Synod at Paris, 1559, Art. 37, Synod at Orléans, 1563, Art. 9, Synod at Paris, 1565.
[148] BN, Ms.fr. 8666, 169v–170r; Mentzer, 'Disciplina', 103, n. 43; Conner, *Huguenot Heartland*, 49.
[149] ADG, 42 J 34, 207v, 10 Apr. 1610.   [150] Mentzer, 'Disciplina', 103, n. 43.
[151] ADG, 42 J 31, 127r, 18 Sept 1596; 42 J 33, 12r, 31 Dec. 1604. This is an interesting counter-example to the usual consistorial blind eye when it came to domestic violence, see pp. 285–292.
[152] ADTG, I 1, 56v, 58r, 27 Sept. 1595.
[153] ADG, 42 J 27, 338r, 27 Jun. 1582; 42 J 28, 312r, 343r, 16 Sept. and 24 Dec. 1587.
[154] For an example of the obscuring of tension between authorities, see Judith Pollmann, 'Off the Record: Problems in the Quantification of Calvinist Church Discipline', *SCJ* 33.2 (2002), 430, 433.

Coterelle had an illegitimate child, was briefly imprisoned by the royal magistrates, and was in the process of appealing against their decision.[155] Again there was some overlap of personnel between the *présidial* and the consistory—in Montauban, for example, two of the consistory's clerks, Jean Delafon and Pierre de la Barthe, were also royal notaries. In Nîmes, Tristan de Brueis, Seigneur de Saint-Chapte, known to us from both the consulate and consistory, was also a royal lawyer in the *présidial* court.[156]

Early on, in 1562, the Nîmois consistory had indicated that it claimed no authority over the city's Catholics. Asked by the lawyer Pierre Chabot to draw up a list of Catholics in the town and to have the most seditious arrested, the consistory responded that they would draw up a list of Catholics, but as to the conduct of the Catholics 'we will send them on the Captain of the town, or to the deputies appointed for the direction of major affairs, as this matter is part of their responsibilities and does not pertain to the consistory'.[157] Yet through their relationships with the magistrates and consuls, the consistory could attempt to influence the outcome of situations between Protestants and Catholics. In 1600 the consistory charged two of its members to speak to 'the criminal [judge] because of a certain judicial process intended by Jonny, Catholic clerk, for certain disputes...against Captain Ferriol...and to remonstrate with him to do justice to the said Ferriol'.[158] This suggests that if the magistrates were Protestant and partial, Catholics in Nîmes may have had a hard time obtaining justice in suits against their Protestant neighbours. Interestingly, however, as we will see, Catholic women seem, ironically, to have used the justice of the consistory fruitfully to their own ends.

At local levels there was often a high level of co-operation and symbiosis between civil and sacral authorities, where records were shared, cases were passed on, and methods of disciplining served complementary functions.[159] Working in union, the net of discipline became particularly impermeable.[160] Nîmes and Montauban are a powerful examples of the possibilities of a Calvinist moral order where both church and public authorities were firmly Protestant.[161] Historian Jacques Boulenger concluded that this continual and harmonious communication and shared personnel meant that 'the government of Nîmes...[was] a pure theocracy', implying the effective dominance of the church.[162] In these primarily Protestant cities, the way in which the Calvinist consuls, councillors, and magistrates worked reciprocally

---

[155] ADG, 42 J 28, 258r (also 372r), 28 Jan. 1587. See Chapter 7.

[156] Tulchin, *That Men*, 77.

[157] Léon Ménard, *Histoire civile, ecclésiastique et littéraire de la ville de Nîmes*, 7 vols (Marseille, 1976, orig. edn, 1750–6), 346.

[158] ADG, 42 J 31, 344r, 19 Apr. 1600.

[159] Raymond A. Mentzer, 'Morals and Moral Regulation in Protestant France', *JIH* 31.1 (2000), 1–20, 17, 19.

[160] Lenman, 'The Limits', 136–7.

[161] Philippe Chareyre, ' "The Great Difficulties One Must Bear to Follow Jesus Christ": Morality at Sixteenth-Century Nîmes', in *Sin and the Calvinists: Morals Control and the Consistory in the Reformed Tradition*, ed. Raymond A. Mentzer (Missouri, 1994), 66.

[162] Boulenger, *Les protestants*, 111, 117.

and collaboratively with the church enabled the consistory to observe, censure, and spiritually punish the population of Languedoc for a wide variety of transgressions.

THE OPERATION OF THE CONSISTORY

Most consistories planned to meet weekly, as was agreed at the first meeting of the consistory of the Reformed church of Nîmes on 23 March 1561.[163] In practice this varied enormously: the long gaps between meetings in the smaller towns of Alès or Meyreuis contrast with the frequency of consistorial gatherings in larger or more enthusiastic towns. In Ganges, the consistory met every Thursday at seven o'clock in the morning.[164] In Nîmes the original intention was to meet on Saturdays at three o'clock in the afternoon but in March 1562 the members adjusted this to meeting on Wednesdays at noon, in the house of one of the elders.

At the end of the Nîmes register of 1583–8 is a numbered list of twenty-five articles, detailing the administration of the consistory.[165] On matters of moral discipline, these established that the minister should chair the meetings, that old matters were to be addressed before new, no one was to speak 'outside his rank' and all business of the consistory was to be carried out in person. People were to be called to the consistory three times by the summoner; then, if they failed to attend, by their deacon and elder; and, finally, by the pastor and their elder. Each Wednesday the summoner was to give an account of those he had been charged to call, which the clerk would record. The clerk was also to maintain a list of all those suspended from the sacrament, which was to be read aloud a month before each quarterly celebration of the Eucharist so that the consistory could encourage those on it to recognize their faults and be reconciled to the church. Finally, all were to investigate each charge as diligently as they were able, and these articles were to be read aloud at each gathering of the consistory.

In addition, other entries indicate that everyone present was required to promise to keep to themselves all matters discussed, 'not to reveal or declare them elsewhere than in the consistory', and 'to keep all secret'.[166] In June 1592 elder Jean Gril was censured for having revealed an allegation of illegitimate pregnancy made in the consistory to the family of the woman in question, thereby breaking this consistorial bond of secrecy.[167] This commitment to secrecy encouraged those who came before them to speak openly and fulsomely about the events of their lives.

In Nîmes the city was divided into ten small districts to facilitate moral surveillance. The districts—Maison de Ville, Temple, La Ferrage, Collège, Chapitre, Corcomayre, Marché, Arènes, Faubourgs and La Bourgade, and La Madeleine—were decided in the first consistorial meeting of 1561 and defined in relation to the gates of the town, major landmarks, and even people's shops and houses. The Arènes district, for example, comprised the area from *Porte de la Couronne* (Crown Gate)—including

---

[163] ADG, 42 J 26, 1v.　　　[164] ADTG, GG 24, 72v.
[165] ADG, 42 J 28, 374r–377r.　　　[166] BN, MS.fr. 8667, 150v, 7 Dec. 1580.
[167] ADG, 42 J 30, 73v, 76r, 82r.

de George's house, the market, and the Roman amphitheatre—to Saint-Antoine's Gate.[168] The survival of some of the landmarks, and the continued existence of Nîmes's old town on the footprint of the sixteenth-century walled city, makes it possible to identify these districts. An adapted version of Philippe Chareyre's plan of the surveillance zones, now also showing the town's landmarks, can be seen in Figure 2.2. Above all, it indicates that each elder—responsible for one district— had an area of a few hundred square metres to oversee: conscientiously policed, such realistically sized districts facilitated the rapid exposure of any sort of visible immorality.

Central to the operation of the consistory, then, was this onus on elders to act as a sort of morality police for the church, and to relay any evidence of iniquity so that the consistory might investigate thoroughly. Certain elders appear to have taken the responsibility especially seriously; one man in particular—Sire Allegre in 1586— carried out an officious one-man campaign against illicit sexuality.[169] Another elder, M. Mazel, found a woman called Valade hiding at Pierre Raymond's house between 5 a.m. and 6 a.m. on 23 December 1587, suggesting that his zealous observation of his neighbours even extended to the early hours of a dark winter's morning.[170] The elders could be stealthy in their methods—planning, for example, to surprise an unmarried woman in her house to see if she was pregnant—and their pursuit of wrongdoers was unflagging—such as with three women seen dancing at a wedding, whom they summoned 'for the third or fourth time'.[171] Their moral zeal was infectious, as attested by the scribe in Montauban's proud note from 1595: 'on the matter which I Barthe denounced...'.[172]

Yet, allegations also reached the consistory through other routes. At times cases were passed on from the consulate, town council, or *présidial*, but denunications by members of the public were also encouraged.[173] These triggered investigations in many cases, suggesting that there existed a fringe of informants, tale-tellers, and do-gooders eager to report their neighbours' misdemeanours. For those less inclined to denounce their peers, pressure could be applied. Baker Pierre Rouviere was summoned in 1612 for having told an elder that he had seen a man and woman having illicit sex but not wanting to name them. Convoked to appear before the consistory, he was accused of abjuring the truth, and harried into revealing their identities.[174] All the evidence suggests a culture that promoted malice, gave credence to spying, nosiness, and ill-report of one's neighbours, and systematized a collective psychology of mutual fear.

Sometimes the consistory began to investigate only when the evidence of misconduct was beyond disguising: Jallette Estienne and Anne Bosquete were both unmarried servants who were convoked to appear before the consistory when they were around seven months pregnant.[175]

---

[168] ADG, 42 J 26, 1v.   [169] ADG, 42 J 28, e.g. 226v.   [170] ADG, 42 J 28, 341r.
[171] BN, Ms. 8667, 183v, 166v.   [172] ADTG, I 1, 26r, 26 Jul. 1595.
[173] ADG, 42 J 29, 65, 5 Oct. 1588.   [174] ADG, 42 J 34, 337v, 11 Apr. 1612.
[175] ADG, 42 J 29, 343, 6 Feb. 1590; 42 J 33, 254v, 21 Jan. 1608.

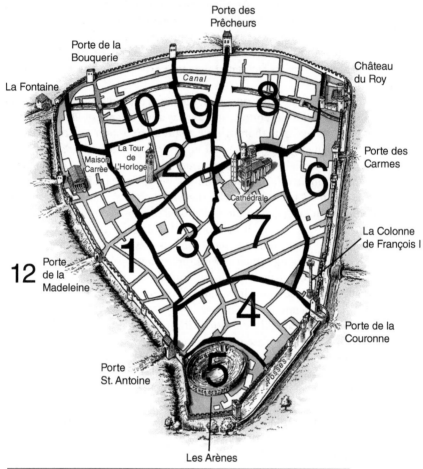

Fig. 2.2. Nîmes, divided into the consistory's surveillance zones (illustrator: Adrian Teal; designer: Lisa Hunter. Adapted from Philippe Chareyre, *Le consistoire de Nîmes de 1561 à 1685* (Thèse de Doctorat, Montpellier, 1987))

At other times cases came to the consistory's attention because people chose to report incidents in which they had some role or interest themselves. Often this was part of a strategic attempt to use the consistory to their advantage. Women especially seem to have come to believe that the consistory could serve as a mechanism for justice. The wife of innkeeper Anthoine Moynier, known as *Figaret*, told an elder that her husband beat and mistreated her and had made their servant-girl pregnant, in the obvious hope that the consistory would act on her behalf.[176] It did.

Such denunciations could be bolstered by rumour and gossip. Apothecary Tanequin Fixor was called to the consistory in May 1591 to be questioned because his maid, Catherine Gillie, had left his house suddenly and 'the noise and public fame is that she left pregnant by him'.[177] It was hearsay that supplied the information used to question Moynier in the investigation that his wife had initiated. Moynier was asked:

> if one day a woman bringing a *fogasse* [slashed flatbread, similar to focaccia] into his house did not find him in his shirt, with his breeches down, sweating, and when she then asked him what had roused [or aroused] him, he did not begin to laugh?

and:

> if he was not at Montpellier with the said chambermaid or if he did not maintain the said chambermaid at...Montpellier and if he was not found behind a door holding the breasts of the said chambermaid in his hands?[178]

Gossip, known as 'common noise', clearly provided fulsome information (which could be used as prosecutorial witnessing in leading questions).[179]

This reliance gave enormous weight to local hearsay, tacitly endorsing the natural rumour and gossip that existed among affinitive neighbours. Marye Lampie's female neighbours said in April 1590 that she had not slept at home for eight days (later varied to six), but had returned several times, once sporting a new grey hat, another time with new yellow breeches, and, on a third, carrying half a bushel of wheat. They also said they had seen her do no work except re-sell a barrel of sardines; the implication was that these goods were the proceeds of prostitution. The neighbours admitted that they had not seen anyone suspicious come to her house nor seen her act badly, yet 'albeit that she had done nothing, this [her apparent new wealth] made them think badly of her'.[180] It was a plausible-enough tale to launch an investigation into Lampie's life.

Feminine socializing was often the place for the exchange of gossip: at *veillées* on winter evenings as married women spun together, they swapped the stories of the day. It was women who might especially know of a maidservant's pregnancy or of

---

[176] ADG, 42 J 28, 10v, 27 Apr. 1583. See Chapter 7 for more details.
[177] ADG, 42 J 29, 645, 657, 658, 675, 29 May 1591.
[178] ADG, 42 J 28, 73v, 18 Jan. 1584.
[179] Bernard Capp, *When Gossips Meet: Women, Family and Neighbourhood in Early Modern England* (Oxford, 2003), 281; Maurice Oudot de Dainville, 'Le consistoire de Ganges à la fin du XVIe siècle', *Revue d'historie de l'Église de France* 18 (1932), 476.
[180] ADG, 42 J 29, 392–3, 19 Apr. 1590.

covert male visits to their neighbours' houses.[181] The consistory's dependence on rumour therefore highlights its paradoxical role in empowering female collectivities and validating an intensely female world of tales and scandal.[182] The separate spheres of life inhabited by men and women raise the question of how the men of the consistory accessed this peculiarly female world of social exchange. It suggests a role for the wives of the ministers, elders, and deacons in reporting back scandalous tit-bits to their husbands.

Once a case had come to their attention, the elders were zealous interrogators of the parties involved. The consistory took its task as seriously as any law court, and there is some evidence that its members modelled their methods on judicial process. They adopted legal terms to describe their procedures and imitated the practice of contemporary criminal and civil justice by gathering and questioning witnesses; taking testimony under oath; cross-examining the accuser, accused, and witnesses; and compelling deponents with differing stories to confront each other. It is perhaps unsurprising in Nîmes especially—a town of notaries—that the consistory would adopt such techniques.[183] There were some distinct differences, however, between the consistory and a court of law: the restorative and penitential goals of the consistory were very different from those of contemporary justice and, crucially, the consistory recognized the validity of women's testimonies, when married women were legally incapable under French law. The consistory was also uneven in the type of information it gathered. Sporadically the ages and occupations of witnesses were noted, but not as a matter of routine. The consistory in Nîmes was also frequently lazy, indifferent, or ignorant when it came to nomenclature, especially for women. Women were often referred to simply as the 'wife of', 'daughter of', or 'maid of' a named man, rather than given their proper name (although this can sometimes be deduced by cross-referencing cases). It may be that as men and women operated in separate, though overlapping spheres, and as women in the Languedoc did not take their husbands' names, the consistory was simply unaware of them, but men, too, were not infrequently referred to by their relationship to another, more prominent, male. The use of nicknames assumed that anyone reading the registers would be familiar with the town's characters: Cephas Bon, for example, first appears in the registers as 'Cefas Castanet', then 'Cephas Castanet', then 'Cephas Brun', and finally as 'Cephas Bon *dict* Castanet' ('Castanet' was, therefore, his sobriquet). People were sometimes recorded only by their first names or surnames—'Donne Blanche, called *La Broquieyre*', 'Blanche Garniere, known as *La Broquiere*', and 'La Brocquiere' are all the same person; 'M. Henry' is later identified as Henry Fabrot. The forenames of many of the elders of the consistory go unnoted—no doubt because everyone present was so familiar with them, and to use titles as a form of respect. This inconsistency in naming provides challenges and riddles to the historian seeking to follow the thread of a case and falls short of contemporary judicial standards of record-keeping. Montauban's

---

[181] Robin Briggs, *Witches and Neighbours: The Social and Cultural Context of European Witchcraft*, 2nd edn (Oxford, 2002), 232.
[182] Capp, *Gossips*, 272–84.   [183] Mentzer, 'Ecclesiastical Discipline', 166.

consistory, by contrast, was far more consistent in its notation of such details, taking the trouble to list the names of the men and women involved in each case in its margin. This suggests that if more years of the Montauban registers had survived than the extant three, these would have been a source for women's history to surpass even the fulsome records of the church at Nîmes. Nevertheless, the information within the surviving registers for all the towns considered is, in some ways, nearly as thorough as that kept by contemporary judicial authorities, and, in others, far superior in its richness and insight.

The way the consistory operated was that when a matter of moral transgression came to its attention, one or two elders were deputized to investigate further or to summon the relevant parties for questioning. Once individuals had been brought before the assembly, the consistory prefaced each examination—which was generally led by a minister—with the requirement that the deponent swear to tell the truth before God; the records are full of such warnings: 'having promised and sworn to tell the truth', 'having been exhorted in the name of God to tell the truth', or, most simply, 'having been exhorted to tell the truth'. Mendacity after this declaration carried significant spiritual implications and swearing the oath was sometimes sufficiently salutary to produce a change of story. The depositions given in response to the consistory's questions were then recorded in the registers by the clerk, in the third person.

A necessity for their system to be operational was that the consistory sincerely believed that the truth was accessible to them. This makes some of their decisions appear naïve: brazen denial while swearing truthfulness won some apparently guilty defendants their acquittal. If in any doubt, the consistory reminded deponents of their oath, and sometimes required them to swear once again that they told the truth.

Depositions were seldom given freely; they were extracted through questions compiled from the consistory's prior knowledge. These questions are recorded in the registers and are sometimes very detailed. The interrogation of merchant Pol Delicat in March 1606 on the charge that he had committed adultery with his wife's niece, Marguerite Pinette, is indicative. Delicat was asked

> if, the said Pinette having left his house, he did not lodge her in a house in this town, with suspect, notorious people, so that he could more easily continue in his frequentation of her and, if he went to see her several times, both during the day and at improper hours of the night?[184]

On at least one occasion the consistory also allowed the accused to question his accuser: as he was a powerful man and she his servant, who had accused him of rape, the consistory's actions speak of either profound credulity or bias, or both.[185] Sometimes the final depositions were read back to the witness, so that they could add anything they had left out. The most powerful weapon in the consistory's arsenal was the confrontation of deponents, by bringing them face to face and testing their stories against each other. In practice, this often resulted in a stalemate where

[184] ADG, 42 J 33, 98r, 22 Mar. 1606.
[185] ADG, 42 J 31, 395v–397r, 23 Feb. 1601; see Chapter 6.

neither side would amend their tale, but recurrent resort to this device suggests the consistory continued to believe in its efficacy to elicit honesty and reconciliation.

The efforts put into investigation varied considerably. Some cases were elaborately pursued and documented, other seemingly equivalent cases were dismissed peremptorily and not, as far as the records show, considered further. Instances taken from the many examples include a brief reference to the pregnant chambermaids of M. de Malmont, M. Lansard, and M. Barthelemy in 1583, who never received further mention, and the alleged fornication by M. Capdur the younger in 1607, which appears not to have been followed up.[186] Such variation confirms the impossibility of arriving at meaningful statistics on the number of cases concerned with any particular sin. Some cases may have been resolved, following the biblical model, off the record. Sometime between 21 March 1607, when Sieur Loys Bonneterre was called to account as head of the household for the pregnancy of one of his servant girls and declared he knew nothing of it, and 25 April 1607, when he appeared at the consistory and was suspended from the sacrament, he had confessed, off record, to having had an affair with the maid.[187] The process of collecting evidence and resolving disputes by deputizing elders to visit witnesses at home and take their testimonies meant that not all evidence heard by, and known to, the consistory appears in written form. Statements given outside the consistorial meetings were not recorded unless the witness appeared to reiterate their evidence before the panel. In the case of an alleged betrothal between Pierre Meynan and Saumette Messe in June 1599, the consistory appointed elders M. Bosquier and Sieur Gril to hear the testimonies of the eyewitnesses but, as these witnesses were never persuaded to appear before the consistory, their evidence was never written down.[188] This supports Judith Pollmann's discovery of a journal from an elder at Utrecht, and comparison of it with the consistorial registers of Utrecht in 1622–8, which demonstrated that disciplinary activity occurred there that was not recorded in the consistorial registers.[189] There are occasional glimpses of activity beyond the pages of the Languedocian registers: in June 1603, while arbitrating a dispute over seats in church, the scribe noted 'seeing the deliberations made on 14th of last month', but while there are records from 14 May, at no point does the record reflect a conversation over pews.[190] Generally, however, and by definition, in the absence of corroborating documents, the extent to which cases were resolved off-stage remains murky.

If some cases were passed over or resolved silently, others attracted the consistory's most dogged pursuit. Between March 1593 and April 1594, for example, delegates from the Nîmes consistory visited and summoned one employer and his pregnant servant twenty times, dropping around unexpectedly to spy on their living

[186] ADG, 42 J 27, 374v; 42 J 33, 244r.
[187] ADG, 42 J 33, 180v, 195v, 21 Apr. 1607. His being deprived of the sacrament is implemented 'seeing his confession'.
[188] ADG, 42 J 31, 292v.
[189] Pollmann, 'Off the Record', 424–38, here 425, and her *Religious Choice in the Dutch Republic: The Reformation of Arnoldus Buchelius (1565–1641)* (Manchester, 1999).
[190] ADG, 42 J 32, 176v, 25 Jun. 1603.

arrangements and even banishing the servant from the town.[191] Given that servant pregnancies were not a rare occurrence, the consistory's singular fixation with this couple is striking. It seems likely that the reason the consistory cared so much was because, unusually, this couple never demonstrated remorse or repentance for their actions: they represented the church's failure to inculcate virtue. Perhaps rapid repentance was the quickest way to disarm the consistory's advances.

An assumption of guilt was not uncommon. M. de la Rouviere was accused of making his maid pregnant in 1591 and denied the charge. The consistory retorted that as the maid had not accused anyone else, and lived in his house, 'it is up to him to justify the contrary'.[192] From the consistory's perspective, the responsibility normally lay on the accused to prove his innocence, rather than on the accuser to prove guilt. It was common for the accused to be suspended from the Eucharist during the period of investigation, or for them to be charged with accepting the sacrament only if their conscience allowed it. In fact, whether a suspect was allowed to continue participating in the Lord's Supper while under investigation spoke volumes about the consistory's presumption of guilt or innocence. Jacques Varlet was allowed to continue 'to approach the Lord's table' after being accused of fornicating with a prostitute in April 1612, but M. Dorthes, despite his declaration of innocence to the charge of making Estiene Charberd's daughter pregnant, was deprived of the sacrament two months later by the same consistory.[193] Maintaining the purity of the Eucharist was paramount, but withholding the sacrament from the accused conveyed a clear and damning message to the community, before guilt had properly been established. Once convinced of a person's sin and relying on their belief that a guilty person would eventually own up, the consistory often tried shock tactics to force a confession, presenting the accused with a blunt statement of their offences, or using the elaborately probing questions of which they were fond, in the hope of provoking repentance. Failing this, they would attempt to recruit further witnesses.[194]

That the goal of discipline was primarily reincorporation into the Eucharistic community meant that the consistory prioritized reconciliation and repentance over punishment, but it also explains the sort of penalties ultimately imposed by the consistory. Discipline followed a graduated series of punishments, each more shameful than the last. These were preliminary reconciliation, private admonition, reparation and repentance before the consistory, public reparation before the whole congregation, temporary suspension from the Eucharist, and, for the obstinately recalcitrant, permanent excommunication.[195] The apparent lightness of punishments, in contrast to contemporary criminal sentences—chiefly corporal or capital punishment—has led some historians to ridicule consistorial discipline as essentially toothless.[196] Yet this is to misunderstand the impact and context of such shaming.

---

[191] This case is further considered in Chapter 6.   [192] ADG, 42 J 29, 673.

[193] ADG, 42 J 34, 345r, 356r.   [194] e.g. ADG, 42 J 29, 178.

[195] Mentzer, 'Marking', 127; Mentzer, 'Notions', 91.

[196] Graham, *The Uses*, 84 and 'Social Discipline in Scotland, 1560–1610', in *Sin and the Calvinists: Morals Control and the Consistory in the Reformed Tradition*, ed. Raymond A. Mentzer (Kirksville, MO, 1994), 156. Particularly critical of the consistory's limited powers to punish was William Naphy,

Private and, especially, public repentance entailed a display of humility that compromised personal honour and was consequently dreaded. In 1597 Pierre Boudou appeared before the consistory in Ganges demanding admission to the Eucharist. He was reminded that he had been accused of having committed *paillardise* with Estienne Amourouse four or five years earlier, and that he needed to make public reparation on the day of the sacrament to receive it. His response was that he was not guilty, that he refused to make public reparation, and that he would rather change his religion than do so.[197] Similarly, in 1589 butcher Jacques Mingaud confessed his adultery with Suzanne Bertrande to the consistory in Nîmes, who ordained that he should publicly repent his adultery and receive the peace of the church the following Sunday before the assembled congregation. He protested vociferously, saying that the consistory was being 'too severe against him' and that he would 'prefer to suffer death immediately than make the said public reparation'.[198] He did, however, eventually—two years later—make the reparation. Anthoine Baudilhon, who confessed to a two-month affair with his maid, went even further. He refused to make public reparation in 1591, cursing the elder sent to urge him to submit to the discipline, and saying that he would kill the next person who talked to him about it. Another time he swore that he would rather be a devil than make the reparation in public.[199] Again, however, Baudilhon finally gave in, after a year in which the consistory sought to have him exiled from the town.[200] There is no need to take these extravagant displays of defiance literally, but they convey vividly the power of public shaming in this community.

There was also no clear distinction between secular and sacred punishment. In Montauban the register of criminal sentences pronounced by the consuls of the town indicates that secular justice also punished fornicators by the '*amande honorable la torche au poing a genoulx*'—that is, a public apology or reparation made by an offender on his or her knees, holding a torch in one hand.[201] These were traditionally made before a church, in a state of undress, with a rope around one's neck; Michel Foucault notes that the attempted regicide Robert-François Damiens was required to 'make the *amende honorable* before the main door of the Church of Paris' in 1757 before his dismemberment.[202] In short, the consistorial sentence of public reparation aped almost exactly a dishonouring punishment used by the criminal courts.

Suspension and excommunication were even more punitive. Following the injunctions of 1 Corinthians to 'purge the evil person' from their midst, to be suspended or permanently disbarred from the sacrament meant the denial of friendship and economic exchange with the faithful—effectively social and economic

---

'Paedophilia and Pederasty in Calvin's Geneva: Attitudes of Children, Parents, Magistrates and the Guilty', unpublished paper delivered Oxford, 12 November 2002; for the counter-argument see Chareyre, 'The Great Difficulties', and Mentzer, 'Marking', 121, both in *Sin and the Calvinists*.

[197] ADH, GG 24, 79r, 6 Apr. 1597.   [198] ADG, 42 J 29, 265, 1 Sept. 1589.

[199] ADG, 42 J 28, 672, 738; 42 J 30, 40v, 16 May 1591.

[200] ADG, 42 J 30, 68r, 15 May 1592.

[201] ADTG, 5 FF 2, e.g. 35r, 36v, 37v, punishments for fornication in 1595–8.

[202] Michel Foucault, *Discipline and Punish: The Birth of the Prison* (London, 1977), 3.

death.[203] In practice, consistories rarely excommunicated their members because they were much more interested in reconciling and reincorporating sinners into the Protestant community than punishing them. One rare exception is Zacarye de Saintes, who, after more than two years of refusing to respond to the consistory's summons on the charge of having an illegitimate child with his maidservant, had allegedly allowed the child to starve to death over the winter of 1598–9, and was finally excommunicated and reported to the judiciary the following spring.[204] Here the gravity of the sin, Saintes' refusal to show repentance, and the sheer length of time that passed together necessitated the consistory's final resort. Rare and weighty, excommunication was so grave because it meant the failure to bring about reconciliation and repentance: in effect, the failure of the disciplinary project itself.

At first, the members of the consistory in Nîmes demonstrated a willingness to submit themselves to censure. On 31 May 1561 members of the consistory were each, in turn, exhorted to amend specific faults or encouraged to continue their pursuit of godliness. Among them, Pierre Chabot was told to attend church services, not to laugh, and not to believe fanciful things; Pierre Maltret, Pierre Malmazet, and Robert Aymes were warned not to get angry; Jehan Bertrand was told to take courage and to fortify himself; and Anthoine Sigalon was instructed not to beat his wife. Neither were the ministers immune to this inspection: M. Mombel was exhorted to reconcile himself to the church for having attended Mass during the time of persecution (meaning the 1550s).[205] This self-censure does not seem to have lasted, or rather, if it continued as a practice, these embarrassing reproofs ceased to be recorded. In later years there is some evidence of continued consistorial arbitration in its members' affairs, but only by invitation. Pastor Moynier in 1600 admitted that there was a breach between his wife and his son, and he asked the consistory to remedy it; three elders were dispatched to his house to do so—but such interventions were extremely rare.[206]

There is partial evidence to suggest that when deacons, elders, or their immediate families were accused of immorality, the consistory reversed its normal stance of presumed guilt. In 1593 the usual suspicions of the employer went unmentioned when maidservant Jehanne Claresse became pregnant. Her employer was Jehan Cabiron, who was serving on the consistory in that very year and had been a town consul five years earlier.[207] Similarly, in January 1596, elder Balthazar Fournier was questioned about a small child whom he was charged with having beaten, and who had later died. Fournier said he knew nothing about it and it was not he who had beaten the child.[208] Nothing more was said on the matter.

While they may have been presumed to be innocent of the worst sins, elders did not always get off scot-free. In four cases in Nîmes men who had, at one time, served on the consistory faced admonishment for failing to ensure morality within

[203] Chareyre, 'The Great Difficulties', 66; Mentzer, 'Marking', 121, and 'Notions', 98.
[204] ADG, 42 J 31, 150r, 165v, 170r, 191r, 250r, 251v, 257r, 259v, 261r, 262v, 264, 280r, 294v.
[205] BN, Ms.fr. 8666, 18r, 31 May 1561.   [206] ADG, 42 J 31, 382r, 27 Dec. 1600.
[207] ADG, 42 J 30, 152v, 10 May 1593.   [208] ADG, 42 J 31, 28v, 24 Jan. 1596.

their households. In three cases this immorality was the pregnancy of a maidservant or tenant, and in the remaining case the evidence suggests the possible prostitution of a daughter by her father. In each the scope for grave accusations of adultery or procuring was disregarded by the consistory in favour of the lesser charge of mismanagement of household morality, in a way that seems unlikely had other people been under scrutiny.[209] Nevertheless, the charge of household mismanagement was not a minor one. To fail to implement patriarchal discipline within their homes was to fall foul of the question for judging the suitability of elders posed in 1 Timothy 3:5—'if someone does not know how to manage his own household, how will he care for God's church?' Reprimand by one's peers that undermined an elder's position of responsibility must have been mortifying.[210] Such evidence raises profound questions about the ability of the discipline to amend society, even within the houses of the devout. The eldership's own fallibility may have desperately impelled them to increased surveillance and discipline.

Far worse than presumed innocence or lessened charges was the possible concealment of offences committed by those in power. Pollmann's findings indicate that in Utrecht there was a process of consciously selective recording, to avoid jeopardizing the honour or reputation of elite and ministerial families.[211] The accusation by Marie Pascalle in 1606 that Sieur Aurias Reynaud's son had tried to rape her may have been quashed because Reynaud senior, a member of the local nobility, had been an elder three times, a town councillor repeatedly in the 1580s and 1590s, and second consul of the town in 1593, while his relation Bernard Reynaud had an even more extensive record of service.[212] The advice given by the Nîmes consistory to M. Filion, the pastor at Aimargues in 1600, to suspend an adulterous elder from the Eucharist and his position—but not publicly—concurs with this suggestion of a defence of consistorial reputations.[213] In Alès the record seems to have been expurgated more vigorously: sections are inked through and vehemently crossed out. It is mainly names that are obliterated, perhaps suggesting an attempt to prevent someone being recorded in their sin for posterity.[214] Elsewhere, by definition, it is impossible to know if information was selectively recorded with any specific agenda. Elite families generally received no quarter from the consistory and it seems reasonable to conclude that while members of the consistory benefited from an assumption of innocence until proven guilty, unlike others, the fact that they were still rebuked on record suggests an ultimate dedication to rooting out sin, rather than entirely masking its incidence.

---

[209] ADG, 42 J 31, 272r; 42 J 33, 180v; 42 J 35, 178r; 42 J 35, 61v.

[210] My thanks to Professor Lyndal Roper for her thoughts on this subject.

[211] Pollmann, 'Off the Record'.

[212] ADG, 42 J 33, 102v; another M. Reynaud, possibly the son, was also to be an elder in 1613; Aurias Reynaud, ADG, E Dépôt 36/130, 140r (1582); E Dépôt 36/131, 154v (1589), 267r (1592), 343r (1593); E Dépôt 36/132, 73r (1594); Bernard Reynaud, ADG, E Dépôt 36/130, 69r (1578), 126v (1581), f 140r (1582), 263v (1585) ADG, E Dépôt 36/131, 33r (1587), 78r (1588), 154v (1589), 230r (1591), 267r (1592).

[213] ADG, 42 J 31, 380r.

[214] ADG, I 2, 2r; in Alès, entries that were later found to be false, or are perhaps paid for, are simply crossed through with a single line. This specific obscuring of names is something different.

Besides moral discipline, the consistory spent much of its time dealing with the distribution of alms to the poor. The articles of 1583–8 state that every deacon and his two elders were to deal with poor relief once a quarter, and one member of the consistory was to act as 'receiver of pennies for the poor', or treasurer.[215] Deacons proposed people for inclusion on the poor list and verified their continued need. The consistory provided assistance in instances of extreme necessity, for some weeks in times of crisis, or as one-off donations. In Nîmes, in 1562, they noted the need of Jehanne Rayole, a poor old woman who was lame or crippled, and very ill. They had already given her two payments of five *sols* but decided to pay her four *sols* a week during her illness.[216] On the same date Fauyer, 'the husband of Daulphine' (an unusual reference to a man by his relationship to a woman), who was so ill that he was insensible, was given two *sols* six *deniers* a week until he recovered.[217] The consistory of 1581 decided to give money to a 'poor blind woman who is in extreme poverty' and similarly in Montauban in 1595 Jean Marty—'not having the means to live or feed his son'—was helped with twenty *sols* a month.[218] They also provided dowry contributions to poor girls—offering two and a half *écus* to Marie Archivyere in 1588—and provided clothing for the destitute—including four *livres* for a robe for a 12-year-old girl, 'seeing her notorious nudity' in 1591.[219] Sometimes the payments were designed to help those who had stumbled get back on their feet, as with the three *livres* paid to M. Marion, a glover, to buy skins in 1605.[220] In Nîmes the standard payment was five *sols* a week, while in the much less prosperous town of Ganges a total of £4 5s. was donated to the poor in 1599, with most payments at around 2s. 6d. to 3s.[221] Immoral behaviour meant that donations could be revoked: in 1601 a blind man called Estienne Pascal was summoned to the consistory on the charge of maintaining prostitutes in his house, and his continued weekly receipt of five *sols* was made dependent on the outcome of the investigation.[222] The distribution and collection of funds for the relief of the poor was one of the few areas where women were involved in the administration of church life. In 1562, at the first meeting of the consistory in Nîmes, four women were appointed to identify the poor and distribute alms.[223] In 1587 the presiding minister in Nîmes suggested that it would be expedient and necessary to deputize 'several honest women' to collect money for the poor of Marveljolz and Albenas, and eight high-status women were chosen for the job.[224] Women were otherwise largely not involved in the running of the church.

The consistory's other responsibilities included the administration and management of the church. An elder was appointed to manage the summoner, the

---

[215] ADG, 42 J 28, 374r–377r.   [216] BN, Ms.fr. 8666, 179v, 21 Nov. 1562.
[217] BN, Ms.fr. 8666, 184r, 4 Jan. 1581.
[218] ADTG, I 1, 5r, 24r, 7 Jun. 1595; BN, Ms.fr. 8667, 159r.
[219] ADG, 42 J 29, 18, 587, 25 May 1588 and 30 Jan. 1591.
[220] ADG, 42 J 33, 37v, 39v, 13 Apr. 1605.
[221] e.g. BN, Ms.fr. 8666, 31r; ADH, GG 24, 35r.
[222] ADG, 42 J 31, 432r–v, 18 Jul. 1601.
[223] BN, Ms.fr. 8666, 3v. The women were 'the wife of M. Guichard, [the wife of] Sire Baudan, the mother of M. Felis and [the mother of] Maltret'.
[224] ADG, 42 J 28, 279v, 16 Jun. 1587.

bellringer, the psalm-singer, upkeep of the temple, and payments for travel to the Reformed's Church synods and colloquies.[225] The consistory considered whether to fund scholars training for the ministry, and deputized deacons (and occasionally women) to visit prisons and hospitals. In times of crisis, the consistory organized special prayers, for instance against the plague in May 1579.[226] Even minor decisions, like whether to open the windows of the temple because of the heat in June 1605 or whether the psalm-singer should sing standing, were decided by the consistory.[227]

Above all, the consistory administered access to the Eucharist. It was the responsibility of the clerk to keep a list at the end of each register of those who had been deprived of the Eucharist or received back into the church.[228] Other elders had special responsibilities on the day of the Eucharist itself, or distributed the *marron* (the token for entry to the sacrament) in advance. This was a sizeable task: in Montauban at Easter 1596, 4,380 people partook of the sacrament.[229] In the same year in Nîmes Thomas Platter thought that 10,000 people took communion at one time.[230]

The consistories also understood part of their role to be communication with other churches, and together the Reformed consistories formed a tight network of interdependence.[231] The local consistory could request help from other consistories in matters of discipline or for advice on doctrinal or theological points of debate. The consistory at Nîmes was often approached by local churches seeking advice. In 1591 it received a letter from the pastors in Montpellier requesting guidance on whether a marriage between a man and his first wife's uncle's widow was permitted, and in 1600 M. Filion, pastor at the church of Aimargues, asked for advice on how to respond to adultery by an elder; both instances suggest that Nîmes was thought to set a moral standard.[232]

This ecclesiastical network was used to pursue investigations beyond the reach of the town. In 1582 the Nîmes consistory wrote to the consistory at Montpezat requesting that they allow one of the Nîmois elders to question chambermaid Jehanne Darbousse, as part of an enquiry into whether Darbousse's employer had made her pregnant.[233] When the servant of M. Percet left his house pregnant in 1607 and went to make her living as a wet-nurse in Aigues-Mortes, the consistory at Nîmes wrote to the pastor of the church at Aigues-Mortes asking him to find out who had fathered her unborn child.[234] The communication went both ways. In 1591 the minister of the church of Sumene wrote to Nîmes to let the consistory know that one Marie Cabanes had been made pregnant by a man called Jehan Brozet and had taken refuge with his relative (also called Jehan Brozet) in Nîmes. Having

---

[225] ADG, 42 J 28, 374r–377r.   [226] ADG, 42 J 29, 76.
[227] ADG, 42 J 33, 51r, 29 Jun. 1605; 42 J 34, 51v.
[228] e.g. ADG, 42 J 28, 372r.   [229] ADTG, I 1, 132v, 13 Apr. 1596.
[230] Emmanuel Le Roy Ladurie and Francine-Dominique Liechtenhan (eds), *Le Siècle de Platter*, vol. 2, *Le voyage de Thomas Platter 1595–1599*, 2 vols (Paris, 2000), 154.
[231] Cf. Margo Todd, *The Culture of Protestantism*, 7.
[232] ADG, 42 J 29, 617; 42 J 31, 380r, 22 Dec. 1600.   [233] BN, Ms.fr. 8667, 337v.
[234] ADG, 42 J 33, 161v, 17 Jan. 1607.

discovered that they had baptized the couple's daughter, the Nîmes consistory decided to investigate.[235] As late as 1612 the consistory in Nîmes was informed by letter that Jean Allegre had committed *paillardise* and adultery in Geneva.[236]

Similarly, other churches could be approached to check out people's stories. The Nîmes consistory wrote to Geneva in 1561 to find out if Bernard Auriol had committed fornication or adultery when living there for a year, and whether Donne Romaine had been excommunicated for leaving her husband.[237] Thirty years later, the same approach still held: in July 1594 they wrote to the church at Aigues-Mortes to find out if a weaver called Anthoine Galaric had cohabited with a woman there.[238]

The Languedocian churches also seem to have had financial ties. The church at Montauban received a letter from the church at Montpellier in 1595 confirming that the church at Geneva had received the 585 *écus* they had together raised for its poor.[239] The church at Nîmes agreed at a provincial synod to pay the church at Alès for the expenses they had incurred to be provided with a pastor, although it took a visit from an elder from Alès in March 1603 to chase it.[240]

As the communication with Geneva indicates, these links were not confined to Languedoc. The consistory of Nîmes also proposed, in April 1584, to write to the 'Scottish churches' to warn them about a book published by the Jesuits of Tournon that equally criticized the Scottish Calvinists and the French Reformed Church. In passing, they also asked whether it was Scottish practice to celebrate baptisms before the regular prayers or at some other point.[241] This communication between the different churches strengthened the system of discipline, for coupled with the requirement that Reformed communicants provide a letter of testimonial when moving to another town, it created a web of surveillance that was hard to elude.

THE CONSISTORY, PATRIARCHY, AND WOMEN

At the heart of the disciplinary enterprise was the regeneration of patriarchy: the pursuit of morality was fundamentally bound up with the governance of women and their bodies.[242] Understanding the consistory's agenda of enforcing patri-archy and its preoccupation with women's appearance and sexuality is vital to recognizing how much women who used the consistory to their own ends defied the odds against them.

At a domestic level, the ministers, deacons, and elders of the consistories of Languedoc sought to implement patriarchy by upholding existing social hierarchies within the household and seeking further to strengthen the authority of husbands

---

[235] ADG, 42 J 29, 599, 20 Feb. 1591.   [236] ADG, 42 J 34, 390r, 14 Nov. 1612.
[237] BN, Ms.fr. 8666, 15r, 47v, 52v, 20 May 1561; 56v, 24 Dec. 1561.
[238] ADG, 42 J 30, 283r, 6 Jul. 1594. See also ADG, 42 J 29, pp. 605, 642.
[239] ADTG, I 1, 31v, 16 Aug. 1595.   [240] ADG, 42 J 32, 1 158r, 19 Mar. 1603.
[241] ADG, 42 J 28, 100r.
[242] Lyndal Roper, *The Holy Household: Women and Morals in Reformation Augsburg* (Oxford, 1989), 2, and 'Gender', 290; Po-Chia Hsia, *Social Discipline*, 8.

and fathers. Admonishments to heads of the family for not paying enough attention to household morals indicate that the consistory held husbands and fathers
accountable for the behaviour of their wives, children, and servants. After M. Guiran's
daughter was made pregnant out of wedlock in 1612 Guiran was summoned
because of the scandal, and required to promise that, thenceforth, he would keep
his family under control with greater diligence.[243] Similarly, when Balthezard
Fornier's daughter fell pregnant before marriage Fornier was exhorted 'to keep better
watch on his family in future'.[244] When fathers failed, brothers were accountable.
Doumergue Gregoire was reprimanded in 1614 for allowing so many men to frequent his daughter Magdalene that their house was 'like a little brothel'. As Gregoire
had been an elder in the church, he was 'grievously censured' for not behaving
better, for not giving a good example to his family, and for not turning his daughter
away from her loose living. In the face of his failure, his son was charged with
taking care of, and watching over the behaviour of, his sister.[245] Even when fathers
fell short, women needed to be put under some form of male oversight and authority.

Heads of households were equally held responsible for the conduct of their servant
girls. In 1607 Sire Boneterre was summoned to the consistory 'to give account as
head of the family for a servant who was made pregnant in his house'.[246] Part of
Boneterre's defence was that during the time the servant lived with him he had not
known that she was pregnant, but this was also cause for consistorial rebuke. They
chided him for being so negligent. Similarly, in 1615 merchant Pierre Granier
admitted that a second of his maidservants had fallen pregnant but declared that
he had known nothing about it because he was so often away from home. The
consistory urged him strongly to 'watch over his family'.[247] When M. Bourholes'
maidservant became pregnant in 1606 Bourholes protested that 'it was not his
fault, for he had watched and watched over his family, but he was little able to
avoid it'.[248] The consistory censured him for not having kept guard over his domestic servants as was his responsibility, and for having retained the servant in his
house after her pregnancy was discovered. Like elders in their districts, heads of
families were to keep a watchful eye over the behaviour of those in their care and
report any transgressions to the proper disciplinary authority.

Although the rule of fathers was paramount, in the absence of male authority
the patriarchal burden fell on women. Mademoiselle Durant, whose chambermaid,
Jeanne La Verde, had committed fornication and become pregnant, was specifically
told 'she must oversee her family because she has no husband'.[249] Similarly, the
widow of M. Ducros was called to the consistory because of the *paillardise* of her
daughter Caterine, and castigated for having 'poorly watched over her daughter, as
was her duty'.[250] Again and again we hear the same refrain. The wife of Sieur Chalas
was summoned in 1603 because her maid had become pregnant in her house, when
she was upbraided for 'not having watched over her house and family, for which

---

[243] ADG, 42 J 34, 361v–363r, 20 Jun. 1612.   [244] ADG, 42 J 34, 296v, 15 Jun. 1611.
[245] ADG, 42 J 35, 61v, 63v–64r, 26 Mar. 1614.   [246] ADG, 42 J 33, 180v.
[247] ADG, 42 J 35, 178r.   [248] ADG, 42 J 33, 130r, 11 Oct. 1606.
[249] ADG, 42 J 34, 14r, 23 May 1608.
[250] ADG, 42 J 34, 10r, 14 May 1608.

she testified she was sorry, saying that she was greatly surprised by it'.[251] Donne Mingaude in 1612 was rebuked for not having governed her daughter, who was now pregnant outside of marriage and Donne Fayette was instructed to supervise the behaviour of her son with her servant in May 1615.[252] Even Mademoiselle de Recolin, who in 1611 had discovered and reported her servant's pregnancy, was, nevertheless, exhorted 'always to watch better and better over her family'.[253] Here we see one of the ways in which women of status were required to be complicit in enforcing patriarchy, and the extent to which the consistory was anxious about lapses in its efficacy.

The Calvinist Church had a clear vision of how women should behave. It was articulated in Alès in 1601 when the consistory told Loyse Ambasse not to visit suspect places at unreasonable hours of the night, but instead 'to comport herself in the fear of God with modesty and humility as is required of honest women'.[254] Honest women were also supposed to be silent. In April 1593 the consistory proposed putting up a wooden grill around the segregated area of women's seats and pews 'because of the noise and debate from them on Sundays at the temple'.[255] It is intriguing to consider what the women were discussing with such vigour: local gossip, the content of the sermon, both? As the only other groups to be chastised for noise that disturbed the sermon were children and adolescent scholars, this proposition makes it apparent that women and children were considered as the same class of persons, and both groups needed their rumbustious natures to be tamed.[256] Men were never instructed to be silent: either—improbably—because they made no noise, or because their noise was not thought to be frivolous. Similarly, decisions in February 1562 about the ministry of the Nîmes church were made 'after the women, children, and strangers have left', designating women as either, like foreigners, irrelevant to the direction of the local church, or like children, incapable of understanding it.[257]

Women's bodies were not only disorderly in the noise they made, but in their appearance.[258] In the late sixteenth century the consistories of Nîmes and Alès waged war on women's immodest and sexually provocative clothing, and equally lascivious cosmetics. In Nîmes, these concerns are clustered between 1582 and 1593, a burst of activity following a letter from the consistory of the church in Orange in November 1582 alerting and reproaching the Nîmois for the fact that the 'lewd garments' of the women and girls of Nîmes were 'causing great scandal

---

[251] ADG, 42 J 32, 197r, 24 Dec. 1603.
[252] ADG, 42 J 34, 365v, 11 Jul. 1612; ADG, 42 J 35, 177r, 3 May 1615.
[253] ADG, 42 J 34, 261r, 11 May 1611.   [254] ADG, I 1, 137v.
[255] ADG, 42 J 30, 168r, 21 Apr. 1593.
[256] ADG, 42 J 28, 222r; ADG, 42 J 31, 443v; ADG, 42 J 32, 5r.
[257] BN, Ms.fr. 8666, 71r.
[258] Raymond Mentzer, 'La place et le role des femmes dans les églises réformées', *Archives de Sciences Sociales des Religions* 113 (2001), 119–32, especially 125; Mentzer, 'Disciplina', 107; Graeme Murdock, 'Dress, Nudity, and Calvinist Culture in Sixteenth-Century France', in *Clothing Culture*, ed. Catherine Richardson (Aldershot, 2004), 130–5; Graeme Murdock, 'Dressed to Repress? Protestant Clerical Dress and the Regulations of Morality in Early Modern Europe', *Fashion Theory* 4.2. (2000), 179–99, especially 191–2. Catholics too denounced women's extravagant and immodest clothing, see Briggs, *Communities*, 249, and James R. Farr, 'The Pure and Disciplined Body: Hierarchy, Morality and Symbolism in France during the Catholic Reformation', *JIH* 21 (1991), 391–414.

and a bad example to all the other churches in all this kingdom of France'.[259] Shocked by the failure to uphold the standards of a holy city, the consistory in Nîmes responded assiduously. It instructed the ministers to use the pulpit to upbraid the women for their scandalous attire and to warn them that those who refused to dress more modestly would be deprived of the sacraments and excommunicated from the Church. Such measures may have worked temporarily, but four years later, town councillor and lawyer M. Galli was noted in the consistorial registers as 'continuing' to express concerns about the immodesty of women's garments, especially their open cleavages, immodest hairstyles, and farthingales—a framework of hoops worn under skirts, which could sway up immodestly. The consistory charged the elders to keep a watchful eye out for those who were being disobedient.[260] The women of Nîmes seem, however, not to have paid a great deal of attention. In April 1590 it was reported that the local Reformed colloquy had complained about the scandalous makeup and clothing of the Nîmoises, especially the immodesty of the '*cache bastardz*'.[261] A *cache-bâtard* or 'bastard-hider' was almost certainly an alternative term for the farthingale, which, holding the skirt out from the waist to the floor, was thought to have been developed to hide unwanted pregnancies.[262] A couple of years later the consistory decided to target the apothecaries who sold outrageous makeup, such as rouge from Spain.[263]

The biggest crackdown, however, was from December 1592 to December 1593. The catalyst was another unfavourable comparison between the women of Nîmes and other Protestant cities. Noting the reformation that had taken place in Montauban, Castres, and elsewhere, the consistory bemoaned: 'the makeup and other vain and dissolute garments of the women and girls, who, daily, are seen giving great scandal to the faithful and despising the honour and glory of God.'[264] The consistory instituted a combined attack of preaching by ministers and surveillance by deacons and elders. From mid-December it was decided that pastors would accompany elders on their rounds to help eliminate such lewd garments, and that a list would be made of those women who continued to wear makeup, immodest clothing, and fancy hairpieces.[265] Over the following weeks many women, mostly of high birth, were summoned to the consistory for their persistent disobedience (though not all attended).[266] In June the scribe noted almost wearily, 'the makeup, high corns, farthingales, exposed breasts, and other vanities of women

---

[259] BN, Ms.fr. 8667, 359r.

[260] ADG, 42 J 28, 236v. Farthingale (also vardingale) or 'vertugalles' is spelt variously in the registers as '*verdugallin*', '*vebduguadins*', and '*vebstgualmer*'. M. Galli was, within a year, implicated in adultery with his wife's maidservant Clarette, so one cannot help but wonder if his sensitivity to women's attire was to do with temptation (ADG, 42 J 28, 331v, 25 Nov. 1587).

[261] ADG, 42 J 29, 384.

[262] In Spanish the same terminology was used: '*guardainfante*' corresponding to '*cache-bâtard*' and '*verdugado*' to '*vertugalles*'. My thanks to Dr Lesley Miller of the V&A for her advice. Cf. also 'Le blason de basquines et vertugalles', Benoît Rigaud (Lyon, 1563), reprinted in *Recueil des poésies françoises des XVe et XVIe siècles*, ed. A. de Montaiglon (Paris, 1885); Viret, *Instruction Crestienne*, vol. 1, 562.

[263] ADG, 42 J 30, 33r.   [264] ADG, 42 J 30, 127v, 3 Dec. 1592.

[265] ADG, 42 J 30, 129v, 131v.

[266] ADG, 42 J 30, 132r, 134r, 136r–v, 137r, 139v, 141r, 142r.

and girls'.[267] In December 1593, however, this eleven-year campaign of preaching, surveillance, and constant convocation of persistent offenders abruptly ended, and the issue seldom arises in the registers again. It seems unlikely that this sudden ending represents a dramatic sartorial shift by the female residents of Nîmes. Instead, it surely suggests the new influx to the consistory pragmatically realized the limits of their power.[268]

The church in Nîmes was not alone in this crusade. The consistory in Alès too expressed reservations about women's clothing. In May 1599 it decided that the minister should caution women against 'wearing such inappropriate farthingales'.[269] At Pentecost, two years later, the consistory reeled off a list of features that offended them: 'false hairpieces and curled hair and large farthingales' and, most shockingly of all, women wearing their décolletage 'so open that you can see the nipples'.[270] It was decided that these offences to God were so great that the women concerned would be refused the sacrament. Men with long hair would also not be allowed to receive the Eucharist—but this is the only objection made to male appearances. Women's appearance was under much more scrutiny for a crucial reason: the regulations against immodest clothing, especially swooping necklines that allowed a glimpse of the nipples, or garments like the farthingale, which could expose a woman's legs or hide an illegitimate pregnancy, were fundamentally sexual restrictions. As the consistory understood it, this was attire designed to attract male attention. Even twisting female hair into high corns was a form of ostentation that invited the male gaze. Long flowing hair had symbolic resonance: it indicated an available woman, either a prostitute or a virgin, while married women hid their hair.[271] Decorative accessories in the hair, or even elaborate headpieces, therefore carried a sexual message of their own.

Consistorial anxiety about women as the source of sexual sin was most obviously manifested in the attempt by the church of Nîmes to solve cases of sexual immorality by drawing up lists of women to banish from the city. There were practical reasons for this too—illegitimate pregnancies produced illegitimate children, whose mothers either needed financial support, or might abandon their children—but there was, nevertheless, a preoccupation with women, expulsion, and sexual sin that seems to outstrip these concerns.[272] The consistory drew up its first list of such women to be 'chased from the town' for the town consuls in September 1580, identifying nine women about whom there was a 'bad noise', that is, rumours of immorality.[273] In 1589 Bauzille Fontfroide, an elder and former town councillor, was deputized to compile another list for the consuls and magistrates, this time of

---

[267] ADG, 42 J 30, 199v; see also 197r, 216r, 216v, 242r. The term for farthingale here is the explicit '*hausse-culz*', so may instead refer to a bum roll, often used instead of a farthingale.

[268] Prestwich, 'International Calvinism', 96.   [269] ADG, I 1, 1r.

[270] ADG, I 1, 80r–v, 6 Jun. 1601. 'False hairpieces' is deduced from '*pauraugues fausses*', following OED entry for '*parrucque*' (1465) under '*peruke*', and Phillipe Camerarius, *Les méditations historiques* (1608), 308.

[271] Mentzer, 'La place', 125.

[272] Conner, *Huguenot Heartland*, 70; see Chapter 6 pp. 263–4 for examples of foundlings.

[273] BN, Ms.fr. 8667, 140r.

procuresses.[274] Some of these lists were clearly directed at operating brothels, such as 'the *putains* [whores] of the suburbs', who were recommended for banishment from Nîmes in April 1601 and again in August 1603, or the enjoinder in December 1589 to expel the woman known as '*l'Archère*', who was frequented by many men and thought to keep an 'open brothel'.[275] Other references are more oblique and seem to cover a wider range of offenders, such as those injunctions in October 1599 'to expel the whoring women, especially her called The Mother'; in December 1601 against 'Bacande and other whores'; and most revealingly, in June 1604 'to punish the whores, fornicators, and procurers'.[276] The reference to fornicators makes it clear that this is not just a list of paid sex-workers, but also of those women whom the consistory simply felt to be morally and sexually reprobate. If the consistory had sought to pursue an even-handed policy of expulsion for sexual misdemeanours, there were obvious candidates among the men of Nîmes, but no men were ever recommended for exile on the basis of their own sexual behaviour.[277]

Sometimes women contested their inclusion on the consistory's lists. Marye Chaudiere, a widow from Provence who had lived in Nîmes for eighteen years, came to the consistory in October 1587 to protest against her place on the 'list of whores', saying she was a good woman and reputed as such. The consistory agreed to examine the truth of her life and morals, and considered whether she had perhaps been confused with another Provençale called Marguerite Charle, but eventually concluded that she was 'very disreputable' and would remain on the list.[278]

In addition to the lists of women to be expelled, there is other evidence of the consistory's conviction that women were the source of sexual wrongdoing. Twice in the register of 1595–1602 the consistory doubted the word of women who claimed men had tried to rape them and launched their investigations into the lives and morals of the women, rather than the men they accused of assault. These instances of immediate supposition of the woman's guilt or dishonesty are remarkable in the clarity with which they reveal a presumption that women were mendacious and responsible for sexual sin. The comment by elder David Guiraud in 1614 that 'Cannet's girls are so abandoned to lubricity that they go often to Corbessas to take by force men to have sex with them' suggests a somewhat extreme, but not unrepresentative, belief in women's concupiscence among the men who formed the Protestant consistories.[279]

[274] ADG, 42 J 29, pp. 216–17. In the registers, he is only given as 'M. Fontfroide', but town council records provide the names of two M. Fontfroides—Jean Fontfroide, who was on the Council in 1559, and Bauzille Fontfroide, who was on the Council in 1586 and 1605, and a consul in 1600, suggesting the latter was likely to be the same man who was an elder in 1589 and 1590.

[275] ADG, 42 J 31, 408v; 42 J 32, 179v; 42 J 29, 312;

[276] ADG, 42 J 31, 304, 449; 42 J 32, 241. The word translated as 'whores' is *putains*, which could be used of both prostitutes and sexually active unmarried women.

[277] Cf. Jeffrey R. Watt, 'Women and the Consistory in Calvin's Geneva', *SCJ* 24 (1993), 431–41, here 429, who suggests the Genevan consistory did not display a double standard with regard to illicit sexuality.

[278] ADG, 42 J 28, 319v, 321r, 322v, 324r.   [279] ADG, 42 J 35, 107r.

CONCLUSIONS

In order to achieve the goal of a pure, reconciled Eucharistic community, the moral discipliners of the French Reformed Church worked to achieve communal and marital harmony, an absence of scandal, the penitence and amendment of sinners, and a society in which sexuality was narrowly trammelled. Convinced of the corrosive power of sin, the pastors, elders, and deacons of the consistory presumed guilt, but strove for perfectibility, and were diligent in their quest, putting time and energy into the pursuit of immorality. This influential caste of men shared a background and ethos, but also drew heavily on the voluntary support of the community, creating an information-gathering culture that tapped into natural currents of rumour and gossip, especially prevalent among women. This was not because they held women in particularly high regard. In fact, there was no break from traditional ideas about the female propensity to lust among Reformed male authorities. As a result, discipline to regulate sexuality was effectively about controlling women: the consistories sought to enforce patriarchy in the home, and to combat sexual sin; they exiled immoral women and pursued campaigns against lewd female clothing. The unashamedly patriarchal mindset of the leaders of the Reformed Church dictated the content of the consistorial registers, and as a result, what can be learnt about women's lives.

Yet because the implementation of moral discipline also, inadvertently, created a mechanism that women could use to their benefit, the records also testify to women's agency in difficult circumstances. The consistory was exceptional in that the testimony of the socially weak, both women and servants, was accepted as valid, given status, and recorded. This has great significance in an age where women's voices had limited status in other judicial courts. The opportunity for women to present cases to the consistory and to know that their voices would be heard and acted upon, constituted an empowering instrument for women. Reformed women may not have sought to challenge patriarchy on a grand scale, but they did try to negotiate their way through it, where necessary by colluding with it, using the disciplinary system to serve their interests and give them some measure of influence over their own lives.[280] That the consistory acted as a useful lever for women of all ages and ranks of society, sometimes against men, must surely have been an unexpected and unintended consequence of Reformed discipline.[281] It was impossible to predict in advance how such a system of discipline would be used, and it is notable that women quickly learnt how to accommodate themselves to the consistory in order to bring change into their domestic lives. 'Power can lodge in dangerous nooks and crannies.'[282]

---

[280] Capp, *Gossips*, 1–25.

[281] Joel F. Harrington noticed that the impact of the Reformation was not always as intended, *Reordering Marriage and Society in Reformation Germany* (Cambridge, 1995), 3; Karant-Nunn, 'Continuity', 28; Grethe Jacobsen, 'Women, Marriage, and Magisterial Reformation: The Case of Malmo, Denmark', in *Pietas et Societas: New Trends in Reformation Social History*, ed. Kyle C. Sessions and Philip N. Bebb (Kirksville, MO, 1985), 75.

[282] Natalie Zemon Davis, ' "Women's History" in Transition: The European Case'; Joan Wallach Scott (ed.), *Feminism and History* (Oxford, 1996), 89.

3

Belief

FAITH

Late sixteenth- and early seventeenth-century Languedoc experienced intense religious upheaval. Even in towns where Protestants were dominant, and where actual warfare was intermittent, the battle for people's souls was ongoing. The consistorial records chart dramatic religious moments of conversion, apostasy, and readmission to the sacrament, the continuing influence of Roman Catholicism, and the prevalence of superstitious practices. As such, used together with notarial records such as wills, the registers allow us to explore women's religious beliefs, attitudes, and behaviour during this tumultuous period.

Conversion to Protestantism

The consistorial registers record triumphal moments when people presented themselves to be received into the Protestant church. The statements made by new converts indicate the mix of reason, piety, and pragmatism that guided sixteenth-century religious decisions. Historians have considered the reasons for female conversion to Calvinism. Max Weber thought women especially receptive to faiths that suited their 'distinctive feminine emotionality'.[1] Nancy Roelker and Natalie Zemon Davis considered the appeal of Protestantism to French noblewomen and city women to be that it complemented and enhanced the independence they already exercised in other spheres, although Barbara Diefendorf doubted the reality of Protestantism's ability to bring autonomy to ordinary, illiterate French women.[2] Menna Prestwich suggested that Protestantism attracted women because it gave a new purpose and identity, and a sense of being part of the elect, while Roelker also stressed the value of having a special sense of God's calling for men and women.[3] Finally, Judith Pollmann has suggested that the austerity of the Reformed church might have been attractive to women because it conveyed respectability and moral probity, while she also highlighted historians' tendency to

[1] Max Weber, *The Sociology of Religion*, trans. Ephraim Fischoff (Boston, MA, 1964), 104–5.
[2] Nancy L. Roelker, 'The Appeal of Calvinism to French Noblewomen in the Sixteenth Century', *JIH* 2.4 (1972), 391–418; Natalie Zemon Davis, 'City Women and Religious Change', in her *Society and Culture in Early Modern France*, 65–95; Barbara B. Diefendorf, 'Gender and the Family', in *Renaissance and Reformation France 1500–1648*, ed. Mack P. Holt (Oxford, 2002), 109–10.
[3] Menna Prestwich, *International Calvinism 1541–1715* (Oxford, 1985), 96; Roelker, 'The Appeal', 404.

look for a 'moment' of conversion in the tradition of Paul and Augustine, which, she argues, was seldom present in the sixteenth century, when conversions were expressed rather as the result of gradual learning.[4]

Conversions reveal both oscillation—the difficulty, perhaps, of making the leap of faith—and a mixture of religious and practical motivations. Marye Camuse presented herself 'to be received into God's church' in 1592. She had once spent time in Geneva but later returned to Roman Catholicism for five years, citing the influence of her relatives. She now repented of her return to Catholicism, asked God's pardon on her knees, and promised to live thereafter in the fear of God.[5] Marguerite Arnaude asked to be received into the Reformed church in 1590 after having attended Reformed services for some time, returned to the Mass, and finally committed to the Reformed church because 'she is at present engaged to François Valeres, who is of the Reformed religion'.[6] Conversion in order to marry was not uncommon. Anne Françoise presented herself 'to be received into the Christian church, desiring to live and to renounce all papistry and idolatry' in March 1595, and after receiving instruction in the faith from a pastor the banns of her marriage to Pierre Verduran were announced.[7] Two months later Jehanne Blancque, engaged to husbandman Rolland Rouz, asked to be received in the church 'saying she renounced all papistry and idolatry with promises to never return to it and to live as long as she lived in the Christian church'.[8] The slight alterations of language suggest that each declaration was tailored by the convert herself: sincere declarations of faith accompanied more obviously strategic motives.

Conversion to marry is hardly surprising, as a woman's faith seems often to have been dictated by her choice of husband. A number of women asked to be readmitted to the Reformed church after years of marriage to a Roman Catholic. Originally Protestant, Pierrette Murarde had attended Mass during the eleven years she was married to François Privat, but in September 1587 wanted to be reconciled to the church.[9] Jeanne Marqueze, having been married in Provence and living in Orange, had been rebellious to the church 'to obey her husband', but now wanted to be received back into the church into which she had been baptized as an infant.[10] Widow Catherine Grimalde showed, paradoxically, both the flexibility of her religious practice and the steadfastness of her religious belief, when in December 1578 she presented herself to be readmitted to the church having renounced and left the faith twice, on account of her two husbands M. Borbat and Pierre Gazelly. Following Gazelly's death, she now sought readmission and made public reparation for her fault, only months before her own death from the plague.[11] While it

---

[4] J. S. Pollmann, 'Honor, Gender and Discipline in Dutch Reformed Churches', in *Dire l'interdit: The Vocabulary of Censure and Exclusion in the Early Modern Reformed Tradition*, ed. Raymond A. Mentzer, F. Moreil, P. Chareyre (Leiden, 2010), 29–42, and 'A Different Road to God? The Protestant Experience of Conversion in the Sixteenth Century', in *Conversion to Modernities: The Globalisation of Christianity*, ed. Peter van der Veer (New York and London, 1996).

[5] ADG, 42 J 30, 133r, 25 Dec. 1592.   [6] ADG, 42 J 29, 497, 26 Sept. 1590.

[7] ADG, 42 J 30, 340r, 24 Mar. 1595.   [8] ADG, 42 J 30, 364r, 31 May 1595.

[9] ADG, 42 J 28, 313v, 23 Sept. 1587.   [10] ADG, 42 J 32, 250v, 3 Sept. 1604.

[11] BN, Ms.fr. 8667, 55r, 4 Dec. 1578. There is this note immediately after her case: 'dead of the plague in the year 1579.'

undoubtedly served their interests, the stress in women's readmission testimonies was on their continuity of belief and, for many, that they had been forced apostates. When Catherine Piallette asked to be received into the church in 1587 she stressed that she had continued to attend sermons since her marriage at a Mass eighteen months earlier.[12] Anthonie Vidalle presented herself before the consistory in Nîmes in August 1581 stating that she had been raised a Protestant, but that during her marriage 'her said husband had forced her to go...to Mass'. Since his death she 'continued to make profession of the Reformed religion' and wished to be publicly received into the church.[13] In 1590 Damoiselle Catherine Crussanelle, 'recognizing frankly her fault' in marrying a Roman Catholic, begged the consistory to consider that she had been unable to be readmitted into the faith before as 'her husband had greatly threatened her...and expressly forbade her from making any public reparation', although he had permitted her to attend Reformed services for six years before she was widowed.[14] Similarly, it was reported in December 1585 that the wife of Pierre de Mercouille had for a long time been 'withdrawn from and deprived of the exercise of the Reformed religion for fear of her husband, who is Catholic, [and who] threatened to mistreat her', but that now she had 'won his heart' and he would finally allow her to return and be readmitted to the church.[15] Some husbands did not merely threaten: the neighbours of a woman identified as Esperance noted in 1601 that her husband had beaten her 'because of her faith'.[16] A succession of husbands—Bonfil, Pastoret, and Anthoine Sere—were challenged by the Nîmes consistory in 1593–4 for beating their Huguenot wives to force them to attend Mass.[17] Marriage seems normally to have meant adherence to a husband's faith for the duration of the union; unless a wife could persuade her Catholic husband to leniency, she had to await his death to practise the faith of her conviction.

The language used by returnees is instructive. Mlle de Rouz stated that she had married before a priest 'against her conscience'.[18] Peyroune Privade emphasized the extent to which her infidelity had been under duress when she declared that in her childhood she had made profession of the Reformed faith but that her father had 'constrained her to take in her first marriage a papist husband and she was also constrained to change her religion and that it was done by force and constraint'. Her threefold repetition of *constraint* as verb and noun emphasized her sense of compulsion. She was engaged to a Protestant and so may have had worldly as well as spiritual reasons for her change of heart, but she also stated that she now wanted to be 'readmitted and reunited into the Reformed church' because 'she recognized it was the truth'.[19] The numerous returnees suggest that many women had a profound sense of attraction to the Reformed church, and felt that suffering the humiliating

[12] ADG, 42 J 28, 309v, 4 Sept. 1587. [13] BN, Ms.fr. 8667, 231r, 2 Aug. 1581.
[14] ADG, 42 J 29, 485, 1 Sept. 1590. [15] ADG, 42 J 28, 198v–199r, 19 Dec. 1585.
[16] ADG, 42 J 31, 429v, 31 Aug. 1601.
[17] ADG, 42 J 30, 209r, 211r, 212r, 28 July 1593; 228r, 229r, 233r, 236r, 20 Oct. 1593; 251v, 264v, 26 Jan. 1594.
[18] ADG, 42 J 28, 358v, 5 Feb. 1588. [19] ADG, 42 J 35, 52r, 5 Mar. 1614.

process of public reparation was worthwhile in exchange for assured salvation and re-inclusion in the community of the faithful.

Women converting in Nîmes were required to attend sermons for a fortnight, be catechized by a pastor, and make public confession of their new faith, no matter how humble and lowly they were.[20] Even chambermaid Anne Durante, who converted in 1598, received the personal instruction of Pastor Moynier. In Montauban too there was concern for women's knowledge of the faith. Anne Vidal had been baptized into the Reformed church, but when her father died and she was left destitute, she had gone to live with her uncle, who, she said, had forced her to attend Mass, and she, not having 'the judgment of discretion because of her age', had done so. Latterly, she had moved to the town of Meusac near Montauban and become engaged to a Protestant man, Anthoine Mariol, whom she wanted to marry if the church would permit it. The consistory required her to make public recognition of her fault and told her, compassionately, to 'ask God the Father's help, praying in the name of His Son, our beloved Saviour, for mercy'. She was permitted to marry Mariol, but was warned not to participate in the Lord's Supper until 'she was better instructed in the faith and knowledge of her salvation'.[21] The consistories seem unperturbed about marital catalysts for religious change, as long as it was to Protestantism; whatever the reason, the church wanted the conversion to be a reformation of heart, mind, and soul.

What of Pollmann's suggestion that conversion happened gradually, rather than as a moment of transition? It is true that in the records of the French consistories men often explained their path to conversion as one of gradual recognition. Anthoine Raymond, from Vans, presented himself to be received into the church in Nîmes in March 1584 and when asked why, said it was because he had heard several sermons recently and found 'the doctrine better'.[22] A few years later Thomas Perdreau of Paris stated similarly that having attended sermons since the death of the late king (Henri III, suggesting that the accession of the Protestant Henri IV had opened up, for some, the possibility of religious exploration) and recognizing 'the purity of the doctrine', he wanted to be received into 'the communion of the church with the truly faithful'.[23] Conversion was not always a momentary decision separating past and present. Nevertheless, the consistory appears to have sought precisely what Pollmann considers lacking in sixteenth-century narratives, a moment of recognition and doctrinal conviction, and some converts couched their story in these terms. Pierre Cardonne was a Catalan monk of the Cordelier order, who 'threw away his habit and left that mire of iniquity'—his monastery in Toulouse—before going to Montauban in 1595. On being questioned by the consistory, he spoke of a moment of conversion—that 'God had touched his heart to leave the idolatry in which he had been for so long'—and said that he wanted now to study to enter the Protestant ministry once he had learnt French properly in order 'to

[20] ADG, 42 J 30, 340r, 52v, 26 Mar. 1592; ADG, 42 J 31, 186r, 9 Jul. 1597 (Suzanne Marcelle's conversion when she was instructed to attend sermons for two weeks and be catechized by M. Moynier before her marriage to Jehan Rogier). ADG, 42 J 31, 225r, 6 Jun. 1598.
[21] ADTG, I 1, 84r–v, 27 Dec. 1595.   [22] ADG, 42 J 28, 96r, 30 Mar. 1584.
[23] ADG, 42 J 30, 100v, 4 Sept. 1592.

serve God and his church'.[24] The church required converts to present themselves for reception into the church, first learning and completing the catechism.[25] For the consistory there was to be, at least, this public moment of ontological change from fallen to saved.

Women's conversion narratives also suggest that Pollmann's model may not suffice. Autense Farelle presented her conversion narrative as a moment of revelation in 1589, stating that:

> having continued to hear the Mass up to the present [time], and, at the present, having the fear of God and knowing [*cogneu*] that the Reformed religion is preferable to her for the health of her soul...she desired to live [in it] from now on, as much as it much pleased God.[26]

Her repetition of 'the present' and 'from now on' stressed that moment as an instant of transition from one state to another. Yet her use of the verb *connaître* can also be understood to suggest experiential knowledge gained by gradual learning— suggesting perhaps that there need be no clear dichotomy between conversions described as momentary or steady. There is another quality here too. Unlike a decision based on the rational appreciation of doctrine cited by Raymond and Perdreau, Farelle's use of *connaître*, with its sense of personal knowledge and familiarity, suggests a more heartfelt conviction—not the intellectual, factual knowledge of *savoir*. Emotion featured in women's conversion testimonies, but this was not uniquely feminine, as is clear from the narrative offered by the former monk Cardonne.

These ideas of conversion as momentary and heartfelt can also be seen in a more detailed narrative from March 1593. Mademoiselle Dianne de Tharaux arrived before the Nîmes consistory seeking reception into the Protestant church. She explained her decision to convert in spiritually charged terms, stating that:

> having made profession of the Roman religion until the present and now knowing [*cognoissant*] the Holy Spirit to have touched her heart, [she] wants to renounce—as from now—to renounce the said religion, declaring she wants to live and die in the Reformed religion.[27]

This conversion narrative also uses the more personal *connaître* and repeats terms of temporal specificity, but the case also goes on to demonstrate ambivalence and the clear practical benefits of (temporary) conversion. Almost as an aside, Tharaux mentioned that Protestantism was the faith professed by her fiancé M. de Forniguet Favier, who had accompanied her to the consistory. He hinted that their marriage rested on her conversion. The assembly concluded that Tharaux was to make public profession of her faith and be received into the church the following Sunday. The following week she was summoned to the consistory and, initially, only her fiancé appeared. Questioned whether Tharaux had been forced to convert, he swore not and declared that she had no intention of returning to Catholicism after the marriage. When Tharaux appeared, the consistory challenged her that one of

---

[24] ADTG, I 1, 12r, 5 Jul. 1595. [25] ADG, 42 J 28, 96r; 42 J 30, 100v.
[26] ADG, 42 J 29, 119, 22 Feb. 1589. [27] ADG, 42 J 30, 159r, 31 Mar. 1593.

their informants had overheard her talking of her public declaration of Protestantism and stating that 'she hadn't promised anything and after she was married, she intended to return to the Mass'. She retorted that they must content themselves with what she had promised and not press her further, as 'until the Holy Spirit touches her heart she did not want to promise more'. Rather surprisingly, the consistory was persuaded by her words, and agreed to await further professions until she had been led by the Spirit, but meanwhile instructed her to attend sermons and prayers, not to attend 'idolatries', and to 'often read the word of God'. A few days later Tharaux returned saying that she was now 'resolved to live and die in the Reformed religion... as her heart had been touched by the Spirit of God and not for any human consideration'. On the basis of this proclamation the couple were permitted to marry. Within a month, however, Favier's new wife was expressing her uncertainty [*l'incertitude*] about the Reformed faith and Pastor Moynier was sent to speak to her. He reported that he hoped for a favourable result. But in September the news broke that Tharaux had once again started going to the Catholic Mass, and her husband was summoned for the scandal his wife had caused to the church. Moynier was again sent to instruct her in the Protestant faith, but the matter was still dragging on in November 1593. The following autumn Favier was summoned because their first child had been baptized into the Roman Catholic Church.[28]

Had Dianne de Tharaux's religious decisions been made purely on the basis of self-serving concerns? It is possible that the entire venture was merely to secure a smooth path to marriage and, in direct contradiction of her protestation, driven wholly by 'human consideration'. That she was allegedly overheard passing off her conversion as a temporary expedient to facilitate marriage, and then later did return to Catholicism, tends to suggest such a strategic use of religious allegiance. If so, Tharaux at least recognized the need to frame her choice in heartfelt spiritual terms, identifying a moment of conviction to help convince the consistory. It is possible, however, that what we see is a genuine oscillation. The evidence of this is Tharaux's hesitancy to say precisely what the consistory wanted her to say when they pressed her to speak in April 1593. Instead, she went away to wait for the movement of God's Spirit; it is possible, but surely not probable, that she asked for this delay deviously and used such language lightly. In addition, her uncertainty a month later about the commitment she had made suggests some genuine misgivings. Finally in March 1594 Favier came before the consistory wanting to 'turn from the marriage he had made'.[29] While there may have been other reasons for this, if Tharaux's conversion was part of their marriage agreement, Favier's perturbation at his wife's apostasy suggests that he had been convinced by her conversion. Tharaux may have been genuine at the time of her conversion, but also genuine in her later uncertainty and return to Catholicism; despite shaping her confession to include a moment of decision, she ultimately found it hard to turn from the faith of her youth.

---

[28] ADG, 42 J 30, 160v–161r, 162, 170v, 193r, 220v, 233r, 236r, 298v, 302r.
[29] ADG, 42 J 30, 257v, 2 Mar. 1594.

What insight do conversion testimonies give us into how women thought and talked about faith, and their reasons for conversion to Protestantism? The repetition of certain phrases gives some sense of the concepts in which women thought about belief. Details of doctrine go unmentioned, but there is a clear distinction between the right (the 'truth' of the Protestant faith) and the wrong ('papistry and idolatry'), which was being actively turned from in an act of renunciation. Women spoke of their 'fear of God' and the 'health of their soul', and more mystically of the movement of the Holy Spirit touching their hearts, suggesting a sense of calling. Together this language suggests a vocation and the attraction of Calvinism's moral fervour, as Roelker posited. There is no mention, however, of wishing to join the elect, but just a corporeal image of being 'reunited' with the church; nor is there any sense of Protestantism offering independence to women, unless we interpret the return of women to the Reformed church after Catholic marriages as such. There is, however, a clear notion of claiming a new identity and purpose, as Prestwich suggested, from a temporally specific single moment, in contradiction to Pollmann's findings. Historians need not invent a conversion moment when sixteenth-century women so readily supplied it in their narratives. They talked repeatedly of 'until the present', 'now', 'as from now', and made vows that suggest that now everything had changed: they 'renounce' the past, they will 'live and die' in the new faith, and they promise 'never to return' to their former selves and ways. Women turned to the Protestant faith because they perceived God to have called them into a clean, fresh start, putting aside idolatry in favour of truth.

It is perhaps a helpful corollary to consider those women who did not choose Calvinism over Catholicism. Many women in Languedoc did not convert to the new religion and, while the consistorial records are understandably hostile to Roman Catholic devotion and necessarily fragmentary in their coverage, there are still glimpses of women's commitment to this alternative faith.[30] One such instance arises in April 1602 when the long-standing engagement between a Catholic girl, Arnouze de Beaucaire, and Sire Aubert's son—the Sire Aubert named here was possibly Noel Aubert, Seigneur de Saint-Alban, and therefore related to an influential Protestant family, the Montcalms—came into question.[31] At the time of their betrothal, Beaucaire's mother had promised that her daughter would join the Reformed church but now Beaucaire announced that 'she would in no wise change her religion for a man'. Calvinism was repugnant to her, she said, because, 'she did not wish at all to see the Bible nor to hear sermons and also she wanted to abstain from meat'.[32] Beaucaire's zeal for her Catholicism, of greater importance to her than marriage, is matched in interest by her reasons: she was repelled by the very things—reading the Bible, hearing sermons, autonomous learning—that are often considered to have attracted women to Protestantism, suggesting that Dienfendorf

---

[30] Jeffrey R. Watt, 'Women and the Consistory in Calvin's Geneva', *SCJ* 24 (1993), 429, 430, 433; Lyndal Roper, *The Holy Household: Women and Morals in Reformation Augsburg* (Oxford, 1989), 261. Most references are like that of the daughter of the late M. de Taraux who, engaged to M. de Clausonne, had not been received into the church and 'does not yet wish to be'—ADG, 42 J 31, 370r, 25 Oct. 1600.

[31] ADG, 42 J 32, 13v, 18, 21 bis v, 25v, 27v.   [32] ADG, 42 J 32, 27v, 10 Apr. 1602.

was right to think the autonomy derived from Bible reading was less relevant for ordinary women, and that Roelker and Zemon Davis's conclusions about the appeal of this for women do not apply in this instance.[33] It is also telling to consider that Beaucaire showed little interest in the alleged austerity of the Reformed church, but rather clung to Roman Catholicism precisely because of *its* austerity: the penitential self-denial of fasting and abstinence from meat on Fridays.

It is also true that new converts to Catholicism used some of the same language as the women who chose Protestantism. Consider Damoiselle Marie de Brenguier. Having been summoned five times to the consistory in Montauban, Brenguier appeared in April 1596 to answer the charge that she had married a Catholic and left the faith. She replied that she had been 'baptized, nourished, and raised in the faith, but she wanted to live and die in the Papist religion'. The consistory suggested that if she was in doubt on any points of doctrine, the pastors would willingly advise her, and admonished her to 'think of her soul' because renouncing Christ before men would result in her being renounced by Christ before God, and that she had fallen into 'false and erroneous opinion and damnable fury'.[34] She nevertheless remained resolute. A fortnight later, the consistory renewed the offer of ministerial guidance on points of doubt. Her response was bold and clear:

> she had nothing to say to the ministers nor to the consistory, and she did not have any doubts in her heart concerning her religion for she had been enlightened about it, but if any of the gentlemen wanted to visit her, she would listen to what they wanted to say and if they asked her why she had changed her religion, she would tell them the reason.[35]

In daring the pastors to come and ask her why she had converted, she raised a challenge which the consistory failed to meet, instead deciding to proceed to her publication as an apostate, and sadly leaving further reasons for her conversion obscure. The influence of her new husband was obviously a factor, but there are two crucial points in Brenguier's testimony that give clues to her reasons: that she had turned her back on the faith of her youth in a radical departure that was decisive—she wanted to 'live and die' in her new faith—and that she spoke of being 'enlightened' (*éclairé*)—she saw with new light, with fresh vision, with unaccustomed clarity. The boldness of these women's convictions, their readiness to confront the powerful men of the church, and their sense of undergoing a transformative change of heart are all powerful indicators of profound faith.

Evidence of Protestant Devotion

While much has been written on why women converted to Protestantism, less scholarship has focused on how ordinary women lived with their choice. Here, consistorial registers and other archival records from Protestant towns can provide evidence of women's devotion to the Reformed cause.

---

[33] Diefendorf, 'Gender', 109–10; Prestwich, 'International Calvinism'; Davis, 'City Women', 82–6.
[34] ADTG, I I, 134r, 137r, 17 Apr. 1596.   [35] ADTG, I I, 148r–149r, see also 144r, 145r.

Women's role in the Calvinist church discloses little of their interior faith. It was designed to be what Wiesner-Hanks has described as 'domestic religion': centred on church attendance, the home, and caring for children and the poor.[36] Women were to have a largely passive role—being catechized, attending the sermons faithfully, and absorbing the church's teaching in silence.[37] Bible reading was encouraged among women. In 1600 Jehan Boutal's wife presented herself at the consistory requiring that her son-in-law give her a Bible he had bought, and the consistory took her part.[38] While this case could represent the desire to own a Bible—a material symbol of piety—rather than to read it, it nevertheless implies that women were expected to possess Bibles. Similarly, women and girls were expected to read and inwardly digest the liturgy of their church.[39] Their intellectual assent to the faith was sought, even as literacy rates remained relatively low among women.[40]

There were some minor duties for women in the church. Some had responsibility for providing religious education for young children, and others were elected to assist the deacons in establishing lists of those eligible for church welfare and collecting and distributing alms.[41] The work was administrative and labour-intensive; personal visits to those on the list also required great tact, empathy, and care. The women chosen and named in 1587 were 'Madamoyselle de Deyron...the widow of Sieur Jehan Deyron, the wife of Sieur Dupin, the widow of Portallier and...Madamoyselle de Clarissi, La Grange, de Monteilz, and de Veyrac'.[42] Seven of the eight can be identified as noblewomen. Two of the eight were widows, as ordained by the early church, and one of these was the widow of Jehan Deyron, who had served on the town council and as a consul. One deaconess was married into the influential Dupin family, so well represented over the years on the consistory and on the town council; another was a Lagrange, and a Simon Lagrange served as a town councillor several times in the 1580s and 1590s, then as consul in 1599. Similarly, Mademoiselle de Montelz's family appeared frequently in lists of councillors and consuls over the 1570s and 1580s, especially Pierre de Montelz, lawyer, advocate, and *accesseur*. In short, as the public face of the church, all were respected, high-status women from important Nîmois families, who had been chosen to handle one of the Reformed church's most important responsibilities—distributing aid to the poor. Women were not, however, to be involved in the consistory itself, or to engage in theological or ethical debate; there is little evidence of protest from women about their exclusion from such lofty realms.[43]

In the consistorial registers there are glimpses of the assimilation of Protestant doctrine. When Catherine Jouve was chastized for not receiving the sacrament in January 1581, she stated that she had not taken it because she was in dispute with

[36] Merry E. Wiesner-Hanks, *Women and Gender in Early Modern Europe* (Cambridge, 2000), 224.
[37] BN, Ms.fr. 8666, 5r, 17 Apr. 1562; ADG, 42 J 28, 72r; 42 J 30, 30r, 168r; 42 J 31, 29v.
[38] ADG, 42 J 31, 363v, 23 Aug. 1600.   [39] ADG, 42 J 33, 136v, 8 Dec. 1606.
[40] Davis noted that at Lyon in the 1570s a significant proportion of Reformed women could not sign their names, 'City Women', 80.
[41] BN, Ms.fr. 8666, 3v; BN, Ms.fr. 8667, 69v; ADG, 42 J 28, 279v, 326r; Jeffrey R. Watt, 'Calvinism, Childhood and Education: The Evidence from the Genevan Consistory', *SCJ* 33.2 (2002), 439–56, here 445, and 'Women', 431.
[42] ADG, 42 J 28, 279v, 16 Jun. 1587.   [43] Davis, 'City Women', 84, 87.

her sister over their inheritance.[44] She seems to have internalized the words of Jesus in Matthew 5:23–4, instructing people not to present themselves at the altar before being reconciled with an estranged sibling. Loise Mingaude also chose to absent herself in 1585 because she was in the midst of a quarrel with her husband and because a long illness had prevented her from being catechized.[45] In 1611 Anthoine Fayn's wife voluntarily deprived herself of participation in the Lord's Supper after she and her husband had allowed their daughter to marry a Catholic.[46] In each case, these women reached their own conclusions on the right state of mind and heart in which to participate in the church's most revered ritual. They removed themselves when stained by disobedience to the church or disharmony in their families, or when insufficiently prepared.

Women also displayed their profound contrition after sin. In 1595 Marguerite Disse told the consistory at Montauban that she had married Guillaume Roziers at Mass, but 'she repented of it and asked pardon from God and recognized her fault, praying that He would be merciful of her faults and sins'.[47] Isabel Bonete, having had two children outside wedlock, prostrated herself on the ground before the consistory and cried that she was 'the greatest sinner that there ever had been in the world'.[48] These women had assimilated the Protestant worldview and displayed remorse and repentance.

Beyond the pages of the consistorial registers, religious devotion can also be read into legacies, wills, and testaments: for example, in 1596 Catherine Lagarde left ten *livres* to the poor of the Reformed church of Nîmes.[49] Other indicators of such provision and of devotion can be found in Huguenot wills, preserved in the notarial archives. In each will a preamble of words of consecration and dedication indicates the denomination of the testator and is followed by a statement of belief. These 'pious clauses' generally followed a formulaic pattern provided by the notary but, as Eamon Duffy and others have shown, the conventionality of wills need not detract from their value as evidence of faith nor imply a second-hand religion.[50] Wills made by notary Jean Ursi the Younger in Nîmes in this period included a poetic statement of belief that read, with slight variations, something like 'firstly, having recommended my soul to our Saviour, who, by the merit of the death and passion of His Son, Jesus Christ, after the separation of the body, desires to meet us in His Kingdom of Paradise'.[51] Wills drawn up by another notary, Jean Guiran, fluctuated more in their opening address, although they often tended to include the phrases 'invoking the name of God', 'in all humility', 'when it pleases Him to

---

[44] BN, Ms.fr. 8667, 168v, 25 Jan. 1581.   [45] ADG, 42 J 28, 173r, 175r, 1 May 1585.

[46] ADG, 42 J 34, 303r, 306v, 14 Dec. 1611.   [47] ADTG, I 1, 34r, 30 Aug. 1595.

[48] BN, Ms.fr. 8667, 19v, 2 Jul. 1578; Raymond A. Mentzer, 'Notions of Sin and Penitence within the Reformed Community', in *Penitence in the Age of Reformations*, ed. Katharine Jackson Lualdi and Anne T. Thayer (Aldershot, 2000), 98.

[49] ADG, 42 J 31, 139v, 20 Nov. 1596.

[50] Eamon Duffy, *The Stripping of the Altars: Traditional Religion in England 1400–1580* (New Haven, CT, and London, 1992), 355; Ariès, *L'homme devant la mort* (Paris, 1977), 187–92; Jacques Le Goff, *La civilisation de L'Occident medieval* (Paris, 1964), 240.

[51] Arc.Not., 2 E 1/312, 1 June 1614, Testament de Catherine Andrieu; cf. 2 E 1/278, 29 Feb. 1590, 2 E 1/312, 5 Jun. 1614.

call him/her from this world', and 'in anticipation of the blessed resurrection'.[52] Yet despite this prescribed content, some still seem to be outliers, with unusually ardent phraseology. One such example is the will of Anthonete Vidalle in 1615. Her testament's preamble is full of little embellishments, including asking for the assistance of the Holy Spirit after invoking God's name, and writing of her hope that God 'will pardon her freely' 'because of Jesus Christ His Son Our Saviour Redeemer'.[53] Is it possible to read piety into these additions? It is not impossible that this Anthonete Vidalle was the very same woman, given as Anthonie Vidalle in 1581, who had returned to the Protestant faith after being widowed by the death of a Catholic husband: this may indicate her devotion to her renewed faith decades later.[54]

Although not exclusive to Protestantism, helping the poor became a central plank of Reformed culture and orthopraxy. The pious clauses inserted by Ursi the Younger ended with the words 'bequeathed to the poor of the Reformed church', followed by a varying sum, which would be a posthumous donation to the Protestant poor-relief fund. Testators were encouraged to make some form of bequest to help those in poverty: in February 1562, the Nîmes consistory reminded the town's notaries to ask all their testators to remember the poor.[55] The amounts, however, varied greatly; there were sometimes specific instructions appended to the legacy; and not every will included a donation, although Tulchin suggests that 'giving became almost universal'.[56]

Such legacies offer concrete examples of women's zeal. In a sample of twenty-six women's wills including a legacy to the poor the bequests varied from twelve *sous* to 200 *livres*, with the average amount being somewhere between five and twenty *livres*.[57] Some sense of proportion can be gained from a comparison with women's other legacies. Catherine de Montcalm, widow of Noel Aubert, Seigneur of Saint-Alban, donated 100 *livres* to the poor and bequeathed her remaining 1,000 *livres* to her daughter—in effect she tithed.[58] Widow Isabeau de Folaquier, noble but evidently impoverished, donated twelve *sols* to the poor and had twenty-five *livres* to divide between her two daughters; her poor-relief donation was both relatively and proportionately small.[59] Widow Françoise de Montcalm gave a significantly greater proportion, donating ten *livres* to the poor and thirty *livres* to her niece, which contrasts with Alix Dupré, also a widow, who promised ten *livres* to the poor and 250 *livres* to her children.[60] Montcalm's quiet charity suggests such a practical piety that it comes as no great surprise to discover that she seems to have been among twenty-four people convicted of heresy for their Protestant faith in 1551, making her an early convert, while her late husband had been Pierre d'Airebaudouze,

[52] Arc.Not., 2 E 1/373, 19 Aug. 1614; 2 E 1/374, 4 Sept. 1615, 19 Nov. 1615.
[53] Arc.Not., 2 E 1/374, 4 Sept. 1615.   [54] BN, Ms.fr. 8667, 231r, 2 Aug. 1581.
[55] BN, Ms.fr. 8666, 76r.
[56] Allan A. Tulchin, *That Men Would Praise the Lord: The Triumph of Protestantism in Nîmes, 1530–1570* (Oxford, 2010) 136–8; Martin Dinges, 'Huguenot Poor Relief and Health Care in the Sixteenth and Seventeenth Centuries', in *Society*, ed. Mentzer and Spicer.
[57] Arc.Not., 2 E 1/: 250, 251, 258, 259, 261, 267, 278, 336, 283, 368, 293, 298, 369, 301, 371, 312, 373, 337, 374; cf. also ADG, 42 J 31, 139v–140.
[58] Arc.Not., 2 E 1/267, 22 Apr. 1579.   [59] Arc.Not., 2 E 1/251, 11 Jul. 1562.
[60] Arc.Not., 2 E 1/261, 28 Aug. 1574, 10 May 1573.

who had been one of the first Protestant preachers in Nîmes in 1552, and minister of the Reformed church in Nîmes from 1564 to 1570.[61] Such a case suggests that the size of a bequest to the poor may not be a poor indicator of commitment to the faith.

The behaviour of Jeanne Destoroffis provides an interesting case. In her will of 1598 she bequeathed twenty-five *livres* to the poor, but she wrote a second testament in 1605 increasing this to fifty *livres*.[62] By contrast, Leonarde de Baudan kept her bequest of twenty-five *livres* constant between her wills of 1592 and 1614.[63] One wonders what had happened to Destoroffis in those seven years. Some women specified causes for their munificence. Catherine de Montcalm divided her 100 *livres* donation into fifty *livres* for the poor of the church and another fifty *livres* 'to poor girls' to enable them to marry, while Catherine Teissier pledged fifty *livres* to the Reformed poor in 1568 and an additional twenty *livres* towards the repair of the Reformed temple.[64] Such precise instructions suggest a heartfelt concern about the objects of their largesse, far beyond any customary contribution. What, then, is one to make of Marie Vaurilhon, widow and innkeeper of *The White Cross* in Générac, and her gift of a measure of wheat 'reduced to cooked bread' to the poor of Générac in 1613?[65] The inventory of her possessions on death does not support the initial suggestion of penury, so the bequest may indicate a practical commitment to helping those poorer than herself. Finally, the will of Claire Espiard in 1592 suggests that women might also have put money towards ensuring their burial within the Reformed church. Her will states that 'she desires to be interred in the church of Saint-André-de-Valabrèque and consecrated fifty-five *écus* to [this] end'.[66] Despite relying on apparently formulaic religious phrases, wills seem to offer evidence of sincere devotion to the Reformed faith, indicating that women engaged with their faith and imprinted, even within the sphere of orthodox belief, their own mark on its practice.

Marrying at the Mass

The close relationship between marriage and faith—already established through those women who converted to Protestantism to marry, or who converted back to Protestantism after years of marriage to a Catholic man—is also indicated by a third category: women who married Roman Catholic men at Mass or before a priest, but still wanted to remain part of the Reformed church. It seems to have been chiefly Protestant women who married Roman Catholic men, rather than the other way around, although there are exceptions, and the evidence may skew in favour of this interpretation, as women's marriages to Catholics seem to have caused greater concern to the church, undoubtedly because women's faith was thought more susceptible to change and more pressure was put on wives to conform to

---

[61] Tulchin, *That Men*, 50–1.
[62] Arc.Not., 2 E 1/368, 21 Apr. 1598; 2 E 1/370, 1 June 1605.
[63] Arc.Not., 2 E 1/337, 27 Nov. 1592, 18 Oct. 1614.
[64] Arc.Not., 2 E 1/267, 22 Apr. 1579; 2 E 1/258, 4 Aug. 1568.
[65] Arc.Not., 2 E 1/371, 21 Oct. 1613.   [66] Arc.Not., 2 E 1/304, 31 Jan. 1592.

their husbands' beliefs. The few instances of men marrying Catholic women that appear tend to be related to another charge, such as Pierre Guiran marrying Catherine Cezargue at the Mass in 1612, which seems to have been contentious mainly because she had given birth before the ceremony.[67]

The practice of women from Protestant families wedding Catholic men in what were known as 'mixed' or 'unequal' marriages appears to have been both relatively common and a regular matter for moral discipline, especially in Nîmes. In 1602 the consistory drew up a list of all Reformed women marrying 'papist men' and the consistory of 1614 felt it necessary to put on record that in such cases they would use every possible exhortation to stop the wedding, and if they could not they would afterwards publicly suspend the culprits from the Eucharist.[68] In fact, their predecessors had long been disciplining women for this practice, summoning all those who married a Catholic or 'at Mass' (the latter term did often mean, in practice, marriage in a Roman Catholic church, but was also used broadly to accommodate any marriage to a Roman Catholic man). In December 1561 Fermine Chambone was chastised for marrying Yllaire Payan at Mass, despite having been received into the Reformed church, and protested that she had done so to obey her husband, who was Catholic, but had not participated in any 'superstition nor idolatry'.[69] Marye Passe and her mother Jaulmette Batte were summoned after the 14-year-old Passe was married to Catholic Anthoine Verdier at Mass, and both were ordered to make public reparation for their fault.[70] The consistory seem to have become aware of such marriages very soon—when Tabitta Pestie married Catholic David Godere before a priest in a room in M. Rozel's house, the consistory knew almost immediately.[71] The consistory was also alert to further misdemeanour: an elder was dispatched to warn the neighbours of Fynes Merianne, known as *La Rabasonne*, to keep watch to see if she started going to Mass after her marriage to the Catholic Tony Bonie.[72]

In most cases, however, the women involved presented themselves to the consistory to seek re-inclusion in the church. Many displayed a profound sense of remorse at their actions: Florane de Rozel appeared in March 1580 to confess to marrying her Catholic husband at Mass, and said she knew the fault she had committed and presented herself to make reparation with 'great regret and displeasure'.[73] Marie Imberte admitted her fault in 1588 and said she had 'acted against her conscience' in marrying P. Pol Laurens before a priest, asked God and the church's forgiveness, and wanted to be received back into the church. (She also, however, claimed to have been advised to marry Laurens by Firmin Bagard and his wife, for whom she had been a servant, which resulted in their convoking, so there may have been

---

[67] ADG, 42 J 34, 374r, 395v, 22 Aug. 1612.
[68] ADG, 42 J 32, 12v, 27 Mar. 1602; ADG, 42 J 35, 84v, 28 May 1614.
[69] BN, Ms.fr. 8666, 187v, 23 Dec. 1561.   [70] ADG, 42 J 29, 586, 30 Jan. 1591.
[71] ADG, 42 J 30, 80r, 86v, first reported on 8 Jul. 1592; on 29 Jul. Pestie said she had married about three weeks earlier.
[72] ADG, 42 J 27, 81v–82r, 25 Nov. 1579. For an additional case, see Damoyselle Catherine Favier and M. Demarez: ADG, 42 J 31, 459r, 23 Jan. 1602.
[73] BN, Ms.fr. 8667, 114v, 20 Mar. 1580.

other motives for her testimony.)[74] Nicollace Commessague presented herself to make reparation for her fault in marrying at Mass 'knowing she had greatly failed and asking God's pardon for her fault', and the same phrase—'greatly failed'—was used by Anne Thomasse four months later, who added that her action had 'deprived her of the company of the faithful'.[75] Gabriele Brune asked to 'repair the fault she had made in marrying a superstitious [man] before a priest' and Mlle de Mourmoyrac 'confessed and asked God's pardon' for her actions.[76] Michelle Meynyere, in 1584, felt such guilt that she presented herself even before her promised marriage to a Catholic man had happened.[77]

Among newly married and repentant women, there were those who had explanations for their behaviour. A sad reason was offered by Gaspare Surre in 1585. She presented herself to the consistory in Nîmes, saying she was 'distressed' because she had married a Catholic—Captain Silhon—before a priest at Mass. Asked why she had done so, she replied that she had previously been engaged to a Reformed man, but that he had left her more than seven years ago, and no other Protestant man had wanted to marry her for that reason.[78] If she wanted to wed she had to accept marriage to a Catholic, despite the cost to her own conscience.

Many women, as we have already seen, reported persuasion and coercion. Bernardine Souveyrasse appeared before the consistory in 1589 some nine weeks after her wedding, without having been summoned, saying she had been constrained by her brother to marry at the Roman Catholic church, but she repented and asked God's pardon.[79] Madame Baudane said she was compelled by her Catholic husband to marry him at Mass, and that her father, father-in-law, and other relatives had collectively persuaded her. She stated that she had 'always been unhappy' about it and appeared before the consistory to repent.[80] Similarly Anne Arnaude in Montauban, having married Anthoine Vignier at the Mass, said she was 'deeply sorry' that she had let herself listen to her husband's persuasions.[81] All these women expressed sincerity of repentance and devotion to the Reformed faith in the face of compulsion.

Similarly, others claimed a breach of promise when it came to matters of faith: Jehanne Conforte presented herself in 1590 saying that she had married a Catholic man at Mass, but it was against her wishes, as he had promised to marry her in the Reformed church, and Mademoiselles de la Baulme and de la Calmette, mother and daughter, presented themselves in similar circumstances in 1584, asserting that the marriage contract between de la Calmette and her husband had specified that the ceremony should take place in the Reformed temple, but that he had renaged when a third party reproached him with the dishonour of changing his religion for a woman.[82] The fullest account of this comes from Astrugue Regine

[74] ADG, 42 J 28, 360r, 10 Feb. 1588.
[75] ADG, 42 J 29, 44, 30 Aug. 1588; 42 J 28, 88r, 22 Dec. 1588.
[76] ADG, 42 J 30, 243v, 24 Dec. 1593; ADG, 42 J 31, 213v, 18 May 1598.
[77] ADG, 42 J 28, 105v, 16 May 1584.   [78] ADG, 42 J 28, 186r, 21 Sept. 1585.
[79] ADG, 42 J 29, 137, 22 Mar. 1589.   [80] ADG, 42 J 29, 623, 3 Mar. 1591.
[81] ADTG, I 1, 140r, 8 May 1596.
[82] ADG, 42 J 29, 559, 26 Dec. 1590; 42 J 28, 78r, 1 Feb. 1584.

who presented herself during her engagement. She claimed that her fiancé, a Catholic man called Delmas, had promised to convert to the Protestant faith, and this stipulation had even been expressly mentioned in the contract of marriage, which she exhibited to the Montauban consistory.[83] She was adamant that she would not marry him if he did not join the Reformed church. Yet a week later, Regine returned and apologetically explained that Delmas no longer wanted to convert because he feared the displeasure of the Vicomte de Bruniguel, whose vassal he was, and that she was therefore constrained to marry at Mass. The wedding, she said, could not be cancelled at this stage as she had given him her dowry, but she wanted to remain part of the Reformed church. Regine's self-presentation on both occasions testifies to her earnest commitment to the Protestant faith, but she was also necessarily guided by pragmatic and economic reasons with which the consistory did not sympathize. Her honesty cost her: the consistory decided that such deliberate waywardness would result in her suspension from the sacraments, and that if she married Delmas at Mass she would be cut off from the church. Such severity probably explains why most people only appeared before the consistory to make amends after the event.

For it is not entirely clear that remorse was deeply felt in all cases. Jannette Bate arrived before the consistory in 1584, saying she was 'very sorry' for marrying her husband 'at the papacy'.[84] Yet 'Jannette Bate' is sufficiently close to 'Jaulmette Batte' in the orthographically diverse world of the consistory to wonder if this is the woman whose daughter, Marye Passe, married a Catholic some seven years later, suggesting that coming to the consistory to ask forgiveness may simply have been known to be a necessary rite to resume normal relations with the church. Countless women appeared to admit, in the words of Suzanne Periere in 1591, that they 'had married at Mass', they 'asked the pardon of God, and to be received back into the church and to reception of the sacrament'.[85] Among them were Anne Julhienne in 1584, Jacquete Maurine in 1585, Maurice Ferrane and Françoise Maurine in 1587, Loise Dufour in 1591, Jeanne Fabresse and Mary Double in 1598, Damoiselle Claude de Robert in 1598, Marguerite Andrine in 1601, and Marye Pradenque in 1609.[86] All voluntarily submitted themselves to the disciplinary procedure of the church and used a fairly formulaic set of words to describe their desire for rehabilitation. The consistory sometimes responded with a harsh reprimand, such as that to the daughter of M. Rochon, who was 'strongly censured' and made to promise 'never again to prostitute herself at the papist church', but all these women submitted to the shameful ritual of re-entry into the church—public reparation—and the matter was closed.[87]

Nevertheless, not everyone was willing to accept the prescribed punishment, either considering it to be disproportionately severe, or fearing the repercussions of

---

[83] ATDG, I 1, 328r–v, 330r, 11 Mar. 1598.   [84] ADG, 42 J 28, 104v, 16 May 1584.

[85] ADG, 42 J 30, 47v, 25 Mar. 1591.

[86] ADG, 42 J 28, 3r, 23 Mar. 1583; 186r, 21 Sept. 1585; 269v, 26 Mar. 1587; 308r, 2 Sept. 1587; 42 J 29, 582, 23 Jan. 1591; 42 J 31, 253r, 21 Dec. 1598 (both Fabresse and Double); 267r, 24 Feb. 1599; 405r, 11 Apr. 1601; 42 J 34, 74v, 137r, 18 Mar. 1609.

[87] BN, Ms.fr. 8667, 42r, 3 Oct. 1578.

doing so. Jehanne de Rozel married her Catholic husband Pierre de la Croix in November 1578 in Croix's house before a priest. She was charged with making reparation, but the prospect of such a public declaration of her error caused great division between husband and wife. The consistory was, nonetheless, unrelenting, insisting on her obedience, and she finally complied.[88] Her three-month delay was nothing compared to M. Galopin's daughter, who married the 'strongly papist' M. Saurin in December 1590 and asked to be received back 'to the bosom of the church' in February 1591, but could only bring herself to face public reparation in January 1592, over a year after the wedding.[89] Mademoiselle Debon, who had been married by a priest, appeared before the consistory in Nîmes several times to be received into the church, and each time sought permission from her husband to make public reparation, but it was never forthcoming.[90] The understandable hostility of Catholic husbands to a public renunciation of the circumstances of their union meant that Protestant women who were sincere in their commitment to their faith and obedient to their husbands were placed in a genuine bind. For some, the immediate consequences were simply too tangible to risk demonstrating such commitment to their faith: when, in March 1584, Anne Paulet, Catherine Roche, and Jehane Juliane were required to make reparation for marrying at Mass, the latter responded 'that she did not want to make the said reparation on Sunday because she had not committed so big a fault'. Ordered to acquiesce to the discipline, she replied that she would not, 'liking better to leave the service than to be mistreated by her husband'.[91]

The consistorial registers also contain multiple references to the mothers of girls and women who had married Catholics, called to the consistory to account for their failure to prevent such 'unequal' unions. Some of these mothers—like Catherine Pierrefort in 1587—came voluntarily to confess to marrying their daughters to Catholics.[92] Others justified themselves by protesting that they had made provision to protect their daughter's faith, such as Donne Grisote in 1594, whose son-in-law had fooled her into believing that the marriage would be per-formed in the Reformed church, or Jehane Audrine, who explained that her daughter's marriage had been agreed on the condition that she would be allowed to continue to attend Protestant services.[93] Most of these mothers, like widow Marguerite Caisergue of Ganges, were required to do public reparation them-selves, but so were fathers, and they, too, made similar excuses for failing to stop the ceremonies.[94]

---

[88] BN, Ms.fr. 8667, 53r, 58r, 59r, 62r, 26 Nov. 1578.

[89] ADG, 42 J 29, 466, 491, 567, 596, 728; 42 J 30, 7r, 26v, 8 Aug. 1590.

[90] ADG, 42 J 31, 42r, 6 Mar. 1596.   [91] ADG, 42 J 28, 93r, 28 Mar. 1584.

[92] ADG, 42 J 28, 333v, 2 Dec. 1587.

[93] ADG, 42 J 30, 293r, 2 Sept. 1594; 267r, 8 Mar. 1594.

[94] ADH, E Dépôt GG 24, 121r, 2 Apr. 1600; other cases include Donne Brauqase: E Dépôt GG 24, 131v, 143v, 25 Aug. 1602; Fulcrand Gourdon: E Dépôt GG 24, 120r, 11 Aug. 1602; Jacques Virac, ADTG, I 1, 217v–218r, 7 Jan. 1598; Jacques de Blausac and his daughter Marie Planiol, ADG, 42 J 29, 342, 356, 6 Feb. 1590; Anthoine Fayn: 42 J 34, 303r, 306v, 14 Dec. 1611; Damoyselle Anne de Nages and her father, who had arranged the condition that the marriage took place at the Reformed

Again, however, some testimonies suggest that much of this may have been rhetoric, for when pressed, not all were willing to undergo the humiliation of public reparation. When M. de Catuzieres and his wife apologized in 1613 for having given their consent to the marriage of their daughter and a Catholic—allegedly on the condition that it was blessed in the Reformed church—their sentence of public reparation was not well received, with Catuzieres's wife 'rejecting the censure with violence and contempt'.[95] The offence was evidently not perceived to be great enough to justify such humiliation. The fault was also made light of by M. de Montelz in 1592 when asked why he had married his daughter, Françoise, to a Catholic. He 'did not think at all that [he] would cause scandal by the said marriage' and stated that such marriages were 'defended by Holy Scripture', citing several biblical passages to the assembly.[96] Meanwhile, in response to the case of Marthe, daughter of Jean Baudan, Seigneur de Vestric, marrying a Catholic and having her marriage blessed by a priest, the consistory sought approval from the next national synod of the Reformed church to insist on public reparation by erring parents.[97] Although content to indicate compliance where possible, many people held a much more flexible and accommodating view of intermarriages than the church authorities.

The prevalence of intermarriages is a reminder that, in this time of war, when Protestant cities were embattled, there could be coexistence between faiths within the walls and even between the sheets. The Reformed consistory did not approve of such unions and considered them acts of faithlessness, but they remained a fact of life and there was never any blanket attempt to prevent them. Protestant women who married Catholic men frequently showed remorse for this disloyalty to the church and God and were squeezed by competing allegiances—to their families, to their new husbands, and to their faith. The moment of marriage was a fraught time for women's faith. Yet marriage to a Catholic was necessary for many Protestant women and it seems likely that some people considered the rite of re-inclusion—appearing before the consistory to ask pardon and the subsequent public reparation—as a necessary obstacle they could contemplate, just as others found it so distasteful that when forced to choose between husband and church they chose domestic peace over eternal verities.

Contact with Catholicism

There are frequent brief references to women in the Protestant community attending the Roman Catholic Mass. In 1592 Mademoiselle de Mormoirac's maid was reprimanded for attending, and the wife of M. Saunier was reported—by her own maid—to have been attending Mass 'for a long time'.[98] The theme of compulsion

---

church, but the bridegroom, M. Rochemaure, had rushed the ceremony: 42 J 28, 248v, 292v, 337v, 26 Dec. 1586.

[95] ADG, 42 J 35, 33v.
[96] ADG, 42 J 30, 104r, 106v, 108r, 116r, 120r, 173, 177r, 220r, 7 Oct. 1592.
[97] ADG, 42 J 30, 377v, 387v, 388r, 395r, 19 Jul. 1595.
[98] ADG, 42 J 30, 36r, 5 Feb. 1592; 60r, 22 Apr. 1592.

quickly emerges. Izabel Verde confessed to attending the Catholic service in Beaucaire when 'constrained by her husband' to do so in 1578.[99] Marie Plantiere reported that her brother 'had forced her to go to Mass and beat her to make her go' when she visited him in Frontignan in 1586.[100] Agnes Jugere held her employer M. de Greniers chiefly to blame, saying 'she had been induced by her said master to accept going to Mass', although she conceded her own 'wicked fault' too.[101]

Others were persuaded: Mademoiselle de Forges was responsible for taking Catherine Mazelle and Bernardine Ariffonne—maidservant to Catholic Charles Rozel—to Mass in 1578 and 1580 respectively. Both Mazelle and Ariffonne recognized their fault, asked God's pardon, and made private reparation before the consistory.[102] Gabriele Olivieyre, known as *Champonoye* (probably a reference to her work in the fields) was reprimanded in Ganges for trying to persuade the unnamed daughter-in-law of one of the church elders of Saint-Bauzille to attend Mass, and was asked why she had so little affection for the faith.[103]

Many could not see anything amiss with what they had done. Claude Bonnette stated that in going to Mass, 'she was not thinking to do wrong'.[104] Inquisitiveness was used as another defence, as it pre-empted accusations of intentional idolatry. When Madame la Baronne d'Alles, Claude de Tuffan, and M. de Malmont's daughter attended Mass in Avignon in 1582, they stated in their defence that they had gone to the Catholic ceremony 'once, out of curiosity...and not from devotion', which is perhaps understandable among these second- and third-generation Calvinists.[105] They feared no spiritual pollution from their visit. Jehanne Marthine similarly explained that she had gone to the 'papists' temple', but 'she only went there out of curiosity', adding that she greatly regretted it.[106] Curiosity probably explained the actions of those women who said they had only gone as far as the Catholic church's door, namely, in Nîmes, Marie Vachiere in 1578 and Marye Dejon in 1587, and Françoise Gaye from Ganges at Saint-Bausille in 1596.[107]

Yet others knew that the church would deem this behaviour sinful. Some simply tried not to be caught, attending Mass away from their hometown: Marie Martine from Ganges and Marie Reyne from Nîmes both attended Mass when visiting Arles.[108] Marguerite Causese was accused of hearing Mass and kissing the ground—the implication being that she had worshipped idolatrously—when visiting Saint-Loup in 1600, but denied it, saying she was simply drawing water from a cistern

[99] BN, Ms.fr. 8667, 10r, 21 May 1578.   [100] ADG, 42 J 28, 247r–v, 24 Dec. 1586.
[101] BN, Ms.fr. 8667, 246v, 28 Sept. 1581.
[102] BN, Ms.fr. 8667, 42v, 3 Oct. 1587; 114r, 20 Mar. 1580.
[103] ADH, E Dépôt GG 24, 126v, 9 Jun. 1602.
[104] BN, Ms.fr. 8667, 310r–v, 4 Apr. 1582.
[105] BN, Ms.fr. 8667, 293r, 294r, 297v, 300v, 303r, 305v, 330r, 331r, 26 Feb. 1582; see Mentzer, '"Disciplina nervus ecclesiae": The Calvinist Reform of Morals at Nîmes', *SCJ* 18 (1987), 13–39. Graeme Murdock, 'The Dancers of Nîmes: Moral Discipline, Gender and Reformed Religion in Late Sixteenth-Century France', unpublished paper.
[106] BN, Ms.fr. 8667, 349v, 5 Sept. 1582.
[107] BN, Ms.fr. 8667, 10v, 21 May 1578; ADG, 42 J 28, 271r, 28 Mar. 1587; ADH, E Dépôt GG 24, 74r, 26 Dec. 1596.
[108] ADH, E Dépôt GG 24, 4r, 25 Mar. 1587; ADG, 42 J 29, 343, 6 Feb. 1590.

and her actions had been misrepresented.[109] Others declared their remorse. M. le Vieulx's wife presented herself before the consistory in 1580 to admit to 'adhering to papal superstitions and going to Mass' and said that she had 'deeply erred', although she baulked at making reparation on her knees, as her husband had forbidden it.[110] Astrugue de Prat also admitted her fault in having often attended Mass and many papal baptisms and funerals while living in Toulouse, which she said she had found 'displeasing to her soul', and so asked God's pardon.[111] Although it may be unlikely that it will be found it in the pages of the consistorial registers, there is no evidence to support Lyndal Roper's hypothesis for Germany, that the reason Protestant women attended Catholic services was because Protestantism was 'relentlessly Christocentric'.[112]

Yet there are signs that some women found Catholic rituals to offer spiritual solace in specific circumstances.[113] In September 1588 a female gardener—or wife of one—called Barronne was chastised for visiting a Catholic hospital in hope of healing for her small child, who was sick with fever. She had been spotted knocking at the door three times, begging the almoner to let her in, and was given a bracelet to attach to her child's arm in order to bring healing. The consistory condemned such practices as 'idolatry and sorcery'.[114] In 1591 Catherine Coueffete confessed that she had attended Mass 'from fear... [because of her] infirmity for two years or more', suggesting that she found comfort and reassurance there that she presumably did not receive from Protestant sermons.[115] The healing benefits of the Mass were also possibly sought by Donne Anthonye Gillie, long-term innkeeper at *The Black Head*, who was rumoured to have had gone to a local healer and had several Masses said for her during her illness in 1605, though she denied the charge.[116] The perception of the health-giving power of the Mass is corroborated by other occasions on which mothers tried to ensure the wellbeing of their children: Pastion's sister was summoned for having had a Mass said for the healing of her young daughter in November 1596, and Marguerite Mourgue admitted in 1608 having had Masses said and sung for the health of her sick child—she recognized that she had been at fault and knelt to ask God's forgiveness.[117]

Here we see an interesting combination: sincere Protestant faith interspersed with the appeal of Catholicism at times of crisis, echoing the findings of Watt, Mentzer, and Blaisdell that people in the Protestant world turned towards the old faith to cope with suffering and catastrophe, as 'many Catholic practices... offered spiritual and psychological comfort to believers, especially women' (although Watt does not consider why women were more tied to Catholic ritual than men).[118] It is

---

[109] ADH, E Dépôt GG 24, 121r, 6 Apr. 1600.   [110] BN, Ms.fr. 8667, 141v, 30 Sept. 1580.
[111] ADTG, I 1, 350v, 26 Aug. 1598.   [112] Roper, Holy Household, 261.
[113] Watt, 'Women', 429, 430, 433.   [114] ADG, 42 J 29, 54, 7 Sept. 1588.
[115] ADG, 42 J 29, 666, 2 Jun. 1591.
[116] ADG, 42 J 33, 30r, 49v, 2 Mar. 1605; E dépôt 36/139, 176r notes *'Anthonye Gillye hostesse'* of *'la teste negre'* on 4 Nov. 1602.
[117] ADG, 42 J 31, 143r, 4 Nov. 1596; 42 J 34, 43r, 5 Nov. 1608.
[118] Mentzer, 'The Persistence of "Superstition and Idolatry" among Rural French Calvinists', *Church History* 65 (1996), 222, 226; Jeffrey R. Watt, 'The Reception of the Reformation in Valangin, Switzerland, 1547–1588', *SCJ* 20.1 (1989) and 'Women and the Consistory', 429, 430, 433;

also possible that those who consulted popular healers were also seeking remedies that included the use of Catholic rituals and shrines.

Perhaps another answer lies in the responsibility of women for childcare, for the consolations of the Mass seem to have been particularly relevant for women in matters involving their children, both in seeking health and in assuring salvation. As well as healing, the other area where some women preferred Catholic ritual to Protestant was in the baptism of infants. In Bédarieux in 1579 Jeanne Lauxeure confessed that she and her husband had, 'without any constraint or solicitation', taken their children to be baptized by a Catholic priest.[119] In October 1595 the wife of a man called Ploumel, who lived near the Protestant college, was reported to the consistory for having her children baptized at Mass, saying that 'if any came to die they would be buried in the manner of the Christian religion'.[120] Similarly, the wife of a man called Tathefaure was suspected of consenting to the confirmation of her child by the Bishop of Nîmes in 1588.[121]

Women also seem to have been especially involved in having babies baptized. In 1562 Jehanne Sabatiere was censured for having baptized a child at the request of his parents.[122] In Pont-de-Camarès, cobbler Jacques Jaques's child was baptized at Barthelemy Formier's house, with the assistance of Magdare's widow as godmother, and the widow was accused of additional 'superstitions done'.[123] Madame Gourgasse was questioned about whether she or her daughter had taken a child to be baptized in the Roman Catholic church, and five midwives—Donne Gabrielle, Claude Gasanhone, Catherine Gardinelle, Donne Fauquete, and Donne Salbette—were reported to have taken children to the Mass (presumably to be baptized) in Nîmes in 1600, implying a veritable industry of women's involvement in this rite.[124] A couple of other women, charged with the same sin, claimed to have been merely carrying the child for someone else, but they came under suspicion because women were associated with illicit infant baptism.[125]

It seems likely that for some women the Reformed faith had a weak spot around assuring salvation for children at baptism. The ancient Catholic ritual of exorcism and baptism that promised such efficacy in protecting children from damnation was resilient and persuasive, even among Protestant communities in the late sixteenth century, some forty years after the Reformed church had been established in

Charmarie Jenkins Blaisdell, 'Response to John H. Bratt, The Role and Status of Women in the Writings of John Calvin', *Renaissance, Reformation, Resurgence* (Colloquium on Calvin and Calvin Studies, Calvin Theological Seminary), ed. Peter De Klerk (Grand Rapids, MI, 1976), 25; see also Olwen Hufton, *The Prospect before Her: A History of Women in Western Europe* (London, 1995), 401.

[119] AN, TT 234, 6, 1r, 12 Jul. 1579.   [120] ADG, 42 J 31, 2v, 4 Oct. 1595.
[121] ADG, 42 J 28, 363v, 17 Feb. 158.   [122] BN, Ms.fr. 8666, 162r, 9 Oct. 1562.
[123] BN, Ars.Ms. 10434, 59r–60r, 8 Apr. 1583.
[124] ADG, 42 J 29, 130, 184, 15 Mar. 1589; 42 J 31, 328v, 23 Feb. 1600.
[125] Francoise Gaye argued that she had not entered the temple at La Roque and was only carrying the child for another woman: ADH, GG 24, 74r, 26 Dec. 1596; Marye Deyson said that her employer Mlle de la Rozel made her take the child into a Catholic church to be baptized, but she was only carrying it, did not go past the second door to the church, and did not attend the baptism: ADG, 42 J 28, 271r, 28 Mar. 1587.

France.[126] Reformed baptisms were probably also unsatisfying for women because they circumscribed the roles that women could play in this familiar and important rite, which was so closely linked to women's role in watching over the health of the family. In the Reformed ceremony it was men who presented babies for baptism.[127] Within Roman Catholicism, as midwives administering emergency baptism, or *ondoiement*, women potentially had an important part to play in ensuring the salvation of children.

Masses for healing and baptism are just two examples of the vestiges of Catholic ritual and practice found in the everyday lives of some Reformed church members. The evidence suggests the existence of tolerant and accommodating believers, shaped by both Catholic and Reformed theologies, prepared to continue interacting with members of each other's church, despite the wider hostility between the faiths in the late sixteenth century. In 1563 Dauphine Ozie—a woman who had been receiving poor relief from the consistory in 1561, and was probably a servant in Mizard Molin's house—testified that she had been doing the washing at the Molin household when, by way of saying grace before their meal, Molin's young niece had spoken the Lord's Prayer, but also added 'the angelic greeting of the Virgin' (the Ave Maria) and the words 'Mother of God, pray for us'.[128] The guileless words of a child tellingly reveal residual Marian faith and the continuing influence of Catholic traditions among first- and second-generation Huguenots. Such influence occurred in parallel with the zealous Calvinism seen in Dauphine Ozie's reaction: she retorted at the time of the prayer that the niece's grace 'spoilt all the soup' and later happily testified against the Molin household.[129]

Yet even much later remnants of Catholic customs survived. Around traditional Roman Catholic burials, a surfeit of ostentatious grief soothed the bereaved and promised to ease the deceased on their way, but Protestants were not to have truck with such superstitions. In 1596 and again in 1597 the pastors were instructed to preach against 'the excesses of deaths, burials, and the clothing of grief', especially the widespread custom of funeral processions 'as in the Roman church', in which men dressed in sheets paraded in front of the corpse.[130] Yet such practices were not easily eradicated. The new minister, M. Suffren, noted in 1601 the continued use of 'certain superstitions at burials which are not tolerable among Christians', particularly drawing attention to the number of women 'who are employed in the funeral processions with the appearance of grief, also...[they] employ four girls to wear sheets...', while five years later he again remarked that many people performed 'extraordinary ceremonies at the sepulchres of the dead', including girls wearing sheets.[131] It seems likely that the 'sheets' were traditional mourning robes, similar to the cowl worn by Catholic penitents or mourners, while the 'girls' may refer to the medieval practice of dressing poor and foundling children in mourning

---

[126] John Bossy, *Christianity in the West 1400–1700* (Oxford, 1975), 14–18; Mentzer, 'Persistence', 229; Duffy, *Stripping*, 280–1.

[127] e.g. ADG, E dépôt 36/696, 146r, 150r, 179v, 196v, 197v, 198v, 231v; Mentzer, 'Persistence', 229.

[128] ADG, 42 J 26, 31r, 3 Sept. 1561.   [129] BN, Ms.fr. 8666, 193v–194r, 13 Dec. 1563.

[130] ADG, 42 J 31, 133r, 192v, 22 Oct. 1595 and 15 Sept. 1597.

[131] ADG, 42 J 31, 448v, 18 Dec. 1601; 42 J 33, 82v, 18 Jan. 1606.

garb to swell funeral processions, as an indication of the piety and generosity of the deceased.[132] Anthropologist Bronislaw Malinowski argued that such mortuary rituals help 'counteract the centrifugal forces of fear, dismay, demoralisation, and provide the most powerful means of reintegration of the group's shaken solidarity'.[133] It is clear that they remained so, despite their Catholic connotations, for many members of the Protestant community.

Even in the Protestant strongholds of the south of France there was no version of Protestantism lived out free from vestiges of, incursions from, or interactions with Roman Catholicism. Either from sheer curiosity or in moments of crisis, danger, or transition—ill-health, infancy, marriage, death—the Catholic system continued to provide well-oiled mechanisms that even the most committed of Protestants might find attractive.[134]

Religious Resistance

In her work on women in sixteenth-century France Susan Broomhall explored whether women accepted religious regulation of their lives and, drawing on the example of the Protestant Charlotte Arbaleste, wife of Philippe Duplessis-Mornay, suggested that 'opportunities to protest [were] based on status and individual circumstances': it was easier to challenge church edicts if of relatively high rank.[135] Marcel Bernos has examined the religious resistance posed by the *religieuses*—female Catholic mystics of seventeenth- and eighteenth-century France, such as Gabrielle Suchon, Jeanne Guyon, and Jacqueline Pascal—who claimed obedience to the voice of heaven over and above the instructions of male ecclesiastical authorities on earth, and he concluded that such resistance was valiant and exceptional.[136] The consistorial registers, in general, supplement and amend this picture of women's resistance to religious authority—suggesting that it was neither exceptional nor limited to women of high status. One consistorial case, in particular, indicates the extent of this resistance over spiritual affairs, as ordinary Huguenot women—like Bernos's famous female Catholic mystics—justified their decision to evade ecclesiastical and societal norms by reference to God's will.[137]

Given that their choice of spouse was so crucial to determining the course of a woman's spiritual life, it is perhaps unsurprising that examples of resistance often occurred in the context of decisions about marriage. As Chapter 4 explores in more depth, there existed a rent between popular and consistorial ideas about the reversibility of betrothal: if convinced that promises to marry had been made with all proper decorum and consents, the Huguenot consistories held them to be thereafter

---

[132] Ariès, *L'homme*, 164–7; Bernard Roussel, '"Ensevelir honnestement les corps": Funeral Corteges and Huguenot Culture', in *Society*, ed. Mentzer and Spicer.

[133] Bronislaw Malinowski, *Magic, Science and Religion and Other Essays* (London, 1948), 53.

[134] Blaisdell, 'Response', 25.

[135] Susan Broomhall, *Women and Religion in Sixteenth-Century France* (Basingstoke, 2006) 2, 39.

[136] Marcel Bernos, 'Résistances féminines à l'autorité ecclésiastique à l'époque moderne (XVIIe–XVIIIe siècles)', *CLIO, Histoire, Femmes et Sociétés* 15 (2002), 103, 109.

[137] See also the case of Gillette de Girardet (Aigues-Mortes, 1580), with which this book opened, for another example.

binding, whereas many outside the church leadership considered engagement to be revocable. In this instance, a woman not only sought to break a purported engagement promise, but did so on claims of divine revelation, giving fascinating insight into women's conceptions of their own right to decide and their relationship with God, and straying some way from consistorial ideas about women's spiritual authority.

Magdaleine Sirmiere was called to the Bédarieux consistory in July 1581 for idolatry—having attended Mass—and dancing.[138] Questioned outside the consistory, she confessed to both faults, and was exhorted to submit herself to the discipline of the church, and to proceed with marriage to her fiancé, tailor Guillaume Puech. She made no answer and was instructed to think well and ask God, then to give the consistory her response within a week. This she did not do. Consequently her mother, Lyonne Martinne, and brother, Antoine Sirmie, were summoned in her stead, and both were ordered to persuade Sirmiere to accept discipline and to marry her fiancé.[139] A week later Sirmiere appeared before the consistory, but when asked whether she would submit to the censure of the church, claimed not to know to what she would be submitting herself. The consistory threatened her with suspension from the sacrament and gave her a week to shape up. A week later she again failed to appear. Her more acquiescent brother presented himself in late August and bore the brunt of the consistory's anger, being threatened with suspension if he failed to persuade her to comply. Finally, when the consistory's patience was running thin, Sirmiere reappeared before the assembly on 2 September, declared herself sorry for having attended Mass and dances, and willing to submit to the authority of the consistory and do as 'will be ordained and advised by the company'. As to Puech, however, she stated that she did 'not wish him harm, but with regard to marrying him, she does not want to do it, because God does not want it'. The consistory quickly retorted that God in fact not only wanted but commanded her to marry Puech and that it was a blasphemy to use the will of God to justify her stubbornness. She was suspended from the Eucharist because of her 'rebellious heart'. Yet Sirmiere clearly persisted in her refusal, for five months later Puech appeared before the consistory to renew his claim to Sirmiere and threatened to appeal to the magistrate. Whether he was ultimately successful in his claims on her is hard to judge: the register of marriages for Bédarieux sadly falls silent between 1582 and 1589, while the baptismal records are no more conclusive.[140]

The records do though give some indication of why Sirmiere might have wanted to terminate the engagement. There are a couple of earlier references to the couple before this series of events. In December 1580 Lyonne Martinne had been instructed to do her motherly duty by instructing her daughter to complete some unnamed task (presumably marriage). Subsequently, in January 1581, the consistory

---

[138] AN, TT 234 6, 16r–v, 17v, 18r, 18v–19r, 20v, 23 Jul. 1581.

[139] Some months earlier, in November 1580, Lyonne Martinne had herself been subject to consistorial investigation on a charge of adultery; see Chapter 7, p. 318.

[140] AN, TT 234 6, 78, 137, 139v (*Registre des batêmes*).

recorded that Guillaume Puech had beaten Sirmiere, and had justified his actions by saying she had told him 'that she did not fear him' and he wanted to remind her that she should do so. As a result she said she did not want to 'yield to the accomplishment of their marriage'.[141] Sirmiere's resistance to marrying had lasted for some time and there were good reasons for it.

Her subsequent interaction with the religious authorities demonstrated the same lack of fear that she had shown to Puech: it was conducted on her timetable, not theirs; she feigned ignorance when wishing to avoid capitulation, but submitted to part of their charge when it was convenient for her to do so; she held to her position on marriage for well over a year, despite intimidations and pressure from the church, her family, and her fiancé; and, above all, she justified her behaviour on the grounds of divine revelation. In so doing, she made an inherently comparative claim about her relationship with God as it stood against that of the consistory. Given a choice between obedience to the church or to God, she chose the latter. In this Magdaleine Sirmiere asserted a spiritual authority that the consistory could not allow her: her untrammelled female piety took a form that did not suit the religious notions of the male authorities (and one which exposed their limited commitment to the Protestant doctrine of the 'priesthood of all believers'). Her faith was one in which God was accessed directly—it was not vicarious or passive—and one that she could use to justify and legitimize her decision to maintain control over the course of her life. It demonstrates that religious resistance to the church was not solely the province of the elites: ordinary women could also have rebellious hearts.

Conclusions

Margo Todd has concluded that the 'interior spirituality' of most women remains outside the historian's compass, but the evidence reviewed here illustrates something of this interiority for women in Reformation Languedoc.[142] What is apparent is women's active engagement with their faith: with their evident devotion manifest in pious clauses or charitable donations in wills, in testimonies after absence or apostasy from the Reformed church, or in vocal defence of their Catholicism. For some, Protestantism was clearly beneficial and empowering; for others, the autonomy of Protestant practice could repel. The evidence of women's faith gives us a complex and not easily resolvable picture of flexibility and steadfastness, sincerity and strategy, contrition and rebellion. Profound Protestant faith was displayed at moments of conversion, in internalization of guilt, in generous legacies to the poor, and even in resistance to authorities who would rather have arrogated all religious revelation to themselves. Women submitted to or resisted religious authorities precisely as their consciences guided them.

For we also see oscillation and inconstancy, especially at the life- and faith-defining moment of marriage, and resort to Catholic ritual and practice in

---

[141] AN, TT 234 6, 13r.
[142] Margo Todd, *The Culture of Protestantism in Early Modern Scotland* (New Haven, CT, and London, 2002), 21.

moments of need. This apparently strategic use of belief need not undermine women's faith; rather, it must be understood as one strand in the skein of reasons determining how a woman acted, sometimes coming to the fore, sometimes necessarily overtaken by life's other exigencies. Yet even when this occurred, women's faith was present, while at times it was formidable, resilient, and resurgent.

MAGIC

Women's faith was not limited to the binaries of Roman Catholic and Reformed Protestant theology. In keeping with the practice of ordinary people across Europe, consistorial evidence suggests that French women resorted to a whole range of rituals, folk healing, divination, and magic that fell outside the orthodoxies of either denomination.[143] Some of this behaviour was the result of carnivalesque licene at times of festivities, when normal restrictions seemed lifted but, generally, the circumstances for such practices were suffering and sickness, unexpected misfortune, such as the loss or theft of goods, or uncertainty, especially decisions and prognostications about marriage. Neither the existence of such practices, nor the Reformed church's hostility to them comes as a great surprise, but the underlying current of popular superstitions into which even those in committed Protestant towns dipped in times of suffering and uncertainty suggests that women, under certain conditions, sought something in these protective and curative practices that neither denomination could supply. There are also instances of more maleficent magical practice: people felt sure that they had been bewitched and sought out their tormentors, while others confessed to participating in rituals to curse their neighbours. In contrast to the situation in many parts of Europe, however, these accusations never manifested themselves in witchcraft prosecutions, and the attitude of the consistories and civic authorities to such accusations is almost certainly key to explaining why—unlike Franche-Comté, Lorraine, the Basque provinces, and even nearby Vivarais—persecution of witches did not become a reality in Protestant southern France, despite the palpable existence of belief in sorcery and magic.

Women were frequently charged with seeking divination in moments of distress. There were several different ways of fortune-telling. In Alès in 1602 Jehanne Pueche was accused of having '*tirer le couvellet*' with her neighbour Jane Brugiere, when they had lost some chickens.[144] This was the homespun method of divination, alternatively referred to as '*tourner le cruvellet*', or '*jouer le cruvellet*'. '*Cruvell*' is Occitan for a circular mesh sieve used to sift grains, later made of steel, but generally, in the

---

[143] Mentzer, 'The Persistence'; Robert Muchembled, *Culture populaire et culture des élites dans la France moderne (XVe–XVIIIe siècles): essai* (Paris, 1978); Keith Thomas, *Religion and the Decline of Magic* (Harmondsworth, 1971); Robin Briggs, *Witches and Neighbours: The Social and Cultural Context of European Witchcraft*, 2nd edn (Oxford, 2002); Lyndal Roper, *Witch Craze: Terror and Fantasy in Baroque Germany* (New Haven, CT, and London, 2004); Stephen Wilson, *The Magical Universe: Everyday Ritual and Magic in Pre-Modern Europe* (London and New York, 2000); Peter Burke, *Popular Culture in Early Modern Europe* (London, 1978); Emmanuel Le Roy Ladurie, *Les paysans de Languedoc*, 2 vols (Paris, 1966), 239–47.

[144] ADG, I 1, 167r, 5 Jan. 1602.

late sixteenth century, made of hair. To turn or play the sieve was to use it to divine the culprit in cases of theft, as recorded by Jean de La Bruyère in the 1690s, by holding the sieve, turning it, naming suspects, and finding it came to a stop when the guilty party was named.[145] Keith Thomas records a slightly different English variant of this in which a sieve was hung by shears or scissors, then those suspected of stealing missing goods were nominated, and the sieve would rotate when the guilty person's name was called.[146] This form of divination by the movements of a hanging sieve to find out persons unknown even has a name: coscinomancy. Some variation of this practice was used in Languedoc to find missing treasure or stolen goods, or to identify thieves. It was a system endlessly open to manipulation and misdirection, and was used with some frequency.

Pueche and Brugiere, in their attempt to identify their chicken-thief, had adopted this method. It seems likely that when mother and daughter Catherine Bertrand and Marye Mazelet were censured for 'having used some charms with certain sieves' in Nîmes in October 1584 they had been doing a similar thing.[147] Suzanne de Fontfroyde and Jacques Fayet's wife were accused of having turned the sieve to divine the location of some lost rings in 1582, although they insisted that they had done it in mockery and only to pass the time.[148] The temptation to experiment must have been too great to ignore and, even if some performed it half in jest, others did it with intent. In February 1599 Jacques Gardiol, nick-named *Borye* or *Borie*; his wife, Anthoine Reynaude; and friends Pierre Collomb and Estienne Rouviere were summoned for having practised coscinomancy to discover who had stolen from them.[149] Borye owned a lodging house in the Faubourg Saint-Antoine, just outside the city walls, called the *Pont du Gard*, and it seems likely that the divination had taken place there.[150] The divination worked, in the sense that the sieve indicated the culprit's name, and its accusation was taken seriously: Borye was simultaneously rebuked for having punched his neighbour, Marguerite Chantagrilhe, and having called her a thief. All four involved were grievously censured, because, as Reynaude was told, coscinomancy 'is a type of magic'.[151]

Beyond these homemade divinatory practices, every now and then a large number of women were reprimanded for consorting with the *bohémiens*, the wandering Romani (although at one point termed 'Egyptian') gypsies who travelled through southern France, setting up camp outside town walls.[152] These *bohémiens* stationed themselves outside Nîmes in the Faubourg des Jacobins beyond the Porte des Prêcheurs for a couple of months in the spring and summer of 1583 and received

[145] Louis Alibert, *Dictionnaire Occitan-Français, d'après les parlers languedociens* (Toulouse, 1965); cf. '*cruvell*' and '*cruvelar*' (*tamiser, cribler*); Jean de La Bruyère, *Les Caractères*, 10th edn (Paris, 1914), 342, n. 2.

[146] Thomas, *Religion*, 253–4; also Mary O'Neil, 'Magical Healing, Love Magic and the Inquisition in Late Sixteenth-Century Modena', in *Inquisition and Society in Early Modern Europe*, ed. Stephen Haliczer (Kent, 1987), 90.

[147] ADG, 42 J 28, 133v, 14 Oct. 1584.   [148] BN, Ms.fr. 8667, 338r, 340r, 27 Jun. 1582.

[149] ADG, 42 J 31, 263r, 264r, 267r, 268v, 3 Feb. 1599.

[150] ADG, E dépôt 36/39, 116r, 176v.   [151] ADG, 42 J 31, 268v, 3 Mar. 1599.

[152] Ladurie, *Les paysans*, 408.

a stream of visitors. Most went to have their fortune told. One of the earliest summer visitors was Jehanne Manuelle, who had been told by her neighbours that the *bohémiens* were in town. In July 1583 she visited them and paid for her palm to be read. One 'took her hand and said [she] would live a long time'.[153] Manuelle had left her husband a few months earlier, which put her in a traumatic and precarious situation, so the psychological appeal of divination in such circumstances is clear.[154] She was followed there by Suzanne de Rozel, the young daughter of the late Jacques Rozel, together with her maidservant, Marye Reboulle, who 'confessed... to having given them money for divination and fortune[-telling]', and at least another fifteen women—the two daughters of Monsieur Lansard, the daughters of M. de Malmont, Monsieur Agullonet's wife, the daughters of Jehan Jacques, Blaize Baudan, Suzanne Periere, Marie Barresse, the daughter and widow of the late M. Villamier, the wife of merchant Sire Jacques Blanc, the daughter of Domergue Ongle, and the eldest daughter of Jehan Deyron—all similarly paid to have their palms read and fortunes told.[155] Many of these women came from well-connected and influential families: Robert Agullonet was an elder and town councillor in 1583; two Baudan men—Guichard and Jacques—were on the town council in 1583 and one ran the *présidial* court in Nîmes; Jehan Lansard had been a town councillor in the previous year, 1582, and Jehan Jacques would be so in 1584; Domergue Ongle had been a church elder in 1580–1, and would be so again in 1590–1; and Jacques Blanc and Jehan Deyron would also subsequently serve on the consistory and as consuls, while Deyron's wife was chosen as a deaconess in 1587.[156] The interaction of their womenfolk with these apparent charlatans, whom the consistory termed 'sorcerers', would have been deeply shameful; all the women concerned were vigorously censured, and required to ask God's pardon on their knees and swear not to return.

Yet there were often good reasons for women's visits. Seeking to know one's fortune is, by definition, an attempt to bring certainty into the unknown and thereby quell anxiety, but there were also specific targets for divination. In late August Loyse Martine paid the *bohémiens* to divine the location of money that she had lost.[157] M. de Savinhargues's niece and daughter had visited them in early September, because the former had a stomach ache—the *bohémiens* knew that before she told them—and the daughter reported being told by one of them that her mother was dead (a statement of fact, rather than a revelation) and that she was well loved by her father.[158] Others went to find out their marriage prospects: Anthoine Bogarelle's fortune-teller told her 'she was of a good father and mother, would be very happy, soon married, and would have five children'—just the sort of fortune that a woman of that period probably wanted to hear.[159]

---

[153] ADG, 42 J 28, 28v, 30 Jul. 1583.
[154] ADG, 42 J 28, 8r, 13 Apr. 1583; she seems likely to be the woman mentioned here and called 'Jehanne Maurelle'.
[155] ADG, 42 J 28, 30r, 31r, 33r, 34v, 15 Aug. 1583; also 372r.
[156] ADG, E dépôt 36/130, 140r, 184r, 201r; ADG, 42 J 28, 279v.
[157] ADG, 42 J 28, 33r, 24 Aug. 1583.
[158] ADG, 42 J 28, 38v, 14 Sept. 1583.   [159] ADG, 42 J 28, 40v, 20 Sept. 1583.

Those visiting the *bohémiens* were almost all female, although there were some rare contacts with the town's men: Loyse Martine was accompanied by Jacques Jullien, who went for the healing of a fever, and Claude Chalas was also suspected of seeking his fortune, although he claimed that the chief of the *bohémiens* had simply asked him for directions to a certain house, and that he had not sought divination from them.[160] The flux of visitors was so great that the consistory asked the ministers to mention in their sermons of 4 September 1583 that all who visited *bohémiens* or sorcerers would be publicly shamed, while a list was kept at the end of the register of those who had had 'recourse to sorcerers and sorceresses' (see Fig. 3.1, opposite)—Jacques Julien is the only male in a list of twenty-one names.[161]

Another season of visits occurred in August–September 1595, when within just one week up to forty-four women visited the *bohémiens* to have their fortunes told.[162] The numbers were so great for two reasons: many of them had very probably—given that reports started coming in on 1 September—gone to the *bohémiens* during the Saint Bartholomew's Day festivities of 24 August. This was a holiday time of revelry and abandon that must have seemed to permit such unorthodox consultation, such ostentatiously harmless fun. The second reason is that, not thinking it harmless, the consistory went into overdrive, specifically asking women to denounce others that they had seen at the fair with the *bohémiens* and summoning the culprits swiftly. Denunciation naturally swelled the numbers of the accused.

Women's reasons for seeking their fortune on this occasion are mostly obscure: most women simply confessed, though a few denied it. Jehanne Maurine was asked if she had given the *bohémiens* a dress and one *écu*—a substantial payment— for their services but said she had not and had simply accompanied a friend.[163] Donne Aubert claimed that she had not sought out the *bohémiens*—they had surprised her and her maid walking to her vineyard. She protested that she had not asked them anything, but that they guessed that her obvious sadness arose from the death of a child—a comment that reminds us of the normality of infant mortality— and she confirmed their supposition.[164]

There were occasional visits by the women of Nîmes to the *bohémiens* when they were stationed elsewhere, such as by Donne Bagarde in December 1584 (she said she went to reclaim money they owed her) and the wife of Captain Ducros in September 1591.[165] In one of these interstitial visits in April 1584 Catherine Formentine visited the *bohémiens* at Bernis along with a poor woman who had several children (Fig. 3.2, p. 136). She pretended that one of the children was hers, but the *bohémienne* knew she was lying, and indicated the actual mother.[166] On every occasion that the *bohémiens'* words are recorded in the registers, they provided pleasing predictions or accurate guesses, suggesting a percipience that fuelled their reputation as soothsayers.

The practice of visiting the *bohémiens* was not confined to Nîmes: in Montauban too in May 1597 a host of women were grievously censured for seeking to have

---

[160] ADG, 42 J 28, 33r, 34r.   [161] ADG, 42 J 28, 35v, 372.
[162] ADG, 42 J 30, 392 bis v, 393v, 394r, 396r–v, 398r, 399v, 1 Sept. 1595. Cf. also ADG, 42 J 31, 8v.
[163] ADG, 42 J 30, 396r, 9 Sept. 1595.   [164] ADG, 42 J 30, 392 bis v.
[165] ADG, 42 J 29, 724r, 4 Sept. 1591.   [166] ADG, 42 J 28, 97r, 11 Apr. 1584.

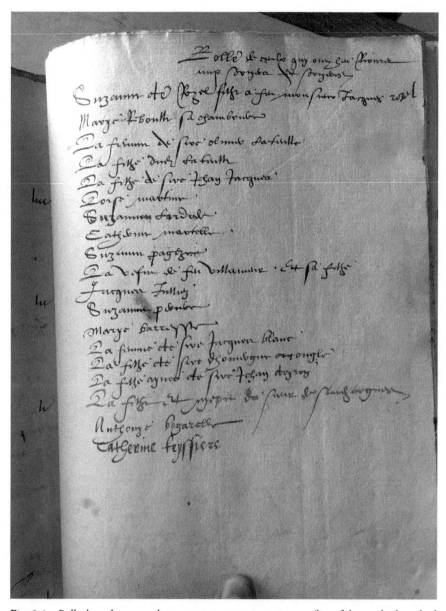

Fig. 3.1. *Rolle de ceulx quy out heu recours aux sorcyers et sorcyeres* (list of those who have had recourse to sorcerers and sorceresses), *Registre des délibérations du consistoire de Nîmes, 1584–8,* Archives départementales du Gard, 42 J 28, 372r

their fortune cast by the *bohémiens*. Marie Delsol was a married woman who seems to have led a group of women—the daughters of Madame de Tenans, the wife of a cobbler called Ybes, her neighbour Astrugue Cappellane, Granier's wife, and a chambermaid called Marie de Talhesre—to have their palms read by the

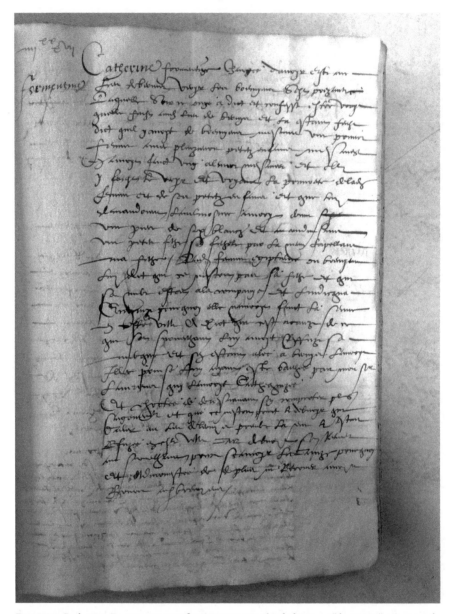

Fig. 3.2. Catherine Formentine confesses to visiting the *bohémiens* ('*boemyens*'), *Registre des délibérations du consistoire de Nîmes, 1584–8*, Archives départementales du Gard, 42 J 28, 97r (11 April 1584)

bohémiens.[167] At the same time a widow called Peyronne Grasse admitted that, on the advice of others, she had turned to the *bohémiens'* palm-reading to disclose the identity of the thief who had burgled her house.[168] A few months later Marie de Vigier went to a female soothsayer in Corbassieu for wisdom. She was struggling with whether to marry Arnaud Ricard, whom she feared might leave or beat her after marriage, and went to see the seer for counsel and 'to know the cause of her grief'.[169] It is not clear whether this soothsayer was a travelling *bohémienne*, but the intent was the same: Vigier needed consolation and guidance at a time of uncertainty and transition.

In Ganges, too, there are records of people visiting the *bohémiens* or soothsayers, but, unusually, the three references are all to men: Jan Rougie went to speak to a 'divine' or folk-doctor in 1587, Pierre Maury confessed to having played cards with the *bohémiens* in 1591, and Jehan Nicoulau went to see a 'sorcerer' in a nearby town after a theft in 1603.[170] It is not clear why it was men rather than women from Ganges who sought out diviners.

An important reason for consulting the *bohémiens* or other local magical healers was the hope of healing. Just as some women attended Mass to seek healing, so too women in the Protestant community were prompted by sickness to solicit the curative powers of unorthodox healers, who offered some hope of redress in a society that had few antidotes to pain. In 1602 Jehane Pueche—who had sought her lost chicken with a sieve—was also reprimanded by the consistory in Alès for having visited a sorcerer in search of a cure for her illness. She confessed that on the recommendation of her father, Claude Pueche, she had gone to a 'soothsayer...and he performed several sorts of magic on her', including a ritual in which an object was passed over her bed.[171]

Many such consultations with folk healers were in the hope of healing sick children, for which women used a desperate mixture of superstitious incantation and popular religion. In April 1597 three women from Saint-Romans-de-Recoudier came to the Protestant town of Ganges carrying with them a sick child, and went to the cemetery to dedicate the infant to St Peter, lighting nine candles, making 'superstitions or idolatries', and offering prayer to the saint, who was esteemed in Catholic tradition to ward off fever.[172] Candles were often suspect—in December 1581 the consistory in Nîmes had ruled against the making of candles, which it called 'a pure superstition and a contravention of our discipline'.[173] Mentzer suggests that this refers to attempts to outlaw the custom of the *chandelle de nadau* or Yule-log, as recorded by Arnold van Gennep, but it may have had a wider application to the creation of candles for use in superstitious ritual, as candles appear elsewhere in equivalent circumstances.[174] The complicity of women from Ganges

---

[167] ADTG, I 1, 256r–v, 257v, 21 May 1597. [168] ADTG, I 1, 256r.

[169] ADTG, I 1, 284r, 20 Aug. 1597.

[170] ADH, E Dépôt GG 24, 8v, 3 Sept. 1587; 21v, 24 Nov. 1591; 144r, 12 Jan. 1603.

[171] ADG, I1, 167r, 5 Jan. 1602. The object is given as '*ung rona*', but I have been unable to discover its meaning.

[172] ADH, E Dépôt GG 24, 80r–82r, 93v–94r, 10 Apr. 1597. [173] BN, Ms.fr. 8667, 267r.

[174] Mentzer, 'Disciplina', 95; Arnold van Gennep, *Manuel de folklore français contemporain* (Paris, 1943), vol. 1, pt 7, 3099–108.

in the 1597 incident was evident in that the women from Saint-Romans were accompanied by a Ganges local called Donne Figuieyresse, who was also known as *La Sauvage*—The Wild Woman—a nickname suggesting her possible reputation as a cunning woman or outsider. Figuieyresse may have been a widow, as five years later one Anne Figuieyresse 'daughter to the late Mathieu' was made to do public reparation (for theft and for losing her temper).[175] Meanwhile Jacquette Vincente, wife of sergeant Bertrand Maury, was responsible for letting the three women into the cemetery, and felt accountable enough to the consistory to appear before the assembly when charged to explain the events. Raymond Mentzer has examined this incident and suggested, plausibly, that Figuieyresse may have presided over the rituals in the cemetery, as the women paid her, while they left Vincente a loaf of bread on her hearth in exchange for her turning a blind eye to their taking a fire-brand.[176] Two years later, in March 1599 in Ganges, a woman called Rondilhonne allowed an unnamed woman to take her sick daughter 'to certain idols' and gave her candles and money towards the healing ritual.[177] This is so similar to the incident from 1597 that one suspects the unnamed woman may have been *La Sauvage*, once again performing curative rites for a desperate mother. A decade earlier in Ganges the wife of Jan Carrieyre had similarly been censured for performing several 'diabolic ceremonies' at the common ovens of the town.[178] The incident of the three women from Saint-Romans is not the only example, either, of consecrating a child to a saint in times of trouble. In Coutras in 1613 Suzanne Bernant was censured for having taken her child to a 'soothsayer' and 'consecrating him with enchantments in the name of the saints'. She denied the charge, assuring the consistory of the contrary, and stated that 'in all her affairs and calamities, her sole recourse is to God', deftly identifying both the consistory's source of concern and precisely the occasions on which women sought help from more obviously visible sources of support.[179]

The world of divination, ritual, and magic could also manifest itself in less benign ways. It was believed that many illnesses, especially children's, could be attributed to sorcery and witchcraft, and needed to be undone by an equivalent magic. In the spring of 1583 a group of six women, led by one called Chantonyelle, had visited the *bohémiens* outside Nîmes to seek healing for Chantonyelle's son, whom she believed to be ill because he had been 'bewitched'.[180] She stated that she 'always well knew' that the *bohémiens*' claim to be able to heal 'was pure deceit', but her anxiety about the magical source of her son's sickness nevertheless drove her to approach them. Others in her group said that 'they did not think they had done any wrong'. In March 1595 a woman living in the Ferrage, to the northwest of Nîmes, was summoned for hearing Mass to heal her daughter, whom she imagined to be bewitched.[181] If ill-health came from curses by witches, then the only reasonable response was to seek a counter-cure.

[175] ADH, E Dépôt GG 24, 136r, 5 Sept. 1602, although this only works if Donne Figuieyresse had adopted her husband's surname.
[176] Mentzer, 'Persistence', 224–8.   [177] ADH, E Dépôt GG 24, 100v, 13 Mar. 1599.
[178] ADH, E Dépôt GG 24, 4r–v, 2 Apr. 1587.   [179] BN, Ars.Ms. 6560, 68v, 30 Aug. 1613.
[180] ADG, 42 J 28, 1r, 16 Mar. 1583.   [181] ADG, 42 J 30, 332r, 1 Mar. 1595.

In September 1584 Claude Jangin's wife and Catherine Nouvelle were both questioned about using a 'certain doctor-sorcerer' or 'enchanter' to heal their sickly children.[182] Jangin's wife admitted that she had heard from a female neighbour that there was a man in the town who could heal all sorts of illnesses, and she invited him round to see her sick little daughter. The healer made several ointments, but she said she could not remember him using any charms. He did, however, use a magical incantation with Nouvelle. Nouvelle's husband, M. Robiac, was the first to appear before the consistory, expressing anger at his wife for consulting the enchanter about the illness of their son. His wife had told him that the healer had put a 'little bell' (*cascavel*) on the fire, made a sign over it, and then laid some paper—on which there were some words inscribed but Nouvelle evidently could not read them—on the kidneys of the boy, who had since died.[183] In giving her account of the events to the consistory Nouvelle, like Jangin's wife, focused on the fact that it was common knowledge in the town that the man made 'lots of cures for lots of illnesses', before explaining how he made divinations with the bell over the fire, and told her that if her child lived for thirteen days there would be hope. But, she mourned, her child had died on the twelfth day. The enchanter had attributed the death to 'some woman who had done her wrong', implying maleficent witchcraft. Nouvelle immediately suspected Jehanne Boissonne, as Boissonne had recently come to her house and said to Nouvelle to 'pray God that all that she loves best may [not?] come to her in grief'. As a result Nouvelle was certain that Boissonne was a 'witch'.[184]

The testimonies of these two women suggest a female information network communicating the presence of the healer, who seems to have used both natural remedies and more ritualistic, magical forms of healing. The difference of opinion between Nouvelle and her husband on the permissibility of such alternative medicine is symptomatic of the divided views of the community about folk magic. This tension could potentially exist even within believers. In Montauban in 1596 Girand Chanderon's wife was interrogated about her recourse to a 'soothsayer' after the death of her son. She too invoked a female network, explaining that her son had died suddenly at seven or eight months old and, as her daughter was also ill, 'by the advice of some woman' she had gone to the soothsayer at Cerdassieu, presumably to find out who was responsible, as sudden or inexplicable illnesses were often associated with witchcraft. Chanderon's wife then claimed to the consistory not to have followed any of the seer's instructions—a puzzling case of ambivalence, but this may have been exaggerated for the benefit of the authorities.[185] The circumstances of her visit to the seer reiterate that women sought external aid and guidance in situations relating to the health and protection of their families.

---

[182] ADG, 42 J 28, 126v, 128v, 19 Sept. 1584.

[183] '*Cascavèl*' is Occitan for a small spherical bell.

[184] The word chosen was '*masque*', meaning 'witch', probably reflecting a belief that witches wore masks on the Sabbath (conversation with Robin Briggs, 17 Oct. 2006), although Mentzer translates '*vielhe masque*' as 'old hag', 'Disciplina', 101.

[185] ADTG, I 1, 213r, 27 Dec. 1596.

These cases also emphasize, of course, the existence of a lively belief in the possibility of maleficent witchcraft and a conviction that harmful witches could be identified. Attributing illness to witchcraft was appealing because it provided logical reasons to explain misfortune, while mechanisms to identify the person responsible for the infirmity tended—like divinatory practices to identify thieves—to confirm the suspicions of the 'bewitched'.[186] The circumstances in which Catherine Nouvelle identified her child's persecutor were precisely those of the classic witchcraft scenario, in which, in the face of disaster, a witch could be identified by her mutterings soon before an apparent act of *maleficium*—evil magic.[187]

As Robin Briggs has argued for the Duchy of Lorraine, reputations for witchcraft took time to build and in Languedoc too some women gained long-standing reputations as witches working for good or for ill.[188] *La Sauvage* is probably an example of a beneficent 'witch' in Ganges. Her counterpoint in Nîmes was a woman known as *La Barbude*—which probably best translates as The Hooded Woman (although The Bearded Woman is also a plausible alternative). In 1587 Marguerite Pynette, when sick, complained that *La Barbude* was the sorceress responsible for her illness.[189] Some twenty years later Sergeant Gallent appeared before the consistory for visiting the house of *La Barbude* because his unwell sister, Donne Mazellete, believed herself to be bewitched. Mazellete had asked her brother to plead with the suspected witch to 'beat a smock belonging to' her, thereby presumably transferring the punishment on to the garment.[190] A reputation for witchcraft could accrue and linger over a long time, each new example only further confirming existing suspicions.

Witchcraft was not only held to be responsible for sickness. In southern France, people were profoundly scared of the *aiguillette*, which could render a marriage frigid, impotent, adulterous, and full of mutual hatred. The *aiguillette*—as described by Thomas Platter in his 1597 visit to Uzès—was created when, at the exact moment that a priest pronounced a couple to be joined as man and wife, a sorcerer or witch tied a knot in a piece of string, said 'and also the devil', and cast a coin over his or her shoulder, thereby binding evil into the marriage.[191] If the coin disappeared the magic had worked. A related sort of magic was wrought in 1614, when Jeanne Brugiere attested to seeing a witch called Lucie Leuziere bring hatred between Sieur de Tournac and his wife, following the death of their firstborn son in Anduze. Encouraged by an enemy of Tournac's, Mademoiselle de Generargues, Leuziere had cut off the end of the dead child's shroud, naming the Father, Son, Holy Spirit, and 'Jesus Maria', and attached it to the mattress where the couple slept. Until the fabric was found and put in the fire by Tournac's daughter, Tournac bore his wife a great hatred, which suddenly ceased when the cutting went up in

---

[186] Thomas, *Religion*, 384–93.
[187] Thomas, *Religion*.   [188] Robin Briggs, *The Witches of Lorraine* (Oxford, 2007), 153.
[189] ADG, 42 J 28, 331r, 25 Nov. 1587; *une barbute* is a riding hood; *barbu* means bearded.
[190] ADG, 42 J 33, 237v, 7 Nov. 1607.
[191] Ladurie, *Les paysans*, 240–1; Mentzer, 'Persistence', 232; Ladurie and Francine-Dominique Liechtenhan (eds), *Le voyage de Thomas Platter 1595–1599*, (2 vols), vol. 2, *Le siècle de Platter* (Paris, 2000), 274–5.

flames.[192] In the Nîmes register of 1595 there is one brief reference to a prostitute who is said to have tied the *aiguillette* against Jehan de Pages, but the consistory did not take it seriously and did not investigate further.[193] They did, however, take quite seriously the accusation levelled against Anthoine Roguere, Seigneur de Clausonne, former president of the *présidial* court and then town councillor, and his wife, in a case stretching over nine folios from late September 1593 onwards.[194]

Clausonne and his wife were summoned—his wife first—to answer to the charge that they had kept a sorcerer, a man from Paris, variously called Simon Boucher or Boschet, at their house and expense, for a fortnight from late September 1593 to untie an *aiguillette* that they believed someone had knotted at their wedding. Reading the consistorial records, it seems more plausible that the relationship was damaged by Clausonne's serial philandering—there is evidence of his having sexual intercourse with at least four different maidservants, in 1588 and 1589, before this incident, and again in 1601 and 1603. On at least one occasion he may have raped a servant, and on another he may have paid for sex.[195] Such behaviour seems sufficient to an outsider to suggest why the marriage may not have been flourishing, but Clausonne and his wife looked for external causes and, suspecting maleficent magic, invited Boucher to stay with them to undo the witch's knot.

Both spouses claimed not to have thought him a sorcerer, despite the rumours. Clausonne said that he understood Boucher to be a 'man of great secrets', 'a man of knowledge', 'a sufficient man...of great experience', and swore that if he had thought him a sorcerer, he would not have kept him in his house. Madame Clausonne said he was 'not a magician nor a sorcerer' but 'a good man', which she judged from the fact that 'he goes to sermons, prays to God often, and sings psalms'. Clausonne admitted that at the end of two weeks he had realized that Boucher was a charlatan and had immediately thrown him out of the house.

The consistory, however, continued to press both to confess what sort of magic Boucher had performed, and the details slowly emerged. Boucher had said that he required three calm and clear days to gather certain herbs, and stayed so long—it being autumn—because they did not have three such consecutive days. Boucher had told them that he needed to gather the roots of the hawthorn tree from the woods on a clear night, a few steps from the path, which he had done one night in Saint-Privat wood. Both spouses protested that Boucher had not used any spells; instead, according to Madame Clausonne, Boucher had spoken a psalm as he split open the hawthorn tree. Clausonne was asked whether he had gone to a cellar at Vigan, deep in the Cévennes, on Boucher's instructions, and admitted that Boucher had indeed told him that if he went to the cellar in Sire de la Vallette's house, near Vigan, he would find a waxen image buried there with two knives crossing it, then once he had removed the knives he would get the healing he sought. He and Vallette had diligently searched everywhere in the cellar, but did not find anything,

---

[192] ADG, 42 J 35, 58r, 22 Mar. 1614.   [193] ADG, 42 J 30, 375v, 12 Jul. 1595.
[194] ADG, 42 J 30, 223r, 224v, 228v, 269r–v, 270r–v, 271r–v, 22 Sept. 1593.
[195] See cases of Catherine Plantade, Alix, Marguerite Fontaniue, and an unnamed maidservant with Clausonne, in Chapter 6.

and it had been the fruitless experience of digging around in the dirt that had made
Clausonne realize that Boucher was a 'braggart' and a charlatan.

The case gives us insight into the magical practices and popular remedies used
by healers such as Boucher. He needed to gather herbs in specific weather conditions and perform his observance at a certain time at night. He sought out the
hawthorn tree, long associated in lore with lovemaking and weddings, but also at
times with evil and faery magic. Like many healers across Europe, he deployed a
mix of religion and magic, repurposing a psalm as an incantation, making magic
into a kind of extension of orthodox religion, as O'Neil also observed in sixteenth-
century Modena.[196] The case also tells us about the magic thought to be used to
bewitch a person. The waxen image may have been some sort of voodoo doll—an
image made in wax, which could then be used to inflict pain on the victim—in this
case by sticking knives in it. This is reminiscent of the testimony of alleged witch
Elizabeth Sowtherns, known as Demdike, in the Pendle witch-trials at Lancaster in
1612, who confessed that 'the speedyst way to take a man's life by witchcraft, is
to make a picture of clay, like unto the shape of the person whom they mean to
kill . . . and when they would have them to be ill in any one place . . . then take a
thorn or pin, and prick it in that part'.[197] We learn also about the magical beliefs
of ordinary people. Clausonne and his wife had taken Boucher into their house
convinced that the discord between them was the result of maleficent magic, and
at first they understood there to be a distinction between Boucher's activities and
sorcery. They protested that he had not used any spells, and was a good man, who
worshipped God, but were also convinced he had esoteric knowledge and was their
only hope of reconciliation.

The consistory was concerned about the scandal that had been caused in Nîmes
and Vigan by Boucher's actions. They asked Clausonne why he had not sought the
advice of the church ministers before employing and housing such a man. They
reminded him that 'most sorcerers are ignorant men', and they required him to
make reparation before the consistory. However, they neither believed in the efficacy of Boucher's magic, nor considered that diabolism underpinned his actions.
When it came to witchcraft they were sceptics.

In fact, the consistorial records are full of accusations of witchcraft and sorcery,
and many suspected witches were identified, but the crucial fact is that ordinary
women and men were far more perturbed by evidence of bewitchment than
the consistory was.[198] When Catherine Nouvelle accused Jehane Boissonne of
witchcraft, the consistory's response was to censure Nouvelle and exhort her to be
reconciled with Boissonne. A dispute between M. Lombard and Donne Ledinare
in 1581 included the accusation that Ledinare was a 'sorceress' who had killed

---

[196] O'Neil, 'Magical Healing', 91; Sara T. Nalle, *God in La Mancha: Religious Reform and the People of Cuenca, 1500–1650* (Baltimore, MD, and London, 1992), 14–15.

[197] Elizabeth Sowtherns, alias Demdike, confession and examination, 2 Apr. 1612, reproduced in Thomas Potts and Robert Poole, *The Wonderful Discovery of Witches in the County of Lancaster* (Lancaster, 2011), 104.

[198] There are also cases only involving men visiting male sorcerers, e.g. ADH, E Dépôt GG 24, 75v, 2 Feb. 1597.

Lombard's child, and Lombard had, as a result, beaten and threatened to kill Ledinare's son; the consistory quietly encouraged the pair to be reconciled with each other.[199] A report in 1594 that Michel Battese's mother-in-law was 'meddling in sorcery' was never investigated.[200]

Ladurie suggested that, in the south of France:

> the Huguenots succeeded... in destroying the web of demonic superstitions and in taking the peasant consciousness in hand... the Calvinist consistories of the Cévennes had only to censure affairs of a benign sort—loaves marked with cabalistic symbols, magic dealings with the gypsies, and so on.

And while 'magic dealings with the gypsies' did indeed feature in ordinary women's activities, not all belief in or dealings with magic were benign. The incidents considered here demonstrate that beliefs in witchcraft certainly persisted and it was only the consistory's general lack of interest in response to claims of bewitchment that prevented the cases escalating further.[201] In 1566 Johann Weyer noted, approvingly, that in Bologna, witches were whipped and exiled, rather than executed.[202] Similarly, the only action occasionally taken by the consistory was to seek the suspect's expulsion from the town. Here they were influenced less by the verse in Exodus that inspired many witchfinders—'Thou shall not suffer a witch to live'—than by Revelation 22:15, where 'the dogs and the sorcerers and the sexually immoral and murderers and idolaters' were found outside the city gates.[203] In 1589 Jehan Arnail, staying in Les Arènes, was ill-famed as a sorcerer. One of the elders reported that he had committed acts of sorcery in Gremont and been evicted from that town, so the decision was taken to denounce him to the magistrates, so that they might discover whether he was practising magic and exile him if so.[204] In February 1605 the consistory sent word to the consuls to banish a 'sorcerer and seer' living in the city.[205] That the remedy—expulsion—was the same as that to be used against *putains* (whores) is even made explicit: when Saumette Malaigne thought Antoinette Contesse had bewitched her children in 1587 the consistory decided to speak to the king's lawyer 'about the *putains* as about the sorceresses'.[206] In fact, in some cases, suspected witches could even turn to the consistory for protection. When a poor old woman called Donne Danie was accused by Captain Audemar and his wife of being a witch and killing their son, she complained to the consistory that she had been defamed.[207] Three years later Jehan Gaillard complained that Donne Danie had bewitched his child, while Anthoine Boyssier, known as *Seigneuret*, and Donne Honorade, known as *Rambalhe*, also accused Danie of witchcraft. Danie again defended herself, saying that they accused her because she had lent them some money that they refused to repay, and instead they beat and tormented her.[208] She again escaped further investigation.

[199] BN, Ms.fr. 8667, 255v, 15 Nov. 1581.   [200] ADG, 42 J 30, 296v, 7 Sept. 1594.
[201] Ladurie, *Les paysans*, 408.
[202] Johann Weyer, *De praestigiis daemonum*, Book VI, Chapter 21 (Amsterdam, 1566); cited by H. C. Lea, *Materials towards a History of Witchcraft*, 3 vols (New York, 1957), vol. 3, 1073–4.
[203] Exodus 22:18; Revelation 22:15.   [204] ADG, 42 J 29, 273r, 13 Sept. 1589.
[205] ADG, 42 J 35, 26v, 9 Feb. 1605.   [206] ADG, 42 J 28, 299r, 300v, 22 Jul. 1587.
[207] ADG, 42 J 28, 105r, 16 May 1584.   [208] ADG, 42 J 28, 299r, 306v, 22 Jul. 1587.

A mechanism for prosecuting witchcraft was therefore denied to French Protestants, but that does not mean that they were sceptical of the existence of witches, sorcerers, and harmful magic. Women and men of the period believed profoundly in the existence of the devil, who revealed himself through malevolent sorcery, bewitchment, and demonic activity. The consistory's lack of enthusiasm for pursuing witchcraft accusations explains why such belief did not manifest itself in these Languedocian towns in the sort of witch-craze seen elsewhere on the continent. This attitude was crucial. By contrast to the French consistories, the Calvinist kirks of Scotland treated accusations of witchcraft extremely seriously.[209] The reaction of authorities to accusations of sorcery, as demonstrated by the well-attested witchcraft epidemics in the rest of France, was decisive in escalating or diminishing the volume of accusations and prosecutions in the late sixteenth and early seventeenth centuries.[210]

Conversely, however, the consistory took very seriously any invocation of Satan in speech: Jehanne Garnie was censured in 1562 for blasphemy for 'having said she had given to the devil that which she had done and damaged the possessions of her children', a slightly curious sentence that implies that she blamed the devil for the fit of anger in which she had damaged her children's things.[211] Mathieu Guilhon was berated in March 1581 for having sworn that 'he would give the devil his body and soul if he could sell more than 200 tiles to Guillaume Guiraud', which he denied, and Catherine Marcoyreze was similarly castigated a couple of months later for swearing that she would 'give her body and soul to the devil' and that she wanted him to carry her away 'in the fire and the wind' if her claim that she had not used counterfeit coinage was untrue.[212] Such casual references to the devil, of which the consistory strongly disapproved, suggest that consistorial and popular views on the devil were somewhat at odds: blasphemy was taken far more seriously by the church authorities than by the populace, the latter casually dropping oaths to the devil into conversation, but when the people feared the devil's emissaries on earth the consistory did little to assuage their fears.

Conclusions

Belief in magic appears unabated among Huguenot communities in this period. Sometimes individuals seemed unaware that what they did, in seeking divination or magical remedies, was illicit, although such actions brought women into conflict with religious authorities. Women's complex and equivocal spiritual beliefs and behaviour cannot easily be compartmentalized. A profound Protestant faith did not rule out resorting to alternative sources of revelation: Catherine Teissiere,

---

[209] Michael F. Graham, 'Social Discipline in Scotland, 1560–1610', in *Sin and the Calvinists: Morals Control and the Consistory in the Reformed Tradition*, ed. Raymond A. Mentzer (Kirksville, MO, 1994), 155.

[210] e.g. Briggs, *Witches and Neighbours*, 291.

[211] BN, Ms.fr. 8666, 101v, 27 Mar. 1562: '*avoyr donne au diable ceulx qui avoyent faict et donne dommage aux biens de ses enfans*'.

[212] BN, Ms.fr. 8667, 192v, 193r, 17 Mar. 1581; 216r, 217v, 12 May 1581.

who donated generously to the poor and the repair of the Reformed temple in her will, was among those who visited the *bohémiens* in 1583.[213] Reformed women particularly turned to traditional curative and divinatory practices at certain key rites of passage or in times of family crisis, such as child sickness, marriage break-down, or the loss of possessions: circumstances in which women were involved in sustaining their families. The Reformed church wanted women's role to be about domestic religion, but it was the concerns of domesticity that prompted women to look beyond orthodoxy. Precisely the modes of spiritual interaction that the Reformers sought to eradicate—healing, divination, and superstitious ritual—were those that women, especially, sought to maintain. Women needed hope and they were willing to pay for it, both financially and, if necessary, reputationally. In their relationship with the divine and the supernatural, as in so many other areas of their lives, women in Languedoc negotiated paths other than those offered by patriarchal and institutional authorities, making their own bricolage of the old and the new.

[213] Arc.Not., ADG, 2 E 1/258, 4 Aug. 1568; 42 J 28, 372r.

4

Social Relations

In June 1597 Jeanne Parette brought a case to the Nîmes consistory against a group of women, namely the widow of M. Naujous and her married daughter; Jeanne Nancelles, wife of Pierre Lacoste, who was sergeant to the consuls of the town; Beatrix de Creuvain, widow of M. Gras; and certain others—that is, at least two widows and two married women, two of whom were related to each other—for saying that Parette was a 'public whore' (meaning a prostitute) and spreading the rumour that a young foundry worker came to visit her in secret.[1] The rumour had started one day when a man called Panse Peyre had knocked on Parette's door and then, discovering it locked and seeing a man inside with her, had cried out to a group of women congregating on the street—including Naujous's widow, her daughter, and Nancelles—that Parette had locked the door from the inside. Peyre's sole action was to alert a group of neighbourhood women to the apparent immorality, and the women's response is instructive. According to their testimony before the consistory, they approached the door and finding that what Peyre had said was true, they then cried out to Parette:

> that she did not act well to stay with a man all alone, and to have closed the door behind them, and that they could not think anything good of her, and that they did not want to put up with such assignations, and that if she continued they would have to denounce [her] to the magistrate.[2]

At that moment Beatrix de Creuvain, who was passing, saw the group assembled in front of Parette's house and asked what was happening, and when told retorted 'it ought not to be endured', suggesting that in her judgement Parette's actions were something that could not be tolerated.

What is striking is that there may have been entirely legitimate grounds for Parette and the young man to be together: since Parette was married to an armourer or cutler, it seems possible that the young metal worker, described also as being 'of

---

[1] ADTG, I 1, 261v, 265v, 4 Jun. 1597. I have elsewhere (Lipscomb, 'Crossing Boundaries: Women's Gossip, Insults and Violence in Sixteenth-Century France', *French History* 25.4 (2011), 408–26) given her surname as Cieuran, on the basis of a nineteenth-century transcription (BSHPF, Ms. 817/1, 448), but consultation of the original register produces this different transcription. Similarly, it is now clear that Monsieur Lacrete and Monsieur Lacoste were one and the same person, and that his wife was Jeanne Nancelles, not Beatrix de Creuvain.

[2] ADTG, I 1, 265v.

her occupation' and 'of her estate', was employed in the marital household workshop. Yet these women were quick to judge their confinement as necessarily sexual, and further, they asserted their right to speak in defence of the moral standards of the community. Their scolding reproof posited their right to delineate the boundaries of acceptable behaviour, while they also assumed a moral responsibility to report scandalous behaviour to the authorities. This group of married and formerly married women defined themselves as respectable by speaking out against apparent adultery—both literally at the time and later through gossip; it is clear that these women had arrogated to themselves a role as moral guardians of the town.[3]

The structural circumstances of urban life meant that neighbours lived cheek-by-jowl, with little privacy and frequent social interaction: conditions that bred deep interest in each other's lives, and inevitably led to gossip, verbal affronts, and even physical confrontation.[4] These incidents served as social entertainment in a world of few other diversions, but also as both catharsis and a means of affirming and remodelling the community's values. Many altercations revolved around the currency of honour and reputation as every woman sought to portray herself as a *femme de bien et d'honneur*—a good and honourable woman—and therefore, by definition, sexually honest.[5]

The existing scholarship has generated several contradictory findings about how neighbourly society functioned, which raise a series of questions. Were neighbours reluctant to intrude on the lives of others, as Julie Hardwick found, or were they happy to intervene in other people's social relations, as David Garrioch reports for late eighteenth-century Paris?[6] Were sixteenth- and seventeenth-century women like those of later centuries, who appear to have policed moral behaviour, as noted by Georg'Ann Cattelona, Roderick Phillips, and Nicole Castan, or did women rarely assume roles of symbolic censure, as Daniel Fabre suggested?[7] Did women

[3] This is an extreme example of the sort of behaviour Cattelona finds for eighteenth-century Marseille, 'Control', 17, 21. Raymond A. Mentzer emphasizes the sense of moral obligation felt by voyeurs, but his examples chiefly involve groups of men, and he does not highlight the large role played by women, see 'Morals and Moral Regulation in Protestant France', *JIH* 31.1 (2000), 1–20, here 14.

[4] David Garrioch, *Neighbourhood and Community in Paris, 1740–1790* (Cambridge, 1986), 32; James R. Farr, *Hands of Honor: Artisans and their World in Dijon, 1550–1650* (Ithaca, NY, and London, 1988), 166; Georg'Ann Cattelona, 'Control and Collaboration: The Role of Women in Regulating Female Sexual Behaviour in Early Modern Marseille', *FHS* 18.1 (1993), 34–49; Julie Hardwick, *The Practice of Patriarchy: Gender and the Politics of Household Authority in Early Modern France* (University Park, PA, 1998), 102–3; Jean-Louis Flandrin, *Familles: parenté, maison, sexualité dans l'ancienne société* (Paris, 1976), 40, 52.

[5] ADG, 42 J 31, 272r; Ian Maclean, *The Renaissance Notion of Woman: A Study in the Fortunes of Scholasticism and Medical Science in European Intellectual Life* (Cambridge, 1980), 16, 22; Robert Muchembled, *Société et mentalités dans la France moderne: XVIe–XVIIIe siècle* (Paris, 1990), 82; Natalie Zemon Davis, *Fiction in the Archives: Pardon Tellers and their Tales in Sixteenth-Century France* (Cambridge, 1987), 91, 96, 98. This is especially charted for later periods, see Marie-Claude Phan, *Les amours illégitimes: histories de séduction en Languedoc (1676–1786)* (Paris, 1986), 144, 155–7; Yves Castan, *Honnêteté et relations sociales en Languedoc (1715–1780)* (Paris, 1974), 164; Garrioch, *Neighbourhood*, 41. Farr, *Hands*, 82 talks of a pan-European moral code.

[6] Hardwick, *Practice*, 102–3; Garrioch, *Neighbourhood*, 19, 79–80.

[7] Cattelona, 'Control', 17, 21; Roderick Phillips, 'Women, Neighborhood, and Family in the Late Eighteenth Century', *FHS* 18.1 (1993), 1–125; Nicole Castan, 'Le public et le particulier', in *Histoire de la vie privée*, 5 vols (Paris, 1985–7), vol. 3, *De la Renaissance aux Lumières*, ed. Ariès, Philippe and

especially use sexualized insults—as Jacques Solé and Castan report—or were such terms used freely by both women and men, as Mary Beth Norton finds for seventeenth-century New England?[8] Did women enthusiastically denounce other women to the authorities—as Laura Gowing finds for England—or did they display a reluctance to denounce others for sexual offences, as Rublack observes in Germany?[9] The consistorial records provide answers.

Previous studies have also reached some conclusions from which the evidence of the consistories diverges. Bernard Capp, Ulinka Rublack, and Garrioch, studying England, Germany, and eighteenth-century France, have argued that gossip was not a particularly gendered activity and have stressed the role played by both women and men in gossip.[10] Gowing concluded that in England, sexualized insults were only 'obliquely related to actual sex', and really represented concerns about financial extravagance, while Rublack found that, in Germany, gossip manifested anxieties about economic independence.[11] Historians such as Robert Muchembled and Stuart Carroll have argued that France in this period was a violent society, but have considered women's violence rare.[12] This chapter will suggest that none of these hypotheses holds for sixteenth- and seventeenth-century southern France. The significant number of consistorial cases concerning social interaction provides a wealth of testimonies that takes us into the heart of neighbourhood life, with all its tensions, competition, and anxieties, and gives us a very different picture of the lives of ordinary women.

Gossip—the exchange of information about the personal lives of third parties— was an important feature of urban life in Languedoc. In a society with few other means of exchanging information, gossip was both diverting and educative. Martin Ingram noted that malice and amusement combined with a voyeuristic interest in other people's lives, and that a feature of English society was 'endemic gossip about sexual reputation, which served...as an outlet for the prurience and spite of the bored and sexually repressed'.[13] The *Oxford English Dictionary* defines gossip as 'to talk idly, mostly about other people's affairs; to go about tattling'—the latter defined as idle or frivolous talk—but gossip was neither simply idle nor frivolous.[14]

Georges Duby (Paris, 1986), 427; Daniel Fabre, 'Familles: le privé contre la coutume', in *Histoire de la vie privée*, 5 vols (Paris, 1985–7), vol. 3, *De la Renaissance aux Lumières*, ed. Philippe Ariès and Georges Duby (Paris, 1986), 556, although he noted that Languedoc might be an exception.

[8] Jacques Solé, *Etre femme en 1500: la vie quotidienne dans la diocèse de Troyes* (Paris, 2000), 148–51; Nicole Castan, 'Les femmes devant la justice: Toulouse, XVIII siècle', in *Femmes et pouvoirs sous l'Ancien Régime*, ed. Danielle Haase-Dubosc and Eliane Viennot (Paris, 1991), 83; Norton, 'Gender', 10.

[9] Bernard Capp, *When Gossips Meet: Women, Family and Neighbourhood in Early Modern England* (Oxford, 2003), 272–3; Ulinka Rublack, *The Crimes of Women in Early Modern Germany* (Oxford, 1999), 22, 218–20; Garrioch, *Neighbourhood*, 23, 25–6; Laura Gowing, *Domestic Dangers: Women, Words and Sex in Early Modern London* (Oxford, 1996), 91, 116, 118.

[10] Garrioch, *Neighbourhood*, 19–27; Rublack, *Crimes*, 26; Capp, *Gossips*, 272–3.

[11] Laura Gowing, *Domestic Dangers: Women, Words, and Sex in Early Modern London* (Oxford, 1996), 59, 90–1, 93, 115, 118; Rublack, *Crimes*, 26.

[12] Stuart Carroll, *Blood and Violence in Early Modern France* (Oxford, 2006), 244–6; Robert Muchembled, *Culture populaire et culture des élites dans la France moderne (XVe–XVIIIe siècles): essai* (Paris, 1978), 67.

[13] Martin Ingram, *Church Courts, Sex and Marriage in England, 1570–1640* (Cambridge, 1987), 305.

[14] Max Gluckman, 'Gossip and Scandal', *Current Anthropology* 4.3 (1963), 307–15, here 312.

It also had vital significance, because gossips dealt in reputations and, in this period, reputations were both crucially important and terribly unstable. A person's good name was innately vulnerable: it was something of no tangible substance and not controlled by its owner, but fundamental to that person's reception in the world.[15] It was because gossip could wound reputations that it was so deeply serious. Gossip was also crucial for maintaining or maiming the trustworthiness on which local economic relationships functioned. Who gossiped, and what they said, were profoundly important.

Gossip was partly an inescapable consequence of geography—people lived crammed into these small walled towns and spilling beyond their gates into the *faubourgs* beyond. The urban population—at a time when most people lived in settlements of a few hundred people—should not, however, suggest that the city was an anonymous place, filled with strangers.[16] Instead, city neighbourhoods can be thought of as 'urban villages'.[17] It seems likely that the division of Nîmes into surveillance districts, each of which could be identified by name—La Ferrage, La Maison de Ville, Le Marché, La Couronne, Les Arènes, Le Chapitre, and so on—represented the intuitively understood, existing *quartiers* of the town. People belonged to a community and were familiar with the lives of the others in that community.[18] In the closed confines of the city—small, crowded houses; narrow roads; cramped shops—much of life was played out on the streets, and even that enacted indoors was known to neighbours, who saw all, and especially heard all, through thin walls and ill-fitting doors.[19] Of eighteenth-century Paris, Garrioch has written that an awareness of one's neighbours' every movement—when they had company, the rhythms of their days and nights, the familiar voices and footfalls providing the soundtrack of life—meant that non-habitual activities and unaccustomed sounds instantly attracted attention and produced a state of high alert, with people displaying 'an almost pathological interest in the lives and doings of those who lived around them'.[20] And once interest in a subject had been raised, it was bound to be discussed. The same is true of the towns of Languedoc in our period. In a world of constant sociability, conversation oiled the wheels of coexistence, and news of, and speculation about, any unusual happenings framed the next day's dialogue. As such, evidence of gossip and slander offers a tremendous opportunity for insight into the mental and social worlds of sixteenth- and seventeenth-century women and men.

Anthropologists have examined the function of gossip in community life. Max Gluckman posited that gossip can too easily be dismissed as pernicious, ungoverned

---

[15] Peter J. Wilson, '"Filcher of Good Names": An Enquiry into Anthropology and Gossip', *Man* 9, 1 (1974), 93–102, here 100.

[16] Philip Benedict, 'French Cities from the Sixteenth Century to the Revolution: An Overview', in *Cities and Social Change in Early Modern France*, ed. Philip Benedict (London, 1989), 16; Garrioch, *Neighbourhood*, 16–18. See also R. Schneider, *Public Life in Toulouse, 1463–1789: From Municipal Republic to Cosmopolitan City* (Cambridge, 1989); Penny Roberts, 'Urban Society', *The European World, 1500–1800*, ed. Bëat Kümin (London and New York, 2009).

[17] Benedict, 'French Cities', 17.   [18] Garrioch, *Neighbourhood*, 16, 27.

[19] Benedict, 'French Cities', 17; Garrioch, *Neighbourhood*, 32.

[20] Garrioch, *Neighbourhood*, 32.

banter of minor importance when, in fact, gossip is 'the very blood and tissue of [community] life', and 'maintains the unity, morals, and values of social groups'.[21] Peter Wilson too concluded that gossip has an essential role to play in reaffirming common bonds and social norms, reinforcing what F. G. Bailey described as the 'quality of intimacy' in small-scale communities.[22] Rather than being damaging to social unity, gossip preserves a sense of community identity. Through defining the morals of the group gossip also acts as a mechanism for controlling socially harmful conduct; by bringing individuals' behaviour under the scrutiny of the group gossip polices behaviour.[23]

In Protestant Languedocian society, gossip was clearly entertaining, sometimes malicious, and often salacious, but it was also fundamentally important in reinforcing and reframing the values of the group. In a context in which existing proclivities towards voyeurism and judgement were encouraged by the church, and when it was considered justifiable and virtuous to enforce morality, prurient gossip could act a way of upholding the social values of the community and the church.[24] This was especially the case as gossip seems to have centred on illicit sexual activity and in this aligned itself, for the most part, with the Protestant Church's agenda of exposing and expunging sexual immorality. The repetition of moral norms through the process of gossip cemented and reaffirmed them. The evidence from the consistories also suggests that women were predominantly those who used, and who were expected to use, gossip to shore up the moral values of the community.

In 1595 Béatrix Cuérande spread a rumour that a woman, known only as Jeanne, had given birth illegitimately. Cuérande's testimony gives an insight into the transmission of the rumour. She said that:

> Madame de Caulet had attested to her that she had heard it from Madame de Gilis, and that the said de Gilis mentioned also that Jean Ampiel, known as *Ginibrières*, [had] told her, so that which Caulet said was supported by the said de Gilis having said it to her and the said Ampiel saying it.[25]

In trying to vouch for the authenticity of her story Cuérande depicted a chain of gossip, from one man—Jean Ampiel—via Madame de Gilis and Madame de Caulet to Cuérande herself. Most members of the chain were women, and the one man involved knew that the effective step to take with reputation-damaging gossip was to tell local women. With this sort of gossip, women asserted the community's proclaimed stance towards sexual immorality.

---

[21] Gluckman, 'Gossip', 308; Robert Paine, 'What Is Gossip About? An Alternative Hypothesis', *Man* 2, 2 (1967), 272–85; Max Gluckman, 'Psychological, Sociological and Anthropological Explanations of Witchcraft and Gossip: A Clarification', Man 3, 1 (1968), 20–34; G. Bailey, 'Gifts and Poison', in *Gifts and Poison: The Politics of Reputation*, ed. G. Bailey (Oxford, 1971); Wilson, 'Filcher'.

[22] Wilson, 'Filcher', 98; Bailey, 'Gifts', 5.

[23] J. A. Sharpe, *Defamation and Sexual Slander in Early Modern England: The Church Courts at York*, Borthwick Papers no. 58 (1980), 19–20.

[24] See Natalie Zemon Davis, 'The Reasons of Misrule', in *Society and Change in Early Modern France* (Cambridge, 1987) for this culture in pre-Reformation French neighbourhoods.

[25] ADTG, I 1, 6r, 14 Jun. 1595.

Further incidents support the idea that gossip in this period was often born of keen interest in the sexual activities of others, was used to designate the community's moral boundaries, and was predominately communicated by women. In April 1586 Donne Loyse was accused of spreading the lurid rumour that M. Grisot's widow had spent a night in the oil mill with three or four men and had been sexually intimate with them all.[26] As the stereotype of the 'lusty widow' was prevalent in sixteenth-century France, widows were easy targets for slander, and the maintenance of a reputation for sexual purity was even more fraught for widows than for most women.[27] This gossip appears to have come to the attention of the consistory because Grisot's widow was demanding that Donne Loyse make reparation for the slander, because it potentially had power to ruin the widow's good name. By summoning Donne Loyse, rather than investigating the accusation, the consistory indicated that they doubted the truth of the rumour. A similar case occurred in 1595 when Jane, Captain Alphanty's widow, complained that her mother-in-law had been spreading a rumour about her to a group of women, including Donne Mazellette—the same woman who, twelve years later, would believe herself to be bewitched by *La Barbude*—that Jane had an eleven-month-old daughter and that her mother-in-law judged 'by this that [the child] was not of [Jane's] late husband'. The sources do not indicate when Captain Alphanty had died, although we know that the couple had probably been married for at least six years before his death, as they had a daughter, Marguerite, baptized in February 1589.[28] Such defaming gossip was a way for the older woman to convey the opprobrium that her daughter-in-law was allegedly sexually active out of wedlock and soon after her husband's death. In the consistory the mother-in-law denied having spread the rumour, but, nonetheless, tacitly admitted wrongdoing when she asked 'forgiveness of God and her daughter-in-law for that which had damaged her honour'.[29]

As these cases make clear, a precious reputation of chastity could be undermined by the words of others, and women were frequently the ones seeking to do so, even though it was other women's reputations that were endangered by their words. These findings contrast with observations made of England, Germany, and eighteenth-century France that gossip was not a gendered activity: in sixteenth-century southern France it seems to have been predominantly female.[30] This is an uncomfortable conclusion, since it appears, at first sight, to echo contemporary misogynistic notions about the garrulity of women.[31] Yet women's talkativeness was not purposeless, for female gossip served the important function of defending social propriety.

[26] ADG, 42 J 28, 222r, 16 Apr. 1586.
[27] Lyndan Warner, 'Widows, Widowers and the Problem of "Second Marriages" in Sixteenth-Century France,' in *Widowhood in Medieval and Early Modern Europe*, ed. Sandra Cavallo and Lyndan Warner (Harlow, 1999), 89; Wendy Gibson, *Women in Seventeenth-Century France* (Basingstoke, 1989), 93–4; Scarlett Beauvalet-Boutouyrie, *Etre veuve sous l'Ancien Régime* (Paris, 2001), 15; Jacques Poumarède, 'Le droit des veuves sous l'Ancien Régime (XVIIe–XVIIIe siècles) ou comment gagner son douaire', in *Femmes et pouvoirs*, ed. Haase-Dubosc and Viennot, 64–6.
[28] ADG, E Dépôt 36/696, 87r; this baptismal register also establishes her first name.
[29] ADG, 42 J 30, 343r, 29 Mar. 1595.
[30] Capp, *Gossips*, 272–3; Rublack, *Crimes*, 22, 218–20; Garrioch, *Neighbourhood*, 23, 25–6.
[31] See, for example, Davis, *Fiction*, 88, 90–1, 101.

Gossip often, therefore, seems to have been about women seeking to convey their disapproval, and through this to delineate the acceptable boundaries of behaviour, especially sexual behaviour. This is a recurring pattern. In 1589 there was a 'certain noise' in Nîmes—that is, people were gossiping—about the frequentation of the Provost with the daughters of M. Grisot.[32] In another entry the Provost is named as M. Rouviere.[33] The rumour was traced back to Marye Boudane, wife of Guilhaume Theron, who said that she had often seen Rouviere coming and going to and from Grisot's house. The last time she had seen this had been a fortnight before she was questioned, and she reported that she had seen him enter but did not know how long he stayed because she had left to report it to Donne Roze, so that she might warn the Provost's wife. Here again is an example of female gossip about sexual misdemeamour and the reporting of such observations to other women, including denouncing the alleged adulterer to his wife. Similarly, in December 1585 it was M. Raymond's wife who disclosed to him—and he, in turn, reported to the consistory—that when she went to an inn belonging to M. de Puechmejan at La Fontaine—just outside the city walls of Nîmes to the north-west—she saw there 'a fornicator with a whore'.[34] It is unlikely she had fabricated this—six months later it was noted, from another source, that there were three or four prostitutes at M. de Puechmejan's inn.[35] Women were also the source of the intelligence passed by Guillaume Codere (known also as *Gramat*) to an elder in Montauban in July 1595 about the immoral behaviour of a hose-maker called Jean Blanc. When they had asked Blanc why he had gone to La Lande he had brazenly told them that he went there to behave badly and that 'he did as much as his virile member would endure'.[36] The consistory was concerned with his 'dirty and villainous words', but the pattern of information-gathering is pertinent: it was a group of women who noticed and asked about Blanc's visit—no doubt anticipating that he had gone there to get up to no good—and his response told them, with some relish, precisely what they had suspected. They then told a man who reported it to the consistory. Similarly, a few months later Susanne Gordonne was found to have been gossiping that Sarra de Bely had committed adultery with a scholar called Alexis Le François, and that Bely had received both money and gold rings from him. The rumours had reached Bely's husband, and he had believed them and threatened to mistreat her. Bely said that Gordonne had committed defamatory libel, although Gordonne denied ever saying anything.[37] In each case women observed the sexual behaviour of others and spoke about it. Their words caused a 'noise'—the hubbub of gossip—that reached both those concerned and members of the consistory, becoming the catalyst for investigation.

The words of female gossipers had the power to make or break reputations. Drivette Sannyere, the widow of Jehan Privat, reported in 1598 that Magdaleine de la Biche had prevented her remarriage by calling her a whore and spreading the

---

[32] The spelling is also given, at one point, as M. Grisol: ADG, 42 J 29, 260, 307, 30 Aug. 1589.
[33] ADG, 42 J 29, 393.   [34] ADG, 42 J 28, 198r, 19 Dec. 1585.
[35] ADG, 42 J 28, 227v.   [36] ADTG, I 1, 21v, 29r, 19 Jul. 1595.
[37] ADTG, I 1, 64v, 1 Nov. 1595.

rumour that Sannyere had given birth to an illegitimate child five or six years earlier.[38] When questioned, Biche claimed 'that she had heard it said' that Sannyere had had a child outside wedlock—a classic formula to anonymize the source of the gossip. Sannyere's assertion that the rumour had had such a direct impact on her chances of remarriage is a testament to the potential gravity of discrediting words.

It is unsurprising, then, that the consistory was frequently resorted to by those hoping to restore their good name, drawing the church authorities into this murky female world of gossip. Many cases of gossip and slander were included in the consistorial registers precisely because the plaintiff hoped, by the process, to reinstate their standing in the community. Sannyere was successful in this: Biche was censured in her presence and required to make reparation and demand pardon from Sannyere.[39] Yet despite Sannyere's success, the incident once again exemplifies a pattern of external female interest and interference in other women's sexual lives.

Three cases show just how easily gossip blurred into denunciation. In May 1562 Donne Robine was reported to the consistory by Catherine Pastre, wife of Anthoine Sigalon; Agnes Servente, wife of Anthoine Paris; Catherine Moldine; and Jehane Buissonete for allegedly keeping a loose woman in her house. Pastre was related to a former church elder—her husband had been one of the elders of the Nîmois consistory in 1561 and their son Mathieu would go on to be an elder in 1584, 1591, 1604, and 1607–9—and her family connections would undoubtedly have increased her credibility before the consistory, as well as adding to her own sense of justification in informing on Robine.[40]

Gossip and denunciation blurred also when in July 1595 Dalphine de Crabol told an elder in Montauban that Pierre Cardonne—the erstwhile Catalan monk—wanted to marry Marie de Petit, 'who lives at his house' (probably as a servant). This was falsified gossip—Cardonne, when questioned, said that he had 'never even thought such a thing' because 'that presupposed that he would make love and he had never thought [to do] it'.[41] He may have stopped being a monk, but he intended to remain celibate, and his denials suggest he would have felt Crabol was a scandalmonger, whose gossip was malicious and defaming.

Finally, the thin line between gossip and denunciation to the consistory can be seen when three elders in Montauban—Messieurs Gautier, Lauzat, and Expert—consulted another woman whose gossip had brought a matter of sexual immorality to their attention. Benacontry's wife was summoned to tell the consistory what she had seen of the behaviour between Gabriel Oliver and his former maidservant Jeanne de Bressanges. She reported that Oliver and Bressanges had often spoken to each other, and that recently her daughter had seen a man dressed only in a chemise lying on Bressanges's bed.[42] She had put two and two together, and the consistory did so too: because of her words the consistory charged an elder to ask the consuls to banish Bressanges from the town, which the consuls promised to do, although this is not recorded in their register of criminal sentences.[43] The story

[38] ADG, 42 J 31, 255v, 258v, 30 Dec. 1598.   [39] ADG, 42 J 31, 259r.
[40] BN, Ms.fr. 8666, 117v, 6 May 1562.   [41] ADTG, I 1, 214r, 24v, 19 Jul. 1595.
[42] ADTG, I 1, 43v, 58v, 60v, 13 Sept. 1595.   [43] See ADTG, 5 FF 2, 34r–v.

had, however, a second act. A month later two elders reported that they had further information about Jeanne de Bressanges's affair. Again, Benacontry's wife 'had said that she had heard it said that' a few days earlier a hatter called Tounellier, who lived close to her, had travelled to 'Casure' (probably Cahors) to buy merchandise, and that Bressanges accompanied him. En route they had stayed at an inn in Molières (some 25 km north of Montauban) belonging to Estienne Besse; the hatter had told Besse that Bressanges was his wife, so the innkeeper had given them one bed where they slept together. The following morning a man from Montauban called Lou Piat arrived at the inn and recognized and greeted Tounellier. When the hostess remarked to him that Bressanges was Tounellier's wife, Piat said that she certainly was not, and that she was estranged from her actual husband. On hearing this the hostess and Piat locked the adulterous pair in two separate bedrooms and went 'that instant' in search of one of Molières's consuls.[44] All this salacious detail—the audacity of the couple pretending to be married, the dismal moment of being recognized by a fellow Montalbanais, the ignominy of being locked in two rooms to await the consuls—came to the consistory in Montauban via Benacontry's wife's gossip.

Beyond denunciation, women's gossip could also mobilize them into action. In May 1588, perhaps in response to the recent compilation of a list of prostitutes in the town and the preaching against 'whoring' from the pulpit, a group of neighbourhood women led by the wife of Guillaume des Arènes and her neighbour Marguerite gathered outside Vidal Raymond's house. Raymond was a maker of packsaddles living in the Arènes, the Roman amphitheatre in Nîmes that had been converted into dwellings. He was possibly a widower, as he is recorded as the father of the new-born daughter to mother Louise Gignand in the baptismal registers in January 1582, but no further children appear to have been born.[45] Judging by the geographical surname, these women were his neighbours. They beat their fists on the door and cried out to Raymond to let them in, saying that they knew he kept a woman inside. Raymond denied that but refused to open the door, so the women forced an entry and found a woman trying to hide herself beneath a pile of straw.[46] They called her a 'whore' and chased her out. In late June Marguerite and Guillaume des Arènes's wife then went on to report the matter to an elder, and weaver Pierre Botelhe, who lived near by, was called to report what he had seen.[47] There was obviously a strong sense of the power and virtue in the female collective and their prerogative to watch over and regulate the sexual behaviour of others by their words and, if necessary, their deeds.

It was not entirely unknown to have gossip spread by men. In May 1595 a cobbler called Pierre Branque told the consistory that three men and four women—Daniel Trapas, Pierre Vezi, David Breil, Anthoinete Tachiere, Marquize de Bructe, Marie

---

[44] ADTG, I 1, 61v–62r.   [45] ADG, E Dépôt 36/696, 188r, Jan. 1582.
[46] ADG, 42 J 29, 19, 21, 27–9, 32–3, 25 May 1588 (this is the date on which the case first appeared in the records; Botelhe testified that the event had happened in May, though he could not remember the exact date); Philippe Chareyre, ' "The Great Difficulties One Must Bear to Follow Jesus Christ": Morality at Sixteenth-Century Nîmes', in *Sin and the Calvinists: Morals Control and the Consistory in the Reformed Tradition*, ed. Raymond A. Mentzer (Kirksville, MO, 1994) 75.
[47] ADG, 42 J 29, 27–8.

de Malras, and Marie de Gineste—had been dancing together, and that Trapas and a woman called Depetit had been having an affair—but the consistory found Branque to have invented it all because of his malice towards Trapas, and rigorously censured Branque for his deceit.[48] It is not clear whether Branque had been gossiping about the alleged immorality, or simply reported his calumny to the consistory. This single case does little, however, to detract from the conclusion that most cases of gossip before the consistories of southern France involved women.

Gossip easily upset the delicate balance of honour and credit that ensured a person's standing in the community, and the consequences of slander could be severe. Yet the consistory endorsed women's cathartic and, at times, malicious, behaviour. Such dependence on the nosiness of others can only have legitimized and encouraged prurient behaviour, while ironically making the all-male, patriarchal consistory reliant on the 'idle chatter' of women.

INSULTS

Women's insults were inventive. In the registers for 1560 to 1615, women were called—mostly by other women—a recorded forty-one different names that can be approximately translated:

arliquyne	inconsequential person
avoir menti	liar
bagasse	baggage, slut, flirt
botefeur	(probably meaning) 'puffed-up'
camuse	flat-nosed
charoupper	good-for-nothing
coquina	loose woman, strumpet
diable	devil
embriague	drunkard
fachilliere	witch, sorceress
gourmande	glutton
ladre	leper/leprous
larrone	thief
malvivante	loose-living
maneffle	toady, flatterer
mange galimes	glutton
masque	witch
meurtriere	murderer
mort de fain	half-starved
paillarde	slut
pezollouer	lice-ridden
pisse au lit	bed-wetter
poisonnieyre	poisoner
puce	flea
putain	whore, prostitute
putain de foire	shitty/diarrhoeic whore

[48] ADTG, I 1, 3r–v, 31 May 1595.

putain maquerelle	bawd for whores
pute	whore, prostitute
putina	whore, prostitute
reballade	slut, whore, prostitute
roisgue cambajon	pork-eater
sac de vin	drunkard; literally, bag of wine
saume	she-ass
soire	old female dog, bitch
sorcyere	sorceress
sotte bauge	wallowing fool, drunk
trainee	slut, whore, prostitute
transportade	slave, convict, criminal
villaine	ugly, wicked
yvre	drunkard
yvrogne	drunkard

Many of these were delivered in dialect—in regional variations of Occitan—and so provide us with an untranslated echo of the words of the street. Listening to these insults we are transported into the heart of women's personal relationships and altercations. Such personal abuse, and the context in which each insult was delivered, show us how foul-mouthed and judgemental women could be, and also how they—and, to a lesser extent, men—assessed female identity and integrity. Above all, it provides a way of unpacking the very notions of gender—of sexual difference—that lay at the root of all these denigrations.

Publicly voiced insults breached the peace of the community, shocked public sensibilities, could ruin reputations, and frequently transgressed commonly held notions of respect and deference.[49] Accusations of slander and reports of insults therefore litter the registers. The reports of invective before the southern French consistories indicate that the majority of insults used against women were sexually dishonouring.[50] For seventeenth-century New England, Mary-Beth Norton noted that women were the target of sexual slander, took sexual slanders seriously, and were more often defamed by men than by other women.[51] For London in 1570–1640, Laura Gowing found that three-quarters of defamation cases were brought by women, and nearly half entirely involved women.[52] In Languedoc sexual insults were directed primarily at women but, unlike New England, women frequently insulted each other, as Jacques Solé and Nicole Castan also found for fifteenth- and eighteenth-century France.[53] Gowing points out that the use of 'whore' in sixteenth-century England indicates women's internalization of the prevalent notion of female unchastity, and in Languedoc too the preferred way to insult a woman, even

[49] Roger Thompson, '"Holy Watchfulness" and Communal Conformism: The Functions of Defamation in Early New England Communities', *New England Quarterly* 56.4 (1983), 504–22.
[50] Sharpe, *Defamation*, 15; Ingram, *Church Courts*, ch. 10; Gowing, *Domestic Dangers*, chs 3–4; Mary Beth Norton, 'Gender and Defamation in Seventeenth-Century Maryland', *William and Mary Quarterly* 44.1 (1987), 3–39; Thompson, 'Holy Watchfulness'.
[51] Norton, 'Gender', 10.
[52] Laura Gowing, 'Gender and the Language of Insult in Early Modern England', *History Workshop Journal* 35, 1–21, here 2.
[53] Solé, *Etre femme*, 148–51; Castan, 'Les femmes', 83.

by another woman, centred on sexual impurity, with instances of the term *putain* outnumbering all other recorded insults.[54] Many seemingly innocuous insults also had sexual connotations. Such insults proffered by women had an inherently comparative claim: by calling another woman a whore, the accuser asserted her own respectability.[55]

Putain—meaning whore or prostitute—was a deeply offensive idiom that served as a discrediting form of abuse in a wide range of circumstances. Even when not used in the context of directly accusing sexual misconduct, it was feared to have such implications. Anne Vallate, wife of Mathieu Corbet, was overheard by witness Estienne Paris calling Olivier Latuelle's wife a *putain*. When called to account for the offensive slander, Vallate said that she did not remember calling her a *putain* but did call her *maneffle*—an Occitan insult meaning 'toady, flatterer, sycophant'— for 'inciting her brother to do his worst' in a civil suit that he had against Vallate. Latuelle's wife maintained that Vallate had called her a *putain* and Paris said he had heard her; Paris also added that Vallate had said, in Occitan, 'the devil appears to her'.[56] Latuelle's wife had squared up to Vallate at this and asked her of whom she was speaking, and Vallate had retorted, 'I'm speaking to you'. This gives us the beginnings of a taxonomy of insults: 'toady' or 'flatterer' was relatively mild, the suggestion that Latuelle's wife entertained the devil was a real slight, but it was *putain* that was the most greatly defaming insult—enough to involve the consistory. The latter insult was, in fact, disturbing enough for Latuelle himself to arrive unbidden before the consistory to explain that his wife had been pregnant since 'three weeks before the last Madeleine'—so since early July 1580, making her eight months pregnant—when they had had 'carnal conversation' with each other; she was, he was maintaining, pregnant by her own husband, and in no way a whore. Vallate had not mentioned any specific sexual behaviour in her accusations against Latuelle's wife, but the insult *putain* was potentially so damaging to a woman's honour that, for fear the mud would stick, Lateulle quickly sought to wash it away. Even the consistory seems to have thought this was unnecessary, as Latuelle's testimony is crossed through in the register.

The link between the insult and sexual conduct could appear relatively tenuous, as shown by examples from all over Languedoc in which *putain* was deployed as non-specific, go-to invective. In Nîmes in October 1562 Maurice Faulquete, wife of a husbandman, confessed that she had called Catholic Jeanne Buingere *putain*. The consistory arranged for the women to be reconciled.[57] The widows of Seranguere and Bernard Belgon appeared before the Pont-de-Camarès consistory in April 1588 after Belgon's widow publicly called the other *putain*. They shook hands to make up.[58] Four women in Montauban in September 1595—Peyronne Maurugue, Marie de Marty, Marthe de Vincener, and Matile de Barthalot—angrily called one another *putains*. They subsequently extended their hands to one another in friendship and

[54] Gowing, *Domestic Dangers*, 1.   [55] Gowing, *Domestic Dangers*, 87.
[56] BN, Ms.fr. 8667, 189r–190r, 17 Mar. 1581; 'lo[u] *diable se [e]la presente*'.
[57] BN, Ms.fr. 8666, 162v, 9 Oct. 1562.   [58] BN, Ars.Ms. 10434, 126r, 7 Apr. 1588.

the matter was settled.[59] In April 1600, in Ganges, Anthoinette Curieyres and Marie Teule insulted each other, each calling the other *putain*, but they were reconciled before the consistory.[60] Women even used the term *putain* to insult their female relatives: in 1581 Couroural's wife was summoned for having called her mother a *putain*, and Jehan Goubin's widow was called five or six times for having said the same of her mother-in-law.[61] In each case, the spat was mild enough for it to be quickly resolved, and reports of substantiating illicit sexual activity were not offered to the consistorial officials, although in each case *putain* was the first and most powerful insult that came to mind.[62]

When women picked their preferred insult to use against another woman, they chose *putain*—for even when sexual slander was not apparently sexual, it nevertheless retained an important potential for ambiguity. As a result, *putain* was never taken lightly by those so labelled, and women regularly appealed to the consistory to contest the slur on their character. In March 1581 Marguerite Blanche approached the consistory in Nîmes to complain that Donne Mingaude had called her *putain* when she had asked Mingaude for her chicken back. Blanche had retorted that Mingaude was *yvrogne*—drunk—and subsequently repented this and said she did not want any bad blood between them: her appearance was as much to clear herself from the accusation as to report her slanderer.[63] Similarly, Marguerite Gautiere presented herself at the Montauban consistory in November 1595 to complain that Matile de Barthalot had called her a *putain*. Barthalot had form, having only two months earlier been in the argument above with three other women.[64] For her, and for many women, the term was in common currency—the most convenient abuse to deploy when angered by another woman. This is significant but should not mean that we conclude, as in Gowing's English research, that sexual insult was only obliquely related to sex. That the gravest and yet most ubiquitous insult for a woman to use against another woman was one that attacked female integrity through implying sexual dishonesty indicated that women primarily evaluated female worth and honour by how they disposed of their bodies. This was a patriarchal idea that the women of sixteenth-century France had fully internalized. Women aligned themselves with the persecutor and persecuted other women on the shameful grounds on which they most feared attack. It is no surprise to find that it was also occasionally used by men against women without providing justification, as when Isaaq Jany called Susanne Montolle a *putain* in Ganges in 1596—but such cases seem to be less common than its generic usage among women.[65]

The power of the term *putain* came from the fact that what it connoted was open to more than one interpretation: it could be general invective or a specific reference to sexually immoral behaviour, and for every use of it as a stock insult, there is another in which it was intended to draw attention to illicit conduct. In this

[59] ADTG, I 1, 38r, 1 Sept. 1588.   [60] ADH, GG 24, 121r, 6 Apr. 1600.

[61] BN, Ms.fr. 8667, 206r, 19 Apr. 1581; BN, Ms.fr. 8667, 210r, 213v, 3 May 1581.

[62] An additional case involves the widow of Jacques Brun Moier and Cotias's wife: BN, Ms.fr. 8667, 7v, 16 May 1578.

[63] BN, Ms.fr. 8667, 195r, 24 Mar. 1581.   [64] ADG, I 1, 66v, 10 Nov. 1595.

[65] ADH, GG 25, 68r–v, 29 Aug. 1596.

way, the use of the term also reflected the profound interest in, and regulation of, the sexual behaviour of others seen in the upholding of community standards with gossip. Marguerite Doumergue and her neighbour Ane Reboulle were summoned to the consistory because Doumergue had called Reboulle a *putain*, and substantiated this by adding that Reboulle had given birth to a bastard child and continually entertained young male servants at her house at night.[66] The wife of surgeon M. Goudin accused Susanne Faveyrolesse of being a *putain* in front of other people, and was entirely unrepentant about it when it came to the consistory's attention. Goudin's wife insisted that 'this fact is extremely true', and that she had reason to say it because Faveyrolesse had given birth to an illegitimate child. This defence was sufficient to persuade the consistory to investigate the 'life and conversation' of Faveyrolesse, taking their lead from Goudin's wife about which witnesses to call.[67] The insult had had its intended effect. It is possible that consul and merchant Jehan Surian intended a similar result when in 1587 before three witnesses he called the wife of M. Chamborigaud a *putain* because she 'ordinarily goes to Colias'. The implications of this allegation are now lost, but it was sufficiently defamatory for Chamborigaud and his wife to consider Surian's words to have 'touched her honour' and to have stirred them to great animosity towards him.[68] Surian had been a town councillor in Nîmes in 1584 and 1585, would be again in 1588, and was third consul in 1587, meaning that he was a person of some standing whose words had power.[69]

The term was also used to regulate sexual behaviour within families. Marguerite Gaudete threw her daughter, Magdaleine Maryonne, out of her house and called her a *putain*, because Maryonne had threatened to bring a man home to sleep.[70] In Ganges in April 1600 Jehan de Tieure called his niece and namesake, Jehanne del Tieura, a *putain maquerelle*—a bawd for prostitutes—for allegedly housing a 'whore' in her house.[71] When faced with genuine grounds for fears of sexual impropriety, Languedocians did not hesitate to use the pyrotechnic term towards their own kin.

Whether the use of *putain* was meant to be reflective of reality, and whether it was intended to be controlling of it, it shaped the way that women's nature was understood. Sexual honesty was a woman's Achilles heel. Any defect could be understood through the prism of a woman's failure to control her body, and such thinking created a way of understanding sexual difference and condemning women further to such ongoing judgement. In 1602 Pierre Tinelly complained that Mademoiselle de Vachières had accused his wife Anne Nouvelle of being *une putain de foire*—a diarrhoeic, shitty whore—while Mlle de Vachières's father, Sieur de Vachières, had called Tinelly *couquin*, *bellitre*, and *feneant*—a knave, a good-for-nothing cad, and an idle do-nothing.[72] The difference of magnitude between the insults directed at a woman and those directed at a man is striking: those against the

---

[66] ADG, 42 J 31, 58v, 17 Apr. 1596.   [67] ADG, 42 J 31, 60v, 18 Apr. 1596.
[68] ADG, 42 J 28, 272r, 273r–v, 8 Apr. 1587.
[69] ADG, E dépôt 36/130, 201r; E dépôt 36/130, 263v; E dépôt 36/131, 33r; E dépôt 36/131, 78v.
[70] ADG, 42 J 30, 360v, 17 May 1595.   [71] ADH, GG 24, 122v, 30 Apr. 1600.
[72] ADG, 42 J 32, 74v, 10 Jul. 1602.

man suggested he was a worthless layabout, but those against the woman suggested shameful incontinence in every way. Vachières's defence was that Nouvelle had been the first to defame, calling his daughter a *villaine provensalle dou diable*—a ugly, wicked Provençal from the devil—an insult that attacked character and focused on foreignness—and an *arliquyne*, an inconsequential person. Mlle de Vachières maintained that she was 'a good and honourable woman, without stain', and so these calumnies had roused her to deliver the bruising slurs against Nouvelle. Two witnesses—women called Mademoiselle de Chambrun and Pellonnye— suggested that she had even gone further. They reported that a Provençale girl had told them that Mlle de Vachières had said that 'if she [Nouvelle] did not look out, her father would take his pleasure with Tinelly's old bitch'.[73] To call someone a whore was to start to think of her as someone who could be—who was, in fact, willing to be—abused.

The insult *putain* was often coupled or exchanged with an allegation of alcoholism. Gillie Michelle called Catherine Fabresse *putain* in June 1593; Fabresse brought the case to the consistory to complain that the insult was offered without provocation, at which Michelle confessed that she had also called Fabresse a drunk.[74] Both were ways of indicating a lack of control and could therefore almost be interchangeable. This was explicitly voiced when Madaleyne Peladane said her sister-in-law, Saumete Audrine, was an alcoholic who was pregnant by someone other than her husband. Peladane had been quarrelling with her husband: he had called her a drunk, and she had retorted 'it was his sister who is a drunk, because drunks are whores'. She added that she had heard it said—by a woman called Donne Marye—that Audrine was pregnant by Monsieur Saurin.[75] There was a causality between the states—being out of control in one way led to a lack of control in the other—and therefore there was almost an equivalence between the insults 'drunk' and 'whore'. In fact, it is possible that *ivrogne* and its variants were just coded ways of accusing a woman of sexual misconduct, or of emphasizing her likely descent into it.

The drunken, whoring woman who failed to control her appetites could also be characterized as animalistic and greedy. In July 1562 the wives of Jehan Pages and Estienne Alies were summoned to the consistory in Nîmes for calling each other *putains*. Pages's wife confessed to also having called the other woman '*saulme et yvrongne*'—a she-ass and a drunk—and of being '*botefeur*', the latter likely to be from the Occitan *botenflar* meaning 'to be puffed up'.[76] Pages's wife was alleging that Alies's wife's whoredom meant she was brutishly out of control and full of herself. In 1599 Susanne Moutolle called Marguerite Ferrigue a '*sotte bauge*'—a wallowing drunk; *bauge* (wallow) was normally used of pigs and wild boars.[77] Merchant's wife Marguerite Valette complained that her daughter-in-law, Madame de Poinet, daily called her '*putain, fachilliere*'—whore, witch—and other insults. It soon emerged, however, that the real culprit here was Valette herself, who had called Poinet '*putain,*

---

[73] '*son pere auroit jouy de la soire de Tinelly*'.   [74] ADG, 42 J 30, 197v, 5 Jun. 1593.
[75] ADG, 42 J 28, 119r, 15 Aug. 1584.
[76] BN, Ms.fr. 8666, 144v, 18 Jul. 1562. *Botenflar, bodenflar, bodenfle*, often used transitively, *se bodenflar*.
[77] ADH, GG 24, 110v, 8 Aug. 1589. *Sotte* can mean fool, but here is most likely to mean drunk.

yvre, gourmande'—whore, drunk, glutton—and, before the consistory, refused to apologize, saying that Poinet was 'nothing but a glutton, and that she had seen her drunk several times'.[78] Here the image of the unbridled woman extended to her over-consumption of food.[79] In September 1599 Claude Cafarelle complained that Yves Mercier had described her as a glutton and a drunk and Sieur Pol had called her a drunk, a *coquina* (a loose woman), and a *putina* (another variant of whore).[80] Cafarelle had retorted that Mercier was a *fripon* (a rascal or rogue). Here we see the yardstick by which to measure the weakness of woman: unable to curb her bodily appetites, she would be reduced to promiscuity. Finally, drunkenness was also associated with villainy. Marguerite Blanche and Marguerite Lausiere had fallen out over a chicken that Lausiere thought Blanche had stolen. Lausiere called Blanche a *sac de vin* and a *villanie*—an ugly, wicked drunkard—literally a bag of wine.[81]

If *putain* was by far the most common insult, and drunkenness carried connotations of lewdness, there were, nevertheless, a range of other terms by which women could be denigrated sexually, many of which were synonyms for *putain*. The term *soire*—used of Tinelly's wife, above—meant old female dog, or bitch. In Ganges in 1602 Janice Barre complained that Jacques Raudon had called her *soire putain* and *pis que soire*—a whore bitch and worse than a bitch. The consistory recognized the severity of the insults and censured Raudon for 'having so little care about Barre's honour'.[82]

Reballade meant slut, whore, or prostitute. A month after her fight with the wife of Jehan Pages, the wife of Estienne Alies was summoned for quarrelling with the wife of Maurice Gentil. According to Gentil's wife, Alies's wife had called Maurice Gentil a thief and a *banard*—a convict—so Gentil's wife had replied that she should '*tire lou bequet*'—pull the beak—a charmingly coarse expression for 'be quiet'. Alies's wife retorted by calling her *putain*, *puce* (flea), *pute* (a short form of *putain*), and *reballade*.[83] Alies's wife's defence was that Gentil's wife had told her to shut up, but had also called her a drunk, and that slur was sufficient to generate the stream of sexually defaming invective with which she responded. *Reballade* was recorded on at least two other occasions. The widow Marguerite Euziere complained in 1587 that Sire Bertrand had defamed her with the words '*putain villaine reballade*' because she had persuaded Bertrand's son to marry against his wishes, ostensibly by refusing to pay back money lent to her late husband.[84] There was obviously a complex story behind this of which the consistory only received a glimpse, but Bertrand's abuse struck right to the quick, while Euziere's against him—she called him a banished thief—was dishonouring, but comparatively less offensive. *Reballade* was also used in 1602, when Magdalene Vernede and Claude Manouelle fell out in

[78] ADTG, I 1, 250r, 23 Apr. 1597.
[79] See also ADH, GG 24, 70r, 13 Oct. 1596, when Anne Marcialle complained that Marguerite de la Fabrique and her daughter, Anthonie Olivete, called her *mange galimes and mange gen*, somewhat obscure insults that seem to suggest gluttony, although they may also draw on the Occitan *galimand*, meaning rascal, knave.
[80] ADG, 42 J 31, 298r–v, 301, 25 Aug. 1599.   [81] BN, Ms.fr. 8667, 202v, 17 Apr. 1581.
[82] ADH, GG 24, 131r, 15 Aug. 1602.   [83] BN, Ms.fr. 8666, 154r, 26 Aug. 1562.
[84] ADG, 42 J 28, 307r, 2 Sept. 1587.

162   *The Voices of Nîmes*

Nîmes. According to Vernede, Manouelle called her *yvronnie*—drunk—and said that it was her own fault her two children had died. Manouelle admitted only saying Vernede was a drunk, but that Vernede had called her *putain* and *villaine reballade*— ugly or wicked slut.[85] Manouelle's suggestion that Vernede was responsible for the deaths of her children was so bruising that it produced the most fearsome slurs that Vernede could think of, and, unsurprisingly, they focused on sexual availability.

Other all-female quarrels add to the number of sexual insults in our lexicon. The wife of cobbler Pierre Legau appeared before the Nîmes consistory in 1578 to complain that the wife of Louis Clovis had called her *bagasse*, *soyre*, and *putain ivrogne*, and said she always went to sleep elsewhere.[86] *Bagasse*, like the contemporary Elizabethan word 'baggage', meant slut, flirt, strumpet, and, ultimately, prostitute. In 1590 an argument erupted among three women—Captain Victour's wife and daughter, and the wife of Charles Aleaume—after Aleaume's wife called Victour's daughter a 'camp prostitute'—*traynee au camp*—because the girl had been a prisoner of the Catholic army, encamped at Caissargues for three weeks. Victour's daughter's retort—that Aleaume's wife was a sorceress and a *putain*—conveys the weight of this defamation.[87]

Yet if *putain*, *pute*, *putina*, *soyre*, *traynee*, *reballade*, *bagasse*, and possibly even *ivrogne*, *yvre*, and other terms for drunkenness all imputed sexual dishonour, there were also more oblique ways of conveying the same message. An intricate story from Nîmes in the winter of 1589 indicates one. The wife of the Provost, known by her nickname of *La Renière*, and her friend, Mademoiselle de Moinier, were passing in front of the house of Anne Grisotte and her husband, Sire Cotellery, when the married couple attacked La Renière with 'infinitely offensive' words, calling her *charoupper* (good-for-nothing), *camuze* (flat-nosed), and 'Broquier's *putain*'.[88] They added that 'she must be very sorry about Broquier's death, and they would send her back to Lyon to find the men she fornicated with'. When called before the consistory, Cotellery admitted that he had been angry because La Renière had cast suspicion on his wife—Grisotte had been interrogated a week earlier about her alleged adultery with the Provost and another man—and had remonstrated with La Renière. La Renière had called him a '*sot*'—a fool or a drunk—and he replied, 'the fools are at Lyon' (her hometown), and that she had 'lost a good friend' since Captain Broquier had died. Grisotte confessed that she had called La Renière *camuze* but denied the other insults. Even *camuze* or *camuse* alone is, however, likely have been sexually insulting. Insults in English included 'flat-nosed whore' or 'saddle-nosed whore', and suspected whores were threatened with having their noses slit.[89] To call La Renière flat-nosed was, therefore, to imply her adultery, as was the suggestion that she had been good friends with Broquier, and that her hometown was full of drunken fools. Inflamed by the sexual suspicion cast on Grisotte, both she and her husband had responded to La Renière with similarly

[85] ADG, 42 J 32, 45v, 22 May 1602.   [86] ADG, 42 J 27, 30v, 13 Aug. 1578.
[87] ADG, 42 J 29, 477, 28 Aug. 1590.
[88] ADG, 42 J 29, 314, 13 Dec. 1589; it may not be irrelevant that *La Renière* means The Denier—she may have been in denial about her husband's adultery.
[89] Gowing, 'Gender', 10.

sexually charged allegations. There is an instructive parallel with a case from London in 1579, when a wife and her adulterous husband united to attack the woman with whom he had committed adultery, yelling insults at her as she walked by.[90] In the Nîmes incident, however, it was the wife who was allegedly adulterous, and she and her husband attacked her alleged lover's wife, in so doing deflecting, denying through attack, and turning the allegations on their head. The consistory understood this: in the aftermath, they chastized Cotellery for not keeping watch over his wife, and for not guarding 'not only against evil, but the appearance of evil'.

Another oblique way of alleging sexual disgrace was to focus—as the insult *putain de foire* had done—on incontinence. The quarrel between Madame de Cavaignac and Madame de Brélie in Montauban in 1596 centred on Cavaignac's assertion that Brélie's daughter, who was on the point of marriage, could not control her urination. Brélie responded by calling Cavaignac a '*putain* from Salitot' (a hamlet near Montauban) and challenged her that if she had something to say to her she should say it directly and not disparage her daughter. Defiantly and maliciously, Cavaignac repeated before the consistory her assertion that Brélie's daughter 'wets the bed every night', inciting Brélie to a stream of insults, including 'whore' and 'drunk', and several others that the scribe noted 'for honour are not to be written'.[91] Although Brélie's use of the ubiquitous *putain* was the most obviously sexual, she was responding to a derogatory suggestion that was in fact sexually dishonouring, because wetting the bed carried notions of both immaturity and a lack of control. It is likely that the allegation that someone wet the bed was also in itself an idiomatic insult. Magdalene Blanche complained to the consistory in Nîmes in July 1597 that Jacques Corrazie had hung a placard on the door of her house that defamed her daughter, Marie Auriole, calling her 'drunk, *roisgue cambajon* (pork-eater), *pisse au lit* (bed-wetter)'.[92] He confessed that he had done this because Auriole had called him *petague*, which seems to derive either from the Occitan *petat*—to be sloshed, plastered—or *petega*, meaning panic-stricken; he was being called either a drunk or a coward (or even, simply, flatulent—from *pet*, meaning 'a fart'). It was his obscenity, however, that was considered so defamatory that to 'repair...the honour' of Blanche and her daughter, and to set an example for others, he was publicly suspended from the sacrament. All the insults dishonoured with their implications of an ungoverned body, but the last slur was the worst.

Another sexual insult was used when Pierre Pue's wife said that a woman Gratiane had called her *pezollouer*.[93] This—from *pezouille*, *pesoulh*, *pou*—means ridden with (pubic) lice or crabs, and so was an inherently sexual denigration implying that Pue's wife had become diseased by being promiscuous. This association with dirt and disease, although common in the contemporary English litany of sexual obscenities, is rare in the Languedocian evidence.[94] *Putain* and its variants may

---

[90] Gowing, 'Gender', 7–8.   [91] ADTG, I 1, 129r, 130v, 12 Apr. 1596.
[92] ADG, 42 J 31, 180v, 23 May 1597. The Occitan for 'to eat' is *ròisser or ròguer; cambajon* is Occitan for ham.
[93] BN, Ms.fr. 8666, 124r, 22 May 1562.   [94] Gowing, 'Gender', 13.

have been the most popular obscenities to use against a woman, but there was a host of others—*soire, reballade, trainee, paillarde, bagasse, camuse, malvivante, pisse au lit, pezoullouer*—that would serve the same purpose.

Sexual jealousy and defamation could also be conveyed without resorting to the stock insults. In 1614 Jeanne Chastelane complained that Sir Jacques Rolland's wife had defamed her at the annual Saint Madeleine fair at Beaucaire. Chastelane said that in the presence of her husband and several others Rolland's wife had addressed a man called Pellet with the words, 'Pellet, here's your daughter', pointing to Chastelane's 5-year-old child.[95] This scandalous insinuation, made by the wife of an elder in the church, and therefore someone whose word had considerable weight, derived strength from its public airing, testifying anew to the dangerous power of words and the potential fragility of reputations. In recognition of this, Rolland's wife denied having said it, claiming that she had in fact said 'Pellet, there's your wife', and that she considered Chastelane a 'a good woman, of honour, and above reproach'. To remove any remaining hint of disgrace, the consistory required her to declare her disavowal in the presence of Chastelane's husband and confirm that she had never heard any rumour about the child's paternity. The quarrel between Sire Pol Delicat's wife and her niece Marguerite Pinette arose from the similarly public intimation by Delicat's wife that the '*malvivante*' (loose-living) Pinette was 'the reason that she [Delicat's wife] is fighting with her husband', thereby implying a sexual relationship between her niece and her husband.[96] This accusation, which bears a resemblance to the contemporary English insult 'my husband's whore', is unusual in the French records, and constituted a seriously damaging claim.[97]

There were a few other possible epithets for women beyond those that were sexually charged. One group related to the practice of witchcraft. We have already seen a reference to the devil and the use of *fachellière*, the Occitan for 'witch'. In a similar vein, in September 1590 in Nîmes, the wives of Sanyet Fornier and Daniel Roche called each other *putains et sorcyeres*—sorceresses—before being reconciled.[98] Women also accused each other of theft. Marguerite Advocate complained that Catherine Plane had called her '*larrone*' (thief), and Plane that Advocate labelled her a drunk.[99] As with *putain*, *larrone* was potent vitriol because it intimated questionable behaviour. The quarrel between widow Donne Cordilhesse and Pierre Anthoine's wife in 1581 was initiated by Cordilhesse's complaint that Anthoine's wife had robbed her of ten *sols*, an accusation that prompted strong retaliatory insults from Anthoine and his spouse.[100] Theft, too, could be tied to sexually defamatory insults, like those exchanged in a quarrel between Jehan Jacques's wife and Anthoine Martin's widow, when Martin's widow complained that Jacques's wife had called her a thief, adding 'that she knows (is familiar with) *écus*'.[101] The insinuation here was probably that Martin's widow received money for sexual intercourse, and it is unsurprising, therefore, that the widow responded with the

---

95 ADG, 42 J 35, 100r, 13 Aug. 1614.　　96 ADG, 42 J 33, 95r.
97 Gowing, *Domestic Dangers*, 112.　　98 ADG, 42 J 29, 489, 7 Sept. 1590.
99 BN, Ms.fr. 8667, 244v, 28 Sept. 1581.　　100 BN, Ms.fr. 8667, 158v, 4 Jan. 1581.
101 BN, Ms.fr. 8667, 223v, 28 Jun. 1581.

sexually insulting claim that Jacques was 'jealous'—in other words, that his wife gave him reason to be.

Finally, women accused other women of criminal and even murderous behaviour. In June 1589 M. Bonnet's wife complained that she had been defamed by Loys Payan's wife (known as *Payane*), who had called her a *meustriere* (murderer) in the middle of the street. Payane explained that she had called Bonnet's wife a murderer because Bonnet's wife had hit her and, later that day, Payane 'had taken herself to bed in panic because of the fruit that she had in her stomach'—she was pregnant and feared that her opponent's blow might cause a miscarriage.[102] Françoise Tartyrane presented herself at the consistory in Ganges in 1598 to complain that, without cause, Astrugue Blaqueyre had called her a *transportade* (slave, convict, criminal), a *meurtriere* (murderer), and a *poisonnieyre* (poisoner), who had 'killed her own sister'.[103]

As Jacques Quet told his mother-in-law, Jane Fage in 1596, 'insults stole honour'—they marred reputations.[104] The fact of being publicly insulted was dishonouring in itself, and cases came to the consistory because defending one's honour against these slurs mattered. Obscenities against women related above all to their sexuality. Not only were sexual insults about sex, in fact nearly all insults seem to have been about sex. The vast majority of insults used against women— normally by other women—were variants of the term *putain* or whore, or focused on some related aspect of sexual incontinence. Insults against men insulted their intelligence, their character, or their ability to offer worth, but they were determinedly non-sexual and comparatively mild. Men's and women's insults against women followed the same logic, because women's insults against other women demonstrated a tendency to internalize the aggressor: they attacked other women's capacity to arouse sexual feelings and reframed that ability to attract as an insult. This was done to take back control over that which shamed them, and they denigrated all evidence of a lack of control—incontinence in various forms, sexual availability, over-consumption—as a way of denying their own weakness and dependency. They also dehumanized other women—using animalistic insults such as bitch or she-ass—and made contrasts with civilized beings in control of their passions and desires. In insulting each other, women aligned themselves with their persecutors, and their insults were accordingly vicious. In so doing they perpetuated the idea that women were weak because of their lack of control, especially over their bodies, and continually constructed and reconstructed gender through their discourse.

DISPUTES

Unavoidably, the picture of social relations represented in the consistorial registers is skewed towards moments of social breakdown, but the evidence nonetheless suggests that sixteenth- and seventeenth-century Languedoc was a disputatious society.

[102] ADG, 42 J 29, 201, 7 Jun. 1589.   [103] ADH, GG 24, 89v, 90, 6 Aug. 1598.
[104] ADG, 42 J 31, 72v.

Visceral disagreements between women, and between women and men, were far from uncommon. The evidence from the consistories suggests that the full extent of this has not been known before now, and that these records capture information about ordinary life that other sources do not, casting light on subjects that have received little attention from scholars. Female physical violence has been treated as rare: Stuart Carroll's otherwise excellent study of violence in France barely mentions female violence, while Robert Muchembled concludes that 'women were very rarely aggressors or victims of interpersonal violence', either vicious verbal exchange or physical assault.[105] Davis too notes how few women were prosecuted for violent crimes (beyond infanticide and witchcraft), and suggests that women's anger was unacceptable in pardon tales (although her findings may indicate that certain parts of French society found women's ferocity unpalatable, rather than indicating that it did not exist).[106] This contrasts with the findings from contemporary Rome and eighteenth-century France that women were quick to anger and aggressive—though their violence is described as tending to be more about 'noise and fury' than causing serious or fatal injury.[107] The testimony of the consistorial records suggests we need a different understanding of women's behaviour in sixteenth- and seventeenth-century France: women were vicious, physical, and aggressive, as well as the recipients of violence.[108] My findings are therefore the opposite of Muchembled's: women were often both aggressors and victims of violence.

In the registers it seems that women were commonly involved in violent argument and physical attack. There are numerous brief references across Languedoc to members of the consistory attempting to reconcile pairs or groups of women and men who were in 'great discord' or 'had differences' with each other, who 'complained against each other', or from whom was heard 'great noise and argument'. Such snapshots include Dame de Ploinhan and Dame de Delvarnée, who in Montauban in December 1595 were so vexed at each other that they refused to greet each other, or the dispute between Marie Panissières, Marie Delsone, and Pierre Compettre in the same month; Jehanne Broussonet and Jehanne Pine, who fell out in Pont-de-Camarès in May 1580; and the big family quarrel involving Claude Boetiere and her father in Nîmes in December 1587.[109] On cases such as these the registers have little information to offer, but these cursory allusions are valuable because they suggest that the fuller instances in the records are not aberrant, but merely the fullest expression of a world of disharmonious scenes, most of which probably never reached the consistory.

The lengthier cases offer insight not only into how women behaved, but into the causes of their actions. The pattern that emerges is of quotidian issues sparking

[105] Muchembled, *Société*, 67; Carroll, *Blood*, 244–6.   [106] Davis, *Fiction*, 81, 83, 102.

[107] Elizabeth S. Cohen, 'Honor and Gender in the Streets of Early Modern Rome', *Journal of Interdisciplinary History* (hereafter *JIH*) 22 (1992), 597–625, here 616, 623; Nicole Castan, 'Criminelle', in *Histoire des femmes en Occident*, vol. 3, *XVIe–XVIIIe siècles*, ed. Davis and Arlette Farge (Paris, 1991), 475; Y. Castan, *Honnêteté*, 172.

[108] Cohen, 'Honor', 616, 623; N. Castan, 'Criminelle', 475; Y. Castan, Honnêteté, 172.

[109] ADTG I 1, 81r, 13 Dec. 1595; ADTG I 1, 87v, 30 Dec. 1595; BN, Ars.Ms. 10434, 10v; ADG, 42 J 28, 339r, 16 Dec. 1587.

altercations with dishonouring insults, which then commonly erupted into an exchange of violence.

People fight over what matters to them, so the catalysts for arguments and fights tell us about women's internal worlds. Frequently such catalysts concerned transgressions of boundaries, notions of authority, attacks on reputation, and infringements of privacy and property. Violence involving women, then, reiterates the importance of authority and reputation in governing social interaction and neighbourly relations.

Fighting in Church

In examining women's fights, two categories of altercation quickly emerge: those that occurred in sacred spaces and those that occurred on profane, non-sacred ground. The former were chiefly perpetrated by women from the socially anxious classes of the provincial gentry and nobility, while street-fights tended to occur among women of the lower social ranks. Pew disputes were also—for reasons that are not entirely clear—a particular feature of the early seventeenth century.

Among women of status, the number of squabbles over seating arrangements on pews in the Reformed church or 'temple' is astonishingly high and provides enormous insight into the mentality of the quarrellers. These temple altercations are not surprising, as the church was one of the few places where women could acquire status in an obvious and highly visible way. Women were seated separately from men on benches and pews directly in front of the pulpit, in sight of the rest of the congregation. This made the contestation of places intensely public. Technically—unlike the places for men, which were assigned by rank—the placement of benches and pews within this space conveyed no inherent status, but in practice the position of pews was evidently thought to signify a woman's social standing.[110] Asserting and maintaining a claim to one's pew therefore became a crucial means of establishing and upholding female honour; the incessant squabbles over pews were really fights about social pre-eminence.[111]

Many of the references to pews in the consistorial registers were therefore petitions to the consistory, requesting admission to their 'list and tariff of pews', as the church strove to keep some semblance of order.[112] M. Vigier's widow asked the Nîmes consistory in 1604 for a place to put a pew in the temple, while Damoyselle de Falguerolles the elder—also a widow, presumably of former minister Claude de Falguerolles—requested a pew for herself and her daughters.[113] Possessing a pew conveyed prestige, and many thought they were entitled to it. Some of those who went without reacted with sulkiness: the wives of Sires de Boutille and de Beraud were summoned for absenting themselves from the sermons and Eucharist on the

---

[110] Raymond A., Mentzer, 'Les débats sur les bancs dans les Églises réformées de France', *BSHPF* 152 (2006), 403; Christian Grosse, 'Places of Sanctification: The Liturgical Sacrality of Genevan Reformed Churches, 1535–1566', in *Sacred Space in Early Modern Europe*, ed. Will Coster and Spicer (Cambridge, 2005), 78–9.

[111] Mentzer, 'Les débats', 393–406.   [112] e.g. ADG, 42 J 33, 21v, 12 Jan. 1605.

[113] ADG, 42 J 32, 254r, 15 Sept. 1604; 42 J 33, 9v, 22 Dec. 1604.

pretext of not having a pew.[114] Other appeals to the consistory focused on the right to make pews more elaborate and prestigious. Sire Combes's wife requested permission to put a *marchepied* (steps or a footboard) on her pew in December 1604, and was granted one three-quarters of the width of her pew.[115] At the same time, the consistory tried to adjudicate in cases where women had pews bigger than that granted to them in the list—accommodating, say, some three or four female relatives, instead of the two permitted.[116] In Montauban, the consistory noted in December 1595 that to stop the 'scandal committed in the temple' by women keeping places in the temple, they would speak to the consuls.[117] Yet, the issue was evidently not settled, as some years later they appealed again to the consuls 'to avoid the tumult and cries made in the temple at services on Sundays, because of the keeping of places'.[118] Pews were a constant place of anxiety about social status.

Such anxiety generated disputes in which piety and status were easily conflated. Nobleman Aulban Petit, Sieur de Boisset, complained in March 1613 that someone had evicted and replaced the pew belonging to his widowed daughter-in-law, Damoiselle Jeanne d'Audifret.[119] Petit argued that she deserved continued possession of the place because, firstly, the pew bore the marks and armorial bearings of his house; secondly, his daughter-in-law had paid money towards the wages of the pastors and towards the repair and construction of a new temple; and, thirdly, she owned two houses and three vineyards in Nîmes and its surrounding environs, denoting her status as a 'true native' of the city. In Petit's reading, wealth and piety were thought to purchase standing, and the family honour was ensured by following patterns of inheritance and nativity. As Carroll has suggested for Catholics in the same period, for Protestants too the church was the primary place in which to display social hierarchy and one's place in it—especially for women, whose possession of a pew and its placement in the church openly signalled their position on the scale of honour.[120]

As status-anxiety turned to envy and hostility, the consistory was drawn into the role of arbitrator of female quarrels. In trying to prove their purity and rank, women degenerated into impiety and spiteful vulgarity. In February 1596, Damoiselles d'Ariffon and Saint Estienne fell out over possession of a certain pew. Saint Estienne complained that Ariffon had called her a simpleton and her husband an imposter, which 'strongly touched their honour', and Ariffon said Saint Estienne had dishonoured her by calling her and her daughters quarrelsome and requiring them to bow to her.[121] Insults were not always sufficient in such disputes, however. The wife of M. Bongrand was summoned to the Nîmes consistory in August 1595 for having violently ousted a poor woman from her place in church.[122]

Such battles for honour could become extremely protracted. The case between Damoiselles Roberti and Ducros, mother and daughter, and Damoiselles de Laval de la Rosselle and Dumolin, also mother and daughter, is an example of an

---

[114] ADG, 42 J 33, 53r, 78r, 10 Aug. 1605.   [115] ADG, 42 J 33, 11r–12r, 29 Dec. 1604.
[116] ADG, 42 J 33, 9v, 11r, 20v, 22v, 22 Dec. 1604.   [117] ADTG, I 1, 82v, 20 Dec. 1595.
[118] ADTG, I 1, 333r, 21 Mar. 1598.   [119] ADG, 42 J 34, 419r, 4 Mar. 1613.
[120] Carroll, Blood, 73.   [121] ADG, 42 J 31, 37v, 50r, 28 Feb. 1596.
[122] ADG, 42 J 30, 381v, 2 Aug. 1595.

especially long-running pew dispute that escalated to open violence and, for a long time, ignored consistorial interventions. Roberti-Ducros had already clashed with two other parties for taking the place of their pews before it was brought to the consistory's attention in June 1603 that the two families were arguing because Rosselle-Dumolin did not want to obey a consistory ruling that the smaller of their two pews should be removed to make space for Roberti and Ducros. Two months later Rosselle-Dumolin were instructed that their smaller pew would again be removed and that of Roberti-Ducros put in its place. By late September—the battle still raging—the consistory again ordered that the Rosselle-Dumolin pew be replaced, noting that 'every time one removes it, it is put back', suggesting a precedence battle of almost farcical proportions, as the alternate pews were removed and replaced each Sunday.[123] As the dispute rumbled on it started to involve others. In June 1604, M. Tempel's wife reported that M. de la Coste's wife had moved Tempel's pew up close to the rostrum and put in its place Rosselle-Dumolin's ousted pew.[124] In August Catherine Mingaude appeared before the consistory to assert that her pew had previously been where Rosselle-Dumolin now put theirs. Her appeal fell on deaf ears, and she was instead reprimanded, because everyone had seen that she had sat on Rosselle-Dumolin's pew and when Dumolin's servant came to claim the pew, Mingaude had punched the servant-girl two or three times to make her relinquish it.[125] Presumably tired of these never-ending disputes, the consistory told Mingaude that Rosselle-Dumolin's pew would stay where it was, and that the list of the pews had been settled. Here we see the consistory attempting to bring the peace, and those directly affected bringing cases to the consistory for arbitration, in outrage at the perceived injustice and hungry to have their status recognized.[126]

Another major dispute broke out in April 1606 between Mademoiselles de Percet and Agullonet the latter the wife of a well-respected man who had repeatedly served as an elder. De Percet had been instructed to make space for Agullonet because her pew was large enough for four, but refused with a succession of excuses, saying that she and Agullonet were enemies, that she had a daughter who also sat with her, and that she would not leave her own pew because it belonged to her. In the circumstances, M. Agullonet insisted that his wife should have the place instead. A week later M. de Percet weighed in, objecting to the consistory's suggestion that his wife make space for Agullonet, 'who is in discord with his wife'. It was concluded that Agullonet would be put between Mlles de Vignolles and Dupin, and that the two of the places taken up by de Percet's pew be bestowed on Mlle de Fons. Rather than attempt to resolve the enmity between de Percet and Agullonet, the consistory unusually chose an easier route around the women's hostility. As luck would have it, a few months later de Percet returned

[123] ADG, 42 J 32, 174v–175r, 176v, 178v, 180r, 184v, 18 Jun. 1603.
[124] ADG, 42 J 32, 239v, 23 Jun. 1604.   [125] ADG, 42 J 32, 248r, 18 Aug. 1604.
[126] Andrew Pettegree and Raymond A. Mentzer concluded, in discussion at the Urban Life in Early Modern France Conference, Stratford-upon-Avon, 10 June 2006, that pew disputes were reported by social inferiors and consistory members, but evidently those directly involved could also report such events.

to complain that de Fons had used the consistorial ruling to justify ousting de Percet's pew and replacing it with her own, which 'entirely occupies her place'.[127] The petty jealousies and squabbles over pews abounded, making it clear that the vagaries of relative status needed to be fought for and defended, and the public arena of the temple provided the perfect location for women of rank to assert themselves.

Nor was fighting in church spaces confined to the pews. In December 1599 in Ganges Damoiselles de Bousquet and de la Baume were summoned for having squabbled and pushed each other as they queued to receive the Eucharist.[128] Such disrespect for the central Protestant rite—which required communal accord and unity, and before which participants were required to be reconciled with their neighbours—was shocking, and the case took several months to resolve. Ultimately, the consistory ordained that at the next Eucharist de Bousquet would go first, and at the next Eucharist after that de la Baume would go first, and so on consecutively. One's physical place in the queue for receiving Holy Communion had become so accepted a way of measuring societal honour that even the consistory bowed to the inevitable. As Carroll has concluded, churches 'were the best environment for impugning an enemy's honour' or for making a public challenge—but what he did not add was that this was especially true for women.[129]

Why Neighbours Fought

Impassioned, long-running, and occasionally violent as women's pew-disputes might have been, they are quickly dwarfed by the apparent frequency and vigour of quarrels and fights in the profane spaces of home and street, many of which had women as their protagonists. The cause of many of these disputes was simply neighbourhood proximity, which produced confined circumstances full of potential for resentment and bitterness to flourish. A typical quarrel arose in December 1562 between Gentile Arnassane, her mother, and her brother, and their neighbour, Anthoine Bordian, and his visitor, François Castaing.[130] Arnassane had a long-running injury, and described how, on this winter's evening as she sat close to the fire, she once again felt the familiar twinge in her leg, which was so painful that she could not help but cry out. Disturbed by her shout, a voice from Bordian's house—which adjoined hers—cried out to Arnassane's mother, 'hit her, beat her up, kill her'.[131] When questioned, Bordian blamed the outburst on his guest Castaing, adding that on hearing Arnassane's blasphemous outburst, Castaing had gone out into the road and started to insult Arnassane's brother. Castaing admitted this, but stated that Arnassane's brother had previously insulted him, calling him 'thief' and 'drunk'.[132] The genesis of this argument may therefore have been a more

---

[127] ADG, 42 J 33, 101v, 132v, 5 Apr. 1606.
[128] ADH, GG 24, 116v–117v, 119r, 119v, 26 Dec. 1599.   [129] Carroll, *Blood*, 68.
[130] BN, Ms.fr. 8666, 191v, 13 Dec. 1562.
[131] '*bat la, bourre bourre tue la*'—*bourrer* has the colloquial sense of 'to beat someone up, to get one's head bashed in'.
[132] BN, Ms.fr. 8666, 191v, 30 Dec. 1562.

long-standing state of hostility between Castaing and Arnassane's brother, but it was catalysed by intensely claustrophobic living arrangements, which meant both Arnassane's cries of pain and Castaing's shouts could be easily heard.

In a manner reminiscent of the catalogue of incidents that preceded an accusation of witchcraft—as demonstrated by Robin Briggs' research on the Lorraine trials—tension between neighbours could build up for a long time before flaring up into fights or denunciations.[133] In January 1593 a woman called Brunelle complained against her neighbour, Anthonye Royayes, saying that some three years previously Royayes had beaten and insulted her, and ever since had wanted to do her harm.[134] In this instance, the consistorial ceremony of embracing as a sign of reconciliation appears to have functioned to dissipate the hostility.

Disputes between neighbours resulted from the fact that such intimately lived lives often led to the transgression of boundaries. Marie Paniesse complained in June 1593 that her neighbour, Donne Saumete Gauffreze, had called her a *putain* and sent her son Pierre Chantozel round to beat her. According to Gauffreze, the reason was that Paniesse's male servant had lately complained that Paniesse beat him, and Gauffreze had told Paniesse that 'she who beat her servant was a whore'. Paniesse was asked whether she had responded by calling Gauffreze *putain* and 'an ugly, wicked, drunk, witch'—she admitted to '*embraigue*' (Occitan for 'drunk') and '*putain*', but explicitly denied 'witch'.[135] Chantozel said he had beaten Paniesse because she insulted his mother.

This litany of insults and the subsequent violence on Gauffreze's behalf stemmed from one central issue: the appropriate boundaries of spheres of authority. The debate over Paniesse's right to discipline her servant and Gauffreze's neighbourly right to interfere brought up the question of how much of life was open to public scrutiny and intervention, and how great an authority a housewife had over her household. In contrast to Hardwick's findings, which suggested that French neighbours were reluctant to intrude, Gauffreze assumed that it was her role to intervene in her neighbour's life.[136] The focus of her indignation is clear: upholding patriarchy, Gauffreze objected to Paniesse's disciplining her male servant and the disorder it brought to social and gender hierarchy. Gauffreze connected the inappropriate handling of household power and gender relations with sexual dishonour, an association that contemporaries would have found familiar. Again we see a link being made between sexual incontinence and a lack of control, here in excessive physical violence. Gowing noted for England that the 'vision of whoredom that was the touchstone of sexual insult had...strong resonances in the area of household and economics'.[137] *Putain* appears to have carried with it connotations of disorderly household management, precisely because whores lacked control. Paniesse's fury sprang from her belief that Gauffreze had overstepped her prerogative as a neighbour. The crux of the altercation between these women was therefore, for both,

---

[133] Robin Briggs, *The Witches of Lorraine* (Oxford, 2007), 153–79.
[134] ADG, 42 J 30, 139r, 12 Jan. 1593.
[135] ADG, 42 J 30, 195v–196r, 5 Jun. 1593: '*vilaine, ivrogne, masque*'.
[136] Hardwick, *Practice*, 102–3.
[137] Gowing, *Domestic Dangers*, 119.

that the other had misappropriated authority. Such cases illustrate that neighbours could have markedly different ideas about the appropriate boundaries of their power, creating circumstances in which infractions of these boundaries might prompt a clash.[138] Gender, appropriate social order, and the extent of permitted interference in the lives of others were contested areas.

If disciplining one's servants was sensitive, how children were treated could be even more delicate. Women reacted badly to interference in how they treated their offspring. In Ganges Anne Marcialle and Marie Marese quarrelled over the punishment of a child.[139] Three months later widow Marie du Cros fell out with Marie Audiberte and her mother after Audiberte's mother told du Cros to treat her small son better and not to beat him so harshly. Du Cros's response was a stream of insults against her challengers.[140] Worse than criticism of one's parenting was mistreatment of one's children by others. In 1582 Jehanne Coderque complained that her neighbour, Domergue Fazendier's wife, had hit one of her daughters, and when she remonstrated with Fazendier's wife, the latter had picked up a shard of broken glass with which to attack her, calling her 'old witch' and other insults, and threatening to kill her. Fazendier's wife said that, on the contrary, it was Coderque's daughter who had beaten and insulted her multiple times, because she had called her a witch. She confessed that she had misspoken but denied threatening to beat up or kill Coderque.[141] All these child-related quarrels reveal, to a greater or lesser extent, an accusation of unwanted and unwarranted intrusion, interference, and influence as their catalyst.

Household boundary infraction and reputational slights were inferred even when other issues were at stake. In May 1582 Honorat Cany's wife punched Donne Coderque (probably the same Jehanne Coderque who quarrelled with Fazendier's wife a month later) and her daughters in the street, drawing blood. Coderque claimed that Cany's wife had just discovered her husband with Coderque's young niece and that she had overheard Cany's wife shouting coarsely at her husband 'that he would just as soon fuck a cow up the arse' (or possibly, more mildly, 'kiss the arsehole of a cow'). In her fury, as she left their house, Cany had lashed out at Coderque and her daughters who were in the road outside.[142] Cany's wife denied having found her husband with anyone, and said instead that, overcome by anger when Coderque and her daughters had called her a 'bad housekeeper', she had hit them.[143] The quarrel might have been the result of a genuine infraction of the marriage by Cany's husband but she reconceptualized it as an infringement by an external party—Coderque's accusation of household disorder. In some ways, the event (if it happened) and the remark (if it was uttered) symbolized for contemporaries the same thing: that only a bad housewife would have caused her husband to stray.

---

[138] Garrioch, *Neighbourhood*, 34.   [139] ADH, GG 24, 103r, 104r, 8 Apr. 1599.
[140] ADH, GG 24, 111v, 2 Jul. 1599.
[141] BN, Ms.fr. 8667, 335v, 20 Jun. 1582. Similarly, widows Louise Robine and Loise Chaironne fought over Robine's corrupting influence on Chaironne's children: ADG, 42 J 28, 43v, 28 Sept. 1583.
[142] '*Il vauldroit aultant baizer le cul duune vache*'.
[143] BN, Ms.fr. 8667, 325v, 2 May 1582.

If fights were often provoked by the interference of others, then such interference often had at its core a profound sense of the right to correct immorality. Messieurs Foulc and Capdur's wives quarrelled and exchanged insults in December 1596, and Capdur even beat Foulc in her own house.[144] The reason was that Foulc had chastized Capdur for allowing an adulterous couple—Benezet and the wife of Laurans, who, rumour had it, had left her husband—to frequent each other in her house. Capdur denied it, but Foulc testified to having seen Capdur waiting for the man's wife to leave his house before calling him to come to hers to meet his lover. Foulc was suggesting that Capdur was acting as that notorious enabler of immorality described in the contemporary term, *commère des fesses*, literally, a 'buttock-gossip'.[145] Foulc was not personally affected by the apparent immorality; she was simply unable to let it occur without comment or consequence. Capdur attacked Foulc because she resented Foulc's intrusion in her household and the discrediting of her reputation. It may have been especially sensitive as Capdur herself had experienced adultery (her husband had made another woman pregnant a dozen years earlier), but any accusation of harbouring immorality was poisonous.[146] Notably, the one accused of immorality was the first to turn to violence, hitting the busybody who accused her.

Arrogation of the right to pronounce on the moral turpitude of others repeatedly triggered violence. Ysabel Bonnete presented herself before the Nîmes consistory to complain that her employer's daughter, Mademoiselle de Lansard, had punched her on the arm and called her a *putain*. Bonnete had retorted, 'the whores are at your house'.[147] Both accusations were well-founded—Bonnete admitted to the consistory that, although she was married, she had not seen her husband for five or six years, and had had two children by different men since—and Lansard's mother was instructed a few months later to 'stop such disorders that have been at [your] house for so long'.[148] Still, pronouncing judgement over the morality of another was linked to quarrels and violence; in objecting, Bonnete was swimming against the tide.

Donne Catherine de Calque complained in October 1587 that Michel La Vye and his wife, who shared a house with her—the couple on the floor above, Calque below—had punched and slapped her. They denied it, but added that she had put 'horns and pieces of hats to profane them' in the cellar.[149] As horns were linked in the popular imagination with cuckoldry, it seems probable that Calque was suggesting that La Vye's wife was an adultereress.[150] This was the ultimate slur, so it is little wonder the couple responded so forcibly. Bernardine Pageze and the wife of Andre Andre quarrelled in December 1584 because Pageze had said that Andre's

---

[144] ADG, 42 J 31, 145v, 18 Dec. 1596.
[145] Randle Cotgrave translated it into English in 1611 as 'a bed-broaker, an arse-gossip, a gossip for all buttock-matches'.
[146] ADG, 42 J 28, 117v, 170v, Estienne Capdur and Françoise Forte.
[147] ADG, 42 J 28, 95r, 30 Mar. 1584.   [148] ADG, 42 J 28, 114v, 18 Jul. 1584.
[149] ADG, 42 J 28, 322r, 21 Oct. 1587.
[150] Cf. Felicity Heal, 'Reputation and Honour in Court and Country: Lady Elizabeth Russell and Sir Thomas Hoby', *TRHS* 6 (1996), 161–78.

wife had sold her wet-nurse (by implication, into prostitution) and wanted to poison her husband. Andre replied that Pageze was *villaine* (ugly, wicked).[151] In this case, the accusation of immorality was ill-founded: Pageze admitted she had said that Andre had tried to poison her husband in anger, after her husband beat her, but she knew it was not true. Nevertheless, true or not, accusations of immorality often preceded a dispute.

In some cases the accuser was directly affected by the alleged misdemeanours. Blanche Garniere, known as *La Broquiere* (suggesting she worked with wood), and Marie Maurine Forniere fought, verbally and physically, in September 1562.[152] Forniere said that she had been on her way to the wheat market when Garniere had openly called her *paillarde, trainee* (whore, slut), and other insults, and both Garniere and her brother had hit Forniere. Garniere denied this, instead accusing Forniere of liberally abusing both her and her brother: Forniere had allegedly reprimanded Garniere's brother for permitting his sister's adultery with Forniere's husband, and Forniere had slandered Garniere by saying that she had found her sleeping with her husband. Garniere said that these were both false accusations; she did, however, admit her retort to Forniere, 'you call me whore, but you are rather the whore and nothing but drunk'. On her second round of questioning, Forniere defended her accusations against Garniere and her brother as 'well deserved'. Some time before, she said, she had spent a whole night outside Garniere's door before seeing her husband exit in the morning. Each women framed her narrative to appear as the wronged party, but only Forniere claimed to have been on the receiving end of violence, suggesting that the physical conflict arose not from a wife's sense of sexual betrayal, but instead, from a mistress who sought to save her reputation by attack (or that Forniere exaggerated her claim against Garniere by adding violence to her list of failings).

Besides interference—the transgression of boundaries of personal authority or accusations of immorality—the tension between intimacy and private space in everyday life also manifested itself in the number of quarrels over material goods. Lending and borrowing possessions was both a necessity of urban life and a potential source of fierce conflict.

Widow Estienne Saurelle quarrelled with locksmiths Jehan de Lacourt and Jehan Suet, and was hit by the latter in May 1580 because Lacourt was demanding payment for a '*coursilhon*' (a small corset or bodice) belonging to his wife that Saurelle had lost. Saurelle responded that she would pay if he also agreed to pay for the missing '*eau ardant*' (a home-made alcoholic spirit) that his son had taken from her.[153] In June 1590, Jehanne de Lafont argued with Madalene Malaisse over Lafont's accusation that Malaisse had stolen a blouse and five *sols* from her. Malaisse asserted that Lafont had simply lost the blouse, but Lafont maintained that it had been stolen and that the thief could not be anyone else because the area outside M. Ferrand's *mas* (farm), where both women lived, had been infected with the plague, so that a quarantine had been in operation. The consistory remonstrated with them for getting

[151] ADG, 42 J 28, 146r, 28 Dec. 1584.   [152] BN, Ms.fr. 8666, 156v, 2 Sept. 1562.
[153] BN, Ms.fr. 8667, 123r–v, 8 May 1580.

angry over 'so little a thing'.[154] Yet, such things were not little for those involved. In 1561 Catherine Molendine and the wife of Jehan Mathieu argued over a table-cloth.[155] In Ganges in 1602 the quarrel between the wives of M. du Cros and Thimotee Boiseyrolles (known also by her surname of Tartayrone) was over who truly owned a *patrinostres*—a paternoster, presumably a necklace or bracelet of ros-ary beads (though curiously not, it seems, a target of Protestant ire). Cros's daugh-ter was wearing it and Tartayrone claimed it was hers; the dispute over this item drew in both husbands and Tartayrone's father.[156] On a larger scale, Catherine Jouve and her sister, M. Banzillion's wife, argued over an inheritance from their mother; Jouve alleged that her sister wanted more than her fair share.[157]

Disagreements over possessions could quickly deteriorate into spiteful invective. Mariette Bernadonne and Marie de Baille fell out over ownership of a goose egg in 1596; Bernadonne accused Baille of calling her 'a leper, from a race of lepers, *putain*, ugly, drunk', while Baille held that Bernadonne had insulted her with the words '*putain*, drunk, starved to death'.[158] Besides a sprinkling of the usual invective, these insults focused on dishonouring appearance and lineage, and tapped into the rare current of disease-associated obscenities. Baille was required to repent and state that she reputed Bernadonne to be from 'a race of good blood', as well as affirming that she was a 'woman of honour and not a whore'. Dishonour could clearly be inherited as well as earned. In 1602 Susanne Sarranne and Marguerite du Ranq quarrelled: Ranq accused Sarranne of stealing a towel, and Sarranne said Ranq had given birth to a bastard.[159] Or the one accusing could express condemnation: Marie Vialarette lost a needle, and accused the pregnant Jehanne Amourcouse of stealing it, adding the curse that she would never deliver the child that she carried.[160] The language of insult used seems wholly disproportionate to the value of goods lost. Material losses created such extreme responses in part because these were people for whom possessions were not abundant and were therefore valuable—but also because in a world where people had only small spheres of influence and control that were theirs, the ownership of goods symbolized much, and their loss was a devastating transgression into that sphere.

Several disputes sparked by the ownership of material goods occurred between women and their former maidservants, where the relationship and shared space forced intimacy. Gillette Mazoiere worked as a maid for Sire Chillac's wife; in September 1587 Chillac's wife claimed to have lost two plates, eleven napkins, a dress, an apron, and various other things, and suspected Mazoiere of stealing them. The wife decided to search her servant's house, and found some of her possessions hidden in an old chest. She remonstrated with Mazoiere, and Mazoiere replied that it was her mistress who was a thief: she said that eleven *livres* were missing from the chest. When the case came to the consistory it emerged that Mazoiere had served Chillac's wife for a long time 'in health and sickness' without receiving payment,

[154] ADG, 42 J 29, 430–1, 8 Jun. 1590.
[155] BN, Ms.fr. 8666, 27v, 19 Aug. 1561.
[156] ADH, GG 24, 133r, 29 Aug. 1602.
[157] BN, Ms.fr. 8667, 168v, 25 Jan. 1581.
[158] ADTG, I 1, 118v–119r, 20 Mar. 1596.
[159] ADH, GG 24, 127v, 30 Jun. 1602.
[160] ADH, GG 24, 103r, 8 Apr. 1599.

and so had decided to take a dress, a plate, and some other items as reimbursement for her missing wages. When the two were reconciled, Mazoiere even admitted that she had lied about Chillac's wife taking the eleven *livres*.[161] The employer's reaction was mild by comparison to the alleged activities of Damoyselle de Gicard: her former servant, the widow of Pigeon d'Alles, complained that not only had Gicard not paid her, but she had sent her son and another woman to beat her up.[162]

The retention of goods could itself be a comment on another's moral standards. Alaissete Petite and her servant-girl Alaissete Bourillone were in dispute in July 1562, because Petite would not give Bourillone back her clothes and possessions.[163] Petite and her mother said that they had found thirty-seven *sous* in Bourrillone's chest, along with a blanket, a dress, and several handkerchiefs, and were not convinced by her explanation that she was looking after the money for another maid, and had bought the things with her New Year's gift-money. They knew she could not have shopped with her wages, as these—twelve *sous* a year—were still due. So, suspecting her of theft, they had retained her possessions. It quickly emerged, however, that their retention was a response to her perceived immorality: Petite accused her servant of having an affair with a man called Dubeton du Boys from Montpellier in Petite's own house. It was a well-played diversionary tactic: the consistory turned to examining the possibility of Bourrillone's sexual indiscretions and it is not clear that her things were ever returned to her.

Female Violence

As several examples so far have demonstrated, women were verbally and physically violent, both with other women and with men. There seems to have been a latent violence underlying women's disputes that could easily be catalysed, and disputes involving women in Languedoc often involved the use of substantial physical force.[164] The examples multiply: Jehanne Laudane and Jehanne Liborde fought in October 1562: Laudane said she had hit Liborde with a stick because Liborde had punched her, and although they apologized to each other and were reconciled, the consistory threatened them with excommunication if it happened again, suggesting that it was perhaps not the first time these two had come to blows.[165] Marguerite Clote and Alys Borrette were reconciled in 1583 following a great argument in which they had hit and insulted each other.[166] The wife of Gregoire Grolier admitted that, as she left church one day in April 1585, she had hit a woman called Bonnelle, because Bonnelle had called her a *putain* in the presence of her husband and many other people. Bonnelle confessed that she had called Grolier's wife a *putain* because—in the classic tit-for-tat—Grolier's wife had called her drunk.[167] Female violence was far from rare.

---

[161] ADG, 42 J 28, 312v, 16 Sept. 1587.   [162] ADG, 42 J 33, 26r, 9 Feb. 1605.
[163] BN, Ms.fr. 8666, 134v; also see 176v, 18 Jul. 1562.
[164] Muchembled, *Société*, 67.   [165] BN, Ms.fr. 8666, 162v, 9 Oct. 1562.
[166] ADG, 42 J 28, 6r, 8 Apr. 1583.   [167] ADG, 42 J 28, 169r, 17 Apr. 1585.

Women acted as if they felt themselves entitled to use violence, and it may be that violence among women was permissible because it carried less grave risks than fights between men, which were more combative, commonly involved arms, and potentially had far more serious consequences, as well as involving the punching and hitting seen in fights involving women.[168] This difference in ethos between male-only fights and those involving women was articulated in a violent quarrel between Astrugue Régine and her daughter, Anne Mossoze, and son-in-law, Arnaud de Loncle. Régine insulted Loncle by calling him a 'coward', 'fat', and a 'louse', and Mossoze responded by punching her mother in the throat.[169] Loncle then told his mother-in-law that 'if she were a man saying these words, he would kill her'.[170] As Castan found in eighteenth-century France, violence between women or between neighbours across the gender divide seems to have represented an acceptable method of handling disagreement, without the fatal consequences threatened by intra-male aggression.[171] Women's violence, where the risks were relatively minor, seems to have provided a tolerable social pressure valve for community tension. When Baroys's wife hit Captain Beufin's wife to alleviate her anger at Beufin's defamatory insults, and then was reconciled with her before the consistory, the pair were enacting a much-rehearsed standard mechanism for defusing brewing hostility, without any real threat of permanent damage.[172]

Yet for all its comparative mildness, the fact remains that fighting between women was considerably more violent and vicious than has been previously realized. This is perhaps most striking when considering incidents of inter-female brutality directed against family members, making manifest *'l'intense haine entre femmes'* (the intense hatred between women) noted by Solé.[173] When Nande de Rossel and her daughter Marqueze de Bruette fell out over a bedcover, Bruette physically attacked her mother, scratching her face and punching her, as she admitted when she asked her mother's forgiveness before the consistory in August 1595.[174] Anthoinette de Carmaing complained about her mother Marguerite Clavariolle in November of that year, saying that, with much swearing and many threats, Clavariolle had tried to stab her, while Marchette and her mother-in-law were reported as fighting 'ordinarily'.[175] Petit's wife and her niece, Martin's wife, threatened to kill each other in response to their mutual exchange of insults.[176] Jehanne Odol complained that her sister Gabrielle

---

[168] See the fight between Captain Allier and Vidal Aulbert (17 Mar. 1581) in which Allier struck Aulbert on the head with a sword: BN, Ms.fr. 8667, 192r; the 'malice mortelle' between Jean de Ranquet and Pinton in Montauban in Nov. 1595 (8 Nov. 1595): ADTG, I 1, 66r; Pierre Jannin stabbing Estene Fenlou in his own garden (6 Oct. 1591): ADH, GG 24, 20v; the swordfight between M. de la Baume and M. le baron de Ganges, because the former would not bow to the latter (20 Jun. 1599): ADH, GG 24, 106v, 107r, 108r; and other examples of combat between men: ADG, 42 J 28, 87v; AN, TT 234, 14v, 5v; BN, Ms.fr.8667, 169r; BN, Ars.Ms. 10434, 92; ADTG, I 1, 41r–42r; ADH, GG 24, 25v, 70r–71v bis, and 136v; Carroll, *Blood*.

[169] She called him *'coyoul, patous, peulions'*—*'coyoul'* is from *'coyon'*, meaning coward or scoundrel; *'patous'* seems to be from *patofle*, meaning plump or fat; *'peulions'* from *'peulhòs'*, meaning louse.

[170] ADTG, I 1, 144v, 22 May 1596.   [171] Castan, 'La criminalité', 93.

[172] ADG, 42 J 29, 198, 31 May 1589.

[173] Solé, *Etre femme*, 153; see also Briggs, *Witches*, 231–3 and Farr, *Hands*, 160.

[174] ADTG, I 1, 32v–33r, 23 Aug. 1595.

[175] ADTG, I 1, 68v, 70v, 15 Nov. 1595; 29r, 9 Aug. 1595.

[176] ADG, 42 J 31, 44r, 18 Mar. 1591.

Odol had hit her and insulted Jehanne's daughter; Gabrielle admitted punching her sister in the head, but denied the insult.[177] It is not too hard to understand why such violence occurred. In a culture where fewer internal checks on force existed, members of a family, often sharing living space, faced the greatest challenges to harmonious coexistence. Most familial conflict occurred between women of different generations, especially between mother and daughter.

Violence was not, however, only between women: no cultural inhibitions existed to deter men from striking women. The consistories offer a range of examples over the period. In September 1588 the Nîmes consistory received reports that on a recent night, outside the house of the weaver Claude Chambon, a poor woman had been fatally hit with a stone, and the neighbours said that she been killed by a man having an affair with Chambon's wife.[178] In 1589 Marie Reyne reported that two soldiers—Pol Costan and Jacques Esparandieu—had threatened to cut her nose, ears, and dress, and she was scared that they would lie in wait for her.[179] The royal councillor M. de Malmont openly punched M. de Ribes's wife in the street, saying he wanted to imprison her because she had insulted his daughter.[180] Marguerite Reynaude reported that when she was in Uzès Theophile Ralli had accused her of stealing his handkerchief; when she had called him a '*villain*' in response he had punched her.[181] In May 1596 Pol Riviere, known as *La Canquille*, attacked the daughter of M. Martel, publicly calling her '*damoiselle d'inniquite*' (Miss Evil) and *putain*, and cutting her dress 'up to her anus'.[182] He was a serial offender: three months later Marguerite Girarde complained that *La Canquille* had insulted and propositioned her with 'vile and dishonest' words that 'stole her honour', and had punched her.[183] Scholar Pol de Falgueyrolles admitted to punching and walloping a poor woman called Jehanne twice on the arms with a bat, leaving her very unwell, perhaps insensate, because she had insulted and used 'dirty words' against his nieces and sister-in-law.[184] In the midst of a quarrel between Miquielle Estoulhe and Jehan Boiseyrolles and his wife Louise Rosette over the non-payment of Estoulhe's husband's wages, Boiseyrolles hit Estoulhe's son and Andre Rosset (Louise's brother) attacked Estoulhe, hitting her 'hard with a bat' and leaving great bruises on her arms.[185] Finally, in May 1609 Marguerite Auvernasse reported that a poor man called Ganozier Ramettie attacked her at two o'clock in the morning near Caissargues bridge as she travelled back from Marseille, hitting her, injuring her, and throwing her in the river.[186] Even if some of these accusations were false, they were thought credible because this was a society in which many men—from the poorest to the most elevated—struck women.

---

[177] ADG, 42 J 28, 127v, 19 Sept. 1584.   [178] ADG, 42 J 29, 57, 19 Sept. 1588.
[179] ADG, 42 J 29, 116, 147, 22 Feb. 1589.
[180] ADG, 42 J 29, 215, 219, 257, 28 Jun. 1589.
[181] ADG, 42 J 29, 514–15, 517, 518, 17 Oct. 1590.
[182] ADG, 42 J 31, 74v, 78r–v, 15 May 1596.   [183] ADG, 42 J 31, 120r, 28 Aug. 1596.
[184] ADG, 42 J 31, 212r, 215v, 14 Mar. 1598.
[185] ADH, GG 24, 132r, 136r, 143r, 29 Aug. 1602.
[186] ADG, 42 J 34, 93v, 27 May 1609. For further examples see: ADG, 42 J 31, 7v; 42 J 34, 412v, 414v.

The acts of violence by men against women reiterate that this was an intensely patriarchal culture. Yet it would be inaccurate to create a picture of women as only ever the victims of male violence. Just as women insulted men, so they sometimes hit back. In September 1587 in Pont-de-Camarès, Jehan Costeplane asserted that his daughter-in-law had hit him on the head with a bat and made him bleed, although she denied this and said he had hurt himself.[187] Claude Rouveyrolle reported in May 1589 that on one recent evening two men called Yssoire and Savin had shouted insults at her, attempted to cut her dress all the way up to her bottom with the words 'as she is a whore' (indicating explicitly that such an attack was sexually violent), and tried to kill her husband. They would have succeeded, she reported, if her neighbours had not helped her. Yssoire said that on the contrary, it was Rouveyrolle who had defended herself: she had hit him with a stone which floored him. She made no attempt to deny it.[188] Such instances are not very common, and in neither case cited here did the woman openly confess to violence against a man, yet in the context of multiple instances of violence by women it seems improbable that this did not sometimes extend to men, even if the dominant narrative of violence between the sexes was one of men assaulting women.

Conclusions

At the heart of women's conflicts was the question about what was theirs, what they possessed, and what agency they had a right to exercise. Disputes came about because of the contested nature of spheres of influence, either as a result of incursions into women's areas of authority, or because women assumed a right to intrude on the lives of others. Women reacted badly to interference by others, but also issued their own accusations of immorality—either could trigger disputes, which quickly degenerated into invective and interpersonal violence. Arguments about simple material possessions—a tablecloth, a towel, a needle, an egg, a dress—linked the question of ownership with morality. Even pew disputes, ostensibly about purity and status, were about the visible ownership of space, the designation of a place—a physical sphere of authority—to call their own.

This survey of social relations among sixteenth-century Languedocian women has shown that they policed one another's behaviour, especially by arrogating to themselves the right to intervene in one another's lives and enforce morality through gossip, sexual insult, and confrontation. Their self-appointed role—recognized by men—was as moral guardians of the community, regulating the moral and sexual behaviour of others through gossip that centred on illicit sexual activity (and could quickly morph into denunciation and aggressive action), sexualized insults, and disputes. Gossip appears to have been an especially female activity, born of prurient interest in the lives of others, and in this age where honour and reputation counted for so much, there was great power in women's critical words. Women commented on how others ran their households, their relationships with men, their use of power, and the extent to which they colluded in the immorality of others.

---

[187] BN, Ars.Ms. 10434, 107r, 17 Sept. 1587.   [188] ADG, 42 J 29, 176, 179, 10 May 1589.

Such gossip defended the moral standards of the community and reinforced the boundaries of acceptable and non-acceptable behaviour. Insults used by and about women were chiefly iterations of *putain*, whore, and its many equivalents. A small number of insults—those relating to witchcraft or murder—were not linked to a women's sexuality and gender, but most were. Sexualized insults were not simply vehicles for other commentary—they really were about sex, as they expressed ideas about gender, namely that women primarily evaluated other women's worth by how they disposed of their bodies. Patriarchy was fully internalized, as women aligned themselves with the persecution they most feared. Sexual dishonesty was conflated with a lack of control, meaning that sexual misconduct was even the subtext of insults and criticism relating to drunkenness, animalistic behaviour, gluttony, incontinence, excessive violence, and a disorderly household. Women continually stressed the weakness of other women—even as their words demonstrated their very strength.

The evidence of pernicious gossip, dishonouring insult, and violent disputes suggests that women were often outspoken, objectionable, and troublesome. Women were not shy in spreading malicious rumours and scandal, and their assumption of the right to judge others volubly, often through a colourful and varied vocabulary of invective, testifies to their vocal participation in community life. It is understandable, perhaps, that women of the period could easily gain a reputation as gossips and scolds (though the men of the period could also be harsh and vulgar). Women's tongue-lashings were frequently coarse and earthy in tone, as exemplified by the foul-mouthed and sexually belligerent comments of Mauret's widow in Philip the tailor's shop in February 1597, who said 'that men who were not able to have children yet did it with their wives six or seven times a night, deserved to be taken to the square and there crucified with a stake up their backsides'.[189] Such a coarse remark epitomizes all the violence and judgement of sixteenth-century Languedocian women's speech and behaviour. Women's words were uninhibited, and they could often be physically aggressive. The cantankerous, spirited, and pugnacious nature of all these interactions and responses suggests a world in which confrontational self-defence was necessary, while women were far from meek and submissive.

[189] ADTG, I 1, 227r, 6 Feb. 1597: '*que les hommes qui ne pouvoient avoir des enfens et que ne faisoient à leurs femmes six ou sept fois la nuict meritoient d'estre admenés à la plasse et illec estre cruciffiés avec un pal par le coul*'.

5

Love and Marriage

COURTSHIP

After his first wife died Guillaume Sallat decided to marry again. Since the woman he chose had a son, and he a daughter, they decided to keep things in the family by arranging the marriage of their two children. On Saint Valentine's Day 1581 Sallat's daughter, Ysabeau Sallade of Nîmes, and Guillaume Bes of Générac, Sallat's son-in-law, were given in marriage in front of a small group of close friends, including Ysabeau's godfather, Monsieur de Saint-Cosme, and Sallat's friend Jean Moynier. The couple exchanged promises to marry in which they stated that they took each other to be husband and wife in 'words of the present [tense]'. A contract of marriage was drawn up by notary Jean Ménard, and Saint-Cosme and Moynier witnessed it. In the years that followed, Bes gave his sweetheart several gifts as tokens of their marriage, including a ring, a purse, and a leather belt adorned with silver.

Since Sallade had only been born and baptized in late 1569, she was roughly a mere 11 years old at the time of the contract. These gifts were given over the years that, by tradition, had to pass before the married couple could live together and consummate their union. As Sallade approached the age when the marriage was expected to come into full effect, now an orphan, she challenged its validity on the grounds that she had never consented to the match. In early 1589 she was questioned three times by the consistory. Accepting that she had not been of sufficient age to give free and full consent to the marriage, they repeatedly asked whether she had not indicated her consent in the intervening eight years: had not the reception of gifts in confirmation of the marriage signalled her willingness to proceed? She stated that she had accepted the gifts but never as an indication that she ratified the marriage; rather, she had received them 'for fear and reverence' of her late father. She offered to return everything. She also swore that she had never given her true consent, neither by word nor by deed, and had 'no affection' for her putative husband. 'In her conscience before God', she added that Bes was a 'poor silly man and has no sense...as one can know and judge as much by his words as his countenance'. She had never intended to marry him and he had always been 'far from her heart'. She begged the consistory to accept that she could not be held to a promise of marriage to which she had never legitimately consented.[1]

Traditionally, the medieval Catholic Church had required engagements and marriages to be made with the couple's mutual consent. If it could be proved that such

[1] ADG, 42 J 29, 111–12, 117–18, 133–7, 15 Feb. 1589.

consent had not been freely made and either party had been forced or induced into the union, the marriage was not binding. Promises to marry could be made in either the future tense, constituting an engagement, or in the present tense, constituting an espousal. The exchange of these words was the one thing necessary. The Church had encouraged couples to seek the consent of their parents, and to exchange these binding words before a priest and witnesses after the publication of banns, but these elements were not obligatory, and a 'clandestine' marriage made in secret, without consent or witnesses, may have been the subject of disapproval, but was still a valid match.[2] Such freely made agreements were binding, although, under canon law, there were various grounds or impediments that could dissolve an engagement, including infancy (being under the age of consent at the time of promising), fornication with another party, or mutual consent of the parties to dissolve the engagement.

One of the Huguenot Church's major concerns was that marriage should be properly contracted between believers, and the Calvinist Church at Geneva established strict regulations around marriage in the Marriage Ordinance of 1546. Engagements made below the age of consent were invalid, unless the parties confirmed them upon reaching the age of majority. Promises had to be made before two witnesses, and required the consent of parents or guardians for boys under the age of twenty and girls under the age of eighteen. If a disagreement existed between the mother and father, the consent of the father or male guardian was decisive.[3] Confusingly, however, Calvin's considered opinion, codified in 1560, was that secret marriages could not be annulled if they had been celebrated and consummated. Clandestine weddings, such as that between noble Captain Cephas Albenas and Damoiselle Suzanne de Paves made in Nîmes in 1589 'without the consent of mother, brother and relatives' and, furthermore, before a Catholic priest, resulted in public penitence, but still remained a marriage.[4] Similarly, Marie de Grenouse and M. Chabot were chastised in 1594 for not having their marriage publicly blessed, but were undeniably husband and wife.[5] Yet parental consent became an essential component of Reformed marriages in Languedoc, for reasons beyond Calvin's jurisdiction.

The French Protestant Church also had French law to consider, under which parental consent had become mandatory. In 1556 a civil statute passed by the chief judicial body of the French kingdom, the *Parlement* of Paris, ruled that the age of consent for men would be thirty and for women twenty-five, and that men and women under those ages who married without parental consent could be disinherited. In 1579 the Ordinance of Blois went further: those marrying without parental approval could be prosecuted for *rapt de violence* (forced abduction) or *rapt de seduction* (willing elopement)—both punishable by death.[6] At an elite level

---

[2] John Witte Jr and Robert M. Kingdon, *Sex, Marriage and Family in John Calvin's Geneva* (Grand Rapids, MI, 2005), vol. 1, *Courtship, Engagement and Marriage*, 28–38.
[3] Witte and Kingdon, *Courtship*, 164–83.   [4] ADG, 42 J 29, 241, 23 Aug. 1589.
[5] ADG, 42 J 30, 245v, 272r–v, 5 Jan. 1594.
[6] Sarah Hanley, 'Family and State in Early Modern France: The Marriage Pact', in *Connecting Spheres: Women in the Western World, 1500 to the Present*, ed. Arilyn J. Boxer and Jean H. Quataert

it was normal that marriages were dictated by parents, that they were arranged, and that they were undertaken, as Mathieu Molé, procureur general of the *Parlement* of Paris put it when talking of the clandestine marriage of Louis XIII's brother to Marguerite de Lorraine, 'not out of consideration for the contracting party, but for the honour and advantage of families...the contract is made not as a private agreement, but one which is common to all the relatives'.[7] Eventually, the French state would expand the definition of a minor to include widows under the age of twenty-five in the Code Michaud of 1629, and then, in a statute of 1639, to require the consent of parents regardless of the age of the marrying parties, but both these regulations occurred after the consistorial cases considered here.

Even under the 1556 ruling, parental consent was made largely necessary for most marriages. Among the Huguenots of Languedoc, however, parental consent was an addition to, not a substitute for, the couple's own consent to the match. Calvin upheld the medieval stipulation that betrothal and marriage promises should be made voluntarily, and not under compulsion. Coerced marriage did not count as true marriage. Promises to marry needed to be made with free and full consent, but also in all seriousness, sobriety, and solemnity—engagements made 'through reckless frivolity' or while drunk would not stand.[8] The ideal betrothal that the consistory expected can be seen in the ceremony between Joseph Simon and Françoise Fagete in August 1578: promises to marry, made soberly and seriously in 'words of the present' tense, were heard by three male witnesses, and the parties indicated their mutual consent in the presence of both sets of parents.[9] All that was ideally needed to complete the union was a formal blessing by a minister.

Love was then theoretically built into the making of Protestant marriages. Yet while the medieval Catholic Church had allowed engagements to be dissolved by mutual consent, the Calvinist Marriage Ordinance did not. Engagement promises were binding and indissoluble. If a couple ceased to feel affection for each other after a properly enacted engagement, they were still required to proceed with the wedding. Mutual consent therefore figured as a one-time-only matter. If it was found that an individual had entered into this serious commitment with more than one person, the consistory sought to determine which engagement or marriage bore more of the marks of a proper and legitimate union and did not concern themselves with which couple would rather be wed. Marriage could also not be made conditional on any grounds that the church considered frivolous, and, after the exchange of promises, the consistory held that engagements should be very short—preferably no more than six weeks. Those who remained engaged a long time, such as Claude Begon and his fiancée, were urged to marry quickly in May

(New York and Oxford, 1987), 56–7; Natalie Zemon Davis, 'Ghosts, Kin and Progeny: Some Features of Family Life in Early Modern France', *Daedalus* 106.2 (1977), 87–114, here 106–8.

[7] Cited by Wendy Gibson, *Women in Seventeenth-Century France* (Basingstoke, 1989), 43, quoting Molé, *Mémoires*, ed. A. Champollion-Figeac, 4 vols (SHF, 1855–7), vol. 2, 227.

[8] Marriage Ordinance (1546), reproduced in translation in Witte and Kingdon, *Courtship*, 51–61, here 53.

[9] BN, Ms.fr. 8667, 28v, 6 Aug. 1578.

1610—in their case, before Pentecost, meaning within a fortnight as Easter was 11 April in 1610 and Pentecost seven weeks later.[10] During this time sexual intercourse between the engaged parties was forbidden, even though a betrothal was as indissoluble as a marriage.

Less essential, but still desirable, were the proper place and personnel for the wedding, and a degree of equity between the marriage partners. In Nîmes the consistory sought to crack down on weddings in the outlying villages rather than in the city temple of the Reformed church.[11] M. Deidier was asked to repent for marrying his wife outside the town and without the proper announcement of banns in 1593.[12] The consistory also discouraged marriage between Reformed believers and Roman Catholics, and where an age disparity existed, although neither constituted sufficient grounds to annul a marriage.

The church's disciplinary ambitions were, therefore, to ensure that marriage promises were reached with mutual and parental consent and were subsequently not breached, with weddings conducted by Reformed ministers, and not preceded by over-hasty intimacy. The contrast between these clear conditions and actual practice offers insight into women and men's thoughts, priorities, and expectations around courtship and marriage, which were often very different to those of the authorities. The women and men of Languedoc seem to have thought questions of choice and parental consent rather more flexible than either the Church or law considered them to be.[13] Ordinary people were obstinate when it came to choosing a life partner: they seemed to expect to love their future spouse all the way up to the ceremony, and parental approval sometimes seemed of little concern.

Ysabeau Sallade was one of those stubbornly focused on making her own choice. With rare exceptions, in the case of a contested engagement, the consistory sought to enforce the sworn promises, and marriage—however distasteful to the participants—was decreed. Sallade was lucky. The consistory paid little heed to her lack of affection for Guillaume Bes or the fact he was a simpleton; they did recognize, however, that her acceptance of the ceremonial gifts had been the result of parental coercion, and that there was no evidence of her free adult consent to the union. Even though her father had consented to the union and it had been accomplished with the proper decorum of witnesses and a notarized contract, her youth at the time played in her favour. She had been a child when the marriage contract was drawn up—she had had neither the intellectual capacity of a mature adult to consent to marriage nor the physical capacity to consummate it. Her childish promise could not stand. She was therefore required to give back the ring and other gifts to Bes, while both were released from their promises and given permission to 'remarry' 'as seems good to them'.[14] This chapter explores the issues raised by their aborted marriage—the

---

[10] ADG, 42 J 34, 180r, 19 May 1610.   [11] e.g. BN, Ms.fr. 8667, 260r, 29 Nov. 1581.

[12] ADG 42 J 30, 240r, 8 Dec. 1593.

[13] Jean Aymon, *Tous les synodes nationaux des Églises réformées de France*, 2 vols (The Hague, 1710), vol. 1, 6–7 (articles 38, 343, synod of Paris, 1559), 75 (article 16, synod of Vertueil, 1567); Jeffrey R. Watt, *The Making of Modern Marriage: Matrimonial Control and the Rise of Sentiment in Neuchâtel, 1550–1800* (New York, 1992), 42, n. 37.

[14] ADG, 42 J 29, 137.

ritual of marriage, attendant gifts, consent, and choice—across a range of cases, thus providing further insights into the mental world of ordinary people.

Gifts and Rituals

Marriage was a contract, expressed both by the verbal exchange that affianced or wed a couple, and by an accompanying document drawn up by a notary. A written contract survives between Jean Combes and Suzanne Rouyere from Nîmes, dating from 10 January 1615, and gives an example of what pertained to the record of a marriage.[15] Theirs was a contract of betrothal: it notes that promises to marry had been made in 'words of the future [tense], to be accomplished if it pleases God'. It was drawn up 'in the name of God', and gave the purposes of marriage to be 'to the praise of God' and the 'multiplication of human lineage'. Jean Combes was identified as the legitimate son of Claude Combes and Margueritte Gaye, both inhabitants of Nîmes, and Suzanne Rouyere as the 'honest daughter' of the late Anthoine Rouyere and Anne Audrigue, also of Nîmes. These appellations are pertinent: the most important criterion for a man was his legitimacy, conveying that he could transmit the blood line of his family; for a woman, it was her honesty—her chastity—ensuring that children born into the marriage would be true heirs of her husband. These labels therefore reaffirm the central purpose of marriage, under law, of safeguarding lineage. The contract then noted the mutual consent of the couple and their intention to solemnize their marriage in the Reformed Christian church. It required banns to be published 'following the ordinance of the king', then noted that it was witnessed by the couple, Jean's parents, and Suzanne's mother and her brother, who was their late father's heir. Her brother's role was chiefly financial: as the inheritor of his father's estate, it fell to him to supply his sister with a dowry of sufficient stature.

The contract was the written confirmation of the interchange of words by which a marriage was promised or occurred. This verbal exchange in which a couple promised to marry each other was known as the *donation de corps*—the 'giving of bodies'. The descriptions of this indicate that the traditional formulation did not require the couple to say, 'I take you as my husband/wife'. Instead, they were asked 'do you give your body to X?'. In Languedoc, marriage was linguistically the gift of two people to each other physically, emotionally, and materially, not the acquisition of another.[16] Much of the popular rite and ritual surrounding betrothal extended this concept of mutual giving, and these attendant customs came for many to signify and validate a marriage in a way that the Reformed Church's new, more regulated version could not.

In Montauban in 1596 objections were raised to the marriage of Jean Pelissie and Susanne de Vernhiol by Pellisie's stepmother, godmother, and his godmother's sister and husband. Even though the marriage had already been contracted, they protested that it had been done without their knowledge or consent, and that

---

[15] ADG, 1 E 284, 10 Jan. 1615.
[16] Lyndal Roper, *The Holy Household: Women and Morals in Reformation Augsburg* (Oxford, 1989), 133.

Pelissie had a prior commitment to another woman, Naude Gabrielle. Gabrielle described the circumstances of Pelissie's proposal to her and their engagement, in a testimony that reads as recorded speech—she gave the direct speech in Occitan and changed pronouns halfway through to address Jean Pelissie directly, and then returned to using the third person:

> It was on a Sunday when they were all eating...and while eating the said Pelissie said to her the beautiful words, 'Naude, would you like me as a husband?' and she replied, 'This is something that I need to think over more.' You gave a response...and for a sign, tore a loaf of bread in half, each [of us] took half, ate it, and afterwards poured wine in a glass, Pelissie having the first sip and the rest he gave to the said Naude, and he made a ring with his fingers and said that, in making it, he [would] make another.[17]

Gabrielle's homely description indicates the rituals of betrothal that were understood by the community: sharing bread and wine together, and the giving of a ring (in this case, symbolic), in front of witnesses. Her testimony of sharing bread and drinking from one cup evoked a regular feature of popular betrothal and marriage: the custom of eating or drinking in the name of marriage, which replayed the symbolism of verbally offering one's body to the other.[18] The man offered his prospective fiancée a cup 'in the name of marriage', from which she then drank, tacitly accepting his proposal through her action. Gabrielle's acceptance of the wine trumped her earlier reticence. Again and again plaintiffs described this familiar ritual of sharing food and drink, often bread and wine, as a testament to their mutual commitment to marry. These symbolic rituals, echoing the central Eucharistic rite of the Church, had great popular significance—Burguière describes them as being understood to be 'invested with a magical force...that contracted an irreversible tie' between the couple—but the church authorities were indifferent to them as valid indicators of a marriage contract.[19] The Montauban consistory considered the promises made between Gabrielle and Pelissie to be 'frivolous' and 'as a result, of null effect', and the marriage to Susanne de Vernhiol continued undeterred.[20] This case indicates the multiple understandings of betrothal that existed, and suggests that a dichotomy existed between religious and popular understandings of what constituted a valid engagement.

Previous studies of France both before and after the Reformation have suggested that this gap should not exist: Solé notes how seriously the fifteenth-century and early sixteenth-century Roman Catholic episcopal tribunal of Troyes took gifts, symbolic offerings, and other popular rituals.[21] Burguière, examining the same sources for 1480 to 1540 and after 1667, also stressed the similarities between

---

[17] ADTG, I 1, 117v–118v, 20 Mar. 1596. The direct speech reads: *Naude voules me per marit* and *Aquo ez une cause que y cal pensa may.*

[18] This is mentioned in the consistorial registers more than James R. Farr finds in *Authority and Sexuality in Early Modern Burgundy (1550–1730)* (New York and Oxford, 1995), and features in Jacques Solé's evidence in *Etre femme en 1500: la vie quotidienne dans la diocèse de Troyes* (Paris, 2000). In one instance, Andre Burguière, in 'Le rituel du mariage en France: pratiques ecclésiastiques et pratiques populaires', *Annales: Economies, Sociétés, Civilisations* 33 (1978), 637–48, 643, finds a man telling his fiancée, 'I put my tongue in your mouth, in [the] name of marriage'.

[19] Burguière, 'Le rituel', 643.   [20] ADTG, I 1, 118v.   [21] Solé, *Etre femme*, 110–11.

popular and religious ritual in the formation of marriage.[22] Farr, drawing on criminal court material from 1582 to 1730 in Burgundy, found that a promise of marriage and an exchange of rings or gifts—in one case, a gift of scissors and some pins—was considered to form a binding contract of marriage.[23] Yet my research suggests more of a discrepancy between popular and religious ritual in Languedoc, with less acceptance by the church of elements of ritual that remained important for most people.

The consistorial cases indicate that gifts remained an important marker of an engagement in the popular imagination. The most important of these was a ring. In July 1562 Pierre Guiraud complained that Jehan Boyer's widow had promised to marry his brother Jacques, and had received a ring from him before witnesses, but had since become engaged to a servant called Vincent.[24] Many years later, Anthonye Reynaude presented herself to protest against the marriage of Jaques Peppilant, and in her defence exhibited a ring that he had given her as evidence of his marriage promise.[25] The strength of the significance of a ring is highlighted by Jacquette Afortide's testimony in 1589. She asserted that, having been promised marriage by Jean Reynaud in the presence of witnesses, she had refused his offer of a ring while she waited for her father's consent. She understood the acceptance of a ring to mean a firmly established commitment and so did her would-be fiancé: her rejection of it—out of deference to her father—led him to believe the promises did not hold, and he contracted marriage with someone else.[26] As the anthropologist Arnold van Gennep noted, the act of giving a gift in betrothal is a 'rite of union'— rejection of the gift indicates a refusal to accede to the union itself.[27]

In addition to rings, other gifts were also exchanged. Jehanne Courtine claimed that Pierre Vidal had given her a silver ring, and a purse and a belt, as indication of his intent to marry her.[28] The consistory dismissed this material evidence without investigating further, and such disregard of gifts when unaccompanied by other proofs contrasts with the earlier Catholic episcopal tribunal at Troyes where a range of gifts—in one example from 1516 a branch from a sloe tree given eleven years earlier in the name of marriage—were accepted as serious symbolic testaments to matrimony.[29]

Lyndal Roper noted the sense of obligation conveyed by betrothal gifts in sixteenth-century Augsburg, and interpreted them less as a symbol of mutual exchange than a transfer of property that focused on the bride's passivity and the groom's aggressive masculinity.[30] Yet in Languedoc women also gave gifts to men. Marguerite

[22] Burguière, 'Le rituel', 638.

[23] Farr, *Authority and Sexuality in Early Modern Burgundy (1550–1730)* (New York and Oxford, 1995), 114.

[24] BN, Ms.fr. 8666, 140r, 18 Jul. 1562.   [25] ADG, 42 J 33, 243r, 21 Nov. 1607.

[26] ADG, 42 J 29, 115, 22 Feb. 1589.

[27] Arnold van Gennep, *The Rites of Passage*, trans. Monika B. Vizedom and Gabrielle L. Caffee (London, 1960), 132–3; Watt, *The Making*, 66.

[28] ADG, 42 J 30, 336v, 22 Mar. 1595.   [29] Solé, *Etre femme*, 111.

[30] Lyndal Roper, 'Mothers of Debauchery: Procuresses in Reformation Augsburg', *German History* 6.1 (1988), 1–19, here 10; Roper, *Holy Household*, 130, 145–8; also see Diana O'Hara, *Courtship and Constraint: Rethinking the Making of Marriage in Tudor England* (Manchester, 2000).

Yssoire stated that she had given François Boissin gifts including 'six handkerchiefs, three collars, a pair of white hose, a garter, and had fed him for three days in her mother's house' as evidence of her claim of a promise of marriage between them at Sommières.[31]

That the exchange of such goods was so frequently mentioned in the testimonies of those seeking to secure a marriage indicates how closely gifts and a commitment to marry were linked in people's minds. The monetary value of these gifts might have been negligible, but something in the giving of one's goods was thought to put oneself in another's possession.[32] By contrast, although the consistory realized that gifts might indicate a decision to marry, they placed no absolute faith in them. People in Languedoc may have continued to valorize betrothal gifts as indicators of commitment in and of themselves, but the Reformed Church's attitudes were markedly different.

Roper's research rightly suggests that gifts indicated the character of marriage as a union of property, as well as a union of persons.[33] The chief gift exchanged at a marriage was the dowry—the portion of property, money, or goods that a woman brought to a marriage. Much of the contract between Jean Combes and Suzanne Rouyere discusses the dowry to be paid by her brother, in this case a sizeable sum of 500 *livres* plus a chest of clothing—the sort of amount offered as a dowry only by wealthy merchants, *bourgeois*, and physicians.[34] The transmission of a dowry was a crucial marker of honourable marriage and has been recognized as such by historians. Hardwick and O'Hara have charted the importance of dowries; Schneider examined the role of dowries, dowers (the portion of property to which a widow was entitled), and inheritance as a primary motive for women's activities in courts in Normandy, and Lebrun concluded that the dowry was obligatory in the Midi, where it represented a commitment to the independence of women and rights of individuals that was distinct from the practices of northern France.[35] This is because in Languedoc the dowry was inalienable and returned to the wife on her husband's death. It was a form of insurance. There was, understandably, a customary and popular attachment to the dowry—it was popularly understood to be an essential part of marriage and was generally paid before a marriage was consecrated in church. In recognition of its necessity, wills from the period testify to benefices 'to the poor girls of Nîmes, to help them to marry', as in Anthoine Augerand's of 1567, Jehan Ravel's of 1581, or Bernardine Rey's of 1601.[36] Yet the consistory focused less on marriage as property transfer

---

[31] ADG, 42 J 32, 190v, 12 Nov. 1603.

[32] John Gillis, *For Better, For Worse: British Marriages from 1600 to the Present* (New York and Oxford, 1988), 31–3.

[33] Witte and Kingdon, *Courtship*, 383.

[34] Allan A. Tulchin, *That Men Would Praise the Lord: The Triumph of Protestantism in Nîmes, 1530–1570* (Oxford, 2010), 21–2.

[35] Julie Hardwick, *The Practice of Patriarchy: Gender and the Politics of Household Authority in Early Modern France* (University Park, PA, 1998), 58–62; O'Hara, *Courtship*, 1–2; François Lebrun, *La vie conjugale sous l'Ancien Régime* (Paris, 1975), 76; Zoë A. Schneider, 'Women before the Bench: Female Litigants in Early Modern Normandy', *FHS* 23.1 (2000), 1–32, 16–17.

[36] Arc.Not., 2 E 1/257, 17 Mar. 1567; 2 E/1 298, 26 Apr. 1601.

and consistently appears to have underestimated the importance of the dowry as a deal-breaker in marriage arrangements.

This is rather inconsistent with the fact that at times the church helped supply the dowry necessary to enable apoor woman to marry. In the 1580s it gave Marie Archivyere two and a half *écus* 'to help her to make her dowry', supplied Françoise Arboussette with six *livres* to assist her to marry a weaver who refused to marry her without it, and gave a 'poor girl who is strongly religious and fears God' ten *livres* so she could marry a young man who worked in the clothing industry.[37] It was also common for those in need to request financial assistance towards their dowries from the consistory, as carter's daughter Catherine Reyne did. She asked for ten *écus* to help towards a dowry of 100 *livres*, and was given fifteen *livres*, which equated to five *écus*—half the sum she had requested (comparative dowries for carters suggest that she was aiming quite high).[38] Not every recipient was honest: in 1587 a servant who had married a young girl called Delange complained that his mother-in-law would not give him the two *écus* that his wife had received from the consistory for her dowry.[39] That the consistory recognized a responsibility to make some form of financial input does not mean, however, that it tolerated the excuse of an unpaid dowry as justification for postponing or cancelling a wedding.

Some men pointedly refused to proceed without upfront payment of the dowry. Jehan Tromel said in 1580 that he did not want to proceed with his promises of marriage to Jacquette Bordure while the dowry remained unpaid.[40] In 1586 Anthoine Favede refused to marry Guilhaumette Privade, to whom he had been engaged for over a year, saying he had been promised a dowry of 140 *livres*, which she now refused to give him.[41] He was deprived of the sacrament for his disobedience in not marrying her without it. When the marriage had still not been solemnized two years later, the consistory threatened to report Favede to the magistrate unless the couple married within a fortnight. Yet delays in the solemnization of marriage because a dowry was not forthcoming were not uncommon. When Jehan Reboul explained the year-long delay in his marriage to Marye Merigne by reference to a promised and unpaid dowry of 142 *livres*, he was told to proceed with the much more paltry sum of thirty *livres* now offered—the sort of dowry exchanged among the poor.[42] This must have been humiliating as well as financially punitive. The retardation of a dowry payment could lead to even more prolonged postponements of marriage: even though weaver Jehan Bertrand and Cassinette lived together, had had a child, and she was again pregnant, Bertrand continued to prevaricate about marrying her, insisting that he receive the money she had promised him before he would proceed with the ceremony. His procrastination lasted for several years.[43] The same applied to goldsmith Jacques Brunet in 1613, who, when chastised for

---

[37] ADG, 42 J 29, 18, 25 May 1588; 111, 15 Feb. 1589; 42 J 29, 155, 31 Mar. 1589.
[38] BN, Ms.fr. 8667, 234r, 9 Aug. 1581.   [39] ADG, 42 J 28, 319r, 320v, 14 Oct. 1587.
[40] BN, Ms.fr. 8667, 93v, 20 Jan. 1580.
[41] ADG, 42 J 28, 210v, 372r, 348v, 364r, 366r, 5 Feb. 1586; Tulchin, *That Men*, 22.
[42] ADG, 42 J 28, 325r, 28 Oct. 1587.
[43] ADG, 42 J 29, 11, 656, 707, 731; 42 J 30, 7r, 13 Apr. 1588.

living with his fiancée and 'giving scandal to his neighbours', explained that, 'it was true that he had neglected the said blessing [of his marriage] but it was [because he was] waiting for the dowry he had been promised'.[44] The consistory insisted Brunet have his marriage blessed within two weeks, yet six months later Brunet and his fiancée remained unmarried.

Financial concerns constituted a profound impediment to prompt nuptials. Anthoine Vialla, engaged to Marguerite Alliere 'for a long time', voiced the problem in February 1581 when he said they were waiting on the dowry promised by Alliere's cousin and employer, Captain Allier, to be able to afford to marry: in the meantime, they would live together.[45] A week later Allier blamed the delay on his cousin having stolen two chests of wheat from him, and consequently offered her only her own clothing and no more as dowry. The consistory determined that the couple would be married that same day. The church might have seen matters differently, but for most ordinary people being able to marry depended on financial resources, the absence of which retarded matrimony, and often encouraged pre-marital cohabitation.[46]

Outside the consistory, the absence of a dowry served as a viable reason for annulling a marriage contract. Although cobbler Pierre Meynan and Saumette Messe had drunk in the name of marriage, Meynan had since promised marriage to Marye Larguiere, and because Messe was not able to pay the 'two hundred *francs* of dowry' that she had promised him, some months later he married Larguiere in the Roman Catholic church.[47] The lack of a dowry could even vitiate a marriage after solemnization: M. Jehan, a lawyer known by his nickname *Esperonnier*, threw his daughter-in-law out of the house in April 1586 as her parents had not paid her dowry, while François Barban similarly expelled his wife because her mother had not provided the promised sum in July 1578.[48] In the popular understanding a marriage without a dowry was no marriage at all. No women presented themselves to complain about a delayed wedding after having failed to provide their dowry, making it clear that the payment of a dowry was commonly accepted as a necessary part of marriage culture.[49] Dowry-culture could be taken advantage of by the unscrupulous: weaver Reymond Pastre from Anduze contracted marriage with both Marie Solieyre and Marie Brossane, in February 1587 and December 1588 respectively, and was accused by hatter Barthelemy Garatz of having promised marriage to both servant-girls in order to extract money from them.[50]

Along with promises and gifts, another important part of the ritual of marriage—as agreed by both popular opinion and ecclesiastical ordinance—was

[44] ADG, 42 J 35, 26r, 48r, 50v, 83r, 23 Oct. 1613.

[45] BN, Ms.fr. 8667, 174v, 178v, 1 Feb. 1581.

[46] Emmanuel Le Roy Ladurie, *L'argent, l'amour et la mort en pays d'oc* (Paris, 1980), 76, 83–4, explores the centrality of this pattern in Occitan literature.

[47] ADG, 42 J 31, 292v, 297r, 301r, 308v, 30 Jun. 1599.

[48] ADG, 42 J 28, 223r–224v, 23 Apr. 1586; BN Ms.fr. 8667, 20r–v, 33r, 9 Jul. 1578.

[49] Lebrun, *La vie conjugale*, 76; Jean-Louis Flandrin, *Les amours paysannes (XVIe–XIXe siècle): amour et sexualité dans les campagnes de l'ancienne France* (Paris, 1975), 60; Hardwick, *The Practice*, 58; Schneider, 'Women', 16–17.

[50] ADG, 42 J 29, 97–8, 18 Jan. 1589.

publicity.[51] In November 1579 a miller called Thomas Sigion testified that he had become engaged to a 30-year-old widow called Claude Rousse. In the house of Donne Francese Rousse in the Jacobins outside Nîmes they had drunk in the name of marriage, promised to marry saying, 'they gave their bodies one to the other', he had given her a ring, and, crucially, they had received the congratulations of many.[52] Rousse denied that they had promised to give their bodies in the name of marriage, drunk in the name of marriage, and been congratulated, and said instead that she was engaged to a man called Foucaran Garaignon. So over the next eleven days the consistory questioned sixteen witnesses. Some, like Rousse's 55-year-old aunt Jehanne Bessede and Francese Rousse, in whose house the engagement had allegedly taken place, were called as witnesses to the promises between Sigion and Claude Rousse. Others, like Guillaume Gaillard, were called as witnesses to Rousse's betrothal ceremony with Garaignon: Gaillard reported that she had a joyful face and accepted the ring Garaignon gave her.

Another group of deponents were asked to give information about what the couple had publicly said about their relationship. Forty-year-old widow Daufine Ferrete stated that 'Claude the widow was [Sigion's] wife and he had no other because he had promised her and given her a ring'. Thirty-five-year-old Claude Tinel testified to seeing Sigion in the Jacobins on a Sunday in June and having asked how come he was there with 'Donne Martelle's widowed niece', Sigion had answered that he hoped she was his wife. Tinel asked if they had exchanged promises and Sigion said they had, but Tinel insisted on asking Rousse herself, who replied that she hoped, if God permitted it, to never have any other for husband but Thomas. Tinel had blessed them and gone on his way. Anthoine Bourras had overheard Claude Rousse telling her servant in July 'that she promised to marry Thomas the Miller'. A woman called Chabanelle had told Sigion off for amusing himself and wasting time with widow Claude, to which he had retorted that she was his wife, that they had made promises to each other, and he had given her a silver ring.

Finally, those of the last category of person interviewed were asked to report on the level of publicity the alleged marriage had generated: Augustere Roque and Donne Chicarde, among others, testified to the 'common noise' that Sigion and Rousse had promised themselves to each other, and that he had given her a ring, a handkerchief, and a blouse—gifts that not even Sigion himself claimed to have gifted. While hearsay would not alone suffice to convince the consistory that a binding contract existed, plaintiffs frequently used public knowledge of an engagement promise in their defence, suggesting that publicity contributed at both the popular and the religious levels to the substantiality of a marriage promise.[53] It was an important part of the ritual. Yet whether it was sufficient to enforce the marriage is unclear: after several folios entitled 'concerning the opposition to the marriage of Thomas Sigion with Claude Rousse', but directly after a mention of the 'marriage to Foulcaran

---

[51] Also noted by Beatrice Gottlieb, 'The Meaning of Clandestine Marriage', in *Family and Sexuality in French History*, ed. Robert Wheaton and Tamara K. Hareven (Philadelphia, PA, 1980), 51.

[52] BN, Ms.fr. 8667, 82r, 29 Nov. 1579.   [53] Gillis, *For Better*, 38.

Granon [*sic*] with Claude', on a fresh line the register's final entry on the subject reads: 'Since the said marriage has been solemnized publicly'. It is frustratingly unclear which of the two marriages this means.

Choice and Consent

How did people in Languedoc choose whom to marry? Was it primarily a decision made by a family or an individual? Evidence for Catholic France has produced contradictory answers—Lebrun and Gibson argue it was primarily a parental choice: Lebrun concludes that 'a marriage of convenience remained the rule and it was mostly dictated by the parents' and that 'marriage was too serious to be a personal choice'.[54] Gibson, focusing on the nobility, notes that parents were not obliged to consult children about their choice of partner.[55] Gottlieb concludes that arranged marriages made sense for the rich (although it is self-evident that money mattered, perhaps even more, for the poor).[56] By contrast, Briggs suggests that the majority of marriages were not arranged and the initiative was often taken by the young themselves, largely because so many parents died before their children married. Using marriage contracts for Nîmes, Tulchin has recently argued the same, although his grounds are practical—low dowries and absent parents—and he notes that such sources give little sense of 'what people's sentiments were'.[57] A sort of midway position is reached by Solé, for an earlier period, when he stresses the role of 'great collective pressure' on individual choice, and Davis similarly concludes that while there was room for compromise and negotiation on the choice of spouse, the need for parental consent was internalized by most young people.[58] Under French law from 1556, parents had to consent to marriages by the young or those marrying faced disinheritance, but how much did parents intervene? How important were personal desire and mutual attraction, or material and social factors? The consistorial cases provide new evidence of how and why ordinary people chose spouses, and whether choices were 'dictated by the parents', were made on the initiative of eligible singles, or represented a compromise between the two.

As the case of Guillaume Bes and Ysabeau Sallade illustrated, some marriages were arranged with minimal consultation of the prospective spouses, or at least of the brides. Sallade's father had evidently considered such an arrangement to be both a legitimate way to contract marriage, and for the good of his daughter. Although Sallade was found to be under age, and not to have subsequently consented, the concept of a father's negotiating a marriage directly with the suitor went unquestioned by the consistory. This mentality must also explain why some parents were summoned to justify allowing their daughters to marry a Catholic: the

---

[54] Lebrun, *La vie conjugale*, 22.   [55] Gibson, *Women*, 47.
[56] Gottlieb, 'The Meaning', 68–9.
[57] Robin Briggs, *Communities of Belief: Cultural and Social Tension in Early Modern France* (Oxford, 1989), 264; Allan A. Tulchin, 'Low Dowries, Absent Parents: Marrying for Love in an Early Modern French Town', *Sixteenth Century Journal* 46.3 (2013), 713–38, here 714–15.
[58] Solé, *Etre femme*, 97; Davis, 'Ghosts', 107–8.

consistory held parents at least partly responsible for the marriages contracted by their children, and expected them to play a major role in their arrangement.

In practice though, many suits were made to the girl alone, even if such behaviour aroused disapproval. For example, Loise Borrette testified that Martin Solignac had pursued her in 1562—he had 'come after her for a long time talking to her of marriage', and Solignac was chastised 'for rather addressing himself to the girl than her parents'. There was clearly attraction between the pair: before the consistory, Solignac said that he had told Borrette that 'he would have none other for a wife than she' and Borrette's response to him had been to say that 'if her mother and relatives wanted [the marriage] she would agree', although she accepted a ring from him before such consent was forthcoming.[59] The initiative came from the couple, but the need for consent had been internalized.

Other marriages were also arranged because of attraction and affection between the parties, with or without the support of their families. A carter called Jean Maynie, known as *Lou Rouge*, and his wife confessed in 1598 that they had sworn a contract of marriage between their daughter and a Catholic peasant, because 'their said daughter did not want any other husband than the said fiancé'. Instructed by the consistory not to proceed to the solemnization of the marriage, they said that they 'could nor would not break off the marriage', and Maynie was suspended from the sacrament for their disobedience.[60] Jeremie Prat and Marie Bouyeyre presented themselves at the consistory of Nîmes in June 1589 saying that they had become engaged eight days earlier and now faced opposition from Bouyeyre's brothers, who threatened that if she married Prat they would throw her out of their house and renounce her as their sister. The consistory asked the pair their ages— Prat was twenty-seven, and Bouyeyre twenty-five, so they did not need familial consent—and then asked whether they could testify in conscience that their marriage would be made to the honour of God and 'to their use'. They replied, rather touchingly, 'that they found that their marriage would succeed in honouring God and [would be] to their profit', and that therefore they wanted to make good on their promises to each other.[61] As far as individuals were concerned, they thought themselves entitled to choose a spouse for romantic reasons.

This is perhaps best illustrated by a couple whom the consistory considered to be 'unequal'. The engagement between Sire Mingaud and Donne Pancye—and the fact that they were sleeping together—caused great consternation because Pancye was 'more than eighty years old' (Mingaud's age is not given), but, as the contract had been passed, the banns read, and the couple had been frequenting each other, it was reluctantly concluded that the marriage ought to go ahead.[62]

Ultimately, however, parental consent was necessary under French law after 1556, and the consistory routinely intervened to uphold this. Promises of marriage between M. Estienne, a Reformed minister in the town of Cayerac, and Helix Vernete were considered to be void in 1561 because the girl's parents did not consent

[59] BN, Ms.fr. 8666, 172r–v, 31 Oct. 1562.
[60] ADTG, I 1, 324v–325r, 326v, 11 Feb. 1598.   [61] ADG 42 J 29, 212–13, 21 Jun. 1589.
[62] ADG, 42 J 28, 335r, 343r, 2 Dec. 1587.

to the union. Estienne was chastised for continuing to pursue Vernete when fully cognizant of her parents' opposition to the match, in fact even after Vernete's father had punched him.[63] When widow Beatris Martine reported her opposition to the marriage of her son, Pierre Estienne, with Susanne Montolle in 1600, the consistory in Ganges took the matter seriously, and decided to seek the advice of the next Reformed colloquy on how to respond.[64] In 1609 the Nîmes consistory flatly denied Barthelemy Turier permission to marry as he did not have the 'express permission' of his father.[65]

Yet for consistories in the cities of Nîmes and Montauban, at times there is something of a tick-box feel to their pursuit of parental consent. If an engagement or marriage had been properly enacted in all other ways, and the couple clearly consented to it, the consistories apparently sought to persuade the parents to agree to it too. In 1595 cobbler Pierre Breil refused permission for his daughter Marie de Breil to marry Yves Cavaillier, despite an engagement of sixteen months. His grounds were that the contract of marriage had been agreed with the condition that the wedding should not be celebrated for two years, as Marie de Breil was only fourteen years old. Although conditional consent was customary under the medieval Catholic Church, the consistory would not accept qualified promises to marry, and preferred a wedding to follow swiftly on from an engagement, so they pressured Pierre Breil to give his consent and for the marriage to be realized as soon as possible. When Breil continued to refuse Cavaillier decided to take the case to the judiciary.[66]

M. Dostaly came to the consistory in Nîmes in 1611 because his son had contracted marriage with Chabaud de Polvetieres's daughter without his consent. He was so incensed that he swore to take the case to the judiciary to have the marriage dissolved. The bride's father defended the marriage by pointing out that the couple had spent time together over three years, it was an equal match, and he knew they had consummated their relationship: what harm was there in a marriage? When it was revealed five days later that his daughter was actually five or six months pregnant, the consistory sent a delegation to M. Dostaly senior, to ask him to reconsider and give his consent to the marriage.[67] The consistory wanted parental consent, but they did not venerate it in the same way that the French statutes did, and were happy for it to be retrospective if all other things were equal. Much like the Catholic Church, they were inclined to uphold marriages without parental consent where the lay elites, concerned about impulsive marriages and the transmission of inheritances, would have wanted to annul them—even though some of their number were elite themselves.

When parental consent was not forthcoming, there were various strategies available to help ordinary couples negotiate the obstacle. The first was to attempt to persuade the consistory that it was not required. One loophole concerned the

---

[63] BN, Ms.fr. 8666, 54r–55r, 57v, 59r–v, 61v, 62r–v, 17 Dec. 1561.
[64] ADH, GG 24, 118v–119r, 12 Mar. 1600.   [65] ADG, 42 J 34, 90v, 20 May 1609.
[66] ADTG, I 1, 79r–v, 30 Dec. 1595.
[67] ADG, 42 J 34, 286v, 298r, 302v, 308r, 4 Sept. 1611.

age of the partners: under French law parental permission was required up to the age of twenty-five for women and thirty for men. Jean Adam and Ysabeau de Tillois said in March 1596 that they had received the consent of de Tillois's father Simon to their engagement, which he had subsequently withdrawn, 'for some fantasy that has come into his head', and had told them, in a series of angry outbursts, that he would not now allow them to marry. De Tillois informed the consistory that she was over twenty-five years old and so did not need her father's consent. As the engagement had initially been made with his approval, and seeing how much they wished to marry— de Tillois 'had begged her father to consent with tears in her eyes'—the consistory sought to persuade Simon to return to his earlier agreement, but he refused. At this point the consistory asked her father to confirm her age; he stated that he could not remember. The consistory sought to ascertain how old she was, and finally agreed that she must be old enough to marry without her father's permission on the basis of two pieces of evidence: 'several notable people' testified that she had been working as a maid for seventeen years, and had started work at the age of about thirteen or fourteen, so must therefore be around thirty years old, and secondly her appearance suggested maturity: 'by bodily aspect she appears to have passed twenty-five years of age', as the consistory delicately put it. The emphasis on de Tillois's age was a successful strategy, but it was probably helped considerably by her father's 'stubbornness', anger, and hostility towards the consistory, which described him as 'capricious'.[68] Similarly, Guiraud Clavel from Marvejols presented himself to the Nîmes consistory in November 1583 saying that he wanted to marry a girl called Suzanne Bate, but that his father did not want to consent to the marriage and wanted him to marry someone else. He turned to the consistory for advice, stating that his father had consented to the marriages of his younger brothers, and that he was over thirty years old. The consistory sought further attestation of his age, which they received five months later from the officers of Marvejols, and the marriage was permitted.[69]

Another strategy was to demonstrate the impossibility of gaining parental consent. Bertrand Maurice, a master gunsmith who was skilled in making long guns called arquebuses—a useful profession in a Protestant town in sixteenth-century France—came from Sedan, a princely enclave on the eastern frontier, now the French/Belgian border. He presented himself to the consistory at Montauban in March 1596 to say that after having lived in the city for more than a year, he wanted to stay and marry Anne Diabonne. Yet he feared that if he made a promise of marriage to her the consistory would refuse to allow him to effect it, because he would not have the consent of his mother, whom he had not seen for six years because she still lived in Sedan. He enumerated the difficulties of obtaining her consent: 'it is impossible for him to go so far, the city being outside the kingdom [of France], and being uncertain whether his mother is alive or not'.[70] This indefatigable logic—and perhaps because he had approached the consistory before making

[68] ADTG, I 1, 111v, 115r–116r, 13 Mar. 1596. [69] ADG, 42 J 28, 62r, 98r, 30 Nov. 1583.
[70] ADTG, I 1, 116v–117r, 20 Mar. 1596.

any promises, indicating goodwill—worked in his favour and the consent of Diabonne's pliant uncle proved sufficient to realize the match.

A more risky alternative was to proceed without waiting for consent. Rostaing Rozel's eldest son and Damoyselle de Colla were summoned in December 1615 for having married without the consent of their parents, having not published banns, and having not been truthful with the pastor of Bocoyran who married them in Dions, a small commune north of Nîmes.[71] They were severely censured for their fault and suspended from the sacrament, but were nevertheless married. The widow of the late Captain Fueillac admitted, on being questioned by the consistory in 1609, that she frequented 'young Daumiere' but said that their frequentation should not cause scandal as they were married, having been contracted by a notary in Avignon. They had not yet dared to publicize it because Daumiere's parents did not want to consent to the marriage. The consistory required documentary proof of the marriage, and ordered them not to spend time together until the marriage had been blessed in a church.[72] Daumiere may have been young, but as the marriage had been promised and contracted, the issue was clearly not serious enough to invite prosecution; it did, however, result in their suspension from the sacrament for their 'clandestine marriage'. Jacques Broche and Bonne Privade chose another popular route that allowed instant gratification. Without the consent of Privade's father, they married in front of a priest, and were suspended from the Eucharist for this grave misdemeanour.[73] Despite French law, it seems that in this instance the Roman Catholic Church turned a blind eye to their lack of demonstrable consent, and such a wedding could be a neat way of avoiding the stringent requirements of the Reformed Church.

Other evidence suggests that some parents could be persuaded to yield to their children's wishes. The many unions between people of different denominations indicate that children could win over their parents under certain circumstances. The Nîmes consistory told Firmin Bagard that it was very strange he had married his daughter to a papist as she and he had long professed the Reformed faith. He replied that 'seeing that his daughter wants it, he did not dare to refuse her'.[74] That parents were responsive to the wishes of their offspring indicates that, as Davis suggested, there was sometimes a symbiosis between parents and children—although less because young people had internalized the need for parental approval than because some parents had internalized the need for their children's happiness.[75]

At times it seems that parents could even try to use the idea of parental consent to support their children's will. Following the marriage contract and official engagement between Jean Court and a woman called de Savynhes (her first name was left blank), Savynhes's mother Marguerite Valese refused to allow the marriage to proceed. She said that Court had threatened to beat Savynhes several times and treated her rudely, rumour had it that he had already been married, and he would not

---

[71] ADG, 42 J 35, 211r, 30 Dec. 1615.
[72] ADG, 42 J 34, 90r, 94r, 100v, 20 May 1609.   [73] ADG, 42 J 34, 258v, 20 Apr. 1611.
[74] BN, Ms.fr. 8667, 105r, 2 Mar. 1580.   [75] Davis, 'Ghosts', 106–8.

demonstrably be able to manage their finances.[76] Valese was clearly acting in line with her daughter's wishes, for Savynhes stated that she did not want to marry Court, because she 'feared his punches'. Unfortunately for her, her mother's belated retraction of permission was trumped by the consent given a week later by Pierre Calvet, Valese's husband and Savynhes's step-father, who had supplied the dowry, and whose word was decisive, despite his lack of blood relationship to Savynhes. On his assent, the consistory ordered that the marriage proceed. The belated nature of this attempt to intervene—after the contract of marriage—partly explains why parental dissent was unsuccessful in this case, although interventions were also bound to be less successful when mothers pleaded and their authority could be invalidated by that of a man.

Parents could act more effectively to implement the wishes of their children by turning a blind eye. The Nîmes consistory discovered that Jehanne de Rozel and M. de la Croix, a Catholic, had married in November 1578 without her parents' consent, after becoming engaged two years earlier.[77] At first Rozel's mother claimed to know nothing of the marriage, saying that she had simply allowed Rozel to dine at Croix's house one night and knew no more; her husband also said, 'if she was married, he knew nothing of it'. Yet it was also recorded that Rozel's father had decided that his daughter's fiancé was 'very good, except for his religion', and Rozel's mother later admitted to knowing that Croix and Rozel had married in his house before a priest. It seems likely that Rozel's parents, despite trying to maintain an appearance of disapproval towards the match, had been fully cognizant that Rozel had gone to Croix's house to marry him, and had allowed the marriage to take place before a priest to avoid the scandal of openly consenting to an interfaith marriage. The interests of parents and children were clearly not always antithetical, and for ordinary people parental consent was something that could often be negotiated, exploited, or even side-stepped.

Conclusions

When it came to courtship, the reformation of marriage regulations put the Calvinist Church out of step with popular tradition. Popular ritual invested gestures and objects with profound symbolic significance, and considered them to valorize an engagement or marriage. When examining the materialism of popular marriage ritual in fifteenth-century Champagne, André Burguière worried that the sources unduly stressed the objects used because they were used to garner reparations; he also thought such ritual was not so important in the Midi.[78] Neither of these points holds true: even when such matters were overlooked by the authorities assessing the validity of marriage, ordinary people in Languedoc continued to cite acts and objects that symbolized giving because they counted in the popular imagination. In a similar way, recognition of the importance of the dowry—for both its symbolic and its practical significance—was almost universal,

[76] ADTG, I 1, 258r–v, 260r–v, 28 May 1597.
[77] BN, Ms.fr. 8667, 53r–v, 56r, 26 Nov. 1578.   [78] Burguière, 'Le rituel', 644–5.

except from members of the consistory (when acting in that capacity, since it seems highly likely that as individuals they gave and received dowries just like everyone else). The Church and public opinion only really coincided on the need for public recognition. When it came to the choice of spouses there was some parental involvement in arranging marriages, but also strong evidence of attraction between marrying pairs who often took the initiative. Ultimately the consistory prized a proper enactment of marriage over parental consent. Parents too could be complicit with their children's wishes. When such consent was not forthcoming, people looked for strategies to circumvent the obstacle and to marry as they wished. What happened when they did not wish it is our next focus.

BROKEN PROMISES

For the Huguenot authorities free consent at the moment of engagement was vital. As we have seen, they sought evidence that promises to marry had been made voluntarily, soberly, and without compulsion, and from that moment on the promise to marry—if made with all due process—was binding. Any later disinclination, even for the most compelling of reasons, was paid little heed. Unless evidence could be found to vitiate the original engagement, the marriage was required to proceed.[79]

Naturally many people coming to the consistory had a very different idea about the revocability of an engagement, and for a very good reason: before the Protestant Reformation, the Catholic Church had been comparatively flexible. Mutual consent of the parties to dissolve the engagement constituted a legitimate impediment to marriage under the medieval Catholic Church. Evidence from an ecclesiastical tribunal in fifteenth-century Troyes suggests that engaged couples who no longer wanted to marry were usually allowed to change their minds on payment of a small fine.[80] The Protestant moral authorities, by contrast (despite ceasing to see marriage as a sacrament), were unusually strict and inflexible.[81] So there existed an expectation-gap between the Church and many of its adherents. Fifty years after the Reformed church was established in Languedoc, Protestant women and men had still not adjusted to the new rules. Many ordinary people continued to expect the right to change one's mind after engagement.

Women Seeking to Break off an Engagement

As the case opening this book demonstrated, women were among those wishing to break off an engagement. For women to seek to do this in an age in which their personal, social, and economic identities were so premised on marriage shows a bold autonomy that is seldom associated with women in this period: not only did they expect to be involved in the decision about whom to marry, they considered

---

[79] Watt, *The Making*, 72.   [80] Gottlieb, 'The Meaning', 63.
[81] Sharon Kettering, *French Society, 1589–1715* (Harlow, 2001), 24.

the decision not to wed theirs as well. But given that marriage had such potential worth for a woman, why might they be the ones to seek the dissolution of an engagement? Previous historiography has been rather quiet on the subject of women changing their minds about marrying, but the cases before the consistory indicate a range of reasons.[82]

The first was a conviction that the men to whom they were engaged were unfit to be husbands. The daughter of Pierre Constantin refused to marry her fiancé in May 1608 because she claimed to have received 'discourtesies, reproaches, and insults' from him. Her father joined her in complaining to the consistory against the invective of her intended, and the couple were not reconciled.[83]

Such complaints of women against their potential spouses indicate what was required of a husband. Dalphine Ginière was a maidservant working for Captain Bessières in early 1597.[84] She was engaged to a tailor called Jean Labourd, who lived a couple of miles outside Montauban, in the small town of Montbeton. With their usual vigilance the Montauban consistory noticed that the couple were taking a long time to marry, and dispatched an elder to investigate. Assuming that Ginière's employer must be delaying the ceremony, they questioned Bessières, who said he had not even thought of such a thing. He explained that it was Ginière herself who was halting the marriage, because of 'certain things' that she had heard others say against her proposed husband-to-be.

Ginière and her fiancé were summoned. Labourd expressed his enthusiasm for the match, pointed out that he had contracted marriage with Ginière according to all the regulations of the Reformed Church, and that their banns had been announced. All that remained was the wedding itself, and he did not know why she was stalling. Ginière was interrogated, and testified that since they had got engaged she had learnt 'that he has given away his possessions, so much so that if she married him, he would not have the means to feed and keep her, as he has nothing in the world'. In addition to this, she had heard it said that 'he killed his first wife because he treated her so poorly'. For these compelling reasons, she did not want to go ahead with the wedding.

The rumours about Labourd identified two aspects of character that cut to the heart of what it meant to be a good husband—how well a man could provide for and would treat his wife. If part of the purpose of marriage was economic provision, a husband who had been impoverishing himself was not up to much. It is unlikely Labourd's dispossession was the result of charitable giving, as the reference to poor treatment often served as a euphemism for tavern-going, gambling, and alcohol-fuelled violence. It may be that Labourd had gambled away his money. Such behaviour would also make sense of the rather cryptic remark that he had murdered his first wife because of his poor treatment. For 'treated her so badly', we should perhaps read vicious assault or starvation.

---

[82] Solé and Gottlieb consider it briefly (Solé, *Etre femme*, 80, 120, 123; Gottlieb, 'Meaning', 59, 64), but the subject is not mentioned by Farr, Capp, Rublack, or others.

[83] ADG, 42 J 34, 15r, 23 May 1608.

[84] ADTG I 1, 223r, 224r–v, 226v, 235v, 237r, 15 Jan. 1597.

The consistory agreed to make enquiries with Labourd's neighbours to see if they knew anything about the alleged mistreatment that had led to Labourd's first wife's death. Several neighbours attested that Labourd had 'poorly treated' his late wife (or possibly, even more seriously, 'late wives'—the text slips into a one-off plural). In response, the consistory tasked Labourd with acting gently towards his fiancée and to 'celebrate and accomplish' their marriage. They also told him that if Ginière continued to refuse to wed, he should have recourse to the magistrates. In a judgment based more on procedure than pathos, the consistory condemned Ginière to marriage with a man whose abuse may have resulted in the death of his previous wife.

Later in the same year, the same consistory reached a similar judgment when another woman hesitated over marriage for near-identical reasons. Marie de Vigier had promised to marry a man called Arnaud Ricard, nicknamed *L'Espagnol*, 'the Spaniard'. The case came to the consistory's attention because Arnaud was complaining that Vigier no longer wanted to see the marriage through, though he stood ready to 'do his duty'.[85]

Vigier was interrogated. Had she agreed to marry him? She answered obliquely that she was afraid that after he had married her he would either desert her and go to Spain, or he would 'beat her and mistreat her, as he had already threatened to do'. Her worries echo Ginière's very closely: a lack of husbandly provision— through abandonment—or violence at his hands. Vigier added that she had also fallen out with Arnaud's sister, and that she had gone with several other women to Corbarieu, a town about five miles from Montauban, to speak to a female fortune-teller, to find out why everything was going wrong for her. She recognized, she said, that in so doing she had sinned.

The consistory seized on this moment of remorse. They remonstrated with her and with Ricard to do their duty and to remain true to their promises to marry. Both declared that they would. The consistory pushed home their advantage: 'and they should marry as quickly as possible'. The couple meekly agreed. To top it off, Vigier was then severely berated for the scandal that she had caused by visiting the fortune-teller. She knelt before the consistory to ask the forgiveness of God and of the church.

From the consistory's perspective this was an absolute triumph. They were unmoved by Vigier's testimony that her fiancé had threatened to assault her. For Vigier this emotional volte-face, caused by her internalization of Protestant doctrine and the external pressure of the church, led to a life-changing act of submission. Ultimately she agreed to marry a man who had expressly threatened to beat her, in order to do the right thing.

A second reason for women seeking to annul an engagement was sexual infidelity. This suggests that it may not only have been female honour that was tainted by promiscuity.[86] The daughter of cobbler Claude Vidal refused to marry her fiancé,

---

[85] ADTG, I 1, 284r, 20 Aug. 1597.

[86] Recent historiography around male honour has conceded that it was imperilled by a wife's sexual dishonesty, and strengthened by the sexual control of women, achieved—it was thought—through

Paulet Hospital, in 1563 even though he could produce their contract as evidence. Her reason was that since their engagement he had carried on an affair with a married woman.[87] Coming near the end of the first register of consistorial cases in Nîmes—after which there is a fifteen-year gap—the outcome of the Hospital-Vidale marriage is unknown, but it demonstrates that women, not just men, thought that sexual infidelity constituted a sufficient betrayal of trust not to marry the betrayer.

For all the cases where seemingly viable excuses like poor behaviour and infidelity were offered, there are plenty more incidences like the case of Jehan Palairet and Jehanne de Bec, who had exchanged promises of marriage which de Bec 'does not now want to consent to'.[88] Yet the most frequent reason why women sought to break off an engagement was that they simply had no affection for their intended. Compelling as it may have been as a reason for those concerned, this found little favour with the consistory.

In October 1597 it became clear that while engagement promises had been made and banns pronounced between Marie de Vigneri and Astorg Cloquet, there appeared to be some delay in their marriage. When Cloquet was summoned before the Montauban consistory he protested that he was not at fault and was ready to marry. Vigneri, however, said 'she did not want to proceed with the marriage, because she did not love the said Cloquet at all'. In fact, she added, 'at the time that she became betrothed to him, she had mislaid her senses, having been suborned into it by several women'.[89] The consistory regarded her lack of love as a secondary concern, but in claiming—in quite strong terms—that she had not freely consented to the engagement and that a group of women had bullied her into the promise, Vigneri was cleverly engaging the consistory on its own grounds. It ought to have been a winning remark, provoking an investigation into whether she had freely consented at the time of engagement. That it did not, that she was instead threatened with suspension, and Astorg was enjoined to take the matter to the magistrates, suggests that there was more to her comment than meets the historian's eye. Yet even in the face of such intimidation she remained adamant. It might not have mattered to the church, but the prospect of a loveless marriage concerned her so much that Vigneri was willing to challenge the authorities, face social exclusion, and even experience the exactitudes of the judicial system to avoid it.

She was not the only one. Jehan del Rieu and Catherine Commessague appeared before the consistory in Nîmes because del Rieu was complaining that Commessague did not wish to enact the marriage contracted between them. When asked why not, she replied simply that, 'she did not want to marry him'.[90] Nothing that was said to exhort her to do so could change her mind. The consistory gave her some

---

sexual potency: Elizabeth A. Foyster, *Manhood in Early Modern England: Honour, Sex, and Marriage* (London and New York, 1999), 4, 9, 39–40, 67–72; Anthony Fletcher, *Gender, Sex and Subordination in England 1500–1800* (New Haven, CT, and London, 1995), 93, 101, 109–10; Roper, *The Holy Household*, 86. This case raises the possibility that it could also be imperilled by a lack of sexual control over one self.

[87] BN, Ms.fr. 8666, 197v, 6 Jan. 1563.   [88] ADTG, I 1, 343v, 13 May 1598.

[89] ADTG, I 1, 295r, 302v, 312v, 322v, 326r, 1 Oct. 1597.

[90] ADG, 42 J 29, 60, 21 Sept. 1588.

days to deliberate and pray to God to direct her wishes, but the couple never returned and it is uncertain what happened between them. Yet not all could resist ecclesiastical pressure. In September 1580 goldsmith Jaques Faget stated that a year earlier he had become engaged and 'given his heart' to Françoyse Codercque, when they had exchanged promises in the presence of witnesses. A notary had drawn up a contract of marriage, which had included the condition that they would marry after twelve months, so that Codercque could first mourn her late husband. Now, she refused to re marry. When she was put under pressure to do so, she said she did not want to marry before the time had elapsed as stated in the contract. When she was told that the time had elapsed and she must rather marry Faget as soon as possible, she said that she would not do so without the consent of her mother. But now she was running out of excuses. The consistory threatened her with suspension, and whether Codercque was content to receive his heart or not, the marriage was duly solemnized.[91]

Sometimes the reasons for wishing to annul an engagement are simply unknown. In April 1609 Madaleyne Valeze was suspended from the Eucharist for refusing to marry her fiancé Ysac Dumas. The register is coy: 'she does not intend to marry the said Dumas for the reasons that she said'; whatever they were, they went unrecorded. Over two years later she sought re admission to the sacrament, but it was only in December 1611 that the consistory finally reconciled her to the church. Again the register notes that the consistory re admitted her 'having heard her reasons for refusing to have the marriage blessed', but for a second time did not note them down.[92] Two incarnations of the consistory apparently thought her reasons sufficiently troubling that they dare not commit them to paper.

The cumulative effect of these cases is to suggest that women living in Languedoc under the Huguenot Church retained a belief in their freedom to change their minds about whom to marry. For ordinary women the right to flexibility, indecision, and self-correction when it came to all-important choices about their life partners was indisputable. The church authorities who regulated their lives did not agree. Never mind whether the reason was a change of heart, a lack of love, the threat of violence, sexual betrayal, or even a claim to have been induced into agreeing to the engagement in a moment of vulnerability, a marriage promised was a marriage made. Such a piebald understanding of engagement and marriage had enormous, life-changing consequences for these women and others besides.

Women Using the Consistory to Try to Enforce Promises

The consistory's unyielding attitude towards engagement promises could, of course, potentially benefit women as well as harm them. What all the women turning to this panel of elders and ministers had in common was the sense that that they might use the institutions of the church for their own ends—even if that meant forcing a recalcitrant man into marrying them.

---

[91] BN, Ms.fr. 8667, 141r, 30 Sept. 1580.
[92] ADG, 42 J 34, 81v, 127v, 373, 304r, 17 Apr. 1609.

At this time, people regularly used courts to resolve social disputes, and in earlier and later centuries we have accounts of French women trying to use episcopal courts to enforce marriage, so resorting to the consistory was not in itself particularly unusual.[93] What makes it distinctive is the circumstances in which women could approach it, and the status of many of those women. In reports from seventeenth-century Burgundy, for example, single women only tried to use the courts to persuade men to marry them when they were pregnant. Only the all-too-obvious nature of a pregnancy could prove that they had succumbed to the advances of their alleged fiancé and help secure them their husband, and only when pregnant with an illegitimate child were they desperate enough to risk the exposure of their immorality in court. There are equivalent cases before the consistories. In May 1583 Catherine Gilliberte confessed to becoming pregnant by George de Saule under a promise of marriage that the Catholic de Saule no longer wished to honour. Although Gilliberte was censured, she was encouraged to keep the child, and the church sent a representative to de Saule to persuade him to deliver on his promise.[94] Conversely, Marguerite Baudriere appeared in October 1562 claiming that her daughter was pregnant by Jehan Paulet, who had promised to marry her. Baudriere assured the consistory that surgeon Guillaume Ribaud, textile-worker Jaques Martin, saddler Domergue Lestant, and a man with a red beard who lived near the Apple Inn were all witnesses to the fact. The consistory promised to investigate, but the case never reappears.[95] Yet most marital cases before the consistory show women seeking to bring a reluctant fiancé to heel in circumstances when the odds were much longer.

Even though not pregnant, when faced with reluctant fiancés refusing to adhere to promises made, women tried to shape their destinies in this crucial question of a spouse. The greater incidence of this before the consistory than other similar bodies is readily explained: the consistory was free of charge to approach. Poor women could take a gamble without incurring the horrendous legal expenses they would face at a judicial court. So women such as Madeleine Pinete, who appeared before the consistory in 1592 asking the elders to persuade her fiancé to marry her, attempted to use the consistory's commitment to upholding engagement promises to implement their own marriage plans.[96] By comparison with other sources, then, the consistory gives us more insight into women's strategies and ambitions. Interestingly, the consistory never seems to have become cautious about this use by women, as judges in Burgundian criminal courts did, which may be because the consistory shared women's goal of enforcing marital promises that could be proved to have been made.[97] This is not how men commonly used the consistory: I have found only two instances, over the fifty-five years of records, of men bringing a case to the consistory in an effort to force a marriage to proceed.[98] There remains the

---

[93] e.g. Martin Ingram, *Church Courts, Sex and Marriage in England, 1570–1640* (Cambridge, 1987), 292; Solé, *Etre femme*, 105; Gottlieb, 'The Meaning', 61–2; Farr, *Authority*, 112.

[94] ADG, 42 J 28, 18v, 25 May 1583.   [95] BN, 42 J 26, 168r, 17 Oct. 1562.

[96] ADG, 42 J 30, 28r, 1 Jan. 1592.   [97] Farr, *Authority*, 92, 101.

[98] Thomas Sigion, see p. 191, and Simon Bourdict, who objected to the marriage of Anne Salles and Pierre Pastrone in October 1603; the consistory ordered that the banns for the marriage proceed nonetheless: ADG, 42 J 32, 187r, 15 Oct. 1603.

possibility that some men found informal ways of getting the consistory to take the initiative in the numerous cases where it coerced reluctant brides.

In a few instances of women's suits the outcome is uncertain, as the cases, for reasons that are unclear, fade out of the records without proper consideration. Marguerite Durante, from Chamborigaud in the Cévennes, presented herself in December 1591 to object to the fact that Pierre de Lacroix had published his banns of marriage with another woman, as he had previously promised to marry her. She could name those who had witnessed their engagement and display his engagement gift to her—a ring of 'gold set in stone'.[99] The consistory decided to question the witnesses to find out the truth of the matter but—whether they did not follow up, or whether the reports were insufficient to warrant notation— Durante's complaint was not satisfied. Suzanne Verilhane claimed that Pierre Peysac had promised to marry her and had given her a ring; in return she had given him twenty-nine *livres*, and yet he had since contracted marriage with a girl in Uzès.[100] She presented herself, with him in tow, to the consistory in December 1604, requiring him to 'do right'. He denied her claims, and the consistory ordered her to produce witnesses to support her story. That the record goes silent suggests that she had no witnesses to call. If nothing came of these cases, at least Durante and Verilhane had some small consolation from having their dissent recognized in this official context.[101]

There were also suits by women that clearly failed. Jehanne Bonnette presented a case against Jehan Berroul in May 1591. She stated that he had promised to take her in marriage three or four years earlier, in the presence of his brother Bernard, Bernard's wife, his son-in-law, and several others, and that they had drunk in the name of marriage. Jehan Berroul had now become engaged to someone else. He admitted to having handed her a glass of wine in the name of marriage, but denied giving her anything else. She, however, had given him a handkerchief and garters, and said that they had 'spent time together' since their engagement, with Berroul repeating his promise less than a month earlier. The consistory took depositions from witnesses, and concluded that as the only basis was a drink in the name of marriage three years earlier, and that there was no evidence that they had since pursued the matter, the objection was not sufficient to prevent Berroul marrying elsewhere.[102]

Some cases seem hopeless and desperate even from the outset. In October 1578 maidservant Gabrielle Lanbonne challenged the marriage of Pierre Dufour to another woman by simply stating that when she was his maid he had promised to marry her and said that he would not have another. She had no other evidence.[103] Jeanne Parvijolle said that Anthoine de Maspoulet had betrothed her but since had become engaged to another woman, and his banns for this second marriage had been published three times. She appeared to protest although she had nothing

[99] ADG, 42 J 30, 20v, 11 Dec. 1591.   [100] ADG, 42 J 33, 5r, 15 Dec. 1604.

[101] Laura Gowing, *Domestic Dangers: Women, Words and Sex in Early Modern London* (Oxford, 1996), 42–3, 53.

[102] ADG, 42 J 29, 647, 654, 16 May 1591.

[103] BN, Ms.fr. 8667, 41r, 1 Oct. 1578.

to prove her claim.[104] Lucie Balzalgete complained in March 1588 that Bastian Flory had become engaged to someone else after having promised marriage to her and had also extorted several items from her. Flory denied having promised anything to Bazalgete, and her inability to produce anything to verify the promise meant that the marriage suit was dropped, but Flory was instructed to return her possessions, which at least represented a small victory.[105]

The failure of many claims should not lead us to conclude that women's suits were not taken seriously by the consistory. An interesting example is that of Jehanne Fontanieue, a servant who presented herself at the consistory in Nîmes in December 1562 to protest the proposed marriage of a carpenter called Jacques Rosilles.[106] Fontanieue claimed that on the promise of marriage she had 'abandoned herself' and submitted to Rosilles's advances, and that since then he had 'known her three or four times a day'—an extravagant story, but one the consistory seems not to have rejected outright. Although she could provide no evidence of the alleged engagement promises, nevertheless the consistory summoned Rosilles, Fontanieue's father, and a man called Lazaire Fazendier, whom Fontanieue had nominated as supporting her claim.

When Rosilles was questioned, he said that one day, when he had been working at the Château de Saint-Genieys where Fontanieue was a servant, another employee, Jehan Dussoyre, had asked him if he had ever thought of marrying Fontanieue, and said that if he did he would stand to gain Fontanieue's parents' wealth via her dowry. According to Rosilles this conversation was only 'in the manner of passing the time and without any intention to marry her at all'. This was male banter in which they assessed the relative merits of women and their financial value. He denied ever having sexual intercourse with her, or making binding promises to marry her before witnesses, but he did admit that he said to Fontanieue that he would marry her if her parents wanted to give her a good dowry. He claimed, however, that this was a statement extracted from him under sufferance, and made when Fontanieue was surrounded by her people whom Rosilles did not want to displease—he was convinced, he alleged, that they meant him ill and would take him prisoner if he did not go along with the plan, and he felt threatened because, not being in his hometown, he had no support.

Yet the consistory had obviously heard rumours that belied his words. They asked whether he had had carnal intercourse with Fontanieue 'behind the old tower of Saint-Genieys', if he had promised to marry her one Sunday in the base court of the château before witnesses, and if he had told her to take care of 'the fruit of her womb'—all of which he fiercely denied. An outraged Rosilles accused Jehan Mantes—whom he said owed him money and was a fornicator, thief, and pimp—of conjuring up these allegations to spite him.

The consistory was confounded by the differences in the accounts, so brought the couple face-to-face and pointedly made them swear to tell the truth.

[104] ADG, 42 J 34, 54r, 24 Dec. 1608.
[105] ADG, 42 J 28, 370v–371r, 9 Mar. 1588.
[106] BN, Ms.fr. 8666, 188r–189v, 192r, v, 23 Dec. 1562.

Fontanieue swore and then put it to Rosilles that he must remember when she had dropped off some white shirts to his workshop and he had 'known' her carnally for the first time. He denied it with the assertion that 'he took God as his witness'.

This planted a seed of doubt, and, after Rosilles had left, Fontanieue was asked who had counselled her to oppose Rosilles's marriage and try to secure him as a husband. These were accusatory terms, to which she responded that her father, her friends, and Lazaire Fazendier had given her such counsel. The consistory called her father, who admitted he had not heard the betrothal promises in person himself, but had been told of them by his daughter. The consistory then sent their summoner to speak to Fazendier. He was just mounting his horse to travel outside the city and spoke only a few words: that he did not have anything to add, and they should look diligently at the evidence and pronounce justice. In short, no one could supply definitive evidence of an engagement, and both men covered themselves rather than supporting Fontanieue. As a final sally, the consistory recalled Rosilles and asked him again 'in the name of God and in all conscience' if he ever promised to take Fontanieue in marriage or slept with her. He again said no, and repeated his powerful assertion that he 'took God as his witness'. In the absence of any concrete evidence it was her word against his, and, while the consistory manifestly felt some hesitancy about making their pronouncement, after much discussion they finally concluded in Rosilles's favour.

Was Fontanieue wronged? Had these two been lovers? Had they sworn to marry each other in the courtyard of the château before an assembled company? Had she promised him a large dowry in exchange for marriage, which he had greedily accepted until a better offer came along? Or was it she who had wronged him? Had she overheard his conversation with Dussoyre, conceived a notion that he wanted to marry her, and got carried away, making up tales of an extravagant sex life and fantasizing about a wedding ceremony to support her claim? And did Rosilles's debtor stitch him up?

Like the consistory before us, we are faced with two conflicting narratives and must make up our minds. In the absence of any further evidence, it seems likely that Fontanieue's claims were deliberately deceptive. When the matter stalled, the older men who had put Fontanieue up to it did not back up her claim and at this point her suit faltered. What is clear, however, is that two factors were decisive: if Fazendier, an influential figure in the town who could have swayed the consistory with his testimony, had not been so keen to set off on his travels but had appeared before the consistory instead, and if Rosilles had not so convincingly brazened his way through the interrogation with the line that he took God as his witness, the case might have turned out very differently indeed.

Even if the complaints were unsuccessful, what is notable about these histories is that low-status women—often maidservants—demonstrated a phenomenal amount of determination in taking their alleged fiancés to task. Their pluck is arguably all the greater if we imagine that they fabricated any part of their accounts, but one gets the impression that they were—for the most part—women with a genuine grievance.

Although the circumstances under which these women's suits prospered or faltered seem somewhat arbitrary, some women did find the keys to success. There appear to have been two ways—though neither failsafe—that led to the result they sought. The first was to provide the consistory with proof.

The most easily available proof was the testimony of eyewitnesses who had seen a promise enacted. In February 1580 Anne Jan Jaques from Montréal, near Joyeuse, presented herself before the consistory to plead for their help in enforcing a promise of marriage made to her by Anthoine Drome. She testified that they had enacted the formal betrothal ceremony and had drunk in the name of marriage in the presence of witnesses. The witnesses were summoned. The baker Pierre Sauyot said he had been unexpectedly pulled in from the street to stand witness to the promises made in a shop beneath the house of M. Mazandier, where Jan Jaques lived (either as a tenant or, more likely, as a servant). The promises had been led by Anthoine Durane, whose wife, when summoned, recalled her husband first being asked to eat with Jan Jaques and Drome. After supper they had gone into the shop under Mazandier's house, where they drank in the name of marriage and Durane had asked them if they wish to give their bodies to each other, following the usual formula. They had both agreed, had kissed, and Drome had given a ring to Jan Jaques. The evidence of the witnesses was compelling, and in the face of it Drome did not deny the series of events. The real problem was that he was dragging his heels. Jan Jaques's ability to resort to the consistory was just the mechanism that she needed. The consistory ordered that banns would be published on the following three Sundays, and the marriage would proceed forthwith, adding ominously that if Drome defaulted, 'they would have recourse to the magistrate to punish him'.[107] Anne had got her man.

Even witnesses, however, would not always swing a case in a woman's favour. In February 1588 Alaysette Forniere presented herself to oppose the marriage of P. Pol Mendre, also known as Christol. She explained that about six years earlier when she had been living at M. Recolin's house, Mendre had lived near by with the butcher Jacques Mingaud, and had promised to marry her. Under this promise, they had had sex and she had given birth to a little girl. As Mendre denied ever promising her, or even knowing her beyond having seen her a few times in the road, Forniere offered to call witnesses. The first, 45-year-old Jehane Bugne, appeared that afternoon to testify that she had known both Mendre and Forniere since the time they lived at Recolin's and Mingaud's houses, that she had often seen Mendre talking with Forniere, and had heard him say to her that he would never have anyone else as his wife but her. Mendre's father had also remarked that he hoped Forniere would be his daughter-in-law. Bunhe remarked that Forniere's child's face greatly resembled Mendre's.

A week later three more women came to depose. Twenty-year-old Marie Imberte said that five years earlier she had often seen Mendre visiting Forniere both day and night. One Sunday evening, when many of the household had gone to Corbessac, he had even stayed a great part of the night with her, had opened up her blouse to

---

[107] BN, Ms.fr. 8667, 96r–v, 3 Feb. 1580.

see her breasts, and then had thrown her on the bed and had sex with her. Imberte, attempting to sleep close by, saw it all. She also added that they regularly sat and talked on Recolin's porch or steps, that when one approached them with a light Mendre would extinguish it, that she had heard him promise Forniere that he would take her in marriage, and that the child looked like Mendre. Curiously the next witness, 22-year-old Anthonye Perote, said—the observed sex aside—almost exactly the same thing: that Mendre visited Forniere day and night, that they were often alone together, if you took a light he extinguished it, and that the child looked like Mendre. Twenty-five-year-old Gillette Franchilhonne repeated the same words, with one original addition: that she had asked Forniere why she 'made such caresses' with Mendre, and Forniere told her that he had promised to take her in marriage. Bunhe, Imberte, and Franchilhonne had also used almost precisely the same formula when describing the child: 'the little girl strongly resembled Mendre in the aspect of her face'. There was clearly a degree of rehearsal between these depositions, given by women who were probably friends, but that does not mean that they were necessarily untrue, even though Mendre denied everything they had said. At this, Bunhe (who had returned) added that one evening, around eight o'clock, she had found the couple on the steps and remonstrated with them that they would do better to speak to their fathers and get married than stay as they were. Mendre said that was false too.

There were several other witnesses, however. Sieur Claude Bessonet, a 40-year-old merchant, said that he had tried to mediate between Forniere and Mendre, after Forniere had the daughter whom she said was Mendre's. Mendre had offered her fifteen *écus* if she left him alone, or to take the child without giving her anything. Forniere had refused to accept even twenty-five *écus*, saying he had promised to take her in marriage. Twenty-one-year-old Anne Verdelhane said that some four or five years earlier, when she lived with Jehan Guyraud as a servant, she saw Forniere bringing her daughter to Guyraud's house, whose wife was breastfeeding the child. Mendre came to join them, took the baby in his arms, and held her for some time. He then offered Forniere five *sols* to buy white bread, but Forniere said she would buy linen to make something for the child. Verdelhane and her sister, 23-year-old Clemence, also each independently told a moving story of an incident that had occurred a few years later, probably in late 1585. Forniere and Mendre's child had died. Anne, Clemence, and Forniere had been on the way to Bonneterre's farm, where her father lived, when they met Mendre. After exchanging greetings, he took Forniere in his arms but also berated her that she was the cause of their young daughter's death. Anne remembered Forniere saying, in tears, that she had done her duty and Clemence reported that Forniere said that 'she was as sorrowful as he at the death of her daughter and that she did all she could to save her', and then started to weep and grieve. Mendre then walked with them all the way to the farm, and told Forniere she should not grieve as he would have no other for wife but her. When they parted from him he had hugged and kissed Forniere, and reiterated his promise. A week after these testimonies, a 45-year-old man called Captain Jehan Solet said that some three or four years earlier Mendre told him he had a child with a woman after having promised to marry her, which he must do or be put in prison, but had instead tried to give her money to pay her off. Finally the minister, M. de Chambrun, reported that he had spoken with two brothers whose father had previously been a *présidial* judge, and to whom Forniere had come complaining that Mendre was the father of her child and had said he would take her in marriage. Several years after this their father had agreed with Mendre a sum of money to pay her if he would not marry her, but nothing came of it.

There is a sad tale in all this—of a woman entirely deceived by a manipulative man's promises, so much so that despite the passing of time, his attempts to pay her off, and, finally, his engagement to someone else, she kept repeating that he had promised to marry her. Maybe he meant it at some stage. There is also the upsetting reality that their daughter, who looked so like him, died at the age of two or three, as so many toddlers did. Contrary to the old idea that people in ages past became inured to death and did not mourn their children, Forniere grieved and cried and, in his grief, Mendre raged against her, suggesting it was her fault. A child's death can break a happy marriage; it is perhaps little wonder that he did not want to marry Forniere after it.

On 9 March 1588 the consistory gathered—pastors, deacons, elders, together with two lawyers—to determine the matter of Forniere and Mendre. For reasons that are entirely obscure, the register says only that they read through the case and it was 'concluded', without recording the outcome.[108] Happily this is an instance in which the baptismal registers come to the rescue. Thirteen months later a son, Jacob, was born to 'Alaysete Forniere' and to a man called Raymond Roux. Over the next eight years they went on to have two more sons and two daughters.[109] Meanwhile Mendre and his new wife Isabeau Bologne had a son, called Pols, in January 1597.[110] It seems likely that the consistory had determined that, despite the wealth of evidence of a relationship between the two, the witnesses could not attest to an official betrothal, and Forniere and Mendre's engagement would not stand. Forniere must have married Roux within months of this decision and, although she may not have got what she hoped from the consistory, her life may have been happier as a result.

The testimony of witnesses to a properly enacted promise could only be surpassed as proof by written evidence—contracts of marriage or receipts of dowry—and as two women discovered in 1598, the more documents that could be produced the better. Catherine Lamberte presented herself at the consistory in Montauban to protest that she and a cordswain called Jehan Picard had made promises of marriage to each other, and had drunk in the name of marriage in the presence of friends and relatives a year or more earlier.[111] She also claimed to have given him 100 *livres* towards her dowry, part of which she had paid in kind with two cows, and the rest in cash. She explained that the marriage had been delayed by her pursuit of a court case, but that the contract of marriage had been drawn up by notary

[108] ADG, 42 J 28, 357r–358r, 360v–363r, 364v–365v, 367r, 369v, 370v, 3 Feb. 1588.
[109] ADG, E Dépôt 36/697, 90v, 133v, 205, 252r, 346r, Apr. 1589, Feb. 1591, Sept. 1593, Feb. 1595, and Sept. 1597.
[110] ADG, E Dépôt 36/697, 360r, Jan. 1597.
[111] ADTG, I 1, 338r–v, 341r–v, 345r, 29 Apr. 1598.

Jehan Lafont with the consent of her fiancé's father Bernard Picard, also a shoemaker. She had since heard that Jehan had contracted marriage with another woman, to which she vehemently objected.

No sooner had Lamberte left the room than Madame de Brassac appeared, saying that Picard had actually first contracted marriage with her daughter Jeanne de Monlauzun. It had been a public engagement and Ramond Picat, a notary—and, she added persuasively, an elder in the church of St Léophaire—had drawn up the contract. The boy's father, Bernard Picard, had consented to the marriage. De Brassac required, therefore—in a speech surely designed to ape the formal language of the consistory itself—that the 'marriage contracted with her daughter be effected and to this end, that they may proceed with the publication of the banns according to the order of the church'.

It was time for the Picards, young and old, to show themselves. Jehan was questioned, and admitted that he and Lamberte had exchanged 'some talk of marriage', but that they could not reach an agreement because Lamberte was a Roman Catholic and he did not want to marry her unless she converted, which she refused to do, instead asking him to leave the Reformed Church. They argued over this so bitterly that they stopped speaking to each other and so he had since contracted marriage with Monlauzun. He denied receiving any dowry—he said she had sold the two cows to his father; admitted that he and Lamberte had drawn up a marriage contract, having been induced to do so by his father; but said that 'ever since the said Lamberte by public act had departed from the contract and had declared that she would not marry him' he wished to marry Monlauzun.

His father Bernard was up next, and seemed to have been genuinely perturbed by his son's potential bigamy. He explained his understanding that the agreement with Lamberte had become null because it was made conditionally on the basis that she converted to Protestantism, which she had not done, so when his son found another woman Bernard had consented to their union. They had haplessly found themselves in a situation where Jehan had contracted two equally valid marriages.

The farce was not over yet. The resourceful Lamberte had a further trick up her sleeve: she appeared brandishing the written contract of marriage between her and Jehan Picard, together with an attestation of the hearing of two witnesses made by M. Esterveru, a notary in the nearby town of Villemur, and a receipt for twenty *écus* (about sixty *livres*), paid by Lamberte to Picard as a down-payment of her dowry. The consistory sent instructions to their sister-consistory in Villemur to verify this with Esterveru and the witnesses and report back.

The Monlauzun camp retaliated. Jehan's other potential bride appeared two days later, insisting that his contract with Lamberte was rather the subsequent and second promise of marriage. Jehan, she said, had promised to have 'no other for wife' than her, and she had promised to have no other husband than him. Her final salvo was to bring with her Ramond Picat, the St Léophaire elder and notary who had drawn up their marriage contract. He attested to the consistory that the engagement had been sworn in 'words of the present', 'following the form observed in the Reformed church'.

Picard did not want to marry the woman who had let their engagement go cold for a year, had stopped speaking to him, publicly called off the marriage, and refused to convert to the Protestant faith. He wanted to marry Monlauzun, from a proper Reformed family, who wanted no other for husband but him. What would transpire? The two women both had written proof of their engagements, drawn up by legal clerks. Monlauzun had the advantage of a witness to her betrothal, but a couple of weeks later a letter back from Villemur, containing the testimonies of three witnesses to the Lamberte betrothal, trumped this.

The crucial question for the consistory was always not what anyone wanted, but what was right. All that mattered was which engagement came first and whether it was valid. The letter from Villemur indicated that Lamberte's claim pre-dated Monlauzan's, and the engagement had been properly contracted, and so it was in view of these proofs—witnesses, contract of marriage, and receipt of the dowry— that the consistory concluded that 'the promise of marriage between the said Picard son and Lamberte would be effected, and the parties would celebrate their marriage according to the order of the church'. The second promise of marriage, made to Jehanne de Monlauzun, was declared null and void. Through dogged persistence, sheer resourcefulness, and by using the Reformed consistory, the Roman Catholic Lamberte got what she desired—at great cost to two Protestants, her husband-to-be and the wife he wanted.

She was not the only Roman Catholic woman to take ingenious advantage of the corrective mechanism that the Protestant consistory offered to members of the female sex. Another Catholic woman who did likewise had witnesses but ultimately her success in confronting the patriarchy was due, ironically, to the preference for male over female authority when it came to familial consent, and to the way she demonstrated constant submission to the Reformed authorities throughout. Her name was Isabel Vielle and in June 1578 she claimed to have exchanged betrothal vows with Claude Dupon, a Protestant wool-carder and weaver from 'Gremon' (probably Gramont, a village outside Montauban), who was said to be between eighteen and twenty years of age.[112] Before the consistory Dupon subsequently denied them, saying rather viciously that 'he would never marry her and that he would rather leave the country than do so!' He pointed out that his mother was fiercely opposed to the match and disapproved strongly of Vielle, as she was 'a papist, a thief and, according to the rumours, a whore'. These were words strong enough to destroy a woman's reputation. He also claimed to have heard that Dupon had recently become pregnant while living in Arles with her aunt.

Vielle was called to give her account. She placidly said that she and Dupon had talked of marriage and she had offered to show him a small vineyard that she owned, which would be part of her dowry. Having nothing else to do at that time, they went to see it, and then after talking together decided to go the house of her uncle Jacques du Bois, where they performed the betrothal ritual of the *donation de corps* before witnesses and drank together in the name of marriage. She was asked again,

---

[112] BN, Ms.fr. 8667, 15v, 15r–v (bis), 16r–v, 17v, 11 Jun. 1578.

'did she promise to marry the said Dupon?' and replied, 'yes, and if it pleased the consistory the said marriage should be effected'.

The consistory tried again with Dupon, with Vielle standing by. Now he amended his story: he did not promise to marry her and he did not perform the *donation de corps*, but they did drink in the name of marriage and he said that he would have to procure the consent of his mother, who lived in his hometown. Since that occasion, he reiterated, he had heard rumours throughout the town that Vielle was pregnant, and he repeated his earlier character assassination, adding that she was also 'a drunk'. He restated his unflattering remark that he would rather leave the country than take her in marriage.

Witnesses were called. Jehanne Dondelle, Vielle's Catholic aunt, said she had been present at the betrothal, while Jacques du Bois, a dressmaker and Vielle's uncle, also confirmed that he had been there when Vielle and Dupon had promised themselves to each other, had drunk in the name of marriage, and performed the betrothal rites.

Two weeks later Dupon's mother, Anthonio Boissete, appeared in furious and voluble spirits, having travelled from Gremon (if this was the village outside Montauban, a journey of some 463 miles or 340 km—a walk of at least eleven days) to have her opinion heard. She was opposed to the marriage, she said, and if her son married the girl she would 'renounce him as her child'. He was far too young to wed, she did not want him to marry a 'papist', and she would never consent to the marriage.

The consistory, evidently troubled, called two more witnesses. François Compte, a neighbour whom Jehanne Dondelle had nominated, swore that he had been present when Dupon and Vielle promised themselves and swore to be loyal to each other. At that time, he tellingly added, Dupon had said nothing about waiting to see what his mother wanted. Guillaume Gorgas, another weaver, said that he too had been present at Jacques du Bois's house when Dupon and Vielle had given their bodies reciprocally to each other and had drunk in the name of marriage.

The consistory was faced with a dilemma. Four witnesses swore that the engagement had taken place, but Dupon's mother refused him consent to marry, she had probably travelled a long way to register this, and Dupon was too young to proceed without it. At this stage other factors were taken into consideration, and it seems likely that the pair's attitudes became of crucial importance.

The consistory had initially assumed, after Dupon's colourful and damaging description of Vielle, that the marriage was a falsehood, only 'pretended' and alleged by her. But as the case wore on and the evidence emerged, Vielle was continually acquiescent to the consistory's authority—despite being a Roman Catholic—and the case slowly swung in her favour. Her opening statement to them, when asked if she wanted to marry Dupon, that 'if it pleased the consistory that the marriage be achieved', set the tone. Such conciliatory comments contrasted with Dupon's misleading and protean depositions, his evident hostility towards his proposed bride, and his humiliating public slanders. It seems likely that when the consistory asked Vielle if she was of the Reformed faith and she replied, 'no, but she had the courage to become so', she won their hearts.

It is worth considering why. If Dupon's abuse of Vielle, though drawn from the stock of insults hurled at women, was based in any truth, and Vielle was known to have a poor reputation, then marriage would have been both hard to secure and of great worth to her. If she were pregnant, then this situation would have been compounded. The fact that despite her Catholicism she was so peculiarly submissive to the consistory's authority, and that her compliance highlighted so effectively Dupon's mendacity, suggests that Vielle was powerfully and subtly influencing the consistory towards her desired end.

She was not the only one. Dupon's abuse of Vielle, situated between saying that he had reserved the decision until he had the consent of his mother, and a continued discussion of his mother's wishes, suggests that it was his mother who first denounced Vielle as a thief and a whore. In court Boissete was thoroughly manipulative—threatening to disown him if the marriage went ahead and giving him a choice between obedience to his mother and responsibility to the vows he had made—Desdemona's 'divided duty'.

It was only when the case was taken to the regional synod of Montpellier, where Dupon's uncle François appeared to confirm that Dupon was old enough to marry and that he gave his consent for him to do so, that the church could finally close the case. Male familial authority eclipsed a mother's resistance. The synod's conclusion that Vielle's version of events was true and that the marriage between them was 'good and valid' meant that the authority of the Reformed church upheld the words of a submissive Catholic girl against a belligerent Protestant man.

If the consistory did not produce the results sought, it seems that women might take their cases elsewhere. Marie Brune and her mother Alis de Falgayrolles presented themselves at the Ganges consistory in September 1602 to protest the recently pronounced banns of marriage of François Coutereau and Jehanne Fabresse, on the grounds that Coutereau had previously promised to marry Brune.[113] Brune testified that they had drunk in the name of marriage—Coutereau had handed her a glass from which to drink—and he had showed her his house, furniture, and merchandise, stored in great chests. Only her mother had been present. Afterwards 'as confirmation of the marriage the said Coutereau had given the said Brune three jars of white radishes'. By contrast, Coutereau said that he had never promised to marry her: he had shown the mother and daughter his furniture, and he had offered them some refreshment before they left his house. Brune had washed the glasses, then given one to Coutereau and one to her mother, and then they drank before Brune drank last. It was not in the name of marriage, as 'he had always said that he was too old for her'. As to the radishes, he gave them to her in the street just as a gift, without any ulterior motive or meaning. The consistory told Brune to gather testimonies of those who knew about the 'marriage', but nothing more was done. Two months later Brune reappeared, again protesting the newly republished banns of François Coutereau and Jehanne Fabresse because Coutereau had 'been condemned by the présidial court to pay her a penalty of thirty *livres* before

---

[113] ADH, GG 24, 133v–134r, 134–5r, 139v–140r, 1 Sept. 1602.

the banns could be announced'.[114] Evidently in the meantime Brune had taken her claim of an engagement to the secular authorities and received a more satisfying response from them than the church had given her—if not the husband she desired. As it is quite by chance that we know this, it is very possible that many other women approached equivalent authorities in pursuit of their suits, without the historical record retaining an imprint of their initiatives. The consistorial records may only reveal the tip of the iceberg.

Conclusions

As there was no charge to approach the consistory, and as people knew how to find it—the consistory meeting at the same time and place every week—everyone from local nobility to poor female servants could take their grievances to the church, and they did. We see women approaching the consistory in the hope of extracting themselves from marriages, or in expectation that the church would force men to honour their marriage promises. In neither case were they always, or even mostly, successful. Yet despite its patriarchal bias, the consistory did generally investigate women's claims, and when evidence and contractual arrangements were in place, they would pronounce the marriage valid—whether a man or a woman had presented the case. To some extent, therefore, the church's judgements were gender-blind.

Although consent—and therefore love—was theoretically written into the formation of a Protestant marriage, the consistory seldom considered the necessity of affection in the making of marriage. They rarely dwelt on who wanted to marry whom or on the miserable years of cohabitation that would follow for an unhappily matched pair. For the Church a properly enacted engagement was absolutely and completely irrevocable. Because people presenting cases expected more leniency and flexibility the gap between these two viewpoints had enormous consequences for individual lives.

Yet the consistory remained a forum that ordinary women could use to air grievances, seek the restoration of honour, or aim for the fulfilment of their hopes, and women could sometimes successfully use the consistory to achieve marriage, without the accompanying pregnancy needed before the other authorities for which records survive. The consistory's commitment to enforcing betrothal could often work in favour of women in Reformed congregations—and sometimes even for their Catholic sisters—demonstrating the achievement of as much recompense and redress as was possible in a patriarchal society.

---

[114] ADH, GG 24, 140r, 17 Nov. 1602.

6

Sex

PAILLARDISE

A great variety of words were used in sixteenth- and seventeenth-century France to describe sexual intercourse, many of which were inherently euphemistic: *malversation, converser mal* (both literally 'evil conversation'), *baiser* (also to kiss, now exclusively a vulgar phrase for sexual intercourse), *jouir* (to enjoy), *abuser* (to abuse), *cognoitre charnellement* (to know carnally), *avoir cognoissance* (to have knowledge of), *s'abandonner* (to abandon oneself), *avoir affaire/affere avec* (to have an affair with), *fornication, frequentation, faire mal de son corps* (to do ill with his/her body), *debaucher* (to debauch), *coucher avec* (to sleep with), *persuader quelqu'un de son honneur* (to persuade someone from his/honour), *cohabiter* (to cohabit, meaning maintaining a sexual relationship), *copulation, forcer* (to force), and *violer* (to rape). But the mostly commonly used were the expression *paillardise* and the verb *paillarder*. Randle Cotgrave's 1611 French–English dictionary translates *paillardise* as 'lecherie, whoredome, venerie...', and *paillarder* as 'to lecher, bitch-hunt it', or, more pertinently, 'to tumble in the straw'. From *paille* for straw, the idiomatic expression almost literally meant 'rolling in the hay' or, more prosaically, pre-marital sex between unmarried heterosexuals. Although it was sometimes extended to cover prostitution, as in Cotgrave's definition, its chief usage was for fornication.

Cases involving apparently consensual pre-marital sex are plentiful in the registers: I found over two hundred between 1560 and 1615. Such a wealth of material certainly reflects the preoccupations of the consistory, but it can also provide an insight into the behaviour and attitudes of ordinary people. Was pre-marital sexual activity common and condoned? Was sex simply a normal part of courting practices and an accepted stage of marriage formation? Was sexual intercourse only likely when a future marriage was (apparently) secured by a promise? How sexually promiscuous were people outside the context of engagement? Was it considered acceptable for unmarried couples to cohabit? Did Reformation ideologies have any impact on popular attitudes in this era of religious upheaval?

While illegitimacy rates were low—suggesting pre-marital sexual activity was limited in both incidence and acceptance—several historians have suggested that it was, nevertheless, not uncommon immediately prior to marriage.[1] Shorter and

---

[1] Jacques Solé, *Etre femme en 1500: la vie quotidienne dans la diocèse de Troyes* (Paris, 2000), 100, 106, 230; James R. Farr, *Authority and Sexuality in Early Modern Burgundy (1550–1730)* (New York and Oxford, 1995), 110; Robert Muchembled, *Société et mentalités dans la France moderne: XVIe–XVIIIe*

Flandrin disagree over how sexually active young people were and whether low
levels of illegitimacy reflect abstinence and suppressed sex drives or the use of non-
coital practices and contraception, but their evidence was largely taken from the
eighteenth century.[2] For earlier periods Ben-Amos suggests that sexual intercourse
'does not appear to have been part of the courting practices of the young, unless a
promise of marriage was given'.[3] Farr, Muchembled, and Rublack argue similarly
that pre-marital sex was likely if it was preceded by the promise of marriage and
followed by matrimony.[4] Fairchilds has concluded that the sexual attitudes of most
women at this time were strongly oriented towards marriage.[5] For many women
it seems to have been, as Solé found for fifteenth-century Troyes, that 'the sexual
act was the bearer of a semblance of betrothal'.[6] Shorter suggested that it was
only after the Reformation that a strict separation between engagement and marriage was recognized, and Gottlieb found in fifteenth-century Champagne that
engagement conveyed a sufficiently strong sense of obligation to appear to permit
sexual intercourse.[7] The sources used previously—whether *déclarations de grossesse*
(eighteenth-century declarations of pregnancy) or court records—are rather biased
towards recounting versions of seduction in which women justified their fornication, and as a result a lacuna has existed in the literature over consensual sexual
relationships between unmarried people, except in Capp's work on England.[8] Farr
dismisses them (which has the unfortunate effect of implying that unmarried
women's expression of their sexuality was never willing) and Phan concludes that
'if feminine pleasure existed, it was not spoken of'.[9] Flandrin suggests that there
was great freedom for sexual activity during courtship whereas Solé urges some
caution, noting that when cohabitation before formal marriage took place it was
not overlooked by the Catholic authorities.[10] Yet Solé, Gottlieb, and Farr find little
evidence of long-term, socially recognized cohabitative unions outside marriage—
Farr found prosecution rates for lay concubinage in Catholic Burgundy, unless involving clerics or accompanied by great scandal, were almost non-existent—although
Gottlieb suggests that the Catholic Church's idea of the correct timetable between

siècle (Paris, 1990), 43; Ulinka Rublack, *The Crimes of Women in Early Modern Germany* (Oxford, 1999), 135–6.

 [2] Edward Shorter, *The Making of the Modern Family* (London, 1976), 79–119; Jean-Louis Flandrin, 'Repression and Change in the Sexual Life of Young People in Medieval and Modern Times', in *Family and Sexuality*, ed. Wheaton and Hareven (Philadelphia, PA, 1980), 32–5.
 [3] I. K. Ben-Amos, *Adolescence and Youth in Early Modern England* (New Haven, CT, and London, 1994), 204.
 [4] Farr, *Authority*, 110; Muchembled, *Société*, 43; Rublack, *Crimes*, 135–6.
 [5] Cissie Fairchilds, 'Female Sexual Attitudes and the Rise of Illegitimacy: A Case Study', *JIH* 8.4 (1978), 627–67, here 642–3 and 654–9.
 [6] Solé, *Etre femme*, 106.
 [7] Shorter, *Making*, 85; Beatrice Gottlieb, 'The Meaning of Clandestine Marriage', in *Family and Sexuality in French History*, ed. Robert Wheaton and Tamara K. Hareven (Philadelphia, PA, 1980), 70.
 [8] Bernard Capp, *When Gossips Meet: Women, Family and Neighbourhood in Early Modern England* (Oxford, 2003), 125, 160.
 [9] Farr, *Authority*, 113; Marie-Claude Phan, *Les amours illégitimes: histories de séduction en Languedoc (1676–1786)* (Paris, 1986), 140, 144.
 [10] Flandrin, 'Repression', 32–4; Solé, *Etre femme*, 100, 106, 230.

engagement and marriage (forty days) was very different from popular notions—a tension that remained the case with Reformed congregations.[11]

The consistory certainly regarded pre-marital sex as a serious moral failing. When a poor woman called Maurice Farnoyze repented of her sexual misdeeds in September 1583 the consistory decided that her public act of reparation should be accompanied by a sermon on the consequences of *paillardise*.[12] In July 1609 the minister Mardochée Suffren gave two sermons on the vices of 'falseness and *paillardise*', thinking them 'too common among the people' and trying to impress on his congregation both the gravity of these sins and the great penalties that could be imposed.[13] Those guilty of fornication generally had to undergo humiliating public reparation in order to receive the Eucharist, as Anne Lironne and Alaisette Ribarde—the latter the mother of an illegitimate child—found in Ganges in the 1590s.[14] This was true even if the couple went on to marry. Gassinete Columbière and her husband Jehan Bertrand had slept together before marriage, and conceived a daughter, who subsequently died. In March 1584 Columbière was instructed to abstain from the sacrament; only in December 1586 did she finally agree to be censured to receive the Eucharist.[15] Earlier that year the consistory had also summoned another married couple—Monsieur and Mademoiselle de Sieure—for having had carnal knowledge of each other before marriage.[16]

In certain cases the consistory also sought to alert the consulate so that the civic penalties for *paillardise* would be activated. In 1598 the consistory in Nîmes sent Suzanne Martine, who was a native of Genolhac and pregnant by Daniel Gausy, to the consuls to ensure the child was fed, and that the mother was punished by the judiciary and exiled from the city.[17] In 1615 a reoffending woman, known only as Durante, was recommended to the consuls for exile.[18] In Ganges, too, the town's consistory instructed the consuls to put Françoise Fauresse out of the town.[19] As noted in Chapter 2, a fifth of the cases in Montauban's register of criminal sentences pronounced by the city's consuls between 1534 and 1606 were concerned with *paillardise*, and sentences ranged from public repentance and substantial fines to banishment.[20] In two cases the consistorial registers note that the royal judicial officers had imprisoned a fornicator. Widow Magdeleine Coterelle gave birth to an illegitimate child while in prison in January 1587, and was probably there because she had had two lovers, Adrian the gardener and Estienne Suas, and could not be sure who the father of her child was; happily, the latter promised to marry her.[21] In 1612 a man called Anric Rudavel was imprisoned after impregnating the daughter

---

[11] Gottlieb, 'The Meaning', 71–2, 67; Farr, *Authority*, 134.
[12] ADG, 42 J 28, 44r, 28 Nov. 1583.   [13] ADG, 42 J 34, 109v, 19 Jul. 1609.
[14] ADH, GG 24, 24r, 94v, 95r, 16 Feb. 1592 and 11 Sept. 1598.
[15] ADG 42 J 28, 94r, 30 Mar. 1584.   [16] ADG 42 J 28, 202r, 203v, 1 Jan. 1586.
[17] ADG, 42 J 31, 215v, 219v, 239v, 241r, 30 Mar. 1598.
[18] ADG, 42 J 35, 181v, 5 Jun. 1615.   [19] ADH, GG 24, 111r, 22 Aug. 1599.
[20] ADTG, 5 FF 2, e.g. 34v, 35r, 36v.
[21] ADG, 42 J 28, 233v, 242v, 250v, 258r, 259r, 20 Aug. 1586. Adrian the gardener had a widow by 1602 (ADG, 42 J 32, 453v, 9 Jan. 1602), so he was presumably married at the time of his encounter with Coterelle.

of one of the elders, M. Guiran; her father's position surely caused this severity.[22] In Calvinist Geneva imprisonment for three days on bread and water was the standard punishment for fornication. By comparison to reports from elsewhere in Huguenot France, however—such as the news that Alyon Gironne had been condemned to death by judges in La Rochelle in 1597 for her 'bad life and lewd misbehaviour'—most of those found guilty of illicit sexual intercourse in Languedoc received relatively light sentences.[23] Yet all such punishments seem to have been a significant step up from those imposed by medieval Catholic authorities, who allowed sexually active couples to marry, but required them first to do penance and pay a small fine—in Troyes, a fine of 20 *sous* and a pound of wax.[24]

Like the Catholic Church, the Reformed discipline urged men and women to marry quickly after engagement, ideally within six weeks. Elders observed and questioned those who had remained engaged for some time, such as Sixmard and his fiancée, who were noticed in February 1596 to have been engaged for a year.[25] Similarly, Suzanne Poteau and her fiancé Guilhaume Malplan were summoned for having remained engaged for a long time in March 1605; they promised the consistory they would marry 'on the first day and as soon as possible', but were still not married by September.[26] Pierre Gourgas was called before the consistory because of his delay in marrying his fiancé: he explained that his business affairs did not permit him to marry yet, but the consistory told him to marry the following week or be publicly suspended.[27]

Investigations into delayed marriages were most commonly initiated by the consistory rather than by popular scandal. Sometimes, though, the evidence suggests external concern about the conduct of unmarried couples. Bernard Peladan, for example, reported to the consistory that his daughter Marie Peladane and Jean Bolon had been engaged for four years.[28]

Suspected *paillardise* could prompt others to turn informant. Pierre de Lhoulive and his fiancée were discovered to be living in the same house, because of the 'common noise among the neighbours that they sleep together'.[29] Neighbours also reported that Jacques Brun and Donne Berriasse's son were sleeping with their fiancées.[30] Fermin Riffard's wife reported her maidservant, Anne Molarede, for having been found with one of her male servants 'kissing and embracing two hours before dawn'. (Molarede admitted it, but said she had been wearing under-garments and they had not had sex; she was nevertheless suspended from the sacrament.)[31] Conversely, the maid of 'the judgess of Sommières' (presumably the judge's widow) reported that her mistress had gone to bed with Sieur Rogier de Meynes. Once asked, the neighbours agreed that there had been 'many signs of misbehaviour'.[32] Neighbours complained too about the frequentation and suspected *paillardise*

---

[22] ADG, 42 J 34, 361v, 362v, 363r; 42 J 35, 30r, 20 Jun. 1612.
[23] ADTG, I 1, 229v, 12 Feb. 1597.   [24] Solé, *Être femme*, 100.
[25] ADG, 42 J 31, 36v, 21 Feb. 1596.   [26] ADG, 42 J 33, 33r, 35r, 59r, 23 Mar. 1605.
[27] ADG, 42 J 34, 247r, 19 Jan. 1611.   [28] ADG, 42 J 33, 68v, 23 Nov. 1605.
[29] BN, Ms.fr. 8667, 135v.   [30] ADG, 42 J 28, 292r, 17 Jun. 1587.
[31] ADG, 42 J 29, 47r, 49r, 30 Aug. 1588.
[32] ADG, 42 J 29, 716, 717; 42 J 30, 5v, 51v, 22 Aug. 1591.

of Sieur de la Caissargues and Damoiselle Suzanne de la Cassaigne. It was also rumoured that Caissargues's sister had taken the couple's illegitimate child to be baptized. Once he finally presented himself to be questioned, some seven months after the case arose, Caissargues admitted that the rumours were true.[33] Such denunciation by others suggests that some in the community had internalized the church's standards of sexual morality.

So too do the rare instances of people presenting themselves to confess to *paillardise*. In September 1605 Marguerite Grille brought herself before the consistory because she had given birth a fortnight earlier to twins, conceived out of wedlock. She gave the father's name as Simon de Dieu and said that one of the children had since died. Grille came to ask 'pardon of God and the church' on her knees.[34] It was decided that de Dieu would be summoned, although he never appeared. Unless Grille had retaliation as a motive, her appearance suggests a profound desire to be reintegrated into the church and a recognition of her guilt.

In some ways, when people denied the facts and defended their reputation against a charge of illicit sex, this also testified to an internalization of the church's moral code. Marye Laupie presented herself before the Nîmes consistory in March 1590 to complain that she was being defamed for 'having slept or had an affair with' Sieur Jehan Pic, and that she was appearing in order 'to purge herself of the said calumny'.[35] Jacquette Sugiere, maidservant to M. de Puechredon, summoned to respond to allegations that she was pregnant by her master, vehemently denied it by saying that 'she had lived all her life as a good girl'.[36] For these women an accusation of *paillardise* was not one that could go unaddressed.

Nevertheless there is also contrary evidence of people acting in support of those who were pregnant outside marriage, possibly suggesting a less severe approach to pre-marital sex. Mademoiselle de Farnoue was called before the consistory in December 1593 for housing a pregnant maidservant called Anthonye. Anthonye had said that she was pregnant by her employer, Sieur Bourdeau, and had stayed with Farnoue for six weeks, before leaving for Saint-Jean-de-Gard. Farnoue was strongly censured for having 'received many debauched people' in her house and in response stormed out of the consistory 'in great anger'. She did, however, return meekly a week later to ask God's pardon for 'keeping a whore in her house'.[37] Pons de l'Escut was summoned in August 1594 for housing Marie Auberte of Montpellier during her illegitimate pregnancy. She had given birth seven or eight months earlier, and Auberte swore that the father was the son of the late Arnaud Vallete, but the consistory suspected l'Escut nonetheless, because rumour said that Auberte was his whore and he had recently been seen dancing, an immoral activity that suggested the capacity for further depravity.[38] But the man Auberte had claimed was the father was further accused, two years later, of making a maidservant called Gasparde Roussone pregnant. In the light of this, and of Auberte and l'Escut's repeated denials of an affair,

<hr />

33 ADG, 42 J 32, 47r, 51r, 66v, 67v, 86r, 127v, 160r, 22 May 1602.
34 ADG, 42 J 33, 59v, 14 Sept. 1605.   35 ADG, 42 J 29, 366, 7 Mar. 1590.
36 ADG, 42 J 31, 86r, 86v, 92v, 29 May 1596.
37 ADG, 42 J 30, 236v, 237v, 239r, 24 Nov. 1593.
38 ADG, 42 J 30, 294v, 295v, 28 Aug. 1594.

it seems likely that l'Escut was simply being hospitable to the pregnant woman or, less altruistically, taking her on as a tenant while unconcerned by her morality.[39] In both cases, then, those offering accommodation to a single, pregnant woman found themselves the subject of censure, but both initially saw little wrong in offering such support.

Suspicious Circumstances

What made people suspicious that *paillardise* was occurring? It seems that a man and a woman were liable to come under suspicion if they spent time alone together, even if there was a good reason for it. The surgeon M. Noguier was accused of *paillardise* with a woman living at M. Merle's house, and when questioned said that he had indeed gone to Merle's house on the previous day because Merle's sister was ill. He was told that to avoid gossip and scandal he should not go to the house for any reason, even when Merle was ill—despite his profession—on pain of being suspended from the sacrament.[40] In 1613 Sire Martin was accused of fornication with Marie Melgesse, servant to M. Bompard, and both gave their accounts of the story. He had gone to Bompard's house to return to Melgesse a panier (he said) or some utensils (she said) that he had borrowed, and had gone into the lower kitchen to do so when Bompard bolted the door and accused him of having slept with his servant. Melgesse's account varied slightly: she said Martin took her by the hand and led her into the stable, at which M. Bompard suddenly appeared and led the pair off to prison. Lending and borrowing was a familiar and necessary daily activity, but this interaction between a man and a woman was viewed as an excuse for the two to communicate illicitly. Why did Martin need to go into the lower kitchen? Why did he take her hand and lead her towards the stable? Only dishonourable intentions could explain it.[41]

Being alone together was compounded by having the door closed. Widow Catherine Telines and Pierre Bernard were suspected in March 1562 when 40-year-old Anthoine Guiraud said that a fortnight earlier he had seen Bernard enter Telines's house, having first made several perambulations to see if there was anyone in the road to stop him, and then had stayed in the house for three hours with the doors closed. Guiraud admitted that the windows had remained open, but added that in his judgement this was so that they could see if there was anyone in the street when Bernard came to leave. Guiraud had informed several women living in the street, who waited and watched. One of them, 25-year-old Perrette de Combas, said that the doors and windows had been closed, and Bernard remained there inside for at least an hour. They may have been suspicious, but the neighbours may also have been right: Telines's mother Aulmureys Melone told the consistory that four or five years earlier, when both women's husbands had still been alive, Melone's late husband had found Bernard and Telines 'knowing each other carnally', and Bernard had promised to take Telines in marriage when she was free, and some

---

[39] ADG, 42 J 31, 134, 137r, 23 Oct. 1596. [40] ADG, 42 J 32, 133r, 136v, 18 Dec. 1602.
[41] ADG, 42 J 35, 22v, 23r, 18 Sept. 1613.

time after the neighbours had seen the couple together, they wed.[42] Textile-worker Jean Bresson was accused of sleeping with Sire Delicat's maid, Jeanne Ratte, in September 1614 because he had attended the morning service one day in June, but then returned to Sire Delicat's house, which he was renting, because he did not feel like going to the other service. He had instead stayed inside and passed the time with Ratte, 'without ever thinking any ill [of it] either that day or other days'.[43] It was the combination of his absence, staying inside on a warm June day, and being alone with a woman while everyone else was at church that created the impression that Bresson and the maid were having an affair. Added to this was the fact that at some stage Delicat said that he had come across Bresson and Ratte engaging in ribald flirtation. From Bresson's perspective Delicat's profound anger at discovering the mild flirtation—so much that he attacked Bresson physically—was so extreme as to suggest to him that it was Delicat having an affair with her; rumour had it, he added, that Delicat was paying for the maintenance of their bastard infant at Galargues.

Some hours of the day were also more questionable than others: being together very early in the morning or late at night made innocent explanations less plausible. On 23 December 1587 elder M. Mazel explained to the consistory that he had found a young man called Pierre Raymond hidden in widow Catherine Valade's house between five and six in the morning, and was convinced that the pair of them were 'up to no good'. Mazel had knocked on the door four times, but no one answered, so he broke it open by force. He found the woman not yet fully clothed, and Raymond hidden between two walls, with his coat and sword elsewhere. He seized them both and dragged them before minister M. Moynier. Raymond confessed that he had been there at her house, which he had entered at seven o'clock the previous night; he had known Valade from childhood. He said that he had slept on some rushes in the shop. Mazel and another elder instantly went to verify what he had said with his brother and sister-in-law, who said Raymond had not slept in their house, and there were no rushes in the shop—but Valade, separately, maintained the same story as Raymond. Although no *paillardise* could be proved Valade was suspended from the sacrament, and only narrowly avoided being denounced to the consuls for exile from the city.[44]

Often the consistory does not relate what exactly was suspicious about the circumstances in which a couple were found. Any action outside that could be construed maliciously was liable to be reported: appearing to signal to each other, inexplicable loitering of one near the other's house, even the manner in which the door was opened could all hint at immorality. A young girl called Marguerite Saurine and carpenter Sergent Cahuc were found together at night 'at a suspect hour' in her house with the door closed. He confirmed that he was passing by and she asked him in to warm himself—nothing further—but the circumstances were enough to raise eyebrows.[45] Lawyer M. Roure was accused of *paillardise* because he had been

[42] BN, Ms.fr. 8666, 86v–89r, 4 Mar. 1562.   [43] ADG, 42 J 35, 112v, 122v, 10 Sept. 1614.
[44] ADG, 42 J 28, 341r, 343r, 350v, 23 Dec. 1587.
[45] ADG, 42 J 30, 38r, 39v, 19 Feb. 1592.

'found in a house alone with a woman at a suspicious time and place'.[46] Merchant M. Boschet was summoned to the consistory for having a conversation 'at an undue hour' with a maid with whom he had previously had a child.[47] The way women and men related to each other was carefully scrutinized and any untoward conduct viewed with suspicion.

One final scenario that understandably led to suspicion was the discovery that a man and woman were sleeping in the same bed, even though the living arrangements of the period made innocuous explanations plausible. Donne Gousette was accused of *paillardise* with her servant Anthoine Livraire, who was contracted to marry her daughter, because they slept in the same bed for seven nights. Both swore it was because he was ill, there was not another bed, and it was in 'all honesty'.[48] Similarly, widow Marguerite Martine was accused of having slept with her servant Anthoine Martin in 1596, and explained that because of sickness she, he, and her daughter were forced to share a bed for a week, but it was 'with all virtue'.[49] It was suspicious enough, however, for someone to notice and report the arrangements to the church.

It seems, then, that there was concern about the sexual behaviour of others, and those accused of impropriety often responded by denial or confession, but not everyone condemned the sexually active as roundly as the consistory. The incidence of pre-marital sex was also not insignificant. As with all the cases under consideration, quantitative analysis would be statistically meaningless, and it is hard to generate a robust sense of typicality, but there is some circumstantial evidence in relation to the cases of pre-marital sex that helps provide a better understanding of social and sexual relations.

Sex after Promises to Marry

For many, as the historiography has suggested, sexual relations before marriage could be justified by betrothal promises. The evidence suggests the existence of a practical folk morality, in which although women remained virgins until the engagement ceremony, a large (if unknown) proportion slept with their intended husbands before the marriage was finalized. A promise of marriage was a great aphrodisiac.

The consistory records are peppered with examples of sex between engaged couples—who were, after all, inextricably bound to each other under the Reformed Church's regulations. Fiancés Jaques Garnier—a baker by profession—and Marie Vedelle were summoned for having sex before the blessing of their marriage and asked God's pardon in May 1608.[50] In October 1609 it was ordered that Jaques le Mignon and his fiancée be questioned about rumours that they had delayed their marriage, and were sleeping together without their banns being published,

---

[46] ADG, 42 J 41, 222v, 224v, 226r, 240v, 22 Apr. 1598.
[47] ADG, 42 J 34, 251v, 26 Jan. 1611.
[48] ADG, 42 J 30, 312v; 42 J 31, 46r, 53v, 55r, 22 Dec. 1594.
[49] ADG, 42 J 31, 58v, 17 Apr. 1596.   [50] ADG, 42 J 34, 11v, 21 May 1608.

nor their marriage blessed.[51] Advocate M. Fontanieu and his fiancée were censured for having 'consummated their marriage before the blessing' in August 1610.[52]

The logical consequence was, of course, pregnancies of single women who had consummated their relationships with men who had promised to marry them. In Montauban in 1597 fellow servants Astorg (no first name given) and Jeanne Bugasagne were chastised for her illegitimate pregnancy, but insisted that they were engaged and wanted to marry.[53] (Their master Bertrand Burquayron was also reprimanded for allowing the couple's *paillardise* to occur in his house.) Catherine Ducros was pregnant by Jacques Berand, and was grievously censured for having had sex on the pretext of their forthcoming wedding.[54] Anne Boyere, known as *Matare*, was questioned for having had an illegitimate daughter whom she called Marie. Boyere claimed that she had slept with Samuel Biadie after a promise of marriage. Happily, notary M. Conyaret could back up the story that she had a written promise of marriage from Biadie and that he had given her a ring.[55] Finally, Jehan Cotelier appeared before the consistory in July 1615, 'miserable and sorry' for having made his bride-to-be Catherine Lafont pregnant, and asking the forgiveness of God and the church.[56] The baptismal registers tell similar stories. Although most babies were born to couples explicitly listed as 'married', some were recorded as being the child of engaged couples, such as Jacques, born to Françoise Rientorte, engaged to Estienne Chambon, in February 1587.[57]

In cases where marriage had subsequently occurred the consistory still reprimanded the parties retrospectively, but the tone was considerably more lenient. Embroiderer Pol Advocat confessed in June 1602 to having made Marie Meyniere pregnant after having promised to marry her, but they had since become formally betrothed. By the time Meyniere appeared before the consistory in March 1603 the couple had married, so although she was reprimanded for her scandalous behaviour, her repentance and their subsequent union meant she was not deprived of the sacrament.[58]

This example demonstrates that some couples even pre-empted their formal engagement with sex. It was reported in May 1601 that Jacques Lateule and Donne Merle de Voz had committed *paillardise* and she had become pregnant. Although he initially denied it, he soon conceded that they had had sex a year or so earlier, before their engagement, and she had since had a child.[59] Pierre Cussac made Daufine Rousse pregnant under the pretext of marriage but in March 1603 was repentant and said he had since become engaged to her.[60] Even in these instances, however, where sexual relations may have been especially precipitate, they still occurred in the context of a future marriage.

[51] ADG, 42 J 34, 129r, 7 Oct. 1609.   [52] ADG, 42 J 34, 213r, 25 Aug. 1610.
[53] ADTG, I 1, 227r, 230v, 231v, 236v, 6 Feb. 1597.   [54] ADG, 42 J 34, 18r, 11 Jun. 1608.
[55] ADG, 42 J 34, 42r, 61v, 64r, 5 Nov. 1608.   [56] ADG, 42 J 35, 188r, 8 Jul. 1615.
[57] ADG, E Dépôt 36/697, 40, 9 Feb. 1587.
[58] ADG, 42 J 32, 36v, 60v, 62r, 156r, 24 Apr. 1602.
[59] ADG, 42 J 31, 413r, 413v–414r, 419r, 426r, 3 May 1601.
[60] ADG, 42 J 32, 156r, 19 Mar. 1603.

Sex therefore often served as a step in the process of marriage-formation. Sometimes this was at the consistory's insistence: the consistory in Nîmes urged Jane Saurine and saddlemaker Jan Robert to repent and to marry after their fornication and her pregnancy in 1596, which Saurine said had happened under the promise of marriage.[61] Anthoine Maurin, who had not married his fiancée before she gave birth in 1599, was instructed to marry her within eight days.[62] In March 1615 the Nîmes consistory ordered Claude Durant to marry Suzanne Sempierre, who had fallen pregnant after Durant's promise of marriage.[63] At other times the consistory only seemed to hinder a natural transition from sexual acquaintance to marriage. Rumours reached the consistory of Ganges in November 1598 that Elisabet Rigailhe and Jehan Tirondel spent 'too much time' together and were having a sexual relationship. By January 1599 it was even being said that Elisabet had given birth to a child, whom she had thrown into a stable immediately after the birth, and 'so was a murderer'. Nothing came of this charge of infanticide and it is likely sheer calumny. What is certain is that at some point the couple agreed to marry. Five months later Elisabet made public reparation for their *paillardise*, while Tirondel's aunts Alaisete Tirondelle and Marie Lironne challenged the engagement as 'clandestine following the king's ordinance'. Eventually, perhaps understandably tiring of the interventions of the Protestant Church, Tirondel and Rigailhe married at the Catholic Mass.[64]

The relationship between having sex and expediting marriage is also illustrated by the convocation of married couples for the premature birth of their children, such as Sire Paulet Truchard and his wife, who had a baby after four months of marriage in 1588, or M. Philip's wife Suzanne, who gave birth after being married for five months in 1591.[65] These marriages were not always swift, though: Mademoyselle de Champanhan, who gave birth four months after marriage, tried to explain her behaviour by pointing out that they had been promised to each other for two years: sex was surely permissible under such circumstances. This also demonstrates that it was probably pregnancy, rather than sex, that led to marriage.[66] Similarly, pregnancy was clearly the spur to marriage between M. de Malmont's chambermaid and Jehan Perier. On hearing that she was pregnant in January 1585, Perier vowed that 'it was his doing' and he wanted to publish their banns of marriage.[67] Yet even when pregnancy was not involved, sex helped encourage a couple into wedlock. Donne Doulce and Guillaume Felines were censured for frequenting each other in May 1561, and subsequently swore that they wanted to marry each other.[68] Sex could simply be part of the marriage-formation process.

The anticipatory link between sex and marriage explains why most unmarried women engaging in sexual intercourse hoped for marriage with some confidence. They consented in response to hearing the magical promise of matrimony. The

---

[61] ADG, 42 J 31, 32v, 35r, 14 Feb. 1596.   [62] ADG, 42 J 31, 273r, 24 Mar. 1599.
[63] ADG, 42 J 35, 163r, 25 Mar. 1615.
[64] ADH, GG 24, 95v, 96r, 98v, 105v, 111r, 114v, 1 Nov. 1598.
[65] ADG, 42 J 29, 20, 1 Jun. 1588; 633, 12 Apr. 1591.
[66] ADG, 42 J 29, 395, 19 Apr. 1590.   [67] ADG, 42 J 28, 153r, 23 Jan. 1585.
[68] BN, Ms.fr. 8666, 14v, 58v, 59r, 20 May 1561.

formula 'under promise of marriage' is repeatedly found in *paillardise* cases, indicating women's hopes, sexual attitudes, and their ideas about what was morally defensible. In confessing fornication, women were quick to indicate that they had had sex only because marriage had been promised. The promise of marriage was a means of justifying their behaviour, presumably with the intention of moderating their sin in the consistory's eyes, and ideally eliciting sympathy and the authoritative weight of the church to insist on the accomplishment of the promises. Marie Longuette, a maidservant, confessed in 1596 to being made pregnant by a manservant, saying that his promises of marriage had long continued. She said she had 'been known and abused under promise of marriage by Doumergue Gan... and he had continued to do so under the said promise for the last seven months'.[69]

Françoise Borrelle, known as *La Poucette*, explained that a man named Boriaut under the 'pretext of taking her in marriage had known her carnally', explicitly delineating the link between his promise and her compliance.[70] Yet promises to marry did not necessarily constitute formal engagement, and the gap between private verbal assent and the prescribed methods of official betrothal exposed women to the risks of illegitimate pregnancy and social ostracism.

The evidence reminds us that sexual intercourse brought no guarantee of 'happy ever after'. Early in 1593 rumours were circulating that M. DeSaliens's maidservant, Jane Deleuze, was having an affair with the locksmith M. Bernard. In November Deleuze was accused of having committed *paillardise* with Bernard in the cellar where he kept wood and wine. She said that he had promised her marriage, and she had given him 100 *écus*, presumably as a down-payment on her dowry. A month later Bernard admitted that what she said was true, and both were deprived of the sacrament, but no move was made to urge them into marriage.[71] Merchant Captain DuGras was accused of *paillardise* with Gillette Ducane in November 1596. She claimed that they had sex on multiple occasions in the house where she served as a maid, and he had promised to marry her. Initially he denied it, saying that he had taken the case before a judge, and that after the judgment he 'would have satisfaction at the faults and sins that a great number of the consistory and other people had done him'. But two months later, when the judicial case had obviously faltered, he took a different tack. He now admitted that he had had sex with Ducane (now called Gillette Duchamp), but the 'truth was that the said Duchamp was a public whore, who had abandoned herself to several'.[72] There was no marriage on the cards for these two. Ramonde Riviere presented herself at the consistory in Montauban to protest that Guillaume Lescure had 'abused and slept' with her and that he had 'always promised to take her as a wife', but when she had demanded that he act as promised he now did not want to do so.[73] In January 1615 François Mazellet was similarly rebuked for having bedded 'one called Arnaude'

---

[69] ADG, 42 J 31, 116v–117r, 14 Aug. 1596.   [70] ADTG, I 1, 30v–31r, 16 Aug. 1595.
[71] ADG, 42 J 30, 154v, 147r, 149v, 153r, 155r, 168v, 171v, 228r, 237r, 241r, 286r, 10 Feb. 1593.
[72] ADG, 42 J 31, 137r, 144r, 152v, 169r, 205, 208r (later references may or may not be to Ducane), 12 Nov. 1596.
[73] ADTG, I 1, 265r, 25 Jun. 1597.

after making her a promise of marriage, and it was ordered that he should be publicly suspended from the sacrament.[74]

Far worse than romantic disappointment was to be left alone to raise a child. Many women in this situation looked to the consistory for help—help that was generally not forthcoming. Marguerite Girarde, from the *cévenol* village of Saint-Estienne-de-Val-Francesque, appeared before the Nîmes consistory in July 1578. She confessed to being pregnant by a servant to M. Menard called Estienne Bertrand, and said that two witnesses—Andrien Castel and Fermin Sambarber—had found them together in a vineyard. She said that she allowed him to sleep with her because Bertrand had promised he would 'behave as a good man'—the implication being that he would marry her. Some months later it was reported that two labourers had indeed found them having sex in a vineyard, but despite this evidence confirming the man's identity, the consistory did not instruct Bertrand to marry her.[75] A woman identified only as Simonne presented herself at the consistory in March 1581 to declare that Anthoine Guibal of Monpezac, currently employed as valet at the Apple Inn, had made her pregnant three weeks prior to the previous Magdaleine (22 July, making her 37 weeks pregnant at the time of her complaint). He had known her carnally following a promise of marriage. Sadly for her, the consistory paid little attention to her charge, but ordered that she would be suspended.[76]

This lack of aid for women who found themselves pregnant outside marriage was a theme across time. Jehane Savaigue appeared at the consistory after having given birth to an illegitimate child following a promise of marriage, but the father was the late Guillaume Cantarelle and the consistory offered her nothing.[77] In August 1584 Françoise Forte appeared to admit that she was pregnant outside marriage, and that she had been made so five months earlier by Estienne Capdur. He had promised to marry her, she said, and had given her an *écu*, with which she had bought the dress she was wearing. Capdur did not appear before the consistory until April the following year, when he denied ever having seen or known Forte. Nothing else came of the case.[78] Suzanne Imberte said she had become pregnant by weaver Loys Bonnaud under the promise of marriage, and claimed she had good witnesses, but nothing came of her claim and she was entered into the roll of those from whom the sacrament had been withheld.[79] She was joined there by Marie Dufour, who also presented herself in January 1586. Dufour named the father of her unborn child as Jehan Vinissac, but her only reward was her suspension from the Eucharist.[80] In 1602, unusually, Pierre Castilhon and Indict Sallesse were both reprimanded for fornication 'under the pretext of marriage', which had left Sallesse pregnant and unmarried.[81] For the most part the consistory provided only rebuke and scant support, and these hapless women were forced to raise their children alone, suffering social stigma and ostracism.

---

[74] ADG, 42 J 35, 153r, 28 Jan. 1615.   [75] BN, Ms.fr. 8667, 26r, 49r, 30 Jul. 1578.
[76] BN, Ms.fr. 8667, 190r, 17 Mar. 1581.   [77] BN, Ms.fr. 8667, 207r, 26 Apr. 1581.
[78] ADG, 42 J 28, 117r, 170v, 18 Aug. 1584.   [79] ADG, 42 J 28, 208v, 372r, 29 Jan. 1586.
[80] ADG, 42 J 28, 209r, 372r, 29 Jan. 1586.
[81] ADG, 42 J 32, 133r, 18 Dec. 1602. For other examples, see ADG, 42 J 30, 229r (Jaquette de St Pierre) and 295v (Gabrielle Fayette).

It seems likely that these male seducers had exploited cheap promises of marriage to have their way with their victims. In modern-day definitions of consent, when consent is given conditionally, and the condition upon which that consent was obtained is not complied with, the act of sex constitutes rape. In May 1595 Ysabel Daubree claimed to be pregnant by Pol Pages, who had promised her marriage, only for him to deny it. By October, however, it became clear that Pages had also made another woman, known as *Brignone*, pregnant.[82] Perhaps the same trick had worked twice.

Just occasionally there is evidence that women recognized their optimistic assumption that marriage would follow intercourse as naïve hopefulness. Jehanne Roze, pregnant by Pascal Bouyer, admitted to 'having been deceived by him under the promise of marriage'.[83] Farr, Muchembled, and Flandrin are right to note that premarital sexual activity was prevalent in France under the promise of marriage: but in truth this situation created great scope for deception and false promises, so that in practice sexual intercourse was far from always followed by matrimony.

Sex outside the Context of Marriage

It might be thought that the Church's focus on marriage would tend to produce only justifications of illicit sexual activity by reference to promises to wed. Yet the consistorial registers are equally full of instances of sex occurring outside wedlock without marriage ever serving as a rationale. In instance after instance it becomes clear that women and men in sixteenth- and seventeenth-century Languedoc also had sex outside the context of proceeding towards marriage—a promiscuity that has seldom been illuminated by the sources. An analysis of the details of these stories therefore promises to be insightful.

In some cases both parties owned up to their behaviour. In November 1578 Bourguine Bosquiere confessed to fornicating with Pestel Mareschal, saying that he came frequently to Oliver Lateule's house, where she worked as a nurse, 'to lie with her'. When she became pregnant Mareschal told her that he would provide for the child. Under interrogation, Mareschal confessed that what she said was true. There is no mention of either party's being married, but neither is there any talk of a subsequent marriage between them. Both were suspended from the Eucharist as punishment for their *paillardise*.[84] In March 1592 rumour had it that Loys Abram had slept with Jehanne Lafont. Abram confessed it frankly and asked God's pardon. By August it was known that Lafont was pregnant and in December she appeared before the consistory to confirm that Abram was the father of her child, and that they had slept together at M. Berrias's house where she lived, from a fortnight before Easter until she moved out to the village of Courbessac. Rumour had it that Abram had since been paying for the upkeep of her and the child.[85] In other instances only the woman admitted their behaviour. Pierre Malbosque, chambermaid to

---

[82] ADG, 42 J 30, 354v; 42 J 31, 4r, 6r, 10 May 1595.
[83] BN, Ms.fr. 8667, 258r, 29 Nov. 1581.   [84] BN, Ms.fr. 8667, 50v, 60r, 63r, 5 Nov. 1578.
[85] ADG, 42 J 30, 41v, 42v, 72r, 96r, 98r, 102v, 125v, 11 Mar. 1592.

M. Fontfroyde, admitted that she had slept with the son of Jehan the painter and had become pregnant some nine or ten days after the previous Magdaleine—around late July 1582.[86] Marriage was never mentioned.

In this scenario, nearly all the women who brought their cases to the consistory were pregnant and evidently admitted their situation in the hope of support. Mathive Theoronde confessed frankly in April 1592 that she had had a child by weaver François de Caveyrac outside marriage.[87] Widow Anne Pagese chose to present herself before the Nîmes consistory in May 1593 claiming that she was pregnant by lawyer Mardochee Lagrange, who had 'debauched' her when she had served as a sick-maid at the house of Donne Jeanne de Morleri. She recognized her behaviour as sinful: she claimed that she had recently not had sex with anyone apart from Lagrange, but admitted that she had 'made another fault'—that is, had had sex with someone else—years ago, before her marriage.[88] Catherine Daudeze stated in January 1595 that she had been pregnant since the feast day of Saint Jean, when she had had sex with her brother's servant Jehan de Langre in the back room where the servants slept. She swore that she had never known another man.[89] Anthonye Pradiere claimed to be pregnant by Jehan Peuch since seven or eight days after the previous Midsummer and said that Peuch had given her many gifts, including an *écu sol*; he denied it completely.[90] Honorade Robert admitted in 1608 that she was six months pregnant by Jean Montelz, who lived, as she did, in Claude Serriere's house. She was forbidden the Easter Eucharist.[91]

Men often acknowledged their sexual activity when challenged by the consistory or caught red-handed. M. Chalas the younger was found in the act of *paillardise*, and subsequently confessed to having made the woman, Beatrix, pregnant, for which he asked God's pardon.[92] Nobleman Jehan de Lageret, Sieur de Queissargues, admitted in April 1600 that he had fornicated with Ysabel de la Cassanhe over a period of some time, and she had subsequently had a child, whom he supported at his cost. He asked God's forgiveness and mercy on his knees before the assembled consistory.[93] Pierre Crozet confessed to having slept with Jehanne Allarie in his father's house; Allarie had subsequently found herself pregnant. She had given birth two months earlier, but the child had died. It was decided that in view of his 'great fault', Crozet would make reparation before the consistory.[94] Lawyer Jean Hubac was more harshly treated when he was accused in June 1614 of having made one of his father's servants pregnant and then passing her off to one of his father's valets. He confessed with regret that it was all true, and was denied access to the sacrament.[95] Doctor and lawyer Jean Jacques Malhan, who was given the honorific title of 'Master', suggesting his elevated status, was nevertheless investigated for having made his father's servant pregnant and, despite confessing and recognizing the error of his ways, he was suspended.[96]

---

[86] ADG, 42 J 28, 9r, 9v, 27 Apr. 1583.   [87] ADG, 42 J 30, 56r, 114v, 8 Apr. 1592.
[88] ADG, 42 J 30, 152r, 10 May 1593.   [89] ADG, 42 J 30, 319v, 18 Jan. 1595.
[90] ADG, 42 J 30, 367v, 7 Jun. 1595.   [91] ADG, 42 J 33, 258v, 13 Feb. 1608.
[92] ADG, 42 J 31, 247v, 249r, 254v, 18 Nov. 1598.   [93] ADG, 42 J 31, 340v, 8 Apr. 1600.
[94] ADG, 42 J 32, 27r, 10 Apr. 1602.   [95] ADG, 42 J 35, 86r, 11 Jun. 1614.
[96] ADG, 42 J 35, 39v, 15 Jan. 1614.

There were always some who denied their guilt. The rope-maker M. Dorthes denied having made Marguerite Chaberte pregnant in June 1612, but she persisted that it was Dorthes's doing, and he was deprived of the Eucharist.[97] M. Baudan's eldest son was convoked for *paillardise* in March 1615, for having made a woman known as Brueysse pregnant, taking the child to be baptized, and for since having been found at M. Gamond's house at an ungodly hour, where he was thought to have fornicated with a servant-girl. Although he admitted he had slept with Brueysse and taken the child to be baptized, he denied being the child's father and swore that he had gone to Gamond's house to talk with him, and to recover something that the servant owed him.[98]

The point of these multiple examples is to demonstrate that in a variety of quotidian situations men and women met and had sexual relations, despite not having any intention to marry—for example in shared houses, with a servant, or while working together. There are many more instances besides—brief references, such as to 'Monsieur Jean Bournet, clerk, accused of making pregnant Alix Marguiere', in October 1604, or to Claude, 'bastard daughter' of François Pilot and Susanne Genoyere, baptized in December 1614.[99] It is impossible from the sources to state how typical this behaviour was among the population as a whole, but it is highly probable that the cases in the archives are the tip of the iceberg. Many of them involved the women becoming pregnant, or the couple being caught in the act; those who were luckier or more discreet had every chance of avoiding discovery.

There is, additionally, evidence to demonstrate that a culture of pre-marital and extra-marital sexual activity existed that was not being fully charted in the consistory's cases. In 1602 a man called Rousset, said to 'ordinarily commit *paillardise*', remarked to the consistory's emissaries that he 'was not at all worried about getting married because he found enough women'.[100] Merchant Sire Feron admitted in September 1607 that before Pentecost he had 'carnally known' a girl, called *La Roirolle*, some three or four times, and she also had sex with others, including the eldest son of *La Rivierée*, one evening in his shop.[101] It was rumoured in June 1611 that wood-worker Jacques Ribot had withdrawn payment for feeding an illegitimate child he was said to have had with a servant of M. de la Farelle two years previously, although he denied having any such child or ever giving any payment for food.[102] There is no earlier mention of the case: if there is truth in the rumours, it suggests

[97] ADG, 42 J 34, 356r, 357r, 6 Jun. 1612.
[98] ADG, 42 J 35, 162v, 18 Mar. 1615. This was possibly Marguerite Brueysse, a rape victim in 1600: see p. 253.
[99] ADG, 42 J 32, 258r, 27 Oct. 1604; ADG, E Dépôt 36/696, 403v, 4 Dec. 1614. Other examples include: Donne Bourgette and Maurier Malpach (BN, Ms.fr. 8667, 129r, 151v, 20 Jun. 1580); M. le Prevost Rouviere and the daughter of Marcellin Grizot (BN, Ms.fr. 8667, 132r, 16 Jul. 1580); François Mazellet and Jeanne Ribote (ADG, 42 J 32, 169r, 169v, 16 May 1603); Mlle de Duranty and Doctor Derbouzes (ADG, 42 J 33, 262v, 5 Mar. 1608); Jehanne Bassoulhette and Anthoine Milanges (ADG, 42 J 34, 97r, 100v, 5 Jun. 1609); Marguerite Hugonne, pregnant maidservant, the father's name is not known (ADG, 42 J 34, 159r, 17 Feb. 1610); Catherine de Clarensac, another pregnant maidservant (ADG, 42 J 34, 231v, 236v, 17 Nov. 1610).
[100] ADG, 42 J 32, 101r, 4 Sept. 1602.
[101] ADG, 42 J 33, 222v, 226r; 42 J 34, 34v, 12 Sept. 1607.
[102] ADG, 42 J 34, 270r, 271r, 15 Jun. 1611.

that sexual relationships flourished and illegitimate children were being born without always being spotted by the elders of the consistory. In May 1612 Susanne Gynouviere claimed to be pregnant outside marriage by 'old Pilot'; two and a half years later old Pilot was summoned, because he was being investigated by the town's judges for a 'second accusation' made against him by 'one called Susanne'.[103] A world of human experience exists behind these two entries. Finally, merchant Sire Pierre Granier was called to the consistory in February 1613 because one of his servants was pregnant; rumour had it that the father was his second cousin, Paul Granier. Pierre Granier's son was also questioned, but the consistory was forced to conclude that they could not 'learn with any certainty' who had made her pregnant, and gave the matter over to the royal officers for justice.[104] Pierre Granier was later convoked when yet another servant left his house with child. The consistory remonstrated with him that this was the third servant in two years (note: we only know of two of these three). He protested that he knew nothing of the misbehaviour because he was mostly away from home. He was firmly told to watch over his family.[105]

From these snippets of information it can be inferred that—in far greater numbers than those reported and investigated by the church—women and men who were not married, and had no intention of marrying each other, engaged in sexual relations. The consequences could be tough: illegitimate pregnancies resulted in children to support, or often the grief of an infant's death; those discovered had to suffer the opprobrium of the church and many in the community; there were potential punishments (both deprivation of the sacrament, and possible criminal penalties)—but despite all this sex outside marriage continued to occur. This challenges and complicates our understanding of the sexual culture of this world: while many trysts occurred after engagement as a stage of marriage-formation, and there were probably many couples who waited until after marriage for sex, the truth is that, outside such circumstances, couples had sex and so played Russian roulette with pregnancy, exposure, and punishment.

The consequences of disclosure led to attempts to cover up affairs. In February 1609, second consul Pierre Galafret reported to the consistory that earlier that day Judict Arboussette had told the judiciary that she was pregnant by a scholar from Dauphiné known as *Durant* and had become so while working as a maid for Sieur de Puechredon. Puechredon agreed that Durant—who had been tutor to his children—had made the servant pregnant. (Puechredon had been accused before of making another maidservant pregnant, but seemingly went unsuspected in this case.) Once Arboussette realized her condition she had left Puechredon's house and had gone to stay with Jehane Reynaude. While there, she said, Sieur Verieu came and tried to blackmail her three times, offering her five or six *écus* to say that the child belonged to a scholar called Barjot. She refused, and Reynaude backed up her story. Verieu argued that he was not asking her to lie, but to tell the truth, as Durant was innocent. The consistory was unconvinced—Verieu was sentenced to abstain

---

[103] ADG, 42 J 34, 355v; 42 J 34, 127v, 30 May 1612 (and 12 Dec. 1614).
[104] ADG, 42 J 34, 413r, 414r, 415r, 6 Feb. 1613.   [105] ADG, 42 J 35, 178r, 20 May 1615.

from the sacrament—and some months later another man tried to present a child for baptism, saying it belonged to Durant and 'Puechredon's servant'.[106]

Apothecary Sire Ravanel was accused of a similar deception. He was said to have made a former servant of Sire Fixor pregnant, but denied having slept with her. His younger brother was summoned and admitted under oath that his brother had asked him to pass off the illegitimate child as his own. He added the conclusive fact that his elder brother paid for the child's food. The younger Ravanel was chastised for wanting to cover his brother's fault and the older Ravanel was suspended from the sacrament.[107]

If paternity could not be passed off on to someone else, an alternative was to seek to persuade the mother to have the child adopted. Supported by her mother Madeleine Sabatieyre, Madaleine du Cros told the Ganges consistory in November 1602 that she had been pregnant since April by the 'carnal operation' of Salomon Rolland. He had offered her six *écus* to give the child away to David (surname missing) and Pierre Melet as soon as she was delivered of it, which she had refused to do. Both mother and daughter were suspended. Pierre Melet denied all knowledge of the arrangements, and Salomon Rolland swore that he had never had sex with du Cros, although she had 'often solicited him to do evil with her', adding that she was known to fornicate. He too was suspended.[108]

Rolland's attempt to slander du Cros as a lascivious woman was a common ploy to shift blame. Anthoine Rousset was summoned for having made Sire Dumas's chambermaid pregnant. He said that he had had sex with her two or three times, and that there were many others before him who had long known her carnally.[109] Jean Bessede admitted to having made an unnamed servant girl at Charles Martin's house pregnant, but said that she had persuaded him.[110] A similar sentiment was expressed by the doctor M. Nycolas. Asked whether he was the father of his maid's unborn child, he replied unpleasantly that 'by common and ancient proverb it is said that never is the [paternity of a] child born to a whore certain', and that, being seduced by his maid, 'he let her school him'.[111]

There was probably seldom much truth in these slurs, but sometimes we have further evidence of their mendacity. In August 1589 Marguerite Pagese was summoned on a charge of *paillardise* and confessed that she had 'erred' with Estienne Barre, clerk to lieutenant Favier, and had been pregnant by him for around six months. She was accused of also sleeping with Guillaume Baudan, which she denied. When Barre appeared, he confessed that he had had 'carnal knowledge' of Pagese, but added, in various iterations, that she had had lots of other men, that the 'common rumour' on the street was that many others had known her, that one of M. Baudan's valets and a young cobbler had been her lovers, that she had previously had another illegitimate child, and that she was a 'public whore', a phrase he repeated. Eighteen months later the consistory proposed to recommend to the

[106] ADG, 42 J 34, 69r, 78r, 79v, 82v–83r, 93r, 18 Feb. 1609.
[107] ADG, 42 J 34, 100r, 153v, 10 Jun. 1609.
[108] ADH, GG 24, 139v, 140r, 140v, 142v, 10 Nov. 1602.
[109] ADG, 42 J 32, 22v, 5 Apr. 1602. [110] ADG, 42 J 34, 107v, 8 Jul. 1609.
[111] ADG, 42 J 28, 165r, 27 Mar. 1585.

consuls that, because of her 'terrible life', Pagese should be exiled from the town. The catalyst for this initiative might have been the news that her child had died, for they had no new evidence, and only recycled the rumour of her previous pregnancy, while reporting that Pagese still said that 'Estienne Barre clerk to Monsieur the lieutenant Favier' had been the father. Yet a year later Pagese presented herself again to receive the peace of the church, following her *paillardise* with, and pregnancy by, 'the late Estienne Barre clerk to Monsieur the lieutenant Favier'. Now, following Barre's death, she was quietly received back into the church and there was no further attempt to slur her as a prostitute. This final outcome suggests that Pagese had very probably chosen, to her misfortune, to have sex outside marriage with a man who subsequently traduced her.[112]

Much of this represented the prevailing view of women's concupiscence, coupled with a desire to shift blame, but of course it may sometimes have been that women initiated sexual relationships. Nurse Marguerite Maurine testified that she was two months pregnant by her employer Maurice Baudan. She also admitted, however, to having had an affair with a 15- or 16-year-old clerk called Bressain with whom she had shared a bed, because he slept in the same bed as the young children of the house, one of whom she was breastfeeding (no mention is made of a husband). When questioned, Bressain declared in tears that one night he had found her lying in his bed, and after 'much licking and touching' she had 'induced him to know her carnally'.[113] The historian must tread the line of recognizing that women's agency could also apply to their sexuality, without falling prey to contemporary theories of female lustfulness.[114]

Cohabitation

If sexual relations before marriage were forbidden, but still practised, the same applies to the cohabitation of unmarried couples. Cohabitation does not appear to have been particularly exceptional: it may be that Farr's evidence of non-prosecution for lay concubinage was part of a tolerance towards such cohabitation when it preceded a wedding, however delayed. Such behaviour was nearly always between engaged couples and represented a prelude to married life, but in practice, this distinction did not prevent the existence of many unmarried couples living together.[115] Far from the timetable of betrothal to marriage of forty days, encouraged by the pre-Reformation Catholic Church, or the analogous six weeks urged by the Reformed authorities, this period could stretch into years of socially recognized pre-nuptial cohabitation.

It is impossible to gauge statistically how common this practice was, but consistorial evidence suggests plentiful examples of engaged couples living together. Many of the examples are very brief references, such as the 1588 reference to 'Durant and

[112] ADG, 42 J 29, 244, 246–8, 590; 42 J 31, 51r, 29 Aug. 1589.
[113] ADG, 42 J 28, 199v–200v, 20 Dec. 1585; Ben-Amos, *Adolescence*, 201.
[114] Capp, *Gossips*, 159.
[115] Gottlieb, 'The Meaning', 71–2.

his wife who will be called for having cohabited together before the solemnization of their marriage[s]', or that to Sire Bodet and his fiancée living together without being married.[116] Some become repeat sagas, demonstrating great obstinacy in the face of the church's appeals, such as in the Bédarieux case of Arnaud Crundillier and Catherine Guine, who remained living together 'day and night', despite a sustained campaign of consistorial interference in 1580.[117] The usual consistorial recommendation was immediate marriage, as when Jacques Meric was ordered to marry his fiancée, with whom he lived, within the week.[118] Jacques Andre, who was summoned in November 1610 for not having married the woman to whom he was engaged, and who lived at his house, meekly promised to do so.[119] Those who had subsequently married were generally still censured. The response given to pin-maker Robert Godin and his 'fiancée'—reprimanded by the Montauban consistory for cohabiting, her subsequent pregnancy, and bringing 'a great scandal to the church'—was to live separately, but only because Robert was already married (until February 1598 when the mayor of La Rochelle condemned his wife to death, and Godin was then permitted to remarry).[120]

There is, of course, little to suggest that cohabitation by betrothed couples was new in 1560. Instead, cases drawn from the very early days of the Huguenot Church suggest a continuing popular tolerance towards pre-nuptial cohabitation that survived the Reformation.[121] M. Bonaud and his fiancée, La Croix, asked permission in May 1561 to be married in church without publishing their banns, seeing that they had lived together for a long time. Marriage was permitted, but they were scolded that living together meant succumbing to the superstitions of the Antichrist.[122] The case of Jehan du Vray reveals a long pre-marital relationship, without much interest from others. Having been received into the Reformed church three weeks earlier, he told the consistory in November 1562 that:

> for nine or ten years, he had maintained the said woman, by whom he had had two or three children without anyone complaining, also they had made no demand to each other to take each other in marriage; that... she had lived as a maid with his mother and father, old and difficult people, [and] had she served them so well that he had promised her that if she would continue to do so, he would take her in marriage, which would be accomplished if God permitted it.[123]

This exposure of a nine- or ten-year relationship and several children before marriage, coupled with the alleged indifference of those around them, is a powerful evocation of the pre-Reformation attitude towards pre-nuptial cohabitation.

Consistorial evidence also suggests that attitudes towards betrothed cohabitation did not change quickly among the Reformed populations of Languedoc, despite

---

[116] ADG, 42 J 29, 329, 10 Jan. 1590; 42 J 29, 16, 18, 4 May 1588.
[117] AN, TT234, 6, 7r–v, 8r–v, 8 [May–Aug., month missing] 1580.
[118] ADG, 42 J 34, 48r, 3 Dec. 1608.
[119] ADG, 42 J 34, 232v, 24 Nov. 1610.
[120] ADTG, I 1, 278v, 279v, 322r, 6 Aug. 1597.
[121] William Naphy, *Sex Crimes from Renaissance to Enlightenment* (Stroud, 2002), 21.
[122] BN, Ms.fr. 8666, 16v, 20 May 1561.
[123] BN, Ms.fr. 8666, 176v–177r, 18 Nov. 1562.

the pressure put on them, suggesting the limited ability of the Church to influence popular sexual and marital behaviour, except in the very long term.[124] Jeanne de Pefrech made the continuing link between engagement and immediate cohabitation explicit in 1596 when she said of her fiancé Ramond Petit, 'he had promised her marriage and as a result of this promise they lived together'.[125] Otherwise it was the unstated assumption guiding people's actions: Barthelemy Gassendon and Fermine Sabatiere saw nothing wrong in presenting themselves in 1589 to explain that 'under promise of marriage and before their engagement' they had lived together, and now sought to have their banns published.[126] The consistory's disciplinary response was unkind: on the day they married they were to make public reparation and ask God's pardon. Yet even the Church formulated doctrines that made the status of fiancés ambiguous: in 1602 the consistory in Nîmes decided that if an engaged person had sexual intercourse with someone other than their fiancé it constituted not fornication but adultery.[127]

Some of these cohabitative unions were distinctly long-term. Anthoine de la Mayes was reported in Montauban in 1595 for having lived '*à pot et à feu*'—an idiomatic expression meaning sharing food and fire, or 'at bed and at board'—with his fiancée for 'a long time' since their engagement, 'to the great scandal of all'.[128] Similarly, later it was reported that Jean Guiran's eldest son was engaged to a girl and cohabited with her for a long time, again 'to great scandal', without having married.[129] What constitutes a 'long time' is relative, so the case of Gaillard Bresson and his fiancée Françoyse Marquese is helpful. They were indicted for having lived together for a year without marrying and were given a month to do so in late February 1602. They had not complied by July, were called again in December, and appeared in January 1603, still attributing the delay to Marquese's completing the 'account of the protective administration of the stuff and children of her first marriage'. In November 1604 they were once again told to have their marriage blessed within a fortnight. When they were eventually suspended they had lived together for almost four years.[130]

Inevitably such long-term cohabitative relationships often produced illegitimate families. In August 1580 M. Yves was told 'he gave great scandal to the church' because he and his fiancée ate, drank, and slept together, and she was pregnant.[131] After months of consistorial exhortations, M. Auzas and his fiancée presented themselves to ask forgiveness for having lived and had several children together without marrying.[132] In February 1599 Jehanne Amourouse and Pierre Cussac, though now married, were summoned before the Ganges consistory for having lived together

---

[124] Gottlieb, 'The Meaning', 67; as R. Po-Chia Hsia found for Germany, *Social Discipline in the Reformation: Central Europe 1550–1750* (London, 1989), 149.

[125] ADTG, I 1, 122r–v, 27 Mar. 1596.   [126] ADG, 42 J 29, 128, 8 Mar. 1589.

[127] ADG, 42 J 32, 91r, 14 Aug. 1602.   [128] ADTG, I 1, 71v, 22 Nov. 1595.

[129] ADG, 42 J 35, 113r, 10 Sept. 1614.

[130] ADG, 42 J 31, 458v, 462v, 473r; 42 J 32, 71v, 132v, 138, 181v, 261, 264; 42 J 33, 3r, 5v, 21 Jan. 1602.

[131] BN, Ms.fr. 8667, 135r, 24 Aug. 1580.

[132] ADG, 42 J 29, 18, 4 May 1588.

before marriage and having had a child six months after their wedding.[133] Anthoine Maurin was chastised for 'not having married his wife' (note the consistory's slippage of language) despite the fact they had a child.[134]

Although most cohabiting couples appear to have been in this liminal situation, there are also a few examples of unmarried and unengaged partners living as man and wife. It was reported in February 1602 that François Mazellet openly kept a woman at bed and at board in a house in the suburbs. Mazellet confessed frankly that two or three years earlier he had bought a house in the suburbs, where he cohabited and slept with this woman—called Loize Plaucharde—'as if she were his wife', and that she had borne him a child whom he recognized as his own. He told the consistory in September that he repented and would put her aside; but two months later he remained 'eating, drinking, and sleeping together' with her.[135] This situation was very similar to that of Gilly Cossard, who was reported to keep a woman at bed and at board. He verified that it was true that two years earlier he had become friends with a girl who lived in Montpellier, and 'since he had maintained her as his wife, having lived with her and had a child, aged a year old'.[136] Although the consistory told him that he was causing a scandal, his honest tale of friendship and cohabitation bears no signs of shame.

Conclusions

There was a clear demarcation in people's minds between what it meant to be engaged and what it meant to be married, but sexual practice did not follow this distinction.[137] The evidence suggests that after engagement, sex, and sexually active cohabitation, were not infrequent and clearly socially acceptable among some parts of society. Sex does seem to have constituted a step in the marriage-formation process for many, and the close association between sex and marriage led many women to allow themselves to be seduced by men's (sometimes false) promises. There were others who adopted the consistory's attitude towards betrothed fornication, and who reported their neighbours for it. Some of the cases in the registers emanated from denunciations, while the consistory's complaints of the scandal caused by such behaviour may not have been merely rhetorical. This was an ambiguous area of social division. There were those who embraced the Reformed Church's disciplined response to pre-marital sex and sought to implement it, those who enjoyed gossiping about such behaviour, and those who held a relaxed approach to pre-nuptial cohabitation. Yet it is likely that the consistorial registers tend towards an impression of scandal and judgement, while representing only a small proportion of those who were sexually active outside marriage.

The records do, however, reveal what other sources have obscured: that people had sex, and even cohabited, wholly outside the context of engagement or an

---

[133] ADH, GG 24, 100r, 121, 13 Feb. 1599.   [134] ADG, 42 J 31, 273r, 24 Mar. 1599.
[135] ADG, 42 J 31, 471r; 42 J 32, 64v, 96v, 103r, 121r, 13 Feb. 1602.
[136] ADG, 42 J 33, 228v, 26 Sept. 1607.
[137] Shorter, *Making*, 85 suggests people did not know the difference between engagement and marriage before the Reformation.

intention to marry. In human terms this is no great surprise, but it has been largely absent from historians' accounts of the period. The evidence of the consistorial registers, therefore, demands some re-thinking of the nature of sexual relations in sixteenth- and seventeenth-century society.

PREY

In July 1595 a Catholic maidservant called Jeanne Gauside—also known as *La Gasconne*, as she was from Gascony—came to the attention of the Montauban consistory.[138] Her name first appeared in the records when a married couple—Raymond Cieurac and Jeanne Malemorque from Reynier, near Bordeaux—brought a child to Montauban to be baptized into the Huguenot faith, stating that Gauside was the child's mother. At the same time, public rumour suggested that Gauside had been making it known that the child's father was Pierre Delhoste, a sailor and the father-in-law of her former employer in Montauban, a Protestant innkeeper called Jean Cotines (who also had a nickname—*Maffre*).[139]

Gauside never testified before the consistory herself, and so we have no auto-biographical account of her sexual encounter with Delhoste, but there are, never-theless, some conclusions that can be drawn. Although Gauside's age was never mentioned, she was likely to be in her teens or early twenties, as life-cycle service was the norm. Delhoste—her master's father-in-law—was sixty years old.[140] There is no evidence of affection or mutual consent between the pair. Delhoste is also mentioned in connection with two other charges of illicit sexual activity in 1595: according to the register of criminal sentences, Marguerite Reyne told the city's consuls that she was pregnant by Pierre Delhoste when they sentenced her to be banished from the city for three years for fornication and in December Delhoste was accused of making another woman pregnant in Gaillac.[141] He seems to have been a sexual predator. The power relations implied by the large age gap, Gauside's 'foreigner' status in Montauban (she spoke 'the language of Gascony', meaning the Gascon dialect of Occitan), and Delhoste's relationship to her employer meant that Gauside was hardly able to resist his advances. When Cotines discovered his father-in-law's behaviour with Gauside he was angry with him. In short, all the evidence implies a case of sexual assault and rape of a young woman by a much older man.

The consistory handled the case by first summoning Cotines. He was admon-ished for his maidservant's having become pregnant under his care, and having left his house three months earlier to give birth in the village of Orgueil, on the out-skirts of Montauban. He was chastised for not reporting her pregnancy to the magistrates, and was additionally accused of advising her to take some medicine to

---

[138] The title of this section is an appreciative imitation of Solé's chapter title, 'Les Proies', Solé, *Etre femme.*
[139] ADTG, I 1, 21r, 22r–23v, 27v, 34r, 37r, 19 Jul. 1595.   [140] ADTG, I 1, 81v.
[141] ADTG, 5 FF 2, 35r, 1595; ADTG, I 1, 80v, 81v, 13 Dec. 1595.

bring on an abortion, and even asking the surgeon Pierre Goby to give her some such potion. When reminded that he would be culpable before God, he confessed that he had done as they said.

The consistory was particularly perturbed by the question of the attempted abortion. Testifying on 2 August 1595 the surgeon Goby (or Goubin, as he gave his name) confirmed that he had seen *La Gasconne*, and she had asked him for some medicine to bring on 'her flowers' (menstruation).[142] He had refused, saying that 'the time was not right', but Cotines and a woman called Astrugue Cappellane had demanded he give it to Gauside.

Cappellane was summoned, and testified that three months earlier Gauside had come to her house in the suburbs to take the medicine that Goby had given her (Fig. 6.1). Cappellane reported that as they lay in bed, she had asked her friend why she needed it. Gauside responded that she had an 'overburdened liver' and that she was planning to take the medicine 'to purge herself'. Cappellane, shocked, passed her hands over Gauside's swollen belly and said to her, in Occitan, 'Jeanne, stop! You cannot say that you are not pregnant?' Gauside immediately—'at that instant'—agreed, saying that she was seven months pregnant by Pierre Delhoste, with just two months left to go, and that she was in 'such great despair' that she had taken a knife and carried it close to her because she had resolved to kill herself and the child she bore.[143] Cappellane told her that she was 'very wretched to want to murder herself, and that she would not only kill herself, but also the creature that she had in her stomach', and by this and other words dissuaded Gauside from suicide.

After many summonses Delhoste finally appeared before the consistory on 1 September, when he admitted freely that he had had sex with Gauside, had made her pregnant, and that she had since given birth. He was told that as the scandal was so well known he must make public reparation for his sins, but he said he did not want to obey and was suspended from the Eucharist.

This is a fascinating glimpse into a female response to a situation that seems to have been far from rare in sixteenth- and seventeenth-century Languedoc. Gauside was an archetypal disempowered woman: probably young, an outsider to the region who sounded different, not surrounded by her kith and kin, and employed as a lowly servant. She was among the least influential of her gender in a male-dominated society.

Through her confession to Astrugue Cappellane it is possible to see something of her feelings about the situation. The way she divulged the truth so quickly—the words almost spilling out of her—suggests that she was deeply relieved by her friend's discernment. She seems to have been heavily burdened by shame. The

---

[142] Women 'were aware of methods of aborting the foetus through herbal remedies', Susan Broomhall, 'Understanding Household Limitation Strategies among the Sixteenth-Century Urban Poor in France', *French History* 20.2 (2006), 121–37, here 127; John M. Riddle, *Eve's Herbs: A History of Contraception and Abortion in the West* (Cambridge, MA, 1997) shows that such methods were not remotely reliable, but not completely ineffective either.

[143] '*Joanne aree non teu podes pas des dire que non sios preine*'. There is a double negative in the Occitan, and the second clause is in the subjunctive. The rustic nature is conveyed by *aree* (*arrê!*)—a word used to stop cattle or animals.

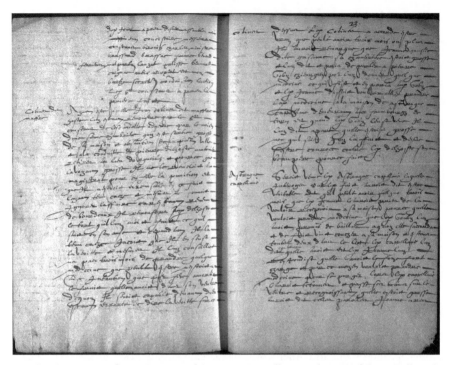

Fig. 6.1. Testimony of Jean Cotines and Astrugue Cappellane, in the case of Pierre Delhoste's assault of Jeanne Gauside, known as *La Gasconne, Registre du consistoire de Montauban, 1595–8*, Archives départementales du Tarn-et-Garonne, I 1, 22v, 23r (26 July 1595)

notion of wanting to 'purge' herself reflected a desire to expel the intruder-foetus from her body, but also expressed a wish to cleanse away sin, to be shriven and purified—feelings concomitant with rape. She had tried to deal with the resultant pregnancy first by ignoring it—she only sought to take abortifacients at seven months, suggesting denial until it was impossible to disregard—then by seeking an abortion, and finally, in despair, by concluding that suicide was her only means of coping with the situation. For many young women the shame, loss of employment, and financial necessity created by sexual abuse were devastating. Delhoste's insouciant admission of his behaviour is in stark contrast to Gauside's distress.

Yet the astonishing thing is that her speech to Cappellane was not the end of the story. Their conversation seems to have marked a shift. Gauside ultimately chose not to take the medicine, but instead manufactured a situation some time later that allowed her to have her baby baptized into the faith of its father, which is how we first hear of her, when the couple brought the baby to Montauban. This was, in part, a manifestation of maternal care—arranging status for her child in the community of its father—but perhaps there was a more calculated purpose behind the baptism: it was through this mechanism that Delhoste was called to account, while the Catholic Gauside never appeared before the consistory. Similarly, public rumour about the child's fatherhood emanated from Gauside herself. Despite her relative powerlessness and the previous abuse, Gauside had successfully manipulated the systems of her society to regain some measure of revenge and control.

There are over a hundred cases of sexual assault—both achieved and attempted—in the manuscripts under study. Some of these conformed to contemporary definitions of rape: the consistory recognized as rape acts of sexual intercourse involving violence by a man against a woman, and referred to them using the verb *violer* (to rape), the verb *forcer*, or said sex had been achieved 'by force'. In such instances the consistory generally referred the case to the king's justice.[144] This historically specific definition of rape does not suffice, however, to cover all the instances of sex by force or coercion that are to be found in these records.[145] Although most women did not physically fight their abuser, they cannot be said to have freely consented to sex. Many cases that the consistory and consuls recognized as *paillardise* occurred in circumstances like Gauside's, in which power was unevenly distributed, and in which the woman was neither able to consent freely nor refuse because of the consequences of resisting. This is what Susan Brownmiller called 'the huge grey area of sexual exploitation, of women who are psychologically coerced into acts of intercourse they do not desire because they do not have the wherewithal to physically, or even psychologically, resist'.[146]

In considering instances where women were prey to predatory men, the consistory cases can contribute meaningfully to the historiography on rape. Many studies of rape have noted the low rates of both prosecution and conviction before the law in the sixteenth to seventeenth centuries.[147] Roy Porter argued that such rare appearances before the courts suggest that rape was not especially common, and that it was severely punished under law by a society that abhorred it.[148] This is surely to misunderstand the evidence. Garthine Walker has demonstrated that the legal requirements of proof in seventeenth-century England meant that a raped woman had to provide the near impossible: tangible proof of active physical resistance.[149] As Shani D'Cruze has observed, it is not possible to consider the 'historical data [of conviction] as in any way reflecting the real incidence of sexual violence'.[150] Daniel Kaiser has pointed out that the severity of punishments might actually have deterred victims

---

[144] See, for example, BN, Ms.fr. 8667, 204r and ADG, 42 J 28, 89v.

[145] Shani D'Cruze, 'Approaching the History of Rape and Sexual Violence: Notes towards Research', *Women's History Review* 1.3 (1992), 377–97, here 388; Garthine Walker, 'Rereading Rape and Sexual Violence in Early Modern England', *Gender & History* 10.1 (1998), 1–25, here 5.

[146] Susan Brownmiller, *Against our Will: Men, Women, and Rape* (New York, 1975), 121.

[147] Nazife Bashar, 'Rape in England between 1550 and 1700', in *The Sexual Dynamics of History: Men's Power, Women's Resistance*, ed. The London Feminist History Group (London, 1983) found 274 cases before the English Assize records in five home counties in 1558–1700 with forty-five guilty verdicts; Miranda Chaytor 'Husband(ry): Narratives of Rape in the Seventeenth Century', *Gender and History* 7.3 (1995), 378–407 found that English Northern Assizes heard a rape case roughly every two years; Manon van der Heijden, 'Women as Victims of Sexual and Domestic Violence in Seventeenth-Century Holland', *Journal of Social History* 33.3 (2000), 623–44, found fourteen accusations for assault and rape in seventeenth-century Delft and Rotterdam.

[148] Roy Porter, 'Rape—Does It Have a Historical Meaning?', in *Rape*, ed. Sylvana Tomaselli and Porter (Oxford, 1986), 217–36.

[149] Walker, 'Rereading Rape', 8.   [150] D'Cruze, 'Approaching', 388.

from filing charges.[151] The cases before the consistory give access to instances of unprosecuted sexual assault that lie beyond the legal statistics, and in which complainants were undeterred by the risk of daunting criminal penalties.

Porter also suggested that sexual assault was practised by marginal young men 'not yet absorbed into patriarchy, with its classic roles of husband and father', and that it was not a symptom of systemic patriarchal oppression.[152] Edward Shorter depicted rape before the French Revolution as the result of a culture in which there was little scope for consensual sex outside (or, even, in his view, inside) marriage, producing a 'huge restless mass of sexually frustrated men'.[153] Jacques Rossiaud found that 85 per cent of rapists in 125 cases in Dijon between 1436 and 1483 were young townsmen—although he differs from Porter in concluding that rape was not rare, but rather 'a normal and permanent aspect of urban life'.[154] Solé too describes sexual aggression as an initiation rite of young men and states that 'the atmosphere of masculine violence was one with which the women of the time were ceaselessly confronted'.[155] Consistory cases suggest that sexual assault may well have been a normal feature of sixteenth- and seventeenth-century French life, but most of the predators were far less marginal—and far more rooted in patriarchy— than these studies suggest.

Many of the sexual assault cases before the consistory involved female servants and their male employers—men well established into patriarchy, as masters, husbands, and fathers. Although I have identified a couple of genuinely consensual relationships between masters and servants, the vast majority were situations of domestic sexual exploitation. Only Farr and Broomhall have—briefly—considered evidence for this in sixteenth-century France, although Solé examined the vulnerability of maidservants in the fifteenth century, and Capp and Ben-Amos considered sixteenth- and seventeenth-century England.[156] The literature is especially abundant for eighteenth-century France, where Nicole Castan, Depauw, Fairchilds, Gutton, Hufton, Maza, Phan, and others noted that young unmarried maidservants often experienced sexual assault by employers.[157] Fairchilds concluded

---

[151] Daniel Kaiser, '"He Said, She Said": Rape and Gender Discourse in Early Modern Russia', *Kritika: Explorations in Russian and Eurasian History* 3.2 (2002), 197–216, here 198.

[152] Porter, 'Rape'.

[153] Edward Shorter, 'On Writing the History of Rape', *Signs* 3.2 (1977), 471–82, here 474.

[154] Jacques Rossiaud, 'Prostitution, Youth and Society in the Towns of Southeastern France in the Fifteenth Century', in *Deviants and the Abandoned in French Society*, ed. R. Foster and O. Ranum (Baltimore, MD, 1978), 1–46, here 12.

[155] Solé, *Etre femme*, 47, 51.

[156] Farr, *Authority*, 110–23; Broomhall, 'Understanding, 121–37; Solé, *Etre femme*, 78; Capp, *Gossips* 129, 144–64, 236–47; Ben-Amos, *Adolescence*, 202. See also Claude Grimmer, *La femme et la bâtard: amours illégitimes et secrètes dans l'ancienne France* (Paris, 1983); Naphy, *Sex*, 24–8; Georges Vigarello's *A History of Rape: Sexual Violence in France from the 16th to the 20th Century*, trans. Jean Birrell (Cambridge, 2001) actually cites very few cases before the eighteenth century. He also works with a definition of rape that only encompasses sexual intercourse involving physical violence and a victim's continuous resistance, which is a product of the case law that makes up his source material (as he explains himself, 40).

[157] Nicole Castan, 'La criminalité familiale dans le ressort du Parlement de Toulouse, 1690–1730', in *Crimes et criminalité en France 17e–18e siècles*, ed. A. Abbiateci, F. Billacois, Y. Bongert, N. Castan, Y. Castan, P. Petrovitch, *Cahier des Annales* 33 (Paris, 1971), 105; Jacques Depauw, 'Amour illégitime

that the circumstances of eighteenth-century France made female day-labourers and domestic servants 'especially vulnerable to such seduction', and Castan recognized how difficult it was for poor girls debauched by rich men to get justice in Toulouse.[158] Much of the evidence from this period is drawn from the *déclarations de grossesse* (declarations of pregnancy). Phan found that 90 per cent of the declarations recorded in eighteenth-century Languedoc came from female servants incriminating their employers.[159] The phenomenon is therefore well known: but because of the nature of the evidence what has been less well established are the circumstances under which assault took place, and the narratives and strategies of both those raped and the rapists.

What this earlier work does provide are some hypotheses to test against the Languedocian evidence. Phan found that women were often surprised by violence—filling their *déclarations* with images of being 'thrown on the floor' and 'known by force', but this may well be a function of the need to stress a lack of consent in these formulaic and calculated documents.[160] Shorter suggests that men did not always use brute force: threats of it, or of dismissal, could be sufficient.[161] Fairchilds goes further: 'force was rarely needed'.[162] Vigarello notes that aggressors were frequently unaware that their actions had been violent.[163] Capp writes of a combination 'of sexual violence and endearments that seems puzzling today but was characteristic of the period': rape often initiated a relationship in which women later acquiesced.[164] This was a frequent model of sexual initiation in literature at the time, in which force overcame resistance, which then yielded to passion.[165] Depauw concludes that maidservants gave way on the promise of financial provision, and Yves Castan notes that women did not consider themselves dishonoured if they ceded under the promise of marriage.[166] The consistorial records show how many of these methods played a role, and that everyday life provided many circumstances that made such sexual relationships almost unavoidable.

The historiography has also suggested methods of analysis. D'Cruze notes that we need to do more than simply record women as victims, and should consider their strategies. Walker urges historians to listen to the narratives and testimonies of both the raped and the rapists, and to heed their historically specific context and content.[167] Manon van der Heijden questions whether twelve raped poor girls

---

et société à Nantes au XVIII siècle', *Annales E.S.C.* 4–5 (1972), 1155–82; Fairchilds, 'Female Sexual Attitudes', and *Domestic Enemies: Servants and their Masters in Old Regime France* (Baltimore, 1984), 627–67; Jean-Pierre Gutton, *Domestiques et serviteurs dans la France de l'ancien regime* (Paris, 1981); Olwen Hufton, *The Poor of Eighteenth-Century France* Oxford: Clarendon Press, 1974), 324–5; Sarah Maza, *Servants and Masters in Eighteenth-Century France: The Uses of Loyalty* (Princeton, 1983), 68, 89–91; Phan, *Les amours* 32, 43, 44 and 'Les déclarations de grossesse en France (XVIe–XVIIIe siecles): essai institutionnel', *Revue d'Histoire Moderne et Contemporaine* 22 (1975), 61–88.

[158] Fairchilds, 'Female Sexual Attitudes', 636; Castan, 'La criminalité', 105.
[159] Phan, *Les amours*, 47.   [160] Phan, *Les amours*, 47, 143.
[161] Shorter, 'On Writing', 475.   [162] Fairchilds, 'Female Sexual Attitudes', 639.
[163] Vigarello, *History*, 25.   [164] Capp, *Gossips*, 144, 143.   [165] Vigarello, *History*, 44.
[166] Depauw, 'Amour illégitime'; Yves Castan, *Honnêteté et Relations Sociales en Languedoc (1715–1780)* (Paris, 1974), 165.
[167] Walker, 'Rereading Rape', 1–5, 18.

bringing a case against their high-status rapist in Holland in 1689 were exceptional.[168] In the seventeenth-century Muscovite courts Kaiser finds a propensity among women to charge men with rape and pursue prosecution, while Capp sees an allegation of rape as a form of leverage by which women could powerfully damage men.[169] How typical are such findings?

The consistorial cases come into their own by offering insight into the strategies employed by both assaulters and assaulted women in sixteenth- and seventeenth-century France. Farr and Broomhall consider abandonment, infanticide, and the use of abortifacients, but Broomhall notes that legal and notarial action was resorted to by few women because of the expense, and we have only 'small scattered pieces of evidence' of poor people's actions and behaviour.[170] The consistorial evidence provides ample material with which to consider both actions and behaviour, and beyond that poor women's accounts of their experience and their attempts to redress and respond to the situation in which they found themselves. The records also demonstrate, as Fairchilds noted, that not all women were innocent victims, and not every allegation was truthful. This section therefore considers a range of encounters including rape, sexual assault, harassment, unwilling sex, conditional consent, attempted rape, alleged rape, and false allegations.

The Identity of Predators

Reports of maidservants made pregnant by their employers are an unrelenting feature of the registers. It was especially hard to resist the advances of an employer, and even when the circumstances of the sexual encounter are not known, the power relations around gender, age, and social and economic status mean that it is reasonable to assume that many of these were situations in which sex was achieved under duress.[171] This is to think in diametrically opposed terms to people at the time when 'the overwhelming conviction that the woman had yielded voluntarily silently prevailed'.[172] Medical beliefs only added to this, because it was thought that a woman needed to reach a sexual climax in order to conceive, which undoubtedly meant that the testimonies of pregnant women claiming to have been raped were going to be heavily discounted from the start. Such convictions tacitly underlay the handling of every case and often limited the extent of the investigation.[173]

The circumstances of sex are therefore often unknown because the consistory did not seek to enquire into them. In their lexicon of sin illicit sex was illicit sex, no matter how it happened. Rumours reached the consistory in 1590 that Jallette Estienne, a maidservant from Ners (some 18 miles or 30 km north of Nîmes), was pregnant by her master Remont de Blausac, a master-gardener. She declared to the consistory that she was indeed seven months pregnant, was reprimanded for her

[168] Heijden, 'Women', 626–8.

[169] Kaiser, ' "He Said" ', 215; Capp, Bernard, 'The Double Standard Revisited: Plebeian Women and Male Sexual Reputation in Early Modern England', *Past and Present* 162.1 (1999), 70–101.

[170] Farr, *Authority*, 112–13; Broomhall, 'Understanding', 127, 128, 137.

[171] Capp, *Gossips*, 144.   [172] Vigarello, *History*, 42.   [173] Vigarello, *History*, 41.

fault, and was ordered to make public reparation the following Sunday.[174] Loyse Felines told the consistory that she was pregnant by Captain Febure, who had 'abused' her the previous May in his house in her hometown of Montinhargues, when she was his chambermaid. The consistory wrote to the pastor of the Montinhargues church to activate the local discipline, but nevertheless denounced her to the magistrates in Nîmes.[175] Violande Frache came to the consistory in August 1595 to confess frankly that she was pregnant by husbandman Jehan Guyon, who had been her master for four months. She swore that she had not had sex with anyone but her master, and was suspended from the sacrament.[176] In each case the woman was chastised, and none of the employers were summoned.

This was not always the case: men were sometimes called to account and could suffer consequences, although temporary suspension from the Eucharist followed by private reparation generally appears to have been the worst punishment they could expect, while the women involved were rarely granted any form of financial assistance, and quite frequently themselves were punished. In February 1591 it was rumoured that Doctor Nicolas's maid was pregnant by him, but when Nicolas was summoned he denied it. The consistory discovered that the woman, Susanne, swore she was pregnant by Nicolas and had had sex with no one else—a claim of sexual innocence, intended to magnify the severity of Nicolas's deflowering. He was summoned and again denied it, although this time he was suspended. Seven months later, however, when he asked to be received back into the church the consistory accepted, taking his repeated denial at face value.[177] In December 1602 it was decided that Robert Del Peuch, known as *Joyeux*, would be summoned to answer to the rumour that he had had sex with his Catholic maid. He admitted that he had and that she was pregnant; he was instructed to dismiss her that day and was barred from the next sacrament.[178] Innkeeper David Vidal, known as *Mazas*, was accused of having made his maid Jehanne Brueysse pregnant. He denied it, claiming that she had left his service five years earlier, and that he had not seen her since. Evidently something about his account did not satisfy the consistory, for they deliberated and decided that he should be warned not to participate in the next Eucharist, while they dispatched an elder to hear witnesses. Their instinct was right: two years later he asked to be received back into the church and confessed that he had indeed made her pregnant. After this private apology he was welcomed back into the fold.[179] Blinded by their belief in women's concupiscence, and the blatant guilt that could be read off pregnant bodies, the consistory censured women while men enjoyed relative impunity. The consistory thus continued to uphold the power relations that had permitted the intercourse in the first place.

There are multiple brief references to suspected or alleged misconduct with a maidservant that hint that those before the consistory were a small sample of a much wider problem. In Ganges, Nichollas Bressou was summoned in 1602 on

---

[174] ADG, 42 J 29, 325, 343, 10 Jan. 1590.   [175] ADG, 42 J 30, 141v, 20 Jan. 1593.

[176] ADG, 42 J 30, 382r, 2 Aug. 1595.

[177] ADG, 42 J 29, 605, 632, 634, 642, 656, 664; 42 J 30, 25v, 27 Feb. 1591.

[178] ADG, 42 J 32, 131v, 138r, 18 Dec. 1602.

[179] ADG, 42 J 34, 291r, 296v, 425v, 28 Sept. 1611.

suspicion of making his servant Jehanne Grosse pregnant; he denied it.[180] The baker Honorat Mille was summoned on account of 'several suspicious charges of adultery and other evil acts with his maidservant' in 1601.[181] Jean Ricard's servant-girl Estienne Ferriere accused him of making her pregnant before both the consistory and the magistrate. Ricard denied it and blamed the pregnancy on Daniel Chalas, but it later emerged that Ricard had contributed fifteen *livres* towards the child's upkeep.[182]

As we saw with Jeanne Gauside, an employer's relatives presented almost as much of a potential threat as masters themselves. The language and behaviour surrounding these cases demonstrates that maidservants had much to fear from the men of the house. In July 1592 the elder Captain Fazendier was furious—at least, so he reported to his fellow members of the consistory—because his wife had seen their maidservant Marie Rouvieyresse with Fazendier's brother, Anthoine Fazendier, with her allegedly pulling down his breeches while he kissed her. The tale was framed by the mistress to suggest Rouvieyresse's sexual initiative, and while it is certainly possible that she had acquiesced or was a willing participant, this was also a trope of the patriarchal culture that many women had internalized, suggesting that the victim must always have behaved seductively. There are also two reasons to suspect that there might be more to the story. Rouvieyresse was a widow with two children (they lived with her aunt in Marmines in the northern Cévennes) and while contemporaries always assumed women's fault in sexual sin, widows were thought to be especially lascivious, having acquired an appetite that was not being sated. Secondly, Rouvieyresse's own framing of the incident was markedly different. When she was questioned she initially denied having had sex with Anthoine Fazendier, but when charged to think of her conscience before God she confessed that Fazendier had regularly 'abused' her in her master's house up until two months earlier, stopping because her mistress had learnt of it and been angry.[183] The consistory used the verb '*abuser*' as a term to signify any sort of sinful sex outside marriage; Vigarello finds that in the eighteenth century it tended to 'signify treachery towards the [woman's] real or supposed guardians' or the use of violence—but in the cases before the consistory it tended to be used by women to designate sex that was shameful and unwilled.

Marthe Privade had lived in Nîmes for nine or ten years by 1594, working as a servant for different households—implying that she was in her early twenties—when she admitted that she was pregnant by Jehan, son of her master, rope-maker Anthoine Mouche, who had 'abused' her six months earlier. When Anthoine was summoned he admitted that the child was his son's and it was 'to his great regret and displeasure' that 'such an abuse' had been committed in his house. The son appeared two months later to be censured by the consistory, but in the same breath—as if equating the sins—they chastized him for the 'high jinks that he gets

---

[180] ADH, GG 24, 128r–v, 30 Jun. 1602.   [181] ADG, 42 J 31, 393r, 395r, 14 Feb. 1601.
[182] ADG, 42 J 33, 262r; 42 J 34, 55v, 62r, 75r, 78r, 79r, 27 Feb. 1608.
[183] ADG, 42 J 30, 86r, 87v, 29 Jul. 1592.

up to at night in the town', implying that his act was not taken as seriously by the consistory as by either Privade or her master.[184]

Other indicators can also suggest the underlying reality of sexual assault. Pierre Bonneterre, accused of having made a girl pregnant—having sent her to give birth at Uzès, and having paid the expenses of feeding the child—presented himself voluntarily to say that he 'had made efforts to enjoy the said girl in his father's house where she lived' a year earlier. The verb—to enjoy (*jouir*)—was that used in association with sex with prostitutes, the so-called 'girls of joy'. Bonneterre was grievously censured for having committed *paillardise*, but the consistory did not have the conceptual framework to recognize that a man making repeated efforts 'to enjoy' a girl as she went about her job might actually constitute rape.[185]

Male servants could also take advantage of the unprotected and often unsupervised situation of maidservants. In February 1588 Captain Molhe blamed the pregnancy of his servant-girl Marguerite, from Marvejols les Gardon, on a servant of his called Ypolite, and no evidence emerged to the contrary.[186]

The story of Jeanne Roueyresse, a nurse who lived at her master Vestric Favier's house, is instructive. In May 1595 she confessed that she was five months pregnant by fellow servant 'Conqueror' Jacques Thomas. She explained that one night during the previous grape harvest Thomas 'had forced her to abandon herself to him' after beating her at midnight in Favier's house, and had 'continued . . . to have her bodily' until she fell pregnant. Since then she had travelled to her hometown, and along the way he had ambushed and attacked her, to try to make her miscarry. Their female employer, who was called as a witness, said that she had found Thomas and Roueyresse in a bedroom in her house acting with 'great friendship and familiarity', and that she had also heard that Thomas had borrowed twenty *livres* from Arnaud Rogier to give to Rouveyresse—presumably to support the child, or pay her off. Once again the mistress's story suggests the seduction was voluntary and contrasts with Roueyresse's account of ongoing physical and sexual assaults. Thomas's nickname suggests that Rouveyresse may not have been the first woman he vanquished. It is easy to see how male servants like Thomas had the occasion and means to intimidate maidservants into compliance, through a combination of constant presence, harassment, and physical force.[187] It is hard to conclude otherwise than that many women lived in an atmosphere of fear.

Although the majority of cases involved servants, the problem was not confined to the workplace. A poor woman called Catherine Pine presented herself in March 1595 to complain against Robert Agullonet, a lawyer who oversaw the town's poor relief, and who had been a deacon on the consistory (as he would be again). He was also probably married.[188] Pine stated that for five years he had tried to solicit her 'from her honour' and most recently had attempted 'to force her [to have

---

[184] ADG, 42 J 30, 250r, 250v, 257v, 26 Jan. 1594: '*des friponeries quil fait de nuit par la ville*'.

[185] ADG, 42 J 31, 405v, 11 Apr. 1601.

[186] ADG, 42 J 28, 354v, 356r, 360v, 27 Jan. 1588.

[187] ADG, 42 J 30, 355r, 356v–357r, 10 May 1595; Capp, *Gossips*, 164.

[188] Robert Agullonet and his wife, Damoiselle Jeanne de Malmont, had a son, Arnaud, baptized in August 1584: ADG, E dépôt 36/696, 222r.

sex] in his house', by hitting her and promising to give her eighteen *sols*. She had started a legal process against him—a potentially expensive gamble that suggests she was probably telling the truth—and said that she had not complained before 'because of the great necessity of the support she receives from him'. He denied it entirely. He said that he had admitted Pine into his house, which he was not obliged to do, still 'less ought he to be called before the consistory on the basis of nothing but her word, without any other proof, and it was nothing by a calumny and pretence, and she had been put up to it'.[189] In the light of his defence and the lack of other proof the matter was dropped. The power relations were all in his favour when it came to challenging the accusation, just as they had been in creating the circumstances in which the attempted rape had allegedly taken place. In her poverty Pine relied on the funds Agullonet controlled; he, she maintained, had sought to make her pay for his generosity.

There appears to be only one single incident, among all those recorded of sexual assault, that conforms to the model proposed by Porter, Shorter, Rossiaud, and Solé: that of an attack by frustrated young men (Fig. 6.2, opposite). Suzanne Cregude was married but her husband, Estienne Giradin, had been absent from Nîmes for three years—the last she had heard, she said, was that he was in Provence. One night in April 1596 two young men—Jacques Gasais and Pol Riviere, known as *La Canquille*—used threats and force to lead her from the house where she worked, through the streets to Gasais's shop, where they each had sex with her. After retelling these events in mid-April, Cregude was required to testify again in Pol Riviere's presence a month later. Riviere admitted going with Gasais to find Cregude around 10 p.m. one night and conducting her to Gasais's house—Gasais in front, Riviere behind, Cregude walking behind them—but said he left the two of them there, and did not have sex with her. Riviere added that he had instead gone into the town square, where he sat and slept on a table for two hours, before returning to the house to find Cregude had gone. Confronted with Riviere, Cregude amended her story to accord with his: both men had conducted her to Gasais's house, but only Gasais had abused her.

A fortnight later Cregude was brought face to face with Gasais. He freely admitted that he and Riviere had walked through the town late one night, gone to Sieur Sigallon's house and met Cregude there, then led her through the streets to his house, where Riviere first had sex with Cregude, then they ate a meal, then Riviere left him alone with Cregude and he took his turn. He added that Cregude had told him that she regularly had sex with Sergent Ysac, who shared her house, and that she was a 'public whore (a prostitute), notorious to all'. Cregude was challenged that her second testimony did not agree with Gasais's confession; she replied that she had been scared to denounce Riviere to his face, and that her first testimony was the truth.

Questioned again, Riviere still denied it and described Cregude as an infamous prostitute. Although the consistory's initial response had been to order an investigation into Cregude's life, morals, and behaviour, and to urge her father to take responsibility for his daughter, they knew that Gasais and Riviere were plausible

[189] ADG, 42 J 31, 47v, 50v, 68v, 20 Mar. 1596.

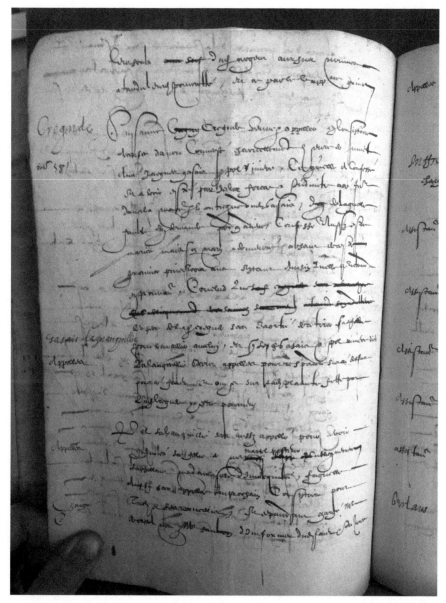

Fig. 6.2. Susanne Cregude testifies to being 'forced' by Jacques Gasais and Pol Riviere, *Registre des délibérations du consistoire de Nîmes, 1595–1602*, Archives départementales du Gard, 42 J 31, 74v (15 May 1596)

candidates for sexual sin. In May Riviere had attacked a girl and cut her dress 'up to her anus'.[190] Both men were also known to roam the streets at night, wearing masks, and performing mummeries and farces. It was decided that all three would be strongly censured, their names published in church, and they would be publicly suspended from the sacrament. Gasais and Riviere tried to challenge this verdict, presenting a statement officially recorded before a notary to the effect that the judgment was 'too harsh', that the circumstances did not merit the publication of their names because Gasais had freely confessed, and that although Cregude was married, they had found her in a public street late at night, and she was a notorious public prostitute. They asked, 'seeing their youth', if they could offer their reparation before the consistory, and threatened otherwise to take the case to the next Reformed colloquy at Montpellier. The consistory decided that their former judgement should stand. The two men presented themselves again at the consistory in August and November, asking to make private reparation, and each time the consistory refused. Eventually, in December, Riviere volunteered to make public reparation after all.[191] Both men ultimately confessed, but the case was never recognized as anything more than adultery between the men and a married woman.

In all these incidents the abusers were known to the women they assaulted. There are rare exceptions to this model, but most women were attacked or seduced by men they knew.[192] In every case the women were servants or of equally low status, and every one of them lacked the protection of a father or husband. This is crucial because it suggests that women were at greater risk when they were not seen to 'belong' to, or be under the protection of, another man.[193] Maidservants also appear to have been in greater danger of sexual assault if they were not local.[194] Many were away from their hometown and had evidently come to the cities in search of work. As foreigners to the region—possibly speaking a different dialect, like Jeanne Gauside—they were isolated from their family networks, and therefore significantly more vulnerable than other women. Their assaulters were mostly men well established in patriarchy, who should have offered paternal guardianship, but instead abused their position to prey on the young women who depended on them.

Circumstances of Sexual Abuse

In April 1596 Jeanne Cappelle was convicted by the consuls of Montauban for the crime of *paillardise* and sentenced to make the *amende honorable*, kneeling with bare feet and holding a torch in one hand, before being banished from the city for three years (see Fig. 2.1, p. 70).[195] No man was named in the register of

---

[190] See Chapter 4.

[191] ADG, 42 J 31, 57r, 58r, 74v, 78v–81r, 86v, 89r–90r, 97r, 98r, 99r–v, 105v, 107r, 109r, 117v, 122r, 141v, 151v, 153r.

[192] See the example in Chapter 1, p. 46, of soldiers groping women in October 1585.

[193] Vigarello, *History*, 47.

[194] Maza, *Servants*, 91; Philippe Chareyre, *Le consistoire de Nîmes 1561 à 1685*, 4 vols (Thèse de Doctorat d'État en Histoire: Université Paul-Valéry-Montpellier III, 1987), 481–2.

[195] ADTG, 5 FF 2, 35r, 21 Apr. 1596.

sentences—women could, it seems, commit fornication all by themselves. The consistory, however, wanted to know the identity of the father of her child, and within a couple of weeks the consistory had sent deputies to investigate. Cappelle told them that the father was a servant, 'who had known her carnally several times'. The servant, Pierre Charles, was summoned and denied it all. A fortnight later Cappelle was summoned to the consistory to make her formal deposition; now she said that Sieur de Philippon's maidservant (whom she described as 'an old wrinkled wrong one') had 'made her say' that the father was Charles, but that she thought that it was Philippon himself. He had locked her in his house for two months to have sex with her, and had since 'known her carnally' and 'abused her' in his other houses 'on various occasions and in various seasons' over a long period of time.[196] She did not, however, let the servant off the hook, for she added that Charles, 'a very short man, who dressed in grey', had lured her to the stables, under the pretext of selling her wine, and then had 'made her fall to the ground in the stable, and at that instant, knew her carnally only the one time'.[197] Ultimately she said she could not say by whom she was pregnant as she 'has had to deal with many', but what she did know was that she was 'very miserable because she was starving'.[198]

Cappelle's testimony about her rape by Pierre Charles is similar in tone to the reports of rape given by women before law courts in England and in the eighteenth-century *déclarations de grossesse*: it very succinctly relates being surprised, the man's use of compulsion and force, and her inertia and passivity, subjected entirely to his violence.[199] In her narrative as a whole, however, it featured only briefly by comparison to the ongoing attentions of Philippon, who had had sex with her over so long and even imprisoned her as his sexual slave. Her concluding thoughts—that she could not identify her child's father because she had been subject to so many advances, and that she had been left utterly miserable and starving—starkly evoke the sobering reality of many poor women's lives. The consistory closed the case by offering her six *sous* towards food, but took no further action against either Philippon or Charles.

Cappelle's case suggests something of the circumstances of sexual assault. Sexual harassment or assault by an employer was particularly hard for a maidservant to avoid, given the nature of his authority and ubiquity of his presence, but there were situations that made the threat more immediate.[200] Being in a domestic space with a man, unobserved by others, was risky. Kitchens and workshops were sometimes the scene of assault, but stables, haylofts, and storerooms were all out-of-the-way places in which a man could take advantage of a woman with the least likelihood of discovery, and with the smallest contrivance, as they were encompassed by the world of a woman's daily chores.

Bedrooms were the setting for such efforts only in cases of extreme nonchalance on the part of the man, assured isolation, or when sleeping arrangements permitted such intimacy without raising too much suspicion. Illness could serve as a catalyst

---

[196] *'Laquelle elle consigne estre une viellie torte, ridee'*. [197] ADTG, I 1, 142v–143r.
[198] ADTG, I 1, 137v, 141v, 142v–143r, 1 May 1596.
[199] Phan, *Les amours*, 140–3; Walker, 'Rereading Rape', 8–9. [200] Maza, *Servants*, 90.

to create this sort of seclusion. Maidservant Marguerite Saurine was interrogated in Nîmes in May 1579 after having given birth to an illegitimate child. She testified that when her employer M. de Savoniargues had been ill she had slept in his room, but in the year after he recovered she continued to sleep there, and sometimes he would call her to come to his bed—a summons that she would scarcely have been in a position to refuse. When she was ready to give birth Savoniargues sent her to Saint-Dézéry in the Cévennes, accompanied by Donne Claude Terraillonne, to stay at M. Fenouillet's house. She raised the child there for two months before returning to Nîmes, where Terraillonne gave the child to a widow to be looked after. Savoniargues paid the widow.[201] This scenario throws an interesting light on the story of Pierre Joly—known as Captain Ducros—who was accused of having made his maid, identified only as 'the daughter of Fortin', pregnant in May 1588.[202] Eighteen months later Joly made a will in which he left an unusually large legacy of sixteen *écus* to his chambermaid Marguerite Fortin for 'good services' to him during his illness.[203] Her services may have gone beyond the normal call of duty.

The absence of a master's wife increased a servant's vulnerability.[204] In March 1580 servant-woman Mamette Hubaque claimed that seven or eight months earlier, shortly after her employer's wife died of the plague, he, Matellin Tiers, had started to 'solicit her to join herself to him' and since that time they had 'behaved badly' together.[205] Catherine Dulhonne had been a maid to Captain de Possasse for two and a half years when she became pregnant by him, which she said had happened in his bed one night when his wife was absent from the town. Possasse denied it all.[206] Marguerite Alcaysse swore that she had been made pregnant by her former employer M. Lause, while his wife was visiting Toulouse the previous May. A neighbour, Bernardine Vallonne, said that Alcaysse had lived with Lause after his wife had gone to Toulouse, and that Alcaysse had told her that Lause was 'difficult to serve and solicited her to do evil'. Vallonne had warned her to leave, cautioning that if Lause found her alone he 'would do her wrong', but Alcaysse had clearly not been able to heed Vallonne's warning in time, and had since given birth to a daughter, whom she said she did not have the means to feed.[207]

If the man was a relative of the master or a servant, the master's absence facilitated the abuse. It was reported in December 1603 that servant Anne Euzasse had left M. de Montelz's house pregnant, and was staying in the suburbs outside Nîmes. Montelz was summoned and accused of committing adultery with her, but he said that it was perpetrated by a relative of his, who shared his surname and had lived in his house for some time. He explained that had not been able to oversee his household because he had spent the previous September in Montpellier, and had returned only for a day before going to court for two months. In due course his

---

[201] BN, Ms.fr. 8667, 6r, 7 May 1579.   [202] ADG, 42 J 29, 11, 13 Apr. 1588.
[203] Arc.Not., 2 E 1/277, 11 Nov. 1589.
[204] Tim Meldrum, *Domestic Service and Gender 1660–1750, Life and Work in the London Household* (Harlow, 2000), 101.
[205] BN, Ms.fr. 8667, 112v, 20 Mar. 1580.   [206] ADG, 42 J 28, 11v, 120r, 13 Jun. 1584.
[207] ADG, 42 J 30, 365v–366r, 369r, 381r; 42 J 31, 33r, 7 Jun. 1595.

relative Daniel de Montelz admitted the child was his.[208] Alayssete Pascalle from near Alès presented herself before the consistory to complain that she had worked as a servant for Captain Privat, but that her master had gone off to fight in the war against the Catholics, leaving her alone with his children and his brother Jacques Privat. One night, towards the end of the previous August, she was in bed with the children when Jacques came to find her and 'enjoyed her', and did so several other times afterwards, as a result of which she was pregnant and Captain Privat had dismissed her.[209]

Outside the house women were vulnerable during any quotidian tasks that left them alone with a man. Boyssette, the wife of a labourer, complained in January 1587 that a fortnight earlier she had gone to Claude Pascal's house to knead bread for him, then Pascal had made his brothers leave, and 'finding themselves alone, he attempted to force' her, with blows and punches, to have sex with him. Her husband was greatly offended and demanded reparation. What Boyssette felt about it is not recorded. Investigations were made among the neighbours and one confirmed that he had seen Pascal punch Boyssette—but nothing further came of the case.[210] In April 1585 Jacques Bodet and Catherine Bastide, the wife of a shepherd called Tholiete, were found *in flagrante* in an olive grove near Saint-Bauzille. In this case we have a rare instance of the narrative of a would-be rapist: Bodet admitted that he had bought the olive grove from Tholiete, who had sent his wife Bastide to show Bodet where it was. Once there he was 'surprised by temptation and wanted to try to do dirty things with the said woman', and he was just attempting to do so when he was interrupted by some labourers. Bastide said that Bodet 'wanted to force her and, as much by his words, he tried to enjoy her'—he had attempted to have her by both violence and persuasion—but had succeeded in little when they were surprised by the men, who found her sitting on the ground with Bodet kneeling close to her, untying his breeches and uncovering 'his shameful parts'.[211] Despite both testimonies the consistory deemed it to be consensual adultery, and both Bastide and Bodet were censured and deprived of the sacrament.[212] Women were, it seems, vulnerable to assault, rape, or attempted rape throughout their everyday circumstances, and in the course of their daily work.

Force and Coercion

Many predatory men simply used violence. Guillaume Eschaubard was accused by Jeanne Plantiere in May 1584 of having raped her the previous Saint Julien's Day (2 August), when his wife was absent from Nîmes: 'he put her on his bed by force and enjoyed her', and when she tried to cry out he 'forced a camisole into her mouth'. She had subsequently had a child. Eschaubard denied it, but Plantiere

---

[208] ADG, 42 J 32, 196r, 199v, 223, 234v, 17 Dec. 1603.
[209] ADG, 42 J 28, 369r, 370r; 42 J 29, 7, 11, 15, 52, 2 Mar. 1588.
[210] ADG, 42 J 28, 256r, 256v, 261r, 21 Jan. 1587.   [211] ADG, 42 J 28, 167v, 3 Apr. 1585.
[212] ADG, 42 J 28, 372r.

maintained that she had not had sex with anyone else, and 'Eschaubard alone had had her youth and [carnal] knowledge of her'.[213] A rapist had taken her virginity.

Jehane Soliere had been a servant in Jehan de Meuran, Sieur de Vachieres's house for one year when her master's son tried to rape her. She said that 'he made efforts to enjoy her and threw her on the bed wanting to take her by force'. She added that 'she did not know if he succeeded'—a testament to her sexual innocence. A few weeks later the son confessed that he had made efforts to have sex with her, but that he was not able to do so.[214] Soliere's story was similar to that of a young servant-girl called Dous Puilhon in Aimargues. Labourers Jehan Pouget and Bertrand Bien reported a conversation they had had with Puilhon in December 1593. Pouget had asked Puilhon if the rumours were true that her master Guillaume Soulie had wanted to rape her, and she had replied that they were: that Soulie had surprised her, thrown her on the bed, and shoved the corner of the bedcover into her throat so that she could not cry out or resist. From further witnesses it emerged that Soulie's wife had discovered the pair on the bed and was furious with her husband. It was also rumoured that Soulie had later bought Puilhon a dress so that she would not report his conduct to the judiciary; she did not need to—her speech to the labourers was enough to publicize the case.[215] Older women could also face such abuse. In 1599 a widow called Drivette Sannyere declared to the consistory that she was five and a half months pregnant by Symon Tabelly, clerk to the town hall in Nîmes, and that he had 'abused' her just once, beating and kicking her several times to make her yield to him. Tabelly had since given her seven *livres* ten *sous* for her upkeep. Tabelly's response when questioned was denial and a character assassination: Sannyere was a whore and a drunk, who could not get along with her employers, and who danced naked before men. Faced with their differing stories the consistory sought witnesses, but the case never re-emerged and we do not know what became of them.[216]

In women's narratives violence happened to them and could seldom be met with resistance (meaning that none of the cases would have qualified as rape before the law courts). One exception is the assault of a young girl called Lucie, a maidservant of a Nîmois tailor, in April 1581. Lucie said that one day three young men— Abraham Vallat, whom she knew well; Jacques le Picard's valet, and a cobbler whose name she did not know—came to her master's house, where she lived and worked, saying that if her master wanted to buy some accessories that they had outside the town she would have to go to collect them. When she got there they showed her some dresses and said she did not need to buy them: they would give them to her for free, providing she let them 'enjoy her'. She refused and so they took hold of her and tried to rape her, and in so doing they 'ruined all her face'— presumably hitting her—and stuffed her mouth with hay to prevent her from crying out. At some point, though, she managed to escape and ran out into the street shouting, where she was seen and heard by two witnesses.[217] The consistory referred this case to the judiciary.

[213] ADG, 42 J 28, 107v–108r, 23 May 1584.   [214] ADG, 42 J 28, 274r, 277r, 8 Apr. 1587.
[215] ADG, E Dépôt GG54, 12r–13v, 15v, 16r, 18r, 19r, 29v, 36v–37r, 46v, 72v, 22 Dec. 1593.
[216] ADG, 42 J 31, 268v, 269r, 3 Mar. 1599.
[217] BN, Ms.fr. 8667, 201v–202r, 204r, 17 Apr. 1581.

Yet force was often only a tiny part of the picture—the sharp end of a system of power relations that compelled women into positions of vulnerability and kept them there. It could be accompanied by threats, coercion, persuasion, and promises, as well as a structural imbalance in socio-economic terms and a conceptual framework that held women to be inherently more sinful than men. To examine the workings of power in the classic scenario of sexual assault, and the narratives of both parties, we will consider one case in detail: that of Marguerite Brueysse, who claimed to be pregnant by her master Anthoine Bonnet in December 1600.[218]

When the matter was first raised in the Nîmes consistory, Bonnet was summoned. He was a man of some substance, who appears on the lists of influential men who gathered at the extraordinary meetings of Nîmes's town council, and given that he and his wife Marguerite Maroisse had presented daughters for baptism in 1572 and 1582, he was probably in his fifties or sixties.[219] He denied the charge and exhibited a declaration that Brueysse had drawn up before a magistrate declaring that she was pregnant by Andre Fauchier, a cobbler who lived opposite Bonnet's house. Bonnet added that she was a 'whore' who conducted herself very badly, both in varying her story and in not behaving well while she was his servant. Her brother Pierre Brueys, who had also been summoned, refuted this and said that he wanted justice for his sister. A couple of weeks later Bonnet returned, triumphantly brandishing a note from the court against his servant, and declaring the consistory to be flatterers and hypocrites who wanted to condemn him.

Two months later Brueysse finally appeared before the consistory to give her side of the story. She told them that her master had made her pregnant, and that he had started having sex with her the previous April two days after his return from Castres. The consistory asked her if Bonnet had given or promised her anything 'to make her yield to his will', and she conceded that he made her great promises, but had never given her more than two or three *écus*. Asked to justify her varying stories, she stated that Bonnet had 'persuaded and induced her by words and by promises'—saying that he would give her fifty *écus* if she made the declaration naming Fauchier as the father, which she did in the house of his son-in-law. The consistory asked her if she would repeat it all in front of Bonnet and she agreed, so a week later the two were brought face to face and Bonnet was permitted to cross-examine Brueysse—a procedure which in modern times has been likened to a re-living of the rape for the victim. This is their full exchange, which allows us to hear their—albeit mediated—voices:[220]

BONNET: Asked her to tell the truth, according to God and her conscience, had he ever treated her badly, or had he rather told her several times to be wise and not err as she did?

[218] ADG, 42 J 31, 375v–376r, 379v, 381v, 393v–394r, 395v–397r, 398v–399r, 401r, 403r, 13 Dec. 1600.
[219] Bonnet's presence at the council's extraordinary meetings e.g. ADG, E dépôt 36/133, 334r (9 Jan. 1603); E dépôt 36/134 (28 Oct. 1604); E dépôt 36/134 (20 Oct. 1608); E dépôt 36/135, 42r (5 Apr. 1609). Baptismal registers: ADG, E dépôt 36/696, 33v, 190r.
[220] I have added punctuation, marked who said what, and removed 'they said' before each name, but otherwise it is as the consistory recorded it, including their use of the third person.

BRUEYSSE: Said that, according to God and her conscience, she had been known carnally and been made pregnant by Bonnet.

BONNET: Enquired in what place he had known her first, and, particularly, what artifices he had used; under what promises, threats, or other inducements, and at what time?

BRUEYSSE: Said that it was the month of April after his return from Castres, one day when she was putting excrement into the ditch in Bonnet's garden [when] on his order she had gone up into the stable to the front, and, there, Bonnet threw her on a pile of rye where he knew her [carnally] by force, putting a handkerchief in her mouth to stop her from shouting out, and, afterwards, he had given her three *écus* in *sous* and made her great promises.

BONNET: Required her to declare if he had ever known her anywhere else?

BRUEYSSE: Said that he knew her in the midden in his garden at the Arènes and at Rodilhan; not elsewhere.[221]

BONNET: Remonstrated that it was not believable that he could force her [to have sex] on a pile of rye, seeing as it was slippery.

BRUEYSSE: Said that the rye was bound together.

BONNET: Required her to tell the truth if he had ever known her inside the house?

BRUEYSSE: Said no.

BONNET: Remonstrated that was it not more convenient inside the house, even during the eight or nine days when his wife went to Uzès to visit her daughter, seeing that Bonnet and Brueysse slept in the same room, in beds close to each other?

BRUEYSSE: Said that he did not have the leisure to attack her inside because his daughter was there when his wife was away, and she [his wife] had not gone to Uzès since that time.

BONNET: Asked to tell the truth if he had not paid her wages during the time she served in his house, and if he had given her any other reason to induce her to evil?

BRUEYSSE: Agreed that he had paid her wages and also that she had received from him three *écus* ten *sols*, as she had said above, and also another time four gold *écus* that he gave her after he realized that she was pregnant and after he made her go to Saint-Gilles to her uncle's house...

BONNET: Said that she knew well the association and familiarity that she had with the cobbler [Fauchier], who had given her a ring, and that it was by his work that she had had the child, as she had declared in her first response, which she would abide by if she had not been made [to act] by her brother.

---

[221] *Crotte* was used to describe a hole, ditch, den, cave, or midden. Rodilhan, now a suburb of Nîmes, was then a village some 4 miles or 7 km outside the city.

BRUEYSSE: Denied the association [with Fauchier] and having received a ring, and insisted that the child was Bonnet's. Said also that Bonnet knew well that by promises and threats he had induced her to attribute the child against the truth and her conscience, to which end he had made her go to his son-in-law's house. Also said that Bonnet or his wife sent for their maid at the Arènes at the house of his aunt, Marie Rosselle, and having spoken to her, she [the maid] took her [Brueysse] to Saint-Gilles where she [the maid] stayed only one night.

BONNET: Required Brueysse to tell the truth where she was known the first time and how many times?

BRUEYSSE: Said [in Occitan] as you wanted, in a ditch of dung, in Rodilhan, a year less a month ago.

BONNET: Said that by her contrarieties the company could judge in what conscience she spoke. Also, that she is a whore, as is attested by the witness of [lists names] whom he required to be heard. Denied ever having known Brueysse carnally nor even having kissed her on the mouth.[222]

About ten days after this interrogation the consistory met to deliberate on the matter. They summoned Bonnet and asked him to tell the truth—he swore he was innocent, and falsely accused. He said he had not been alone with Brueysse in the stable, but he had been:

alone with her a hundred times whether at Rodilhan or in his garden or in other places and they slept in the same room, there being two beds, his wife being absent, he was alone with his servant-woman and his little girl.

He then left and the consistory began to discuss the case, but were interrupted by Bonnet bursting back into the temple to warn them that he suspected the scribe of the consistory M. Barre of having set him up and that he would start a criminal process against him. This did not help him, because the consistory told him coldly that Barre did not offer his opinions in the meeting. They then reached their decision: unanimously they agreed that the investigation against Bonnet would continue, and that he would be suspended from the sacrament. They summoned him to declare their decision, and he responded, 'in all passion and anger... that they did him a great wrong to believe a whore rather than a good man', swearing that he would appeal to the national synod. That is the last we hear of the case.

There is no definitive proof either way about whether Bonnet or Brueysse told the truth, but the power relations in the relationship and around her decision to relate this story were such that her version of events seems convincing. There is an earthy, quotidian quality to the story told: she was taking human excrement outside to put in a ditch when she was attacked by Bonnet, who ordered her to enter the stable, and threw her on to a pile of rye. His wife was away, but he did not attack her inside, as his little daughter might have seen them. Unluckily for him

---

[222] ADG, 42 J 31, 395v–397r.

(and her), Brueysse became pregnant, and subsequently Bonnet had attempted to pay her off—giving her money at the time of the rape and promising her vast sums, then giving her more after discovering she was pregnant—and, failing that, had coerced her into making a declaration that someone else was the father. He denounced her as promiscuous in his first appearance at the consistory and was amazed that the assembly did not take his word immediately. When he interrogated her, he tried to catch her out—suggesting the stable would have been impracticable as rye was slippery, that the house would have been a more logical place, and asking her twice about the details of the first incident. He made her admit his wise instruction and financial provision, and tried to plant the idea that she was wronging him, having been manipulated by her brother. He sought to present himself as a good and paternal employer and Brueysse as untrustworthy, illogical, and unreasonably biased by her brother's persuasion. Deciding to question her himself was a risky strategy because, in asking her leading questions about the case, he unwittingly provided evidence against himself, but he was so convinced of his own power and superiority that he was overconfident.

Brueysse had bowed to his coercion at every stage until she had the child, when, supported by her brother, she decided to make the truth known. She was brave to maintain her truth when face to face with her employer and rapist. Her calm and logical recitation of facts in an immensely stressful situation was impressive; she seems to have remained unflustered until he repeated his earlier question—as if he were planning to question her all over again—when, speaking from the heart, she dropped angrily into dialect. It worked: the affair and process had been immensely bruising for her, but at least the outcome was in her favour—to the extent that she was believed.

It is clear from this case that coercion was not just used to intimidate women into sex, but featured in the aftermath of such encounters. The theme of a culpable man intimidating a woman into transferring the blame to a scapegoat is echoed elsewhere. One such murky tale of deceit and intimidation emerged in late November 1580, when a rumour reached the Nîmes consistory that joiner Amins Esperit, promised in marriage to Anthonie Coderque, had got engaged to the daughter of his fellow carpenter Charles Coste.[223] Two weeks later the consistory discovered that Coderque was pregnant and she was summoned. Coderque claimed that she had been pregnant by her former employer, court clerk Arnaud Guiran, since the previous wine harvest. Asked how many times she had had sex with him and whether she had any proof, she said that it had happened several times, and she had no proof because it had happened secretly in Guiran's house. A week later both she and Guiran appeared. Guiran said that Coderque had provided childcare for him, but denied having sex with her, and said he had 'not even thought any evil' towards her. She was asked how long she had known she was pregnant (since late August) and whether she lived at Guiran's house (she did not normally do so, only during the harvest), and again whether she had any proof. She was told to give

---

[223] BN, Ms.fr. 8667, 151r, 151v, 152v, 153v, 154v, 161r, 167v–168r, 179r, 181r–v, 311r, 312r, 30 Nov. 1580. She is also, at times, called Anthonie Vincente.

more details: she said the first time he abused her was when she went to his house to ask for some wheat, and he accosted her and led her to the hayloft and abused her, then repeated this several other times in the storeroom, cellar, and kitchen. He persisted in his denial. The consistory questioned her about the rumours that Amins Esperit had given her a dress and a ring in the name of marriage, before witnesses who confirmed the event. She swore that they had not gone through the formal *donation de corps*, nor drawn up a marriage contract. A few days later Coderque's landlady was asked if she knew anything about the engagement. She said that Guiran had told her to instigate it, providing wheat and wine, and the next day had produced a notary to draw up a contract of marriage. But when Coderque had declared that she was pregnant the marriage had stalled.

In late January Guiran and Coderque were called again. He now declared that he had seen Coderque showing her breasts to a servant, and he assumed that the two had had sex. He added that Coderque had asked a townswoman whether a pregnant woman could be prevented from attributing the child to a man who was not its father. He asserted that she accused him falsely and that she was 'lustful', abandoning herself to all; he claimed that she had already had three illegitimate children. Coderque denied all the accusations, saying that only Guiran had 'enjoyed her, to her great regret', and that he had always promised that he would marry her. The consistory pressed her again to say where the sex had taken place, to which she replied that he had always 'enjoyed her' in his house, as he did one day when she was collecting meat, another time in the shop, another in the hayloft where she had gone to get some bags for wheat, when Guiran's wife had been sick in bed. That time, she said, Guiran's wife had heard her cry out to try to defend herself, and there were many other times that she could not perfectly recall. Guiran had always told her that he would marry her in future, and she should want for nothing. She said he had once given her nineteen *sous* six *deniers*. He still denied everything. Even when Guiran was asked about the arranged marriage, he dismissed his gifts of wheat and wine as customary for a master to give a servant, and continued to protest that 'before God and in all conscience', he was innocent. This ongoing, brazen denial foxed the consistory.

The case went silent until Coderque's child—a daughter called Anne—was born and baptized on 12 June 1581. Unusually, no father's name was given in the baptismal register.[224] But, there was one further twist in the tale. In April 1582 Guiran was summoned to explain why he fed Coderque's child at his expense. He replied that Coderque had turned up on his doorstep after the birth and said she would bring the girl repeatedly to his door until he paid her. His relatives had, he said, advised him to contribute to the costs of the child's food to avoid this inconvenience. The consistory was unconvinced, and warned him to examine his heart before returning to the Lord's Table, but he insisted that he had never had a 'carnal affair' with Coderque. At the same time, however, the consistory agreed to allow Coderque to receive the sacrament, noting that 'she had previously given birth to a bastard by copulation with M. Arnaud Guiran, clerk, having been a nursemaid in his house'.

---

[224] ADG, UU92, 179v, 12 June 1581.

Guiran had assaulted his maidservant through a combination of force, compulsion, and promises. He had then tried to neutralize her with money, besmirched her sexual reputation, and attempted to blame the pregnancy on someone else. He had attempted to arrange a marriage for her before the pregnancy showed, and his final—almost successful—gambit was persistent denial. For married men who could not claim the sex had been consensual, these were the classic responses. Yet Coderque had a brazen resilience of her own. She publicly announced the pregnancy and refused to be married off. She pestered Guiran for money to support the child, which he eventually granted. Above all, she continued to tell her version, and such persistence must explain why the consistory seems, ultimately, to have accepted her word over his. (Incidentally, her fate also seems ultimately to have been a happy one: she subsequently married Jacques Fayet, and they had a son—Anne's half-brother—who was baptized in March 1586.)[225]

Our final examples of sexual assault involving force and coercion are those of men who repeatedly took advantage of the power dynamics of the master-servant relationship. In Montauban the worst culprit was Pierre Larroque, known as *Lacroquette*, who was accused of two assaults within two months in 1595. First, Larroque was accused of having had sex with his servant Aime Alzonne, who had become pregnant and given birth to a girl. In December 1597 Larroque would finally admit this, and ask to be received back into the church, but meanwhile he made a deal with Alzonne's brother to stop him going to the judiciary, giving him ten *écus* and the lease of a horse, and in return the brother swore silence before a notary called Boneau.[226] Larroque tried a similar trick in September 1595, when it became known that he had made another servant-girl, Anthoinette Siniolle, pregnant.[227] As soon as the pregnancy started to show he had quickly married her off to a boy called Jacine Plazon, and paid her dowry.[228] He eventually admitted to this too.

In Nîmes Guilhaumette Gaujouse reported in August 1590 that Cephas Bon, known as *Castanet*, had made her pregnant since she had stayed and worked in his house, from March onwards. In October he confessed, and was required to make reparation. Two years later Gaujouse returned to the consistory to complain that Bon had again 'tried to force her from her honour', and as she had not wanted to submit to his advances he had beaten her and her child, and grievously injured them both. The child in question was probably their 2-year-old.[229]

One of the worst offenders in Nîmes was, however, Anthoine Roguere, Seigneur de Clausonne, former president of the *présidial* court and town councillor (who has already come to our attention because he and his wife employed a sorcerer). In May 1589 a young servant-girl called Catherine Plantade complained that Clausonne and M. de Saint-Cezaire had attempted to 'take her by force' at Clausonne's house. Saint-Cezaire declared it to be the girl's 'invention', because he had not paid part of her wages.[230] The next month Clausonne was overheard

---

[225] ADG, E Dépôt 36/697, 24v.   [226] ADTG, I 1, 26r, 28r, 314r, 26 Jul. 1595.
[227] Her name is later given as Catherine Siniolle.
[228] ADTG, I 1, 44v, 54v, 56r, 66r, 67r, 86v, 110v, 18 Sept. 1595.
[229] ADG, 42 J 29, 475, 489, 491, 493, 518, 522, 22 Aug. 1590; 42 J 30, 97r, 26 Aug. 1592.
[230] ADG, 42 J 29, 176, 184, 10 May 1589.

boasting of the *paillardises* he had committed, including the 'ransacking' of a poor girl called Plantade.[231] A couple of months later a known procuress called Florette Gentille testified that Clausonne gave Plantade fifteen *livres* to sleep with him. Gentille added that Clausonne had fathered a child on a probable prostitute called Jeane.[232] In April 1590 the consistory also noted that Clausonne maintained a woman called Chaye (probably Gaye) as his mistress. Clausonne confessed to Jeane's pregnancy, but denied all the others as invented by the malevolence of his enemies.[233] This is not the last we hear of him. In January 1601 his former servant Alix was found to be pregnant, allegedly by him, and in June 1603 Marguerite Fontanieue also accused him of making her pregnant.[234] Clausonne denied Fontanieue's accusation as pure calumny, and said Fontanieue was a 'public whore, as is said in all corners and crossroads of the town'. This could, of course, more accurately have been said about him.[235] Across fifteen years five women that we know of—several of whom can be identified as his servants—had accused him of having sex with them; he admitted two instances, and at least one of those, of which he was overheard to boast, was a brutal rape of a poor young girl.

Conditional Consent

Many of the cases considered involved not only physical force and threats, but also promises to marry or never be allowed to want, or gifts of money. A stark differentiation between sexual assault and consensual sex would be ahistorical: there was a fluid boundary between the two, where employers offered incentives, persuasions, and promises that maidservants were induced into accepting. Sometimes it seems that rape might initiate a sexual relationship that then continued because the women, who could see some benefit and whose alternatives were severely restricted, acquiesced.[236] These were not freely made choices, but they may have constituted consent given conditionally under a promise that was often not subsequently fulfilled.

A compelling inducement was a promise of marriage. Marriage was the hope of many servants, and so powerful an incentive that a maid could use it to justify to the consistory, and to herself, her involvement with her employer, even when the relationship began with rape and the master's wife was still living.[237] In September 1587 a hosier called M. Henry was accused of having had sex with his servant, Marye Vernesse from Saint-Privat-de-Vallongue in the Cévennes, after they had been seen together several times in a garden. Vernesse swore that she had not been with her master, but with a man who had been courting her, who wore a violet coat and happened to resemble Henry, but four witnesses—all market-gardeners living and working in the gardens—Françoise Guerine, Jehan Lacombe, Jean Andre, and Guilhaumette Castagnolle—testified that they had seen the two together in Jehan

[231] '*Le destroussement dune pouvre fille nommee Plantade*': ADG, 42 J 29, 207.
[232] ADG, 42 J 29, 234.   [233] ADG, 42 J 29, 382, 4 Apr. 1590.
[234] ADG, 42 J 31, 389r, 398r, 17 Jan. 1601; ADG, 42 J 32, 172r, 4 Jun. 1603.
[235] ADG, 42 J 32, 257v, 27 Oct. 1604.   [236] Capp, *Gossips*, 145; Maza, *Servants*, 92–3.
[237] Fairchilds, 'Female Sexual Attitudes', 641; Maza, *Servants*, 68–72.

Burnet's garden. Lacombe said that he had twice seen the couple enter the garden, and then the gardener had left so that the two were alone behind a closed door. Guerine said that Vernesse had told her that the man was her master M. Henry, who wanted to speak to her of marriage. Castagnolle—the wife of Jehan Burnet—testified that Henry had come three or four times to the garden with Vernesse; one time Fabrot had given her three *sols* to go away and leave them alone, saying he wanted to talk to his servant about marriage. When Castagnolle said this to the consistory in front of Henry he told her that she was an evil woman. Although Henry was still denying the charge in June 1588, he was entered into the list of those deprived of the sacrament. What is clear is that Henry and Vernesse had spent time alone together; they may have just have talked, but it is possible that the promise of marriage meant further intimacy, for which they needed a closed door and no prying eyes.[238]

The promise of marriage also worked, of course, when deployed by fellow servants. Marguerite Mazalle confessed to having become pregnant by Guillaume Gallabert, servant of cobbler Jehan Allen for whom she also worked as a maid, as Gallabert had promised to marry her and had given her a silver ring.[239]

Otherwise promises could be less specific and more capacious. In October 1602 Gillette Fabresse accused Jehan Rouviere, known as *Ballounayre*, of having tried both to persuade her into sex and to rape her.[240] She said that a year earlier at Saint Jehan Ballounayre had come into her shop at night, and tried to 'persuade her' to have sex with him, promising 'to give her all that she wants' if she would yield to his 'carnal wishes'. He defended himself with the claim that he had helped her to move some sacks of wheat and to close her shop, and that they were there when a man called M. Fermin arrived and she started to tell him that Rouviere's intentions were evil. She countered that on 'several and diverse occasions she was persuaded by the said Rouviere to adhere to him' and talked of 'the efforts he made to take her by force', even giving her money, a gold *écu*. Both agreed, however, that they never had actually had sex, and the case was put aside for lack of evidence.[241]

It seems possible that in rare instances the woman could regulate the development of a sexual relationship with a master. In September 1588 one of the elders saw apothecary Jehan Pic kissing his maidservant Jehanne Girarde in his shop and bedroom. Girarde confessed to having kissed her master once in the shop and twice in the bedroom, and a witness said he had seen them embracing between nine and ten at night, but differentiated between having seen them kissing (*baiser*)

[238] ADG, 42 J 28, 315r, 317v–318r, 322r, 327r, 335v, 340v, 342r, 349r, 359r, 372r; 42 J 29, 13, 24–30 Sept. 1587. Only identified as 'M. Henry' throughout this case, ADG, 42 J 30, 26r suggests that 'M. Henry' may have been Henry Fabrot, who arises in a case with Marie Gibernesse in 1596, below. In the case with Vernesse, M. Henry is identified as a *chaussatier* (a hosier), a *cousturier* (a clothesmaker), and a tailor. On 42 J 30, 26r, Henry Fabrot's occupation is given as a *cousturier*; in the case with Gibernesse, he is identified throughout as a merchant. By late 1591, Henry Fabrot was married, but to whom? His wife's name goes unrecorded: ADG, 42 J 30, 21r. It is possible—even probable—that Vernesse and Gibernesse, who hailed from the same town in the Cévennes, were the same person. One final piece of evidence comes after an adultery case involving a woman called Jane (almost certainly her sister), whose surname is given as both Gibernesse and Yvernesse (ADG, 42 J 31, 150r, 27 Dec. 1596).
[239] BN, Ms.fr, 8667, 362v, 22 Dec. 1582.
[240] She is also called Suzanne at one time, but clearly gives her name as Gillette.
[241] ADG, 42 J 32, 114r, 116r–117r, 16 Oct. 1602.

and not knowing whether they fornicated (*paillarder*), although he also added that he had seen Pic pulling up his breeches. Pic said, rather implausibly, that he had kissed Girarde to find out if she had eaten all the biscuits from a jar in his shop. It seems that she may have imposed boundaries on the physical nature of their relationship. If Girarde had a policy of limiting their sexual involvement, it could be understood to have worked: her subsequent pregnancy was delayed for a year.[242]

There are also some rare examples of what appear to be fully consensual and genuinely affectionate sexual relationships.[243] The promise of marriage made to Anthonie Chalaisse by cobbler François Nycolas, her master, was honoured by him publicly in the consistory, where he admitted to sexual intercourse with her and stated that 'if she was pregnant he wanted to take the child, and still to cover his fault, he wanted to marry and take her as his legitimate wife'. This ardent declaration was not quite as altruistic as it sounds: it may have been partly prompted by the fact that Nycolas was engaged to nursemaid Marguerite Dugua, whom he said he did not now want to marry because he had been warned that she was a 'whore'. By October Chalaisse had given birth and in November, defying the consistory's injunction to keep to his first betrothal, Nycolas procured an ordinance from the *sénéchausée* court, which declared the engagement between him and Dugua null. Although the records go silent as to whether he and Chalaisse did then marry, there is some hope that this may have been a rare promise fulfilled.[244]

A clearly consensual relationship between Captain Alexandre Carrière and his maid Anne Bollette was first reported in January 1593 (though it must have started somewhat earlier). Carrière was a widower: his late wife Alix Toulouse had died after giving him at least two sons, and the marriage had seemingly not been a happy one; Toulouse was recorded as shouting at and insulting her husband in the street in July 1592.[245] She died soon after, and Carrière began an affair with his servant. In March 1593 Bollette testified that she had lived with Carrière for three months, and that three weeks earlier he had promised to marry her, as a result of which promise she had slept in his bed. She admitted that she had earlier slept in his bed when he was ill with a stomach ache, but remained clothed. This may have been something of a fudge—she was already pregnant, and promises to marry probably followed rather than pre-empted pregnancy. The consistory ordered Carrière to dismiss his servant, threatening to pronounce in church that Bollette was a concubine and a rebel to the church, and to alert the magistrate. Their child was born in June, and from this point on Carrière refused to respond to the ongoing consistorial demands. When elders visited his house some days later they found Carrière cradling the child whom Bollette had just breastfed. This evidence of them living as a family contrasts with increasing consistorial endeavours to bring them to

[242] ADG, 42 J 29, 62, 65, 289, 28 Sept. 1588. Capp, *Gossips*, 159; Girarde used the verb *baiser*, defined in Randle Cotgrave, *A Dictionarie of the French and English tongues*... (London, 1632), and Louis Chambaud and J. B. Robinet, *Nouveau dictionnaire François-Anglois, et Anglois-François*... (Paris, 1776) as 'to kiss', although in modern French, it is a crude term for 'to have sex'.
[243] Fairchilds, 'Female Sexual Attitudes', 640.
[244] ADG, 42 J 32, 70r–v, 74r–v, 76r, 78v, 80v, 114v, 125r, 3 Jul. 1602.
[245] ADG, E Dépôt 36/696, 196v; E Dépôt 36/697, 71v.

repentance—between March 1593 and April 1594 the Nîmes consistory visited or summoned Carrière and Bollette twenty times, and in July 1593 tried to orchestrate her banishment from the town. Nevertheless, despite the consistory's best efforts, by December reports reached them that Carrière had married Bollette. In April 1594 Carrière told an elder that he and his wife had left the church.[246] Yet the couple subsequently returned to the Protestant church, and we can therefore chart the success of their marriage in longevity and procreativity. Their second child Guillaume was born 10 December 1596 and baptized into the Protestant faith in January 1597, and another son was born and baptized in November 1602.[247] They prospered: in the same month as their second son was born, Captain Carrière was granted a licence for an inn called the *Gal Rouge* (The Red Cock).[248] What these cases reveal is that there were occasionally maids and masters who developed, after long periods of living in such proximity, a mutual fondness and a consensual relationship.

Consequences

For most women in sexual relationships with their masters, or otherwise sexually assaulted, the circumstances and the consequences were decidedly less pleasant. Loss of employment was almost inevitable, as there was a cultural imperative—encouraged by the church—to dismiss a servant found to be living immorally. Dismissal was insisted upon even when evidence was scant. After the rumour of an affair with his maid Maurice Guitard was told to dismiss her to avoid scandal.[249] This was the biblical injunction to 'expel the immoral person from your midst' operating on a domestic level.

Worse could befall such women. Pierre Laval confessed that he had made his servant pregnant in early 1609. She had given birth at a farm outside town and the child had lived for only a few hours. The woman had retired to Lédignan, some 19 miles (30 km) away towards the Cévennes, where she too had died, probably of complications following the birth.[250]

Rebeca Cognete, maid to M. Bonet, had been made pregnant by Bonet's clerk, Boniol. She gave birth to a daughter all alone one evening in late December 1587. When Bonet found her he could see that she had been 'greatly tormented in childbirth'. She asked Bonet to help her keep the child out of the sight of her older daughter, and he called a female neighbour to come to help her. Then the next morning, without the elder daughter being aware, he asked the neighbour to find a wet-nurse for the infant, which she did. Bonet agreed to pay the wet-nurse four *livres*, half in advance.[251] For helping her Bonet was suspended from the sacrament,

---

[246] ADG, 42 J 30, 157v, 159r, 164v–165r, 195r, 195v, 198v–199r, 203v, 204v, 205v–206r, 206r, 207r, 208r, 210r, 212v–213r, 238v, 239v, 240v, 242r, 264v, 266r–v, 24 Mar. 1593.

[247] ADG, E Dépôt 36/697, 358v; E Dépôt 36/698, 7 Nov. 1602.

[248] ADG, E dépôt 36/39, 176v, 15 Nov. 1602.   [249] BN, Ms.fr. 8667, 143r, 12 Oct. 1580.

[250] ADG, 42 J 34, 82r, 64r, 92r, 95v, 166r, 21 Jan. 1609. Laval was suspended from the sacrament and publicly made reparation in May 1609.

[251] ADG, 42 J 28, 351r, 353r–v, 354r, 356v, 358v, 370r, 372r; 42 J 29, 45, 48, 53, 13 Jan. 1588.

but how much worse it would have been if he had not. We can only imagine the horror experienced by women in this situation, going into labour alone, experiencing a difficult birth, trying to hide what had happened, and arranging for the child to be spirited away.

If both mother and child survived, for an unemployed woman without a bene-factor the financial demands of feeding a new child soon added to the gravity of her situation. Custom and the necessity of finding more work meant that the child would generally be sent to a wet-nurse at between one and three months of age. The rate seems to vary considerably: a contract between a mother and a nursemaid from 1613 gave a rate of twenty-one *livres* for six months, but Savoniargues's pay-ment of twelve *livres* to Marguerite Saurine was designed to feed their illegitimate child for a year in 1579, and Bonet agreed a rate of four *livres* for a month in 1587.[252] For those without support this was a vast sum of money, significantly more than a maid's yearly salary.

Not all unwanted children were treated so favourably. In the years after Zaccarye de Saintes's maidservant became pregnant by him in 1596, the baby was first fed by a wet-nurse at Saint-Gilles, but after its return to Nîmes witnesses testified in May 1599 that the child was barely clothed and starving to death in de Saintes's house; those responsible for poor relief were alerted (and de Saintes was reported to the judiciary).[253]

It is little wonder that one of the responses of women in this situation was to abandon their children. The records are full of such instances: the consistory noted in July 1589 that a small child, son to the late Jehan Thomas, had been abandoned, and no one knew where his mother was.[254] In June 1587 a baby girl, christened Marguerite, was found at the *Porte de la Coronne* (Crown Gate), and in August 1591 a small baby girl was discovered, bearing a letter saying she belonged to M. Milly.[255] Some were left in fields, like Marguerite, found near the Faubourg des Jacobins in May 1608.[256] Others were left in locations that suggested their paternity, such as the child left outside the house of Sieur Camerarius, a professor of philosophy in the College.[257] Some were anonymously placed with wet-nurses, like the child that Jehanne de Lomme fed in October 1608 without knowing the identity of his mother or father.[258] Some were recorded as bastards in the register of baptisms, especially in that from 1602–16, with hopeful spaces left as to identity and date of birth, such as 'Pierre, bastard, outside of marriage, son of [blank]' from July 1613 or Marie, a girl 'born out of marriage' in March 1614.[259] Many were intended to be discovered, like all the girls left at the door of the city hospital, the Hôtel-Dieu in the Faubourg Saint-Antoine, which was known for taking in abandoned children: a girl called Catherine in December 1614, and another Catherine in April 1615;

[252] Arc.Not., 2 E 1/371 (*Mise en nourrice*, Françoise Serre), 21 May 1613. BN, Ms.fr. 8667, 6r, 7 May 1579.
[253] ADG, 42 J 31, 150r, 165v, 170r, 191r, 250r, 251v, 256r, 257r, 259v, 261r, 262v–263r, 264r, 280r, 294v, 27 Dec. 1596.
[254] ADG, 42 J 29, 223, 26 Jul. 1589.
[255] ADG, E Dépôt 36/697, 89r, 22 Jun. 1587; ADG, 42 J 29, 716, 22 Aug. 1591.
[256] ADG, E Dépôt 3/698, 216r, 3 May 1608.   [257] ADG, 42 J 34, 94v, 3 Jun. 1609.
[258] ADG, 42 J 34, 38r, 15 Oct. 1608.
[259] ADG, E Dépôt 3/698, 368r, 27 Jul. 1613; 384r, 15 Mar. 1614.

Anne in September 1615, and Jeanne a month later.[260] A widow called Jacquette Richarde was accused of having abandoned her child at the hospital in Beaucaire, and tried to pass it off as simply having forgotten her son.[261] The consequence of child abandonment was not always the care of others or a reunion with a 'forgetful' parent: in January 1605 two foreigners to Nîmes reported that they had found a hog eating a dead child, half-hidden in a midden near the Arènes.[262]

Women's Strategies

Although women were vulnerable to abuse by men, they were not passive. They looked for ways in which they could negotiate their circumstances and influence their destinies: some tried to resist rapes, some accommodated involvement to reap rewards, others attempted to negotiate the conditions under which intercourse occurred.[263] Afterwards they were faced with another choice, chiefly whether they would stay silent or disclose the affair. Many women recognized that their words could be their strongest retaliatory weapon, and the choice of to whom to talk presented a range of different, if not easy or reliable, strategies by which they could attempt to harness support and influence the course of their own lives.

In the case of sexual abuse by a master, the most immediate candidate for disclosure was their mistress. This was a high-risk strategy and had mixed results. Some wives informed the consistory of their husband's involvement with the maid.[264] Yet when a wife heard a servant's claims, even if she knew them to be true, the preferred response was usually to pretend ignorance—until forced to acknowledge it—and to assume that the other woman was to blame, prioritizing the marriage union above all. In such a case the maidservant represented a threat and the simplest response was to seek her dismissal.[265] An alternative and effective tactic could be to tell the neighbourhood.[266] As the consistory relied on gossip and rumour for intelligence, this could indirectly be an important route to prosecution. While it is unlikely that every woman who complained to neighbours or family about a man's behaviour anticipated that by doing so she might trigger ecclesiastical justice, some of those considered above deliberately galvanized public opinion to shame and castigate men who had wronged them.[267] A more daring strategy was to speak directly to the authorities. Many of the cases before the consistory emerged because women who had suffered abuse made the fact known to the church. As such a declaration could mean immediate dismissal and public opprobrium, this was a hazardous route, chosen with specific objectives in mind.

For some women the crucial goal was to discharge their conscience. Marguerite L'Hermitte confessed before the Nîmes consistory that she had given birth to a

---

[260] ADG, E Dépôt 3/698, 406v, 30 Dec. 1614; 420r, 26 Apr. 1615; 434r, 6 Sept. 1615; 437r, 3 Oct. 1615.
[261] ADG, 42 J 35, 50r, 19 Feb. 1614.   [262] ADG, 42 J 33, 20v, 22v, 12 Jan. 1605.
[263] Meldrum, *Domestic Service and Gender*, 59.
[264] For example, BN, Ms.fr. 8667, 294v, 28 Feb. 1582.
[265] Capp, *Gossips*, 146.   [266] Meldrum, *Domestic Service*, 112.
[267] For example, Jeanne Gauside and Dous Puilhon, pp. 236, 252.

child in Sommières, and that the father was her master Estienne Flory. She also admitted to having accused Hector Crinally of Garrigues near Sommières before a magistrate 'at the solicitation and request of her said master', but subsequently felt the weight of having unjustly accused an innocent man: 'in order not to burden her conscience [she] wanted to declare the truth.'[268] Pascalle Fabresse, an orphaned girl from Marguerittes, who worked as a servant for a female innkeeper called Bogarelle at The Red Hat, presented herself to the consistory in October 1587. She said that her late father Nicolas Fabre had been 'of the religion' (a Protestant) and she wanted to be so also, but that she had been 'debauched', 'abused and forced' by a young servant. This was rape, even by the consistory's own definition. Rather than pursuing his punishment—he is not even named—she sought her own shriving, declaring to the consistory that she recognized her fault, asked God's pardon, and promised to live better in future.[269]

A desire for honesty also drove Marie Gibernesse. A 30-year-old native of Saint-Privat-de-Vallongue, she presented herself at the Nîmes consistory in May 1596 to name the father of her illegitimate unborn child as the son of her employer M. Vallette. Vallette was a procurer to the king, and his son an advocate in the *Parlement*, who had stayed with his father in Nîmes for three months in the house where Gibernesse worked as a servant. Challenging men of such status was daring, and it is not surprising that the consistory sought to establish her credentials, asking her whether she had ever had sex before. She replied in startlingly frank terms that she had been 'debauched' by her previous employer Captain Duranc in Montpellier, where she had lived for six years, and had had a child. Rumour had it that she had also been 'persuaded from her honour' by M. Henri Fabrot, a Nîmois merchant.[270] She said that it was true that Fabrot had often tried to 'debauch' her, attracted to her because she was 'little', and making 'beautiful promises' to her over four months, but that he had never succeeded. (Fabrot was later questioned and denied ever having had sex with Gibernesse, 'although', he stated, 'she is a little wench'—she had correctly surmised why he wanted her.) She had originally blamed the pregnancy on a man in Alès, but she said that this was because Vallette had threatened her to whip her if she accused him or anyone in his household, and because she did not want to give shame to her parents. She said she recognized her fault and asked God's pardon. Gibernesse represented her divulgence as a virtuous and brave defiance of the script that her employer had written for her, in the hope of shaping her life more favourably. Despite—or because of—her candid admissions to the consistory, her resistance did not achieve the desired result. Her employer was never called to testify, and Gibernesse herself was required to do public reparation and suspended from the sacrament.[271] She seems to have been particularly unfortunate, because most denunciations did at least result in the accused man being questioned.

---

[268] ADG, 42 J 28, 280v, 15 Jun. 1587.   [269] ADG, 42 J 28, 321r, 322r, 21 Oct. 1587.
[270] See n.238 —it seems possible, even probable, that Marie Gibernesse and Marye Vernesse are one and the same, and M. Henri and M. Henri Fabrot are too. This rumour, then, would be about events nine years previously.
[271] ADG, 42 J 31, 86v–87r, 90v–91r, 29 May 1596.

Beyond correcting a wrongful attribution and seeking their own peace of mind, abused women also approached the consistory in order to have their versions of events heard and to seek restitution of their honour.[272] Jehanne Moyniere presented herself at the consistory in March 1606 complaining that Captain Engarran had 'persuaded her to abandon herself to him', and asking the consistory to 'receive her complaint and hear her testimony'. They did: they questioned Engarran on points of Moyniere's statement. He admitted being at Gaussen Taboul's house and having spoken to Moyniere. He said that he had found her hidden under the bed, and had asked to see a ring she wore, but denied having stolen it. He admitted having given her a small slap as she left, but said he had not done her any harm, and he denied having debauched her. It is possible to imagine the spaces in this testimony: she hid from him—was there a history? He harassed her, saying he wanted to look at her ring, then perhaps taking it and refusing to return it. He admitted hitting her, but thought it no great deal; did he also rape her? Unsatisfied with the consistory's response, Moyniere reported the matter to the magistrate, and the consistory summoned Engarran again. He said her claim to be pregnant by him was false and calumnious, and added that she was a 'girl of bad fame' and a 'public whore', in an attempt to discredit her testimony.[273] Yet it is his name that repeatedly appears in the consistorial registers: he was under suspicion for keeping a prostitute in the suburbs in 1604, and in 1607 it was said that he kept 'whores' at his farm.[274] Moyniere was probably telling the truth. Her testimony was heard and recorded, but in the face of his denial and disparagement no more was done to give her justice.

Little more was done for George Mouleze. She was a Catholic who presented herself before the consistory to claim that she was pregnant by doctor and lawyer Pierre Rozel. When he was summoned he said it was a false accusation, without proof and from a 'papist', implying that she could not be believed. Although the consistory said that they would look into it further there are no records to suggest that they did, and they allowed Rozel to continue receiving the sacrament.[275] This may have been because he was from an influential family—there was a Rozel on the town council almost every year for which we have records between 1560 and 1615, with this Rozel himself probably serving in 1604 and 1610.[276] Similarly, the son of Aurias Reynaud—another man privileged by family status—was accused by Marie Pascalle in April 1606 of attempting to 'debauch and force her' while she lived with Donne Baudinelle; she added that he had beaten her, and when he came across her in the town had called her a 'whore' and other insults, for which she wanted reparation—but little appears to have been forthcoming.[277]

---

[272] Elizabeth S. Cohen has demonstrated that honour still mattered to those of little standing— even prostitutes in early modern Rome fought to maintain their honour, in 'Honor and Gender in the Streets of Early Modern Rome', *JIH* 22 (1992), 597–625, 610.

[273] ADG, 42 J 33, 101r, 103r, 129v–130r, 29 Mar. 1606.

[274] ADG, 42 J 32, 253r, 10 Sept. 1604; 42 J 33, 224v, 12 Sept. 1607.

[275] ADG, 42 J 31, 401r, 406v, 21 Mar. 1601.

[276] ADG, E Dépôt 36/127–36/134.   [277] ADG, 42 J 33, 102v, 5 Apr. 1606.

Although few women received justice, that did not stop them approaching the consistory in the hope of it—any feedback loop that existed did not deter them. Maidservant Anne Rocquiere told the consistory in December 1614 that a few days earlier she had been attacked and 'grievously beaten' by four or five young men, who wanted to 'force her' from her honour. She brought a witness to testify on her behalf, Claude Martine, the wife of journeyman Pierre Borne, who reported that she had seen several young men from the town following Rocquiere, who was going towards the *Porte de la Coronne*, and that they did not stop harassing her until she was right up to the door of her master's house, 'using against her evil and insolent words'. The consistory asked Rocquiere why the men had followed her, and she repeated with tears in her eyes that the men wanted to force her from her honour, which they could not do because of her resistance, so they had beaten her horribly. She asked the consistory 'to administer justice for her in view of her poverty'. They charged a deacon and an elder to investigate further, but if they did they did not write their findings down.[278]

Others approached the consistory in the hope of more tangible recompense, and with marginally more luck. Marguerite Solière brought herself to the consistory to complain against the eldest son of her employer François Bony, Sieur de Castanet, for having made her pregnant at around the time of the last Saint Madeleine. In February 1584 the son was refusing to pay the sum of eighteen *livres* for her maintenance during her pregnancy. Solière's gamble paid off, literally—as the consistory decided that he was required to give her money, but there were also consequences for speaking out. Shortly afterwards her employer reportedly beat her for complaining about his son, although he denied having done so. Solière would have been seven months pregnant at the time.[279]

There is also evidence of women approaching other authorities besides the consistory, in the hope of recognition of their innocence, of justice, or of financial aid. Catherine Bécharde approached notary Jean Guiran in September 1611 to make an act of retraction of a previous declaration she had made asserting that apprentice Pierre Luquet was responsible for her illegitimate pregnancy. Bécharde now stated on record that the father was in fact her employer Thimothée Chilliac, who had 'used and corrupted her to misbehave with him' only a few days after she entered his service.[280] When she became pregnant her master had forced and bribed her through a combination of 'promises, persuasions, threats, beatings, and bad treatment' into denouncing Luquet before the royal councillor. Now she had bravely approached the notary, wanting to make it known that this accusation was 'calumnious and against the truth'. She required from Chilliac provision of food for her and the child she carried, and her wages as his servant for six and a half months.[281] The impassioned nature of Bécharde's deposition suggests her retraction was motivated by rage. She now made the monumental decision to break out of the paradigm in which she had been confined when forced to go along with her employer's plans,

---

[278] ADG, 42 J 35, 141r, 17 Dec. 1614. [279] ADG, 42 J 28, 76v, 79v, 88r, 88v, 1 Feb. 1584.
[280] The verb *malverser*—to misbehave—was exclusively used for illicit sex.
[281] ADG, Arc.Not., 2 E 1/371, 22 Sept. 1611.

by turning authorities similar to those that her master had used to uphold his position against him. This case did not come before the consistory, and the notarial records give no clue as to whether Bécharde was successful in her suit.

Alongside notaries, as we have already seen, another forum for denouncing abusers lay with the magistrates or royal officers of the law. Marguerite Ytiere complained in March 1588 that her widowed employer Leonard Chalas had made her pregnant some nine months earlier, and that he had started to abuse her on 15 May 1587—an unusually precise recollection—and 'enjoyed' her several times afterwards. When he realized she was pregnant he had sent her to a farm rented by relatives of his, where he kept a chest in which there were fifty *livres* in silver. Yet he refused to give her money to provide for their child. The consistory had actually suspected Chalas back in December 1587, nevertheless they took his denial at face value and in April 1588 Ytiere took the case to the magistrate, asking for the means to feed the child she had borne.[282] When Anne Bourrombe's complaint to the consistory that Daniel Guiran had made her pregnant resulted only in his denial and no further action, she reported the matter to the royal officers, and took with her a witness who claimed that Guiran had boasted of having had sex with her. On the strength of this charge the consistory proceeded to question Guiran again, asking him whether it was not true that he had been seen by three guards in a vineyard with Bourrombe. He admitted it was, but that he had not had carnal knowledge of her and had only wanted to do so. Such a desire was sufficient sin to mean that Guiran was required to ask God's pardon on his knees, with his head uncovered, but yet again the question of her child's paternity seems to have gone unanswered.[283] Perhaps she had more luck with the royal authorities, although it seems doubtful.

These examples of women approaching other authorities indicate that the attitudes and behaviours that drove women to ask the consistory to intervene were not those of particularly exceptional or unusual women: the consistorial cases probably represent only a thin sliver of all those women who spoke out and approached authorities for help. That they let women initiate cases, and that the documents recording what the women said survive, simply gives us more insight into this mechanism than can be found elsewhere. The generally feeble reaction of the elders and ministers also indicates how little help was actually forthcoming—but women went on asking nonetheless.

It is worth considering why. It is likely that, besides the value of expressing one's feelings and having one's testimony put on record, approaching authorities like the consistories was itself part of a strategy to put pressure on the other person. Women who had been sexually assaulted may not have hoped for much, but any gesture of help—be it the provision of a wet-nurse, money for food, or even help to get a new position—could make a great difference to the lives of unemployed women with illegitimate children. Airing their allegations in public might just have produced this—we know that many fathers of illegitimate children did in fact pay for their child's sustenance. As the consistory did not charge, there was no incentive for a

[282] ADG, 42 J 28, 339v, 344v–345r; 42 J 29, 9, 11, 13, 16 Dec. 1587.
[283] ADG, 42 J 34, 18r, 219r, 26 May 1610.

woman in this position not to plead her case, nor to withdraw it part way through. For those dishonoured by pregnancy outside marriage there was nothing to lose.

Women who testified before the authorities had already decided that public exposure could not further decrease their honour—in fact, they may have believed that it would mitigate the dishonour of their circumstances. It was no less a strategy, however, to defend their own reputation, or increase their bargaining strength, by admitting nothing. In a few places in the baptismal registers it is clear that the mothers refused to disclose the fathers' names, so we have 'Marguerite natural daughter' to Catherine Grangiere, baptized in April 1572, and 'Madeleine daughter to Jaquette who lives in Jean Valat's house', baptized in February 1583—no fathers are named.[284] Silence could be a way of earning favour and continued provision. In January 1593 it became known that a nursemaid called Catherine from Saint-Etienne-de-Valfrancesque in the Cévennes, who worked for the *patissier* (pastry-cook) Vidal du Vray, was pregnant. Vidal (as he was called throughout the case) was questioned and said that he did not know that she was pregnant, while he had sent her away because she stole from him. The elders discovered that she was taking refuge at M. Petit's farm outside the town, and went to ask her the paternity of the child. She refused to tell them, adding that she 'would never say' who made her pregnant, as 'she would lose much if she declared it'. The consistory worried at the problem like a dog with a bone. They continued to put pressure on her, and as the months went by tried to find out the name of the father from the woman with whom Catherine now stayed, and then from Anne Crespine, the wet-nurse to whom the baby was sent. Crespine said that she had only seen the mother once, and she had not wanted to say who the father was, but did name the woman who had first brought the baby to her—Jehane Clavele, known as *La Bourciere*—none other than Vidal's sister-in-law. Clavele was summoned, questioned, and soon gave away that Vidal was indeed the father. Catherine's silence had been in vain. In late May Vidal was summoned for the second time, and confessed to the consistory that he had taken umbrage the first time they spoke to him, but that it was true that he had had sex with Catherine a week after the death of his wife Sibille Clavelle, and during the month that followed. When she became pregnant he had given her eighteen *livres* and sent her to his brother's farm to give birth, and had subsequently sent the child to a wet-nurse via his sister-in-law.[285] Whether by their words or their silence, women tried to direct the outcome of events.

False Accusations

Although passing the buck was a stock response to a charge of rape or assault, inevitably there were occasional cases where the accusation can be shown to have been false. Sometimes such allegations did not go very far. Marguerite Julianne had told her female friend Claude Jaquiere that her master M. Bresson had tried to rape

---

[284] ADG, E Dépôt 36/696, 33v, 195v.
[285] ADG, 42 J 30, 142v, 147v, 149r, 156r, 167v, 168v, 170v, 175v 176r, 176v, 179v, 194v, 196v, 197v, 27 Jan. 1593.

her several times, as Jaquiere testified to the consistory in January 1563. Called before the consistory herself, however, she denied that he had ever tried to rape her, although she said he had hit her twice—once for not having his dinner ready, and once for not pulling his boots off. She had also slept outside one night because he had beaten her.

Eventually she confessed that she had told Jaquiere that Bresson had tried to rape her, but that it was not true.[286] She had magnified his crimes in her anger at his mistreatment, but could not sustain the lie in the face of consistorial questioning.

One woman, however, tried to keep a deception going for much longer. In August 1590 goldsmith Jacques Fayet was summoned to the Nîmes consistory to answer to the popular rumour that his maidservant Jehanne Vinhesse was pregnant by him. Fayet was married (as luck would have it, to Anthonie Coderque). He said that Vinhesse's accusation was not true and that she had previously made a declaration before the magistrate M. Roberti, instead accusing Fayet's valet Guillaume Rogier of making her pregnant. Called to the consistory, Vinhesse said that she was pregnant by her master, and that he had 'known her carnally many times' since the previous May. She denied having had sex with anyone else, and said she was induced to make the declaration before the magistrate. Fayet was summoned again and stated that Vinhesse was a 'fornicator'.

So far this sounded much like any case of denial, coupled with a denigration of the woman's sexual reputation. But then Fayet added that he had overheard Vinhesse talking with Rogier, and that Rogier had said to her, 'Come on, Jehanne, I've only ever had pleasure with you once or twice'. At this Fayet said he had beaten both his servants for their immorality. He added that he had no doubt that she had been put up to accusing him by his enemy, M. Ribes's wife. Vinhesse responded that it was true that Rogier had pursued her keenly and said such evil words, which had been heard by her master, so he had beaten them both, but she had never had sex with the valet, only her master. She added that she could not be pregnant by Rogier, as he had left Nîmes on 14 May, and she had only been pregnant for about four months. Fayet confirmed that Rogier had indeed left his house on that day, but continued to protest his innocence, adding that 'God would judge him if he spoke anything other than the whole truth'.

Vinhesse was required to swear once again to tell the truth, and now varied her story. She admitted that she had had sex with Rogier, but, she said, with Fayet first, and the pregnancy was Fayet's doing, as it had happened since 14 May. The notary who had drawn up the declaration was asked to appear, and testified Vinhesse had made the declaration two and a half months earlier, suggesting that by her reckoning she would have been only a month-and-a-half pregnant at the time.

Matters stood there for some time, with Fayet regularly called back to the consistory, instructed to tell the truth, and protesting his innocence. He was suspended from the sacrament for his obduracy, but his luck was soon to turn. It came to the consistory's attention in April 1591 that Vinhesse had now made another declaration before the court at Villevielle that accorded with her first declaration before M. Roberti,

---

[286] BN, Ms.fr. 8666, 207r–v, 20 Jan. 1563.

naming Guillaume Rogier once again as the father of the child that had been born on 1 February (meaning she might have become pregnant before 14 May 1590). When recalled she still insisted that Fayet was the father, but the consistory obtained access to the declaration that she had made at Villevielle, and with the proof in their hands permitted Fayet to receive communion again. It was not until another five months later that Vinhesse appeared at the consistory and admitted that she had lied. She was charged to make public reparation for her fault, which she finally did in May 1592. By this point she worked as a nursemaid for M. Ribes, suggesting that Ribes had rewarded her with employment for making the false accusation.[287]

These are the only cases that I have found in which women admitted a false allegation, but there were almost certainly others where they did not admit it. There is a handful of cases that seem difficult to determine either way.[288] This serves as a salutary reminder that it is not always easy to know 'what actually happened', and highlights that the allegation of rape by an employer lay sufficiently within common experience to render women's chances of being believed worth risking a false allegation, if it could be in some way to their advantage.

Conclusions

What does the evidence from the consistories contribute to our knowledge of rape, sexual assault, and coercion, and the lived experience of ordinary women?

Sexual violence and rape, as classified by the legal authorities, may have been perpetrated by young men—and there are sufficient examples of male servants harassing female servants, or groups of young men attacking girls, to corroborate Rossiaud and Solé's findings—but it did not stop there. Both sexual violence that conformed to the limited contemporary definition of rape, and non-consensual sex obtained by means including, but not limited to, force, continued to be committed by men well-established in the patriarchy—masters, husbands, and fathers. Such men could do so without suffering injurious consequences. Men were subject to more scrutiny before the consistory than before secular authorities such as the consuls— the consistory at least wanted to know the identity of those who had fathered illegitimate children, and temporarily suspended those who were guilty from the Eucharist—a practice that provoked many objections from the men in question, who expected to be believed at face value. Nevertheless, the men of the consistory retained the conceptual filters of their age, and understood most cases of coerced sex that came before them as fornication, in which the women had acted willingly or had initiated proceedings. The consistory understood fornication to be a grave sin, but did not recognize these examples as anything more. They certainly did not perceive them to be rape, and their assumption of female willingness (often,

---

[287] ADG, 42 J 29, 467, 482–3, 502–7, 665; 42 J 30, 4r, 63r, 8 Aug. 1590.

[288] Marie Dauson and M. de la Roviere (ADG, 42 J 29, 641, 644, 673, 25 Apr. 1591); Jehanne Claresse, Abraham Cabiron, and Daniel Martin (ADG, 42 J 30, 149v, 152v, 164r, 167v, 171v, 193r, 360r, 3 Mar. 1593); Anne Hebrarde and Jehan Chantozel (ADG, 42 J 34, 230v, 242v, 10 Nov. 1610); Sieur Montmejan and servant (ADG, 42 J 34, 374v, 386r, 395v, 22 Aug. 1612); Jeanne Ratte and Pol Delicat (ADG, 42 J 35, 48r, 78v, 85r, 90r, 112r, 113r, 122v, 133r–135r, 136v, 144v, 12 Feb. 1614).

as they believed, attested by subsequent pregnancies) hampered the integrity of their investigations. The status of the man could also act in his favour: some men, especially those of high status, could get away with repeated instances of sexual harassment and assault of their dependants.

As historians have found for contemporary England and eighteenth-century France, young female servants were especially vulnerable to such attacks, because they were poor, unmarried, and were not thought to 'belong' to any other man, had often travelled to the cities for work and so lacked a local support network, and were constantly in the orbit of predatory men. There was much to fear in the domestic workspace from men they knew—employers, relatives of their employers, and male servants. Whether in the house or garden, stable or outhouse, they ran the gauntlet of men's efforts to 'enjoy' them. Chores that took them outside the home were little safer. Being alone with a man was dangerous, and mistresses—despite the fact that they themselves had probably been servants at one time—were of little help, tending to believe (in support of their own status quo) that the other woman acted seductively.

Men used the combination of violence and affection that Capp identified, but also and above all a range of coercive techniques. They made 'beautiful promises' of money and marriage, and sweeping offers of meeting every need and desire, so that through constant harassment and unrelenting pressure they physically and psychologically strong-armed women into sex. The rare examples of consensual sex between master and maid probably only contributed to this general coercion, working as urban legends by suggesting that women who yielded might just find it the route to a husband, status, and wealth otherwise beyond their reach.

In practice the consequences of being raped were rarely marriage and prosperity. Women's honour was badly tarnished. Pregnant servants were dismissed and faced a perilous, lonely childbirth. Maternal death was not rare; infant mortality was common. If the baby survived, the cost—financial and emotional—of raising it was considerable. That women considered late-term abortion, suicide, or made the heartrending choice to abandon their children indicates quite how desperate and wretched their situation was.

Men who had raped and abused continued their coercion after sex and pregnancy. They discredited their victim's sexual reputation and logic. They depicted women as untrustworthy liars, who had been coached or manipulated into bringing an honest man into disrepute. They scapegoated other, lower-status men, coercing women into making formal declarations of false paternity. They married off and paid off and beat up their victims, and they lied and denied for as long as they could get away with it.

Women rarely said that they had been 'raped'. They talked of being abused, enjoyed, forced, taken by force, forced to abandon themselves, known carnally, solicited to do evil, debauched, and persuaded from their honour. Their language, almost without exception, portrayed them as passive, inert victims. The instances of women claiming in their narratives that they had resisted are few, but their choices of verbs continually professed their lack of willingness or agency. They were prey.

Yet women's response to sexual assault was far from passive. Women with some character and initiative could still seek ways to shape their lives after such a pregnancy. Van der Heijden wondered whether an instance of girls bringing a case against their high-status rapist was exceptional—it would not have been in Languedoc. There were repeated instances of women galvanizing public opinion or telling a range of authorities what had happened to them, in the hope of discharging their consciences, to be heard, to receive financial aid, to seek restitution of their honour, and in a quest for justice.[289]

Sufficient representations were made before the consistory to suggest that some analyses of the reasons for the scarcity of complaints of and convictions for rape in sixteenth- and seventeenth-century France have been misguided. This does not seem to have been a crime that women were reluctant to denounce because of the cost to their honour.[290] Although the consistory castigated them hardly less than other authorities, and maintained a similar attitude towards assuming their guilt, women commonly reported sexual abuse there. Instead, it seems likely that there were at least two important reasons why there were few legal convictions for rape, despite the evidence that rape probably occurred often: first, the consistory may have acted in favour of men of power, but they did allow them to be challenged, as courts seldom did; and second, few instances of sexual assault, as it was practised in women's homes and workplaces, fitted the qualifying legal definition of rape as being achieved by violence, which a woman had to have continued resisting forcibly.

In practice women deployed their speech to discredit the men who assaulted them, albeit with varying degrees of success. The myriad cases before the consistory and the evidence of this happening before other authorities, from the consistorial and notarial records, suggest that this probably happened many, many more times than indicated here. That justice was rarely equally distributed does not seem to have greatly impeded its pursuit.

---

[289] Although not mentioned, maybe disclosure also meant, like the later *déclarations de grossesse* (Phan, 'Les déclarations'), that a woman could not be held responsible for infanticide if the child later died.

[290] Vigarello, *History*, 28; Jean-Louis Flandrin, *Les amours paysannes (XVIe–XIXe siècle): amour et sexualité dans les campagnes de l'ancienne France* (Paris, 1975), 221.

7

The Trials of Marriage

DISHARMONY AND VIOLENCE

In one month, August 1593, the Protestant church in Nîmes celebrated four weddings: yeoman Anthoine Mentfort and Jeane Bastide, Estienne Froment and Isabeau Burnette, Pol de Virs and Marthe Baulouine, and Andre Rodré and Jeane Martine.[1] Four weddings in one month was nothing special—from 1585 to 1602 the Protestant church in Nîmes recorded 350 marriages in its register—but what is notable about these four couples is that we never hear any of their names again.

What this tells us is that, while they may have endured unhappiness in private, they were probably decent, companionable relationships. 'Happiness writes in white ink on a white page'.[2] That sort of marriage seldom came before the consistory; the marriages about which we know more were marked by argument, violence, and adultery. The consistorial tales of conjugal woe give us an insight into the causes and circumstances of marital disagreements, and how wives especially responded to such situations.

Broken Marriages

There is relatively little literature on the experience of marriage breakdown among ordinary people, and that which exists for France draws only on northern French examples, using research on Cambrai, Dijon, and Nantes.[3] Information about the experience of marriage elsewhere, therefore, immediately fills a void. The northern material does however provide some initial points of enquiry, as do studies of other parts of Europe.

For England Bernard Capp charts women's complaints against their husbands, namely violence, adultery, and failure to provide, often accompanied by spending

---

[1] ADG, E Dépôt 36/697, 522v (inverse).

[2] 'Le bonheur écrit à l'encre blanche sur des pages blanches', Henry de Montherlant.

[3] Julie Hardwick, 'Seeking Separations: Gender, Marriages, and Household Economies in Early Modern France', FHS 21.1 (1998), 157–80; Alain Lottin, 'Vie et mort du couple: difficultés conjugales et divorces dans le Nord de la France aux XVIIe et XVIII siècles', XVIIe siècle 102–3 (1974), 59–78', and La désunion du couple sous l'Ancien Régime: l'exemple du Nord (Paris, 1975); James R. Farr, Hands of Honor: Artisans and their World in Dijon, 1550–1650 (Ithaca, NY, and London, 1988); François Lebrun, La vie conjugale sous l'Ancien Régime (Paris, 1975) draws on Lottin's research. There is more for higher levels of society, e.g. Wendy Gibson, Women in Seventeenth-Century France (Basingstoke, 1989), 59–69.

the family's limited resources on alcohol.[4] Manon van der Heijden echoes this with the observations that women before the Dutch consistories also claimed that drinking greatly hindered a man's ability to work and provide for the family, but she warns, too, that the stories women told would have been fashioned for maximum effect on their audience.[5] Julie Hardwick, in the separation cases before the Nantais provost court, and Alain Lottin in the Cambrai *officialité* of 1670–1774, found that the themes of mistreatment and physical violence were common.[6] What stories did French women tell, and how did men for their part complain about their wives?[7] How could women respond to unhappy marriages? Capp examines a range of responses by English women: attempts to persuade, scolding, tears, anger, threats to leave, shaming an erring spouse, approaching the other woman, seeking official intervention, abandoning the marriage, and even murder.[8] How far are these strategies reflective of the actions of women in Languedoc?

Reconciliation was one of the primary goals of the French consistory and this was true within marriage too. This meant that the consistory regularly acted as marriage counsellors, determined to bring argumentative spouses to heel. In October 1578 Laurens Banduron was summoned before the consistory for the 'bad household' that existed between him and his wife. A month later the couple appeared before the consistory, were reprimanded for their disagreements, and were reconciled.[9] Master Lortigne was called in June 1586 for having evicted his wife from their home, and said that the truth was—to his regret—that she had left him. The consistory summoned both to find out the truth, and Lortigne was meanwhile urged to care for his wife.[10] Couples who remained in discord were barred from receiving the sacrament—sometimes to their surprise. Donne Romaine Vallone angrily approached the consistory to ask why she had not received the token for the Eucharist, and was told it was because she had left her husband and insulted him publicly, saying among other things that she hoped the 'evil plague killed him'.[11] Benet's wife complained that her husband had thrown her out of their house, and the consistory required them both to appear for what had happened between them and they were then exhorted to live together in concord. When they did not want to heed this plan, the consistory threatened them with suspension from the sacrament.[12] The consistory considered quarrels between spouses to contravene the word of God, as the Montauban consistory said in 1597.[13] Couples

[4] Bernard Capp, *When Gossips Meet: Women, Family and Neighbourhood in Early Modern England* (Oxford, 2003), 84.

[5] Manon Van der Heijden, 'Domestic Violence, Alcohol Use and the Uses of Justice in Early Modern Holland', *Annales de démographie historique* 130 (2015), 69–85, here 75, citing Natalie Zemon Davis, *Fiction in the Archives: Pardon Tellers and their Tales in Sixteenth-Century France* (Cambridge, 1987).

[6] Hardwick, 'Seeking Separations', 164–5; Lottin, 'Vie', 68–9.

[7] This latter subject is only considered briefly by Capp, *Gossips*, 84; Hardwick, 'Seeking Separations', 159, 163–8; for a later period, Lottin, 'Vie', 68–72; Davis, *Fiction*, considers the causes for female homicide, 92–5.

[8] Capp, *Gossips*, 86–125.   [9] BN, Ms.fr. 8667, 47r, 22 Oct. 1578.

[10] ADG, 42 J 28, 228v, 13 Jun. 1586.   [11] BN, Ms.fr. 8667, 94v, 27 Jan. 1580.

[12] ADG, 42 J 29, 56, 69, 7 Sept. 1588.

[13] ADTG, I 1, 259r, 28 (23) May 1597.

were instructed instead—like Pierre Causse, known as *Bragayrat*, and his wife—to 'live in peace, union, and concord, like true spouses'.[14] Husbands were reminded that wives were gifts of God, and wives were told to be obedient to their husbands.[15]

Causes of Disharmony

Married couples were convoked by the consistory when their arguments spilled out into the public domain: a wife had slept outside, a couple lived separately, a pair had been seen quarrelling in the street. The sound of fighting attracted attention, like that from the glover and his wife whose violent, acrimonious argument in early August 1582 was heard through the walls by their neighbour, the elder Sire Dupin.[16] The cases that reached the consistory—some 150 of them, including marital violence—were therefore typically not mere quotidian marital squabbles, but heated rows that led to voluble fights and separations.

The stories that spouses offered about why they fought may seem unreliable—testimonies framed and altered to suit their audience—but the context in which information was given to the consistory suggests less of this than we might imagine: because of neighbourhood interest, the consistory tended to have advance information about marital disharmony, which was then used to question the couple. In consequence the information that emerges under consistorial questioning was generally less guided by the agenda of those responding than by what was already known about his or her life, and is consequently relatively trustworthy. In responding to these questions women and men revealed the ways in which they were disappointed in their spouses.

Spousal complaints were generally presented antiphonally: he said, she said. In December 1586 yeoman Pierre Abeille, known as *L'Escarrabilhat* (from the Occitan *escarrabilhar*, meaning to perk up, to waken; perhaps an equivalent might be 'bright spark') was summoned for having mistreated his wife Catherine D'Airevielle, but the couple did not show up for arbitration until July 1587. The consistory noted 'the argument and noise between them' and asked them why. Abeille had three complaints against his wife: that she never served or honoured him, that she had wanted to poison him, and that 'she is in thrall to, and lets herself be governed by, wine'—she drank too much. He said he never wanted to live with her again. D'Airevielle retorted that she had never thought of poisoning him, and that her husband hit her. She could name three people who could stand witness to her husband's marital violence. After the couple had departed the consistory was just deliberating how to investigate their claims when D'Airevielle burst back in to complain that her husband had punched and slapped her as they left the consistory. She was followed in by three women who attested that they had seen Abeille hit her, and one man, a cobbler called M. Chivallier, who had put himself between the two to separate them. In the light of such proof the consistory informed the

[14] ADTG, I 1, 295r, 24 Sept. 1597.
[15] ADG, 42 J 35, 124v, 5 Nov. 1614; 42 J 33, 131r, 18 Oct. 1606.
[16] BN, Ms.fr. 8667, 343v, 1 Aug. 1582.

magistrate about Abeille's behaviour, but things did not improve—by early August witnesses attested that D'Airevielle would no longer live with her husband.[17]

Abeille's claim that his wife drank too much is unusual in the cases under study: normally men were represented as the problem drinkers. In other ways, however, their accusations are characteristic of those made by other spouses. Women complained about their husbands' violence, and men complained about their wives' failure to serve and obey them. Pierre Gebelin was asked to explain why his wife had slept outdoors the previous night and said that she did not come immediately when he called her while she was in the street talking with a female neighbour.[18] Jean Bruette, whose repudiation of his wife Marguerite de Calhacy in January 1596 reportedly caused much scandal, said that his wife was a hypochondriac, and subject to many weaknesses, 'which he could amply recite', and so did not do her duty. He was given a week to be reconciled with her, but two months later had not done so.[19]

A lengthy case illustrates the standard dynamic. Catherine Vidallote and her husband, mason Jacques Soisson, had been married for six years when they were summoned in September 1602 for their widely known dissension. Vidallote complained that her husband spoke harshly towards her and regularly hit her. She said that he addressed her as *putain*, rather than using her name of Catherine, that when he entered her house he said that 'he was entering hell', and when he saw her that 'he saw a devil'. She then added—perhaps with her audience in mind—that he did not permit her to take the sacrament, except once when he beat her afterwards, and that he did not give her anything to live on. Soisson responded by saying that he may have allowed himself to insult her a few times when he was angry, but that that was because of her 'poor housekeeping', and that she left the house for several days without reason or permission. They were exhorted to be reconciled 'with friendship and concord, like true spouses', or be suspended. Her charges against him were violence in speech and behaviour, a lack of provision, and spiritual deprivation, while his against her were about the way she kept the house, and a lack of respect for him, as manifested by her disappearance.

In subsequent years Soisson's behaviour grew worse. Seven months later he was summoned and censured for having committed adultery with a prostitute, and for going to taverns. In December 1604 the consistory recommended to the magistrate that he be imprisoned for 'treating his wife poorly'—a euphemism for violence and, as few men were referred to the magistrate, indicative of a serious problem. In January 1606 the couple appeared before the consistory again to be questioned about their troubled relationship. Soisson was asked why he treated his wife badly, and why he had made her leave their house. He replied that his wife 'ruins him, having ransacked his house, so he had hit her'. The consistory also asked—based on their prior intelligence—whether he had not ill-treated his wife because she had

---

[17] ADG, 42 J 28, 246v, 297v, 299r, 10 Dec. 1586. Pierre Abeille had, six years earlier, lived with a woman called Marye Blanche, 'giving great scandal to the neighbours', but because she was his cousin, they were forbidden from marrying.

[18] BN, Ms.fr. 8666, 102r, 27 Mar. 1562.   [19] ADTG, I 1, 97r, 113r, 31 Jan. 1596.

rebuked him for 'frequenting *cabarets*' (taverns), whether he had not ripped his wife's dress, and whether he had slept with a prostitute lying in bed between him and his wife. He said that he did occasionally go to taverns, and sought to correct that in himself. He added that 'he denied the rest', but went on to confirm that he had torn his wife's dress because she had bought it without his consent, and then told a tall tale about having met a prostitute who was travelling through the town: he had tied her up and kept her in his house one night until he could put her in the consuls' hands, but had not intended anything immoral towards her. He was told to take back his wife of ten years, but refused, and when Vidallote was asked to respond to his answers she did not deign to reply. The consistory threatened Soisson with suspension from the sacrament, and having his name published in church, but he still refused to live with Vidallote again.[20]

Soisson's complaints were still to do with his wife's household management: his allegation was that she was a spendthrift and had stolen from him, and he continued to resent her lack of deference—she had not sought his permission to buy the dress, so he had damaged it. In turn, the charges against him were squandering resources and time on drinking and whoring, throwing out his wife, and physical violence towards her.

Similar accusations were made in another marital dispute, between Jehan Poudaigne and Jehanne Pradelle, who were summoned for arguing in July 1602. Poudaigne complained that his wife 'had ruined him, having stolen all that he had', and added that she had a reputation as an adulteress. Pradelle responded that she had always lived as a good woman, had never taken or stolen anything from her husband, and that, 'on the contrary, without cause, her husband had thrown her out at night'. Poudaigne retaliated that when he had been ill his wife had hit him, and repeated that it was widely said that she was committing adultery. Pradelle's rejoinder did not exactly respond to these charges. She said that she had 'never thought anything against her husband', but now admitted that when her husband had thrown her out of the house she had taken with her some pieces of furniture that she had offered for sale. Poudaigne was told to take her back, while Pradelle was instructed to return the furniture to her husband and be faithful and loyal to him, which she promised to do. He, however, refused to have her back. Pradelle's hackneyed answers do not give much away about the real stakes here, and Poudaigne's contention that she had stolen and sold his stuff appears only to relate to the period after he had thrown her out. Perhaps her alleged adultery—a charge the consistory appears not to have taken seriously—was the crux of the matter. All Poudaigne's allegations related to the ways in which Pradelle had transgressed her wifely role by taking furniture from the family house, by stealing his honour through her alleged sexual liaisons, and by hitting him.[21]

Suspected adultery by wives was often at the heart of men's allegations. Jacques Reboul was reconciled to his wife in August 1561, even though he said he had found her in *paillardise* (here meaning adultery). Ramond Costeplane of Pont-de-Camarès

[20] ADG, 42 J 32, 110r, 148r; 42 J 33, 12r, 84v, 25 Sept. 1602.
[21] ADG, 42 J 32, 83r, 31 Jul. 1602.

was less forgiving in April 1581: it was reported that he had left his wife and they now lived separately, because Costeplane had found his wife with Bernard Ramond, known as *Campalbne* (from the Occitan, *campal*, meaning one who works outside), and had threatened him.[22] Jacques du Bec, master locksmith of Nîmes, presented himself at the consistory in December 1588 to request a formal separation from his wife and permission to marry someone else, as his wife had 'left him and abandoned him and abandons herself to many'—an almost poetic play on the word 'abandon'. Bec added that his wife had even had a bastard child by Sieur de la Calmette. The consistory informed Bec that he should report his wife to the judiciary, but that he could not meanwhile be formally divorced from her, nor marry another.[23] Pierre Couget's allegation of adultery in October 1574 concerned a different sort of infidelity. He contested that his wife was 'an adulteress' because she was Roman Catholic, while he was Protestant, and as she did not want to convert he wanted the marriage to be dissolved. The Pont-de-Camarès consistory referred him the secular judge for deliberation.[24]

The mason Andre Bacand was summoned in April 1584 for blaspheming and mistreating his wife. He told the consistory that his wife had been fraternizing with a weaver called Carriere, even though he had instructed her not to: in recent days, he had found them together at the door to M. Jaussard's house. He confessed to having sworn and blasphemed, and asked God's pardon for that fault. When his wife Claude Pradon was called she said that her husband treated her badly and had hit her, and while it was true that her husband had found her with Carriere, she had not been up to any wrong. The couple were exhorted to live in peace; Pradon was instructed not to speak any more with Carriere because of Bacand's suspicions, while Bacand was admonished not to treat her badly ('and, above all, not to blaspheme the name of God') and they both promised to obey. Bacand may have had grounds for his violent anger, however: five years later it was reported that weaver Jean Carriere had become engaged to Bacand's widow.[25] But we should not imagine that all these allegations of adultery were truthful. Ramond Ruelle del Sol and his wife were called to the Montauban consistory because of their arguments: Del Sol had made it known that his wife had committed adultery, but he now admitted that it was a false report and the couple were reconciled.[26]

Men also often focused on women's hurtful words. When M. Borges was summoned for having beaten his wife he said that when his brother wanted him to go out (perhaps to a *cabaret*), his wife had insulted him and called him a thief—perhaps a reference to squandering household monies—and threatened him several times, so he punched her: 'just a single punch, and nothing more'.[27] Weaver Loys Colin was summoned in April 1604 for having fought publicly with his wife and his in-laws. He said that the cause of the argument was that his wife had despised him for a long time, called him a knave, and said she was fed up with his company.

---

[22] BN, Ars, Ms. 10434, 37v, 41r, 42r–v, 17 Apr. 1581.
[23] ADG, 42 J 29, 90, 28 Dec. 1588.   [24] BN, Ars.Ms. 6563, 8v, 12 Oct. 1574.
[25] ADG, 42 J 28, 97v, 111r; ADG, 42 J 29, 254, 11 Apr. 1584.
[26] ADTG, I 1, 300r, 29 Oct. 1597.   [27] ADG, 42 J 28, 124r, 5 Sept. 1584.

She also often left the house without having first asked his permission. For these faults of impertinence, unkindness, and disobedience, he had complained to his in-laws, M. Ralli and his wife, but rather than urging their daughter to behave with decorum, they had taken her side and had threatened Colin. In late May, Ralli informed the consistory that Colin had sent his wife—Ralli's daughter—home to live with her parents, and in subsequent months the case descended into a legal wrangle over her possessions and the dowry that had been promised.[28] The insults, unkindness of speech, and lack of respect towards him had driven Colin to seek a permanent separation.

Relationships with in-laws were cobbler Jacques Guiraud's complaint in 1589. Despite being the son of the consistory's summoner, Guillaume Guiraud, Jacques was charged with having beaten his wife, and then having scandalously evicted her and his child from the family home. He explained that his father-in-law, Sieur Bagard, had failed to deliver on a promise to give him part of his rents and bene-fices, and now Guiraud said he was not of a mind to take his wife back, even if Bagard were to pay up. He said that he would 'rather leave the town and go live in Rome', and would take their child with him. The consistory was taken aback by his obstinacy and demanded to know his reasons, but Guiraud was determined to remain silent, saying 'he had many reasons which at present he did not want to say, neither here, nor elsewhere, but it was his resolution'. His silence may have been because of his father's presence in the room, or perhaps because he was con-currently pursuing the case with the judiciary. The consistory threatened him with public suspension, but it was not enough to change his mind. In September the consistory were still pursuing the couple's reconciliation and by December Guiraud had reportedly hit his father-in-law several times, while appealing the consistory's sentence to the national synod. Eventually Guillaume Guiraud acknowledged that his son had acted as a rebel to the consistory, had broken the ties that ought to bind a man to his father-in-law, had abandoned and evicted his wife without cause, and 'continued in his mischief'. Jacques Guiraud was given one final opportunity to explain himself, but again declined, simply stating that he would never take his wife back. The sentence against him was pronounced.[29]

Women's grievances seldom mention in-laws, but the male equivalent to poor housekeeping—poor provision—was a regular complaint. M. Bernardy's wife had left him and moved from Alès to Nîmes, where he came to find her in April 1598. In response to his accusation that she had been 'behaving badly' at M. Auzas' house, where she had been lodging, she replied that 'the truth is that for a long time he [her husband] had not kept her as a husband should his wife', and therefore she could not live with him. Bernandy now promised to treat her better.[30] Jehanne Martinelle and her husband Pierre Ruelle were summoned to the Montauban

[28] ADG, 42 J 32, 228r, 232r, 234r, 23 Apr. 1604.
[29] ADG, 42 J 29, 106, 127, 130, 192, 224, 272, 289, 551, 558–9, 566–7, 1 Feb. 1589. Early in the case, Guiraud is referred to as 'Anthoine Guiraud', but his forename silently changes to 'Jacques', while the attendant facts (being Sire Bagard's son-in-law, having sent away his wife and child etc.) remain the same.
[30] ADG, 42 J 31, 222r, 22 Apr. 1598.

consistory, because Ruelle complained that his wife had abandoned him four years earlier. His charge was that 'she better liked to serve masters than to live with him and do him service'. She replied that he did not have the means to feed her, so she had been forced to go into service. The consistory's response was to order her back to live with her husband or be deprived of the sacrament.[31] Sometimes women complained of a man's unwillingness to provide for children by a former husband, in an age when remarriage was common. Françoise Graveyrole said that she had left her husband because he treated her badly and did not want to feed a child whom she had by a previous marriage, despite having promised to do so in their marriage contract.[32] Captain Cade's wife complained of her husband's poor treatment of her daughters by her first husband: her father had left each fifty *livres* to cover their livelihood and nourishment until they married, but Cade had thrown his step-daughters out of the house and deprived them of this. When called to answer to the charge, Cade got angry, swore at the minister, and stormed out. He later explained that he was annoyed because he was 'greatly vexed' by his wife.[33]

Just as the charge against Jacques Soisson had been attending taverns and entertaining prostitutes, failing to provide was clearly linked in people's minds with squandering familial resources, alcohol abuse, and immoral activity. Jehan Chappeau and M. Nicollas were summoned in June 1592 for having regularly 'debauched' at taverns and having mistreated their wives.[34] Claude Roueyrolle complained that her husband's philandering had had devastating consequences: he had given her and their 5-year-old child the pox—syphilis. When she left him and took their children to Bellegarde, he had threatened to kill her on the way.[35] His surname was Ysnard; he may well be the Pestel Ysnard who was found in a hemp field with a prostitute eighteen months later.[36] In October 1602 Claude Andrienne had complained to an elder that her husband Claude Lacroix had wanted to prostitute her to another man, so three weeks later she had left him.[37] Only Guillaume Coste's wife proffered the opposite complaint. Asked why his wife had left him in March 1582, Coste replied that his wife 'was always terrible to him' and had left him 'because he had the inability of a man'—by which he presumably meant that he was impotent.[38]

The stories told to explain the breakdown of a marriage are, in some ways, reflective of those told by women in England and Holland. Women's complaints focused on the familiar themes of violence, lack of provision, alcohol consumption, tavern-going, and adultery—but there are incidental details that move us out of stereotypes, and remind us of the reality of this lived experience—insulting speech, a ripped new dress, the pox, attempted prostitution, and impotence. We learn that men's complaints centred on disobedience and disrespect, a wife's poor housekeeping or service, on leaving the marital home without permission, adultery, and verbal abuse, with added charges of physical violence, excessive alcohol

---

[31] ADTG, I 1, 343v, 13 May 1598.   [32] ADG. 42 J 34, 44r, 19 Nov. 1608.
[33] ADG, 42 J 28, 128r, 129v, 26 Sept. 1584.   [34] ADG, 42 J 30, 80v, 83r, 22 Jul. 1592.
[35] ADG, 42 J 30, 67r, 13 May 1592.   [36] ADG, 42 J 30, 225r, 6 Oct. 1593.
[37] ADG, 42 J 32, 118v, 120r, 20 Oct. 1602.   [38] BN, Ms.fr. 8667, 295v, 28 Feb. 1582.

consumption, and complications with in-laws. These are charges that tell us about ideals of gender and expectations of marital roles, and real spouses' failure to fulfil them.

These narratives also give us an insight into women's strategies when faced with marital conflict. To prevent the break-up of their household, maintain family cohesion, and evade the economic destitution that accompanied abandonment, many chose to endure the situation. Catherine Vidallote, after giving one testimony, subsequently remained silently with her husband, as his abuses grew ever worse; the consistory's later interventions relied not on her complaints, but on public rumour.[39] This meant tolerating all manner of abuses for the sake of peace and shelter. Marguerite de Calhacy's response to her husband Jean Bruette's charge that she failed to serve him and was a hypochondriac was to offer to 'return to serve her husband, whom she promised in future to obey faithfully and [she] asked him to pardon her fault, even if he starved her or was angry with her'.[40] She sounded as if she was describing a familiar situation, and yet promised ongoing patience in return for his forgiveness of her failings.

For those who were not content to remain silent in such circumstances, an alternative strategy was to express grievances and find cathartic relief. A primary means was through publicly voiced insult. Captain Alexandre Carriere's first wife, Alix Toulouse, was reprimanded in July 1592 because she 'is often angry with her husband in the open street, using cruel insults'.[41] It was the public nature of her words that gave them such power to wound and defame. Sarra de Bely was chastised by the Montauban consistory in April 1596 for acting 'like a wild beast... being angry with her neighbours... and treating her husband with contempt to the scandal of many good people'. She was told to live in peace and not to 'make the world think badly by wronging her husband'.[42] Claude Tourelle's wife publicly said to her husband in November 1561, 'the devil break your neck'.[43] Such insult and defamation undoubtedly served as a cathartic expression in response to mistreatment and was a form of revenge that attempted to generate public support, but was of limited value in repairing a breach or escaping marital discomfort, and could actually exacerbate the situation. Proctor Ramond Coffinhal and his wife Ysabeau de Fornier fell out in May 1597: Fornier blamed Coffinhal's frequentation of another woman—Anne de Verdiere—but according to Coffinhal, for the previous three years Fornier had 'not ceased to defame him everywhere and to be angry with him at home'. He added that she was 'nothing but a fool' and he had thrown her out of their house. Even when she repented before him in the consistory, he granted only that he would give her a pension to live on, but refused to take her back. Only a month later when the consistory put him on the list of those who would not receive the sacrament did he finally relent.[44]

---

[39] ADG, 42 J 32, 110r; 42 J 33, 12r, 84v.   [40] ADTG, I 1, 97r, 113r, 31 Jan. 1596.
[41] ADG, 42 J 30, 80r, 8 Jul. 1592.   [42] ADTG, I 1, 130v, 13 Apr. 1596.
[43] BN, Ms.fr. 8666, 47r, 22 Nov. 1561.
[44] ADTG I 1, 256v–257r, 259r, 261v–262r, 269v, 23 May 1597.

A more extreme measure was to flee. As these cases have shown, women did abandon their husbands. In November 1601 Marguerite Roudil, wife of merchant Pierre Messe, drew up her last will and testament, in which she declared that for two or three years she had been been 'daily molested' by her husband to make her will and 'leave her possessions to his profit', and that two days before the date of the will she had been:

> beaten and tormented by her husband so much that she was constrained, for fear of being killed, to run away, leaving her husband and abandoning her children, to her great regret and displeasure.

She left ten *livres* to the poor of the church and a sizeable 200 *écus* to her violent husband, after which she presumably fled.[45] The inclusion of these remarks in her will must have served as a cathartic and just riposte to him for posterity.

In fact many marital arguments ended in separation. These were not, for the most part, separations achieved under customary law, and so are unlikely to feature in other historical records such as petitions to a court.[46] They sometimes emerged when the abandoned spouse sought redress. Despite the passion they had shown during their courtship ten years earlier (or perhaps because of it—'these violent delights have violent ends'), Jeremie Prat approached the consistory in April 1599 to report that his wife Marie Bouyeyre had left him without reason.[47] He asked for her to be summoned to the consistory to explain why she had left, in the hope that she might come back to live with him, but she never appeared.[48] In October 1613 the scribe noted that Anric Rudavel, from Saine, had similarly approached the consistory asking them to help him to have his wife returned to him. She had left him and come to stay with her father, Jehan Guiran, and Guiran refused to appear at the consistory while his son-in-law was in the town.[49] In other instances, the one who had been left sought to cut his losses. Joseph Ressongles presented himself at the consistory in Montauban in January, February, and again in October 1596, saying that his wife, Jeanne de Cos, had left him two or three years earlier to go to Toulouse, where, he alleged, she was an adulteress. He had asked her several times 'to come and serve him', but she did not want to do so, so he approached the consistory asking for permission to marry someone else. This the consistory could not give. They advised him to seek evidence of his wife's adultery, and to proceed against her via the judiciary. When he did so the results were not quite what the consistory had anticipated. A year later Ressongles presented them with an attestation on parchment from the *présidial* court in Toulouse, signed by the clerk, dated 20 August 1597, and made before Jehan de Rossel, royal councillor of the court. It was a certificate of death, declaring that his wife, de Cos, had been killed by sword or dagger in the town of Villefranche de Lauragais (some 22 miles or 35 km southeast of Toulouse), as was testified by two witnesses. There is no mention of her murderer but Ressongles certainly benefited from her death. Now officially

---

[45] ADG, 2 E 1/369, 29v–31v, 22 Nov. 1601.
[46] See Hardwick, 'Seeking Separations', for these in Nantes, 1598–1710.
[47] William Shakespeare, *Romeo and Juliet*, II.6.9.   [48] ADG, 42 J 31, 278r, 21 Apr. 1599.
[49] ADG, 42 J 35, 30r, 23 Oct. 1613.

free, he presented himself in October 1597 once again to seek the consistory's permission to remarry.[50] It was granted.

Some separations were ostensibly involuntary. The Montauban consistory remonstrated with M. Alias in September 1595 for having remained separated from his wife for a long time, and neither living with her, nor visiting her, nor providing for her. He had also reportedly said to neighbours who had reprimanded him for his conduct 'that God had created the commandments back-to-front', but he denied this before the church authorities. Alias told them that as he worked as a servant he could not visit his wife often, but claimed that he continued to send her money.[51]

Separations were the unofficial answer to marital strife. Sieur Allegre appeared with his two sons before the Nîmes consistory because some thirteen or fourteen months earlier he and his wife had quarrelled, and she had left him. According to Allegre she left 'without reason or occasion', but not only was he exhorted to take her back and keep her 'like a true husband', his sons were also instructed to treat her with honour and respect. She had probably left after being bullied by both her husband and step-sons.[52]

Such separations could become semi-permanent. Benoyt Feste and his wife had remained separated for ten years when they were reportedly reunited and reconciled in October 1584 (though they maybe simply supplied the consistory with the platitudes sought).[53] Jehan Bertrand, a schoolmaster in Sumène near Ganges, and Catherine Cheysse had been married for twenty-one years and had four children together by July 1592, but had spent eleven of those years apart. Bertrand testified that this was because they had lived in Angroigne, in Piedmont (now Northern Italy), where a decade earlier Protestants had been greatly persecuted, so he had been obliged to flee to Languedoc, taking his children with him. Some time afterwards, when he thought it was safe, he had returned to the marital home in Angroigne to collect his wife and bring her to Languedoc, but 'she did not want to obey'. Subsequently he had presumed her dead. Then, a month before Bertrand appeared at the consistory, Cheysse had arrived in Languedoc. She had been told by a nephew, who wanted to seize his possessions, that her husband and elder son were dead, and so came to see for herself. Bertrand said that he and his son had asked her to stay and live with them, 'which she did not want to do', rather preferring to return to Piedmont. There is little to glean of the emotions of either Bertrand or Cheysse, except for the curious report that Bertrand had told the minister in Ganges that 'she was not his wife, but the wife of a Piedmontese man in need of money'. Asked why he had said this, he replied that it was, 'because his wife was badly dressed'.[54] Is there the slightest whiff of sour grapes?

All these cases rest on the testimony of men who had left or been abandoned. Only the faintest hints exist of what befell abandoned women. We have already learnt of what happened to Susanne Cregude, whose husband had been absent for

[50] ADTG, I 1, 92v, 99r, 197v, 300v, 17 Jan. 1596. Her name is also later given as Johanne DuCas.
[51] ADTG, I 1, 41r, 16 Sept. 1595.   [52] ADG, 42 J 35, 124v, 5 Nov. 1614.
[53] ADG, 42 J 28, 136r, 24 Oct. 1584.   [54] ADG, 42 J 30, 84r–v, 85r–v, 27 Jul. 1592.

three years when she was raped by two young men in Nîmes. In April 1562 deacon Guerin Deleuziere reported that in his quarter there was a woman with four children who had been abandoned by her husband and was in 'great necessity', and asked for support from the poor-relief fund.[55] Women without the protection and provision of men faced an uncertain and fraught path.

Marital Violence

All too often the people from whom women needed the most protection were their husbands. As many of the cases considered so far have suggested, violence by husbands towards wives was far from uncommon. Contemporaries generally considered that a certain amount of physical discipline of wives by husbands was acceptable. Hardwick notes that, legally, marital violence could be used to justify separation only when 'beyond the norm or without cause'.[56] What is less clear is what was 'the norm' and what was considered excessive. For England Capp argues that there was an unwritten code for marital violence—that it be applied with moderation, for good cause, and in private, and Hardwick notes the same for France, although this begs the question of what 'moderation' and 'good cause' meant in practice.[57]

This is linked to the question of what sort of violence was sufficiently public, excessive, or unjustified to be reported to the authorities, and who reported it. Farr notes that neighbours in Dijon often intervened to stop husbands beating their wives, while Hardwick (and Garrioch for eighteenth-century Paris) found a reluctance to interfere in neighbours' marital relationships, unless the quarrels spilled out on to the streets and caused disturbance.[58] Of Holland, Manon Van der Heijden notes that neighbours complained 'for both moral and practical reasons': they disapproved of domestic violence and felt it reflected poorly on their community, but also had tired of the noise.[59] Van der Heijden also finds that neighbours initiated the majority of criminal prosecutions for violent behaviour towards wives; few battered women reported it themselves.[60] To what extent was this true of Languedoc? How much would neighbours intervene to stop domestic violence?

The attitudes of the Church are also of interest. Lottin argues that Catholic authorities in Cambrai were supportive of abused women, and concludes that 'the defence of marriage was identified with defence of the woman', but Jacques Solé

[55] BN, Ms.fr. 8666, 110r, 6 Apr. 1562.
[56] Hardwick, 'Seeking Separations', 165, and *The Practice of Patriarchy: Gender and the Politics of Household Authority in Early Modern France* (University Park, PA, 1998), 86; also Susan Dwyer Amussen, 'Being Stirred to Much Unquietness: Violence and Domestic Violence in Early Modern England', *Journal of Women's History* 6 (1994), 70–89. See Jacques Solé, *Etre femme en 1500: la vie quotidienne dans la diocèse de Troyes* (Paris, 2000), 185–96; and Roderick Phillips, 'Women, Neighborhood, and Family in the Late Eighteenth Century', *FHS* 18.1 (1993), 1–12, 8, for similar evidence from either side of the period under study.
[57] Capp, *Gossips*, 106; Hardwick, 'Seeking Separations', 165.
[58] Farr, *Hands*, 166, 170; Hardwick, *Practice*, 102–3; David Garrioch, *Neighbourhood and Community in Paris, 1740–1790* (Cambridge, 1986), 79; cf. Capp, *Gossips*, 84.
[59] Van der Heijden, 'Domestic Violence', 74.
[60] Van der Heijden, 'Domestic Violence', 73.

notes that in Troyes women asking for a separation after being beaten were generally instructed to return to their violent husbands.[61] For Protestant authorities, Lyndal Roper finds that the Reformed church in Augsburg upheld the right to domestic violence, and Van der Heijden observes, by contrast, that Dutch consistories supported battered wives and kept abusive husbands from the Eucharist, but would not countenance separations or divorces, and were rarely inclined to report such behaviour to judicial authorities.[62]

The French consistories were not deaf to charges of marital violence, and recognized it to be a sin: they told Jacques Bois in August 1561 to 'treat his wife peaceably without beating her, as is taught … by the word of God'.[63] Nevertheless, their response to marital violence was not especially robust. There are therefore many indications that such violence occurred, about which, however, we have only simple statements of fact. In Nîmes Nicholas Motard was to be summoned in 1561 'for having beaten and mistreated his wife' and M. Jouquet, known as *Berrasson*, was admonished 'not to beat his wife but rather repose peaceably with her'.[64] In December 1587 M. Benezet was summoned for 'beating and defaming' his wife.[65] The same day a cobbler called François was reported to have beaten and hit his wife after she had been absent from him, and two elders were sent to reconcile the spouses.[66] Dispatching elders to initiate a spousal reconciliation was also deployed after Loys Abraham had reportedly given his wife a beating, and the elders were also charged with speaking to 'a brigadier that beats his wife too'.[67] In Montauban the consistory's notes were often even more concise: in October 1596 innkeeper Laurant Parrison 'for having beaten and mistreated his wife, after having been vigorously censured, was exhorted from now on to live in peace with his wife which he promised'.[68] Such brief notices indicate the frequent occurrence of marital violence, the tendency for some of this behaviour to attract enough attention for it to be reported, and—as many of these cases were not followed up—an approach by the church of pacifying battered wives, papering over broken marriages, and being seen to act, without having any serious ambitions to amend the immutable.

In part this expressed a consistorial, and more broadly societal, ambivalence towards the physical disciplining of wives. By sixteenth-century standards, violent men could justify their behaviour because their wives gave them 'strong and great reasons' for it, as hatmaker M. Blary put it in April 1596.[69] Some of the explanations given illustrate a conviction that even minor infringements might warrant violent chastisement. When Roland Valat was asked by the consistory in May 1562 why he had beaten his wife and how it had happened, he calmly explained that he had punched his wife in the head because she had reproached him for having beaten

---

[61] Lottin, 'Vie', 77–8; Solé, *Etre femme*, 196.
[62] Lyndal Roper, *The Holy Household: Women and Morals in Reformation Augsburg* (Oxford, 1989), 193; Van der Heijden, 'Domestic Violence', 74–5.
[63] BN, Ms.fr. 8666, 27v–28r, 9 Aug. 1561.
[64] BN, Ms.fr. 8666, 41v, 27 Sept. 1561; 31r, 5 Sept. 1561.
[65] ADG, 42 J 28, 335v, 2 Dec. 1587.   [66] ADG, 42 J 28, 335r, 2 Dec. 1587.
[67] ADG, 42 J 28, 357r, 14 Feb. 1588.   [68] ADTG, I 1, 195r, 197r, 2 Oct. 1596.
[69] ADTG, I 1, 127v, 10 Apr. 1596.

her father.[70] The consistory did not rebuke him, and Valat's logic was obviously not lost on some of his listeners. Jean Vernet, an elder in the Nîmes consistory that year, had an argument with his wife a month later about bread-making and beat her—making her strip so he could do so—because in his words 'she had treated him badly, not paying him as much attention as she would a servant'.[71] The cobbler Langre was a repeat offender, being summoned in December 1604, April 1610, and July 1613 for beating and mistreating his wife. He justified his behaviour in 1610 by saying that 'he had hit his wife for having spoken badly'.[72] Violent correction could be justified then on the grounds of impertinent or disrespectful speech and not paying a husband enough attention. These complaints were often collected together under the theme of disobedience, which, as we have seen, was peppered throughout men's narratives of their conduct.[73] In practice it seems likely that men actually hit women for a range of reasons, including in compensation for their own misdeeds: Langre was twice accused of and once confessed to adultery and was twice suspended from the sacrament on this charge. The Montauban consistory themselves made the link in 1595, summoning Ramondy Rodier on the grounds that he 'beat his wife because of a *putain* that he keeps'.[74]

As Van der Heijden found in Rotterdam and Delft, battered women themselves did not make many complaints to authorities. There are, however, a few instances in which women chose to turn to the consistory to report their violent husbands. Maurice Carreyrone, wife of Benoict Ganhayre, appeared of her own initiative before the Nîmes consistory in March 1562 to report that her husband was 'a drunk that beats and mistreats her because of that'. The consistory remained suspicious that Carreyrone must have done something to justify Ganhayre's actions, scolding her to be reconciled with her husband and only to take the sacrament if she had a clean conscience. They planned to rebuke Ganhayre too: they summoned him twice, but it was reported that he did not want to attend the consistory. They threatened to report him to the magistrate if he did not show up again, but whether this happened is not recorded.[75]

This response was mirrored in Montauban. The wife of coachman Simon Tillois presented herself to the consistory in October 1596 complaining that her 'husband does nothing but beats and mistreats her'. Both were called before the consistory a week later, and the register records: 'Simon Tillois and his wife, for having been angry and fighting together, after having been vigorously censured, were exhorted from now on to live in peace, on pain that the magistrate will be warned.' Two elders were appointed to report back if the disturbance recurred.[76] There was no apparent recognition that one of the couple could have been more to blame.

At least these women received some response. A woman identified only as the mother of Captain Allier approached the Nîmes consistory in November 1580 and

---

[70] BN, Ms.fr. 8666, 121r, 6 May 1562.   [71] BN, Ms.fr. 8666, 132r, 27 Jun. 1562.

[72] ADJ, 42 J 33, 12r, 20r, 31 Dec. 1604; 42 J 34, 166r, 7 Apr. 1610; 42 J 35, 10r, 3 Jul. 1613.

[73] Laura Gowing, *Domestic Dangers: Women, Words and Sex in Early Modern London* (Oxford, 1996), 27, calls this 'the rhetoric of household order'.

[74] ADTG, I 1, 33v, 38r, 23 Aug. 1595.   [75] BN, Ms.fr. 8666, 101r, 27 Mar. 1562.

[76] ADTG, I 1, 195r, 197r, 2 Oct. 1596.

was asked why she had left her husband. She said that the reason was that 'he did nothing but beat her and is a blasphemer of God's name'. The consistory told her to return to him, but she 'persisted in her opinion not to return'. They deputized an elder to speak to her husband and ask him to appear before the consistory, but he did not show and the case was silently closed.[77] Another barely identified woman—'the wife of the servant of M. Lansard'—complained to one of the elders in July 1602 that her husband had evicted her from their house 'for a certain jealousy that he has without cause and that he has beaten her several times'. The consistory dispatched another elder to make enquiries with the husband to find out why he had hit his wife and evicted her, and report back to the next consistory. If he did, it was not put on record.[78]

In another case a husband's aggression was noted in passing during a female quarrel. Bernardine Pageze and the wife of Andre Andre had an argument in December 1584 because Pageze had defamed Andre's wife as a poisoner. Pageze later admitted that it was not true, but that 'she said it in anger having been beaten by her husband'. The consistory censured and reconciled the two women, and required Pageze to do reparation for her 'outrageous words'; her husband's violence was entirely overlooked. The few instances in which women did come forward to report their husband's violence suggest that the overall deficit of reports by battered wives probably had less to do with a lack of resourcefulness and drive on their part than with the paucity of the response they received.

Therefore most cases in the archives only emerged as a result of public concern. There are several brief indications of neighbourly outrage. In August 1582, for example, innkeeper M. Ricard was reported to have 'beaten his wife and injured her, about which all the neighbours are scandalized'.[79] There are also indications that neighbours thought more often about reporting abusive husbands than they acted on it. In December 1608 a locksmith called M. Olivier was summoned for 'having beaten his wife black and evicted her', blaspheming while he did so.[80] He was exhorted to live in peace with his wife and with his neighbour, M. Jaumar's wife, 'who wanted, during their domestic quarrels, to raise how badly he treated his wife'.[81] It is not clear whether she wanted to raise it with him or the authorities, but, either way, the consistory's response was to send an elder to reconcile the couple.

Given that most cases were the product of neighbourly solicitude, they indicate, therefore, the point at which the limits of public toleration towards such behaviour were reached.[82] As such, they help identify what behaviour transgressed socially acceptable boundaries on the physical chastisement of spouses.

Attention was attracted when the violence was felt to be unduly extreme. Anthoine Roueyran was summoned in September 1581 for 'having beaten his wife

---

[77] BN, Ms.fr. 8667, 148v, 30 Nov. 1580.   [78] ADG, 42 J 32, 71v–72r, 3 Jul. 1602.

[79] BN, Ms.fr. 8667, 345r, 15 Aug. 1582.

[80] *'Pour avoir battu et chasse sa femme noire avec blasphemes'* (ADG, 42 J 34, 58r)—there is a small possibility that this actually means that his wife was black.

[81] ADG, 42 J 34, 58r, 31 Dec. 1608.

[82] Hardwick, 'Seeking Separations', 165, *Practice*, 86; Solé, *Etre femme*, 185–96, and Phillips, *Women*, 8, find similar evidence from either side of the period under study.

so much that she was almost insensible', and confessed that he had done so because 'she had not wanted to obey him'. The consistory told him to live in peace with her and contain himself, but several elders present remarked that Roueyran was known for his scandalous, dissipated lifestyle—he squandered his money on gambling and tavern-going—and that it was possible Roueyran had beaten his wife because she had remonstrated with him about his behaviour. This would classify as physical discipline 'without reason' and the consistory resolved to investigate, and suspend him from the sacrament if it had been unjustified.[83] The consistory's underlying assumption was that most violence was justified, but the wider community had obviously considered his extreme brutality grave enough to be worthy of comment. Jacques Guiraud—who would evict his wife and child over his father-in-law's failure to share part of his rents—was first reported in February 1589 for his mistreatment of his wife and his daily beatings that left her 'bleeding from several places on her body'. The minister and elders were sent to ask her and the neighbours about it, suggesting the source of their intelligence. The neighbours reported that 'Guiraud does nothing but beat and misuse his wife'.[84] In Montauban, a man called Artine was summoned five times to be instructed not to beat his wife Astrugette 'so violently'.[85]

Not only neighbours, but relatives too, were emboldened to report violent men when the results of their brutality were devastating. The mother-in-law of a goldsmith (and cantor in the church) called Toussans Rouvier presented herself to the consistory in July 1612 to complain that Rouvier had beaten his wife—her daughter—so 'extraordinarily' that, as a result, she gave birth prematurely, and died three days later. Her mother was categorical: 'Rovier was the cause of her death because he mistreated his wife'. By November the consistory was still investigating whether Rouvier had occasioned his wife's death, as well as whether he had connived in the prostitution of his daughter, but although he was suspended during the investigation, he remained in his position as cantor and received his quarterly wages of twenty-seven *livres*. He was pronounced innocent of all faults in March 1613.[86] Such explicit references to 'extraordinary' violence, inflicting grievous bodily harm—or even death—show the sort of behaviour that overstepped the public's conventional standards and tolerable limits of physical correction.

Men could also transgress societal norms by beating their wives too often. Physical admonishment was not to be a common or daily occurrence. Jacques Berzam and M. Boulhet were told not to beat and mistreat their wives as they were 'accustomed' to do.[87] In March 1593 it was decided that Guillaume Divie would be privately censured because he 'beats his wife ordinarily', and two elders were sent the following month to speak to M. Lyeuron because he 'continues to beat and torment his wife every day'.[88]

[83] BN, Ms.fr. 8667, 245r, 28 Sept. 1581.
[84] ADG, 42 J 29, 106, 127, 130, 192, 224, 272, 289, 551, 558–9, 566–7, 1 Feb. 1589.
[85] ADTG, I 1, 69r, 15 Nov. 1595.
[86] ADG, 42 J 34, 365v, 388v, 393r, 403r, 422r, 18 Jul. 1612. His name is also spelt Rovier and Rouyer, and his first name is identified on 417r.
[87] BN, Ms.fr. 8666, 17r, 31 May 1561; BN, Ms.fr. 8667, 292r, 26 Feb. 1582.
[88] ADG, 42 J 30, 151r, 3 Mar. 1593; 42 J 30, 14v, 10 Apr. 1593.

Nor should the beating be public. The silversmith M. David Somard was summoned four times in fifteen years for beating his wife and committing adultery, including a specific reprimand for having 'wanted to beat his wife publicly at ten o'clock in the morning'.[89] Joseph Cassard repented 'for the scandal he had committed' by having broken his fiancée's girdle in anger on the day of the Eucharist. He was especially reprimanded for having done this in the most public and sacred place: in the temple on the day of the sacrament.[90]

Above all, neighbourly concern was aroused by violent episodes that followed alcohol consumption. The violence of Anthoine Laguarde came to the consistory's attention because Laguarde's neighbour had remonstrated with him for having beaten his wife the day before the Pentecost Eucharist in May 1583. Laguarde was asked why he 'comported himself so badly with his wife', and said, predictably, that it was because she failed to obey him. Unusually, his wife Marguerite Nongeyrole testified that:

> she is obedient to him, but he is subject to drink and then the wine governs, and from that come their altercations... from anger [and] at everything she says, he throws now a knife, now a loaf, now a staff... everything that fall into his hands.[91]

Once her husband drank, wine ruled his behaviour, and he attacked her with whatever he could lay hold of. The consistory remonstrated with both spouses, who repented and promised to live in peace and friendship. Eighteen months later, however, Nongeyrole presented herself to complain that her husband continued to beat her frequently, and, even worse, had tried to poison her. She said that the poison in her soup had been identified by two men—Leroy Courrayeux and Sire Dutou—the latter a reputable apothecary. When the consistory summoned Laguarde, he said that these charges 'were nothing but things invented', and it was rather his wife who was a 'scold', and then he stormed out of the consistory in anger. It was probably this insolence, rather than his behaviour towards his wife alone, that prompted the consistory to report him to the magistrate.[92]

The association between alcohol and violence was often made. A cobbler called Carriere was admonished in November 1561 'not to frequent taverns and beat his wife, but to live soberly in his house with her and his family'.[93] A furrier called Pierre Leroy was similarly chided for frequenting taverns and beating his wife, and was told to do otherwise.[94] Anthoine Danton confessed in January 1588 to having beaten his wife after gambling—an activity that often accompanied drinking.[95] It was also neighbourly gossip about Vidal Aulbert's tendency to do 'nothing but beat his wife and haunt the taverns' that made the consistory send two elders to him, to 'make such admonitions as they think are necessary'.[96] Reports in November 1591 also suggested that Leonard Petit, who would later be found in a hemp field with

---

[89] ADG, 42 J 31, 184v; 42 J 33, 245r, 42 J 34, 16v, 169r, 395v, 25 Jun. 1597 (through to 12 Dec. 1612). His name is given as M. David *orpheure*, David Saumard *orpheure*, M. David Somard, and M. David Somart, *orfeuvre*.

[90] ADTG, I 1, 23r–v, 26 Jul. 1595.   [91] BN, Ms.fr. 8667, 219r–v, 31 May 1581.

[92] BN, Ms.fr. 8667, 361v–362r, 22 Nov. 1582.   [93] BN, Ms.fr. 8666, 44r, 15 Nov. 1561.

[94] BN, Ms.fr. 8666, 121v, 6 May 1562.   [95] ADG, 42 J 28, 350r, 13 Jan. 1588.

[96] ADG, 42 J 29, 77, 19 Nov. 1588.

a prostitute, drank so much of his money away at the taverns that he made 'his wife and children endure hunger'.[97] Finally, public gossip and outrage at the dissolute behaviour of ten merchants in April 1602 led to their summonses. Pierre Granier, M. Coulomb, M. Bon, M. Bessede, M. Tampeau, M. L'Hermitte, Pierre Fontanieu, M. Saunier, M. Daulau, and the familiar M. Henri Fabrot were charged with having become rowdily drunk, yelling and shouting in the street at night, and because of this debauchery returning home to beat their wives. Five of them reported that Fabrot had given several cuffs to his wife, daughter, and maid because his wife did not want to open the door to him after he had knocked several times. When asked if he had hit his wife because he had been drunk, Coulomb replied that he had several differences with his wife for other reasons, not because of his drunkenness: he did not deny hitting her, only disputed why. L'Hermitte said he did nothing scandalous, and was astonished the consistory should have called him and his friends 'for so little a thing that was not worth talking about'. All were firmly reprimanded, especially L'Hermitte for his arrogance towards the consistory, and were threatened with suspension if they did anything similar 'that brought scandal'.[98] The scandal had arisen because violence in the context of drunkenness was evidently not a reasonable, measured response to disobedience, but instead indicated ill discipline and poor husbandry, in both senses of the word.[99]

For the consistory, far worse than simple domestic violence was its use to facilitate spiritual deviancy. When a Catholic called Bonfil forced his wife to go to the Mass, 'beating and tormenting her ordinarily with great blasphemy and swearing', the consistory informed the criminal judge and asked him to exile Bonfil from the city.[100] The consistory reported Anthoine Sere to the magistrate for having 'oppressed his wife to make her go to Mass [and] beating her to this end'.[101] It is curious that weaver Julian Dufesc remained unpunished: in February 1592, he beat his wife and 'forced her to give herself to Satan', but nothing came of this report.[102]

Unlike the Catholic authorities of eighteenth-century Cambrai, and more like those of fifteenth-century Troyes or Reformed Augsburg, the consistory showed very limited sympathy towards abused women.[103] Van der Heijden has shown that drunken and abusive husbands in Holland were summoned, allowed to return home without repercussions if they showed remorse, and were suspended if they relapsed. They were rarely reported to the magistrates. The French consistory's response was even less exacting. In fifty-three alleged instances of marital violence (some involving the same man) the consistory's response is known. In nine cases the men were called or promises were made to investigate, but there was no follow-up. In thirty-eight cases the men were verbally censured. (In many cases wives were equally reprimanded.) In one case that involved an elder, the culprit was fined five *sous* for failing in his duty. There were four instances of suspension from the sacrament, but, in each case there was an aggravating cause beyond violence to a wife: Langre twice suspended for violence and adultery, Rovier for permitting his daughter's

[97] ADG, 42 J 30, 16r, 17v, 13 Nov. 1591; for the prostitution, cf. 225r.
[98] ADG, 42 J 32, 33v, 17 Apr. 1602.   [99] Hardwick, 'Seeking Separations', 165–7.
[100] ADG, 42 J 30, 209r, 28 Jul. 1593.   [101] ADG, 42 J 30, 251v, 26 Jan. 1594.
[102] ADG, 42 J 30, 38v, 19 Feb. 1592.   [103] Lottin, 'Vie et mort', 77–8.

prostitution, and Jacques Guiraud for his impertinence to the consistory. The only two men reported to the magistrate were Sere and Bonfil, who had used their violence to force their wives to the Mass. (The only additional example is Jacques Soisson, and again there were aggravating reasons.) The response to an exclusive charge of marital violence was therefore a summons and verbal censure, at worst. Men were neither suspended nor referred to the magistrates merely for beating their wives, and recidivists appear not to have been punished any more severely than one-time offenders. Consistorial interest in marital violence was also not sustained at the same intensity over time. The earliest consistorial register in Nîmes, of 1561–3, contains more than a quarter of all the known cases in the city over the fifty-five-year period. There were other bursts of activity, but the church did not pay consistent attention to the problem of domestic violence.

Conclusions

This survey of broken marriages has shown that men complained, above all, that their wives did not obey them, or lacked respect and deference, did not keep their houses well, committed adultery, or were rude in their speech. Wives complained that their husbands provided poorly for them or their dependants, squandered their time and money at the taverns and in drink, were violent, and committed adultery. Women chose to respond, as far as they had a choice, with silent endurance (probably in many more instances than the consistorial registers show) and with cathartic expression of their grievances. In cases of domestic violence, some few women told the consistory of their troubles, but it was not a forum that gave them any great relief, and their reports had limited results.

A certain level of domestic discipline was expected and tolerated. It was considered proper and correct to beat a woman in the pursuit of a disciplined household, and the consistory assumed that there had been cause unless there was strong evidence to the contrary. Most referrals to the consistory seem to indicate the concerns of neighbours over certain types of domestic violence—that which failed the test of moderation by excessive force or great frequency, that which was performed in public, but, above all, that which was alcohol-fuelled, as the latter undermined the justification that there was good reason. All these instances met with public disapproval, while the consistory was provoked more by religious implications. Neighbours only rarely intervened to stop marital violence, but they did talk directly to offenders, gossip about its occurrence, and report it to elders. That the punishments meted out were frequently little more than verbal censure, focusing primarily on any accompanying misdemeanour, reveals that the presence of these cases in the consistories was a testament to public pressure, rather than consistorial zeal.

ADULTERY

Jacques Ursi was an early convert to Protestantism, who had suffered persecution in the years before the faith was legally permitted, and he was a notary of some standing in the Protestant community (his records survive to this day and provide some of the source material for this book). It was therefore especially galling for the church when he was found to be having sex with a married woman in March 1562.

Two witnesses testified. Jehan Maurin, a 50-year-old locksmith in Nîmes, said that he had heard rumours some four or five years earlier that Ursi was having sex with Estienne Le Sourd's wife, and had remonstrated with him about it at the time.[104] Then, six months earlier, he had heard that they were at it again, and a week before he testified, someone—whom he did not want to name—had told him that the woman was at Ursi's house.

Very early the next morning, at around 4 a.m. on a Thursday, he had woken his neighbour M. Symon, a spit-roaster, and told him to come with him without explaining why. They concealed themselves outside the shop under Ursi's house and kept watch for half an hour. A little before daybreak Ursi emerged and, sensing them near by, called out, 'Who's there?' Maurin identified himself, but before Ursi had time to warn his lover, she also came out of the house, and Symon jumped up and grabbed hold of her. Ursi offered the men ten *livres each*, asking them, as Symon reported, 'to pardon him this time and to let her go and to take money to the church and he would not do it again, and his wife was sick and if she knew it would cost her her life'. But Maurin was not to be swayed, and both spies led the woman to the house of second consul Vidal d'Albenas, and she was subsequently imprisoned.

A few weeks later Ursi confessed his fault before the consistory, admitting that the affair had lasted seven or eight years (although he said they had not had sex on the morning she had been discovered leaving his house). He asked the consistory to pardon him, and promised to submit himself to whatever punishment the church saw fit. Given his public standing as a Protestant, and that the woman was also married, he was publicly 'excommunicated' (suspended) from the church for two months.[105]

As with other instances of sexual immorality, cases of adultery feature regularly in Languedoc's consistorial records, with around seventy-five cases in the registers under study. These are especially valuable to the historian because, for lack of pertinent sources, adultery has been little studied in this period. Assumptions have filled this void, such as Julie Hardwick's startling assertions—on the basis of separation cases before the provost's court in Nantes—that when it came to conjugal breakdowns, we must recognize the 'unimportance of adultery as an issue in France' and that 'neither judges nor communities in France were much inclined to regulate sexual morality'.[106] Such conclusions surely result from a failure to recognize the limits and biases of her sources: male adultery was not legal grounds for separation and therefore necessarily received little attention before the provost's court. The consistorial cases indicate that it was an important issue in the lives of French spouses, and those such as Ursi's suggest that both ecclesiastical judges and the communities from which they came were keen to regulate and denounce any

---

[104] 'Le Sourd' may be his surname, or it may mean 'the deaf'.
[105] BN, Ms.fr. 8666, 95r–v, 96r–v, 99r, 101v, 115r, 116r, 21 Mar. 1562.
[106] Hardwick, 'Seeking Separations', 168, n. 23, 180.

form of sexual immorality, especially when it broke the bonds of marriage. The lack of legal evidence about women's responses to their husband's adultery also makes the insights of the consistorial cases extremely valuable.[107]

Even though a woman's adultery was sufficient grounds for legal separation, it too has received relatively little historical attention. Female adultery gets only brief mentions by Nicole Castan, Wendy Gibson, and Solé; James Farr and Laura Gowing do not discuss it, Capp considers only male adultery, and only Ulinka Rublack, for Germany, seriously examines the phenomenon.[108] Yet female adultery was considered by contemporaries to be gravely serious. Edicts such as that of 1560 'openly charged women with potential wreckage of the family and, by analogy, the state through adultery (an act of treason)'.[109] Judges punished adulteresses by confinement in convents or prison for two years, at which point a husband could be reconciled with his wife and welcome her home, or leave her detained in the convent, excluded from civil society, for life.[110] As we have seen, the *sénéchaussée* court of Quercy sentenced Marye Barryere to be whipped for her adultery in 1597, while Alyon Gironne, former wife of Robert Godin of Montauban, was condemned to death by judges in La Rochelle for 'her bad life and lewd misbehaviour'.[111] The consistories often turned female adultery cases over to the secular authorities to initiate judicial proceedings. In the light of these fearsome penalties and the historiographical lacunae, consistorial evidence plays an immensely valuable role in accessing the mentalities and experience of women and men who committed adultery or who suffered the betrayal of their spouses, as well as alerting us to existing attitudes towards such behaviour.

Male Adultery

Male adultery was the flipside of many of the cases considered in Chapter 6: most men who sexually assaulted maidservants were married. There are also many cases in which both parties were married. Such behaviour did not go unobserved or disregarded by their peers, and it is through eyewitness reports and denunciations, as well as gossip, that many instances of adultery by men were made known to the church.

Three months before his wife Catherine Cauelle gave birth to a daughter, Isaac Gardiol, known as *Boria* or *Borye*, was suspected of committing adultery with

---

[107] Lebrun, *La vie conjugale*, 53. The evidence complements that found by Lottin, 'Vie et mort', 71 and Capp, *Gossips*, 93–103.

[108] Nicole Castan, 'La criminalité familiale dans le ressort du Parlement de Toulouse, 1690–1730', in *Crimes et criminalité en France 17e–18e siècles*, ed. A. Abbiateci, F. Billacois, Y. Bongert, N. Castan, Y. Castan, P. Petrovitch, *Cahier des Annales* 33 (Paris, 1971), 95–6; Gibson, *Women*, 64–5; Solé, *Etre femme*, 157–62; Capp, *Gossips*; Ulinka Rublack, *The Crimes of Women in Early Modern Germany* (Oxford, 1999), 213–22.

[109] Sarah Hanley, 'Social Sites of Political Practice in France: Lawsuits, Civil Rights, and the Separation of Powers in Domestic and State Government, 1500–1800', *American Historical Review* 102.1 (1997), 27–52, here 32.

[110] Gibson, *Women*, 64; Hanley, 'Social Sites', 39; Gibson, *Women*, 64; Lebrun, *La vie conjugale*, 79.

[111] ADTG, I 1, 231v, 229v, both 12 Feb. 1597.

Suzanne Blavignague (Fig. 7.1, p. 296), the wife of a locksmith (and referred to as a locksmith herself).[112] Both she and Gardiol had been in M. Bourguet's house on the same day; Gardiol swore that he had been there for some business affairs he had with Bourguet and denied having seen her; she said that she had been seated close to the fire and Gardiol did not speak to her. But neighbours M. du Pont and Sieur Gallofre had suspected enough to wait on the street for two hours after Gardiol entered the house, until they saw him leave, followed by Blavignague. They had then reported their suspicions to the consistory, and because of the rumours, Blavignague and her husband had quarrelled.[113]

Peer judgement on a man's adultery is also seen in an argument between two scholars—Launay and Alexis—at the College in Montauban in September 1595. Alexis admitted to the consistory that they had quarrelled because Launay had received a letter telling him that Alexis had taken a married woman, Sarra de Boly, as a mistress. It added that she lived near to the College, Alexis loved her ardently, and that one day Alexis had almost been caught by her husband, having to jump out of her house to escape in the nick of time. Launay would not say from whom the letter came, but Alexis's immorality provoked a fierce argument between the two friends.[114]

Men's adultery could also create gossip in the community that reached the consistory, as happened in December 1595 when it was rumoured that Bregnier Ormieres was frequenting widow Sarra Gausailhe's house. As he was married and his wife was in Toulouse, this behaviour 'gave scandal', and they were forbidden from visiting each other. Three months later, when it became known that Ormieres's wife had died, the consistory still insisted that because of the scandal surrounding their previous association, Ormieres and Gausailhe should not spend time together.[115] In Ganges in 1602 there was a common rumour that Sieur Pierre Fabre and his servant Jehanne Bosquette were committing adultery. It had probably been circulated by Pierre Roland and Sire Calvas, who had appointed themselves as moral spies: they reported to the consistory that a few days earlier they had seen that Fabre's garden was not locked and had tried to enter it, but could not open the door because there was a stone propped against the inside, and Fabre cried out to them not to enter. Their suspicions roused, they climbed up on to the walls of the town to see if there was anyone in the garden with him, and soon saw him leave by the *Chemin des Treilles* (still a street in Ganges, close to the Hérault River), and then saw Jehanne Bosquette walking the same road. They supposed the two had been in the garden together, although they admitted that they had not actually seen any mischief.[116]

The other primary way that cases of men's adultery reached the consistory was through their wives' testimony. Such denunciations give a fascinating insight into women's responses and reactions to infidelity. Women seeking redress for their husband's adultery might be expected to have had the advantage of aligning themselves

---

[112] ADG, E Dépôt 36/697, 8r, May 1585.
[113] ADG, 42 J 28, 159v–160r, 161r–v, 27 Feb. 1585.
[114] ADTG, I 1, 55v, 27 Sept. 1595.   [115] ADTG, I 1, 83r, 113r, 20 Dec. 1595.
[116] ADH, GG 24, 132v, 29 Aug. 1602.

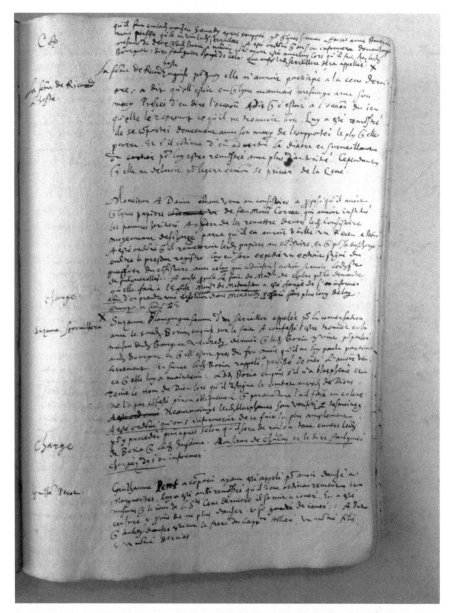

Fig. 7.1. Suzanne Blavignague is questioned about her alleged adultery with Isaac Gardiol, known as *Borie* or *Boria*, *Registre des délibérations du consistoire de Nîmes, 1584–8*, Archives départementales du Gard, 42 J 28, 160r (27 February 1585)

with the church's objectives of reconciling estranged couples and eradicating sexual sin and scandal. In practice, however, appealing to the consistory was a strategy that carried no guarantee of success, and women's attempts to take control in response to a husband's infidelity were seldom wholly profitable.

The consistory were first alerted to the adultery of Anthoine Moynier, known as *Figaret*, innkeeper of the Scissors (the inn was known both by the French word *Ciseau* and by the Occitan *Talhants*) in April 1583, when his wife, Marguerite Pradiere, reported to one of the elders that her husband had made their maid pregnant and had beaten her when she remonstrated with him.[117] When the couple appeared before the consistory in August Pradiere explained that she had found him having sex with the maid, on a chest pressed against the bed, with his breeches around his ankles. He protested his innocence. In January 1584, however, the consistory had more evidence from independent sources. A woman delivering bread to the house said she had found him sweatily dressed only in a shirt, and when she had asked him what had awakened him—using a verb that can also mean 'to arouse'—he had started to laugh. Reports said that he had been seen with the maidservant in Montpellier and had been discovered hidden behind a door with her, fondling her breasts. A man called Blaize from Provence reported that *Figaret* had given him bags to carry to the maid; another from Saint-Hippolyte-du-Fort said that he had carried the maid's child to Moynier's house. Moynier denied all these accusations.

Five years passed before Moynier presented himself at the consistory asking to be received to take the sacrament. He still denied making his maid pregnant, but evidence emerged that Moynier had been giving money to Blaize to cover the cost of the child's food since her birth. His continued denials left him suspended from the sacrament. The consistory concluded that he was a 'rude man without feeling' to have 'remained so long in his wickedness'. Only in June 1590 would Moynier finally confess that he had made the woman pregnant, and that the child was his.[118]

His wife Pradiere's complaint to the consistory had evidently been a step taken only when the usual process of internal resolution between husband and wife had broken down or proved inadequate: reprimanding him directly had resulted in her being beaten. Telling the authorities was not, however, particularly effective in this case, because Moynier persistently denied his adultery over the course of seven years. Nor did his wife adopt this approach again. In March 1601 it was rumoured that *Figaret* was committing adultery with another maid, whom he had sent secretly to stay in some place outside the town. It was similarly reported in December 1604 that the innkeeper of the *Tailans*, 'Thony Moynier', had made a girl pregnant at his house and in October 1606 he was said yet again to have a 'whore' in his house.[119] These charges—which were barely investigated—all reached the church by public rumour; Marguerite Pradiere had evidently learnt that, for her needs, the consistory was ineffectual.

---

[117] Anthoine Moynier is sometimes called Anthoine Martin; later in life he became known as Thony Moynier. *Figaret* means a place where fig-trees grow, or a type of chestnut—the reasoning behind this moniker is lost. *Talhants* is Occitan for tailors' scissors, and the inn was most commonly referred to as the *Tailhans* (*Tallions*, *Talhans*, *Talheurs*, *Tailans*), although also as the *Ciseau* or *Sizeaulx*. This case was mentioned in Chapter 2 (p. 89).

[118] ADG, 42 J 28, 10v, 18r, 25r, 32r, 73v, 76r; 42 J 29, 148, 162, 178, 254, 428, 27 Apr. 1583.

[119] ADG, 42 J 31, 402v, 413v, 28 Mar. 1601 and 3 May 1601; 42 J 33, 3r, 130v, 8 Dec. 1604.

In fact, there is no evidence that the consistory was ever successful in properly reconciling a couple after a husband's adultery. Market-gardener Adrian Vero was reported in October 1585 for allegedly abusing a servant-girl in his house, and for his association with Catherine Formentine, an infamous prostitute. In January 1587, Magdeleine Coterelle had given birth and claimed that Vero was one of her lovers, but it was only in June 1587 that his wife approached the consistory to 'complain greatly that her husband maintains and haunts Formentine's house ordinarily, where he spends all that he owns and, afterwards, returns to their house and does nothing but torment and beat her.'[120] The consistory decided to question her further to find out if she had sufficient evidence of this behaviour, but nothing more came of her charge. Perhaps it was impoverishment caused by her husband's profligate and adulterous behaviour that explained why, after his death, Vero's widow became a prostitute.[121]

Perine Panysse was no more successful in using the consistory to bring her husband Gabriel Pastel to task. Rumours of her husband's poor behaviour had reached the elders almost a year before Panysse approached the consistory in April 1595 to complain that her husband committed adultery and treated her poorly. Turning to the consistory seems to have been a final resort. Panysse's purpose was probably in part to justify her decision to leave him, which she said she had been forced to do, but if she also hoped that consistorial pressure would result in a reconciliation, her efforts were in vain. The consistory's actions were not those best designed to achieve a reunion: they asked the judge to put Pastel's name on the list of people to be expelled from the town, they threatened him with criminal justice if he refused to have his lover exiled, and they publicly announced him as an adulterer and whore-monger for three Sundays in a row. In July 1595 Pastel declared that he would rather leave his wife than 'the whore he keeps'.[122]

The records also provide examples of women reacting to their husbands' infidelity outside the consistory. Like Panysse, Gros Bonnet's wife had left her husband in March 1562 because of his well-attested adultery. We know this because she questioned why she had not received a token for the sacrament and was told that it was because she was not living with her husband, but that if she took him back she could have the token. She offered to receive him if he would agree to join her.[123] Sieur Jehan Surian's wife also left him in December 1581, after growing jealous at his relationship with a female servant. Reports were that he had hit his wife with a staff. A minister, deacon, and elder were deputized to reconcile them, but there is no record of whether they were successful.[124] The 'great divorce' between Captain Bimarc and his wife 'because of a certain maidservant' also presumably referred to the wife's suspicion over Bimarc's sexual impropriety with the maid.[125]

Yet the consistorial records also reveal more complex and more concrete ways in which women expressed the jealousy, anger, and pain caused by a husband's

[120] ADG, 42 J 28, 190v, 233v, 242v, 250v, 258r, 259r, 281r, 19 Oct. 1585.
[121] ADG, 42 J 31, 453v, 457r, 462r, 9 Jan. 1602.
[122] ADG, 42 J 30, 281v, 349r, 377r, 15 Jun. 1594.
[123] BN, Ms.fr. 8666, 100v, 27 Mar. 1562.   [124] BN, Ms.fr. 8667, 267v, 23 Dec. 1581.
[125] BN, Ms.fr. 8667, 7r, 4 May 1579.

infidelity. Catherine Andrienne presented herself at the consistory in August 1589 to complain that when she had been a servant for the notary Jean Petit, he had abused her several times in an upper chamber of his house where he kept the flour, and as a result she found herself pregnant. A few months later, a nurse who also lived at the Petit house related to the consistory that several times in one evening she had called Catherine, who eventually replied in a low voice, whereupon the nurse— wanting to see where she was, so she could brush the child's hair—went with a light into the child's room, at which a man suddenly stood up and extinguished the candle, making her cry out in surprise and run in fear to tell her mistress. The mistress, unable to find her husband anywhere near by, started to cry, saying over and over, 'My husband! My husband!' Andrienne's account of the evening's events echoed the nurse's testimony, saying that she had heard Petit's wife crying out, 'My husband, where are you?' and then loudly shouting Andrienne's name. Petit's response was to deny that he was the man in question, saying instead that he had been in bed with his wife that night, and having heard the nurse cry out and seen the light snuffed, he got up to go see what was going on. The following year Andrienne's child was born, and the consistory discovered that Petit had sent her money to cover the child's food and upkeep in an attempt to fob her off, as Andrienne had warned that she would bring the child into Nîmes if he did not, and Petit's wife threatened 'to poison her husband or use a little pen-knife to kill him' if she did.[126] In July 1590 it was reported that Petit was still paying for the child's wet-nurse, 'despite his wife's anger'. Before the consistory, however, as late as November 1591, Petit swore that the accusation of adultery was pure calumny, and he had never had sex with Catherine Andrienne.[127] Petit's wife had reacted with dismay and distress, but also with fierce anger and threats of violence.

Betrayed wives also expressed their sadness and anger through public speech and in more than mere threats of violence. In Montauban in June 1595, according to the testimony of two witnesses and reports of neighbourhood gossip, Anne de Valaty discovered her husband Pierre Cordiny trying to have sex with their maid, and reacted with violence in both word and deed. This case highlights the possibilities of wifely redress and is worth exploring at some length, for it sheds light on how women might react and seek to remedy marital disharmonies outside the consistory.[128]

Pierre Arnaud, known as *Balafrat* (which probably relates to the Occitan, *balar*, to dance) was an armourer in François Miguot's workshop, and had been working there one day around Wednesday 28 June 1595, about a fortnight before he testi-fied, when he had seen Valaty coming out of her house crying and had heard her speaking to her neighbours. According to Arnaud, she had told her friends that

---

[126] '*La femme dudict M. Petiti le menassoit de lempoisonner ou tuer avec un ganivet son dict mary.*' An alternative reading was that Petit's wife was threatening to poison or stab the baby.

[127] ADG, 42 J 29, 227, 252–3, 255–6, 288, 328, 338, 344, 374, 378, 389–91, 445, 452–3, 457–8, 565, 575, 618, 628, 695, 700; 42 J 30, 5r, 18v, 20v, 2 Aug. 1589. The maid is also called Audoiere and Andrin, and the nurse is identified as Ysabel and Marguerite, so it is not clear what her name is. Petit (or Petiti)'s wife is not named.

[128] ADTG, I 1, 17r, 17v, 18v–19r, 59v–60v, 83v, 12 Jul. 1595.

her husband had tried to have sex with their maid, and that she had found them lying on a sack that he had brought from Lagarde, but that she had stopped them before they could succeed. Arnaud remembered her saying in Occitan, '*Naurio jamay penssat que mon marit aguesse fach aqueste acte*', which means, 'I would never have thought my husband would do this act'. Arnaud had also heard that the maid had since been dismissed.

According to the consistory's sources, this was not the only time that Valaty had found her husband up to mischief with the maid. When Cordiny was called to the consistory on 19 July he was charged with having tried to commit the 'abominable sin' of adultery several times, each time having been stopped by his wife. The consistory questioned him about an incident during the service on the previous Sunday, 16 July, when Cordiny's wife and her sister, the wife of Arnaud Desmastins, had found Cordiny with the maid in the room where meal was boulted. On discovering them Valaty had taken up a sieve and hit the maid with it several times, and had thrown her out of the house, as several neighbours had observed. (Cordiny was a merchant, and the boulting room, sack, and sieve suggest he traded grain.) Cordiny denied the accusation and said that his wife had conceived a jealousy of the maid for no good reason after one night when he went to bed, and his wife was not there, but later came in and found the maid near the bed. This could reflect the sleeping arrangements of the period, but could also suggest that Cordiny had started his advances towards the maid earlier. Since that night, Cordiny said, his wife had done nothing but 'murmur and prattle' about the evil he thought and might commit. As to the incident in the boulting room—which seems to have been beneath the living quarters of the house—he said that he had been going downstairs to church, and because his wife had hidden herself in that room, she had seen him, soon followed by the maid, descending the stairs; this had 'augmented her jealousy' and she had then dismissed the servant. In short, Cordiny's response was total denial and that the story was a product of his wife's jealous imagination. The consistory decided to speak to Valaty, to her sister, and to the neighbours, including the wife of François Miguot, known as *Poitevin* (this nickname may suggest, from the Occitan noun *poitre*, that he was short and fat or simply that he was from Poitou).

Neither Valaty nor her sister chose to be heard by the consistory at this stage, and it was not until mid-October that two of the neighbourhood women came forward, with contradictory stories to tell. François Miguot's wife Marthe de Praissac, who was around thirty years old, explained that some time ago she had seen Cordiny's wife sitting on the street and had spoken with her. Praissac said Valaty had told her that she 'should keep watch on her maid so that her husband does not do [with her] as Cordiny did with his', and when Praissac asked what Cordiny had done, Valaty said that she had found him with their maid lying on a sack in the boulting-room 'behaving badly together', at which point she grabbed the sieve and made Cordiny and the maid get up, while at another time she and her sister found Cordiny and the maid together. In Praissac's account memory conflated the two discoveries into one, with all the features of the boulting-room, sack, and sieve rolled into the first incident, and the second incident undescribed.

An element of doubt was introduced, however, with the testimony of the other neighbourhood woman, Astruguette Dauzieu, wife of Guillaume Baure. She said that she had never heard Cordiny's wife or Poitevin's wife speaking of the matter, and that Praissac had said it 'from malice conceived against Cordiny's wife'. This was the line also taken by Valaty when she now finally appeared to answer the consistory's demands. She denied that any of this had happened and said that Praissac had invented the tales of attempted adultery out of spite, to put her in discord with her husband.[129] She admitted that she had dismissed the maid, however, saying she had learnt 'she was not well-reputed'. This comfortable version is the one that the consistory chose to believe, and Praissac was grievously censured on what strikes the modern reader as wholly unconvincing grounds.

The discovery of her husband's infidelity seems to have been very distressing to Valaty, who was described by Arnaud as being 'completely grief-stricken' (the verb, *esplorée*, can also mean overcome with anguish, broken-hearted). Even Cordiny's version of events portrayed Valaty as 'driven by jealousy'. Valaty's reaction to her husband's infidelity was a combination of anger and tears—suggesting the betrayal and breakdown of an affectionate marriage—and shame and dishonour. Yet Valaty did not only weep. Rather than responding passively to the situation, Valaty used her speech and her authority in the public arena to influence the course of events as they proceeded. We can hear Valaty's voice refracted through the testimony of others, and in both instances Valaty used her network to invoke female support to denounce and humiliate her husband, holding Cordiny up for public inspection and finding him wanting. For the shame he brought on her by his adultery, Valaty shamed Cordiny with her words. She also acted: hitting the maid and/or her husband with the nearest object to hand and using her power as housewife to dismiss the girl. If any of Cordiny's testimony is to be believed, Valaty had been lying in wait for him in the boulting-room, suggesting a level of premeditation and guile designed to expose her husband's misdemeanours. Finally, it seems likely that even the cancellation of charges brought by Valaty in October 1595—though, of course, frustrating, as shutting out the consistory closes our view too—is a fascinating indication of the means women could use to direct events. It seems likely that Valaty's testimony in October was a face-saving exercise, maybe part of a private deal between husband and wife, burying the hatchet.[130] As such, it was a manoeuvre designed to dispense with the court of public opinion when its work had been done; Valaty did not tolerate further intrusion into her family life when exposure had brought about the desired goal of reconciliation. Maybe here too she drew on her female network: Astruguette Dauzieu's testimony (which was not what the consistory expected to hear) supported Valaty's claims and made the whole incident sound like a petty intra-female quarrel. Ultimately the consistory ended the case by charging two elders to reconcile Praissac and Valaty.

[129] It is only because she appeared before the consistory that we learn her name: until this point every speaker had simply referred to her as 'Cordiny's wife'.

[130] A similar decision was made by the wife and daughter of alleged adulterer Pierre Vincens, known as *Petiton*, in Coutras in June 1583, Alfred Soman, and Elisabeth Labrousse, 'Le registre consistorial de Coutras, 1582–1584', *BSHPF* 126 (1980), 193–228, 213–15.

302   The Voices of Nîmes

Valaty's case is not a lone exception. Mademoiselle de Galli, wife of M. Galli, also discovered her husband's adultery with their maidservant Clarette the hard way, and reacted with similarly vociferous protests and intemperate action.[131] In mid-November 1587 the scholar Pierre Serres went to Galli's house at around 3 or 4 p.m. on a Thursday to instruct him in a lawsuit. When he entered the house, he saw Galli through an open door kissing and 'passing time with' a woman (a lovely euphemism for sexual activity) near the couch. Having only seen the sleeves of her dress and heard her voice, he presumed the woman to be Galli's wife. Embarrassed, Serres left quickly without saying a word. Outside on the street he bumped into M. Nicolas, and told him that he would never pass Galli's house without laughing, as he had walked in on Galli and his wife and in his mortification had left without instructing him. He asked Nicolas not to repeat to anyone what had happened, but the story was too good for Nicolas to keep quiet. The next day Nicolas came across Mlle de Galli in a group of women and children and teased her with the words, 'nine months from yesterday you'll have another child'.[132] She did not reply, but a few days later at M. de Caissargues's house she came across Nicolas and asked, 'Why did you say that?' Nicolas gleefully told her that she had been seen having sex with her husband, but she said that she had been somewhere else that Thursday afternoon, and that it must have been her 'rascal' of a maid.

It was at this point that Mlle de Galli started to act in ways that brought the case to the consistory's attention. On 25 November it was noted that Galli's wife had 'complained of it in several places and before many people' and had also beaten and dismissed her maid. In the preceding week, when asked by the baker Jehan Menoes why she had beaten her maidservant, Galli told him that her husband had been found embracing a woman, and she knew it was the maid because Clarette had previously complained to her that Galli had made advances. Mlle de Galli had then beaten and dismissed the maidservant, and complained to her husband, who had told her it was nothing—but the latest incident revealed the truth. Mlle de Galli told Menoes that her maid had betrayed and disappointed her, and that her husband had made her wear (cuckold's) horns.[133]

By 2 December, however, Mlle de Galli's story had changed. She now would not be drawn—M. Clericy, sent by the consistory to question her, said he could not 'pull' much from her—except that she had dismissed the maid for stealing some bracelets. Two weeks later the maid, Clarette, maintained the same story: that after working for the Gallis for two years, some three (probably more like four) weeks earlier Mlle de Galli had beaten and dismissed her, complaining that she had stolen

---

[131] Her forename is never given—even in the baptismal register. In August 1581, 'Marguerite daughter to Monsieur Gally' was registered, but her mother's name is, unusually, not given (ADG, E Dépôt 36/696, 181r).

[132] One account says he said to her, 'Ah well, a few days ago you had a child, and in nine months, you'll have another!' but the version above is as Nicolas related it.

[133] '*Sa chambriere luy avoyt faict ung faux bon son mary luy fesant porter les banes.*' To 'faire un faux bond' (to make a false leap, originally from a racquet game, when a ball bounced badly or not where it was thought) means to betray someone, disappointing someone's hopes and expectations; *banet* and *banèl* in Occitan mean horns (of a goat or sheep).

from her, and so she could not complete her term of service. She herself maintained that Galli 'had never done evil with her, and she was a poor girl but a very good girl'. To protect her reputation, Clarette had adapted Galli's story to depict a wrongful allegation of theft as the cause of her dismissal.

Mlle de Galli's initial response to her husband's adultery was explosive and voluble anger, and a willingness to complain and humiliate him in front of anyone who would listen, but as time passed another strategy seemed preferable. Despite Clarette's previous complaints to her mistress about her master's unwanted advances, Mlle de Galli ultimately had no choice but to hold the maid responsible, and to patch up her marriage by telling an alternative story to explain the maid's departure. Husband and wife can be seen to have closed ranks; neither again responded to calls to come before the consistory.[134] Such transitions were not rare. Donne Marnasse's daughter was reported to have voiced complaints to her husband (only identified as a glover) about his sexual misconduct with a servant in October 1587. Between public complaint and consistorial query, however, this wife too chose to become silent.[135]

After their initial outbursts of castigatory speech and violence towards the 'other woman', these women chose restorative silence for the sake of marital appeasement. But not all women responded actively and aggressively to their husband's adultery in the first place. There were those—maybe most aggrieved wives—who stood by their husbands from the outset, asserting the innocence of their spouses in the face of possible sexual betrayal. No doubt many such instances of support remain unrecorded, but on occasion we have evidence that wives spoke in the street or appeared in the consistory to defend their husbands.

In February 1613 the cantor Toussans Rouviere's daughter accused Sieur Jean Geofret of being alone in his house with his servant Jeanne at the time of the Sunday service while his wife was absent—the implication being, of course, that he had had sex with her. In early March Geofret's wife accosted an elder in the street and told him that the consistory had received false witnesses against her husband and had given them 'licence to speak words against his honour'. Her words were taken as such an affront that three weeks later she was required to appear before the consistory to admit that she had spoken 'angry and violent words' against the church. Her instinct had been to defend her husband from defamation.[136] When M. Molin was accused of having made his maid Jehanne de Rochegude pregnant in February 1591, it was his wife who turned up to excuse him, saying he could not appear because of his business affairs and that Rochegude was pregnant by a man from her home region: Molin's wife seemed confident enough in her husband's fidelity to make a public declaration of his innocence. When Molin finally appeared two months later he asserted that his maid had assured his wife, in the presence of neighbours, that it was not his doing and these combined testimonies meant that he continued to be admitted to the sacrament. His wife's trust in him was, however,

---

[134] ADG, 42 J 28, 331v, 332r–v, 334v, 338r, 338v, 25 Nov. 1587.
[135] ADG, 42 J 28, 319r, 320v, 14 Oct. 1587.
[136] ADG, 42 J 34, 417r–v, 421v–422r, 27 Feb. 1613.

misplaced. In September elder M. Guiraud found a baby boy left at the town gate on the road leading to Beaucaire (the *Porte des Carmes*) with a note on him saying he belonged to M. Molin. The baby must just have been set down as Guiraud managed to identify a woman from Beaucaire at the gate, who said that she had fed the child for two months, having been paid two *écus* by Molin's maid, and had been told by the maid that Molin, the child's father, would pay the rest. She had approached Molin for the sum, which he did not want to pay in full, although he had given her two pieces of silver. Guiraud had promptly taken the child to Jean Dupin, the second consul, who had spoken to Molin, and Molin had promised to take the child and feed him.[137]

In all probability Molin's wife knew he was guilty: women's loyalty to their husbands was not necessarily dependent on their innocence. In practice we must suppose that wives may have chosen to defend their menfolk, despite compelling evidence of adultery, for the sake of domestic peace and security, as appears to have happened in the case of Jacques Gardiol. Gardiol—known (as his brother confusingly was as well) by the nickname *Borie* or *Borye* (probably meaning 'farmer', from the Occitan *bòria*, 'farm')—was the innkeeper of the *Pont du Gard* (named after the famous local Roman aqueduct) in the Faubourg Saint-Antoine.[138] He was married to Anthoine Reynaude, and they had at least three children, daughters born in 1582 and 1584, and a son born in 1592.[139] At the very end of 1596 and again in January 1597 their maidservant, Jane Gibernesse, approached the Nîmes consistory to say that since the last Saint Michel she had been pregnant by Gardiol, for whom she had worked for three or four years.[140] She had also been engaged to Mathieu Bague for three weeks, and he now wanted their betrothal declared null. Both Gardiol and his wife denied Gibernesse's accusation, but a woman called Claude Rousse, known as Donne Garagnonne, said that Borie's wife had wanted her to take the child: the implication was that both husband and wife had acted together to cover up his mess.

The consistory summoned everyone together at the end of January. Gibernesse maintained that she was pregnant by Gardiol and no one else, and that he had forced her to get engaged to Bague when he realized that she was pregnant 'to cover his fault'. Her sister, probably Marie Gibernesse, related that Reynaude had instructed Garagnonne to feed the child and had tried to persuade her to tell Jane to give the child away. Garagnonne agreed that Reynaude had told her to persuade Gibernesse that it 'would be more honourable to give the child to a journeyman than a married man'. Reynaude insisted that she had helped Gibernesse by supplying Garagnonne to feed the child, but that it meant nothing more. At every interstice Gardiol denied the charge.

---

[137] ADG, 42 J 29, 60, 633, 736, 20 Feb. 1591.

[138] Permission was given for 'Jacques Gardiol called Borie to put a sign on his inn in the Faubourgs Saint-Antoine with a picture of the *Pont du Gard*', ADG, E Dépôt 36/39, 116r, 15 Nov. 1599.

[139] ADG, E Dépôt 36/696, 189v, 222v; E Dépôt 36/697, 164v.

[140] Also spelt Yvernesse, she was almost certainly the sister of Marie Gibernesse, both from Saint-Privat-de-Vallongue, in the Cévennes.

The consistory pressed Gibernesse once more to tell the truth, and she now said that she and Gardiol had had sex for a year before she got pregnant, adding that Reynaude had even found them doing so. At this Reynaude demanded that Gibernesse retract her words, and kneel and say that Gardiol was a good man, while Gardiol repeated his denial. Poor Mathieu Bague, listening to all this, finally spoke up and asked to be set free from the contract of marriage he had entered not knowing that Gibernesse was already pregnant. Contrary to usual practice but in the face of compelling circumstances, the consistory allowed the engagement to be declared null, and Gibernesse was publicly suspended from the sacrament.

A year passed. In January 1598, Gardiol was summoned for feeding his maid's bastard child at his expense—the specific reparative gesture that gave so many guilty men away. It is unlikely that this revelation came as any great surprise to Anthoine Reynaude, who seems to have been conscious throughout that her husband had committed adultery, and had tried to conceal his wrongdoing. It is almost painful to read, then, that by September 1598 Gardiol was again accused of making another maid pregnant—which he denied—and that in September 1599 Jehanne Lanteyresse presented herself to be publicly received back into the church after having given the birth to an illegitimate child whose father was none other than Jacques Gardiol, called *Borye*.[141]

Reynaude's defence of her husband is echoed by the behaviour of the baker Jean Benezet's wife in January 1603. Benezet had made a maidservant called Catherine pregnant and at the end of 1602 Benezet's wife had taken the child to be baptized. When summoned, Benezet denied being the father and portrayed his wife's intervention as a caring act that did not imply guilt. The consistory urged him to tell the truth, saying that there were several pieces of evidence against him, not least that he had been spied caressing the maid, but he continued to deny it. Similarly, his wife said she knew nothing of any sexual activity between her husband and maid and, when asked if she had provided for the child's upkeep, said she had given a mere fifteen *sols* towards bread and nothing more. Whether this was deliberate concealment or true innocence is uncertain: in December 1603, after being suspended from the sacrament for nearly a year, Benezet presented himself to be reconciled to the church, and still maintained his innocence. This endurance under questioning impressed the consistory, which decided that he should be permitted to take the Eucharist, absolving him of any guilt.[142] Women's words could be used to support as well as revile their partners.

When it came to distinguishing the guilty from the innocent, perhaps the consistory should have learnt from the example, eight years earlier, of Sieur Jacques de la Farelle. Farelle, a doctor and lawyer, was questioned about his frequentation of a Catholic woman called Damoiselle Brocquiere in August 1595. The consistory instructed him not to spend any more time with her but within ten days he had once again been seen entering her house. When he was summoned again on

---

[141] ADG, 42 J 31, 150r, 155v, 158v, 160v–162r, 163r, 202v, 204v, 240r, 241r, 299r, 27 Dec. 1596.
[142] ADG, 42 J 32, 141r, 144r, 145v, 147v, 153v, (168v), 200v, 8 Jan. 1603.

the same charge he said he had gone to the consistory once and would not return. Nevertheless, after much badgering by the elders, he did eventually appear in January 1596 and was told again to stop visiting Brocquiere as it caused 'great scandal' to the church. He replied that 'he would not desist from her company, because she is a woman of honour…that he is married, and she is too', suggesting that their time together was perfectly innocent. When told that he would be suspended if he failed to obey, he said he would appeal to the next colloquy. This drew the matter out until the colloquy decided in the consistory's favour in May, and when summoned in June Farelle said that he did not want to listen to the 'villainous words' of the consistory. For saying this and for refusing to appear over the next few months, the consistory continued to threaten to suspend him. Eventually, in October 1596, he appeared and 'promised to desist from frequenting Brocquiere', saying he would only speak to her in future at times of the day that would not scandalize others, and in the presence of other people. The consistory noted that 'all the neighbours' were complaining, but Farelle still maintained that they had done no wrong. Despite this promise, however, he continued to visit her and on 24 November 1596, some fifteen months after first calling him, the consistory suspended him from the Eucharist 'for frequentation and scandalous conversation with a woman' and the 'dirty, injurious, and profane words' he had used against them. He protested his innocence when he asked to be received back into the church in October 1597, but refused to make public reparation. Finally, in March 1599, he was found alone in bed with Brocquiere at eleven o'clock at night—well past the hour at which most people had returned to their homes to sleep. Despite this apparently damning evidence of (at least eventual) guilt, he nonetheless professed his innocence.[143] Constant denial did not necessarily equate to enduring innocence.

Not all men were so brazen: there is evidence of men being willing to confess to their sins. In Ganges in December 1599 Pierre Rossy confessed to committing adultery with Remon Miquiel's daughter and giving her the pox.[144] In April 1606 Sieur Anthoine Janin denied having had sex with a prostitute in his house but, when accused of committing adultery with his servant five months later, he admitted that he had done so—to a point: he said it was she who had 'surprised and incited him to have sex with her', alleging that because she had been pregnant by his valet, 'to cover her fault, [she had] induced to him to have sex with her'. This sexist and illogical reasoning did not, however, prevent him from crying as he asked God's and the church's pardon on his knees for the scandal he had caused.[145]

Confession could also serve a purpose. Guillaume Baudan presented himself to the consistory in September 1607, declaring that he had committed adultery with his children's nurse and wished to confess his sin, making any reparation the company deemed right to be reconciled with God. As he had 'frankly and voluntarily' presented himself without being summoned, the consistory decided that, after

---

[143] ADG, 42 J 30, 383v, 385r, 386v, 390; 42 J 31, (4v), 29r, 456, 88v, 93v, 94v, 98v, 108v, 111v, 113r, 117v, 126r, 128v, 129r, 129v, 130r, 135r, 138v, 140r, 196v, 273v, 278v, 285v, 9 Aug. 1595.
[144] ADH, GG 24, 116v, 121r, 26 Dec. 1599.   [145] ADG, 42 J 33, 102r, 125r, 5 Apr. 1606.

being suspended for a time, he should make reparation before them alone, not in the humiliatingly public arena of the Sunday service.[146] Innkeeper Corporal Jean was denounced for making his maid pregnant in August 1614, but his voluntary confession of his 'great fault' and his demonstration of extreme regret led the consistory to conclude that he too would be privately suspended from the sacrament.[147] As ever, the consistory were happy to see evidence of emendation and improvement, and convincing them of this was a clever strategy to avoid public damage to personal honour.

Female Adultery

It is noticeable that many of the cases of female adultery cluster in four consistorial registers: in Nîmes in 1561–3, 1588–91, 1591–5, and in Montauban in 1595–8. This may be coincidental but could also suggest a particular preoccupation in these years with eradicating sexual sin, and that, in the eyes of the church at least, sexual sinners could be blamed for the divine punishments of plague, dearth, and religious war affecting Languedoc at these times. These cases provide evidence of popular attitudes, the consequences of these attitudes for social behaviour, and the mentalities of the women and men both involved in and affected by adultery.

Prevailing cultural attitudes towards female sexuality meant that cuckoldry was seriously worrying for men. A wife's adultery was deeply galling as it was taken as evidence of a husband's lack of sexual dominance, authority, and patriarchal control.[148] In line with this, the consistory also often held men responsible for their wives' actions. In the summer of 1588 Jehanne Saurine, wife of weaver Claude Chambon, and clothes-maker François Deluc were summoned because they had been found together alone at eight o'clock on a Sunday evening and the assumption was that they had had sex. Deluc's excuse—that he had simply been collecting from Saurine some laundry that she had whitened—only served to ensure that he was deprived of the sacrament. Their affair seems likely to have continued, however, as in September there came an alarming report from the neighbours that 'Chambon's wife's lover' had killed a poor woman outside Chambon's house (she had been hit by a stone). Had Deluc perhaps thought that the poor woman would tell on them and taken this drastic step? The consistory's response was to ask the town authorities to exile Chambon and Saurine—not Deluc—from the town. They also barred Chambon from the Eucharist. He subsequently appeared to request reception back into the church and was exhorted 'to think of his conscience and not to conceal such wickedness by his wife'. He was told that if Deluc ever entered his house again all three of them would be charged.[149]

[146] ADG, 42 J 33, 222r; 42 J 34, 26v, 7 Sept. 1607.

[147] ADG, 42 J 35, 99v, 13 Aug. 1614.

[148] Elizabeth A. Foyster, *Manhood in Early Modern England: Honour, Sex and Marriage* (London and New York, 1999), 4–9, 72; Roper, *Holy Household*, 86; Anthony Fletcher, *Gender, Sex and Subordination in England 1500–1800* (New Haven, CT, and London, 1995), 93, 101, 110; Rublack, *Crimes*, 218.

[149] ADG, 42 J 29, 23, 41–2, 57, 131–8 Jun. 1588. Chambon's forename is initially given as Jehan.

In the contemporary view, a wife's adultery was ultimately her husband's fault and responsibility.

Nevertheless, some men reported their wives' adultery, both in an attempt to dissociate themselves from such behaviour and confine moral opprobrium to their wives alone, and from their sheer anger and hurt at the betrayal. Jehan Merle presented himself at the Nîmes consistory in November 1561 stating that 'he wanted to leave his wife because she was a *paillarde*'. His wife said that she had told her husband she had had sex with Estienne de Rodilhan because he had wanted to beat her, but it was not true: she had not committed adultery with de Rodilhan or anyone else. She had two female friends—Donne Bone and Cardeue's wife—who could attest to her having told them this, and consequently the couple were simply told to be reconciled.[150] Given that the stakes were so high, it seems odd that Merle's wife had taunted her husband with the idea that she had slept with another man, but she was not the only one. In December 1587 weaver Anthonye Galary was reported to have 'inflicted beatings upon his wife's body' because his servant had 'outraged and injured him'. He was told to treat her better and promised to live in peace with her from then on, but three months later the justification for his extreme violence became clear—his male servant had been bragging that he had had sex with Galary's wife Suzanne Bonyere, and Bonyere too had told her husband that her servant had 'enjoyed her'. She told the consistory that this was not true, but she had said it because her husband had 'abandoned' her for three months, not 'giving her any help, beating her and mistreating her ordinarily, [and] making her sleep in the cellar... [while her husband slept] in the bed with the servant'. He had also forced her to leave her small child—she does not say where or with whom.[151] The accusation of sexual betrayal, and of a husband's inability to curb his wife's appetite, was so potent that women used it as a final provocation, even when it could only exacerbate their situation.

Men who thought themselves wronged were vehement in their denunciations. A 44-year old lawyer, Jehan Alesti, reported in February 1562 that he had great suspicions of his wife.[152] He related how a week earlier he had asked his daughter where her mother was, and been told that she was at 'Costone's house'. This he doubted, because he had seen her passing Bodet's house in the Bourgade des Precheurs, and then standing outside the house of a weaver called Anthoine Cabane, known (almost exclusively) as *Commessari*. He promptly had gone to Commessari's house and the weaver's wife, who was sitting outside, had closed the door as he approached. He asked her to open up, but she did not want to and he told the consistory that since that day he had been warned that his wife was in that house, behind the closed door, with the scholar Claude Maiffre. He asked the consistory's counsel on how to govern her, but also said that he was not willing 'to endure *paillardise*'.

The irony is that there is a good chance that Alesti's wife was not committing adultery, but the depositions made by Maiffre and Commessari's wife made her

---

[150] BN, Ms.fr. 8666, 45v, 22 Nov. 1561.   [151] ADG, 42 J 28, 333r, 368r, 2 Dec. 1587.
[152] His name, age, and occupation can be learnt from BN, Ms.fr. 8666, 15r, 203v, 209r, 271v.

appear guilty. Alesti's wife said that she had gone to Commessari's house to make some lace and to speak with Maiffre, because she had been told that he had news of her absent son. She admitted that she and Maiffre had left the house by the back door, because Commessari's wife had warned them of Alesti's arrival and they feared her husband's fury. This sounded very plausible but, unfortunately for her, when Commessari's wife was questioned she said that Alesti's wife had come to her house to ask for payment for some shoes that Alesti had sold to her husband and denied knowing who Maiffre was. Urged to tell the truth, she then confessed that Maiffre had been in her house and that he and Alesti's wife had talked alone together for two hours, and that this was not the first time it had happened. Maiffre made matters worse when he was questioned and denied having been alone with Alesti's wife in Commessari's house or having ever spoken to her with news of her son. He and Alesti's wife were consequently brought face to face, when he admitted that they had spoken in the house, sitting on a chest in an upper room, and had left by the back door when Alesti approached. Both denied having had sex, and did so repeatedly: in late March, when it was decided that Maiffre, Alesti's wife, and Commessari would be publicly suspended from the sacrament, Maiffre said that he 'took God as his witness that he had never behaved badly' with her, and Alesti's wife said that she was a good woman. In late May, when Maiffre tried to be reconciled with the church, he was refused because he maintained that 'Alesti's wife was a good woman and not an adulteress'. Unfortunately the contradictory and protean nature of their depositions lent them the appearance of guilt; it is not clear what subsequently occurred between Alesti and his wife.[153]

Other men did not immediately report their wives' behaviour but made sufficient fuss that the attendant gossip sparked an investigation. This happened in June 1604 when Pierre Sannier, known as *Friquenelle*, became convinced that his wife was having an affair with the barber Pierre Brunel. He told the consistory that Brunel had given him fifty *sols* to gather a pile of granite stones from his vineyard and build a small wall, and when part way through the work he needed shade, he had headed to take shelter in the hut in Sieur Forment's vineyard.[154] Near Forment's vines he had found Brunel and his wife, the latter lying on the ground, and it seemed to him that if Brunel had not yet 'enjoyed' her he was about to do so. Sannier got angry at the wrong that Brunel had done him, and although Brunel asked him not to say anything to anyone, Sannier told a goldsmith called Captain Bruant on his way home and seems to have continued to report the story to all and sundry. By July Sannier's wife no longer lived with him, 'ranging', he said, 'now here, now there'. When Brunel appeared in September he denied the charge of adultery and was received into the church, but the damage to Sannier's marriage had already been done.[155]

The husband of a woman called Bugnone discovered his wife with the journeyman Jacques Roche in December 1598. After spending seven or eight hours together

---

[153] BN, Ms.fr. 8666, 77v–80r, 89v, 103v, 116r, 116v, 117v, 28 Feb. 1562.
[154] '*A sortir de sa vigne du gres ung clapas et bastir une petite murallie.*'
[155] ADG, 42 J 32, 237r, 239v, 240r, 242v, 251v, 9 Jun. 1604.

in Bugnone's house, the illicit pair were 'surprised by her husband and several others, around seven o'clock in the evening and [Roche] escaped over the roof', as he later admitted to the consistory. The only reason her husband did not report the affair to the consistory or other officials was that Roche had bribed him, giving him and his friends seven *livres* not to charge him—but the case still reached the consistory, suggesting that either Bugnone's husband or his friends saw fit to disseminate the information more informally. Roche was suspended from the sacrament.[156]

As these responses show, men demonstrated great anxiety about the possibility of their wives' infidelity and displayed a natural suspicion concomitant with their beliefs about female lustfulness. Andre Roc grew convinced that his wife Marie Girarde was having an affair with their male servant in 1602 and threw her out of the marital home. Girarde swore that she had never even thought of such a thing, that she always lived in the fear of God as a good woman, and that her husband was greatly mistaken, but Roc maintained that 'he knew well by many indices' that she was faithless, and refused to take her back despite the consistory's talk of the 'sacred bonds of marriage' and the commands of God's word.[157]

Men testifying before the consistory had often gone to great lengths to corroborate their suspicions. In December 1598 Jammette Rigonelle alerted her son Jean Del Peyron to her suspicions that his wife was committing adultery with their lodger. Rigonelle had noticed that Peyron's wife Anne de Feutrie seemed to be suffering from morning sickness, while Peyron had long been absent from Montauban to avoid his creditors. Peyron was shocked at the allegation and decided to 'test the behaviour and actions of his wife'. He snuck into the house and hid himself behind the bed, where he remained while his wife and the lodger, a scholar called *Le Saige* (meaning 'the wise'; this may be a sobriquet), had breakfast together.[158] He saw Le Saige kiss his wife, leave the house, saying he was going to the College, and come back a few hours later for lunch. Peyron remained in hiding. Now Feutrie and Le Saige again ate together, during which they twice sent the maidservant for oysters, and, according to Peyron, while the girl was absent and after they had eaten, his wife went to urinate, and then 'Le Saige dropped his breeches and his wife put herself against the bed, and lifted the front of her dress, being one against the other'. At this Peyron jumped out from hiding, grabbed both miscreants by the head, and jeered at Le Saige saying, 'Are these the commandments of God that you read daily? You are a *paillard*.' This taunt was presumably a reference to Le Saige's clerical education, although it sounds as if it may have been partially reformulated for the benefit of the consistory. Nevertheless, Peyron's protracted observation of his wife and her lover from a cramped position behind the bed—the very execution of which involved a dangerous visit to the town of his creditors—indicates the profound sexual jealousy and fear of cuckoldry that characterized manhood, a concern that was entirely justified in Peyron's case.

---

[156] ADG, 42 J 31, 254r, 256r, 21 Dec. 1598.   [157] ADG, 42 J 31, 476v, 27 Feb. 1602.

[158] '*Lo dejunar*' is the Occitan equivalent of *le petit déjeuner* (breakfast), while '*lo dinnar*' is the mid day meal.

Predictably, another rich vein of allegations about women's infidelity emanated from neighbours and the surrounding community. The culture of prurient scrutiny that produced these should by now come as no surprise, nor should the fact that those who came forward to offer testimony tacitly claimed a right to interfere in other people's sexual lives and pass judgement on the tell-tale signs that they gathered as evidence.

In April 1589 the story of the adultery of Suzanne Bertrande and butcher Jacques (or Jehan—he is called both) Mingaud reached the consistory first by public report and subsequently, on the basis of neighbourly intelligence, by her husband Loys Ouillier's denunciation. Ouillier said that his wife had called him names (including *pissechaud*, meaning 'gonorrhoetic'), had stolen from him, and had committed adultery: it was said that the previous Sunday Bertrande and Mingaud had spent three hours alone together in Mingaud's sheep-pen (*jasse*).[159] Bertrande was questioned and claimed that the previous Sunday after going to Donne Chabanelle's house to eat she had gone out of town to the *faubourgs*, and had never gone to Mingaud's sheep-pen, nor had she been with him. Baker Jacques Andre was called as a witness and said that 'Guillaume the butcher' had pointed out Ouillier's wife leaving Mingaud's sheep-pen. In response to this Bertrande admitted that she was near the sheep-pen, but claimed that she did not visit, enter, or leave it. The consistory pressed her to tell the truth and in her third variation Bertrande said that Donne Chabanelle had told her that Mingaud would be in his sheep-pen, and that he promised to pay her if she had sex with him, so she had gone there after lunch, when he had 'enjoyed and abused her' for half an hour and had paid her ten *sols*.

At the next consistory a week later, further witnesses were called and the full scale of neighbourly observation, comment, and interposition became clear. Weaver Anthoine Taboul said that he had seen Bertrande at Mingaud's sheep-pen just outside the '*Porte la Boucarie*' (Porte de la Bouquerie), entering at around noon and leaving at 1 or 2 p.m. Guillaume the butcher had pointed them out and had remarked, 'There is a butcher who leads a cow into his sheep-pen without giving a damn!'[160] Taboul said that when he had seen Bertrande leave the pen he had followed her and asked her who she had been with at the pen, and she said that it was Mingaud. Mingaud was summoned and denied it, saying that Taboul was his enemy, as they had quarrelled when Taboul was drunk, implying that Taboul invented the whole story. Mingaud stated that Bertrande only passed by his sheep-pen but did not enter. More witnesses were called. Anne Palhiere said that during the time she learnt to sew at Donne Chabanelle's house she had often seen Mingaud and Bertrande together. Guillaume Ytier, the butcher whom both Andre and Taboul had mentioned, also appeared and said that two weeks earlier, as he watched people play *quills* (bowls) on the wall above the Porte de la Bouquerie, he had seen

---

[159] A *jasse* was a covered shelter for keeping sheep: Marcel Lachiver, *Dictionnaire du Monde Rural: Les mots du passé* (Paris, 1977).

[160] '*Voila ung bouchier que mest dans sa jasse une vache sans [s'en] fichairon.*' An alternative reading would be 'without tying her up', but it makes rather less sense.

'Jacques Mingaud' enter his sheep-pen outside the gate, followed by 'Suzanne, the wife of weaver Loys Ouillier' and they stayed inside for two hours. He too remembered his remark to Taboul and others about a butcher and a cow, but added, with either tact or pointed ignorance, that 'he did not know why they were there'.

At the beginning of September, some four months later, 'Jehan Mingaud' finally appeared before the consistory to confess his adultery with Suzanne Bertrande. He said that he had previously denied it because Bertrande's brother had threatened to kill him. His story was, however, different from hers: he said that Donne Chabanelle was not involved at all, and that he had never met Bertrande at Chabanelle's house. He said that he and Bertrande had had sex twice, both times at his sheep-pen. He asked God's pardon, but when told he would be publicly suspended as an adulterer and rebel against the church, and would only be received back into the church after demonstrating his repentance, he claimed that the consistory was being too severe on him and that he would 'rather endure death' than make the public reparation they demanded. Faced with the full consequences of his actions, Mingaud had subsequently threatened to kill Guillaume Ytier for his part in making their affair known. Two months later Chabanelle appeared and backed up Mingaud's story, claiming not have had anything to do with the affair; she reiterated this twice the following year. It was natural that Chabanelle would deny her part in it, but why Mingaud thought it better not to admit prostitution or why Bertrande thought it better to do so is unclear. It was not until March 1592 that Mingaud finally made public reparation for his sins. Two months after that Loys Ouillier asked the consistory for a copy of the part of the register containing his wife's adultery to present to the consistory at Orange to facilitate his remarriage.[161] What happened to Suzanne Bertrande is less certain: a woman of her name, married to a man called Reymond Cathalan, gave birth to a daughter in January 1614.[162] It was twenty-five years after the event, but it is just possible that it was the same Suzanne Bertrande. The daughter was called Loyse—perhaps in memory of the husband she had betrayed? What is clear is that the voyeurism and interest of neighbours alerted both the wronged husband and the consistory to the affair, with devastating consequences.

This is far from an isolated case. In March 1562 widow Marguerite Velue approached the consistory stating that she had often seen a young journeyman visiting Claude, the wife of cobbler Anthoine Combeter. On several occasions when the couple could not 'do their business' in Combeter's house, they had retired to Estienne Payse's house near by. Velue reported that the neighbours were 'greatly scandalized' by this behaviour, especially as Claude was a member of the Reformed church, and that one, Donne Pierre Tribie, knew the name of Claude's lover. Tribie did: she said that 'as a close neighbour', she had once found a young journeyman-cobbler called Pierre alone in Combeter's house with Claude, which she thought 'a great scandal'.[163]

[161] ADG, 42 J 29, 162–5, 170, 174, 226, 263, 274, 304, 329, 398, 431, 453, 455; ADG, 42 J 30, 52v, 68r, 12 Apr. 1589.
[162] ADG, E Dépôt, 36/698, 380v.   [163] BN, Ms.fr. 8666, 94v–95r, 21 Mar. 1562.

Similarly, in May 1589, Donne Estrugue, wife of the fourth consul, Jean Gril, reported her suspicions about Suzanne, wife of Laurens Bastie, and their lodger, Estienne, who was servant to Sieur Aulras Rainaud. When Bastie was asked what he knew about his wife's alleged adultery he said he knew nothing of it, but he 'held his wife to be a good and honourable woman, who served and honoured him as a wife should her husband'. This did not satisfy Estrugue. Determined to pursue immorality whatever the cost to the Bastie marriage, Estrugue said that she had recently seen Estienne and Suzanne entering the house together, where they remained enclosed for a long time (a story told with little regard for the fact that, as a lodger, Estienne lived there). She also said that one night, when Bastie was in bed asleep, his wife had called out to her lover, 'Estienne, the ass is asleep!' Two other female neighbours were called, and one of them, Sarra, confirmed that she had heard Suzanne at night going to find Estienne in his bed on the ground floor, when Bastie was asleep at the top of the house. Sarra at least had the grace to add that she did not know whether Suzanne and Estienne had 'behaved badly with their bodies'.[164] These cases remind us of the extensive knowledge that people possessed about the lives of their neighbours: they knew every creak of the stairs, whom they entertained, when they went to sleep, when they went out, and when they came in—all indicators that could be used to detect immoral behaviour.

There also appears to have been no sense of shame or being inappropriately invasive of other people's domestic arrangements: all was open to comment and query. When Delains the younger was suspected of having an affair with Anne de la Garrigue, wife of Sieur Bartent de Saincte Grace, in May–June 1597, among those questioned was a 64-year-old widow called Jeanne Roberte, who stated that two years earlier when she had stayed at Garrigue's farm for three weeks, she observed Delains often visiting and when Garrigue's stomach grew swollen and Roberte asked her if she was pregnant, Garrigue said that she was and by Delains.[165] Roberte does not seem to have considered that this information might have been shared confidentially; private blended into public, and the elders of the church found many willing accomplices in the business of moral surveillance and upholding patriarchy. For those who reported others, there was surely something persuasive in the honour and respectability conveyed by being a witness and the drama and prestige of having one's quotidian observations recorded.

In June 1562 many spectators were keen to register testimonies that Catherine Baudane, wife of Remond Dombier, had been unfaithful with a Catholic priest called Estienne Mazoyer from Rodilhan (some 4 miles or 7 km east of Nîmes) and had recently been arrested by the royal judicial officers and imprisoned in the château.[166] Thirty-eight-year-old Loys Solignac said that 'as a neighbour' he knew that 'Master Estienne' normally visited Dombier and Baudane's house, and had done so for four years, at all hours of the day and night, whether Dombier was present

---

[164] ADG, 42 J 29, 189–90, 18 May 1589.
[165] ADTG, I 1, 259v, 261r, 262r, 28 May 1597.
[166] This may have been the same 'Estienne de Rodilhan' that Jehan Merle's wife had taunted him by mentioning, as he is often referred to as such, or 'M. Estienne'.

or not. He added that recently he had seen Mazoyer waiting in the *Chemin de la Coronne* for Dombier to leave the house one morning and as soon as he did Baudane had immediately opened the door to Mazoyer, who was—'to the sorrow of all the neighbours who saw the villainy'—soon after seen sucking Baudane's breasts. Fifty-year-old widow Isabel d'Asperes said that she had heard rumours about the affair for four or five years, and had several times seen Baudane entering Mazoyer's house or him entering hers. Perhaps concerned that these did not seem like sufficiently robust charges, she added that these visits happened both during the day and at night, while Baudane's husband was absent, and at all hours, while she had heard a maid who worked at Mazoyer's house say he and Baudane sang lascivious songs together. Twenty-year-old Isabel Lanteyresse, married to mason Anthoine Cappon, said that ever since she had lived on that road she had heard 'by common noise and public fame' that Baudane behaved badly with Mazoyer, and had seen them acting 'too familiarly' together. Twenty-five-year-old Jehanne Bermonde said that she had seen Baudane make signs to Mazoyer to come to her house in her husband's absence. Twenty-eight-year-old Bernardine Bermonde said that Mazoyer's maid was jealous of Baudane, and so had followed Mazoyer one time when he said he was going to Matins, only to find that he actually went to Baudane's house. Finally, 23-year-old scholar Anthoine Duplan said he had had observed Mazoyer entering Baudane's house between four and five in the morning, quietly pushing the door open without announcing himself, and later that morning heard that her husband had gone to Marguerittes. All the witnesses in this case spoke from a history of observing, noting, and interpreting the smallest actions of their neighbours, and felt entitled to draw conclusions and act on them. In this they did not overestimate the power of their words, which were dignified and given value by the authorities, who welcomed and depended upon such curiosity. It was indeed neighbourly intervention that was responsible for the couple's eventual discovery by the magistrates: after the final affront of the breast-sucking incident, the neighbours had informed a number of women, including Baudane's sister-in-law and the wife of a royal officer, about the affair, and these women had alerted the magistrates, who found Mazoyer hiding upstairs in the servants' room in Baudane's house.[167] Despite this culture of judgement and tittle-tattle, however, it should be noted that these neighbours had also tolerated and tacitly colluded with the adultery for years before it was reported. Perhaps neighbours kept quiet until it became obvious that a scandal was brewing, and then denounced immorality to avoid any attendant blame themselves.

In some instances the testimony of neighbours seems to have been deliberately inflammatory. Marguerite Tortoulhe protested her innocence in the face of her husband's accusation that she was having an affair with mason Michel Candellier. Her husband Mathieu Rogeyron said that one day his daughter told him that she had seen Candellier kissing and embracing her mother. Rogeyron had beaten his wife, forbidden her from seeing Candellier again, and denounced her to the consistory. Enquiries among the neighbours did not help matters. Anthonyete

---

[167] BN, Ms.fr. 8666, 104r, 126r–128r, 187r, 190r, 27 Mar. 1562 (interrogations on 3 Jun. 1562).

Barry and Anthoneye Alyere seem to have taken pleasure in saying how 'notorious' the frequentation was, that Tortoulhe had often been admonished by neighbours but showed no regret, and that Candellier had been found having sex with her in a ditch in the fields near the livestock's watering-hole. They added that Rogeyron had even seen her lying down with a man—an indication that their stories were far-fetched, for not even Rogeyron had claimed this. When Tourtoulhe herself was finally questioned, she explained that Candellier and his wife had lived with them for a time, but she had never had an affair with him. She added that her neighbours suspected her—not because she had done it, she said it was 'evil put against her'— but because she had accused one of her neighbours of a similar crime. Two months later, however, Candellier was still reputed to be her lover and Rogeyron was said to have leprosy.[168]

Tortoulhe's protestation of innocence was the narrative adopted by many women charged with adultery. Like men accused of infidelity, many women stalwartly denied any wrongdoing. In December 1561 Donne Romaine Vallone was under suspicion of having left her husband in Geneva to commit adultery with Arnaud Alizot in Nîmes. Although she confessed that they had spent time together, she maintained that they had not had sex, and claimed that her separation from her former husband was entirely legitimate because he was impotent. The Nîmes consistory wrote to Geneva to find out if the church there could shed light on the situation, but their response was inconclusive. Five months later Vallone appeared before the consistory with a surgeon from Provence, Nicolas Tabys, who could testify why her marriage had ended. Tabys stated that he knew Vallone, her parents, and her husband, and that the latter 'did not have power to know his wife'— but had, nevertheless, remarried. On the strength of this, Romaine asked permission to marry Alizot.[169]

Ysabel Pages, wife of Mathieu Bonaud, presented herself at the consistory in March 1596 after being charged with committing adultery with Provost Besserier, in whose garden she and her husband lived. She said that she 'presented herself at the consistory to purge...the bad rumours' imposed on her. She denied any wrongdoing, although she admitted having visited Besserier's house several times. The elders told her and her husband to change their lodging within a week, but her bold protestation of innocence appears to have persuaded them of her virtue.[170] Both these women took pains to erase the stain of adultery from their reputation.

Catherine Martelle, known as *Sabatierette*, adopted a variation on this approach when she hoped to convince the consistory that her visible pregnancy was not the result of adultery. Her husband, Claude Roux, had been absent from the town for eight years, and Martelle argued in February 1591 that she had been informed of his death. Like Vallone she called on witnesses. Merchant Anthoine Andre, known as *Le Redon*, declared that he knew Roux had left the town in 1583 and had not been seen since, but did not know whether he was dead or alive. Elder Jehan Gril

---

[168] ADG, 42 J 29, 236–7, 243, 281, 13 Aug. 1589.
[169] BN, Ms.fr. 8666, 56v, 109r–v, 158r, 24 Dec. 1561.
[170] ADG, 42 J 31, 36v, 44v, 21 Feb. 1596.

said that he had last seen Martelle's husband eight years ago near Marseille, when Roux had asked Gril how his wife was and said that he wanted to come to see her soon, but he had not returned since. The lack of confirmation of his death was sufficient grounds for the consistory to ordain that Martelle and her fiancé should make reparation for the scandal they had caused, and their licence to marry should be withdrawn from the magistrate. Some days later, however, a sub-committee of elders gathered to consider the matter more fully. This time, they concluded that as Martelle did not give Roux cause to leave and they did not part in strife, as his previous sea-voyages had taken him away for three or four months at most, and as Martelle had shown due diligence in searching for her husband, she should be allowed to re marry—after having done public reparation for her pregnancy.[171] What caused this change of heart is unrecorded, but this conclusion displayed a sensitivity and realistic appraisal of the situation that was sometimes lacking from consistorial decisions.

Denial by the guilty was not always successful. Many people revealed themselves by failing to get their stories straight. This was the case with Catherine Mative and carpenter Gros Jehan ('Big John') in February 1590. When asked why she had entered Gros Jehan's house and been alone with him with the door closed, Mative told the consistory that she had gone there to ask Gros Jehan to come and saw the legs of her bed, which he promised to do if she would wait a while, inviting her inside out of the cold to warm herself by the fire. She declared that she never went to the upper room of his house, but stayed by the fire and chatted with Gros Jehan's daughter when she dropped by. Mative's story, however, did not ring true, because when Gros Jehan was questioned as to why he had been alone with Mative during his wife's absence, he said that Mative had come to buy a bed, had gone to the upper room to look at some for sale, and did not stay by the fire. A month or so later the pair were brought together, and the consistory pointed out with implacable logic that their stories did not match, and that as neither had Gros Jehan sawed the legs of Mative's bed, nor had Mative bought a bed, neither of them could be telling the truth, and there must have been another reason for their being alone together. They were then questioned separately again, but had still not worked out a consistent tale. Mative maintained her line about staying by the fire, but Gros Jehan crumbled and confessed to committing adultery with her just the once, and said he was greatly sorry. Mative was told of his confession and was exhorted to tell the truth, but perhaps finding the challenge of admitting immediately to falsehood too great for her pride, persevered with her version of events. As the scandal of their adultery was not well known—and the consistory determined that it would be more harmful than edifying to publicize the details—Gros Jehan was allowed to make reparation on his knees before the consistory, but Mative's obstinacy meant that the church decided to investigate her life more fully.[172] A significant reason for their failure to hoodwink the consistory was that their narratives were each undermined by the contradictory testimony of the other party.

---

[171] ADG, 42 J 29, 586, 589–90, 598, 603, 30 Jan. 1591.
[172] ADG, 42 J 29, 337, 340, 346, 370–2, 24 Jan. 1590.

There were women who chose to confess their adultery. Loyse Famuere was questioned about why she had invited the male (and Catholic) servant of her neighbour, Sieur Chicard, to stay with her while her husband was out of town and had tried to 'cover her fault' by inviting a maidservant to sleep in the bed too. (The idea of three people having sex never seems to have crossed their minds.) After being admonished at some length to tell the truth, Famuere confessed to having had sex with the servant in the company of the young maid, and asked God's pardon in tears.[173]

For others confession served a practical purpose, such as reconciliation with their husbands when the evidence of guilt was undeniable. Catherine Dossaire, wife of Dimanche Millet, confessed frankly in August 1589 to having committed adultery two years earlier with a weaver called Luc, and declared that they had had a child. She stated that her husband had lived apart from her for three years at that stage, and Luc had promised to take her in marriage because she believed her husband must be dead. But Millet had returned in the summer of 1589 to find a stranger's child in his house. Dossaire was instructed to be reconciled with her husband, 'which he did not want to do'. The consistory's solution to this was to suspend her publicly from the sacrament until she demonstrated evidence of her repentance before the whole church—attempting to heal the breach by helping Millet save face and quashing any gossip by public ownership of the fault.[174]

Several of these women appear to have started an extra-marital affair in circumstances that make their adultery more explicable.[175] Many of their husbands were absent for extended periods of time: Dossaire's husband had been absent for up to three years and she believed him to be dead, Martelle's husband had been away for eight years, Feutrie's husband had left the town four months earlier to avoid his creditors. Similarly, weaver Guillaume Fontanieu was accused in 1590 of visiting by day and night a married woman whose husband was at war.[176]

As with *paillardise*, all these adultery cases demonstrate the circumstances that were viewed as suspicious, and the impact that attitudes towards morality had on social behaviour. Inter-gender friendships were not encouraged or understood outside marriage. Women and men needed a good reason to visit each other's houses unchaperoned, and such adequate and credible reasons were difficult to come by. Being seen after dark in the company of someone of the opposite sex to whom one was not married was especially suspicious. In Ganges in September 1587, Perrine Moutolle was instructed to tell the truth about whether she had received anyone in her house at night, during her husband Guillaume Cause's absence. She said that no one had entered her house, except Pierre Nadal, who came around eight o'clock in the evening. As a result of this admission, she was suspended from the Eucharist.[177] (A decade later the now widowed Moutolle was found guilty of adultery with a married man, but it was not Pierre Nadal.)[178] Similarly, merchant

---

[173] BN, Ms.fr. 8666, 34v–35r, 27 Sept. 1561.   [174] ADG, 42 J 29, 230–1, 6 Aug. 1589.
[175] Rublack, *Crimes*, 214.   [176] ADG, 42 J 29, 327, 10 Jan. 1590.
[177] ADH, GG 24, 9v, 10r, 10 Sept. 1587.
[178] ADH, GG 24, 95r, 97v, 120r, 18 Oct. 1598.

Sieur Pol Delicat was under suspicion of committing adultery with his wife's niece Marguerite Pinette, because he had been seen going to her house 'both night and day at undue hours', and had given Pinette financial assistance. He said that Pinette had been sick with pleurisy and he had supported her in her sickness as 'he was obliged as a relative', and had occasionally visited her and stayed for the evening until 8 or 9 p.m. to pray for her.[179] Ramond Coffinhal was summoned in February 1596 for having been at the lodgings of M. Monge and his wife Dartis at ten o'clock at night; it was assumed that he had been there to commit adultery with Dartis. Coffinhal was affronted by the suggestion and reprimanded the consistory fiercely that he was there only to demand from Monge some money that was owed to him, as he proved by a document to that effect. The consistory, nevertheless, bitterly censured him both for being at the house at a 'nocturnal and suspect hour', and for the audacity of his criticism.[180] In Bédarieux in October 1580, Lyonne Martinne was reprimanded because Jean Arnail, known as *Farettes*, had been found at her house around midnight one night. Both Martinne and Arnail said that he had only been there to speak with her, but the consistory concluded that, because of 'the circumstances of time and place, and, above all, the number of other times he had interacted with her, it was not believable that he went to her house for any other reason but to have sex'.[181]

Conclusions

The ample evidence of adultery and reactions to it in the communities of Languedoc must undermine any suggestion that marital infidelity was not an issue in France, or that neighbours and authorities were not much inclined to regulate sexual morality. The adultery of both married men and women caused community scandal and provoked self-appointed regulation. Incident after incident shows people spying on their neighbours early in the morning or late at night, watching every coming and going, and reporting those thought guilty. The consistory did not need to rely on its elders to learn of the townfolk's immorality: the women and men of Languedoc were willing accomplices in the enforcement of moral justice, eager to have their quotidian observations recorded for posterity.

Both women and men reacted with pain and anger to their spouses' deceit. Women sometimes reported unfaithful husbands to the consistory as a last resort, though this had little positive impact. Otherwise they responded with violence in word—castigatory speech and humiliating discourse—and action, especially towards the 'other woman'. They also drew extensively on their female support network. Nevertheless, many women were faced with little choice but to defend their husbands, whether innocent or patently guilty, using their words to defend as well as undermine their men.

Although blamed for their wives' adultery, husbands still reported it to the consistory or gossiped about it, and women knew that a claim of adultery was

---

[179] ADG, 42 J 33, 95r, 98r, 122r, 150v, 22 Mar. 1606.
[180] ADTG, I 1, 103r–v, 14 Feb. 1596.   [181] AN, TT 234 6, 8v, 9r, 10r, 30 Oct. 1580.

the ultimate provocation. Men showed great and sometimes justifiable anxiety about being cuckolded, and were supported in this by neighbourhood voyeurs. Most people accused of committing adultery understandably claimed to be innocent, while the guilty often revealed themselves with protean stories and inconsistent facts. There must, however, have been many more people who, somehow, despite the watchful eyes of their neighbours, got away with it. If Guillaume Ytier the butcher had not been watching his friends play bowls on the wall of the town, he would never have seen Suzanne Bertrande slip into Mingaud's sheep-pen.

Conclusion

The Languedoc of the sixteenth and early seventeenth centuries was beset with religious warfare, bouts of plague and disease, and years of famine and hardship. The women who lived through this tumultuous time were largely very ordinary women—women who worked as maids, nurses, and market-gardeners; whose husbands were merchants, carpenters, and weavers; and who spent their days baking bread, washing laundry, and looking after children. It was an intensely patriarchal society where the odds were stacked against women conceptually, economically, and legally; they were 'afflicted in every way, but not crushed'.[1] Nor can they now be reduced to neat categories. They were, at times, inventive, sincere, hopeful, desperate, mendacious, persuasive, violent, loving, resourceful, hardy, silent, and deafening. For a brief time, we have glimpsed their lives, and heard snatches of their conversation. What have they told us?

We have learnt that in Languedoc between 1560 and 1615 gender, like religion, was contentious. Although the Reformed consistory was in no way predisposed towards women, its interactions with the women of the towns and cities of Languedoc influenced the operation of gender and patriarchy. This study of women's narratives, mentalities, and behaviour has demonstrated how such women understood and deployed sexual difference, and how they participated in patriarchy. Above all, the records have testified to the gendered culture beyond the consistory: a community of unexceptional women whose power was far from hidden, despite their decreasing power before the law and the decline in female earnings over this period.

This study has argued that the goals of the French Protestant consistory were restoration, unity, reconciliation, and repentance, and that the consistory relied heavily on the voluntary co-operation of the community to achieve these. Membership of the Reformed Church was attractive to many in Languedoc because it conveyed respectability, moral probity, and honour. The Reformation regenerated patriarchy, and the men of the consistory, like everyone in the period, were patriarchal in their outlook. The consistory's interest in punishing and eradicating sexual sin was shared by secular authorities, and in line with contemporary theory the consistory blamed women for that sin. Controlling morality was therefore effectively about controlling women.

Serving on the consistory was a burdensome responsibility, but nevertheless most elders and deacons served more than once. They formed an influential cadre

---

[1] 2 Corinthians 4:8.

of men—a strong body of lay leaders with a shared ethos and mentality. They operated handinglove with the municipal authorities of consuls and council—in fact, most consuls and councillors at some time also served as elders. This stranglehold on governance made the Protestant leaders of these southern French towns uncommonly powerful, as did their interlocking system of support among churches. Yet—as they probably would not have admitted to themselves—sin clung to the members of their church with remarkable persistence, their attempts to eradicate immorality were constantly thwarted, and behavioural change occurred at a sloth-like pace, if at all. The decade-long campaign against women's immodest attire in Nîmes probably ended because the consistory realized the limits of its reach, rather than because women changed their habits and covered up their bodies.

In an unexpected and unintended consequence of Reformed discipline, the existence of the consistory provided a useful mechanism for women of the society to wield against men and against one another. The consistory's interest in women's domestic and sexual lives, and the fact that the existence of the consistory created an environment in which even poor women could have their testimony recorded, mean that the registers are rich in women's narratives about faith, love, marriage, sex, and society.

Firstly, these narratives have led us to recognize women's active engagement with their faith and provided us with new information about how women lived with their religious choices in the early years after the Reformation. We have seen evidence of women's devotion and inculcation of Protestantism, and of their profound attraction to the Reformed Church, especially manifested in an eagerness to re-join the Church after sin or apostasy. There were also those who chose the Protestant Church for social advantage or marital prospects. There were moments—and journeys—of conversion, suggesting that women who chose Protestantism did so with a sense of receiving new identity and purpose, of choosing the truth and acting in the fear of God, and of being moved in their hearts by the Holy Spirit. They never spoke of being part of the elect, but they did talk about being united or reunited with the Church—community was very important in religious choice, as was marriage. Yet, there is also a sense of continuity and mutability in many of the testimonies of apostates, and even these Reformed registers testify to the strong, enduring allegiance of many women to Roman Catholicism. For at least some of those who chose Catholicism, Protestantism repelled for precisely the same reasons for which it has been thought to attract other women: autonomy, Bible-reading, and sermons. Nor did any women mention these as pull-factors: their engagement with their faith was just as much about the heart as the head. The consistorial evidence suggests that narratives of Protestantism's appeal to women have perhaps been too biased by elite attitudes.

It was also not unusual for women to maintain ties to both confessions, resulting in complex and equivocal religious behaviour. The large numbers of mixed marriages suggest that, even in this age of religious war, there was quotidian coexistence, while many tolerant Christians took a flexible view of intermarriage and social intermingling between Protestants and Catholics. There is evidence that some Protestant women attended the Mass out of curiosity, and that others sought spiritual solace there in moments of crisis, danger, or transition. In similar circumstances women turned to popular ritual, magic, and divination. Whether coping with rites of passage or times of family crisis, women sought external aid and guidance beyond the Reformed Church in situations of domestic anxiety, when faced with suffering, sickness, unexpected misfortune, or uncertainty. For most ordinary women even profound Protestant faith did not rule out resorting to alternative sources of revelation. Ordinary women and men also believed in, and were sometimes perturbed by, evidence of magic and bewitchment, but they found a sceptical audience in the Protestant consistory, whose attitude was crucial to halting witchcraft accusations in their tracks and preventing them from becoming prosecutions. Even in the Protestant strongholds of the south of France, there was no version of Protestantism lived out free from vestiges of, incursions from, or interactions with Roman Catholicism and popular heterodoxy. Women in this era, shaped by both Catholic and Reformed theologies, boldly carved out their own spiritual paths and created their own amalgams of old and new.

The consistory's pursuit of morality promoted and tapped into a culture of voyeurism, prurience, nosiness, malice, and even collective fear. The registers contain abundant evidence to indicate that sixteenth- and seventeenth-century women (and to a lesser extent men) policed and regulated each other's sexual behaviour, arrogating a right to define acceptable conduct, and chastising those who failed to meet these standards. Women's role in creating, fomenting, and disseminating gossip and scandal was central to bringing such affairs under communal scrutiny and before the authorities. As many cases before the consistory were based on rumour, this made the consistory paradoxically empowering to the female voice. Women's cathartic or malicious words about others, in their self-appointed role as moral guardians of the community, therefore regulated the sexual and moral behaviour of others in multiple ways. Women also denounced each other directly to the consistory.

There are several reasons why the consistorial registers reveal this aspect of popular culture so fully when other sources have only been able to hint at it, and they are all linked to the nature of the judicial system. Firstly, women could initiate cases in the consistories, and although their words were not always given the same status as those of men, they were recorded and acted upon to a far greater extent than in French secular courts. In addition there were no costs for using the consistory, as there were for other judiciaries or notaries, so a whole swathe of poor women could bring cases against other women and men without paying for the right to do so, as they could not elsewhere. A third important factor was the lack of corporal or capital punishment for those condemned for sexual offences by the consistory; harsh punishments may have deterred people from making denunciations to secular authorities. Shaming punishments, by contrast, were satisfying to the community. Lastly and crucially, the Reformed Church and consistory were voluntary institutions, willingly subscribed to by a minority community and dependent upon community consent. Women's choice to be part of a moral society under authority, and in effect to be recognized as part of the pious community, gave them a serious impetus for denouncing others. These four factors produced increased denunciations by women. Yet it seems likely that the consistory was only providing a formal mechanism for (and in the process empowering and encouraging) an existing culture of female judgement, moral reprimand, and authority. This behaviour was almost certainly a feature of women's lives elsewhere in France, and presumably Europe, but few other sources bring it to light as clearly as the consistorial records.

Evidence of women's gossip, insults, and fights has also revealed a culture of belligerent and foul-mouthed judgement, in which women, above all, brutally assessed the identity and integrity of other women. Women's invective against other women demonstrated a tendency to internalize the aggressor: they attacked other women's capacity to attract sexual feelings and reframed that ability as an insult; they focused on other women's weaknesses as a way of denying their own. In insulting one another, women internally aligned themselves with male persecutors, and their insults were accordingly vicious. Sexual insults—and, indeed, nearly all insults, whether sexual at first glance or not—were *about* sex: they expressed ideas about gender, specifically that a woman's worth was assessed by how she disposed of, and controlled, her body. Most insults used against women were variants of the term *putain*, or whore, or focused on some related aspect of sexual availability. To call someone a whore was to start to think of her as someone who was willing to be abused. Sexual dishonesty was conflated with a lack of control, and sexual misconduct was therefore the subtext of insults relating to drunkenness, animalistic behaviour, gluttony, literal incontinence, excessive violence, and a disorderly household. In their speech women perpetuated the idea that other women were weak because of their lack of control, and continually constructed and reconstructed gender through their discourse. Such thinking created a way of understanding sexual difference and condemned women to ongoing judgement on the very grounds where they felt most vulnerable.

Other sources have been quiet about women and physical violence, if anything suggesting it was rare. The registers in fact demonstrate that women were often both aggressors and victims of violence, and were considerably more vicious, both verbally and physically, than has been previously realized. Neither did any cultural inhibitions exist to deter men from hitting women, and women sometimes hit back, but violence between women was common, especially within families. Pew disputes were chiefly perpetrated by women from the socially anxious classes of the provincial gentry and nobility, while street-fights occurred among women of the lower social ranks, but both were concerned with the questions of what was theirs, what they possessed, and what agency they had a right to exercise. The claustrophobic conditions of urban life, the few material possessions that people owned, and their small spheres of influence and control made both the transgression of boundaries and unwanted intrusion by neighbours bitterly sensitive, and understandably so, as such interference often had at its core a sense of the right to correct perceived immorality. The prerogative to intervene in a neighbour's affairs was therefore contested and quarrels frequently related to the mismanagement of possessions or dependants, household power, sexual relationships with men, areas of authority, or inversions of the gendered social order. The way women challenged one another defined the ideal woman, who was sexually chaste, financially honest, judicious in household management, properly submissive, and responsible. Yet in their behaviour towards one another (and men) ordinary women were often not submissive, but belligerent and confrontational.

To the Protestant authorities they may have seemed this way when it came to marriage, too. There was a marked discrepancy between what the Church understood to be a properly enacted engagement—promises to marry made with free and full consent of the parties (and, to a lesser extent, their parents), in all seriousness, sobriety, and solemnity, in the presence of witnesses—and what was popularly understood to be one—the *donation de corps* ceremony, accompanied by rituals of sharing food and drink, and the exchange of gifts, including rings and ultimately a dowry. For the consistory promises to marry were a verbal contract that could not be broken, but for ordinary women and men they were a gift of oneself that could always be withdrawn. The Church also failed to understand the financial, practical, and psychological importance of the dowry: its absence could retard marriage for years or even vitiate a marriage after solemnization.

Despite changes in French law, the consistorial registers demonstrate that ordinary people prioritized affective, romantic reasons when it came to choosing a spouse. Women expected to be involved in the decision about whom they would marry, and if the men to whom they were engaged were shown to be unfit they considered the decision not to wed to be theirs as well. The grounds upon which women and men rejected their fiancé/es say much about gender ideals. Men scorned women who drank or stole, or were sexually active; women turned down men who threatened to mistreat them or failed to provide for them, and women too considered sexual infidelity sufficient cause to break off a betrothal. The most common reason why women sought to break an engagement was, however, that they simply did not care for their intended—an argument that won little favour with the consistory. Both women and men demonstrated their belief in the revocability of engagement, despite the Protestant Church's firm stance on the immutability of marriage promises. That this was still an area of contention more than thirty years after the Reformed Church was established in France testifies to the fact that Reformation ideals of marriage and sexuality were only adopted with painful slowness, and could at times be hard to detect among the Reformed congregations of Languedoc.

The consistories therefore show something almost entirely obscured by other sources: women choosing not to marry and seeking release from previous promises. These women prioritized their own sense of what was right over the marriages that the consistory sought to enforce. They used religious rhetoric and called on divine authority to support their choice. For ordinary women, the right to flexibility, indecision, and self-correction when it came to choosing their spouse was imperative. The church authorities who regulated their lives did not agree.

Other women, however, whether Protestant or Catholic, quickly discovered how the consistory might serve their own ends when it came to upholding marriage promises made by now-reluctant men. The greater incidence of this before the consistory than other similar bodies seems evident and explicable: the consistory was free of charge. Poor women could take a gamble without incurring the horrendous legal expenses they would face at a judicial court—even when they were not pregnant, and when objectively speaking they had little chance of securing a successful marriage. It is nevertheless very possible that many other women approached equivalent authorities in pursuit of their suits, without leaving any records of their initiative. Low-status women demonstrated phenomenal determination and shrewdness in taking their alleged fiancés to task. To succeed they required proof—eyewitnesses to the actual betrothal ceremony (normally drawn from their family or female peer group) or written evidence of a contract of marriage, or receipts of dowry. Few had such resources, but nevertheless the consistory normally investigated women's claims, and when evidence and contractual arrangements were in place they would pronounce the marriage valid— whether a man or a woman had presented the case: in some instances, the consistory enforced the marriage promises these women claimed. That women could use the consistory in this way was a highly significant achievement in this patriarchal society.

The consistorial records have shown how during the period of engagement many felt that anticipatory sexual relations were entirely justified by their betrothal promises, which inextricably bound a couple to each other under the regulations of the Reformed Church. Sex often served as a step in the process of marriage-formation and could precipitate its solemnization. Society generally accepted pre-marital sexual activity after promises to marry had been exchanged, even if the Church disagreed. Many couples were summoned for the premature births of their children soon after a wedding. The role played by sex in courtship meant, however, that there was scope for deception and false promises. Many women consented to sex under the promise of marriage, but it brought no guarantee of a wedding, and could leave women alone to raise illegitimate children, if the child lived, and dishonour either way.

The registers also, however, demonstrate that much sexual activity occurred outside the context of proceeding towards marriage—a promiscuity that has seldom been illuminated by other sources. It is impossible to state how typical this behaviour was, but it is highly probable that the cases in the registers were the tip of the iceberg. Many of them resulted from the women becoming pregnant, or the couple being caught in the act; quite a lot of illicit sexual activity surely failed to produce children and happened without others noticing it, or choosing to report it. These permutations challenge and complicate our understanding of the sexual culture of the sixteenth and seventeenth centuries.

So too does the fact that cohabitation of unmarried (though nearly always engaged) couples does not appear to have been particularly exceptional. Such socially recognized pre-nuptial cohabitation sometimes continued for many years, and children were born into it. There are also a few examples of unmarried and unengaged partners living as man and wife. This was not a function of blurred boundaries between engagement and marriage: there was a clear demarcation in people's minds between what it meant to be engaged and what it meant to be married, but sexual practice did not necessarily follow this distinction. The evidence suggests that after engagement, sex and sexually active cohabitation were not infrequent and clearly socially acceptable among parts of society. These attitudes seem likely to have pre-dated the Reformation and their continuation shows again that popular sexual and marital behaviour did not change quickly, despite the pressure of Protestant authorities. This is not to suggest that everyone felt this way: many of the cases came to the consistory's attention because neighbours were willing accomplices in the business of moral surveillance. Nevertheless the evidence of the consistorial registers demands a re-thinking of the nature of sexual relations in this society.

The cases before the consistory also give access to instances of unprosecuted sexual assault that lie beyond the legal statistics, and in which complainants were undeterred by daunting criminal penalties. This evidence suggests that sexual assault may well have been a normal feature of sixteenth- and seventeenth-century French life, and that most of the predators were far less marginal and far more rooted in patriarchy than previous studies suggest. Most women were attacked or seduced by men they knew; many of the cases involved female servants and their male employers, the employer's relatives, or male servants, in situations of domestic sexual exploitation. Such men had the occasion and means to intimidate maidservants into compliance, through a combination of constant presence, harassment, persuasion, and physical force. Young female servants were especially vulnerable to such attacks, because they were poor, unmarried, and were not thought to 'belong' to any other man; they had often travelled to the cities for work and so lacked a local support network; and they were constantly in the orbit of predatory men. Many young women must have lived in a suffocating atmosphere of fear. It has been important to recognize that physical force could be accompanied by the carrot (persuasion and promises) as well as the stick (threats and coercion). Women may have appeared to consent in circumstances where their psychological and physical scope to refuse consent was severely limited. It was assumed by the consistory (and many others involved) that the victim must always have behaved seductively, and indeed because pregnancy was thought only to result from a female sexual climax, women's willing participation could be read off their bodies. As a result the consistory censured the women in these situations, but the men were accorded relative impunity, and so the power relations that had permitted sexual assault in the first place were upheld. In responding to such treatment women sought ways to negotiate their circumstances and direct their destinies. They could choose to stay silent or to disclose the affair to their mistress, neighbours, or the authorities. Although speech could be an opportunity to discharge one's conscience, express one's feelings, and have one's testimony recognized, both strategies ultimately shared the same central goal: the provision of resources to help them cope with their distressing circumstances. Women were vulnerable, but their responses to sexual assault were far from passive. Finally, on rare occasions there also seem to have been fully consensual and affectionate relationships between servants and their employers, and it is important to recognize these as well.

Finally, the consistorial registers have borne witness to quarrels and violence between married couples, and incidents of adultery. Couples were called before the consistory when their arguments became public, so these cases give us unusual insight into the circumstances and causes of conjugal disagreements. The consistories had little excuse for their frequent failures to admit that marital conflict, alongside decisions not to marry someone, had at its heart a spouse's failure to fulfil gender ideals and marital roles. Women complained about their husbands' violence, lack of provision, alcohol consumption, and adultery. Men's complaints centred on disobedience and disrespect, a wife's poor housekeeping or service, absences from the marital home without permission, adultery, and hurtful words, with occasional added charges of physical violence, excessive alcohol consumption, and complications with in-laws. Women compared their husbands to patriarchal ideals of masculinity, just as men used ideals of womanhood to castigate their wives. Faced with marital conflict, many women simply chose to endure the situation; others expressed their grievances through publicly voiced insult; some fled. The cases have shown that women did abandon their husbands, and that separations, without recourse to law and at risk of becoming semi-permanent, were the unofficial answer to marital strife.

Violence by husbands against wives was not uncommon. Corporal discipline of wives was commonly expected and permitted if in private and for good cause and, although the consistory recognized it to be a sin, their approach tended towards pacification and papering over the cracks. In so doing they expressed a broader societal ambivalence towards physical disciplining. Battered women themselves made few complaints to the consistory, and the response they received demonstrates why. The consistory showed very limited sympathy towards abused women: husbands charged with mere marital violence received a summons and verbal censure at worst. Men were neither suspended nor referred to the magistrates merely for beating their wives, and recidivists appear not to have been punished any more severely than first-time offenders. Men justified their behaviour on the grounds of impertinence, disrespect, or a lack of attention, although much violence actually occurred in the context of drunkenness, and in compensation for (and projection of) men's own misdeeds.

Neighbours only rarely intervened to stop marital violence, but they did talk directly to offenders, gossip about its occurrence, and report it to the elders. Most cases emerged in the registers because of public concern: the consistorial cases show, therefore, the limits of public toleration towards domestic discipline and the socially determined boundaries of such violence. Popular opinion quickly became vocal when violence was too brutal or extreme, too frequent, in public, or administered while drunk. This behaviour was unacceptable because it was unreasonable and unmeasured.

Male adultery also did not go unobserved by neighbours. It is through eyewitness reports and denunciations, as well as gossip, that many instances of adultery by men were made known to the church, while otherwise men's adultery came to light through the testimony of their wives. Betrayed wives expressed their sadness and anger through public speech and violent action. There is strong evidence of women using female networks to denounce, discredit, and humiliate their abusive or adulterous husbands through castigatory speech. More destructive than constructive, this tactic was seldom wholly profitable, but such activism is testament to women's attempts to achieve revenge and redress outside the consistory. Yet other wives chose to use their voices in defence of their husbands, presenting a united front that maintained their husbands' innocence even when they knew that to be untrue, and even women who initially responded actively and aggressively later chose restorative silence and marital appeasement. The reactions of women faced with a husband's adultery were frequently strategic and ingenious.

Cuckoldry was a source of deep anxiety for men. The accusation of sexual betrayal, and of a husband's inability to curb his wife's appetite, was so potent that women used it as a final provocation in arguments, even when it could only exacerbate their situation. Men who thought themselves wronged were vehement in their denunciations, and men testifying before the consistory had often gone to great lengths to corroborate their suspicions. Others who did not report their wives' behaviour made enough noise for public rumour and gossip to force an investigation. Another rich vein of allegations about women's adultery came from neighbours and the surrounding community. These denunciations reveal the depth of knowledge that people possessed about the lives of their neighbours and the impact that attitudes towards morality had on social behaviour. Inter-gender friendships were not encouraged. Men and woman came under suspicion if they spent time alone together, especially if they did so behind closed doors, even though houses often served as workshops. Being together very early in the morning or late at night made innocent explanations less plausible. Reporting the behaviour of one's neighbours apparently occasioned no sense of shame, and played instead into the culture of judgement, which saw the community participate in the business of moral justice and self-appointed regulation. Nevertheless, neighbours also tolerated and colluded with adultery, sometimes for years, suggesting that they may only have denounced illicit sex when it became sufficiently scandalous that a failure to condemn it might have reflected badly on them.

Overall, then, there are two main findings from this study. The first concerns women's agency and power. The Reformed Church inadvertently created a mechanism that women could use to their benefit, and so the consistorial registers testify to women's agency and resourcefulness, whether pursuing revenge and redress for wrongs done to them or in their eclectic approaches to religion, whether using Reformed institutions, or through their local social networks. The registers provide a more substantial picture of women's strategies than other sources have been able to do, with evidence that is sustained and voluminous. This is chiefly because the consistory was the ideal environment for women to initiate cases, seek redress or denounce others, while consistorial evidence also allows us to glimpse the workings of similar processes outside the judicial or ecclesiastical systems. These cases have made it clear that the ability to protest authority was not dependent upon status. Ordinary women could exercise power, and it seems that a previous historiographical skew towards elites and structures, using evidence from courts where it cost money to sue, has obscured this. There were many opportunities for poor women to take action in Languedoc in the sixteenth and seventeenth centuries, and undoubtedly elsewhere too.

This helps us think about the nature of female power. Barbara Diefendorf suggested that women exercised private power to compensate for public powerlessness. Natalie Zemon Davis portrayed the wife of Martin Guerre, Bertrande de Rols, as deviously manipulative and 'self-fashioning', 'using all the leeway and imagination she had as a woman', or as Robert Finlay summarized Davis's conclusions, 'an instance of the ingenuity and calculation commonly shown by peasant women who must manoeuvre within a patriarchal system'.[2] Other historians concurred with this portrayal, emphasizing women's tendency to conform outwardly through obedience and submission, but secretly to dissemble, manipulate, shirk, malinger, mock, and criticize men, and in other ways conspire with female allies to 'camouflage their non-compliance'. The consistorial registers demonstrate that women did indeed display independence, ingenuity, and imagination; they were often skilful manipulators and were aware of strategic possibilities. Invisible patterns of influence are seen in the way their speech shaped consistorial investigations, their resistance in how they gossiped with their friends about their husbands' failings, and outward submission in how they complied with the consistory in pursuit of their goals. Yet it is wrong to contrast public and private power, and ascribe to women only this silent, devious, and manipulative influence. The women found in these pages also displayed an activism that was bold, public, and vocal. Urban women living at the same time as Bertrande de Rols assumed great direct power and demonstrated this in the streets. Their suits were not always successful, but they continued to agitate for what they wanted, and were a voluble and obvious presence in urban society. These women were not exceptional: it is simply that the nature of the consistorial records and the narratives contained within them bring women's agency into sharper focus than other sources have been able to do.

The second major finding of this study is that patriarchy was not exactly 'contested' by women: they challenged patriarchy, but also entirely adopted it. Patriarchy itself needs to be reconceived in the light of the consistorial evidence. It has emerged that the successful maintenance of patriarchy rested both on women's firm commitment to gender ideals within a gendered, social hierarchy, and on their agency: their aggressive pursuit of other women, their tendency to report misdemeanours and gossip about immorality, and their defamation of unworthy men. This illustrates perfectly Bennett's dictum about women simultaneously being victims and agents.[3] Female strategies for resisting authorities supported the patriarchal order on which authorities' power rested. Women's ways of challenging patriarchy and colluding with patriarchy were often indistinguishable. Challenge and collusion collided: in maidservants reporting their masters' unwanted sexual advances by using the consistory; the wives of adulterous husbands spreading defamatory rumour among their female networks to humiliate their husbands into fidelity; and the importance of a man's conformation to male gender

---

[2] Natalie Zemon Davis, *The Return of Martin Guerre* (Cambridge, MA, and London, 1983), 60, 118, 28; Robert Finlay, 'The Refashioning of Martin Guerre', *American Historical Review* 93.3 (1988), 553–71, here 556.

[3] Judith M. Bennett, 'Feminism and History', *Gender and History* 1 (1989), 251–72, here 262.

ideals in determining whether a woman wanted to marry him or stay married to him. Above all, women colluded as accomplices in surveillance by appointing themselves as moral guardians (appropriating the role of male elders) and contributing to a culture of scrutiny. They colluded by defaming one another in ways that persecuted other women for the very aspects of their nature that they feared, by perpetrating the ideas that women were weak, lacked control, and were willing to be abused, and by requiring each other to conform to contemporary female ideals—seeking in each other the 'humility and modesty' the consistory required even as they themselves acted immodestly and proudly, asserting their right to judge. In the context of late sixteenth- and early seventeenth-century France, when women were under tremendous pressure—with war bringing incursions and taking away husbands, economic hardship creating extensive female pauperization, increasing legal restrictions on women's rights, contemporary ideas about women's propensity for sin, pressure to shift religious and social allegiances, and the continual interrogation of their behaviour—it was actually women who increased the pressure on one another.

Finally, therefore, this work helps us to understand the impact of the Reformation on women. Gender was central to the Reformation not because there were radical new ideas about the position of women or new ways of relating between the sexes—cultural change was glacial and popular attitudes about the social order, sexuality, and marriage were, in the short term, practically unchanged by Reformed moral codes—but because the pattern of challenge and response in interactions between the Reformed institutions and ordinary women enabled and shaped both women's agency and patriarchy. What the consistorial registers give us is an unrivalled snapshot of how gender evolved in the torrid years of the early French Reformation, and the distant echoes of the voices of women who lived four hundred years ago.

APPENDIX I

Glossary: Occitan, Patois, and Early Modern French Terms

Legend	
ADJ.	Adjective
NF	Feminine noun
NM	Masculine noun
O	Occitan
pl.	Plural
V	Verb

abeurador (abeuradoux)	**O NM** watering-place for livestock
amende/amande honorable	**NF** public apology and reparation after a crime, with torch in hand and a rope around the offender's neck
aguèsse	**O V** (he/she) would have/had—third-person imperfect subjunctive of *aver* (to have)
aqueste/acqueste	**O** this one
aquò	**O** this
arliquyne	**NF** harlequin, inconsequential person
aree (arrè!)	**O** stop! (used for stopping cattle, animals)
assemblar	**O V** to join
aurio (auriái)	**O V** (I) would/will have—first-person present conditional of *aver* (to have)
bagasse	**NF** baggage, slut, flirt, strumpet, whore
banard	**NM** convict, criminal
bane (banet, banèl)	**O NF** small horns (of a goat or sheep)
baume	**O NF** grotto or troglodyte dwelling
bavard	**ADJ.** vain
becquet (bequet)	**NM** beak
bellitre (bélitre)	**NM** good-for-nothing cad, rascal, worthless person
bòria	**O NF** farm
botefeur	**O V** to get puffed up—from *botenflar, bodenflar, bodenfle*
botelha	**O NF** bottle
brocquier/brocquière	**NM/NF** wood-worker

cache-bastard (-bâtard)	NF 'bastard-hider', farthingale
cambajon	O NM ham
caler	O V to need to
camuse/camuze	ADJ. flat-nosed
canebièra (canebière)	O NF hemp field
capitèl (capitelle)	O NM/F hut (in a vineyard), often equipped with a tank
cascavèl	O NM small, spherical bell
castèlnau	O NM new castle
causa	O NF object, thing, matter
charoupper	NF good-for-nothing
clapàs	O NM pile of stones
coullaretz (colaret/collerette)	NF collar, ruff (*colaret* in Occitan)
commère	NF originally godmother; later, gossip, chatterbox
commère des fesses	NF 'buttock-gossip', one who enabled sexual sin
commun bruict (bruit)	NM 'common noise', rumour, gossip
coquin, coquine	NM knave, rascal NF loose woman, strumpet
coursilhon/corsilhon/coursillon/	
corsillon	O NF small corset/bodice/camisole
coyoul	NM coward, scoundrel—from *coyon*
crotte	NF hole, ditch, den, cave, midden
cruvell	O NM circular sieve mesh to sift grains
dejunar	O NM breakfast
dinnar	O NM lunch/dinner (meal at midday)
donation de corps	NF formal engagement ceremony in which the couple promised to 'give their bodies' to each other
dròlle	O NM/NF child
eau ardant	NF home-made alcoholic spirit, aqua vita
embraçar	O V to kiss
embriagar	O V to get drunk, inebriated
embriague	O ADJ. drunk
escarrabilhar	O V to perk or buck up, to waken, to warm up, to tantalize or titillate
espasier	O NM armourer (from *espasa*, sword)
fachilhièra, fachilièra, fachillière	O NF witch
fach	O NM fact (as noun), V done—past participle of *fàser* (to do, make)
faubourgs	NM suburbs

faudilh (faudalz)	O NM small apron
feneant	NM idle do-nothing, lazybones
figaret	O NF (from *figa*, fig-tree) a place planted with fig-trees, or a type of chestnut
filha	O NF young girl, daughter
filhòl	O NM baptism, godson, godchild
foet	NM whip, scourge
fogasse	O NF flatbread (like focaccia)
fouger	O V to stir up ordure
fraire	O NM brother, elder
frippon/fripon	NM a ragged or tattered rascal, an unworthy fellow, given to base tricks, rogue, knave
friponnerie	NF prank, mischief
gal	O NM cock, cockerel
ganivet	NM a little pen-knife
gounelles (gonnelles)	NF **pl.** petticoats in which the bodies and skirts are attached to each other
gres	O NM granite
grollier	NM cobbler
jamai	O never
jarretière	NF garter
jasse	NF a covered shelter for keeping sheep
Jean/Jehan, Saint	NF annual feast day and festival of Saint John or Midsummer's Day (24 June)
ladre	O NM leper, **ADJ.** leprous
lheste (lhesta)	O N choice, election
Madgaleine/Madeleine, Saint	NF annual feast day and festival of Saint Mary Magdalene (22 July)
mai/may	O more, further
manesfle (manèfle/maneffle)	O **ADJ.** fawning, smarmy, toadying, sycophantic NM/NF toady, flatterer, sycophant
mange galimes	NM glutton
maquerelle	NF bawd, pimp, panderer
marchepied	NM step, footboard
marit	O NM husband
mas	O NM farm
masque	NF witch
Michel, Saint	NF Michaelmas—annual feast day and festival of Saint Michael (29 September)

mort de fain (faim)	**ADJ.** half-starved ['dead from hunger']
paillardise	**NF** fornication
paillard/e	**NM/NF** fornicator, slut
parrucque/perruque (pauraugues)	**NF** hairpiece, wig
passarilhas	**O NF pl.** raisins, dried cherries
passadoire/passadoira/passador	**O NM** sieve
patous (patofle)	**O ADJ.** plump, fat, chubby
patrenotres	**NM pl.** paternosters—devotional beads
pellisou/pellison	**N** bolero jacket
pensar	**O V** to think
petague	*Uncertain—probably either:*
	from petat **O V**—to be drunk, sloshed
	from petega **O**—ADJ. panic-stricken
	from pet **O NM**—a fart
peulions (peulhós)	**O NM** louse
pezollouer	**O ADJ.** lice-ridden—from *pezouille, pesoulh, pou*
pisse (au lit)	**V** urinates (in bed)
pissechaud (pisse-chaude)	**NF** gonorrhoea, gonorrhoetic (literally, 'hot piss')
pòder	**O V** to be able to
prat	**O NM** meadow
prensa	**O NF** pregnancy
prens	**O ADJ.** pregnant
prestidou (prestidor)	**O NM** kneading trough, boulting tub, or room to boult meal in
pute	**NF** whore, prostitute
putain de foire	**NF** shitty/diarrhoeic whore
putain maquerelle	**NF** bawd/procurer for prostitutes
putina	**NF** whore/prostitute
radelle	**O NM** raft, or timber boat
reballade	**O NF** slut, whore, prostitute—from *rebalar*
ròisser (ròguer)	**O V** to eat
rouvière	**O** where the oak grows
saume/sauma	**O NF** she-ass
sios (sísa)	**O V** be/are—second-person present subjunctive of *eser* (to be)
soire, soyre, soira	**O NF** old female dog, bitch
sorcyere	**NF** witch
sot	**NM** fool, drunk

sotte bauge	**NM** wallowing fool, drunk
talhans	**O NM pl.** tailors' scissors
tigne	**NF** scurvy
trainee	**NF** prostitute
transportade	**NM** slave, criminal
veillées	**NF pl.** spinning bees
vielh	**O NM** old man, **ADJ.** old
villaine	**ADJ.** ugly/wicked/coarse
voler	**O V** to want
yvrogne (ivrogne), yvre (ivre)	**ADJ.** drunk

APPENDIX II

Chronological Conspectus

The conspectus lists every one of 1,210 cases on which this study has been based in date order. Each case is designated by a category, identified by town and participants, and cited with full archival references, to assist future scholars. It can be found online at: <http:// suzannahlipscomb.com/the-voices-of-nimes-chronological-conspectus/>.

Bibliography

MANUSCRIPTS AND ARCHIVAL SOURCES

Bibliothèque de l'Arsenal, Paris

Ms 6559 Livre du concistoire de Coutras (Gironde), 1581–92

Ms 6560 Papier du consistoire de l'eglise réformée de Coutras (Gironde), 1603–21

Ms 6563 Actes du consistoire de l'église chrestienne et réformée de Jésus Christ du Pont de Camarez (Camarès, Aveyron), 1574–5

Ms 6563 Les actes du consistoire de l'église chrestienne et réformée de Jésus Christ du Pont de Camarez (Camarès, Aveyron), 1576–8

Ms 10434 Registres des délibérations de L'église Réformée de Pont-de-Camarès (Camarès, Aveyron), 1580–96

Ms 10434 Registres des délibérations du consistoire de Saint-André-de-Sangonis (Hérault), 1585–1602

Bibliothèque nationale de France, Paris

Ms.fr. 8666 Registre de deliberations du consistoire de l'église réformée de Nîmes. Registre du consictoire de l'église chrestienne de la ville de Nismes (Gard), 1561–2

Ms.fr. 8667 Le livre du consistoire de l'esglise reformée de Nismes (Gard), 1578–83

Bibliothèque de la Société de l'Histoire du Protestantisme Français, Paris

Ms 5 Livre du consistoire de l'esglize réformée de St. Jean du Bruel (Aveyron), 1615–24

Ms 453 Registre des délibérations du concistoire de Meyrueis (Lozère), 1587–92

Ms 566 Synodes provinciaux du Bas Languedoc, 1561–82, copy made by Pasteur Louis Auzières, 1876–8

Ms 817/1 Registre du consistoire de Montauban (Tarn-et-Garonne), 1595–8, copy made in the nineteenth–twentieth centuries by Capitaine Rey-Lescure and H. Aubert

Archives nationales, Paris

TT 234 6 Registre des batêmes, marriages de sepultre & de lieu de Bédarieux (Hérault), 1574–1622

TT 234 6 Registre de consistoire de l'église réformée de Bédarieux (Hérault), 1579–86

TT 235 16 Registre du consistoire de l'église réformée de Boissezon (Tarn), 1570–94

TT 241 2 Registres du consistoire de l'église réformée de Chizé (Deux-Sèvres), 1598–1663

TT 241 12 Livre du consistoire de l'église réformée de Codognan (Gard), 1607–16

TT 250 1 Registre de baptemes et de mariages, Loudun (Vienne), 1566–82

TT 250 2 Registre du concistoire de l'église réformée de Loudun (Vienne), 1589–91, 1591–4

TT 252 5 Livre du consistoire du Mas de Verdun ou Granier (Mas-Grenier, Tarn-et-Garonne), 1590–5

TT 275ᴬ 15 bis Livres des actes du consistoire de l'église de Verteuil (Verteuil-sur-Charente, Charente), 1576–81

TT 275ᴬ 12 Papier du consistoire de l'église réformée de Verteuil (Verteuil-sur-Charente, Charente), 1581–93

TT 275ᴬ 16 Registre des Concistoires de églizes réformées de Verteuil et Ruffec (Verteuil-sur-Charente, Charente), 1601–7

Archives départementales du Gard, Nîmes

B 113 Registres du conseil, civil (Nimes) 1560–1

B 121 Registres du conseil, civil (Nimes), 1577–82

B 211 Registres du conseil, criminel (Nimes), 1606–9

B 212 Senechausee juge criminel 1610

I1 Consistoire d'Alès, délibérations (Alès, Gard), 1599–1601

I2 Consistoire d'Alès, délibérations (Alès, Gard), 1600–2

I2 Consistoire d'Alès, délibérations (Gard), 1602–12

42 J 26 Registre de délibérations du consistoire de l'église réformée de Nîmes (Gard), 1561–3, copy made in nineteenth century of Ms.fr. 8666, Bibliothèque Nationale, Paris, by Pasteur Louis Auzières

42 J 27 Registre de délibérations du consistoire de l'église réformée de Nîmes (Gard), 1578–83, copy made in nineteenth century of Ms.fr. 8667, Bibliothèque Nationale, Paris, by Pasteur Louis Auzières

42 J 28 Registre de délibérations du consistoire de l'église réformée de Nîmes (Gard), 1583–8

42 J 29 Registre de délibérations du consistoire de l'église réformée de Nîmes (Gard), 1588–91

42 J 30 Registre de délibérations du consistoire de l'église réformée de Nîmes (Gard), 1591–5

42 J 31 Registre de délibérations du consistoire de l'église réformée de Nîmes (Gard), 1595–1602

42 J 32 Registre de délibérations du consistoire de l'église réformée de Nîmes (Gard), 1602–4

42 J 33 Registre de délibérations du consistoire de l'église réformée de Nîmes (Gard), 1604–8

42 J 34 Registre de délibérations du consistoire de l'église réformée de Nîmes (Gard), 1608–13

42 J 35 Registre de délibérations du consistoire de l'église réformée de Nîmes (Gard), 1613–19

42 J 7 Actes des synods provinciaux de Bas-Languedoc, 1596–1609

Archives notariales

(Deposited at the Archives départementales du Gard)

2 E 1/271–308 Jean Ursi le Jeune, 1582–1610

2 E 36/556–62 Michel Ursi, 1595–1602

2 E 1/315–29 Jean Corniaret, 1591–1615

2 E 1/336–60 Marcelin Bruguier, 1591–6, 1608–15

2 E 1/270 Robert Restaurand, 1580–2

2 E 1/250–67 Jacques Ursi, 1561–79

2 E 1/268 Jean Mombel, 1560–82

2 E 1/368–74 Jean Guiran, 1594–1615

Archives communales de Nîmes

(Deposited at the Archives départementales du Gard)

E Dépôt 36/17 Troubles religieux à Nîmes, du XIIIe au XVIIe siècle, pardons et rémissions accordés par le Roi à ce sujet, 1562–83

E Dépôt 36/18 Troubles religieux à Nîmes, du XIIIe au XVIIe siècle, pardons et rémissions accordés par le Roi à ce sujet, 1585–1652

E Dépôt 36/38 Police de la ville et du territoire de Nîmes, 1541–72

E Dépôt 36/39 Police de la ville et du territoire de Nîmes, 1586–1612
E Dépôt 36/40 Livres et Registres des actes politiques de la maison conseillier de Nismes, 1613–21
E Dépôt 36/84 Acts et contrats de la ville, livre des contracts et arrentementz, 1561–80
E Dépôt 36/127 Administration communale, 1554–64
E Dépôt 36/128 Administration communale, 1563–70
E Dépôt 36/129 Administration communale, 1571–5
E Dépôt 36/130 Administration communale, 1576–85
E Dépôt 36/131 Administration communale, 1586–93
E Dépôt 36/132 Administration communale, 1594–5
E Dépôt 36/133 Administration communale, 1599–1604
E Dépôt 36/134 Déliberations du conseil, 1604–8
E Dépôt 36/135 Déliberations du conseil, 1609–12
E Dépôt 36/136 Déliberations du conseil, 1612–20
E Dépôt 36/433 Compoix terriers, 1544
E Dépôt 36/434 Compoix terriers, 1596
E Dépôt 36/490 Comptes des deniers municipaux et extraordinaries, 1564–79
E Dépôt 36/491 Comptes des deniers municipaux et extraordinaries, 1600–11
E Dépôt 36/492 Comptes des deniers municipaux et extraordinaries, 1612–26
E Dépôt 36/606 Registre de baptêmes, mariages et décès (catholique)
E Dépôt 36/696 Registre de baptêmes protestants (Nîmes, Gard), 1571–84
E Dépôt 36/697 Registre de baptêmes et mariages protestants (Nîmes, Gard), 1585–1602
E Dépôt 36/698 Registre de baptêmes et mariages protestants (Nîmes, Gard), 1602–16

Archives communales d'Aimargues
(Deposited at the Archives départementales du Gard)
E Dépôt GG30 Registre du consistoire d'Aimargues (Gard), 1584–91
E Dépôt GG54 Livre des délibérations du consistoire d'Aimargues (Gard), 1593–1601

Archives départementales de l'Hérault
Archives communales de Ganges
(Deposited at the Archives départementales de l'Hérault)
E Dépôt GG24 Actes du consistoire de Ganges (Hérault), 1588–1603 [says 1609, but actually ends January 1603]

Archives départementales du Tarn-et-Garonne
I 1 Registre du consistoire de Montauban, 1595–8

Archives communales de Montauban
(Deposited at the Archives départementales de Tarn-et-Garonne)
5 FF 2 Registre des sentences prononcees en matiere criminelle par les Consuls de la Ville de Montauban de 1534 a 1606
2 BB 29 Registre des deliberations consulaire de Montauban, 1595

Bibliothèque de l'Eglise Réformée de Nîmes
Copies made in the nineteenth century (1866–75) by Pasteur Louis Auzières of the originals at ADG.
8604 A Registre de délibérations du consistoire de l'église réformée de Nîmes (Gard), 1561–3
8604 D Registre de délibérations du consistoire de l'église réformée de Nîmes (Gard), 1578–83

8604 B Registre de délibérations du consistoire de l'église réformée de Nîmes (Gard), 1583–8

8604 C Registre de délibérations du consistoire de l'église réformée de Nîmes (Gard), 1588–91

8604 E Registre de délibérations du consistoire de l'église réformée de Nîmes (Gard), 1591–5

8604 F Registre de délibérations du consistoire de l'église réformée de Nîmes (Gard), 1595–1602

8604 G Registre de délibérations du consistoire de l'église réformée de Nîmes (Gard), 1602–4

8604 H Registre de délibérations du consistoire de l'église réformée de Nîmes (Gard), 1604–8

8604 I Registre de délibérations du consistoire de l'église réformée de Nîmes (Gard), 1608–13

8604 J Registre de délibérations du consistoire de l'église réformée de Nîmes (Gard), 1613–19

(N.B. These were originally classified under the codes B91 1–13.)

No code *Oeuvres des pasteurs de l'église de Nîmes* (List of pastors 1559–1896)

PRINTED PRIMARY SOURCES

Amyraut, Moyse, *La morale Chrestienne à Monsieur Villarnovl* (Saumur, 1654)

Anjubault, M. M. and H. Chardon (eds), *Papier et Registre du Concistoire de l'Eglise du Mans, réformée selon l'évangile, 1560–1561 (1561–1562 nouveau style)*, in *Recueil de pièces inédites pour servir à l'histoire de la Réforme et de la Ligue dans le Maine* (Le Mans, 1867)

Aymon, Jean, *Tous les synods nationaux des Églises réformées de France*, 2 vols (The Hague, 1710)

Histoire ecclésiastique des Eglises Réformées au Royaume de France, ed. G. Baum and E. Cunitz, 3 vols (Paris, 1883–9)

Calvin: Theological Treatises, trans. Rev. J. K. S. Reid (London, 1954)

Calvin, John, *The Institutes of the Christian Religion*, trans. Henry Beveridge (London, 1957)

Calvin, John, *1 Corinthians*, trans. and ed. John W. Fraser, David W. Torrance, and Thomas F. Torrance (Michigan, 1960)

Calvin, John, *The Epistles of Paul the Apostle to the Galatians, Ephesians, Philippians and Colossians*, trans. and ed. T. H. L. Parker, David W. Torrance, and Thomas F. Torrance (Michigan, 1965)

Letters of John Calvin: Selected from the Bonnet Edition with an Introductory Biographical Sketch (ed. anon.) (Edinburgh, 1980, first published 1855–7)

Calvin, John, *1, 2 Timothy and Titus*, ed. Alister McGrath and J. I. Packer, (Illinois, 1998)

Calvin, John, *Genesis*, ed. Alister McGrath and J. I. Packer, (Illinois, 2001)

Calvin, Jean, *Institution de la Religion chrétienne*, ed. Jacques Pannier, 4 vols (Paris, 1936–9)

Calvin, Jean, *Sermons sur la Genèse Chapitres 1, 1–11, 4*, ed. Max Engammare (Neukirchen-Vluyn, 2000)

Camerarius, Philippe, *Les meditations historiques* (Paris, 1608)

Drelincourt, Charles, *Recueil de sermons sur divers passages de l'Escriture saincte* vol. 1 (Geneva and Tournes, 1658–64)

Falloppio, Gabriele, *Observationes anatomicae* (Venice, 1561)

Francillon, François (ed.), *Livre des délibérations de l'Eglise réformée de l'Albenc (1606–1682)* *(Paris, 1998)*

Gibson, Thomas, *The Anatomy of Human Bodies Epitomised* (London, 1682)

Kingdon, Robert M., Thomas A. Lambert, Isabella M. Watt, and Wallace McDonald (eds), *Registres du consistoire de Genève au temps de Calvin. Tome III 3 (1547–1548)* (Geneva, 2004)

La Bruyère, Jean de, *Characters*, Jean Stewart (ed.) (Harmondsworth, 1970, orig. edn, 1668–94)

Ladurie, Emmanuel Le Roy Ladurie and Francine-Dominique Liechtenhan (eds and trans.), *Le Siècle de Platter*, 2 vols (Paris, 2000), vol. 2, *Le voyage de Thomas Platter 1595–1599*

Leroux, Alfred, Emile Molinier, and Anthoine Thomas (eds), 'Extraits du premier Registre consistorial de Rochechouart, 1596–1635', in *Documents historiques bas-latins, proven-çaux et français concernant principalement la Marche et le Limousin*, 2 vols (Limoges, 1883–5), vol. 2

Montaiglon, A. de (ed.), *Recueil des poésies françoises des XVe et XVIe siècles* (Paris, 1885)

Nicole, Pierre, 'Pensées diverses', *in Essais de morale*, 6 vols (Desprez, 1755), vol. 6

Quick, John, *Synodicon in Gallia Reformata: Or the Acts, Decisions, Decrees and Canons of Those Famous National Councils of the French Reformed Churches in France*, 2 vols (London, 1692)

'Registre du consistoire de l'église réformée de Melle (Deux-Sèvres) 1660–1669', *BSHPF* 25.2 (1876), 61–74

Soman, A. and E. Labrousse, 'Le Registre consistorial de Coutras, 1582–1584', *BSHPF* 126 (1980), 193–228

Vallette, Jean, 'Les actes du consistoire de l'Eglise réformée de Mussidan de 1593 à 1599', *Bulletin de la Société Historique et Archéologique du Périgord* 115 (1988)

Vicary, Thomas, *The Anatomy of the Body of Man* (London, 1548)

Viret, Pierre, *Du vray Ministère de la vraye Église de Jésus Christ et des vrais sacremens d'icelle, et des faus sacremens de l'eglise de l'Antechrist, et des additions adjoustées par les hommes au sacrement du baptesme* (Lyon, 1560)

Viret, Pierre, *Instruction chrestienne en la doctrine de la loy et de l'evangile* (Geneva, 1564)

REFERENCE WORKS

Alibert, Louis, *Dictionnaire Occitan-Français, d'après les parlers languedociens* (2nd edn, Toulouse, 2016)

Cayla, Paul, *Dictionnaire des institutions des coutumes et de la langue en usage dans quelques pays de Languedoc de 1535 à 1648* (Montpellier, 1964)

Chambaud, Louis and J. B. Robinet, *Nouveau dictionnaire François-Anglois, et Anglois-François. Contenant la signification et les differens usages des mots, les constructions, idiomes, façons de parler particulières, et les proverbes usités dans l'une et l'autre langue...* (Paris, 1776)

Cotgrave, Randle, *A Dictionarie of the French and English Tongues. Whereunto Is Annexed a Dictionarie of the English Set before the French* (London, 1632)

Haag, Eugène et Émile, *La France protestante ou vies des protestants français qui se sont fait un nom dans l'histoire depuis les premiers temps de la Réformation jusqu'à la reconnaissance du principe de la liberté des cultes par l'Assemblée nationale*, 10 vols (Paris, 1846–59)

Lachiver, Marcel, *Dictionnaire du Monde Rural: les mots du passé* (Paris, 1997)

Lagarda, Andrieu, *Vocabulari occitan* (Toulouse, 2013)

Laux, Christian, *Dictionnaire français-occitan: languedocien central* (Toulouse, 2017)

Ménard, Léon, *Histoire civile, ecclésiastique et littéraire de la ville de Nîmes*, 7 vols (Marseille, 1976, orig. edn 1750–6)

PRINTED SECONDARY WORKS

Acker, Joan, 'The Problem with Patriarchy', *Sociology* 23.2 (1989), 235–40

Alexander, Sally and Barbara Taylor, 'In Defence of "Patriarchy"', in *People's History and Socialist Theory*, ed. Raphael Samuel (London, 1981)

Amussen, Susan Dwyer, '"Being Stirred to Much Unquietness": Violence and Domestic Violence in Early Modern England', *Journal of Women's History* 6.2 (1994), 70–89

Ariès, Philippe, *L'enfant et la vie familiale sous l'Ancien Régime* (Paris, 1960)

Ariès, Philippe, *L'homme devant la mort* (Paris, 1977)

Ariès, Philippe and Georges Duby, *Histoire de la vie privée*, 5 vols (Paris, 1985–7), vol. 3, *De la Renaissance aux Lumières* (Paris, 1986)

Armstrong, Brian G., '*Semper Reformanda*: The Case of the French Reformed Church, 1559–1620', in *Later Calvinism: International Perspectives*, ed. W. Fred Graham (Kirksville, MO, 1994)

Arnaud, E., *Histoire de Protestants de Provence*, 2 vols (Paris, 1884)

Aughterson, Kate (ed.), *Renaissance Woman: Constructions of Femininity in England* (London and New York, 1995)

Bailey, F. G., 'Gifts and Poison', in *Gifts and Poison: The Politics of Reputation*, ed. F. G. Bailey (Oxford, 1971)

Bainton, Roland, *Women of the Reformation* (Minneapolis, MN, 1971)

Baldwin, Claude-Marie, 'Marriage in Calvin's Sermons', in *Calviniana: Ideas and Influence of Jean Calvin*, ed. Robert V. Schnucker (Kirksville, MO, 1988)

Barstow, Anne Llewellyn, 'The First Generations of Anglican Clergy Wives: Heroines or Whores?', *Historical Magazine of the Protestant Episcopal Church* 52 (1983)

Bashar, Nazife, 'Rape in England between 1550 and 1700', in *The Sexual Dynamics of History: Men's Power, Women's Resistance*, ed. The London Feminist History Group (London, 1983)

Baulant, Micheline, 'The Scattered Family: Another Aspect of Seventeenth-Century Demography', in *Family and Society: Selections from the Annales: Economies, Sociétés, Civilisations*, ed. Robert Forster and Orest Ranum, trans. Elborg Forster and Patricia M. Ranum (Baltimore, MD, and London, 1976)

Baumgartner, Frederic J., *France in the Sixteenth Century* (New York, 1995)

Bayley, Peter, *French Pulpit Oratory, 1598–1650: A Study in Themes and Styles, with a Descriptive Catalogue of Printed Texts* (Cambridge, 1980)

Beauvalet-Boutouyrie, Scarlett, *Etre veuve sous l'Ancien Régime* (Paris, 2001)

Bels, Pierre, *Le mariage des Protestants français jusqu'en 1685: Fondements doctrinaux et pratique juridique* (Paris, 1968)

Ben-Amos, I. K., *Adolescence and Youth in Early Modern England* (New Haven, CT, and London, 1994)

Benedict, Philip, *Rouen during the Wars of Religion* (Cambridge, 1981)

Benedict, Philip (ed.), *Cities and Social Change in Early Modern France* (London, 1989)

Benedict, Philip, *The Huguenot Population of France, 1600–1685: The Demographic Fate and Customs of a Religious Minority* (Philadelphia, PA, 1991)

Benedict, Philip, *The Faith and Fortune of France's Huguenots, 1600–85* (Aldershot, 2001)

Benedict, Philip, *Christ's Churches Purely Reformed: A Social History of Calvinism* (New Haven, CT, and London, 2002)

Bennett, Judith M., 'Feminism and History', *Gender and History* 1 (1989), 251–72

Bernos, Marcel, 'Résistances féminines à l'autorité ecclésiastique à l'époque moderne (XVIIe–XVIII 3e siècles)', *CLIO, Histoire, Femmes et Sociétés* 15 (2002), 103–10

Berriot-Salvadore, Evelyne, *Les femmes dans la société française de la Renaissance* (Geneva, 1990)

Bertheau, Solange, 'Le consistoire dans les Eglises Réformées du Moyen-Poitou au XVIIe Siècle', *BSHPF* 116 (1970), 332–59 and 513–49

Biéler, André, *L'homme et la femme dans la morale calviniste* (Geneva, 1963)

Blaisdell, Charmarie Jenkins, 'Response to John H. Bratt, The Role and Status of Women in the Writings of John Calvin', in *Renaissance, Reformation, Resurgence* (Colloquium on Calvin and Calvin Studies, Calvin Theological Seminary), ed. Peter De Klerk (Michigan, 1976)

Blaisdell, Charmarie Jenkins, 'Calvin's Letters to Women: The Courting of Ladies in High Places', *SCJ* 13.3 (1982), 67–84

Blaisdell, Charmarie Jenkins, 'The Matrix of Reform: Women in the Lutheran and Calvinist Movements', in *Triumph over Silence: Women in Protestant History*, ed. Richard L. Greaves (Westport, CT, 1985)

Blaisdell, Charmarie Jenkins, 'Calvin's and Loyola's Letters to Women', in *Calviniana: Ideas and Influence of Jean Calvin*, ed. Robert V. Schnucker (Kirksville, MO, 1988)

Bloch, Marc, *Les rois thaumaturges* (1924, new edn Paris, 1983)

Bloch, Marc, *Apologie pour l'histoire, ou, Métier d'historien* (Paris, 1949)

Bossy, John, *Christianity in the West 1400–1700* (Oxford, 1975)

Boulenger, Jacques, *Les protestants à Nîmes au temps de l'Edit de Nantes* (Paris, 1903)

Bourdieu, Pierre, 'Marriage Strategies as Strategies of Social Reproduction', in *Family and Society: Selections from the Annales Economies, Sociétés, Civilisations*, ed. Robert Forster and Orest Ranum, trans. Elborg Forster and Patricia M. Ranum (Baltimore, MD, and London, 1976)

Boyle, Leonard E., 'Montaillou Revisited: *Mentalité* and Methodology', in *Pathways to Medieval Peasants*, ed. J. A. Raftis (Toronto, 1981), 121–31

Bratt, John H., 'The Role and Status of Women in the Writings of John Calvin', in *Renaissance, Reformation, Resurgence* (Colloquium on Calvin and Calvin Studies, Calvin Theological Seminary), ed. Peter De Klerk (Michigan, 1976)

Braudel, Fernand, *La Méditerranée et le monde méditerranéen à l'époque de Philippe II* (Paris, 1949)

Braudel, Fernand, 'Histoire et sciences sociales: la longue durée', *Annales: Economies, Sociétés, Civilisations* 17 (1958), 725–53

Bridenthal, Renate, Claudia Koonz, and Susan Stuard (eds), *Becoming Visible: Women in European History*, (2nd edn, Boston, 1987)

Bridenthal, Renate, Susan Stuard, and Merry E. Wiesner (eds), *Becoming Visible: Women in European History*, (3rd edn, Boston, 1998)

Briggs, Robin, *Early Modern France, 1560–1715* (Oxford, 1977)

Briggs, Robin, *Communities of Belief: Cultural and Social Tension in Early Modern France* (Oxford, 1989)

Briggs, Robin, *Witches and Neighbours: The Social and Cultural Context of European Witchcraft*, (2nd edn, Oxford, 2002)

Briggs, Robin, *The Witches of Lorraine* (Oxford, 2007)

Broomhall, Susan, 'Identity and Life Narratives among the Poor in Later Sixteenth-Century Tours', *Renaissance Quarterly* 57 (2004), 439–65

Broomhall, Susan, '"Burdened with Small Children": Women Defining Poverty in Sixteenth-Century Tours', in *Women's Letters Across Europe, 1400–1700: Form and Persuasion*, ed. Jane Couchman and Ann Crabb (Aldershot, 2005)

Broomhall, Susan, 'Understanding Household Limitation Strategies among the Sixteenth-Century Urban Poor in France', *French History* 20.2 (2006), 121–37

Broomhall, Susan, *Women and Religion in Sixteenth-Century France* (Basingstoke, 2006)

Brownmiller, Susan, *Against our Will: Men, Women, and Rape* (New York, 1975)

Brunelle, Gayle K., "Dangerous Liaisons: Mésalliance and Early Modern French Noblewomen', *FHS* 19.1 (1995), 75–103

Bruston, H., 'La portée universelle de la pensée calviniste', in *Calvin et la réforme en France* (Aix-en-Provence, 1944)

Burguière, André, 'Le rituel du mariage en France: pratiques ecclésiastiques et pratiques populaires', *Annales: Economies, Sociétés, Civilisations* 33 (1978), 637–48

Burke, Peter, *Popular Culture in Early Modern Europe* (London, 1978)

Burke, Peter, *The French Historical Revolution: The* Annales *School, 1929–89* (Cambridge, 1990)

Burke, Peter (ed.), *New Perspectives on Historical Writing* (Cambridge and Oxford, 1991)

Cameron, Euan (ed.), *Early Modern Europe: An Oxford History* (Oxford, 1999)

Cameron, J. K., 'Godly Nurture and Admonition in the Lord: Ecclesiastical Discipline in the Reformed Tradition', in *Die danische Reformation vor ihrem internationalen Hintergrund*, ed. Leif Grane and Kai Hørby (Göttingen, 1990)

Capp, Bernard, 'The Double Standard Revisited: Plebeian Women and Male Sexual Reputation in Early Modern England', *Past and Present* 162.1 (1999), 70–101

Capp, Bernard, *When Gossips Meet: Women, Family and Neighbourhood in Early Modern England* (Oxford, 2003)

Carroll, Stuart, *Blood and Violence in Early Modern France* (Oxford, 2006)

Castan, Nicole, 'La criminalité familiale dans le ressort du Parlement de Toulouse, 1690–1730', in *Crimes et criminalité en France 17e–18e siècles*, ed. A. Abbiateci, F. Billacois, Y. Bongert, N. Castan, Y. Castan, P. Petrovitch, *Cahier des Annales* 33 (Paris, 1971)

Castan, Nicole, 'Le public et le particulier', in *Histoire de la vie privée*, 5 vols (Paris, 1985–7), vol. 3, *De la Renaissance aux Lumières*, ed. Philippe Ariès and Georges Duby (Paris, 1986)

Castan, Nicole, 'Les femmes devant la justice: Toulouse, XVIIIe siècle', in *Femmes et pouvoirs sous l'Ancien Régime*, ed. Danielle Haase-Dubosc and Eliane Viennot (Paris, 1991)

Castan, Nicole, 'Criminelle', in *Histoire des femmes en Occident*, vol. 3, *XVIe–XVIIIe siècles*, ed. Natalie Zemon Davis and Arlette Farge (Paris, 1991)

Castan, Nicole and Yves Castan (eds), *Vivre ensemble: ordre et désordre en Languedoc (XVIIe–XVIIIe siècles)* (Paris, 1981)

Castan, Yves, *Honnêteté et Relations Sociales en Languedoc (1715–1780)* (Paris, 1974)

Cattelona, Georg'Ann, 'Control and Collaboration: The Role of Women in Regulating Female Sexual Behaviour in Early Modern Marseille', *FHS* 18.1 (1993), 34–49

Cavallo, Sandra and Lyndan Warner (eds), *Widowhood in Medieval and Early Modern Europe* (Harlow, 1999)

Chareyre, Philippe, '"The Great Difficulties One Must Bear to Follow Jesus Christ": Morality at Sixteenth-Century Nîmes', in *Sin and the Calvinists: Morals Control and the Consistory in the Reformed Tradition*, ed. Raymond A. Mentzer (Kirksville, MO, 1994)

Chaunu, Pierre, *Eglise, culture et société. Réforme et Contre-Réforme (1517–1620)* (Paris, 1980)

Chaytor, Miranda, 'Husband(ry): Narratives of Rape in the Seventeenth Century', *Gender and History* 7.3 (1995), 378–407

Clark, Elizabeth A. and Herbert Richardson, 'The Protestant Reformations and the Catholic Response', in *Women and Religion: The Original Sourcebook of Women in Christian Thought*, (2nd edn, New York, 1996)

Cohen, Elizabeth S., 'Honor and Gender in the Streets of Early Modern Rome', *JIH* 22 (1992), 597–625

Cohen, Thomas V. 'The Politics of Jeopardy in Monte Rotondo', *Comparative Studies in Society and History* 33.4 (1991)

Collins, J. B., 'The Economic Role of Women in Seventeenth-Century France', *FHS* 16.2 (1989), 436–70

Collinson, Patrick, 'The Protestant Family', in *The Birthpangs of Protestant England: Religion and Cultural Change in the Sixteenth and Seventeenth Centuries* (London, 1998)

Collomp, Alain, *La maison du père. Famille et village en Haute-Provence aux XVIIe et XVIIIe siècles* (Paris, 1983)

Collomp, Alain, 'Tensions, Dissensions, and Ruptures inside the Family in Seventeenth- and Eighteenth-Century Haute Provence', in *Interest and Emotion: Essays on the Study of Family and Kinship*, ed. Hans Medick and David Warren Sabean (Cambridge, 1984)

Conner, Philip, *Huguenot Heartland: Montauban and Southern French Calvinism During the Wars of Religion* (Aldershot, 2002)

Coster, Will and Andrew Spicer, *Sacred Space in Early Modern Europe* (Cambridge, 2005)

Cottret, Bernard, *Calvin: A Biography*, trans. M. Wallace McDonald (Grand Rapids, MI, Cambridge, 1995)

Courthial, Pierre, 'The Golden Age of Calvinism in France, 1533–1633', in *John Calvin: His Influence in the Western World*, ed. W. Stanford Reid (Michigan, 1982)

Cranny-Francis, Anne, Wendy Waring, Pam Stavropoulos, and Joan Kirkby, *Gender Studies: Terms and Debates* (Basingstoke, 2003)

Crawford, Patricia, *Women and Religion in Early Modern England 1500–1750* (London and New York, 1993)

Cressy, David, 'De la fiction dans les archives? Ou le monstre de 1569', *Annales E.S.C.* 48 (1993), 1309–29

Cressy, David, *Travesties and Transgressions in Tudor and Stuart England: Tales of Discord and Dissension* (Oxford, 2000)

Crouzet, Denis, *Les guerriers de Dieu. La violence au temps de trouble de religion, vers 1525–vers 1610*, 2 vols (Paris, 1990)

Cunningham, Andrew and Ole Peter Grell, *The Four Horsemen of the Apocalypse: Religion, War, Famine and Death in Reformation Europe* (Cambridge, 2000)

Darmon, Pierre, *Mythologie de la femme dans l'ancienne France* (Paris, 1983)

Darnton, Robert, *The Great Cat Massacre and Other Episodes in French Cultural History* (London, 1984)

Davies, Joan, 'Persecution and Protestantism: Toulouse, 1562–1575', *HJ* 22.1 (1979), 31–51

Davies, Joan, 'The Politics of the Marriage Bed', *French History* 6.1 (1992), 63–95

Davis, Natalie Zemon, 'Ghosts, Kin and Progeny: Some Features of Family Life in Early Modern France', *Daedalus* 106. 2 (1977), 87–114

Davis, Natalie Zemon, 'Women in the Crafts in Sixteenth-Century Lyon, *Feminist Studies* 8.1 (1982), 46–80

Davis, Natalie Zemon, *The Return of Martin Guerre* (Cambridge, MA, and London, 1983)

Davis, Natalie Zemon, *Fiction in the Archives: Pardon Tellers and their Tales in Sixteenth-Century France* (Cambridge, 1987)

Davis, Natalie Zemon, *Society and Change in Early Modern France* (Cambridge, 1987)

Davis, Natalie Zemon, 'Women's History in Transition: The European Case', in *Feminism and History*, ed. Joan Wallach Scott (Oxford, 1996)

Davis, Natalie Zemon and Arlette Farge (eds), *Histoire des femmes en Occident*, vol. 3, *XVIe–XVIIIe siècles* (Paris, 1991)

Dawson, Jane, '"The face of ane perfyt reformed kyrk": St Andrews and the Early Scottish Reformation', in *Humanism and Reform: The Church in Europe, England and Scotland, 1400–1640: Essays in Honour of James J. Cameron*, ed. J. Kirk (Oxford, 1991)

D'Cruze, Shani, 'Approaching the History of Rape and Sexual Violence: Notes towards Research', *Women's History Review* 1.3 (1992), 377–97

Delteil, Frank, 'Institutions et vie de l'église réformée de Pont-de-Camarès (1574–1576) in *Les eglises et leurs institutions au XVIeme siècle: hommage solennel a la mémoire du Professeur Jean Boisset*, ed. Michel Péronnet (Montpellier, 1978)

Delumeau, Jean, *La peur en Occident XIVe–XVIIIe siècles* (Paris, 1978)

Depauw, Jacques, 'Amour illégitime et société à Nantes au XVIII 3 siècle', *Annales E.S.C.* 4–5 (1972), 1155–82

Diefendorf, Barbara B., 'Widowhood and Remarriage in Sixteenth-Century Paris', *Journal of Family History* 7.4 (1982), 379–95

Diefendorf, Barbara B., *Beneath the Cross: Catholics and Huguenots in Sixteenth-Century Paris* (Oxford, 1991)

Diefendorf, Barbara B., 'The Huguenot Psalter and the Faith of French Protestants in the Sixteenth Century', in *Culture and Identity in Early Modern Europe (1500–1800). Essays in Honour of Natalie Zemon Davis*, ed. Barbara B. Diefendorf and Carla Hesse (Ann Arbor, MI, 1993)

Diefendorf, Barbara B., 'Gender and the Family', in *Renaissance and Reformation France, 1500–1648*, ed. Mack P. Holt (Oxford, 2002)

Diefendorf, Barbara B., *From Penitence to Charity: Pious Women and the Catholic Reformation in Paris* (Oxford, 2004)

Dinan, Susan E. and Debra Meyers (eds), *Women and Religion in New and Old Worlds* (New York and London, 2001)

Dinges, Martin, 'Huguenot Poor Relief and Health Care in the Sixteenth and Seventeenth Centuries', in *Society and Culture in the Huguenot World, 1559–1685*, ed. Raymond A. Mentzer and Andrew Spicer (Cambridge, 2002)

Dinges, Martin, 'The Uses of Justice as a Form of Social Control in Early Modern Europe', in *Social Control in Europe, 1500–1800*, ed. Herman Roodenburg and Pieter Spierenburg (Columbus, OH, 2004)

Douglass, Jane Dempsey, *Women, Freedom and Calvin* (Philadelphia, PA, 1985)

Duby, Georges and Michelle Perrot, *Histoire des femmes en Occident*, 5 vols (Paris, 1991)

Duffy, Eamon, *The Stripping of the Altars: Traditional Religion in England 1400–1580* (New Haven, CT, and London, 1992)

Eisenbichler, Konrad, *The Premodern Teenager: Youth in Society 1150–1650* (Toronto, 2002)

Estèbe, J., 'Les Saint-Barthélemy des villes du midi', in *Actes du colloque l'amiral de Coligny et son temps* (Paris, 1974)

Fabre, Daniel, 'Familles. Le privé contre la coutume', in *Histoire de la vie privée*, 5 vols (Paris, 1985–7), vol. 3, *De la Renaissance aux Lumières*, ed. Philippe Ariès and Georges Duby (Paris, 1986)

Fairchilds, Cissie, 'Female Sexual Attitudes and the Rise of Illegitimacy: A Case Study', *JIH* 8.4 (1978), 627–67

Fairchilds, Cissie, *Domestic Enemies: Servants and their Masters in Old Regime France* (Baltimore, MD, 1984)

Farge, Arlette and Michel Foucault (eds), *Le désordre des familles: lettres de cachet des archives de la Bastille aux XVIIIe siècle* (Paris, 1982)

Farr, James R., *Hands of Honor: Artisans and their World in Dijon, 1550–1650* (Ithaca, NY, and London, 1988)

Farr, James R., 'The Pure and Disciplined Body: Hierarchy, Morality and Symbolism in France during the Catholic Reformation', *JIH* 21.3 (1991), 391–414

Farr, James R., *Authority and Sexuality in Early Modern Burgundy (1550–1730)* (New York and Oxford, 1995)

Farr, James R., *A Tale of Two Murders: Passion and Power in Seventeenth-Century France* (Durham, 2005)

Febvre, Lucien, *Le problème de l'incroyance au XVIe siècle: la religion de Rabelais* (Paris, 1947)

Fildes, Valerie, *Wet Nursing: A History from Antiquity to the Present* (Oxford, 1988)

Finlay, Robert, 'The Refashioning of Martin Guerre', *American Historical Review* 93.3 (1988), 553–71

Finley-Croswhite and S. Annette, *Henry IV and the Towns: The Pursuit of Legitimacy in French Urban Society, 1589–1610* (Cambridge, 1999)

Flandrin, Jean-Louis, *Les amours paysannes (XVIe–XIXe siècle): amour et sexualité dans les campagnes de l'ancienne France* (Paris, 1975)

Flandrin, Jean-Louis, *Familles: parenté, maison, sexualité dans l'ancienne société* (Paris, 1976)

Flandrin, Jean-Louis, 'Repression and Change in the Sexual Life of Young People in Medieval and Early Modern Times', *Journal of Family History* 2 (1977), 196–210

Flandrin, Jean-Louis, 'A Case of Naïveté in the Use of Statistics', *JIH* 9.2 (1978), 309–15

Flandrin, Jean-Louis, 'Repression and Change in the Sexual Life of Young People in Medieval and Modern Times', in *Family and Sexuality in French History*, ed. Robert Wheaton and Tamara K. Hareven (Philadelphia, PA, 1980)

Fletcher, Anthony, *Gender, Sex and Subordination in England 1500–1800* (New Haven, CT, and London, 1995)

Forster, Robert and Orest Ranum (eds), *Family and Society: Selections from the Annales Economies, Sociétés, Civilisations*, trans. Elborg Forster and Patricia M. Ranum (Baltimore, MD, and London, 1976)

Foucault, Michael, *Discipline and Punish: The Birth of the Prison* (London, 1977)

Garrioch, David, *Neighbourhood and Community in Paris, 1740–1790* (Cambridge, 1986)

Garrisson-Estèbe, Janine, *Les protestants du Midi, 1559–1598* (Toulouse, 1980)

Garrisson, Janine, *L'Homme protestant* (Paris, 1980)

Geertz, Clifford, *The Interpretation of Cultures* (New York, 1993)

Geremek, Bronislaw, *The Margins of Society in Late Medieval Paris*, trans. Jean Birrell (Paris and Cambridge, 1987)

Gibson, Wendy, *Women in Seventeenth-Century France* (Basingstoke, 1989)

Gillis, John, *For Better, For Worse: British Marriages from 1600 to the Present* (New York and Oxford, 1988)

Ginzburg, Carlo, *The Cheese and the Worms: The Cosmos of a Sixteenth-Century Miller*, trans. John and Anne Tedeschi (London, 1980)

Ginzburg, Carlo, 'The Inquisitor as Anthropologist', in *Clues, Myths and Historical Method*, trans. John and Anne Tedeschi (Baltimore, MD, and London, 1989), 156–64

Gluckman, Max, 'Gossip and Scandal', *Current Anthropology* 4.3 (1963), 307–15

Gluckman, Max, 'Psychological, Sociological and Anthropological Explanations of Witchcraft and Gossip: A Clarification', *Man* 3 (1968), 20–34

Goody, Jack, *The Development of the Family and Marriage in Europe* (Cambridge, 1983)

Gottlieb, Beatrice, 'The Meaning of Clandestine Marriage', in *Family and Sexuality in French History*, ed. Robert Wheaton and Tamara K. Hareven (Philadelphia, PA, 1980)

Goubert,Pierre, *La vie quotidienne dans les campagnes françaises au XVIIe siècle* (Paris, 1982)

Gowing, Laura, 'Gender and the Language of Insult in Early Modern England', *History Workshop Journal* 35 (1993), 1–21

Gowing, Laura, *Domestic Dangers: Women, Words and Sex in Early Modern London* (Oxford, 1996)

Gowing, Laura, 'Secret Births and Infanticide in Seventeenth-Century England', *Past and Present* 156 (1997), 87–115

Gowing, Laura, *Common Bodies: Women, Touch and Power in Seventeenth-Century England* (New Haven, CT, and London, 2003)

Graham, Michael F., 'Social Discipline in Scotland, 1560–1610', in *Sin and the Calvinists: Morals Control and the Consistory in the Reformed Tradition*, ed. Raymond A. Mentzer (Kirksville, MO, 1994)

Graham, Michael F., *The Uses of Reform: 'Godly Discipline' and Popular Behaviour in Scotland and Beyond, 1560–1610* (New York, 1996)

de Greef, W., *The Writings of John Calvin: An Introductory Guide*, trans. Lyle D. Bierma (Michigan, 1993)

Greengrass, Mark, 'Review Article: The Psychology of Religious Violence', *French History* 5.4 (1991), 467–74

Greengrass, Mark, 'Informal Networks in French Protestantism', in *Society and Culture in the Huguenot World, 1559–1685*, ed. Raymond A. Mentzer and Andrew Spicer (Cambridge, 2002)

Grell, Ole and Robert Scribner (eds), *Tolerance and Intolerance in the European Reformation* (Cambridge, 1996)

Grimmer, Claude, *La femme et la bâtard: amours illégitimes et secrètes dans l'ancienne France* (Paris, 1983)

Grinberg, Martine, 'L'obsédante absence des femmes: réponses rituelles et juridiques', in *Femmes et pouvoirs sous l'Ancien Régime*, ed. Danielle Haase-Dubosc and Eliane Viennot (Paris, 1991)

Grosse, Christian, 'Places of Sanctification: The Liturgical Sacrality of Genevan Reformed Churches, 1535–1566', in *Sacred Space in Early Modern Europe*, ed. Will Coster and Andrew Spicer (Cambridge, 2005)

Guggenheim, Ann H., 'The Calvinist Notables of Nîmes during the Era of the Religious Wars', *SCJ* 3.1 (1972), 80–96

Gutton, Jean-Pierre, *Domestiques et serviteurs dans la France de l'ancien régime* (Paris, 1981)

Haase-Dubosc, Danielle, 'Ravie et enlevée au XVIIe siècle', in *Femmes et pouvoirs sous l'Ancien Régime*, ed. Danielle Haase-Dubosc and Eliane Viennot (Paris, 1991)

Haase-Dubosc, Danielle and Eliane Viennot (eds), *Femmes et pouvoirs sous l'Ancien Régime* (Paris, 1991)

Hacke, Daniela, *Women, Sex and Marriage in Early Modern Venice* (Aldershot, 2004)

Hanley, Sarah, 'Family and State in Early Modern France: The Marriage Pact', in *Connecting Spheres: Women in the Western World, 1500 to the Present*, ed. Arilyn J. Boxer and Jean H. Quataert (New York and Oxford, 1987)

Hanley, Sarah, 'Engendering the State: Family Formation and State Building in Early Modern France', *FHS* 16.1 (1989), 4–27

Hanley, Sarah, 'Social Sites of Political Practice in France: Lawsuits, Civil Rights, and the Separation of Powers in Domestic and State Government, 1500–1800', *American Historical Review* 102.1 (1997), 27–52

Hanlon, Gregory, *Confession and Community in Seventeenth-Century France: Catholic and Protestant Co-existence in Aquitaine* (Philadelphia, PA, 1993)

Hardwick, Julie, 'Widowhood and Patriarchy in Seventeenth-Century France', *Journal of Social History* 26 (1992), 133–48

Hardwick, Julie, *The Practice of Patriarchy: Gender and the Politics of Household Authority in Early Modern France* (University Park, PA, 1998)

Hardwick, Julie, 'Seeking Separations: Gender, Marriages, and Household Economies in Early Modern France', *FHS* 21.1 (1998), 157–80

Harrington, Joel F., *Reordering Marriage and Society in Reformation Germany* (Cambridge, 1995)

Harrison, Brian and James McMillan, 'Some Feminist Betrayals of Women's History', *Historical Journal* 26 (1983), 375–89

Heal, Felicity, 'Reputation and Honour in Court and Country: Lady Elizabeth Russell and Sir Thomas Hoby', *TRHS* 6 (1996)

Hendrix, Scott, 'Masculinity and Patriarchy in Reformation Germany', *Journal of the History of Ideas* 56.2 (1995), 177–93

Hendrix, Scott H. and Susan C. Karant-Nunn (eds), *Masculinity in the Reformation Era* (Kirksville, MO, 2008)

Herlihy, David, 'Review: Ladurie, Montaillou', *Social History* 4.3 (1979), 517–20

Hogrefe, Pearl, 'Legal Rights of Tudor Women and the Circumvention by Men and Women', *SCJ* 3.1 (1972), 97–105

Holt, Mack P. (ed.), *Renaissance and Reformation France 1500–1648* (Oxford, 2002)

Hoskins, W. G., 'Harvest Fluctuations and English Economic History (XVIth/XVIIth Centuries)', *Agricultural History Review* 12.1 (1964), 28–46

Hsia, R. Po-Chia, *Social Discipline in the Reformation: Central Europe 1550–1750* (London, 1989)

Hufton, Olwen, 'Le travail et la famille', in *Histoire des femmes en Occident*, ed. Georges Duby and Michelle Perrot, 5 vols (Paris, 1991), vol. 3, ed. Natalie Zemon Davis and Arlette Farge

Hufton, Olwen, *The Prospect before Her: A History of Women in Western Europe* (London, 1995)

Hunt, David, *Parents and Children in History: The Psychology of Family Life in Early Modern France* (New York, 1970)

Ingram, Martin, *Church Courts, Sex and Marriage in England, 1570–1640* (Cambridge, 1987)

Irwin, Joyce, *Womanhood in Radical Protestantism* (New York, 1979)

Jacobsen, Grethe, 'Women, Marriage, and Magisterial Reformation: The Case of Malmo, Denmark', in *Pietas et Societas: New Trends in Reformation Social History*, ed. Kyle C. Sessions and Philip N. Bebb (Kirksville, MO, 1985)

Jelsma, Auke, *Frontiers of the Reformation: Dissidence and Orthodoxy in Sixteenth-Century Europe* (Aldershot, 1998)

Johnson, Allan G., *The Gender Knot: Unraveling our Patriarchal Legacy* (Philadelphia, PA, 2005)

Jones, Colin, 'Plague and its Metaphors in Early Modern France', *Representations* 53 (1996), 97–127

Joukovsky, Françoise (ed.), *Images de la femme au XVIe siècle* (Paris, 1995)

Kaiser, Daniel, '"He Said, She Said": Rape and Gender Discourse in Early Modern Russia', *Kritika: Explorations in Russian and Eurasian History* 3.2 (2002), 197–216

Karant-Nunn, Susan C., 'Continuity and Change: Some Effects of the Reformation on the Women of Zwickau', *SCJ* 13.2 (1982), 17–42

Karant-Nunn, Susan C. and Merry E. Wiesner-Hanks (eds), *Luther on Women: A Sourcebook* (Cambridge, 2003)

Kelly-Gadol, Joan, 'Did Women Have a Renaissance?', in *Becoming Visible: Women in European History*, ed. Renate Bridenthal, Claudia Koonz, Susan Stuard (2nd edn, Boston, 1987)

Kermode, Jenny and Garthine Walker (eds), *Women, Crime and the Courts in Early Modern England* (London, 1994)

Kettering, Sharon, 'The Patronage Power of Early Modern French Noblewomen', *Historical Journal* 32 (1989), 817–41

Kettering, Sharon, 'The Household Service of Early Modern French Noblewomen', *FHS* 20.1 (1997), 67–78

Kettering, Sharon, *French Society, 1589–1715* (Harlow, 2001)

Kingdon, Robert M., *Geneva and the Coming of the Wars of Religion in France, 1555–1563* (Geneva, 1956)

Kingdon, Robert M., *Geneva and the Consolidation of the French Protestant Movement, 1564–1572: A Contribution to the History of Congregationalism, Presbyterianism and Calvinist Resistance Theory* (Madison, WI, 1967)

Kingdon, Robert M., 'The Control of Morals in Calvin's Geneva', in *The Social History of the Reformation*, ed. L. P. Buck and J. W. Zophy (Columbus, OH, 1972)

Kingdon, Robert M., 'The Control of Morals by the Earliest Calvinists', in *Renaissance, Reformation, Resurgence*, ed. Peter De Klerk (Grand Rapids, MI, 1976)

Kingdon, Robert M., 'Calvin and the Establishment of Consistory Discipline in Geneva', *Nederlands archief voor kerkgeschiedenis* 70 (1990), 158–72

Kingdon, Robert M., 'The Geneva Consistory in the Time of Calvin', in *Calvinism in Europe, 1540–1620*, ed. Andrew Pettegree, Alastair Duke, and Gillian Lewis (Cambridge, 1994)

Kingdon, Robert M., *Adultery and Divorce in Calvin's Geneva* (Cambridge, 1995)

Kümin, Bëat ed., *The European World, 1500–1800* (New York and London, 2009)

Labrousse, Elisabeth, *Pierre Bayle, Du pays de foix a la cite d'erasme* (The Hague, 1963), vol. 1

Labrousse, Elisabeth, 'Les mariages bigarrés: unions mixtes en France au XVIIIe siècle', in *Le couple interdit entretiens sur le racisme: la dialectique de l'altérité socio-culturelle et la sexualité*, ed. Léon Poliakov (Paris, 1980)

Labrousse, Ernest, *Histoire économique et sociale de la France*, 3 vols (Paris, 1970–9)

Le Goff, Jacques, *La civilisation de l'occident medieval* (Paris, 1964)

Le Goff, Jacques, *La naissance du purgatoire* (Paris, 1981)

Lea, H. C., *Materials Towards a History of Witchcraft*, 3 vols (New York, 1957)

Lebrun, François, *La vie conjugale sous l'Ancien Régime* (Paris, 1975)

Lenman, Bruce, 'The Limits of Godly Discipline in the Early Modern Period', in *Religion and Society in Early Modern Europe 1500–1800*, ed. Kaspar von Greyerz (London, 1984)

Leneman, Leah and Rosalind Mitchinson, *Sin in the City: Sexuality and Social Control in Urban Scotland 1660–1780* (Edinburgh, 1988)

Léonard, Emile G., *Histoire générale du protestantisme*, 2 vols (Paris, 1961)

Le Roy Ladurie, Emmanuel, *Les paysans de Languedoc*, 2 vols (Paris, 1966)

Le Roy Ladurie, Emmanuel, *Histoire du climat* (Paris, 1967)

Le Roy Ladurie, Emmanuel, 'Huguenots contre papists', in *Histoire du Languedoc*, dir. Philippe Wolff, ed. Edouard Privat (Toulouse, 1967)

Le Roy Ladurie, Emmanuel, 'Système de la coutume: structures familiales et coutumes d'héritage en France au XVIe siècle', *Annales E.S.C.* 4–5 (1972), 825–6

Le Roy Ladurie, Emmanuel, *Le territoire de l'historien* (Paris, 1973)

Le Roy Ladurie, Emmanuel, *Montaillou, village occitan 1294 à 1324* (Paris, 1975)

Le Roy Ladurie, Emmanuel, *Le carnival de Romans* (Paris, 1979)

Le Roy Ladurie, Emmanuel, *L'argent, l'amour et la mort en pays d'oc* (Paris, 1980)

Lewis, Gillian, 'The Geneva Academy', in *Calvinism in Europe 1540–1620*, ed. Alastair Duke, Gillian Lewis, and Andrew Pettegree (Manchester, 1992)

Lipscomb, Suzannah, 'Subjection and Companionship: The French Reformed Marriage', *Reformation & Renaissance Review* 6.3 (2004), 349–60

Lipscomb, Suzannah, 'Refractory Women: The Limits of Power in the French Reformed Church', in Raymond A. Mentzer, Philippe Chareyre, and Françoise Moreil (eds), *Dire l'interdit: The Vocabulary of Censure and Exclusion in the Early Modern Reformed Tradition* (Leiden, 2010), 13–28

Lipscomb, Suzannah, 'Crossing Boundaries: Women's Gossip, Insults and Violence in Sixteenth-Century France', *French History* 25.4 (2011), 408–26

Loats, Carol L., 'Gender, Guilds and Work Identity: Perspectives from Sixteenth-Century Paris', *FHS* 20.1 (1997), 15–30

Lottin, Alain, 'Vie et mort du couple: difficultés conjugales et divorces dans le Nord de la France aux XVIIe et XVIIIe siècles', *XVIIe siècle* 102–3 (1974), 59–78

Lottin, Alain, *La désunion du couple sous l'Ancien Régime: l'exemple du Nord* (Paris, 1975)

Lougée, Carolyn, *Le Paradis des Femmes: Women, Salons and Social Stratification in Seventeenth-Century France* (Princeton, NJ, 1976)

Maag, Karin, *Seminary or University? The Genevan Academy and Reformed Higher Education, 1560–1620* (Aldershot, 1995)

Maag, Karin, 'The Huguenot Academies: An Uncertain Future?', in *Society and Culture in the Huguenot World 1559–1685*, ed. Raymond A. Mentzer and Andrew Spicer (Cambridge, 2002)

MacCulloch, Diarmaid, *The Reformation: Europe's House Divided* (New York and London, 2003)

Maclean, Ian, *The Renaissance Notion of Woman: A Study in the Fortunes of Scholasticism and Medical Science in European Intellectual Life* (Cambridge, 1980)

Malinowski, Bronsilaw, *Magic, Science and Religion and Other Essays* (London, 1948)

Mandrou, Robert, *Introduction à la France moderne: essai de psychologie historique 1500–1640* (Paris, 1961)

Martin, François, 'Ganges, action de son consistoire et vie de son église aux 16e et 17e siècle', *Études évangeliques* 2 (Revue de théologie de la faculté libre de théologie protestante, Aix-en-Provence) (1942)

Matheson, Peter, *The Imaginative World of the Reformation* (Edinburgh, 2000)

Matthew Grieco, Sara F., 'Amour et sexualité', in *Histoire des femmes en Occident*, ed. Georges Duby and Michelle Perrot, 5 vols (Paris, 1991), vol. 3, ed. Natalie Zemon Davis and Arlette Farge

Maza, Sarah, *Servants and Masters in Eighteenth-Century France: The Uses of Loyalty* (Princeton, 1983)

McGrath, Alister E., *A Life of John Calvin: A Study in the Shaping of Western Culture* (Oxford, 1990)

McGrath, Alister E., *Reformation Thought: An Introduction* (Oxford, 1998)

Meldrum, Tim, *Domestic Service and Gender 1660–1750, Life and Work in the London Household* (Harlow, 2000)

Mentzer, Jr, Raymond A. "'Disciplina nervus ecclesiae": The Calvinist Reform of Morals at Nîmes', *SCJ* 18.1 (1987), 13–39

Mentzer, Jr, Raymond A., 'Le consistoire et la pacification du monde rural', *BSHPF* 135 (1989), 373–91

Mentzer, Jr, Raymond A., 'Ecclesiastical Discipline and Communal Reorganisation among the Protestants of Southern France', *European History Quarterly* 21 (1991), 163–84

Mentzer, Jr, Raymond A., 'Organizational Endeavour and Charitable Impulse in Sixteenth-Century France: The Care of Protestant Nîmes', *French History* 5.1 (1991), 1–29

Mentzer, Raymond A., 'Marking the Taboo: Excommunication in French Reformed Churches', in *Sin and the Calvinists: Morals Control and the Consistory in the Reformed Tradition*, ed. Raymond A. Mentzer (Kirksville, MO, 1994)

Mentzer, Raymond A. (ed.), *Sin and the Calvinists: Morals Control and the Consistory in the Reformed Tradition* (Kirksville, MO, 1994)

Mentzer, Raymond A., 'The Persistence of "Superstition and Idolatry" among Rural French Calvinists', *Church History* 65.2 (1996), 220–33

Mentzer, Raymond A., 'Morals and Moral Regulation in Protestant France', *JIH* 31.1 (2000), 1–20

Mentzer, Raymond A., 'Notions of Sin and Penitence within the Reformed Community', in *Penitence in the Age of Reformations*, ed. Katharine Jackson Lualdi and Anne T. Thayer (Aldershot, 2000)

Mentzer, Raymond A., 'La place et le rôle des femmes dans les églises réformées', *Archives de sciences sociales des religions* 113 (2001), 119–32

Mentzer, Raymond A., 'Acting on Calvin's Ideas: The Church in France', in *Calvin and the Church*, ed. David Foxgrover (Grand Rapids, 2002)

Mentzer, Raymond A., 'Laity and Liturgy in the French Reformed Tradition', in *History Has Many Voices*, ed. Lee P. Wandel (Kirksville, 2003)

Mentzer, Raymond A., 'Sociability and Culpability: Conventions of Mediation and Reconciliation within the Sixteenth-Century Huguenot Community', in *Memory and Identity: The Huguenots in France and the Atlantic Diaspora*, ed. Bertrand Van Ruymbeke and Randy J. Sparks (Columbia, SC, 2003)

Mentzer, Raymond A., 'Fashioning Reformed Identity in Early Modern France', in *Confessionalization in Europe, 1555–1700: Essays in Honor and Memory of Bodo Nischan*, ed. John M. Headley (Aldershot, 2004)

Mentzer, Raymond A., 'Les débats sur les bancs dans les Églises réformées de France', *BSHPF* 152 (2006), 393–406

Mentzer, Raymond A. and Andrew Spicer (eds), *Society and Culture in the Huguenot World, 1559–1685* (Cambridge, 2002)

Mentzer, Raymond A., Françoise Chevalier, Christian Grosse, and Bernard Roussel, 'Anthrolopogie historique: les rituels réformés (XVIe–XVIIe siècles)', *BSHPF* 148 (2002), 979–1009

Millet, K., *Sexual Politics* (London, 1977)

Monter, E. William, 'The Consistory of Geneva, 1559–1569', *Bibliothèque d'Humanisme et Renaissance* 38 (1976)

Monter, E. William, 'Women in Calvinist Geneva (1550–1800)', *Signs* 6.2 (1980), 189–209

Monter, William, E. 'Protestant Wives, Catholic Saints, and the Devil's Handmaid: Women in the Age of Reformations', in *Becoming Visible: Women in European History*, ed. Renate Bridenthal, Claudia Koonz, and Susan Stuard, (2nd edn, Boston, MA, 1987)

Monter, E. William, 'Crime and Punishment in Calvin's Geneva, 1562', in his *Enforcing Morality in Early Modern Europe* (London, 1987)

Moreil, Françoise, 'Le Collège et l'Académie réformée de Nîmes', *Bulletin de la Société de l'Histoire du Protestantisme Français* 122 (1976), 77–86

Morgan, Edmund, *Visible Saints: The History of the Puritan Idea* (New York, 1992)

Muchembled, Robert, *Culture populaire et culture des élites dans la France moderne (XVe–XVIIIe siècles): essai* (Paris, 1978)

Muchembled, Robert, Société et mentalités dans la France moderne: XVIe–XVIIIe siècle (Paris, 1990)

Murdock, Graeme 'Dressed to Repress? Protestant Clerical Dress and the Regulations of Morality in Early Modern Europe', *Fashion Theory* 4.2. (2000), 179–99

Murdock, Graeme, *Calvinism on the Frontier 1600–1660: International Calvinism and the Reformed Church in Hungary and Transylvania* (Oxford, 2000)

Murdock, Graeme, *Beyond Calvin: The Intellectual, Political and Cultural World of Europe's Reformed Churches, c.1540–1620* (Basingstoke, 2004)

Nalle, Sara T., *God in La Mancha: Religious Reform and the People of Cuenca, 1500–1650* (Baltimore, MD, and London, 1992)

Naphy, William, *Calvin and the Consolidation of the Genevan Reformation* (Manchester, 1994)

Naphy, William, *Sex Crimes from Renaissance to Enlightenment* (Stroud, 2002)

Neuschel, Kristen B., 'Noble Households in the Sixteenth Century', *FHS* 15.4 (1988), 595–622

Neuschel, Kristen B., 'Noblewomen and War in Sixteenth-Century France', in *Changing Identities in Early Modern France*, ed. Michael Wolfe (Durham and London, 1996)

Norton, Mary Beth, 'Gender and Defamation in Seventeenth-Century Maryland', *William and Mary Quarterly* 44.1 (1987), 3–39

O'Hara, Diana, *Courtship and Constraint: Rethinking the Making of Marriage in Tudor England* (Manchester, 2000)

Otis-Cour, Leah, *Prostitution in Medieval Society: The History of an Urban Institution in Languedoc* (Chicago, IL, 1985)

Oudot de Dainville, Maurice, 'Le consistoire de Ganges à la fin du XVIe siècle', *Revue d'historie de l'Eglise de France* 18 (81) (1932), 464–85

Ourliac, Paul, *Histoire du droit privé francais de l'an mil au Code Civil* (Paris, 1985)

Ozment, Steven, *The Reformation in the Cities: The Appeal of Protestantism to Sixteenth-Century Germany and Switzerland* (New Haven, CT, and London, 1975)

Ozment, Steven, *Reformation Europe: A Guide to Research* (St Louis, MO, 1982)

Ozment, Steven, *When Fathers Ruled: Family Life in Reformation Europe* (Cambridge, MA, and London, 1983)

Ozment, Steven, *Magdalena and Balthasar: An Intimate Portrait of Life in Sixteenth-Century Europe Revealed in the Letters of a Nuremberg Husband and Wife* (New Haven, CT, and London, 1989)

Ozment, Steven, *Protestants: The Birth of a Revolution* (New York, 1993)

Ozment, Steven, *Ancestors: The Loving Family in Old Europe* (Cambridge, MA, and London, 2001)

Paine, Robert, 'What Is Gossip About? An Alternative Hypothesis', *Man* 2 (1967), 272–85

Pardailhé-Galabrun, Annik, *La Naissance de l'intime: 3000 foyers parisiens XVIIe–XVIIIe siècles* (Paris, 1988)

Parker, Geoffrey, 'The "Kirk by Law Established" and Origins of "The Taming of Scotland": Saint Andrews, 1559–1600', in *Sin and the Calvinists: Morals Control and the Consistory in the Reformed Tradition*, ed. Raymond A. Mentzer (Kirksville, MO, 1994)

Parker, T. H. L., *Calvin's Preaching* (Edinburgh, 1992)

Peachey, Stuart, *Single Women 1580–1660: The Lifestyles of Spinsters, Singlewomen, Maidservants and Maidens* (Bristol, 1998)

Pellegrin, Nicole, 'L'androgyne au XVIe siècle: pour une relecture des savoirs', in *Femmes et pouvoirs sous l'Ancien Régime*, ed. Danielle Haase-Dubosc and Eliane Viennot (Paris, 1991)

Pettegree, Andrew, *Reformation and the Culture of Persuasion* (Cambridge, 2005)

Pettegree, Andrew, Alastair Duke, and Gillian Lewis (eds), *Calvinism in Europe, 1540–1620* (Cambridge, 1994)

Phan, Marie-Claude, 'Les déclarations de grossesse en France (XVIe–XVIIIe siecles): essai institutionnel', *Revue d'Histoire Moderne et Contemporaine* 22 (1975), 61–88

Phan, Marie-Claude, *Les amours illégitimes: histories de séduction en Languedoc (1676–1786)* (Paris, 1986)

Phillips, Roderick, 'Women, Neighborhood, and Family in the Late Eighteenth Century', *FHS* 18.1 (1993), 1–12

Phillips, Roderick, *Family Breakdown in Late Eighteenth-Century France: Divorces in Rouen, 1792–1803* (Oxford and New York, 1980)

Pillorget, René, *La tige et le rameau: familles anglaises et française 16e–18e siècle* (Paris, 1979)

Pollmann, J. S., 'A Different Road to God? The Protestant Experience of Conversion in the Sixteenth Century', in *Conversion to Modernities: The Globalisation of Christianity*, ed. Peter van der Veer (New York and London, 1996)

Pollmann, J. S., *Religious Choice in the Dutch Republic: The Reformation of Arnoldus Buchelius (1565–1641)* (Manchester, 1999)

Pollmann, J. S., 'Off the Record: Problems in the Quantification of Calvinist Church Discipline', *SCJ* 33.2 (2002), 424–38

Pollmann, J. S., 'Honor, Gender and Discipline in Dutch Reformed Churches', in *Dire l'interdit: The Vocabulary of Censure and Exclusion in the Early Modern Reformed Tradition*, ed. Raymond A. Mentzer, Philippe Chareyre, and Françoise Moreil (Leiden, 2010)

Porter, Roy, 'Rape—Does It Have a Historical Meaning?', in *Rape*, ed. Sylvana Tomaselli and Roy Porter (Oxford: Basil Blackwell, 1986), 217–36

Porterfield, Amanda, 'Women's Attraction to Puritanism', *Church History* 60.2 (1991), 196–209

Potts, Thomas and Robert Poole, *The Wonderful Discovery of Witches in the County of Lancaster* (Lancaster, 2011)

Poumarede, Jacques, 'Le droit des veuves sous l'Ancien Régime (XVIIe–XVIIIe siècles) ou comment gagner son douaire', in *Femmes et pouvoirs sous l'Ancien Régime*, ed. Danielle Haase-Dubosc and Eliane Viennot (Paris, 1991)

Prestwich, Menna (ed.), *International Calvinism 1541–1715* (Oxford, 1985)

Ranft, Patricia, *A Woman's Way: The Forgotten History of Women Spiritual Directors* (New York, 2000)

Ranum, Orest, 'Review Article of Yves Castan, *Honnêteté et Relations Sociales en Languedoc (1715–1780)*', *Eighteenth-Century Studies* 9 (1976), 608–14

Rapley, Elizabeth, *The Devotés: Women and Church in Seventeenth-Century France* (London, 1990)

Reid, W. Stanford, 'The Transmission of Calvinism in the Sixteenth Century', in *John Calvin: His Influence in the Western World*, ed. W. Stanford Reid (Michigan, 1982)

Riddle, John M., *Eve's Herbs: A History of Contraception and Abortion in the West* (Cambridge, MA, 1997)

Roberts, Penny, 'Urban Society', in *The European World, 1500–1800*, ed. Bëat Kümin (London and New York, 2009)

Roelker, Nancy L., 'The Appeal of Calvinism to French Noblewomen in the Sixteenth Century', *JIH* 2.4 (1972), 391–418

Roper, Lyndal, 'Mothers of Debauchery: Procuresses in Reformation Augsburg', *German History* 6.1 (1988), 1–19

Roper, Lyndal, *The Holy Household: Women and Morals in Reformation Augsburg* (Oxford, 1989)

Roper, Lyndal, *Oedipus and the Devil: Witchcraft, Sexuality and Religion in Early Modern Europe* (London, 1994)

Roper, Lyndal, 'Gender and the Reformation', *Archiv für Reformationsgeschichte* 92 (2001), 290–302

Roper, Lyndal, *Witch Craze: Terror and Fantasy in Baroque Germany* (New Haven, CT, and London, 2004)

Roper, Michael and John Tosh (eds), *Manful Assertions: Masculinity in Britain since 1800* (London and New York, 1991)

Rossiaud, Jacques, 'Prostitution, Youth and Society in the Towns of Southeastern France in the Fifteenth Century', in *Deviants and the Abandoned in French Society*, ed. R. Foster and O. Ranum (Baltimore, MD, 1978), 1–46

Rossiaud, Jacques, *La prostitution médiévale* (Paris, 1988)

Roussel, Bernard, 'La discipline des églises réformées de France en 1559: un royaume sans clergé?', in *De l'humanisme aux Lumières, Bayle et le protestantisme: Mélanges en l'honneur d'Elisabeth Labrousse*, ed. Michelle Magdelaine, Maria-Cristina Pitassi, Ruth Whelan, and Antony McKenna (Paris and Oxford, 1996)

Roussel, Bernard, '"Ensevelir honnestement les corps": Funeral Corteges and Huguenot Culture', in *Society and Culture in the Huguenot World, 1559–1685*, ed. Raymond A. Mentzer and Andrew Spicer (Cambridge, 2002)

Rowbotham, Sheila, 'The Trouble with "Patriarchy"', in *People's History and Socialist Theory*, ed. Raphael Samuel (London, 1981)

Rublack, Ulinka, *The Crimes of Women in Early Modern Germany* (Oxford, 1999)

Ryrie, Alec (ed.), *Palgrave Advances in the European Reformations* (Basingstoke, 2006)

Samuel, Raphael (ed.), *People's History and Socialist Theory* (London, 1981)

Sauzet, Robert, *Contre-Réforme et Réforme catholique en Bas-Languedoc: Le Diocèse de Nîmes de 1598 à 1694* (Bruxelles, Louvain, and Paris, 1979)

Sauzet, Robert, 'Huguenots et papists a Nîmes, du XVIe siècle au XVIIIe siècle', in *Histoire de Nîmes*, ed. Xavier Gutherz (et al.) (Aix, 1982)

Schilling, Heinz, '"History of Crime" or "History of Sin"? Some Reflections on the Social History of Early Modern Church Discipline', in *Politics and Society in Reformation Europe: Essays for Sir Geoffrey Elton on his Sixty-Fifth Birthday*, ed. E. I. Kouri and Tom Scott (Basingstoke, 1987)

Schilling, Heinz, 'Calvinism and the Making of the Modern Mind: Ecclesiastical Discipline of Public and Private Sin from the Sixteenth to the Nineteenth Century', in *Civic Calvinism in Northwestern Germany and the Netherlands: Sixteenth to Nineteenth Centuries* (Kirksville, MO, 1991)

Schilling, Heinz, 'Reform and Supervision of Family Life in Germany and the Netherlands', in *Sin and the Calvinists: Morals Control and the Consistory in the Reformed Tradition*, ed. Raymond A. Mentzer (Kirksville, MO, 1994)

Schneider, R., *Public Life in Toulouse, 1463–1789: From Municipal Republic to Cosmopolitan City* (Cambridge, 1989)

Schneider, Zoë A., 'Women before the Bench: Female Litigants in Early Modern Normandy', *FHS* 23.1 (2000), 1–32

Scott, James C., *Domination and the Arts of Resistance: Hidden Transcripts* (New Haven, CT, and London, 1990)

Scott, Joan Wallach, 'Gender: A Useful Category of Historical Analysis', *American Historical Review* 91 (1986), 53–75

Scott, Joan Wallach, *Gender and the Politics of History* (New York, 1988)

Scott, Joan Wallach (ed.), *Feminism and History* (Oxford, 1996)

Segalen, Martine, *Mari et femme dans la société paysanne* (Paris, 1980)

Sharpe, J. A., *Defamation and Sexual Slander in Early Modern England: The Church Courts at York*, Borthwick Papers no. 58 (York, 1980)

Sharpe, J. A., '"Such Disagreement betwyx Neighbours": Litigation and Human Relations in Early Modern England', *Disputes and Settlements: Law and Human Relations in the West*, ed. John Bossy (Cambridge, 1983)

Sharpe, J. A., *Crime in Early Modern England 1550–1750* (2nd edn, London, 1999)

Sherwood, Jessie, 'The Inquisitor as Archivist: or Surprise, Fear, and Ruthless Efficiency in the Archives', *The American Archivist* 75.1 (2012), 56–80

Shorter, Edward, *The Making of the Modern Family* (London, 1976)

Shorter, Edward, 'On Writing the History of Rape', *Signs* 3.2 (1977), 471–82

Solé, Jacques, *L'amour en occident à l'epoque moderne* (Paris, 1976)

Solé, Jacques, *Etre femme en 1500: la vie quotidienne dans la diocèse de Troyes* (Paris, 2000)

Soman, A., 'Sorcellerie, justice criminelle et société dans la France moderne', *Histoire, économie et société* 12 (1993), 177–217

Soman, Alfred, 'The Anatomy of an Infanticide Trial: The Case of Marie-Jeanne Bartonnet (1742)', in *Changing Identities in Early Modern France*, ed. Michael Wolfe (Durham and London, 1996)

Spierling, Karen E., 'Insolence towards God? The Perpetuation of Catholic Baptismal Traditions in Sixteenth-Century Geneva', *Archive for Reformation History* 93 (2002), 97–125

Spierling, Karen E., *Infant Baptism in Reformation Geneva: The Shaping of a Community, 1536–1564* (Aldershot and Burlington, 2005)

Spooner, Frank, *The International Economy and Monetary Movements in France, 1493–1725* (Cambridge, 1972)

Stauffenegger, Roger, 'Le mariage à Genèva vers 1600', *Mémoires de la société pour l'histoire du droit* 27 (1966), 133–64

Stone, Lawrence, *The Family, Sex and Marriage in England 1500–1800* (London, 1977)

Stretton, Tim, *Women Waging Law in Elizabethan England* (Cambridge, 1999)

Stuart, Kathy, *Defiled Trades and Social Outcasts* (Cambridge, 1999)

Sunshine, Glenn. S., 'Reformed Theology and the Origins of Synodical Polity: Calvin, Beza and the Gallican Confession', in *Later Calvinism: International Perspectives*, ed. W. Fred Graham (Kirksville, MO, 1994)

Tanner, Deborah, *You Just Don't Understand Me: Men and Women in Conversation* (London, 1990)

Taylor, Larissa, *Soldiers of Christ: Preaching in Late Medieval and Reformation France* (New York and Oxford, 1992)

Thayer, Anne T., *Penitence, Preaching and the Coming of the Reformation* (Aldershot, 2002)

Thomas, Keith, 'A Double Standard', *Journal of History of Ideas* 20 (1959), 195–216

Thomas, Keith, *Religion and the Decline of Magic* (Harmondsworth, 1971)

Thompson, John Lee, *John Calvin and the Daughters of Sarah: Women in Regular and Exceptional Roles in the Exegesis of Calvin, his Predecessors, and his Contemporaries* (Geneva, 1992)

Thompson, John Lee, *Writing the Wrongs: Women of the Old Testament among Biblical Commentators from Philo through the Reformation* (Oxford, 2001)

Thompson, Roger, '"Holy Watchfulness" and Communal Conformism: The Functions of Defamation in Early New England Communities', *New England Quarterly* 56.4 (1983), 504–22

Todd, Margo, *The Culture of Protestantism in Early Modern Scotland* (New Haven, CT, and London, 2002)

Tulchin, Allan A., 'The Michelade in Nîmes, 1567', *FHS* 29.1 (2006), 1–36

Tulchin, Allan A., *That Men Would Praise the Lord: The Triumph of Protestantism in Nîmes, 1530–1570* (Oxford, 2010)

Tulchin, Allan A., 'Low Dowries, Absent Parents: Marrying for Love in an Early Modern French Town', *SCJ* 44.3 (2013), 713–38

Turner, James Grantham, *Sexuality and Gender in Early Modern Europe: Institutions, Texts and Images* (Cambridge, 1993)

Valeri, Mark, 'Religion, Discipline and the Economy in Calvin's Geneva', *SCJ* 28 (1997), 123–42

Van der Heijden, Manon, 'Women as Victims of Sexual and Domestic Violence in Seventeenth-Century Holland', *Journal of Social History* 33.3 (2000), 623–44

Van der Heijden, Manon, 'Domestic Violence, Alcohol Use and the Uses of Justice in Early Modern Holland', *Annales de démographie historique* 130 (2015), 69–85

van Gennep, Arnold, *Manuel de folklore français contemporain* (Paris, 1943)

van Gennep, Arnold, *The Rites of Passage,* trans. Monika B. Vizedom and Gabrielle L. Caffee (London, 1960)

Vigarello, Georges, *A History of Rape: Sexual Violence in France from the 16th to the 20th Century,* trans. Jean Birrell (Cambridge, 2001)

Vogler B. and J. Estèbe, 'La genèse d'une société protestante: Étude comparée de quelques Registres consistoriaux languedociens et palatins vers 1600', *Annales: Economies, Sociétés, Civilisations* 31 (1976), 362–88

Walker, Garthine, 'Rereading Rape and Sexual Violence in Early Modern England', *Gender and History* 10 (1998), 1–25

Warner, Lyndan, 'Widows, Widowhood and the Problem of "Second Marriages" in Sixteenth-Century France', in *Widowhood in Medieval and Early Modern Europe,* ed. Sandra Cavallo and Lyndan Warner (Harlow, 1999)

Watt, Jeffrey R., 'The Reception of the Reformation in Valangin, Switzerland, 1547–1588', *SCJ* 20.1 (1989), 89–104

Watt, Jeffrey R., *The Making of Modern Marriage: Matrimonial Control and the Rise of Sentiment in Neuchâtel, 1550–1800* (New York, 1992)

Watt, Jeffrey R., 'Women and the Consistory in Calvin's Geneva', *SCJ* 24 (1993), 431–41

Watt, Jeffrey R., 'Calvinism, Childhood and Education: The Evidence from the Genevan Consistory', *SCJ* 33.2 (2002), 439–56

Weaver, F. E., 'Women and Religion in Early Modern France: A Bibliographic Essay on the State of the Question', *The Catholic Historical Review* 57.1 (1981), 50–9

Wheaton, Robert, 'Recent Trends in the Historical Study of the French Family', in *Family and Sexuality in French History,* ed. Robert Wheaton and Tamara K. Hareven (Philadelphia, PA, 1980)

Wheaton, Robert, 'Affinity and Descent in Seventeenth-Century Bordeaux', in *Family and Sexuality in French History*, ed. Robert Wheaton and Tamara K. Hareven (Philadelphia, PA, 1980)

Wheaton, Robert and Tamara K. Hareven (eds), *Family and Sexuality in French History* (Philadelphia, PA, 1980)

Wiesner, Merry E., *Working Women in Renaissance Germany* (New Brunswick, 1986)

Wiesner, Merry E., 'Beyond Women and the Family: Towards a Gender Analysis of the Reformation', *SCJ* 18 (1987)

Wiesner, Merry E., 'Luther and the Death of Two Marys', in *Disciplines of Faith: Studies in Religion, Politics and Patriarchy*, ed. Jim Obelkevich, Lyndal Roper, and Raphael Samuel (New York, 1987)

Wiesner, Merry E., 'Women's Response to the Reformation', in *The German People and the Reformation*, ed. R. Po-Chia Hsia (New York, 1988)

Wiesner, Merry E., 'Nuns, Wives and Mothers: Women and the Reformation in Germany', in *Women in Reformation and Counter-Reformation Europe: Public and Private Worlds*, ed. Sherrin Marshall (Indiana, 1989)

Wiesner, Merry E., *Women and Gender in Early Modern Europe* (Cambridge, 1993)

Wiesner-Hanks, Merry E., *Christianity and Sexuality in the Early Modern World: Regulating Desire, Reforming Practice* (London and New York, 2000)

Wiesner-Hanks, Merry E., 'Women, Gender and Sexuality', in *Palgrave Advances in the European Reformations*, ed. Alec Ryrie (Basingstoke, 2006)

Wilson, Peter J., 'Filcher of Good Names': An Enquiry into Anthropology and Gossip', *Man* 9 (1974), 93–102

Wilson, Stephen, *The Magical Universe: Everyday Ritual and Magic in Pre-Modern Europe* (London and New York, 2000)

Witte, John, Jr, and Robert M. Kingdon, *Sex, Marriage and Family in John Calvin's Geneva* (Grand Rapids, MI, 2005), vol. 1, *Courtship, Engagement and Marriage*

Wolfe, Michael (ed.), *Changing Identities in Early Modern France* (Durham and London, 1996)

Wolff, Philippe (dir.), *Histoire du Languedoc*, ed. Edouard Privat (Toulouse, 1967)

UNPUBLISHED THESES AND PAPERS

Chareyre, Philippe, *Le consistoire de Nîmes de 1561 à 1685*, 4 vols (Thèse de Doctorat d'État en Histoire: Université Paul-Valéry-Montpellier III 3, 1987)

Guggenheim, Ann. H., 'Calvinism and the Political Elite of Sixteenth-Century Nîmes', Ph.D. thesis (New York University, 1968), 274

Kmec, Sonja, *Noblewomen and Family Fortunes in Seventeenth-Century France and England: A Study of the Lives of the Duchesse de La Trémoïlle and her Sister-in-Law, the Countess of Derby*, D.Phil. (University of Oxford, 2004)

Mentzer, Raymond A., 'Urban Piety and the French Reformed Churches', Urban Life in Early Modern France Conference, 10 June 2006, unpublished paper

Murdock, Graeme, 'The Dancers of Nîmes: Moral Discipline, Gender and Reformed Religion in Late Sixteenth-Century France', unpublished paper

Tulchin, Allan A., *The Reformation in Nîmes*, Ph.D. (University of Chicago, 2000)

Wanegffelen, Thierry, 'Un cléricalisme réformé : Le protestantisme français entre principe du sacerdoce universel et théologie de la vocation au ministère (XVIe–XVIIe siècles)', Reformation Studies Colloquium, April 2004, unpublished paper

Index

Abeille, Pierre (*L'Escarrabilhat*) 276–7
abortion 69, 237–8, 272
Abraham, Loys 286
Abram, Loys 64, 227
Adam, Jean 195
Advocat, Pol 223
Advocate, Marguerite 164
Afortide, Jacquette 187
Agulhonnet, Mlle d' 169
Agullonet (Agullonnet/Agulhonet), Robert 78, 133, 245–6
aiguillette 140–1
Airebaudouze, Pierre d' 73, 117
Albenas, Captain Cephas 182
Albenas, Vidal d' 293
Alcaysse, Marguerite 250
Aleaume, Charles 162
Alesti, Jehan 308–9
Alexis, M. 295
Alias, M. 284
Alies, Estienne 160–1
Alix (servant) 259
Alizot, Arnaud 315
Allarie, Jehanne 228
Allegre, Jean 99
Allegre, Sieur 284
Allegre, Sire 87
Allen, Jehan 260
Alles, Mme la Baronne d' 124
Alles, Pigeon d' 176
Allier, Captain 190, 287
Allier, Jacques 35, 83
Alliere, Marguerite 190
alms distribution 97
Alphanty, Captain 150
Alphanty, Jane 151
Alyere, Anthoneye 315
Alzonne, Aime 258
Ambasse, Loyse 101
amende (*amande*) *honorable* 94, 248
Amourcouse, Jehanne 175
Amourouse, Estienne 94
Amourouse, Jehanne 234
Ampiel, Jean (*Ginibrières*) 150
Andre, Andre 173–4, 288
Andre, Anthoine (*Le Redon*) 315
Andre, Jacques 233, 311
Andre, Jean 259
Andrienne, Catherine 299
Andrienne, Claude 281
Andrine, Marguerite 121
Annales school 27
Anthoine, Pierre 164

Anthonye (servant) 219
Arbaleste, Charlotte 128
Arboussette, Françoise 189
Arboussette, Judict 81, 230
Archiveyre, Marie 97, 189
Arènes, Guillaume de 154
Argentier, Antonie 57
Argentier, Drivette 57
Arguisan, Foralguier 66
Ariès, Philippe 11–12
Ariffon, Damoiselle d' 168
Ariffonne, Bernardine 124
Aristotle 49
Arnail, Jean (*Farettes*) 318
Arnail, Jehan 143
Arnassane, Gentile 170–1
Arnaud, Bernard, Seigneur de la Cassagne 35
Arnaud, Pierre (*Balafrat*) 299–301
Arnaude (woman) 225
Arnaude, Anne 120
Arnaude, Marguerite 108
Artine, M. 289
Asperes, Isabel d' 60, 314
Astorg (servant) 223
Aubert, Donne 134
Aubert, Noel, Seigneur de Saint-Alban 113, 117
Auberte, Marie 219
Audemar, Captain 143
Audiberte, Marie 172
Audifret, Jeanne d' 168
Audrigue, Anne 185
Audrine, Jehane 122
Audrine, Saumette 160
Augerand, Anthoine 188
Augsburg 187, 286, 291
Aulbert, Vidal 290
Auriol, Bernard 99
Auriole, Marie 163
Auvernasse, Marguerite 178
Auzas, M. 234, 280
Aymes, Robert 95

Bacand, Andre 279
Bagard, Firmin 119, 196
Bagard, Sieur 280
Bagarde, Donne 134
Bague, Mathieu 304–5
Bailey, F. G. 150
Baille, Marie de 175
Balauzau, M. de 64
Baldit, Marguerite 57

Index